THE CAMBRIDGE HISTORY
OF
ENGLISH LITERATURE

VOLUME IV

PROSE AND POETRY
SIR THOMAS NORTH TO MICHAEL DRAYTON

The Cambridge History
of
English Literature

Edited by

A. W. Ward, Litt.D., F.B.A.
Master of Peterhouse

and

A. R. Waller, M.A.
Peterhouse

Volume IV

Prose and Poetry

Sir Thomas North to Michael Drayton

New York: The Macmillan Company
Cambridge, England: at the University Press

1932

Printed in the United States of America

NOTE

VOLUMES V and VI of *The Cambridge History of English Literature* will deal with the history of dramatic writing in England to the closing of the theatres under the puritan rule, that is to say, to about the middle of the seventeenth century.

Volume VII, *Cavalier and Puritan*, will be concerned with non-dramatic literature, mainly of the period between 1625 and 1660. Its contents are in an advanced stage of preparation, and we hope to be able to publish this volume before the end of 1910.

It was originally intended to continue, in the present volume, the account of scholars and scholarship in England from the point reached in Volume III; it has been decided, however, to postpone this continuation until Volume VII.

A. W. W.
A. R. W.

CAMBRIDGE,
29 *September*, 1909.

CONTENTS

CHAPTER I

TRANSLATORS

By Charles Whibley, Jesus College

CHAPTER II

THE "AUTHORISED VERSION" AND ITS INFLUENCE

By Albert S. Cook, L.H.D., LL.D., Professor of the English Language and Literature in Yale University

CHAPTER III

SIR WALTER RALEGH

By Louise Creighton

v

Contents

CHAPTER IV

THE LITERATURE OF THE SEA

From the Origins to Hakluyt

By Commander CHARLES N. ROBINSON, R.N.,
and JOHN LEYLAND

CHAPTER V

SEAFARING AND TRAVEL

The Growth of Professional Text-Books and Geographical Literature

By Commander CHARLES N. ROBINSON, R.N.,
and JOHN LEYLAND

CHAPTER VI

THE SONG-BOOKS AND MISCELLANIES

By HAROLD H. CHILD, sometime Scholar of Brasenose College,
Oxford

CHAPTER VII

ROBERT SOUTHWELL. SAMUEL DANIEL

By HAROLD H. CHILD

Contents

CHAPTER VIII

THOMAS CAMPION

By S. PERCIVAL VIVIAN, sometime Scholar of St. John's College, Oxford

CHAPTER IX

THE SUCCESSORS OF SPENSER

By HUGH DE SÉLINCOURT, University College, Oxford

CHAPTER X

MICHAEL DRAYTON

By HAROLD H. CHILD

CHAPTER XI

JOHN DONNE

By HERBERT J. C. GRIERSON, M.A., Chalmers Professor of English Literature in the University of Aberdeen

CHAPTER XII

THE ENGLISH PULPIT FROM FISHER TO DONNE

By the Rev. F. E. HUTCHINSON, M.A., Trinity College, Oxford; Chaplain of King's College, Cambridge

CHAPTER XIII

ROBERT BURTON, JOHN BARCLAY AND JOHN OWEN

By EDWARD BENSLY, M.A., Trinity College; Professor of Latin, University College of Wales, Aberystwyth

CHAPTER XIV

THE BEGINNINGS OF ENGLISH PHILOSOPHY

By W. R. SORLEY, Litt.D., LL.D., F.B.A., Fellow of King's College, and Knightbridge Professor of Moral Philosophy

CHAPTER XV

EARLY WRITINGS ON POLITICS AND ECONOMICS

By the Ven. Archdeacon CUNNINGHAM, D.D., F.B.A., Fellow of Trinity College

CHAPTER XVI

LONDON AND THE DEVELOPMENT OF POPULAR LITERATURE

Character Writing. Satire. The Essay

By Harold V. Routh, M.A., Peterhouse; Professor of Latin in Trinity College, Toronto

CHAPTER XVII

WRITERS ON COUNTRY PURSUITS AND PASTIMES

Gervase Markham

By H. G. Aldis, M.A., Peterhouse; Secretary of the University Library

CHAPTER XVIII

THE BOOK-TRADE, 1557–1625

By H. G. Aldis

Contents

CHAPTER XIX

THE FOUNDATION OF LIBRARIES

By J. BASS MULLINGER, M.A., Formerly Librarian of St. John's
College

The Cambridge History of
English Literature

CHAPTER I

Translators

THE translators of Elizabeth's age pursued their craft in the spirit of bold adventure which animated Drake and Hawkins. It was their ambition to discover new worlds of thought and beauty. They sailed the wide ocean of knowledge to plant their colonies of the intellect where they might, or to bring back to our English shores some eloquent stranger, whom their industry had taught to speak with our English tongue. Holland justly describes his enterprise as a conquest. He "would wish rather and endeavour," says he in the preface to his translation of Pliny, "by all means to triumph now over the Romans in subduing their literature under the dent of the English pen, in requitall of the conquest some time over this Island, atchieved by the edge of their sword." And, harbouring this sentiment of conquest, the translators were strongly impelled also by the desire to benefit their native land and its rulers. They had learned from the classics deep lessons of policy and statecraft, which they would impart to their queen and her magistrates. Their achievement was, indeed, the real renascence of England, the authentic recovery of the ancient spirit. That they were keenly conscious of what they were doing is clear from their dedications and their prefaces. The choice of the great personages to whom they presented their works was made with a deliberate purpose. When North and Holland asked the queen's protection for their masterpieces, it was in the full hope and knowledge that Plutarch and Livy would prove wise guides unto her footsteps. Nor was it with the mere intent of flattery or applause that other translators offered the fruits of their toil to Cecil, Leicester and Christopher Hatton. They wished to give counsel where they deemed it useful. Thomas Wilson, for instance, the translator of Demosthenes, thought that every good subject should compare the present and the past; that, when he heard of Athens and the Athenians, he should remember England and Englishmen; that, in brief, he should learn from the doings of his elders how to deal with his own affairs. John Brende, who Englished Quintus Curtius, in presenting his book to the duke of Northumberland, thus explained his purpose:

"There is required in all Magistrates," says he, "both a faith and feare in God, and also an outward pollicie in wordly thinges:[1] whereof, as the one is to be learned by the Scriptures, so the other must chiefly be gathered by reading of histories."

Wherever you turn, you find the same admirable excuse; and, as the translators gave to England well nigh the whole wisdom of the ancients, they provided not merely grave instruction for kings and statesmen, but plots for the dramatists, and entertainment for lettered ease.

As their interest lay chiefly in the matter of their originals, they professed little desire to illustrate a theory of translation. They had neither the knowledge nor the sense of criticism, which should measure accurately the niceties of their craft. They set about their work in a spirit of sublime unconsciousness. In their many prefaces, and they delighted in prefaces, there is scarce a hint that they are pursuing a delicate art. The most of them were indifferent to, or ignorant of, Horace's maxim:

Nec verbum verbo curabis reddere fidus
Interpres,

though, for the best of reasons, they followed the poet's liberal counsel. They would not have understood the scientific care with which Dryden presently distinguished metaphrase and paraphrase. Chapman, it is true, knew the end at which he aimed, and, in the preface to his *Homer*, lucidly describes what should be the ambition of the translator:

"The work of a skilfull and worthy translator," says he, "is to observe the sentences, figures and formes of speech proposed

[1] Geffraie Fenton showed his approval of this sentiment by borrowing it word for word in his preface to the *Tragicall Discourses.*

in his author, his true sence and height, and to adorn them with figures and formes of oration fitted to the originall in the same tongue to which they are translated."

And one W. R., in an eloquent epistle, addressed to the translator, wittily defends Lodge against the charge that he had not parrot-like spoken Seneca's own words and lost himself in a Latin echo. But both Chapman and Lodge's defender wrote when the art of translation had been pursued for two generations and was falling, not unnaturally, into a habit of self-criticism. In general, the translators of the heyday were accurate neither in word nor in shape. They followed the text as remotely as they imitated the style of their originals.

I have said that North and his colleagues were inspired by a love of adventure. They resembled the pioneers of our empire also in a splendid lack of scruple. As the early travellers cheerfully seized upon the treasure of others, painfully acquired, and turned to their own profit the discoveries of Spaniard and Portuguese, so the translators cared not by what intermediary they approached the Greek and Latin texts. Very few were scholars in the sense that Philemon Holland was a scholar. Like Shakespeare, the most had little Latin and less Greek. When Thomas Nicolls, citizen and goldsmith of London, set out to translate Thucydides, he went no further than the French of Claude de Seyssel, and Claude de Seyssel made his version not from the Greek but from the Latin of Laurentius Valla. Between Thomas North and Plutarch stands the gracious figure of Jacques Amyot. Thomas Underdowne derived his *Aethiopian Historie* from the Latin of Stanislaus Warschewiczki, a Polish country gentleman, who translated the Greek of Heliodorous, *rure paterno*, in 1551. Thus Adlington, in interpreting *The Golden Ass*, was misled by *Lasne Dore* of Guillaume Michel. Thus Aristotle came into our speech through the French of Leroy, and even Bandello crossed from Italy to England by the courtly bridge of Belleforest.

The result of this careless method is that the translations of Elizabeth's age (in prose, at any rate) are unsoiled by pedantry. They do not smell of the lamp; they suggest nowhere the laborious use of the pedestrian dictionary. They call up a vision of space and courage and the open air. That they are inappropriate seems no fault in them. If they replace the restraint of the classics with the colour and sentiment of romance, it is because the translators have done their work thoroughly. They have turned the authors of Greece and Rome not merely into a new language but into the feeling of another age and clime. In other words, their books carry with them the lively air of brave originals. And this natural impress is the deeper, because translation was not an exclusive craft, pursued in the narrow spirit of mere scholarship. Many of the most ingenious craftsmen were men of the world, who made their versions to beguile a leisure snatched from the conduct of affairs. Sir Thomas Hoby, who gave us *The Courtier*, was an ambassador; Danett, who put Commines in an English dress, practised the art of diplomacy loftily exemplified in his original; with a fine sense of propriety, Peter Whitehorne translated Machiavelli's *Arte of Warre* when he was in Barbary with the emperor, "at the siege and winning of Calibbia"; Thomas North himself played his part as a magistrate in the policies of the larger world. Even those who, like Holland and Golding, adopted translating as a profession practised a style all untrammelled by the schools. The reproach of Dryden, that "there are many who understand Greek and Latin, and yet are ignorant of their mother-tongue," might not be brought with justice against them. Few men of the century knew Greek and Latin. Many were masters of English, which they wrote with an eloquence and elaboration rarely surpassed.

The translators' range of discovery was wide. They brought into the ken of Englishmen the vast continent of classical literature. Only a few provinces escaped their search, and, of the few, one was the province which should have had the quickest attraction for them. It is not a little strange that the golden age of our drama should have seen the translation of but one Greek play. Of Aeschylus and Sophocles there is nothing. A free paraphrase of the *Phoenissae*, presented at Gray's Inn under the name of *Jocasta* in 1566 by George Gascoigne and Francis Kinwelmersh, and made not from the Greek but from the Italian of Ludovico Dolce, is the Elizabethans' only and fragile link with Euripides.

Plautus fared not much better: we have no more than the *Menaechmi* of William Warner (1595), which may have given Shakespeare a hint for *The Comedy of Errors*. More popular were Seneca and Terence—Seneca, no doubt, for his ingenious maxims, and Terence because he was appointed to be read in schools. Of the historians, both Greek and Latin, there is a long list. An unknown translator, who hides his name under the initials B. R., and who may be Barnabe Rich, published two books of Herodotus in 1584, and Thomas Nicolls, already mentioned, gave to England a complete Thucydides in 1550. Of Livy, we have a fragment by Antony Cope (1544), and a version of all that remains by the incomparable Philemon Holland (1600), to whose industry also are due Suetonius (1606), Ammianus Marcellinus (1609) and Xenophon's *Cyropaedia* (1632). Sallust, as might be expected, was a favourite of Tudor England. His *Catiline* was translated by Thomas Paynell (1541), his *Jugurtha* by Alexander Barclay (1557), and both histories by Thomas Heywood, the dramatist (1608). Golding's *Caesar* (1565), Brende's *Quintus Curtius* (1553), and Stocker's *Diodorus Siculus* (1569), by no means complete the tale. What Sir Henry Savile did for the *Histories* and the *Agricola* of Tacitus (1591), Richard Greenwey did for the *Annals* and the *Description of Germany* (1598), and there is no author Englished for us in fuller and worthier shape than the wisest of Roman historians. Xenophon found other translators besides Holland, and Plutarch's *Lives of the Noble Grecians and Romans* fell happily into the hands of Sir Thomas North, whose skill gave them a second and a larger immortality.

The philosophers and moralists of the ancient world chimed with the humour of Tudor England. Their simple disputations possess the charm of freshness and curiosity. The problems of conduct posed by Cicero and Plutarch are of a kind that found an eager solution in the minds of men, still simple enough to love casuistry for its own sake. Such questions as how a man may praise himself without incurring envy or blame, or whether philosophers ought to converse with princes and rulers, were met, it is certain, with many arguments and various answers. And the translators supplied those ignorant of the dead languages with a mighty armoury of intellectual weapons. Of Plato, to be sure, there is little enough. Besides Sir Thomas Elyot's *Of the Knowledge which maketh a wise man* (1533), distantly inspired by the philosopher, immediately suggested by Diogenes Laertius, there is but a version of the *Axiochus*, a doubtful dialogue. Aristotle received more generous treatment. His *Ethics* were translated from the Italian by John Wylkinson (1547), and, as has been said, one J. D. made a version of the *Politics* from the French of Loys Leroy, *dit* Regius (1598). Far more popular were Cicero and Seneca, the chief instructors of the age. Tully's *Offices*, translated by Robert Whittington, laureate in grammar (1533), and by Nicholas Grimald (1555), were confidently commended to rulers, schoolmen, orators and rhetoricans:

"At few words," says the ingenious Grimalde, "al men, that of wisdome be studious, may gette sommewhat herein to sharpe the wyt, to store the intelligence, to fede the minde, to quicke the sprite, to augment the reason, to direct the appetite, to frame the tounge, to fashion the maners."

Nor were the two treatises on *Friendship* and *Old Age* overlooked. The one was translated by John Harington (1550), the other by Thomas Newton (1569), and both have as handsome an appearance in their English dress as any books of the time; and, in 1561, John Dolman "englysshed these fyve Questions, which Marke Tullye Cicero disputed in his Manor of Tusculanum." Upon Seneca, also, Whittington tried his hand, to whom we owe *The Fame and Rule of Honest lyvynge* (1546) and *The Remedyes against all casuall Chances*. For the rest, Arthur Golding translated *The Woorke concerning Benefyting* (1558), and, in 1614, Thomas Lodge published his monumental version of Seneca's prose, a work undimmed by comparison even with Holland's translation of Plutarch's *Morals* (1603).

The modern world yielded as rich a spoil as the ancient. The Italianate Englishman, bitterly reproached by his contemporaries, brought back from Italy, with his fantastic costume and new-fangled manners, a love of Italian literature and of Italian romance. From across the Alps came our knowledge of the court, of arms and of the arts. In a famous passage, Ascham deplored the encroaching influence. Evil as he thought the *Morte Arthure*, "the whole pleasure of which booke standeth in two speciall poyntes, in open mans slaughter, and bold bawdrye," he declared that "ten *Morte Arthures* do not the tenth part so much harme as one of these bookes, made in Italie, and translated in England." Yet their growing popularity could not be gainsaid:

"That which is most to be lamented"—again Ascham speaks— "and therefore more nedefull to be looked to, there be mo of these ungratious bookes set out in Printe within these fewe monethes, than have been sene in England many score yeare before."

Ascham wrote in 1567, and there is no doubt that he had in his mind William Painter's *Palace of Pleasure*, of which the first volume was published in 1566, the second in 1567, and Geffraie Fenton's *Certaine Tragicall Discourses* (1567). Few books of the time had a more immediate and profound influence than these. They entertained the court and were an inspiration to the poets. Had it not been for Painter, the English drama would have taken another path. The stories of blood and desire, appropriate to the ferocity of the Italian republics, were eagerly retold by our dramatists, avid of the fierce emotions which Elizabeth's peaceful England did not encourage in act. The tale of borrowings from Painter's *Palace* is a long one. Shakespeare and Webster, Marston and Massinger, all owe a debt to the ingenious writer whom Ascham savagely condemned. And they could not have gone for their plots to a better source. For Painter was a true child of his age. His ambition, like the ambition of the chroniclers, was encyclopaedic. He aimed, not at telling one story, but at telling all stories. He began at the beginning and carried his work to the very end. It would be difficult to find a plot that has not its origin, or its counterpart, in Painter's treasure-house. His earliest stories are taken from Livy, Herodotus and Aulus Gellius; and, presently, he seeks his originals in the works of queen Margaret and Boccaccio, of Bandello and Straparola. Whatever were the origin and substance of his tales, he reduced them all to a certain plainness. He had a ready talent for story-telling; he cultivated a straightforward style; and, unlike the most of his fellows, he avoided embroidery. His popularity, therefore, is easily explained: his work was quickly intelligible to simple folk, and the dramatists had no difficulty in clothing

his dry bones with their romantic imagery. But they acknowledged their debt with a difference. Shakespeare did
not scruple to borrow the very words of North and Holinshed.
He took no more than the plot from Painter's version of
Rhomeo and Julietta.

Ascham's judgment of Painter and Fenton, foolish and
unjust as it is, seems to have been anticipated by the translator
of the *Tragicall Discourses* of Bandello. Fenton, indeed,
securely defends himself against the detraction of the puritan.
In an epistle dedicatory, addressed to the lady Mary Sidney,
he professes that his choice of stories was made with the best
motive. He had no other desire than to improve the occasion.

"Albeit, at the firste sighte," says he, "theis discourses maye
importe certeine vanytyes or fonde practises in love, yet I doubte
not to bee absolved . . ., seinge I have rather noted diversitie of
examples in sondrye younge men and women, approvynge sufficient-
lye the inconvenience happenynge by the pursute of lycenceous
desyer, then affected in anye sorte suche uncerteyne follyes."

If Bandello incurred censure, what sentence would have been
passed upon Boccaccio? Though his *Decameron* was involved
in the harsh judgment passed upon Painter's *Palace*, though
some stories found a place in Turbervile's *Tragical Tales*, it
was not known to England, save in fragments, until 1620.
His *Philocopo* was translated in 1567 by H. G., and, twenty
years later, Bartholomew Young did into English the *Amorous
Fiammetta, wherein is sette doune a catalogue of all and singular
passions of love and jealosie incident to an enamoured yong
gentleman.* Of the other Italian books, thus early done into
English, the most famous was Castiglione's *Il Cortegiano,* of
which Hoby's version won the difficult approval of Ascham
himself. This book, he said, "advisedlie read, and diligentlie
folowed, but one yeare at home in England, would do a yong
gentleman more good, I wisse, then three yeares travell abrode
spent in Italie." And then came Machiavelli, whose *Arte of
Warre,* as has been said, was Englished by Peter Whitehorne
(1560), and of whose *Florentine Historie* we owe an excellent
version to Thomas Bedingfield (1598). But there is no *Prince*
in English until 1640, and thus we are confronted by a literary
puzzle.

No work had a profounder influence upon the thought and policy of Tudor England than Machiavelli's *Prince*. It was a text-book to Thomas Cromwell; its precepts were obediently followed by Cecil and Leicester. The mingled fear and respect in which its author was held converted him into a monstrous legend. No writer is more frequently cited, generally with disapproval, than Machiavelli, and it is always the *Prince*, which was not translated, and not the *Arte of Warre* and the *Florentine Historie*, which were, that arouses the ire of Englishmen. A German scholar has counted more than three hundred references to the *Prince* in the works of the dramatists alone, and has traced them to the celebrated treatise of Gentillet: *Discours sur les moyens de bien gouverner et maintenir en bonne paix un royaume ... contre N. Machiavel le Florentin* (1576), a work translated into English by Simon Patericke (1602). Thus the hostility of the Elizabethans against the Florentine was inspired not by the study of the original but by the violent partisanship of a Huguenot. However, if the accident which took the *Arte of Warre* and left the *Prince* remains unexplained, the preference of French to Italian is natural enough. The truth is, French was the language best understood by the English of the sixteenth century. Not merely was it the avenue through which many of the classics passed into our language and our literature; its familiar use tempted the translators to make known in England the learning and philosophy of France. The French books which we find in English are many and of many kinds. First in importance is Florio's *Montaigne* (1603), after which may be placed Danett's *Commines* (1596), a finished portrait of the politician, which partly atones for the absence of the *Prince*.[1] The indefatigable Arthur Golding translated the *Politicke, Moral and Martiall Discourses*, written in French by Jacques Hurault (1595), while Henri Estienne, La Noue and La Primaudaye all found their way into our English speech. And France, also, like Italy, has her paradox. As we have no *Prince* before Dacres,

[1] That masterpiece of satiric observation, de la Sale's *Les Quinze Joyes de Mariage*, should surely have found a translator in the sixteenth century. And, though the earliest version noted bears the date 1694, it is a fourth edition, and earlier in style than the year of its publication. See Volume III of the present work, p. 10c.

so we have no Rabelais before Sir Thomas Urquhart. The influence of Gargantua, now the legendary giant, now Rabelais's own creation, and of Pantagruel, is plain for all to see. They are among the commonplaces of our dramatists, and, but for the example of Rabelais, at least two masters of prose, Nashe and Harvey, would have written far other than they did. But, though a version of *Gargantua his Prophecie* is entered in the Stationers' registers (1592), either it was never published or it has disappeared, and those who studied the style and gospel of Messer Alcofribas must have studied them in the original.

There remains Spain, united to England in the bonds of enmity, and then, as now, the land of curiosity and romance. Her influence, widely felt, was deepest in the realms of discovery and mysticism, of manners and chivalry. The great masterpieces, Cervantes's *Don Quixote* and *Exemplary Novels* and the *Celestina* of Fernando de Rojas, came to England, when the Stewarts sat upon the throne. But the sixteenth century knew no more popular book, no more potent influence than *The Diall of Princes*, translated from Guevara by Thomas North (1557), in which may be detected the first seeds of euphuism. Vives taught philosophy, rhetoric and civil law orally at Oxford, and, by his translated works, to England. The "spiritual and heavenly exercises" of Granada brought comfort and inspiration to the devout; it was through Spain that Amadis and Palmerin came to England; and many of the bravest adventures, chronicled in Hakluyt's treasury of voyages, were sought and found in the peninsula. The earliest example of the picaresque novel, *Lazarillo de Tormes*, was "drawen out of Spanish" by David Rowland (1576), and, among many others, Bartholomew Young, already mentioned as a scholar in Italian, translated from its native Spanish the *Diana* of George Montemayor.

Thus it will be seen that the translators into prose of Elizabeth's reign were impartial, as they were courageous, in their choice. They were appalled neither by the difficulty of strange tongues nor by the freedom of foreign tales. And, various as was their excuse, their style is uniform. As I have said, they made no attempt to represent the niceties of the original in their own tongue. They cut and clipped French and Roman, Spanish and Greek, to the same form and shape.

Some were simpler than others; some were less cunning in the search after strange words. William Adlington, for instance, who might have found in Apuleius an opportunity for all the resources of Elizabethan vigour and Elizabethan slang, treated his author with a certain reserve. But, for the most part, the colour of the translations is the colour of the translator's time and country, and if we study the method of one or two chosen examples, we shall get an insight into the method of them all.

The most famous, and, perhaps, the best, of Elizabethan translations is Sir Thomas North's *Lives of the Noble Grecians and Romans* (1579). That Shakespeare used it in patient obedience, borrowing words as well as plots, is its unique distinction. But if Shakespeare had never laid upon it that hand of Midas, which transmuted whatever it touched into pure gold, the version had yet been memorable. It is not Plutarch. In many respects it is Plutarch's antithesis. North composed a new masterpiece upon Plutarch's theme. As I have said, he saw Plutarch through Amyot's eye. And the result is neither Amyot nor Plutarch. No book, in truth, ever had a stranger history. There came out of Chaeronea in the first century after Christ a scholar and a writer who was destined to exert a powerful, if indirect, influence upon the greatest of our poets. Thus was Boeotia avenged of her slanderers; thus did a star of intelligence shine over despised Thebes. The Boeotian wrote a book, which, in due time, fell into the hands of Jacques Amyot. What Amyot did with the book, Montaigne, himself a humble debtor, shall proclaim:

" *Je donne avec raison*," he writes, "*ce me semble, la palme à Jacques Amyot, sur touts nos escrivains françois. . . . Nous, aultres ignorants estions perdus, si ce livre ne nous eust relevé du bourbier; sa mercy, nous osons à cett' heure et parler et escrire: les dames en regentent les maistres d'eschole: c'est nostre breviaire.*"

And Plutarch's good fortune did not rest here. Amyot's book, which was Montaigne's breviary, came to Thomas North, who embellished Amyot, as Amyot had embellished Plutarch. North's Plutarch is as far from Amyot's as Amyot's is from its original. Not merely the words, but the very spirit is transformed. Change the names, and you might be reading in North's page of Philip Sidney and Richard Grenville, of

Leicester and of the great lord Burghley. For North, though he knew little of the classics, was a master of noble English. He was neither schoolman nor euphuist. As he freed his language from the fetters which immature scholars had cast upon it, so he did not lay upon its bones the awkward chains of a purposed ingenuity. He held a central place in the history of our speech. He played upon English prose as upon an organ whose every stop he controlled with an easy confidence. He had a perfect sense of the weight and colour of words; pathos and gaiety, familiarity and grandeur resound in his magnificently cadenced periods. It was his good fortune to handle a language still fired with the various energy of youth, and he could contrive the effects of sound and sense which had neither been condemned nor worn out by the thoughtful pedant. Above all, his style had a dramatic quality which suggests to the reader a constant movement, and the value of which, no doubt, was candidly recognised by Shakespeare. An example will best illustrate this peculiar skill of the translator. Here is the prelude to the immortal discourse of Coriolanus:

It was even twy light when he entred the cittie of Antium, and many people met him in the streetes, but no man knewe him. So he went directly to Tullus Aufidius house, and when he came thither, he got him up straight to the chimney harthe, and sat him downe, and spake not a worde to any man, his face all muffled over. They of the house spying him, wondered what he should be, and yet they durst not byd him rise. For, ill-favoredly muffled up and disguised as he was, yet there appeared a certaine majestie in his countenance, and in his silence: whereupon they went to Tullus who was at supper, to tell him of the straunge disguising of this man.

The beauty of this passage is incontestable, and yet it is hard to explain. There is no striving after effect. There are no strange words. If it has a modern air, it is because the words used are of universal significance, and belong neither to this age nor to that. And, simple as they are, they breathe the very spirit of romance. They move and throb with life, as if they were not mere symbols, but were the very essence of drama and of action. Now turn to the French of Amyot, and you will discern the same quality sternly subdued to the finer classicism of the language:

Ainsy s'en alla droict à la maison de Tullus, là où de primsault il entra jusqu'au fouyer, et illec s'assit sans dire mot à personne, ayant le visage couvert et la teste affublée: de quoy ceulx de la maison jeurent bien esbahis, et neantmoins ne l'oserent faire leiver: car encores qu'il se cachast, si recognoissoit on ne sçay quoy de dignité en sa contenance et en son silence, et s'en allerent dire à Tullus, qui souppoit, ceste estrange façon de faire.

At first sight the economy of the French is apparent. The words are fewer and are held together by a firmer thread than in the English version. But North has contrived by a touch here and there to give a picturesqueness to the scene which neither the French nor the Greek warrants. For instance, "they of the house spying him" introduces a new image. *Ceulx de la maison* is in Amyot's version, and corresponds to οἱ κατὰ τὴν οἰκίαν. But the spying is North's own legitimate invention. And again, the words "ill-favoredly muffled up and disguised as he was," which give an accent to the whole passage, represent no more than a particle in the Greek (ἦν γάρ τι καὶ περὶ αὐτὸν κ.τ.λ.), and are far more finely dramatic than the French: *encores qu'il se cachast*. Moreover, the last words of the English passage, "the straunge disguising of this man," find their excuse neither in French nor in Greek. There is a commonness of phrase in τὴν ἀτοπίαν τοῦ πράγματος as in *ceste estrange façon de faire*, which finds no echo in North's splendidly inaccurate rendering. He instantly calls your attention from the thing to the man, and asks you to look once again at the strange muffled figure sitting by the hearth. And this, perhaps, is one of his secrets: an intent always to flatter the eye as well as the ear, and to reveal in pictures the meaning of his author. At any rate, there are few who, were the choice given them, would not rather read Plutarch in the noble English of North than in the restrained and sometimes inexpressive Greek of Plutarch. North, it is true, turned Plutarch's men into heroes of English blood and bone, but, in separating them thus ruthlessly from their origin, he endowed them with a warm, pulsing humanity, of which their author dreamed not.

Philemon Holland was a translator of another kind. His legendary pen was apt for any enterprise. He was a finished master *utriusque linguae*, and so great was his industry that he

is not the hero of one but of half a dozen books.   It was not
for him to ask the aid of French or Italian.   He went straight
to the ancient texts—Greek or Latin—and brought back with
him to his native English spoils which were legitimately his
own.   His whole career was a proper training for the work of
his mature years.   Born in 1552, he was educated at Trinity
College, Cambridge, and, having studied medicine, settled
at Coventry in the practice of his profession.   But humane
letters had laid a stern hand upon him, and, while he cured
the poor in charity, he became usher in the Coventry Grammar
School, and gave his life to scholarship and the muses.   Fuller,
who had a genius for devising names, called him "the Translator Generall in his age," and it is thus that he will be remembered unto the end of time.   As I have said, his knowledge of
Greek and Latin was accurate and profound.   Still rarer was
his knowledge of English.   True, he did not possess the tact
and simplicity of North.   He could not produce wonderful
effects by the use of a few plain words.   His was the romance
not of feeling, but of decoration.   He loved ornament with
the ardour of an ornamental age, and he tricked out his authors
with all the resources of Elizabethan English.   The concision
and reticence of the classics were as nothing to him.   He was
ambitious always to clothe them in the garb which they might
have worn had they been not mere Englishmen, but fantastics
of his own age.   Like all his contemporaries, he was eager to
excuse his own shortcomings.

"According to this purpose and intent of mine," he wrote, "I
frame my pen, not to any affected phrase, but to a meane and
popular stile.   Wherein, if I have called againe into use some old
words, let it be attributed to the love of my countrey language: if
the sentence be not so concise, couched and knit togither as the
originall, loth I was to be obscure and darke: have I not Englished
every word aptly? ech nation hath several maners, yea, and tearmes
appropriate by themselves."

His phrase is never affected; his style is neither mean nor
popular; and thus far he speaks the language of convention.
The rest of the passage is the soundest criticism.   Holland
had a natural love of the old words and proverbs which distinguished his country language.   His sentences are seldom

concise or knit together, and his translations, though not apt
to their orginals, are apt enough to the language of their
adoption. If he seldom echoed the sound of Greek and Latin,
he never missed the sense, nor did he fear a comparison of his
own work with the classical texts. When it was said that his
versions were not in accord with the French or Italian, he
knew that he was in the right of it. "Like as Alcibiades said
to one"—thus he wrote—"*πάταξον οὖν καὶ ἄκουσον, i.e. strike
hardly (Euribiades) so you heare me speake:* even so I say;
Find fault and spare not; but withal, read the original better
before you give sentence." Let his own test be applied to
him, and he will not fail. Take, for instance, a famous passage
in the fifth book of Livy, which describes the salvation of the
Capitol from the Gauls. Here is the Latin, simple and straightforward:

*Anseres non fefellere, quibus sacris Junonis in summa inopia cibi
tamen abstinebatur. Quae res saluti fuit; namque clangore eorum
alarumque crepitu excitus M. Manlius, qui triennio ante consul fuerat,
vir bello egregius, armis arreptis simul ad arma ceteros ciens vadit.*

Holland's English, close as it keeps to the text of Livy, has its
own colour and quality:

"But they could not so escape the geese"—thus it runs—
"which were consecrated unto *Juno*, and for all the scarcitie of
victuals were spared and not killed up. And this it was that saved
them all. For with their gagling and fluttering of their wings,
M. Manlius, who three yeares before had been Consul, a right
hardie and noble warriour, was awaked. Who taking weapon in
hand, speedily went forth and raised the rest withall to take armes."

The English has a plainness to which Holland very rarely
attains; but it is not its plainness nor its perfect harmony that
gives it a character of its own. In the first place, "gagling"
arrests the ear so sharply, that the reader is as wide awake
as M. Manlius himself. And then how admirable in sound and
sense is the equivalent of *vir bello egregius*—"a right hardie
and noble warriour"! It is by such touches as this and by a
feeling of what is musical in prose, which never deserted him,
that Holland produced his effects. His failing from a pedantic
point of view is an excess of ornament. He was not always

content to say what he had to say once. He delighted to turn
a statement about—to put it now in this light, now in that.
"*Jacta est alea*," writes Suetonius. "The dice be thrown,"
says Holland; "I have set up my rest; come what will of it."
His variety and resource are endless. In a single passage he
makes Vitellius his own contemporary.

"Being given most of all to excessive bellie cheere and crueltie,"
he writes, "he devided his repast into three meales every day at
least, and sometime into foure, to wit, Breakfast, Dinner, Supper,
and rere-bankets."

From this, the last drop of Latin austerity is squeezed. And
you can hear Vespasian rioting with his friends when Holland
writes:

given exceedingly hee was to skoffs, and those so skurrile and filthy,
that he could not so much as forbeare words of ribaudrie. And
yet there be many right pleasant conceited jests of his extant.

In such terms as these might Rabelais have composed the
lives of the Roman Emperors. Excellent in tone and movement as is the *Suetonius*, in some respects his *Pliny* is Holland's
masterpiece. The difficulty of this enterprise was far greater.
If the obstacle in the way of a familiar rendering might have
seemed insuperable, Holland has easily surmounted it. He
has thawed the frigid original at the fire of his romantic temper.
"Sirrah (quoth he) remember you are but a shoemaker, and
therefore meddle no higher I advise you than with shoes."
The mere *Sirrah* carries you leagues away from Apelles and
the shoemaker whom he bade look to his last, and reminds you
of the truth that Holland, like the old painters, put the noblest
of his Greeks and Romans into doublet and hose.

His industry was universally applauded. He composed
folios with as little toil as other men give to the writing of
pamphlets. The two largest of his works are separated by a
bare year. It was said that he wrote the whole of Plutarch's
Morals with one pen—a pen which became mythical. "It
seemed that he leaned very lightly on the Neb thereof," says
Fuller, "though weightily enough in another sense, performing
not slightly but solidly what he undertook." Fuller, with his
usual good sense, puts his finger upon the truth. It was the

solidity of Holland's achievement, not its extent, which was remarkable. His industry was always well directed. Few writers have ever kept so consistently at a high level of excellence. He was no master in the art of sinking. His narrative never flags; his argument knows no failure. His style was apt alike for history or reflection. And if he did not accurately represent in English the prose of Livy and Plutarch, of Suetonius and Pliny, he left us a set of variations upon ancient motives to which we may listen with an independent and unalloyed pleasure.

John Florio's *Montaigne* holds a place apart. This translator had neither the sentiment of North nor the scholarship of Holland. He brought to his task that which neither the one nor the other of these masters possessed—a curious fantasy, which was all his own. He was of the stuff whereof pedants are made. He delighted in eccentricity and extravagance. His prefaces are masterpieces of pomp and decoration. Asking, in a breathless refrain, "Madame, now do I flatter you?" he exhausts the language of adulation, until at last he falls back upon ecstatic repetitions. He dedicates the first book of his *Montaigne* "to the Right Honourable my best-best Benefactors, and most-most honored Ladies, Lucie Countesse of Bedford; and hir best-most loved-loving mother Lady Anne Harrington." He plays upon words; he lets sound take the place of sense; he cultivates alliteration, and pleads guilty to "a jirke of the French jargon." A plain simplicity is beyond his reach; he fetches his frequent images from afar. He declares that in his translation he serves "but as Vulcan, to hatchet this Minerva from that Jupiter's bigge braine." When he contemplates his finished work, he strikes an attitude of valiance. "I sweat, I wept, and I went-on, til now I stand at bay." He is modest only when he thinks of his original. "Him have I set before you," says he, "perhaps without his trappings," and his "meate without sauce." But he keeps a stern face even in the presence of his "peerlesse, and in all good gifts unparagonised Ladies"; he tells his reader that he is "still resolute John Florio"; and there is always more of Bobadil in his bearing than of Holofernes.

Upon his version of Montaigne's *Essays* he exhausted his gifts and lavished his temperament. He loved words for their own sakes with a love which Montaigne would not have appreciated, and which will be easily intelligible to all who know Florio's famous *Worlde of Wordes*. Turn where you will in his translation, and you will find flowers of speech, which grow not in the garden of the original. "*Je n'y vauls rien*," says Montaigne, and Florio interprets: "I am nothing worth, and I can never fadge well." For *soufflet* Florio can find nothing simpler than "a whirret in the ear"; for *finesses verbales* he gives us "verbal wily-beguilies," surely a coinage of his own. *Fade* becomes "wallowish," and *crestez* is admirably rendered by "pert and cocket." The "jirke of the French jargon," already mentioned, is evident in such borrowed words as "tintamare," "entrecuidance," "friandize" and "mignardize." He is as fond as Montaigne himself of proverbial phrases. "I will have them to give Plutarch a bob upon mine own lips" has precisely the same sense and sound as the French "*Je veux qu'ils donnent une nazarde à Plutarque sur mon nez.*" And, though the metaphor is changed, "he hath had the canvas" (as who should say "he hath had the sack") is an excellent match for "*cettuy-cy aura donné du nez à terre.*" It will be seen that Florio's method was neither just nor accurate. He made no attempt to suppress himself as we are told a good translator should. The reader never forgets that "resolute John Florio" is looking out from the page as well as Montaigne. He is often inaccurate, and not seldom he misses the point. But compare his version with Cotton's, and you will not hesitate to give the palm to Florio. Cotton's translation is a sound and scholarly piece of work; Florio's is a living book.

The translations in verse made in the age of Elizabeth may not be compared with the translations in prose. For their inferiority there are many plain reasons. Only a poet can render in another tongue the works of a poet, and even a poet cannot ensure a just interpretation. Between one language and another there are obstacles of metre and style, of temper and music, which are most often insuperable. Moreover, in the sixteenth century, the translating of prose was governed by so wise a convention, that mere journeymen could attempt a delicate task without risking conspicuous failure. The secret of verse could not be thus easily imparted, and much that won the approval of its own time appears to us the saddest of doggerel. The enterprise was yet further hampered by a vain love of experiment. An age which desired to leave nothing untried did its best to introduce the hexameter into English verse, and, as Vergil and Ovid composed their poems in hexameters, it seemed proper to some translators to follow an alien example. Ascham began the controversy both by practice and precept. In his *Toxophilus*, he gave the world some poor specimens of the kind. The exercise of some ingenuity may scan the lines which follow:

> What thing wants quiet and meri rest endures but a smal while.
> Both merie songs and good shoting deliteth Apollo.

His precept was better than his practice. He condemned the English hexameter far more effectively than he wrote it. *Carmen exametrum*, said he, "doth rather holte and hoble than run smothly in an English tong." The question, once posed, was hotly debated. Gabriel Harvey wished no other epitaph than this: "the inventor of the English hexameter." Spenser gave Harvey a ready approval, and Nashe, of course, took the other side. "The Hexameter verse," says he, with excellent sense, "I grant to be a gentleman of an auncient house (so is many an English begger); yet this clyme of ours hee cannot thrive in." Time has proved the justice of Nashe's opinion. The experiments of Spenser and Harvey were long since forgotten, and those who turned Vergil and Ovid into their own measures are remembered only as curiosities.

By far the bravest of them was Richard Stanyhurst, who, in 1582, published "the First Foure Bookes of Virgil his Aeneis translated intoo English heroical verse." Whether he wrote in prose or verse, he surpassed in a fantastic eccentricity the vainest of his contemporaries. Never was there a stranger mixture of pedantry and slang than is to be found in his work. His criticism is his own and expressed in his own terms. The verses of Ennius, he says, "savoure soomwhat nappy of thee spigget," and he classes him with Horace, Juvenal and Persius among a "rablement of cheate Poëtes." Vergil, on the other hand, "for his peerelesse style, and matchlesse stuffe doth beare thee prick and price among al thee Roman Poëts." He declares that, if any hold that Phaer's version lightened his enterprise, they "are altogeather in a wrong box." He offers to go over these books again and give them a new livery, which shall neither "jet with Mr. Phaer his badges, ne yeet bee clad with this apparaile wherewith at this present they coom furth atyred." Indeed, he makes light of his labour. Phaer took fifteen days to translate the fourth book. He "huddled up" his in ten. And for this he asks no praise but pardon, adding, characteristically, that "forelittring bitches whelp blynd puppies." But, though he wasted not his time, he did nothing at haphazard. He expounds his theory of the hexameter with great care, and gives every syllable its proper quantity, varying its length according to its termination and to the consonant or vowel which follows it. His labour is lost. Even if his theory were admissible, it would not save his version from ridicule.

Yet, absurd as it is, Stanyhurst's *Vergil* is worth examination. It is a work which owes no debt to anything save to its author's perverted ingenuity. Orthography, metre, vocabulary are each unique. Stanyhurst aimed, not merely at a new prosody, but at a new language. He invented a set of onomatopoeic symbols, which you cannot match elsewhere in literature. What can we make of such lines as these:

Theese flaws theyre cabbans wyth stur snar jarrye doe ransack.

Now doe they rayse gastly lyghtnings, now grislye reboundings
Of ruffe raffe roaring, mens harts with terror agrysing,
With peale meale ramping, with thwick thwack sturdelye thundring?

Not content with these mimicries of sound, he invented whatever new words seemed useful for his purpose. "Mutterus humming," "gredelye bibled," "smacklye bebasse thee," "boucherous hatchet"—these are a few of his false coins. And he used the slang which was modern in his day for the interpretation of Vergil without scruple or shame. Imagine Dido, queen of Carthage, asking in fury: "shall a stranger give me the slampam"! With an equal contempt of fitness he renders *pollutum hospitium* by "Paltock's Inn," and so pleased is he with "Scarboro warning," for the blow before the word, that he uses it with no better excuse than *incautam*, and, in another place, he is guilty of "Scarboro scrabbling" without any excuse at all. As little did he hesitate to mar the epic dignity of Vergil with the popular proverbs of every day, such as "in straw there lurketh some pad," or "as wild as a March hare." And, being bound in the chains of the hexameter, he distorts the order of the words out of all semblance to English, until his version is wholly unintelligible without the friendly aid of the Latin. Yet his monstrous incongruities pleased the taste of his time. Harvey is proud to have been imitated by "learned Mr. Stanyhurst": and Phaer fell, that this "thrasonicall huffe snuffe" might rise. Richard Carew mentions him in the same breath with Sir Philip Sidney, and Francis Meres cites him without disapproval. But critics there were who saw through his pretence. Nashe, above all, rated him at a proper value; and Barnabe Rich did him ample justice in few words: "Among other Fictions," says Rich, "he tooke upon him to translate Virgill, and stript him out of a Velvet gowne into a Fooles coate, out of a Latin Heroicall verse into an English riffe raffe." The question of the English hexameter has received a final answer, and, for us, Stanyhurst is but an episode in the history of literature. And what an episode! His very gravity makes him the more ludicrous, and his only pupils are Charles Cotton, Thomas Bridges, captain Alexander Radcliffe and the other writers of burlesque.

To Stanyhurst, Thomas Phaer was an insignificant competitor. But he had enjoyed twenty years of fame before Stanyhurst's version was printed, and, though momentarily depressed, he survived the absurd fashion of the hexameter in the esteem of his contemporaries. Webbe praises his "most gallant verse," and chooses him as an example to prove "the meetnesse of our speeche to receive the best forme of poetry." The proof is deficient. Phaer was no poet, and very ill-skilled to present the beauty of Vergil in English verse. As Anthony à Wood says, he was "a person of a mutable mind," who addicted his muse to many studies. Educated at Oxford, he studied law, wrote a work *Of the Nature of Writts* and presently adopted medicine as his profession. In brief, translation was his pastime, and, doubtless, his knowledge of the healing art was profounder than his knowledge of English or Latin. His *Vergil*, composed in lines of fourteen syllables, like Golding's *Ovid* and Chapman's *Homer*, never rises above a facile mediocrity. The translator constantly sacrifices taste and sense to the demands of rime, and mixes in a kind of familiar jingle the easy stateliness of the original. Even in the rare passages which display some movement and energy, he descends suddenly upon the wrong word, and sets the reader on his guard. Here, for instance, is his rendering of the celebrated lines, *Monstrum horrendum ingens*, etc., in the fourth book:

A monster gastly great, for every plume her carkas beares
Lyke number leering eies she hath, like number harckning eares,
Lyke number tounges and mouthes she waggs, a wondrous thing to
　　speake;
At midnight fourth she flies, and under shade her sounde doth
　　squeake.

If the first two lines might pass muster, no word can be said in defence of the others. With the word "squeake," Phaer descends into bathos, and the best that can be said for him is that, while Stanyhurst always lets his reason go, Phaer is sometimes sane.

　　The best loved of all the ancient poets was Ovid, whose popularity is attested by many translations of varying worth. The first version in point of date is *The Fable of Ovid treting of Narcissus, translated oute of Latin into Englysh Mytre, with a moral therein to, very pleasante to rede.* This was followed, five years later, by the first edition of Arthur Golding's work (1565), of which more will be said presently. In 1567, George Turbervile printed *The Heroycall Epistles of the learned Poet Publius Ovidius Naso*, and, in 1577, there came from the press two versions of *Ovid his Invective against Ibis*, one of which is the work of Thomas Underdowne, to whom, also, we owe the *Aethiopian Historie* of Heliodorus. Marlowe turned the *Elegies* into rimed couplets, and George Chapman, in 1595, published *Ovid's Banquet of Sauce, a coronet for his Mistress Philosophy, and his amorous Zodiac.* *De Tristibus* was Englished by Churchyard, and Francis Beaumont gave proof of his skill in a lively version of *Salmacis and Hermaphroditus*. The cause of Ovid's popularity is not far to seek. He was an efficient guide to the Greek and Roman mythologies, and he furnished the poets with theme, sentiment and allusion. Of all the translations, by far the most famous was Arthur Golding's rendering of the *Metamorphoses*. The first edition (1565) contained but four books. In 1567, the work was complete. It is described on the title-page as "a worke very pleasaunt and delectable," and a stern couplet warns the reader against frivolity:

> With skill, heede, and judgement, thys work must be red,
> For els to the reader it stands in small stead.

Golding's motive, in truth, was above suspicion. His work was "pleasaunt and delectable" by accident. He wished to improve the occasion before all things. In a long epistle, addressed to Robert earl of Leicester, he clearly sets forth his purpose. There is no fable of Ovid which does not make for edification. For instance:

> In Phaeton's fable untoo syght the Poet dooth expresse
> The natures of ambition blynd, and youthful wilfulnesse.

And a little ingenuity will interpret every book in a sense most profitable to the reader. That Ovid and his heroes were paynims he confesses with regret, and takes heart in the reflection that they may all be reduced "too ryght of Christian law." In the same spirit, he hopes that the simple sort of reader will not be offended when he sees the heathen names of feigned gods in the book, and assures him that every living wight, high and low, rich and poor, master and slave, maid and wife, simple and brave, young and old, good and bad, wise and foolish, lout and learned man, shall see his whole estate, words, thoughts and deeds in this mirror. It is a bold claim of universality, which Ovid himself would not have made. But it was in tune with the temper of the age, and, doubtless, added to the popularity of the work.

The chief characteristic of the translation is its evenness. It never falls below or rises above a certain level. The craftsmanship is neither slovenly nor distinguished. The narrative flows through its easy channel without the smallest shock of interruption. In other words, the style is rapid, fluent and monotonous. The author is never a poet and never a shirk. You may read his mellifluous lines with something of the same simple pleasure which the original gives you. Strength and energy are beyond Golding's compass, and he wisely chose a poet to translate who made no demand upon the qualities he did not possess. He chose a metre, too, very apt for continuous narrative—the long line of fourteen syllables—and it is not strange that his contemporaries bestowed upon him their high approval. Puttenham paid him no more than his due when he described him as "in translation very cleare and very faithfully answering his author's intent." He won the rare and difficult praise of Thomas Nashe, and he was honoured by Shakespeare, who did not disdain to borrow of his verses. The lines which follow will recall to everyone a celebrated passage in *The Tempest*:

Ye Ayres and windes: ye Elves of Hills, of Brookes, of Woods alone,
Of standing Lakes, and of the Night approche ye everychone.

And Golding was by no means a man of one book. He turned Latin and French into English with equal facility. Had it not been for Holland, he might justly have been called the "Translator Generall in his age." A friend of Sir Philip Sidney, he completed that poet's translation of De Mornay's *Woorke concerning the trewnesse of the Christian Religion*. To him we owe our earliest and best version of Caesar's *Gallic War* (1565), besides *The abridgemente of the Histories of Trogus Pompeius, gathered and written in the Latin tung by the famous Historiographer Justin* (1570), several works translated from Calvin and the *Politicke, Moral and Martial Discourses written in French by M. Jacques Hurault* (1595). In brief, he tried his hand at many enterprises and failed in none, and Webbe's panegyric might still stand for his epitaph:

 For which Gentleman surely our Country hath greatly to gyve God thankes: as for him which hath taken infinite paynes without ceasing, travelling as yet indefatigably, and is addicted without society by his continuall laboure to profit this nation and speeche in all kind of good learning.

 Though Ovid and Vergil were the favourites, the other poets were by no means neglected. Another reign saw the completion of Chapman's vigorous and faithful *Homer*, which Pope should never have displaced, but he published a translation of seven books of the *Iliad* in 1598, and a word must be said here of his splendid achievement. To do full justice to Chapman's work a continuous reading is necessary. It shines less brightly in isolated passages than in its whole surface, various and burnished, like the shield of Achilles. It is a poet's echo of a poet —loud and bold. Justly may the same indulgence be granted Chapman which he would claim for Homer: he "must not bee read for a few lynes with leaves turned over caprichiously in dismembred fractions, but throughout, the whole drift, weight, and height of his workes set before the apprensive eyes of his judge." Then shall we perceive the true merit of Chapman's masterpiece. From end to end it gives proof of an abounding life, a quenchless energy. There is a grandeur and spirit in Chapman's rendering, not unworthy the original, "of all bookes extant in all kinds the first and best." The long, swinging line of fourteen syllables, chosen for the *Iliad*, is the fairest representative of Homer's majestic hexameters, and it is matter for regret that Chapman preferred the heroical distich in his rendering of the *Odyssey*. Moreover, Chapman claimed an advantage over his fellows in that he translated his author without a French or Latin intermediary. His knowledge of Greek was not impeccable. Errors due to ignorance or haste are not infrequent, nor need they cause us surprise, if it be true, as he asserts, that he translated the last twelve books in fifteen weeks. As little need they incur our censure. If Chapman, the scholar, sometimes nodded, Chapman, the poet, was ever awake, and his version of Homer will ever remain one among the masterpieces of his age and country.

In his prefaces, he vindicates both Homer and himself from the detraction of enemies. Admitting proudly that his manner of writing is "farre fecht, and, as it were, beyond sea," he defends, as well he may, his "varietie of new wordes." If "my countrey language were an usurer," says he, "hee would thanke me for enriching him." Chaucer had more new words than any man since him need devise,

and therefore for currant wits to crie from standing braines, like a broode of Frogs from a ditch, to have the ceaseless flowing river of our tongue turnde into their Frogpoole, is a song farre from their arrogation of sweetnes.

And, ready as he was, in his "harmlesse and pious studie," to esteem the policies and wisdoms of his enemies at no more value than a musty nut, he was readier still to champion the

fame of Homer, especially against the "soule-blind Scaliger"
and his "palsied diminuation." He did not belittle the beauty
of the *Aeneid*, but, with perfect truth, declared that Homer's
poems were "writ from a free furie," Vergil's out of a "courtly,
laborious, and altogether imitatorie spirit." In brief, he was
loyal alike in commentary and interpretation, and, as he
hailed Homer "the Prince of Poets," so he himself may justly
be styled the prince of poetical translators. But even he had
his forerunners. In 1579, Thomas Purfoote gave to English
what he calls *The Croune of Homer's Works, or The Battel of
the Frogges and Myce*, and, in 1581, Author Hall, M.P. for
Grantham, translated ten books of the *Iliad* from the French.
Of Horace, Thomas Drant Englished both *Satires* and *Epistles;*
Marlowe turned a book of Lucan into blank verse; and Timothy
Kendall's *Flowres of Epigrammes* (1575 and 1577) were gathered out of sundry authors and particularly from Martial. The
deficiency in Greek drama, as has been said, was made up for
by many versions of Seneca, and there was no reason why
an Englishman of the sixteenth century, who had not the
ancient tongues, should have been deprived of a fair knowledge
of the Greek and Latin poets.

Of modern poets there is not so long a tale to tell. Dante
was unknown, and Petrarch was revealed for the most part
surreptitiously under the names of his translators. The most
widely read of them all was Du Bartas, styled by Gabriel Harvey "the Treasury of Humanity and the Jewell of Divinity,"
whose *Divine Weekes and Workes* was translated into rimed
decasyllabic verse by Joshua Sylvester (1590–2). The popularity which this version enjoyed is not easily intelligible, and
the fact that Milton sought therein some sort of inspiration
is not enough to tempt a modern curiosity. Tasso's masterpiece found two translators in Edward Fairfax and Richard
Carew, and Sir John Harington, at the behest of queen Elizabeth, made a version of Ariosto's *Orlando Furioso* (1591) in
eight-lined stanzas. His translation, like the other verse
translations of the time, displays care and fluidity without distinction. Its rapid course knows neither check nor variety.
Its style is rather familiar than dignified, and Harington errs
like Stanyhurst in the use of modern slang. Such lines as

They tooke them to a fort, with such small treasure,
And in so Scarborow warning they had leasure,

suggest the barbarism of the barbarous *Aeneid*. Harington,
moreover, embellished his text with a set of notes, in which he
extols his family and his friends. In brief, he was a pedant
and a courtier, who took to letters as a pastime, and practised
them after the fashion of his kind. In a characteristic preface,
he defended the craft of the poet, his chosen author, and his
own enterprise. Though the craft, as he knew well enough,
needed no apology, he could not refrain from breaking a lance
with Puttenham, whose treatise had recently been published,
and who had withheld the "high and supernatural" title of
maker from mere translators. In his defence of Ariosto,
Harington appeals to authority and to sound morals. The
Italian poet, says his translator, follows the rules of Aristotle.
More than this, he follows Vergil with a patient fidelity. "Virgill extolled Aeneas to please Augustus; Ariosto prayseth
Rogero to the honour of the house of Este." And does not
Alcina beguile Rogero, as Dido beguiled Aeneas? It is clear,
therefore, that Ariosto should share the common eulogy of
Vergil. Indeed, he may claim a higher praise, because there
may be found in his many writings passages of which Vergil
was incapable—such as the Christian demeanour of Charle-
magne in the 14th book, and the conversion of Rogero to the
Christian faith in the 41st. Briefly, Harington treats Vergil
as Golding treated Ovid, and reproves him, in sorrow rather
than in anger, for his inevitable paganism. As for the mention
of himself and his kinsmen in his notes, to which Harington
pleads guilty, he made them because Plutarch blamed Homer
for nowhere explaining of what stock he was, of what town,
or of what country. "Excuse me, then," says he, "if I in a
work that may perhaps last longer than a better thing, and
being not ashamed of my kindred, name them here and there
to no man's offence." No excuse is necessary. Who would
blame a whimsical scholar for chattering of himself and for
interrupting a serious work with amiable anecdotage?

Besides the translations openly made and avowed, there
are others which masquerade as fresh, unborrowed works. In
his *Elizabethan Sonnets*, Sidney Lee has traced to their origin

in France or Italy a vast number of English sonnets. He has
proved the debt which the poets of the sixteenth century
owed to their predecessors. He has set side by side in a close
parallel the sonnets of Lodge and Ronsard, of Daniel and
Desportes. He has shown most clearly what Wyatt and many
others took from Petrarch. He has illustrated the "influence"
of Marot, du Bellay, de Pontoux, Jacques de Billy and Durant
upon our bards, great and small. As an episode in the history
of translation this "influence" is of the greatest interest. We
should not consider its moral aspect too censoriously. In
Puttenham's despite, the Elizabethans do not seem to have
regarded plagiarism as a heinous sin. If they had, who would
have escaped condemnation? No doubt Southern, who pilfered from Ronsard, and spoiled what he pilfered, deserved
all the censure which the critic heaped upon him. But there
are indications not merely that plagiarism was thought respectable, but that a translator might claim as his own that
which he had put into English. "I call it mine," says Nicholas
Grimald of his translation of Cicero's *De Officiis*, "as Plautus
and Terence called the comedies theirs which they made out of
Greek"; and, doubtless, Wyatt, Daniel, Lodge, Spenser and
the rest called the sonnets theirs which they had made out
of French and Italian, because they had made them. Ben
Jonson did not think it worth while to give Philostratus credit
for his "Drink to me only with thine eyes," and he left it for
the critics of a later age to track every chapter of his *Discoveries*
to its lair. In neither case need the morality of his method be
discussed, and Dryden's defence of him may stand as a defence
for all save for such burglars as Southern: "He has done his
robberies so openly, that we may see that he fears not to be
taxed by any law. He invades authors like a monarch; and
what would be theft in other poets, is only victory in him."

CHAPTER II

The "Authorised Version" and its Influence

IF the *Authorised Version*[1] of the Bible be the first English classic, as seems by all competent authorities to be allowed, two enquiries suggest themselves: first, what is meant when it is called a classic, and, secondly, what are the qualities that entitle it to be ranked as the first classic in English? In other words, it will be necessary first to examine the Bible as literature, irrespective of any translation whatever; and, secondly, to examine its diction in the standard English translation, in order to see whether the choice of words, the mould of sentences and the harmonious disposition of sounds are such as deserve the highest praise, in comparison with the choicest productions of native English genius.

These two enquiries, however—the one into the nature of the Bible considered as literature, and the other into the nature of the English in which our standard version is written—will, of necessity, imply some consideration of the successive stages by which what we call the Bible grew into being, and of the successive stages by which the English of our Bible was gradually selected, imbued with the proper meanings and associations, and ordered into a fit medium for the conveyance of the high thoughts and noble emotions in which the original abounds. Especially is it true of our second enquiry that no adequate conception of the language employed in the Jacobean version can be formed, save through at least a brief survey of the series of English translations which led up to it. Their indebtedness to their predecessors is recognised most clearly

---

[1] Notwithstanding the current use of this term, the Jacobean revision was never publicly authorised by parliament or convocation, privy council or king. The acceptance which it has enjoyed has been won chiefly on its merits.

by the translators of the *Authorised Version*, who say in their preface:

Truly, good Christian reader, we never thought, from the beginning, that we should need to make a new translation, nor yet to make of a bad one a good one; . . . but to make a good one better, or out of many good ones one principal good one, not justly to be excepted against—that hath been our endeavour, that our mark.

The Bible either proceeds from divine inspiration, as some will have it, or, according to others, is the fruit of the religious genius of the Hebrew race. From either point of view, the authors are highly gifted individuals, who, notwithstanding their diversities, and the progressiveness observable in their representations of the nature of God, are wonderfully consistent in the main tenor of their writings, and serve, in general, for mutual confirmation and illustration. In some cases, this may be due to the revision of earlier productions by later writers, which has thus brought more primitive conceptions into a degree of conformity with maturer and profounder views; but, even in such cases, the earlier conception often lends itself, without wrenching, to the deeper interpretation and the completer exposition.

The Bible is not distinctively an intellectual achievement. Like all other great works of literature, it springs from, and addresses, human nature as a whole. It has no more to do with intellect than with sensibility, imagination, or will. In fact, if it be more concerned with one of these faculties than another, sensibility, the sphere of the emotions, is the one that has pre-eminence over the rest.

The character of the Bible as a whole is best understood by regarding the Old Testament as its representative, and devoting attention primarily to that. It is the Hebraic temper, and the achievements of the Hebrew genius, that give the Bible a unique place among books; and these racial traits were much less subject to modification by alien influences—such as that of Greek culture—in the period covered by the Old Testament, than during the epoch in which the composition of the New Testament was effected. Much of the difficulty, for example, encountered in the adequate rendering of St. Paul's

epistles into another tongue is due to elements in his writing
which are not common to him and the writers of the Old
Testament, but belong specifically to him as one who had
received a tincture of Greek learning, which, in modifying his
thought, had also modified his speech. The tone of the Bible,
then, is given to it by the Old Testament, which, therefore,
may be considered as the type of the whole.

Its themes are the greatest that literature can treat. They
may be reduced to three—God, man and the physical universe.
The physical universe is regarded as subordinate and even
subject, to man, within the measure of his capacity and needs,
while man, in his turn, is subject to God. The visible creation
reveals the wisdom, power and skill of its Maker. Man's
constitution being related to that of the world about him, he
finds in the latter provision for his physical wants, and a
certain satisfaction, falling, however, short of the highest, for
his spiritual cravings. The relations of one human being to
another, and of all spiritual existences among themselves, are
partly matters of positive ordinance, and partly to be inferred
from their relations to God. Thus, if God is the Father of all,
all men are brethren. God is represented as desiring to draw
man into closer and closer union with Himself, or as restoring
man to his original condition of friend and trustful child. Such
eventual and complete restoration is to be effected through
the agency of the Hebrew people, but particularly of certain
leaders—patriarchs, prophets and others—who, accordingly,
are made the subjects of more or less extended biographies.

Speaking generally, the three species of literature in the
Old Testament, succeeding one another in the order of time,
are: narrative, poetry—chiefly lyrical—and prophecy. In the
New Testament, the epistles may be said to represent prophecy,
and the *Revelation* to be partly of a prophetic, and partly of
a poetical, character, so far as these two can be distinguished.

Narrative, then, comes first in order of time, as in order of
books. It deals with the early history of mankind, and the
great epochs, especially the earlier, in the history of the Hebrew
race. As suggested above, it delineates history largely under
the form of biography, its most universally interesting form,
and these biographies are full of ups and downs, of lights and
shadows, both in characters and events. Conceived as affect-

ing the ultimate destinies of all mankind, and, indeed, of every individual soul, these lives, presented in bold and picturesque outlines, are among the most enthralling of stories.

Next in order to the narrative books, thus filled with matter of deepest import and overwhelming interest to the race, come the poetic books, of which the *Psalter* is the chief. Some of the psalms are founded upon chapters of the national history, and all presuppose an acquaintance with the national religion. In turn, the psalms of an earlier period are subject to reworking at a later epoch, to express more perfectly the sentiments of the individual or the religious community. The same staple of matter thus reappears in a variety of forms, all of them charged with sincerity, fervour, or even passion.

The prophetic books form the third main division. After story and song come monition and reproof, mingled with predictions of a better time. The prophet has much in common with the poet, but is more didactic, and is concerned with the national life rather than with the individual. Like the poet, the prophet rehearses or alludes to God's dealings with His people, so that continuity of motive is maintained throughout. A projection into the future opens up occasional vistas of limitless range and surpassing beauty, which give scope and direction to such hopes as men are prone to conceive for themselves or their descendants.

The first condition of great literature is a unity of theme and concept that shall give coherence and organisation to all detail, however varied. By this test the Bible is great literature. One increasing purpose runs through the whole, and is reflected in the widening and deepening thought of the writers; yet it is a purpose which exists germinally at the beginning, and unfolds like a bud. Thus, all the principal books are linked and even welded together, and to the common consciousness form, as it were, but a single book, rather τὸ βιβλίον than τὰ βιβλία.

By far the greater part of the books which the world has agreed to call classic—that is, permanently enjoyable and permanently helpful—are marked by dignity of theme and earnestness of treatment. The theme or themes of the Bible are of the utmost comprehensiveness, depth and poignancy of appeal. In the treatment there is nowhere a trace of

levity or insincerity to be detected. The heart of a man is felt
to be pulsating behind every line. There is no straining for
effect, no obtrusive ornament, no complacent parading of the
devices of art. Great matters are presented with warmth of
sentiment, in a simple style; and nothing is more likely to
render literature enduring.

Another trait of good literature exemplified by the Bible
is breadth. Take, for example, the story of Jacob, the parable
of the Prodigal Son, or St. Paul's speech on Mars' hill. Only
the essentials are given. There is no petty and befogging
detail. The characters, the events, or the arguments stand
out with clearness, even with boldness. An inclusive and
central effect is produced with a few masterly strokes, so that
the resulting impression is one of conciseness and economy.

Closely associated with this quality of breadth is that of
vigour. The authors of the Bible have no time nor mind to
spend upon the elaboration of curiosities, or upon minute and
trifling points. Every sentence, nay, every word, must count.
The spirit which animates the whole must inform every particle.
There is no room for delicate shadings; the issues are too
momentous, the concerns too pressing, to admit of introducing
anything that can be spared. A volume is compressed into
a page, a page into a line.

And God said, Let there be light, and there was light.

Jesus wept.

It would not be difficult to show how all these qualities
flow necessarily from the intense preoccupation of the Biblical authors with matters affecting all they held dear, all their
hopes and fears with respect to their country, their family and
themselves, at the present and in a boundless future. Even
when the phrases employed seem cool and measured, they
represent a compressed energy like that of a tightly coiled
spring, tending to actuate effort and struggle of many kinds,
and to open out into arts and civilisations of which the Hebrew
never dreamed.

In a sense, then, it is the lyrical faculty that distinguishes
the Hebrew author. Yet he is not an Aeolian harp, delicately
responsive to every zephyr of sentiment. His passions are few
and elemental, and, as we have seen, are prone to utter them-

selves energetically. One is tempted to compare the great lyric, as it has been called, of the Hebrew, with the effusions, or rather the creations, of Sappho and Pindar. Yet Sappho and Pindar must suffer in the comparison. Addison speaks of Horace and Pindar as showing, when confronted with the *Psalms*, "an absurdity and confusion of style," and "a comparative poverty of imagination." As for Sappho, her longest extant production, while intense, shows, in conjunction with the shorter fragments, that her deeper emotion is limited in range, and, because of this limitation, and the tropical fervour displayed, is less universal in its appeal than the best lyrical outpourings of the Hebrew genius. These include, not only the *Psalms*, but much of *Job*, the best of the prophets, a good deal of the *Apocalypse*, occasional passages of St. Paul, and even parts of the narrative books, especially those which report the utterances of notable persons.

It has been asserted that the Hebrews of the Old Testament were incapable of producing either drama or fiction, and, one might add, the leisurely developments of the epic. This is only another way of affirming their lyrical intensity and preoccupation. The destruction of Sennacherib's host is related with exultation, and the historian of *Exodus* rejoices over the destruction of the Egyptians in the Red Sea. He is no more dispassionate than Tacitus in excoriating Nero, or Joinville in his devotion to St. Louis. Events are never displayed in that "dry light" so dear, as they supposed, to Heraclitus and Francis Bacon. There are always postulates which nothing could induce the writer to discard. There is always a presumption in favour of monotheism, of God's protecting or punitive care for the people of Israel, of their eventual deliverance and full entrance upon their divinely ordained mission. The poet or prophet could never be brought to admit that there might be gods many, nor that the Hebrew people were not fore-ordained to pre-eminence over Philistines and Assyrians.

But this egoism, this racial pride, which manifest themselves by a strong colouring and a decided tone, and which are at the furthest possible remove from scientific indifferentism, do not prevent the Bible from possessing a universality which has placed it at the foundation, or the head, or both, of all modern literatures. There are several reasons for this. Every one is interested in the origin of the world and of man. It may be urged that no other literature gives so plain and coherent an account of these origins, and of the early history of mankind, as the book of *Genesis*. Next, the Bible emphasises the conception that all nations are of one blood, and that all men are brethren, since their Father is one. This, in satisfying the social instinct, has tended more and more to draw tribe to tribe, and kingdom to kingdom, as well as individual to individual, and, indirectly, has appealed to national and personal ambition. Thirdly, the morality of the Bible, even where it takes the form of statutory enactments, keeps in view the interests of individual happiness and social well-being. Fourthly, the Hebrew race is presented as, in some sort, the prototype, or the beneficent elder brother, of all other races and nationalities, so that any of its experiences are likely to find a parallel in subsequent history, or even to help in making subsequent history. Fifthly, the future of mankind is regarded in the Bible as bound up with the general acceptance of Hebrew principles and ideals. Sixthly, the utmost fulness of individual life is represented as conditional upon the acceptance of that God who first distinctly revealed Himself to the Hebrews, upon obedience to Him and upon spiritual union with Him. With this is associated the Messianic hope of a Deliverer, who, greater than His brethren, yet even as they, should serve to bring God down to man, and lift man up to God. These, perhaps, are reasons enough why, notwithstanding the lyric note which is everywhere heard throughout the Bible, it possesses also a character of universality, and, one might also say, of impersonality. Thus, the *Psalter*, the most lyrical part of the Bible, is perhaps the widest in its appeal of any, simply because the cry of the individual believer, however impassioned, finds an echo in every other believing soul, and is not without some response from the most apathetic.

As to form, in the sense of order and proportion, it is often assumed that the Greeks alone possessed its secret in antiquity, and bequeathed some hint of it to the modern world. Perhaps, in an endeavour to vindicate for the Hebrews a sense of form, we may best appeal to authority; and, if so, we can hardly decline to accept the judgment of a man who, classically educated, and possessed of a Frenchman's love of order and beauty, was a Semitic scholar of unusual scope and insight. It was Renan who said:

Israel had, like Greece, the gift of disengaging its idea perfectly, and of expressing it in a concise and finished outline; proportion, measure, taste were, in the Orient, the exclusive privilege of the Hebrew people, and because of this they succeeded in imparting to thought and feeling a form general and acceptable to all mankind.

It is true that, if we regard the technicalities of literary construction, a book of the Bible will not infrequently seem to fall short; but this is because the author is not intent upon structure of a patent and easily definable sort. If he secures unity of impression with variety in detail, it is often by the use of other means, and especially through an intrinsic and enthralling power which pervades his whole composition. Structure in the more usual sense is, however, to be found in limited portions, such as the story of Joseph, a single prophecy, or a speech from the *Acts of the Apostles*.

An attempt has been made above to show what there is in the constitution and qualities of the Bible entitling it to be called a classic. In what follows, the aim will be to consider the process by which it became an *English* classic, and the influence it has exerted, and continues to exert, in that capacity. Before attempting this directly, however, we shall need briefly to examine the problem which it presents to the translator.

The nature of the Hebrew language first demands consideration. Its most noticeable feature is its deficiency in abstract and general terms. It has no philosophical or scientific vocabulary. Nearly every word presents a concrete meaning, clearly visible even through a figurative use. Many of its roots are verbal, and the physical activity underlying each word is felt through all its special applications. Thus, to take a single example, there is a Hebrew word variously rendered in the following passages by *bud, east, spring, outgoing, going out*.

Job xxxviii, 27: To cause the *bud* of the tender herb to spring forth.

Psalm lxxv, 6: For promotion cometh neither from the *east* nor from the west.

2 *Kings* ii, 21: And he went forth unto the *spring* of the waters.

Psalm lxv, 8: Thou makest the *outgoings* of the morning and evening to rejoice.

2 *Sam.* iii, 25: Thou knowest . . . that he came to deceive thee, and to know thy *going out* and thy coming in, and to know all that thou doest.

In every one of these cases the Hebrew word means "going out" or "going forth," and the Hebrew so understands it; but the "going forth" of the sun is one thing, and that of the waters another. Now, if we could suppose the word "bud" or "east" in English to present to the imagination, as transparently as "spring" does, the original activity which the word records, we should better understand what is true of practically all Hebrew words. Everywhere we are face to face with motion, activity, life. Of the Hebrew words for pride, one presents the notion of mounting up, one of strutting, and one of seething, as a boiling pot. What fundamental idea of similar concreteness does the English word "pride" suggest?

There were not many abstract ideas to be conveyed in Biblical Hebrew; the absence of the words is a sign of the absence of the ideas. Such a sentence as "The problem of external perception is a problem in metaphysics," or "The modifications produced within our nervous system are the only states of which we can have a direct consciousness," would be untranslatable into ancient Hebrew. It is hardly too much to say that every generalisation —or, better, every general truth —expressed by the Hebrew is rendered with the utmost directness, and in phraseology as pictorial, as elemental, as transparent, as stimulative to imagination and feeling, as could possibly be. Such a language is the very language of poetry. The medium through which poetry works is the world of sensible objects—wine and oil, the cedar of Lebanon, the young lion, the moon, the cloud, the smoking hills, the wild goat, the coney and the stork; or, if we turn to Homer rather than the Psalmist, a plane-tree, the bright water of a spring, a snake blood-red on the back, the cheeping brood of a sparrow, or beaked ships and well-greaved Achaians. What is necessary in order to make poetry out of such materials is intensity of feeling, with elevation and coherence of thought. These, we have seen, were the endowment of the Hebrews. On the one hand, they were close to nature; they had not parcelled out their human constitution into separate and independent faculties; they had not interposed a cloud and hubbub of words between themselves and things; they had not so dissipated their powers in minute and laborious analysis that they were incapable of naïve views, powerful sensations and vigorous convictions. On the other hand, they had, as tending to coherence and elevation of thought, what to them was a sufficient explanation of all the wonders of the universe, and a sufficient impulse to lift up their hearts: these they found in their overmastering belief in God the Creator, God the Maintainer, and, for those who trust and love Him, God the Deliverer.

But not only were their words concrete—the structure of their sentences was simple, while of the paragraph, in the Greek sense, they had hardly any conception, until, in the New Testament, we find their diction fallen under Greek influence. Their chief connective was "and"—hence the periodic sentence was, virtually, beyond their scope. The verse was their stylistic unit; and a sequence of verses, or of sentences about the length of what we understand by the average Biblical verse, was all that they aimed at achieving in composition.

Their poetry was measured, not by feet, as in ancient Latin and Greek, but by word-accents, as in the most ancient poetry of many nations, including that of our English ancestors. Moreover, Hebrew poetry was dominated by the principle of parallelism of members. Often these members are arranged in couplets, but sometimes they include several lines. The three primary forms of parallelism are the synonymous, the synthetic and the antithetic. Thus, synonymous:

Psalm xv, 1: (*a*) Lord, who shall abide in thy tabernacle? (*b*) Who shall dwell in thy holy hill?

Synthetic (a succeeding line or lines supplementing or completing the first):

Psalm xiv, 2: (*a*) The Lord looked down from heaven upon the children of men, (b) to see if there were any that did understand, and seek God.

Antithetic:

Prov. x, 1: (a) A wise son maketh a glad father, (b) but a foolish son is the heaviness of his mother.

Besides these, there are variations, such as climactic parallelism, where an expression in the first line is repeated in one or more that follow:

Psalm xxiv, 8: (a) The Lord strong and mighty, (b) the Lord mighty in battle.

The formation of the strophe, and devices such as the refrain, are less important. What is chiefly to be noted is, first, that Hebrew poetry has a decided accentual rhythm, and, secondly, that the dominant principle in the union of lines into larger groups is that of parallelism. The controlling rhythm is, therefore, the rhythm of meaning, what Watts-Dunton has called "sense-rhythm," this, as he observes, being the rhythm of nature. Stanley eloquently says:

"The rapid stroke as of alternate wings," "the heaving and sinking as of the troubled heart," which have been beautifully described as the essence of the parallel structure of Hebrew verse, are exactly suited for the endless play of human feeling, and for the understanding of every age and nation.

Much of Hebrew prose was poetical, in the sense that it employed these devices to a greater or less extent, and all of it was poetical in the sense described above in the discussion of the Hebrew vocabulary. The prophets, in particular, frequently rise into a strain which is hardly distinguishable from poetry.

The qualities, then, which fitted the Bible, beyond any other book of the world, for translation, are, among others, these:

(a) Universality of interest. There is much in it for the meanest and most illiterate, and its treasures are not to be exhausted by the wisest. It touches every person at more points than any other book that can be named.

(b) The concreteness and picturesqueness of its language, appealing alike to the child and the poet, while suggesting abundant reflection to the philosopher.

(c) The simplicity of its structure, which requires little more from the translator than that he shall render with fidelity one brief clause at a time, and follow it by the next.

(d) A rhythm largely independent of the features, prosodical or other, of any individual language — a rhythm free, varied and indeterminate, or, rather, determinate only by what has been called "the energy of the spirit which sings within the bosom of him who speaks," and therefore adaptable to every emotion, from the most delicate to the most energetic.

It follows that the sway of the original is so powerful that hardly any translation will be devoid of merit, while infinite room is still left for felicities of detail, according to the character of the medium and the skill and taste of the translator.

Among the qualifications of a good translator, the first, undoubtedly, is that he shall be penetrated by a sense of the surpassing value of his original, and a corresponding sense of the importance of his task. This will preserve him from flippancy and meanness, by imbuing him with earnestness and humility. It will make him ready to follow wherever he is led by the text, and will prevent him from pluming himself upon prettiness of phrase, or any fancies of his own. Such a translator will strive with all his might after fidelity to word and sense, and after the utmost clearness and simplicity of rendering, avoiding, on the one hand, the trivial, and, on the other, the ornate or pompous. He will conform to the genius of his own tongue while endeavouring to transfer to it the treasures of another; and, besides possessing naturally, he will cultivate, in every proper way, a sensitiveness to that music of the phrase, which, in the case of the Bible, is but another name for the music of the heart. Only a few translators have united these endowments in a just proportion, but among them must be counted Jerome, the first of the great translators whom we know by name, the author—though he called himself rather the reviser—of the Latin *Vulgate*.

Of Jerome's fitness for his task the following illustration will serve. It is worthy of attention, moreover, as presenting the verses contained in the various English specimens which follow:

Exod. xix, 16, 18, 19: *Jamque advenerat tertius dies, et mane inclaruerat, et ecce coeperunt audiri tonitrua, et micare fulgura, et nubes densissima operire montem, clangorque buccinae vehementius perstrepebat, et timuit populus qui erat in castris. . . . Totus autem mons Sinai fumabat, eo quod descendisset Dominus super eum in igne, et ascenderet fumus ex eo quasi de fornace; eratque omnis mons terribilis. Et sonitus buccinae paulatim crescebat in majus, et prolixius tendebatur.*

The language into which the Bible can be most perfectly rendered will, in the first place, be popular, in distinction from artificial or scholastic. Its vocabulary will consist of such words as ordinary people would naturally use to describe objects or utter their emotions. It will abound in concrete expressions, and need but few learned or recondite terms. The words should, if possible, exhibit their primitive meaning on their face, or, at least, suggest immediately a single central meaning which can be accepted as radical and primary. They must, in general, while racy and vernacular, be free from degrading or belittling associations, so that they may be equally suitable for the middle or ordinary style and for passages of any degree of elevation up to the highest. A considerable proportion of them must possess sonority, or contain such admixtures of vowels and musical consonants as will ensure, according to the need, a scale of melodious effects ranging from serene and quiet harmonies to rich and rolling *crescendos* — but all without appearance of effort, instinctively responsive to the situation, and to the feeling which the situation evokes. If the rhythmical effects of a language are attained through the alternation of stressed and unstressed syllables, such a language will so far resemble the Hebrew, and serve as a natural medium for the transmission of the original effects.

The influences which moulded the English language into a proper vehicle for so stupendous a literary creation as the Bible must next be briefly considered. Early in the eighth century, Bede was making a translation into Old English of the *Gospel of John*, and, about the year 800 A.D., the language was already capable of such poetry as this from the *Christ* of Cynewulf : [1]

Thereupon from the four corners of the world, from the uttermost regions of earth, angels all-shining shall with one accord blow their crashing trumpets; the earth shall tremble under men. Glorious and steadfast they shall sound together over against the course of the stars, chanting in harmony and making melody from south and from north, from east and from west, throughout the whole creation. All mankind shall they wake from the dead unto the Last Judgment; they shall rouse the sons of men all aghast from the ancient earth, bidding them straightway arise from their deep sleep.

Throughout the Old English period, most of the literature produced was strongly coloured by Biblical diction. Even a work like Bede's *Ecclesiastical History of the English People* was under this influence. By about the year 1000, the language was able to render the Latin of Jerome, as given above, in the following form [2] (*Exod.* xix, 16, 18, 19):

þā cōm se þrydda dæg, and līgetta and þunor and þicce genip oferwrēh þone munt, and bȳman swēg wæs gehīred, and eall þæt folc him ondrēd þe wæs on þām fyrdwīcon. . . . And eall Sinai munt smēac, forþamþe Drihten wæs uppan him on fȳre; and se smīc ārās of him, and eall se munt wæs egeslic. And þære bȳman swēg wēox swā leng swā swīðor.[3]

Before we leave this part of the subject, it may be added that, according to the computations of Marsh, about 93 per cent. of the words of the *Authorised Version*, counting repetitions of the same word, are native English.

Ormulum and *Piers Plowman* will suggest the influence exerted by the Bible on English diction during the period between A.D. 1000 and 1400—roughly speaking, between the age of Aelfric and that of Wyclif. The poetry near the end

---

[1] Ll. 878–889, Whitman's translation.

[2] The vowel-sounds of either Italian, French, or German will be sufficiently close. The characters ð and þ represent *th;* g before or after *e* or *i* is usually like *y*. Final *e* is pronounced somewhat like that in *liveth*, or the final *e* of German. The macron indicates length of vowel.

[3] Aelfric's versions of the same passage may be found in his *Homilies*, ed. Thorpe, I, 312; II, 196, 202.

of this period is better able than prose to cope with the difficulties of translation.   Thus, Chaucer[1] has:

> Caste alle awey the werkes of derknesse,
> And armeth you in armure of brightnesse;

where the second Wyclifite version reads:

Rom. xiii, 12:   Therfor caste we awei the werkis of derknessis,
and be we clothid in the armeris of liʒt.

Though this second version, that of Purvey (1388), is,
in general, much less pedantically literal than the first, made
some eight or nine years earlier, yet such words as *derknessis*
and *armeris*, for the Latin plurals *tenebrae* and *arma*, illustrate
the chief defect of both the Wyclifite translations, namely, a
failure to attain perfect English idiom.

Purvey seems to have been quite conscious of the excessive
literalness of the earlier version (1380), and of the awkwardness
due to the close following of Latin idiom.   In his prologue,
after describing how he had toiled, in association with others,
to obtain a true Latin text, and to elucidate its difficulties, he
proceeds to lay down important principles of Biblical translation, which have never been superseded.   Among them are:

First, to translate as clearly as possible according to the
sense, and not merely according to the words.

Secondly, to make the sentence at least as "open" in
English as in Latin, that is, to have due regard to English
idiom.

Nevertheless, it may be affirmed that both Wyclifite
versions are far inferior in ease and idiomatic character to the
Old English.   It cannot be said that scholars are agreed as to
the influence of the Wyclifite versions upon Tindale and
the *Authorised Version;* but it is pretty clear that Tindale was
influenced by them to a moderate extent, and that expressions
of great force and beauty have, occasionally, been appropri-
ated from Wyclif by the *Authorised Version*, either mediately
or directly.   One or two instances may suffice: *John* iv, 14,
"a well of water springing up into everlasting life" comes,
through Tindale, from both the Wyclifite versions; 1 *Cor.* ii, 10,
"the deep things of God," which Tindale renders, "the bottom

---

[1] *Second Nun's Tale,* 384–5.

of God's secrets," and the Rheims version, "the profundities of God." How easy it is to go stylistically astray in such matters is shown by the fact that two versions, both published within the last ten years, have, respectively, for the first passage above, "a spring of water . . . welling up for enduring life," and "a fountain . . . of water springing up for the Life of the ages"; and, for the second, "the profoundest secrets of God," and "the depths of the divine nature."

The Wyclifite version of *Exod.* xix, 16, 18, 19 is subjoined, the spelling being modernised, and modern renderings being indicated:

WYCLIF (earlier).

And now the third day was come, and the morning [*morewe*, morrow] tide was full cleared; and lo! thunders began to be heard and lightnings [*leytes*, from the Old English word above] to shine, and the most thick cloud to cover the hill; and the cry of the trump more hideously made noise, and the people dreaded that was in the tents. . . . And all the hill of Sinai smoked, because [*for thi that*] the Lord descended upon it in fire; and the smoke rose [*steyde*] up of it as of a furnace, and all the hill was full fearful; and the sound of the trump little by little [*litil mele*] sprang into more, and longer was stretched.

A hundred years later than the Wiclifite versions (20 November, 1483), Caxton published his *Golden Legend*, in which he had inserted considerable portions of the *Pentateuch* and the Gospels, on the basis, probably, of Peter Comestor's *Historia Scholastica*. Caxton's theory of translation, if we may judge from the preface to his *Eneydos*, was to seek a mean between "fair and strange terms," by some regarded as "over curious," and such "old and homely terms" as were now strange and almost disused. His aim lay in the wish to be generally understood. The clearness and beauty of the passage from *Exodus* will be readily seen.

CAXTON's *Golden Legend* (spelling modernised).

When the third day came, and the morning waxed clear, they heard thunder and lightning, and saw a great cloud cover the mount; and the cry of the trump was so shrill that the people were sore afraid. . . . All the mount of Sinai smoked, for so much as our Lord descended on it in fire; and the smoke ascended from the hill as it had been from a furnace. The mount was terrible and dreadful, and the sound of the trump grew a little more, and continued longer.

It will be evident that the vocabulary of Caxton is drawn from the same source as Tindale's, while it does not greatly differ from Wyclif's, these sources being native English and Old French, with a very slight admixture of words coming directly from the Latin.

It is agreed on all hands that the English of the *Authorised Version* is, in essentials, that of Tindale. Minor modifications were made by translators and revisers for the next eighty years or so; but, speaking broadly, the *Authorised Version* is Tindale's. The spirit of the man passed into his work, and therefore it is of moment to ascertain what that spirit was. He himself may tell us:

(*a*) His version was to be made for all the people, even the humblest:

If God spare me life, ere many years I will cause the boy that driveth the plow to know more of the Scriptures than you [a theologian] do.

To the same effect is his preference of *favour* to *grace*, *love* to *charity*, *health* to *salvation*.

(*b*) His surrender of himself to God. Writing to a friend and fellow-labourer, Frith, he says:

The wisdom and the spirit of Stephen be with your heart and with your mouth, and teach your lips what they shall say, and how to answer to all things. He is our God if we despair in ourselves, and trust in him; and his is the glory. Amen.

(*c*) His theory regarding the meaning to be conveyed:

Believing that every part of Scripture had one sense and one only, the sense in the mind of the writer.

(*d*) On Greek and Hebrew with reference to English:

The Greek tongue agreeth more with the English than with the Latin. And the properties of the Hebrew tongue agreeth a thousand times more with the English than with the Latin. The manner of speaking is both one, so that in a thousand places thou needest not but to translate it into the English word for word, when thou must seek a compass in the Latin, and yet shalt have much work to translate it well-favouredly, so that it have the same grace and sweetness, sense and pure understanding with it in the Latin as it hath in the Hebrew. A thousand parts better may it be translated into the English than into the Latin.

(e) His scrupulous fidelity:

I call God to record against the day we shall appear before our Lord Jesus Christ to give reckoning of our doings that I never altered one syllable of God's word against my conscience, nor would to this day, if all that is in earth—whether it be honour, pleasure, or riches—might be given me.

The observation of Augustus Hare, in speaking of the Jacobean revisers, is applicable to Tindale: "They were far more studious of the matter than of the manner; and there is no surer preservative against writing ill, or more potent charm for writing well." And so Goldsmith: "To feel your subject thoroughly, and to speak without fear, are the only rules of eloquence." Elsewhere he says: "Eloquence is not in the words, but in the subject; and in great concerns, the more simply anything is expressed, it is generally the more sublime."

(f) His humility:

And if they perceive in any places that I have not attained the very sense of the tongue, or meaning of the Scripture, or have not given the right English word, that they put to their hand to amend it, remembering that so is their duty to do.

Again, he speaks of himself as "evil-favoured in this world, and without grace in the sight of men, speechless and rude, dull and slow-witted."

If we add that he was an assiduous and minute student, went directly to the originals, and employed the best helps attainable, all that is needful will have been said.

TINDALE.

And the third day in the morning there was thunder and lightning, and a thick cloud upon the mount, and the voice of the horn waxed exceeding loud, and all the people that was in the host was afraid. . . . And Mount Sinai was altogether on a smoke, because the Lord descended down upon it in fire; and the smoke thereof ascended up, as it had been the smoke of a kiln, and all the mount was exceeding fearful. And the voice of the horn blew, and waxed louder and louder.

Before we pass from Tindale to the *Authorised Version*, three other translations must be mentioned. Coverdale's nature may be indicated by the fact that it is he who introduced into the language the expressions "loving kindness" and "tender mercy." Tindale's nature was masculine, Coverdale's of a more feminine cast. His translations, of which the Prayer Book [1] version of the *Psalter* is the most generally known—possess a more flexible and musical rhythm than Tindale's. Tindale wrote (*Luke* ii, 12): "And take this for a sign; ye shall find the child swaddled, and laid in a manger." When this has passed under Coverdale's revising hand, it stands: "And take this for a sign; ye shall find the child wrapped in swaddling clothes and laid in a manger." Westcott has truly said of Coverdale that he

allowed himself considerable freedom in dealing with the shape of the original sentences. . . . There is in every part an endeavour to transfuse the spirit as well as the letter into the English rendering.

A peculiarity of the Genevan version is that it attains a special accuracy. One example will suffice. Tindale translates *Luke* xi, 17: "One house shall fall upon another." The Genevan Bible has: "A house divided against itself, falleth."

The Rheims and Douay versions inclined to Latinise, whereas earlier versions had sought to employ simpler words, generally of native origin. Thus, Tindale had written (*Rom.* x, 10): "To knowledge [*i.e.* acknowledge] with the mouth maketh a man safe." The Rheims version has: "With the mouth confession is made to salvation"; the second Wyclifite version

---

[1] The Prayer Book excels in the music of its phrasing. One of Cranmer's collects, that for the first Sunday in Advent, will serve as a specimen (*c.* A.D. 1546): "Almighty God, give us grace that we may cast away the works of darkness, and put upon us the armour of light, now in the time of this mortal life, in which Thy Son Jesus Christ came to visit us in great humility; that in the last day, when He shall come again in His glorious majesty to judge both the quick and the dead, we may rise to the life immortal, through Him who liveth and reigneth with Thee and the Holy Ghost, now and ever."

Coverdale has been regarded by some as the originator of the tendency to translate the same word in different ways at different times; but this tendency existed as far back as the Old English period.

had rendered the same Latin by: "By mouth knowledging is made to health." The translators of the *Authorised Version* endeavoured, out of the English renderings with which they were acquainted, compared with the originals and the principal versions into other tongues, ancient and modern, to frame one which should surpass them all, by appropriating the chief excellences of each—so far, at least, as these excellences could be harmonised with one another. In so far as it did thus reconcile pre-existing differences, it became a powerful agent in establishing unity throughout the English nation, for, to borrow the words of Gardiner: "In its production all sectarian influences were banished, and all hostilities were mute." Whereas previously, one Bible had been read in church, and another at home, now, all parties and classes turned with one accord to the new version, and adopted it as their very own. It thus became bound up with the life of the nation. Since it stilled all controversy over the best rendering, it gradually came to be accepted as so far absolute that, in the minds of myriads, there was no distinction between this version and the original texts, and they may almost be said to have believed in the literal inspiration of the very words which composed it.

It must not be overlooked that the *Authorised Version* profited by all the controversy regarding previous translations. Practically every word that could be challenged had been challenged. The fate of a doctrine, even the fate of a party, had, at times, seemed to depend upon a phrase. The whole ground had been fought over so long that great intimacy with the Bible had resulted. Not only did the mind take cognisance of it, but the emotions seized upon it; much of it was literally learned by heart by great numbers of the English people. Thus, it grew to be a national possession; and literature which is a national possession, and by its very nature appeals to the poor and lowly, is, in truth, a national classic. No other book has so penetrated and permeated the hearts and speech of the English race as has the Bible. What Homer was to the Greeks, and the Koran to the Arabs, that, or something not unlike it, the Bible has become to the English. Huxley writes:

Consider the great historical fact that, for three centuries, this book has been woven into the life of all that is best and noblest in

English history; that it has become the national epic of Britain, and is as familiar to noble and simple, from John-o'-Groat's House to Land's End, as Dante and Tasso once were to the Italians; that it is written in the noblest and purest English, and abounds in exquisite beauties of pure literary form; and finally, that it forbids the veriest hind who never left his village to be ignorant of the existence of other countries and other civilisations, and of a great past stretching back to the furthest limits of the oldest civilisations of the world.

The classical, yet popular, character of the Bible has been already insisted on. Two or three comparisons will further illustrate this. Chateaubriand, rendering the pathetic address of Ruth to Naomi in the Homeric manner, shows how prolix and comparatively languid Homer can be. It might be objected that Chateaubriand has travestied Homer, but it cannot be said that Thucydides, the consummate Greek historian, travesties himself. Compare the close of a Thucydidean speech, being about one-sixth of the harangue of Brasidas to his soldiers before their engagement with the Illyrians (Thuc. IV, 126), with the whole of Gideon's address to his men before their encounter with the Midianites (*Judges* vii, 17, 18):

If you repel their tumultuous onset, and, when opportunity offers, withdraw again in good order, keeping your ranks, you will sooner arrive at a place of safety, and will also learn the lesson that mobs like these, if an adversary withstand their first attack, do but threaten at a distance and make a flourish of valour, although if he yields to them they are quick enough to show their courage in following at his heels when there is no danger.

Look on me, and do likewise; and behold, when I come to the outside of the camp, it shall be that, as I do, so shall ye do. When I blow with a trumpet, I and all that are with me, then blow ye the trumpets also on every side of all the camp, and say, The sword of the Lord, and of Gideon.

The speech of Jahaziel (2 *Chron.* XX, 15–17) seems real. It is thus that an energetic man would speak. It runs (with modernised punctuation):

Hearken ye, all Judah, and ye inhabitants of Jerusalem, and thou king Jehoshaphat. Thus saith the Lord unto you: Be not afraid nor dismayed by reason of this great multitude, for the battle is not yours, but God's. To-morrow go ye down against them. Behold, they come up by the cliff of Ziz, and ye shall find them at the end of the brook, before the wilderness of Jeruel. Ye shall not need to fight in this battle. Set yourselves, stand ye still, and see the salvation of the Lord with you, O Judah and Jerusalem. Fear not, nor be dismayed. To-morrow go out against them, for the Lord will be with you.

Coleridge was so impressed with the vigour of Biblical style as to affirm:

After reading Isaiah, or St. Paul's Epistle to the Hebrews, Homer and Virgil are disgustingly tame to me, and Milton himself barely tolerable.

Shakespeare, by common consent, is the first name in English literature. Of Shakespeare's prose, Churton Collins makes five classes, the last being what he calls highly wrought poetical prose. "This," he says, "is the style where Shakespeare has raised prose to the sublimest pitch of verse." As the first illustration of it he chooses *Hamlet*, act II, sc. 2, 310–321:

This goodly frame, the earth, seems to me a sterile promontory, this most excellent canopy, the air, look you, this brave o'erhanging firmament, this majestical roof fretted with golden fire, why, it appears no other thing to me than a foul and pestilent congregation of vapours. What a piece of work is a man! how noble in reason! how infinite in faculty! in form and moving how express and admirable! in action how like an angel! in apprehension how like a god! the beauty of the world! the paragon of animals! And yet, to me, what is this quintessence of dust? Man delights not me.

This, indeed, is fine rhetoric, but how apostrophic it is, and how repetitious! "Canopy"—"firmament"—"roof"—thus it is amplified. Again, even if we can distinguish between "noble in reason," "infinite in faculty," and "in apprehension . . . like a god," how shall we make clear to ourselves the difference between "moving" and "action"? And what an anticlimax—"the paragon of animals"!

This is Shakespeare, though, to be sure, Shakespeare putting words into the mouth of a dramatic character. And now, merely as a composition, compare *Psalm* viii, 3–8:

When I consider thy heavens, the work of thy fingers, the moon and the stars which thou hast ordained, what is man, that thou art mindful of him? and the son of man, that thou visitest him? For thou hast made him a little lower than the angels, and hast crowned him with glory and honour. Thou madest him to have dominion over the works of thy hands; thou hast put all things under his feet: all sheep and oxen, yea, and the beasts of the field; the fowl of the air, and the fish of the sea, and whatsoever passeth through the paths of the seas.

Does "moon and stars" appeal less forcibly and pictorially to the imagination than "golden fire"? Shakespeare's "majestical roof" is unrelated to man; the "heavens" of the Biblical passage are knit up into the same fabric with him. In the psalm there is no exaggeration. Man is not, as a matter of fact, "infinite in faculty," nor may we assume a universal consensus that he is, above everything else, "the beauty of the world." In the psalm he is subordinated to the heavens, only to be exalted over the creatures, and, when he is said to be "a little lower than the angels," the moderation of tone is more permanently effective than Shakespeare's "in action how like an angel!" which seems merely a piece of somewhat hysterical exaggeration —though, perhaps, dramatically in keeping—to one who has formed his conception of angels from the Bible, Dante, or Milton, from the Hermes of the ancient poets, or even from Shakespeare's own line in this same play,

And flights of angels sing thee to thy rest.

Milton does not scruple to affirm: "There are no songs to be compared with the songs of Zion, no orations equal to those of the prophets." As Sir Walter Scott drew near his beautiful and affecting end, he requested Lockhart to read to him. When asked from what book, he replied: "Need you ask? There is but one." To Wordsworth, "the grand storehouses of enthusiastic and meditative imagination . . . are the prophetic and lyrical parts of the Holy Scriptures."

Ruskin ascribed the best part of his taste in literature to his having been required by his mother to learn by heart certain chapters of the Bible, adding: "I count [it] very confidently the most precious, and, on the whole, the one *essential* part of all my education." Carlyle said: "In the poorest cottage . . . is one Book, wherein for several thousands of years the spirit of man has found light, and nourishment, and an interpreting response to whatever is deepest in him." Newman speaks of the Scriptures as "compositions which, even humanly considered, are among the most sublime and beautiful ever written." Macaulay regarded the Bible as "a book which, if everything else in our language should perish, would alone suffice to show the whole extent of its beauty and power"; and elsewhere, he says of Bunyan: "He had studied no great model of composition, with the exception—an important exception undoubtedly—of our noble translation of the Bible." Froude speaks of its "mingled tenderness and majesty, the Saxon simplicity, the preternatural grandeur." Swift writes, almost exactly a hundred years after the date of the *Authorised Version:* "The translators of our Bible were masters of an English style much fitter for that work than any which we see in our present writings, which I take to be owing to the simplicity that runs through the whole"; and again, of the changes which had been introduced into the language: "They have taken off a great deal from that simplicity which is one of the greatest perfections in any language."

Hallam, though he admits that the style of the *Authorised Version* is "the perfection of our English language," has often been censured for declaring that the English of the Jacobean version "is not the English of Daniel, of Raleigh, or Bacon"— in fact, that "it is not the language of the reign of James I." Yet this is strictly true, and for the reason that he assigns, namely, "in consequence of the principle of adherence to the original versions which had been kept up since the time of Henry VIII." It is true, in a sense, that no great writer's diction is of his age, any more than he himself is of his age. Coleridge declares of Shakespeare, "His is not the style of the age," just as Ben Jonson declared of the poet himself, "He was not of an age." Indeed, it seems as though this were the necessary condition, at least in the case of great writers, of being "for all time," that one shall not be too much "of an age." Great thought and great feeling draw their own appropriate diction to themselves, somewhat as the magnet attracts steel filings; and, after the appropriate diction has thus been attracted, the union between it and the substance of discourse seems to be almost indissoluble. It is as if a soul had been clothed upon with flesh. From that moment, nothing can be changed with impunity; if you wrench away a word, it is as if a portion of the life-blood followed it. Now the time when the soul of the Bible began to take upon itself flesh for us was nearly three-quarters of a century before the work of the Jacobean revisers. But, since the life-process, so to speak, did not absolutely begin with Tindale, it really extended over a considerably longer period than that named above, especially if we consider that Wyclif was concerned in it; for, if the Wyclifite versions be included, the *Vulgate* can hardly be ignored, so that eventually the *Septuagint* must be regarded as having initiated a process which the Jacobean revisers completed. If the substance of the Bible may thus be compared to a soul which was to be fitted with a body, it will follow that the diction will differ somewhat from member to member, even as it did in the Hebrew and Greek originals; but it will also follow, in proportion to the assumed relation and interdependence of these parts of members, that this diction will have a certain homogeneity, so that a radical change in the vocabulary at any point would be likely to throw that part out of keeping with the rest. The truth of this was recognised by Ellicott, when, in 1870, he advised future revisers to

limit the choice of words to the vocabulary of the present [Authorised] version, combined with that of the versions that preceded it; and in alterations preserve as far as possible the rhythm and cadence of the Authorised Version.

It is not a little remarkable that the effects wrought by the English Bible should require so few words. The editors of the *New English Dictionary* reckon the words in A to L, inclusive, as 160,813, of which number 113,677 are what they call main words. Shakespeare, it has been estimated, employs about 21,000 (others say 15,000, or 24,000); Milton, in his verse, about 13,000. The Hebrew (with the Chaldee) of the Old Testament, according to the computations of Leusden, comprises 5,642 words, and the New Testament, it is said, has 4,800, while the whole English Bible, if we may trust Marsh, employs about 6,000. Making all due allowances for the "myriad-mindedness" of a Shakespeare, there is still room for the conclusion that the capacities of words, especially of the simpler words, are much greater than is believed by those who use a large and heterogeneous vocabulary. In this respect there is not so much difference between native English and Norman-French words as is commonly supposed. In the following examples, the words *clean*, *pure*, and *clear* translate the same Greek adjective, and all seem equally expressive, or nearly so:

Rev. xv, 6: "And the seven angels came out of the temple, . . . clothed in *pure* and white linen."

Rev. xix, 8: "And to her was granted that she should be arrayed in fine linen, *clean* and white."

Rev. xxi, 18: "And the city was pure gold, like unto *clear* glass." That, in this sense, they are fairly interchangeable may be seen by comparing *Job* xv, 15, "Yea, the heavens are not *clean* in his sight," with Tennyson's

> Make thou my spirit *pure* and *clear*
> As are the frosty skies.

This brings us to the question of the influence of the *Authorised Version* upon subsequent English literature—an influence which cannot always be precisely distinguished from that of the Bible in some earlier form. When Spenser or Shakespeare, for instance, uses the Bible, it is, of course, not the Jacobean version, and now and then the same thing will be true at a later period, as in some of Milton's writing. The more important modes in which the Bible has affected English literature are these:

(*a*) The themes are Scriptural, and the language partly, at times even largely, Scriptural. Such is the case in sermons, versified psalms, paraphrases of Scriptural narrative, devotional essays, and the like. An excellent example is Bunyan's *Pilgrim's Progress*. This book apart, however, there are few, if any, examples of a work which has been accepted as pure literature employing Biblical diction to anything like such a degree. Other attempts, such as the *Book of Mormon*, tend to the grotesque or ludicrous, because of the disparity between the language and the ideas suggested. A diction resembling that of the Bible in its concreteness and simplicity, and in its slightly archaic character, has, however, of late been employed with good effect in prose versions from authors like Homer.

(b) Quotations from the Bible are introduced, sometimes slightly changed, into secular writings. The object is to substantiate a statement, or to awaken a train of associations favourable to the author's purpose. These can be found in almost any author, but they are more common in the nineteenth century than earlier, being especially used by writers who have at heart the reform or elevation of society or individuals.

(c) Allusions, or considerably modified quotations, are introduced freely, and may be found on the editorial page of many a newspaper. Thus, one reads: "The full measure of justice is not meted out to them"; "They sold their birthright for a mess of pottage"; "They have fallen among thieves." In the last three books which the present writer has read for amusement, he has been interested to note quotations and allusions of this nature. In one of them, a recent book on life in an Italian province, 63 references were found; in the second, a recent work on the life of wild animals, 12; in the third, a novel by Thomas Hardy, 18.

(d) Many phrases have grown so common that they have become part of the web of current English speech, and are hardly thought of as Biblical at all, except on deliberate reflection. For instance: "highways and hedges"; "clear as crystal"; "still small voice"; "hip and thigh"; "arose as one man"; "lick the dust"; "a thorn in the flesh"; "broken reed"; "root of all evil"; "the nether millstone"; "sweat of his brow"; "heap coals of fire"; "a law unto themselves"; "the fat of the land"; "dark sayings"; "a soft answer"; "a word in season"; "moth and rust"; "weighed in the balance and found wanting"; even such colloquialisms as, "we are the people" (cf. *Job* xii, 2). Many more of these might readily be quoted.

(e) Other influences, less definitely measurable, but more important, remain to be mentioned.

Of the Bible in its relations to religion, individual conduct, and ideals political and social, this is not the place to speak; yet these affect literature to an incalculable extent, if they do not even provide its very substance. Of such matters as fall within the scope of this chapter—matters of vocabulary, grammar, idiom, and style—something may briefly be said.

In the first place, the literary influence of the Bible, like that of any classic, is distinctly conservative. The reading of it tends to keep alive a familiarity with the words and constructions which were current when the English Bible grew up, or, rather, of such of these words and constructions as proved most conformable to the genius of the Hebrew and Greek employed in the sacred writings. As hinted above, this influence, in conjunction with that of the Bible in the sphere of thought and emotion, seems to have culminated, if its culmination be not rather a matter of the future, in the latter half of the nineteenth century. The result is that many terms formerly regarded as awkward, or alien to the genius of the language, are now understood and accepted. Soon after the *Authorised Version* was issued, Selden thus criticised the rendering:

The Bible is rather translated into English words than into English phrases. The Hebraisms are kept, and the phrase of that language is kept.

A typical Hebraism is the use of *of* in such phrases as "oil of gladness," "man of sin," "King of kings"; but who has any difficulty with them now? In the first half of the nineteenth century, Hallam could say:

It abounds, . . . especially in the Old Testament, with obsolete phraseology, and with single words long since abandoned, or retained only in provincial use.

At present this is no truer of the Bible than of Shakespeare, if as true. Our earlier English has been so revived, and rendered so familiar, that much which needed elaborate explanation in the eighteenth century is now intelligible to every one. As Lightfoot said of other objectors:

The very words which these critics would have ejected from our English Bibles as barbarous, or uncouth, or obsolete, have again taken their places in our highest poetry, and even in our popular language.

Like the course of a planet round the sun, the movement of English diction, which, in the seventeenth and eighteenth centuries, was, on the whole, away from that of the Bible, now returns with ever accelerating speed toward it. That the movement really began at a much earlier date, though inconspicuously, is shown by the counsels and practice of Swift, and by the circumstance that Challoner's Roman Catholic version of 1763–4 abandoned many of the Latinisms of the Rheims and Douay translations in favour of the simpler language of the *Authorised Version*.

The use of concrete words has grown in favour. The colourlessness, vagueness and obscurity of abstract terms, and of conventional phraseology whether abstract or not, have been discredited. Vividness, the sense of reality, have more and more prevailed in literature—that is, in non-technical writings.

Simplicity has always been recommended by the example of the *Authorised Version*, and, especially since the age of Wordsworth, is more and more gaining upon bombast and meretricious ornament. The concreteness and simplicity of the *Authorised Version*, and its use of the homely vernacular, have steadily appealed to plain people, as distinguished from those who have had more abundant opportunities of education. But the love of the humble for the Bible is largely due to its message of cheer and hope. Huxley has even gone so far as to call the Bible "the Magna Charta of the poor and the oppressed." Two men, Bunyan and Lincoln, who educated themselves largely by means of the Bible, may serve as examples of many who have become known to posterity for their inestimable services to their race. Both are famous as writers, and the best writing of both is alive with the spirit of the Bible. Bunyan has already been mentioned. Of Lincoln it has been said that he

built up his entire reading upon his early study of the Bible. He had mastered it absolutely; mastered it as later he mastered only one or two other books, notably Shakespeare; mastered it so that he became almost "a man of one book"; . . . and he left his life as part of the crowning work of the century that has just closed.

Of Walt Whitman, the American who wished to be known as the poet of democracy, it has been authoritatively said:

His own essential model, after all is said, was the rhythmical patterns of the English Bible. Here was precisely that natural stylistic variation between the "terrific," the "gentle," and the "inferior" parts, so desired by William Blake. Here were lyric fragments, of consummate beauty, imbedded in narrative or argumentative passages. . . . In this strong, rolling music, this intense feeling, these concrete words expressing primal emotion in daring terms of bodily sensation, Whitman found the charter for the book he wished to write.

The elevation and nobility of Biblical diction, assisted by its slightly archaic tinge, have a tendency to keep all English style above meanness and triviality. In the words of Coleridge "intense study of the Bible will keep any writer from being vulgar in point of style."

The Bible teaches that emotion should not habitually be divorced from thought, nor thought from emotion; certainly not in literature. Wherever simple language is charged with noble feeling, stirs the imagination, is directed by steady and comprehensive thought, is adapted to actuate the will in the direction of social and individual good, and is concise and pregnant, Biblical style is approximated, and, very probably, Biblical influence is dominant.

Finally, the English Bible is the chief bond which holds united, in a common loyalty and a common endeavour, the various branches of the English race. The influence of the Bible can be traced through the whole course of English literature and English civilisation, and, more than anything else, it tends to give unity and perpetuity to both.

CHAPTER III

Sir Walter Ralegh

NOTHING, perhaps, is more remarkable with regard to
Sir Walter Ralegh's [1] literary career than the fact that
a man of his nature should have won for himself a
place in the history of letters.   He was, pre-eminently, a man of
action, a man who loved the stir and bustle of life, the excitement of adventure; and his proud, ambitious character made
him keen to play a foremost part in the affairs of the world.
But his intellectual activity was as great as his physical
energy.   Neither his mind nor his body could rest.   All the
periods of enforced leisure in his life he used for study or
writing; yet the chance of an active enterprise could always
win him away from his books.

At the age of 14 or 15, Ralegh, who was born in 1552,
at Hayes Barton, Budleigh, Devon, went to Oxford, where he
stayed for about three years.   According to Anthony à Wood,
"he became the ornament of the juniors, and a proficient in
oratory and philosophy."   He passed from Oxford quickly
to seek more stirring adventures in the Huguenot army in
France.   But, wherever he went, he was gathering knowledge.
Sir Robert Naunton says "he was an indefatigable reader,
whether by sea or land, and none of the least observers both of
men and the times."   On his sea voyages, he took always a
trunk of books with him, and spent the long hours, when he
had nothing to divert him, in reading.   He is said, by an
early biographer, to have slept but five hours, so as to gain

[1] Ralegh's name may be found spelt in some seventy different ways.   His
own signature varied very considerably till 1584, after which he used no
other signature but Ralegh; he never used the common modern form Raleigh.
His pronunciation of his name is clear from the fact that in his early days he
often wrote Rauley.

daily four hours for reading. His knowledge of literature helped, no doubt, to give him that command of words, that incisive way of stating a question which called Elizabeth's attention to him when he discussed Irish affairs over the council table with lord Grey. He had, says Naunton, "a strong natural wit and a better judgment, with a bold and plausible tongue, whereby he could set out his parts to the best advantage." He retained a decided Devonshire accent all his life; but his parliamentary speeches were distinguished by good style and pointed utterance. He seems to have shown a tendency towards liberal views. In a debate about the Brownists, in 1583, he spoke against religious persecution. But his was neither the speech nor the nature by which a man wins ready popularity, for in everything, though he showed himself a lover of liberty, he showed, also, his proud and contemptuous character. Perhaps that proud and contemptuous character showed itself also in the extravagance of the language of compliment and adulation with which he addressed Elizabeth. Such language was fashionable at the time, but it seems strange in the mouth of a man like Ralegh, and we are inclined to think that it was his ambition and desire to get on which made him put no limit to his exaggeration, in scornful contempt of the vanity that could be pleased by such language.

That Ralegh must have early been known as a writer of occasional verse is shown by the fact that he contributed some introductory verses, *In commendation of the Steel Glass*, to George Gascoigne's satire, published in 1576. In these lines he describes Gascoigne's poems in one of his concise, pointed phrases:

> This medicine may suffice
> To scorn the rest, and seek to please the wise.

Elizabethan poets appear to have had little desire to see their works in print. They wrote to please their friends, or for their own delight, not for the general public. Their poems were passed about in manuscript or read to their friends, and then might, perhaps, find their way into some of the popular miscellanies of verse. Few of Ralegh's poems appeared with his name during his lifetime, and it was long after his death before any attempt was made to identify or collect his scattered verses. Some of them had appeared in *England's Helicon* with the signature "Ignoto," and it was, in consequence, at first assumed that all the poems so signed in that collection were his. More critical examination has rejected many of these, and Hannah's carefully edited collection, published in 1892, gives some thirty pieces which have reasonably been supposed to be Ralegh's.[1] These are enough to justify fully the judgment passed on him in Puttenham's *The Arte of English Poesie*, "For dittie and amourous ode I find Sir Walter Ralegh's vein most lofty, insolent and passionate."

Ralegh seems, at many crises in his life, to have sought expression for his feelings in verse. When, after his rapid rise to favour at court, he was driven into temporary disgrace by the jealousy of Essex, he employed himself in composing a long elegy expressing his devotion to Elizabeth, and his despair at her anger, in which he addressed the queen as Cynthia. We hear of this poem first in Spenser's verses *Colin Clout's Come Home Again*. During this temporary disgrace, Ralegh revisited Ireland, where he had served some years before. There, he either began or renewed at Kilcolman his friendship with Spenser, then lord Grey's secretary. The poets seem to have passed some delightful days in reading their verses to one another. Spenser says of Ralegh in *Colin Clout:*

> His song was all a lamentable lay
> Of great unkindnesse, and of usage hard
> Of Cynthia the Ladie of the Sea,
> Which from her presence faultlesse him debard.

Ralegh's delight in *The Faerie Queene* led him, as soon as he was restored to favour, to introduce Spenser at court. Spenser, in his turn, was full of admiration of Ralegh's work and wrote:

> Full sweetly tempered is that Muse of his
> That can empierce a Princes' mightie hart.

He returns to it again in the beautiful sonnet addressed to Ralegh which appeared attached to *The Faerie Queene*, where

[1] See *post*, the chapter on the "Song Books."

he says that, compared with Ralegh's, his rimes are "un-savory and sowre," and concludes:

Yet, till that thou thy Poeme wilt make knowne,
Let thy fair Cinthias praises be thus rudely showne.

Cynthia was never published; we do not know that it was ever presented to Elizabeth. It was thought to be entirely lost, when a fragment of it was discovered among the Hatfield MSS. and first printed by Hannah in 1870. This fragment is entitled *The twenty-first and last book of the Ocean to Cynthia.* Spenser used to call Ralegh "The Shepherd of the Ocean," and, hence, Ralegh took to calling himself "the Ocean." Hannah published this fragment as *A continuation of the lost poem Cynthia*, and imagined that it was composed during Ralegh's imprisonment in the Tower under James I. But it has been conclusively shown that it must be a portion of the earlier poem.[1] If the other twenty books were of the same length as this canto, the whole poem must have consisted of ten to fifteen thousand lines. It is written in four-lined stanzas, alternately rimed. Judging from the fragment that remains, there appears to have been no action or narrative in this long poem, yet Gabriel Harvey describes the part of it which he saw before 1590 as "a fine and sweet invention." There are many fine passages, none finer than the line

Of all which past the sorrow only stays.

The stately, dignified sonnet by Ralegh, which was appended to the first edition of *The Faerie Queene*, in 1590, is worthy of an age when the sonnet attained rare distinction. Brydges, the first editor of a collection of Ralegh's poems, says:

Milton had deeply studied this sonnet, for in his compositions of the same class, he has evidently more than once the very rhythm and construction, as well as cast of thought of this noble though brief composition.

Other of the poems by Ralegh show more of the impetuous and daring spirit which was compelled to find an utterance.

---

[1] This point has been clearly demonstrated by Edmund Gosse from internal evidence, in two letters printed in *The Athenaeum* for the first two weeks of January, 1886. See, also, *Sir Walter Ralegh*, by W. Stebbing, p. 73.

The ringing scorn of "The Lie" depicts the man who knew fɪom personal experience courts and their meanness. The disenchantment with life expressed in several of his poems led to the assumption that they were written on the night before his death; but of only one can this be true, the fine lines found in his Bible at the gate-house, Westminster:

> Even such is time, that takes on trust
> Our youth, our joys, our all we have,
> And pays us but with earth and dust.

The others, such as *Like Hermit Poor*, and *The Pilgrimmage*, were, probably, written at moments when his impatient spirit was filled with disgust of life. No poem of his has greater charm than *The Pilgrimmage*, whether for its form, its fancy, or for the deep seriousness underlying its light grace. Among the authenticated poems of Ralegh there are few love poems, and those few are singularly free from sentimentality or the precious conceits popular at the time. In his reply to Marlowe's song *The passionate Shepherd to his Love*, he by no means responds to the passion of the appeal, but shows his disbelief in the possibility of the permanence of the shepherd's love in a world full of fears of "cares to come."

The authenticity of many of Ralegh's prose works is almost as difficult to decide with any certainty as that of his poems. He seems to have written papers on many varied subjects, but only two of them, and *The History of the World*, were published during his lifetime. Ralegh manuscripts were collected by literary men, were to be found in many libraries, and were much valued. It is said in the *Observations on the Statesmen and Favourites of England*, by David Lloyd, published in 1665, that John Hampden, shortly before the Civil Wars, was at the charge of transcribing 3452 sheets of Ralegh's writing. Archbishop Sancroft speaks of "a great MS. in folio," by Sir Walter, lent to him by Mr. Ralegh, the author's grandson. He also possessed another MS., a *Breviary of the History of England under William I*, which he attributed to Sir Walter Ralegh, and which he said had been "taken from the papers of an old Presbyterian in Hertfordshire, which sort of men were always the more fond of Sir Walter's books, because he was under the disfavour of the Court." One of his MSS., called *The Arts of Empire*, was first printed by Milton in 1658, under the title of *The Cabinet Council by the ever-renowned knight, Sir Walter Ralegh*. It does not seem as if Ralegh, ambitious in other respects, aspired to the fame of an author. He read and wrote for his own delight and recreation. He loved books and the society of men of letters of all kinds. He was a friend of Sir Robert Cotton, the antiquary, who collected the famous library at Cotton House, which became the meeting place of the scholars of the day. There and elsewhere, Ralegh consorted with the other men of learning of his times. He was a member of the Society of Antiquaries, which archbishop Parker had founded in 1572, and which lasted till 1605, and he is said to have suggested those gatherings at the Mermaid tavern, in Bread street, where Shakespeare, Ben Jonson, Beaumont and other playwriters met the antiquaries and literary men of the day, such as Cotton, Selden and Donne. Here began Ralegh's friendship with Ben Jonson, which led him, later, to choose him as travelling tutor for his son. Always of an open mind and liberal views, Ralegh also mixed freely with sceptical and freethinking men. He often met together with Marlowe, Harriot and others for discussions, in which religious topics were treated fearlessly and without reserve. A Roman Catholic pamphleteer, writing in 1592, says that the meetings of this little group of friends were called "Sir Walter Rawley's School of Atheism." In 1593, the attention of the privy council was called to their discussions, and a special commission was appointed to examine Ralegh, his brother Carew and others as to their alleged heresies. What was the result of this investigation we do not know, but it is impossible to read Ralegh's writings without being convinced of the depth and sincerity of his religious convictions. Sir John Harington says of him in *Nugae Antiquae:* "In religion he hath shown in private talk, great depth and good reading."

Ralegh was, at all times, a generous patron of learning. He advised Richard Hakluyt with regard to his great collection of voyages, and assisted his enterprise with gifts of money and manuscripts. He was with the fleet that, under the command of the earl of Essex, made, in 1596, a descent upon Faro in Portugal, and it was, no doubt, he that suggested the seizure and careful preservation of the great library of bishop Hieron

Osorius, which was afterwards given, probably, again, at Ralegh's suggestion, to the library newly founded at Oxford by Sir Thomas Bodley. The Bodleian library was opened in 1602, and, in 1603, Ralegh showed his love for books by making it a gift of fifty pounds.

The first work published by Ralegh was a quarto tract issued in 1596, called *Report of the Truth of the Fight about the Iles of the Açores this last sommer*. It appeared anonymously, but was republished by Hakluyt, as Sir Walter Ralegh's. It describes the doings of the little fleet in which, at the last moment, Ralegh had been prevented from sailing himself, and ends with an account of the famous fight and death of his kinsman Sir Richard Grenville, on *The Revenge*. In forcible and vigorous prose, Ralegh tells with great simplicity the story of what actually happened. But, both before and after his story, he gives vent to violent denunciation of the Spaniards, at all times the object of his bitterest hatred. He speaks of "their frivolouse vain glorious taunts" as opposed to the "honourable actions" characteristic of the English. It seems to have been this kind of language which counted as patriotism in Elizabethan days, and helped to give Ralegh his high reputation as a lover of his country. The account ends with a touch of poetry when, after describing the terrible storm which followed the fight of *The Revenge* and caused the destruction of many ships, he says: "So it pleased them to honour the buriall of that renowned ship the Revenge, not suffering her to perish alone, for the great honour she achieved in her life time."

It was partly his natural love of adventure, partly his desire to regain the favour at court which he had temporarily lost, that led Ralegh to undertake his first expedition to Guiana, in 1595. When he returned, full of tales of what he had seen, his enemies attempted to cast discredit on him by asserting that he had never been to Guiana at all. To defend himself, he at once wrote an account of his *Discovery of the large, rich and beautiful Empire of Guiana, with a relation of the great, and golden city of Manoa*. This appeared in 1596, with a dedication to "my singular good Lord and kinsman Charles Howard and to the Rt. Hon. Sir Robt. Cecil"; in which Ralegh says that in his discourse he has "neither studied phrase, forme, nor fashion." The simple story of his stirring adventures, told in pure and nervous English, won immediate popularity, and was translated into German, Dutch and Latin, running through many editions. His sentences are long and sometimes involved, but he tells his story admirably and his adventures live, whilst his descriptions of scenery are graceful and attractive, and he urges the advantages of the colonisation of Guiana in glowing and eloquent words. His allusions to the tales that the natives told him of tribes of Amazons, and other strange beings, led Hume to characterise his whole narrative as "full of the grossest and most palpable lies"; a criticism which his most careful editor, Sir Robert Schomburgh, who has himself visited Guiana, says "we can now regard with a smile." Besides these two tracts, nothing was published by Ralegh during the reign of Elizabeth, though one or two of his letters, especially that written to Robert Cecil on the death of his wife, in 1596, and the one giving *A relation of the Cadiz Action*, in the same year, well deserve to be counted amongst literary productions. In the letter to Cecil, we find these fine words:

The minde of man is that part of God which is in us, which, by how mich is it subject to passion, by so mich it is farther from Hyme that gave it us. Sorrows draw not the dead to life, but the livinge to death.

Ralegh's life of stir and adventure, his enjoyment and hope of court favour, all came to an end with the death of Elizabeth and the accession of James I. He found himself, only just reprieved from the scaffold, a prisoner in the Tower, the victim of the prejudice and suspicions of the king. Conscious of the falseness of the accusation of treason upon which he had been convicted, still full of schemes of active enterprise and, especially, of the idea that he would be able to win for England a possession of boundless wealth in Guiana, he could not, at first, believe that his captivity would last. But, as his hopes of a speedy release slowly passed away, it became more and more necessary for him to use his energies in work of some kind. For the most part, the conditions of his captivity were not rigorous. He had rooms in the Bloody Tower, with sufficient accommodation to enable his wife and son to be with him. His friends visited him freely. His rooms opened out on a terrace, where he could take exercise, and below was a little garden, where he was allowed to turn a former hen-house into a laboratory for the chemical experiments in which he delighted. At first, it was to his scientific studies that he devoted most of his time. But he also wrote a great deal. Prince Henry, the promising eldest son of James I, was a great admirer of Ralegh and declared that no one but his father would keep such a bird in such a cage. He was only a boy of nine when Ralegh was committed to the Tower, but he had always loved the society of those older than himself, and, as time went on, he consulted Ralegh on many points that interested him, especially on naval and military matters. Several of the papers which Ralegh wrote in the Tower were composed specially for prince Henry. Among others, there is a treatise called *Observations concerning the Royal Navy and Sea Service*, which is full of interest as throwing light on the condition of the ships by means of which the great Elizabethan seamen carried out their famous exploits. When there was a proposal, very distasteful to prince Henry, to arrange a marriage between him and a daughter of the house of Savoy, Ralegh wrote a vigorous treatise in which he clearly pointed out the disadvantages of the match. It was also for prince Henry that he planned his greatest work, *The History of the World*.

It is a testimony to the extent of Ralegh's belief in himself as well as to the soaring nature of his imagination, that he, a prisoner in the Tower, in broken health and already over fifty years of age, should have projected a work of such gigantic scope. History, as a branch of literature, did not then exist in England; indeed, except for the work of the antiquaries, the Elizabethan age is specially poor in historical work of any kind. The age of the great chroniclers was over. There were some writers of historical poems, some annalists, many industrious antiquaries. But the annalists and the antiquaries still wrote in Latin. Only Richard Knolles had produced his *Generall Historie of the Turkes*, published in 1603, and John Speed a *Historie of Great Britaine*, published in 1611, in English. Ralegh's plan was on an entirely different scale from anything that had been dreamt of before. He wished to bring the history of the past together, to treat it as a whole, to use it as an introduction to the history of his own country; and his great book was to be for the people, not only for the learned. It was written in the pure strong English of which he had such easy command. Not quite free yet from the habit of using too long sentences which, sometimes, have a tendency to become involved, he is free from elaborate and fanciful conceits. The subject seems to command the style. He can tell a story well, he can sketch a character with force and vigour. He shows at least some sense of the unity of history, for the motives of men in the past are judged by him in the same way as the motives of men in the present, and, at all events when he began, his intention was to lead up from the past to the present. But, though he had the mind to conceive a work on such a vast scale, he had not the experience or the training to enable him to plan it out in such a way that, under any circumstances, it would have been possible to complete it. The large folio which he did complete, and which consisted of five books, began with the Creation and reached only to 130 B.C., when Macedonia became a Roman province. He projected two other folio volumes, but these do not seem even to have been begun. After the publication of the first volume, his mind was diverted to other schemes, to his hope of regaining his liberty and accomplishing a second voyage to Guiana. The death of prince Henry, in 1612, also deprived him of one of his chief motives for writing the history.

We do not know in what year he actually began to write, but, on 15 April, 1611, notice was given in the registers of the Stationers' company of "*The History of the World* written by Sir Walter Rawleighe."

It was published, according to Camden, on 29 March, 1614; but it is possible that it may not really have been published till the beginning of 1615. Many scholars and learned men were ready to help him in his work. Sir Robert Cotton freely lent him books from his great library. Robert Burhill, a divine of wide learning and acquainted with Greek and Hebrew, languages unknown to Ralegh, was frequently consulted by him. John Hoskins, a wit and scholar and also a prisoner in the Tower for a supposed libel on James I, is credited, by tradition, with having revised the book for him. The fact that Ben Jonson was, also, for a short time a fellow prisoner in the Tower, and was known to have been connected with Ralegh, led some to believe his boasts, made some years later over his cups, that he had contributed considerable portions of the *History*. But there is no evidence for these assertions, which rest only on his own word.

In his search for accuracy, Ralegh frequently consulted Thomas Harriot the mathematician, an old friend of his, on points of chronology and geography. But, though no doubt he profited by the advice and learning of his friends, no one can read the *History* without feeling that it is the work of one man, inspired by one mind and purpose. Moreover, though he naturally read and studied much specially for it during his years in the Tower, we see in it also the result of the reading of his whole life. In *The History of the World*, as well as in his occasional writings, we are struck with the freedom with which Ralegh handles his material, with the ready hold that he has on the resources of his vast reading. About the middle of the nineteenth century, some old books, amongst them Peter Comestor's *Historia Scholastica*, were found behind the wainscot of a room in Ralegh's favourite Irish house at Youghal. Comestor is one of the authors quoted by Ralegh, and, though it is possible that these old books were placed in their hiding-place before his day, yet it is by no means improbable that his study of Comestor may have begun at Youghal during the months he spent in Ireland. It has been computed that six hundred and sixty authors are cited by him in his *History*, and there exists a letter to Cotton asking for the loan of thirteen books, none of which is included amongst the works of the six hundred and sixty authors quoted.

In writing his history, Ralegh was inspired by a distinct purpose. He says in his preface, that he wishes to show God's judgment on the wicked; to him all history was a revelation of God's ways. His preface is to us now, perhaps, the most interesting part of the book. In it he runs through, and passes judgment upon, the kings of England from the time of the Conquest, then makes a rapid survey of the history of France and of Spain. From the teaching of history he draws his philosophy of life:

For seeing God, who is the author of all our tragedies hath written out for us and appointed us all the parts we are to play;

and hath not, in their distribution been partial to the most mighty
princes of the world . . . why should other men, who are but
as the least worms, complain of wrongs? Certainly there is no
other account to be made of this ridiculous world, than to resolve,
that the change of fortune on the great theatre is but the change
of garments on the less: for when on the one and the other, every
man wears but his own skin, the players are all alike.

As we think of the picture of his own times, of the account
of Elizabeth and her court, of the stirring tales of adventure
that the ready pen and quick insight of Ralegh might have
given us had he spent his time in prison in writing his own
memoirs, we can but be filled with regret that he should have
chosen, instead, to have written long chapters on the Creation,
the site of the Garden of Eden, the ages of the patriarchs.
But Ralegh had not done with life, his ambitious, restless
spirit still aspired to play a part in the world outside and his
book was intended to add to his friends, not to his enemies.
In his preface, he explains his choice of subject:

I know that it will be said by many, that I might have been
more pleasing to the reader, if I had written the story of mine own
times. . . . To this I answer, that whosoever in writing a modern
history, shall follow truth too near the heels, it may happily strike
out his teeth. There is no mistress or guide that hath led her
followers and servants into greater miseries. . . . It is true, that
I never travelled after men's opinions, when I might have made
the best use of them; and I have now too few days remaining to
imitate those, that, either out of extreme ambition or extreme
cowardice, or both, do yet (when death hath them on this shoulders)
flatter the world between the bed and the grave. It is enough for me
(being in that state I am) to write of the eldest times; wherein also,
why may it not be said, that, in speaking of the past, I point
at the present and tax the vices of those that are yet living in their
persons that are long since dead; and have it laid to my charge.
But this I cannot help, though innocent.

It is but seldom that he even illuminates his pages with
any illustrations drawn from his own experiences. Sometimes,
he indulges in a digression, as when he breaks forth into a
dissertation on the nature of law, after telling of the giving
of the law to Moses, or when, in a later book, he makes long
dissertations on the way to defend the coast, on the nature

of government, on mercenary soldiers, on the folly and wicked-
ness of duels and the false view of honour they involve. He has
a long digression, also, about the bands of Amazons, said to
be living in the districts round Guiana, and gives his reasons
for believing in the possibility of their existence.

The first two books of the *History*, containing twenty-eight
chapters, are occupied with an account of the Creation and
the history of the Jews. Side by side with that history, they
give the contemporary events in Greek mythology and Egyp-
tian history. The questions treated of, and the method of
treating them, alike show how different were the interests of
his day and ours. His discussion as to the nature of the
two trees in the Garden of Eden is enlivened by a description
of *Ficus Indica* as he had seen it in Trinidad, dropping its
roots, or cords, into the sea "so as by pulling up one of these
cords out of the sea, I have seen five hundred oysters hanging
in a heap thereon." In none of Ralegh's writings do we find
any sign that he possessed a sense of humour; had he done so,
he would not, perhaps, have indulged in such an elaborate
disquisition as to the capacity of the ark to hold all the animals
which were driven into it. Naturally, no thought of criticising
the Bible narrative entered his mind, as he said "Let us
build upon the scriptures themselves and after them upon
reason and nature." But there is some attempt at criticism
in comparing one author with another, some attempt to
trace the development of thought, and to bring things together,
a remarkable feat in his day, as we may realise when we remember that, before him, there was practically no attempt
at critical history in English. He was much interested in
questions of chronology, and provided his book with elaborate
chronological tables as well as with many maps. But it is a
relief when he passes from his discussions on chronology
to tell a story, such as the story of the Argonauts, which he
does simply and well.

The book moves more freely as he reaches Greek and
Roman times. The characters of some of the great men are
given with much insight and point, and he brings his commonsense to bear in criticising the conduct of leaders and generals.
As the book goes on, his references to modern history in
illustration of his story grow more frequent. We feel that

not only has he read much, but that he has weighed and pondered what he has read in the light of his own experience. In reflecting on the end of Hannibal and Scipio, he says:

Hence it comes, to wit from the envy of our equals, and jealousy of our masters, be they kings or commonweals, that there is no profession more unprosperous than that of men of war and great captains, being no kings. . . . For the most of others whose virtues have raised them above the level of their inferiors, and have surmounted their envy, yet have they been rewarded in the end either with disgrace, banishment, or death.

Whenever he touches upon any matter of personal experience, the interest at once quickens and the writing appears at its best. War is always his main theme; to him, history is an account of wars and conquests. Questions as to methods of government or the social conditions of the people have little interest for him, though he seems to see the importance of combining geography with history by the descriptions he gives of the nature of the countries, the towns and cities of which he writes. On the whole, the best part of the book is his account of the Punic wars; there he feels fully the interest of his story. Curiously enough, he misses the tragic interest of the Athenian expedition to Sicily, which, in his telling, he even manages to make dull.

Never does he lose sight of his moral purpose. His whole object in writing was to teach a great moral: "it being the end and scope of all history to teach by example of times past, such wisdom as may guide our desires and actions." So he carries us through the history of the "three first Monarchies of the world"; leaving off when the fourth, Rome, was "almost at the highest." He ends with these noble words on death:

O eloquent, just and mighty death! Whom none could advise, thou hast persuaded! What none have dared, thou hast done! And whom all the world hath flattered, thou only hast cast out of the world and despised! Thou hast drawn together all the far fetched greatness, all the pride, cruelty and ambition of men; and covered it all over with these two narrow words: Hic jacet.

Though, in his preface, Ralegh said of James I that

if all the malice of the world were infused into one eye, yet could it not discern in his life, even to this day, any one of those foul spots, by which the consciences of all the fore named princes (in effect) have been defiled; nor any drop of that innocent blood on the sword of his justice, with which the most that forewent him have stained both their hands and fame,

James I was displeased with the book. Perhaps he was clever enough to discern the value of this fashionable language of adulation; perhaps, as some said, he thought that Ralegh had criticised too freely the character of Henry VIII, when he said "if all the pictures and patterns of a merciless prince were lost in the world, they might all again be painted out of the story of this king." To the fanatical believer in the divine right of kings, any censure of princes was, in itself, a crime. James appears, in consequence, to have tried to suppress the book. In a letter written to Venice on 5 January, 1615, it is said, "Sir Walter Ralegh's book is called in by the King's commandment, for divers exceptions, but specially for being too saucy in censuring princes." There is, also, a letter from the archbishop of Canterbury, dated 22 December, 1614, to the Stationers' company, saying that he had received "expresse directions from his Majestie that the book latelie published by Sʳ Walter Rawleigh, nowe prisoner in the Tower, should be suppressed and not suffered for hereafter to be sould." The book mentioned in this letter can be none other but the *History*. But the suppression seems not to have been carried out; at any rate, the royal command did not affect the distribution of the book. The first two editions appeared anonymously without any title-page, but with an elaborate allegorical frontispiece, representing *Magister Vitae*, standing on Death represented by a skeleton, and Oblivion as a man asleep. Experience, as an old woman, and Truth as a young woman, hold aloft a globe, on one side of which *fama bona* and, on the other, *fama mala* are blowing trumpets. On the other page is a sonnet, presumably by Ben Jonson, as he afterwards published it under his name, containing these lines:

> From death and dark Oblivion (neere the same)
> The Mistresse of Man's life, grave Historie
> Raising the world to good or Evill fame
> Doth vindicate it to Æternitie.

The book seems to have been immediately popular. From

1614 to 1678, ten separate folio editions of it appeared, and of the first edition, certainly, and probably of others, there were several distinct issues. For the first time, English readers could enjoy an account of the Persian, Greek and Punic wars, written in the finest prose, as well as learned and yet popular discussions of those questions of biblical history and chronology which then interested the reading public. Wilson, in his life of James I, written in 1653, says "Rawleigh while he was a Prisoner, having the Idea of the World in his contemplation, brought it to some perfection in his excellent and incomparable history." The moral purpose of the book also commended it to many. It was a favourite book amongst the puritans of the next generation. Oliver Cromwell recommended it to his son Richard, saying, "Recreate yourself with Sir Walter Ralegh's *History;* it is a body of history, and will add much more to your understanding than fragments of story."

No doubt the popularity of the *History* was increased by the sudden revulsion of feeling in favour of Ralegh, which was called out by his tragic end, and the noble manner of his death. Men were glad to find in it the mind of one of the most distinguished amongst the soldiers and statesmen of the great days of Elizabeth. Many of the reasons which led to the popularity of the *History* no longer prevail with us. We value it, chiefly, as a noble monument of Elizabethan prose, and as a revelation of the character and mind of its author. But its place in the development of English historical writing should not be overlooked.

None of the political treatises written by Ralegh during his imprisonment were printed during his lifetime. *The Prerogative of Parliaments*, written in 1615, was circulated in manuscript copies and was presented to James I. In spite of the usual adulatory preface, James was much displeased by this treatise, which, in the form of a dialogue between a counsellor of state and a justice of the peace, demonstrates the advantage of raising money through parliament, instead of by benevolences and other exceptional means. For his day, at least, Ralegh's views were liberal—at any rate they were too liberal for James I. *The Prerogative of Parliaments* was not printed till ten years later, at "Midelburge." The manuscript of *The Cabinet Council*, a treatise on state-craft, passed into the hands of Milton, and was by him published in 1658. Its numerous quotations from the classics show the wide range of Ralegh's reading, and the treatment of the subject, as well as many allusions, shows his intimate acquaintance with the writings of Machiavelli. *The Maxims of State* is a shorter treatise of somewhat the same kind, wise and sensible enough, but, on the whole, it cannot be said that there is any distinctive flavour or charm of style about these two treatises. Ralegh's lack of humour gives a certain heaviness to his moral and political writings. They are wanting in terse and epigrammatic sayings, and give us the sense of being almost too wise. We are tempted, as we read, to think that he followed too closely his own precept, quoted in a paper called *The Loyal Observer*, printed in the *Harleian Miscellanies*, "It is an observation of judicious Ralegh 'Nothing is more an enemy to wisdom than drollery and over sharpness of conceit.'" Ralegh's papers dealing with naval and military affairs, such as *A Discourse on War in General* and *Observations on the Navy and Sea Service*, are much more living and full of interest, as written by a man having close personal acquaintance with what he is writing about. A paper on *Trade and Commerce* shows that he had studied modern conditions with the same care as the history of the past. In the paper on *A war with Spain* we have an interesting study of the relative strength of the European powers at that time, bringing out the great importance of the Dutch as a maritime power.

In all these occasional papers, we have constant evidence of Ralegh's wide knowledge, and of the way in which he had his knowledge at his command. Always there is a remarkable freedom in the use of historical allusions and illustrations.

The growing interest in Ralegh after his death led to the issue of various collections of his shorter papers. The most popular of these collections was *The Remains of Sir Walter Ralegh*, which first appeared in 1651, and of which there are many subsequent editions, varying slightly in their contents. Another interesting sign of the popular feeling for him was a little tract of six pages, which appeared in 1644, called *To-day a man, To-morrow none, or Sir Walter Rawleigh's Farewell to his Lady with his advice concerning Her and her Sonne.*

Besides this last letter to his wife, the tract contains the beautiful lines beginning "Like hermit poor," and the striking poem found in his Bible in the gate-house at Westminster, written on 28 October, 1618, the night before his execution.

CHAPTER IV

The Literature of the Sea

From the Origins to Hakluyt

THE great movement which stirred the minds of men in the days of the renascence, born in a love of the intimate life of nature, and in an abundant zeal for the glories of classic art and letters, received a new impulse and was inspired with a fresh tendency by the enlargement of the known world and a widening of the horizon of the nations. There was an eager desire to learn more, both of things at home and of the new lands which were being disclosed by the enterprise of merchants and seamen. Curiosity and patient zeal in search of the unknown began, indeed, at home. We may read in *The laboriouse Journey and Serche of Johan Leylande*—his new year's gift to Henry VIII—how he had been possessed with such a desire to see the different parts of the realm that there was

almost neyther cape nor baye, haven, creke or pere, ryver or confluence of ryvers, breches, washes, lakes, meres, fenny waters, mountaynes, valleys, mores, hethes, forestes, woodes, cyties, burges, castels, pryncypall manor places, monasteryes, and colleges, but I have seane them, and noted in so doynge a whole worlde of thynges verye memorable.

But the change now wrought in the outlook of the nations went far outside the narrow bounds of any one country, and was more vast than any the world had seen since the fall of the Roman empire. If it has been recognised more often in its intellectual character, its practical effects were seen in the discovery of new lands and the planting of new colonies. Copernicus had revealed the mystery of the universe. Portuguese and Spanish navigators had traversed the unknown seas, and John Cabot had touched the shores of cape Breton or Labrador. Nothing now seemed strange to any one, and, in every part of the world, there were new seas and lands to explore, and new approaches to be discovered to the Spice islands and Cathay. More, in his *Utopia*, opened a fresh view in the realm of speculation beyond the narrow bounds of knowledge. The most romantic poetic imaginings were exceeded in wonder by the things discovered and made known, and no marvel in *The Faerie Queene* exceeded the strange experiences that storm-tossed mariners told every day on 'change to the merchant adventurers of the Muscovy and Levant trades. "The nakedness of the Spaniards, and their long hidden secrets, whereby they went about to delude the world," as Hakluyt says, "were espied." Seamen were to make literature; upon their experience was to be built much of the literature that followed; their expressions and words were to descend into the common speech of the land. But, save, perhaps, in the instances of Gilbert and Ralegh, English seamen, pioneers of our maritime supremacy, were not in their own persons stirred by the intellectual movement. Rather they were its unconscious and often dumb instruments, while taking part in the vast material and political change which resulted from the direction of the capital and enterprise of merchants into fresh channels of intercourse and trade.

It would be true to say that the foundations of England's naval greatness were laid almost in silence, and that, though the peculiar genius of the nation for maritime adventure was recognised in the days of the early Henrys,[1] hardy seamen were opening communications with the Baltic, and driving their keels into unknown seas, long before any writer set himself to narrate their experiences or their exploits. Monastic chroniclers had collected the legendary lore of their predecessors, records of kings and annals of their own time, but voyages of exploration and discovery lay, mostly, outside the range of their experience or their opportunities of knowledge. It is mainly from narratives of pilgrimages and crusades that

[1] Cf. *The Libel of English Policy*, etc., referred to in Vol. II of the present work.

we learn how the known world was being widened in those early times. The brilliant chronicles of Giraldus Cambrensis, the quick-witted historian who records the conquest of Ireland, are not altogether barren of reference to events at sea, and there is some reflection of seafaring life in the pages of Geoffrey of Monmouth. Hakluyt, indeed, has included in the *Principall Navigations* the legendary conquests of Arthur and of Malgo from the chronicles of Geoffrey, the achievements of Edwin of Northumbria from Bede and the navigations of Edgar from Roger of Hoveden, Florence of Worcester and others. There are in existence various narratives of journeys to Palestine, like that of Saewulf of Malmesbury, who went overland to Italy in 1102, sailed thence to the Ionian islands and took ship along the coast to Joppa, where he re-embarked, but dared not venture into the open sea for fear of the Saracens. The voyages of Saewulf, and of Adelard, a little later, and the exploits of the crusaders in 1147 and 1190 on the coasts of Spain and in the Mediterranean, present a view of English enterprise that cannot be passed by without mention, because in them we trace the beginnings of a permanent marine, and of mercantile enterprise, which constituted the mainspring of the exploration of the world and, therefore, of the literature of discovery. But the seamen of Venice and Genoa, as well as Portuguese and Spanish navigators, were, in the fifteenth century, more enterprising than Englishmen, both in discovery and in the systematic recording of voyages.

The journeys of Marco Polo had aroused interest in the study of geography in England at the close of the thirteenth century, and the "travels" recorded by the Mandeville translators, considered in a previous chapter, had their well-deserved popularity in the early days of English prose. But the literature of travel by sea was unbegotten, and the achievements of the captains of prince Henry, "the navigator," and of Columbus and his companions, made far more sound in the world than anything done by British seamen until the time of Drake and Hawkins. A seaman named Thylde, whom William of Worcester mentions, preceded Columbus by some twelve years, as we ought not to forget, sailing from Bristol in 1480, but he battled vainly with the storms of the north Atlantic, and the world knows infinitely more of the great

navigations of the "admiral of the ocean" and of the bold
seaman Vasco Nuñez de Balboa, who first set eyes upon the
Pacific, and of Ojeda and Nicuesa, who were his equals in
courage and enterprise.

It is sometimes said that the great age of English discovery
really opened with John Cabot, who, in his effort to discover
a north-west passage to India, discovered the mainland of
America in 1497, and of him more is known than of the earlier
Bristol mariners; but even his discoveries may be accounted
foreign to the national instincts of the time, and, being himself
a seaman from the Mediterranean, his voyages seem rather to
belong to the age of Columbus and Vasco da Gama than
to that which saw the northern enterprises of Willoughby,
Chancellor and Burrough. The scanty particulars which
Hakluyt could bring together concerning the explorations of
John Cabot and his son Sebastian are a very striking illustration of the paucity of literary materials relating to the early
history of English maritime discovery.

The literary impulse to the recording of voyages came from
the continent, as was inevitable, since foreigners were the
pioneers in exploration, adding new links to the long chain of
seafaring enterprise which stretched back to the beginning
of Mediterranean history. Angiolo Poliziano, professor of
Greek and Latin literature at Florence, in a letter addressed
to king John II, tendered the thanks of the cultivated world
to Portugal for dragging from secular darkness into the light
of day new seas, new lands and new worlds, and offered his
services to record great voyages while the materials should be
fresh and available. At Seville, in 1522, Peter Martyr of
Anghiera, was instructed to examine all navigators who returned, and to write the history of Spanish explorations. He
threw his whole mind into the task, was the first historian
of the discovery of America and became known as a great
cosmographer. The first *Decade* of his *De Orbe Novo* was published at Seville in 1511, but appears to have been surreptitiously anticipated at Venice in 1504. Three of the *Decades*
followed at Alcalà in 1516, and other editions, largely augmented, were printed in 1530 and 1532, and were subsequently translated or became the basis of editions and works
published in Italy, France and Germany. Giovanni Battista

Ramusio published collections of voyages, which went through several editions, and told the story of Magellan's voyage as recorded by Antonio Pigafetta. Meanwhile, the printing of the *Sumario de la natural y general Hystoria de las Indias* of Gonçalo Hernandez de Oviedo y Valdes was completed at Toledo in 1526 and was followed, in 1552, by the *Istoria de las Indias y conquista de Mejico* of Francisco Lopez de Gomara. These, and other works, illuminated the new world for the benefit of the old, and, working like a ferment in the minds of scholars in every centre of learning in Europe, were a new inspiration of Englishmen, and set in motion the navigators who issued from English ports to conquer the mystery and win the spoils of new lands beyond the sea.

The first English book relating to America is said to have been printed in 1511, probably at Antwerp, by John Doesborch or Desborowe. It has been reprinted by Arber, in his *First Three English Books on America*, 1885, and is entitled *Of the newelandes and of ye people founde by the messengers of the Kynge of Portyngale named Emanuel;* but it is an arid tract, which relates chiefly to the ten nations christened by Prester John, and reflects the legends of the Middle Ages rather than any real knowledge of more recent explorations. More interesting are the references in a *New Interlude and a Merry of the nature of the Four Elements*, printed by John Rastell between 1510 and 1520. Here we have an account of the route to the new lands, and of how men could sail "plain eastwards and come to England again." The object was to cast scorn upon English mariners who had relinquished the enterprise, with assumed reference to a supposed failure of Sebastian Cabot in 1516-7.

In the literature of English navigation and discovery, a notable place must be given to Richard Eden, not, indeed, as an original narrator, but as a diligent interpreter of the work of others. His object was to make known to his countrymen what the Portuguese and Spaniards had done, and with that object he translated and published in 1553, from the Latin of Sebastian Münster's *Universal Cosmography*, *A Treatyse of the newe India with other new founde landes and Islands, as well eastwarde as westwarde, as they are knowen and founde in these our dayes*. He followed this, in 1555, with a translation from

Peter Martyr: *The Decades of the Newe Worlde or West India, conteyning the Navigations and Conquestes of the Spanyardes, with particular description of the most ryche and large Landes and Islandes lately found in the West Ocean.* These *Decades* are narratives of the voyages of Columbus and his companions, of Pedro Affonso, of Vincenzo Pinzon and of Nicuesa and others, and Eden added translations from Oviedo and matter descriptive of some other Spanish explorations. His object was national and patriotic; and, in presenting to his countrymen some record of the achievements of Spanish navigators, he censures the timidity of his times, and makes an eloquent appeal to seamen and merchants to quit the well-worn tracks of trade and commerce and to adventure boldly to the coasts of Florida and Newfoundland. Eden was born about the year 1521, and was a student at Cambridge under Sir Thomas Smith. He was a good Latin and Italian scholar, and tells his readers that, in his youth, he had read "the poet Hesiodus." He was minded to translate the whole of the *Pyrotechnica* of Vannuccio Biringaccio, but, having completed only a few chapters, he lent them to a friend to read, and they were lost. In the introduction to his tranlsation of the *Decades* of Peter Martyr, he expresses contempt for the previous issue, entitled, *Of the newe founde landes*, as "a shiete of printed paper (more worthy so to be called than a boke)." He had witnessed the splendours of the marriage procession of Philip and Mary, and was moved by its "within significance" for the future of England. His rendering is simple, direct and forcible, and, in a poetical epilogue entitled "Thinterpretours excuse," he says he has not been very curious to avoid "the scornes of Rhinoceros nose," nor "the fyled judgment of severe Aristarchus."

> I am not eloquent I know it ryght well;
> If I be not barbarous I desyre no more;
> I have not for every woorde asked counsell
> Of eloquent Eliot or Syr Thomas Moore.
> Take it therefore as I have intended;
> The faultes with favour may soon be amended.

Eden was not content to point out merely what foreigners had accomplished; he desired to show what were the fruits of their discoveries and to explain the secrets of land, sea and stars which must be known to those who would follow in their footsteps. Accordingly in 1561, at the expense of certain members of the Muscovy company, he published, under the title of *The Arte of Navigation*, a translation of Martin Cortes's *Breve compendio de la Sphera y de la arte de navigar*, printed at Seville in 1556. He likewise busied himself with gathering together the records of the Muscovy voyages, which formed so valuable a part of the subsequent collection of Hakluyt.

With the writings of Richard Eden, we reach the great age of maritime discovery, though still the stream of literature is small and intermittent. Two years before he published or wrote, Sir Hugh Willoughby, with the object of reaching Cathay, had sailed, in 1553, upon that voyage to the north-east in which he perished. Hakluyt has preserved the records of that great effort, and he presents to us the striking picture of Sebastian Cabot, as "governour of the mysterie and companie of the Marchants adventurers," laying down his wise ordinances and instructions for the intended voyage. The captain-general, the pilot-major (who was Richard Chancellor), the masters, merchants and other officers were to be

so knit and accorded in unitie, love, conformitie, and obedience in everie degree on all sides, that no dissention, variance or contention may rise or spring betwixt them and the mariners of this companie to the damage or hindrance of the voyage.

Regulations were laid down for the discipline and conduct of the fleet, and, in relation to the records of adventure, merchants and other skilful persons were to put into writing daily their observations of navigation, of day and night, lands, tides, elements, altitude of the sun, course of the moon and stars and other matters, and these were afterwards to be collated, discussed and placed upon record. Again, it was ordered that the liveries in apparel given to the mariners were to be kept by the merchants and not to be worn except by order of the captain when he should see cause to muster or show his men in good array, for the adornment and honour of the voyage, and then they were again to be delivered to the keeping of the merchants.

Willoughby perished, but Clement Adams wrote in Latin an account of the navigation, which was conducted by Richard Chancellor, and Hakluyt has given a translation. Amongst other things he tells how Henry Sidney came down to the ships and eloquently addressed the masters before they departed from the Thames. He contrasted the hard life of the seaman, and its dangers and uncertainties with the quiet life at home. He spoke of the duty of keeping unruly mariners in good order and obedience, and concluded by saying,

With how many cares shall he trouble and vex himself? with how many troubles shall he break himself? and how many disquietings shall he be forced to sustain? We shall keep on our coasts and country; he shall seek strange and unknown regions.

We now see the spirit of enterprise thoroughly aroused. English seamen were not only seeking to reach Cathay and the Spice islands by the north-east or the north-west, but were resolved to make an end of the barriers that were set up by Portuguese and Spanish monopolies and partitions. William Hawkins had broken with the old trade routes in his three voyages to Brazil and the coast of Guinea in the time of Henry VIII, and the successive voyages of his son, the celebrated Sir John Hawkins, in 1562, 1564 and 1567, made a great mark upon the history of the time and practically led, together with the actions of Drake, to the breach with Spain. Of his third voyage, Hawkins himself wrote an account, published in the year of his return, entitled *A True Declaration of the Troublesome voyage of Mr. John Hawkins to the parts of Guinea and the West Indies in the years of our Lord 1567 and 1568*. It is a vigorous and direct narrative of experiences, full of shrewd observations, and with a notable reflective quality. "If all the miseries and troublesome affaires of this sorrowfull voyage should be perfectly and thoroughly written," says the author, "there should neede a paynfull man with his penne, and as great a time as hee had that wrote the lives and deathes of the martirs." Other accounts were written by Miles Philips, Job Hartop and David Ingram, all survivors of the fight at San Juan de Ulloa, and their narratives have been printed by Hakluyt. For the record of the great navigations of Drake in 1570 and 1572 and his wonderful voyage of

circumnavigation in 1577, we have to consult mostly the collection of Hakluyt and certain volumes published in the seventeenth century.

The project of passing by the north-west to Cathay and the
Spice islands had long inspired Sir Humphrey Gilbert. His
Discourse of a Discoverie for a new passage to Cataia was issued
in April, 1576, in a black letter tract of great rarity, written
some seven years before. In a prefatory note, it is introduced
to the reader by George Gascoigne, a friend of the author,
who tells us that a worshipful knight, Sir Humphrey's brother,
was "abashed at this enterprise," because he had no heir but
the author, and that to him the enterprise seemed "unpossible
unto common capacities." The brother, therefore, misliked
Sir Humphrey's resolution, and sought to dissuade him, and
it was in order to overcome his objections that this *Discourse*
was prepared. Gascoigne, being on a visit to Gilbert at his
dwelling at Limehouse, had a sight of the *Discourse*. Being
a short essay, and Martin Frobisher (whom he calls "Four-
boyser, a kinsman of mine") having engaged in the same enterprise, it seemed to him that it would be useful to make public
the tract. He compared it with the tables of Ortelius and
sundry other cosmographical maps and charts, and said it was
approved by the learned Dr. Dee, whose house at Mortlake
was the seat of astronomical and nautical knowledge. In this
remarkable letter, Gilbert tells his brother that he might
have charged him with an unsettled head if he had taken
in hand the discovery of Utopia, but Cataia was no country
of the imagination, and the passage thereto by sea on the
north side of Labrador had been mentioned and proved by the
most expert and best learned amongst modern geographers.
To Gilbert, the continent of America was an island representing
the Atlantis of Plato and of other writers of antiquity. If
Atlantis were an island, the cataclysm in which it had been
partly overwhelmed, would, said Gilbert, make more practica-
ble the navigation of its northern coasts. He was confirmed
in his opinion by Gemma Frisius, Münster, Regiomontanus,
Peter Martyr, Ortelius and other modern geographers, as well
as by the experience of certain navigators, including Othere
in king Alfred's time and others more recent.

Sir Humphrey Gilbert's tract remains amongst the most

notable literary contributions to the subject of exploration which preceded the publication of the monumental work of Hakluyt. At the conclusion of his discourse, he writes: "He is not worthy to live at all who, for fear of danger or death, shunneth his country's service or his own honour, since death is inevitable and the fame of virtue immortal." This discourse has the true ring of a scholarly and patriotic Englishman, and there is much freshness in its persuasive earnestness.

This great Englishman made his first voyage of discovery to North America, with his half-brother, Sir Walter Ralegh, in his company, in 1578. Hakluyt has preserved a narrative of Gilbert's last enterprise, in 1583, in which he perished; and there are few more striking pictures in English narrative literature than that of the old seaman, on the September afternoon upon which his vessel, the "Squirrel," was overwhelmed, sitting abaft on his quarter-deck with a book in his hand, hailing the men in the "Golden Hind," which was following in the wake, whenever she came within hailing distance, with the old seaman's phrase, uttered, says the narrator, with signs of joy, "We are as near to heaven by sea as by land." These were the last words of this good Englishman before he went down. A speech, says the narrator, "well beseeming a soldier resolute in Jesus Christ, as I can testify he was."

Meanwhile, the valiant Martin Frobisher had also been battling with the icy approaches to the north-west, in 1576 and 1577; and, in the following year, captain George Best, Frobisher's trusted friend, printed in black letters *A true discourse of the late voyages for the finding of a passage to Cathaya by the north-weast, under the conduct of Martin Frobisher, Generall.* Hakluyt has collected narratives of all these voyages, but none are so lively and vigorous as those which captain Best has given us in his volume. What could be more direct and forcible than a letter which Frobisher wrote in August, 1577, to certain Englishmen who were held captive by truculent natives, and whom he was resolved to set free?

In the name of God, in whom we all believe, who, I trust, hath preserved your bodies and souls amongst these infidels, I commend me unto you. I will be glad to seek by all means you can devise for your deliverance either with force or with any commodities within my ships, which I will not spare for your sakes, or anything else I can do for you.

After telling them that he has some natives on board whom he would exchange, he proceeds,

Moreover you may declare unto them that if they deliver you not I will not leave a man alive in their country. And thus, if one of you can come to speak with me, they shall have either the man woman or child in pawn for you, and thus unto God, whom I trust you do serve, in haste I leave you, and to Him we will daily pray for you. . . . Yours to the uttermost of my power, Martin Frobisher.

An appetite for further knowledge now existed throughout the land, and eager enquirers were demanding information as to the voyages of the navigators and the riches of the new-found lands. In 1577, a new edition of Eden's *Decades of the Newe Worlde* appeared under the title of *The History of Travayle in the West and East Indies, and other countreys lying either way towards the fruitfull and ryche Moluccaes . . . with a discourse of the North-west Passage*. It was augmented and finished by Richard Willes, who says that he was moved to place in an orderly manner what Eden had "confusely gyven out." He omitted some things which he thought superfluous, and added to the three decades of Peter Martyr, and to the fourth, which is given under another title, four others, besides including many additional accounts of voyages relating to Japan and the Guinea coast, Muscovy voyages and travels, the exploits of Magellan and the explorations of Sebastian Cabot. The most interesting of his additions is his argument regarding the projected passage by the north-west. First, he gives the arguments advanced against the project, and then attempts to show the reasonableness of it. "M. Frobisher's prosperous voyage and happy returne wyl absolutely decide these controversies."

Eden and Willes were the precursors of Hakluyt, and lived in a time when many seamen were leaving our ports to penetrate the mysteries of the unknown world. Hakluyt's first book, a voyage of discovery to America, was published in 1582, and he issued a new edition of Peter Martyr's *De Orbe Novo* in

1587. He was preparing himself then for his great work. The imperial imagination was stirred, and the importance of colonising and developing the new-found lands was in all men's minds. Ralegh received his charter of colonisation in 1584, and three expeditions were despatched to the new colony to which he gave the name of Virginia. In the introduction to the second book of *The Faerie Queene*, Spenser bids the man who does not know "where is that happy land of Faery," in which he has drawn his immortal allegory, to see how little of the world he is acquainted with.

> But let that man with better sence advize,
> That of the world least part to us is red;
> And daily how through hardy enterprize
> Many great Regions are discovered,
> Which to late age were never mentioned.
> Who ever heard of th' Indian Peru?
> Or who in venturous vessell measured
> The Amazon huge river, now found trew?
> Or fruitfullest Virginia who did ever vew?

Thus did the spirit of discovery make its influence felt in literature. What had been achieved was being recorded or made known by rumour and report, and the bold work of navigators made a profound impression upon thinking men at home, who, by speech and pen, impelled them to new conquests in the unknown. In the record of these achievements, no name stands higher than that of John Davys, the famous voyager, beloved by his comrades, who made three Arctic voyages and gave his name to Davis strait. All these expeditions of Davys are related in the pages of Hakluyt's *Principall Navigations*. The narratives of the first and third voyages were written by John James, and of the second by Davys himself, the detached voyage of the "Sunshine" being narrated by Henry Morgan, the purser. Davys had, of course, kept logs during all these voyages, but the log of his third voyage is the only one that has been preserved. Davys was also the author of *The Seaman's Secrets*, published in 1594, and several times reprinted. It is a valuable treatise on navigation, devoted to "the three kinds of sayling, horizontall, paradoxall, and sayling upon a great circle," and including a tide table and a "regiment" for finding the declinations of the sun. Davys's Arctic voyages were all made with the object of discovering the north-west passage, in the navigability of which he was a firm believer, and his name, with those of Gilbert and Frobisher, will ever be associated with the early efforts to penetrate the icy barrier and discover a direct route to Cathay and the Spice islands. His arguments in favour of it will be found in his volume, *The Worlde's Hydrographical Description*, a black letter treatise, published in London in 1595, wherein he sought to show that the earth was habitable in all its zones, and navigable in all its seas. In his fervid imagination, difficulties disappeared, and he draws a glowing picture of the advantages which would accrue to England from the discovery of a passage by the north-west. He sets forth the arguments against the passage, and then, with cumulative force, endeavours to prove them untenable, and he quotes Isaiah from memory (lxv, 1, "They seeke me that hitherto have not asked for me; they find me that hitherto have not sought me").

Another remarkable contribution to the literature of maritime discovery is the description of his adventures by Sir Richard Hawkins, only son of Sir John Hawkins, a storehouse of information of all kinds concerning the lives and ideas of the early navigators. It is entitled *The Observations of Sir Richard Hawkins, Knight, in his voiage into the South Sea; anno Domini*, 1593 (printed 1622). In this volume, Hawkins shows strong descriptive power, imagination and skill, besides natural sagacity and a just judgment of affairs. He enforces the need of experience for the successful conduct of enterprise at sea, adding "and I am of opinion that the want of experience is much more tolerable in a general on land than in a governor by sea." The ship in which he sailed was built in the Thames in 1588, and he tells us that his mother, craving the naming of the ship, called her the "Repentance." He expostulated with her for giving the vessel that "uncouth name," but never could have any satisfaction, save that "repentance was the safest ship we could sail in to purchase the haven of heaven."

In the halls of merchant companies, in the parlours of enterprising traders and in the chambers of students, problems of the new world, and the means of reaching its treasures, were being discussed. The genius of the nation for colonisation was now aroused, and new lands were to be developed by men of English blood. Seamen had begun to speak in literature, and the thoughts and language of the sea, by tongue and writing, were being grafted into the conceptions and the language of men who never knew the salt breath of the ocean. Lyly has a mariner strongly emphasised in his *Galathea*, 1592; Lodge, himself a sailor, wrote his *Rosalynde*, 1590, "in the ocean, where every line was wet with a surge, and every human passion counterchecked with a storm"; his *Margarite of America*, 1596, was begun in the strait of Magellan, on board ship, where "I had rather will to get my dinner than win my fame." The new spirit in literature is seen in the poems of Spenser and it had a profound influence upon Bacon. Above all, it is reflected in the writings of Shakespeare; the sea sings in his music, and the anger of its storms thunders in the rush of his invective; the magic and romance of discovery and strange tales of the navigators are reflected in the witchery of his language. Ralegh wrote of the "Ewaipanoma race," who had eyes in their shoulders, and mouths in the middle of their bowels, and it is with such marvels that Othello beguiles the ear of Desdemona, who would "seriously incline" to his moving story of wonders,

> And of the Cannibals that each other eat,
> The Anthropophagi, and men whose heads
> Do grow beneath their shoulders.

Though he rarely deals with the sea directly, Shakespeare never uses nautical language except correctly and aptly. His seamen speak as with the voice of the sea, his allusions all have the knowledge of the sea. In *Twelfth Night* (III, 2) Maria says of Malvolio that "he doth smile his face into more lines than are in the new map with the augmentation of the Indies." This was the map published with Hakluyt's *Voyages*, bearing the marks of Davys's hand, showing the geographical knowledge of the time, his discoveries in the north-west, and those of Magellan, Drake, Sarmiento and Cavendish in the south; the imaginary strait of Anian between Asia and America disappears, and, in its place, is the Pacific, as traversed by the Spanish captain, Francisco de Gali, whose narrative was translated into Dutch by Linschoten, and then into English under the title of *Discourse of the East and West Indies*, 1598. In *The Tempest*, Shakespeare speaks of the "still vexed Bermoothes," doubtless with reference to the sufferings and shipwrecks of explorers, and, perhaps, particularly to the expedition of Sir George Somers, which was driven on the coast of the then unknown Bermudas in 1609. But to Shakespeare, as to his predecessors, the sea still remained rather a barrier than a pathway; it was the "moat defensive to a house," of which John of Gaunt speaks in *Richard II*, "against the envy of less happier lands."

Many illustrations might be given of Shakespeare's knowledge of the sea and seafarers. Was it a mere coincidence that Ancient Pistol, hauled off to the Fleet with Falstaff in the last scene of *Henry IV*, part II, uses a phrase which is employed in *The Observations of Sir Richard Hawkins*, referred to above, existing in manuscript, we presume, when Shakespeare wrote the play? Or, rather, were not Shakespeare and Hawkins quoting from a common original in the speech of the people? *Si fortuna me tormenta spero me contenta*, says the Ancient. When Hawkins loses his pinnace at Plymouth he, also, exclaims, *Si fortuna me tormenta, esperança me contenta*. In *The Comedy of Errors*, old Aegeon of Syracuse, recounting his woes in the storm, says,

> The seas wax'd calm, and we discovered
> Two ships from far making amain to us.

To "make amain" or "wave amain" was the signal of surrender by striking sail or flag (*amener le pavillon*). Sir Richard Hawkins, off Ushant, sights a great hulk, and his men, eager to make a Spanish prize, "without speaking to her wished that the gunner might shoot at her to cause her to amain"—a bad custom, says Hawkins, "to gun at all whatsoever they discover." *The Tempest* has many nautical allusions; in *Romeo and Juliet* it is "to the high top-gallant of my joy" that Romeo climbs by "a tackled stair"; in *As You Like It*, we find the figure, "Dry as the remainder biscuit after a voyage"; in *The Merchant of Venice* there is much of the ventures of the traders, and thus says Solanio, if he had such ventures,

> I should be still
> Plucking the grass to know where sits the wind;
> Peering in maps for ports and piers and roads.

It is to Richard Hakluyt that we are indebted for our knowledge of many matters that have been alluded to above. Shakespeare undoubtedly studied his pages. Scattered treatises and manuscript descriptions alone existed when Hakluyt set to work. He had long been amassing material, and his writings, as we have mentioned, began to appear in 1582, while the first edition of the *Principall Navigations* was published in 1589. The latter is the first great body of information we possess relating to the voyages of the sixteenth century. Purchas and others followed in his steps, and carried on the task, but the nation and its literature owe a debt to Hakluyt which is imperfectly recognised even now. His whole life was given up, with a singleness of purpose that has rarely been matched, to the literature of navigation and discovery. When he undertook his labours he set himself an arduous task. Proceeding to France as chaplain to Sir Edward Stafford, ambassador to the French court, in 1583, he learned much of foreign discoveries and enterprises at sea, but, in Paris, he found the English noted of all others for "their sluggish security." Eden had been but an interpreter of what others had done; and it was because Hakluyt heard much obloquy of our nation, and because few or none were able to make reply, that, with the object of "stopping the mouths of our reproachers," he determined forthwith to undertake the work, which others, he said, owing to the heavy labour involved, and the small profit that would result, had rejected. One cause of the state of things which Hakluyt deplored must not be overlooked. It was that English voyages and expeditions had been undertaken mainly with a commercial purpose, and with the object of gain, and that merchants who invested their capital in these enterprises were not always anxious that the results of their discoveries should be made known for the advantage of others. The guild of the merchant adventurers did much to extend the range of discovery, and gave a fresh impulse to seamanship and navigation, particularly in the east, but it did not promote the general knowledge of those operations which were its especial privilege, and nowhere can we discern any direct encouragement to the publication of the records of maritime discovery.

All honour, therefore, is due to Richard Hakluyt for his lifelong devotion to the subject he made his own. His writings are informed with the qualities of his enthusiasm, and he has brought together an immense mass of original material, without which our knowledge would have heen restricted and our understanding of the maritime events of his time uncertain. He has himself told us, in the dedication to Sir Francis Walsingham of the first edition of his *Principall Navigations*, how he was attracted to the subject which afterwards engrossed his attention until his death. He was born about the year 1553, in London, as is conjectured, but belonged to a family long seated at Yatton, in Herefordshire. He was one of the queen's scholars at Westminster school, that "fruitful nursery," as he describes it, and it was his fortune, he tells us, to visit the chamber of his cousin, Richard Hakluyt, a gentleman of the Middle Temple, who had greatly interested himself in maritime discovery and the science of navigation, in relation to the ventures and expeditions of the Muscovy and Levant merchants. The writings of Peter Martyr and Pigafetta, the translations of Eden and the works of the great cosmographers had, doubtless, been his study. The Westminster boy found lying open upon a board in his cousin's room certain books of cosmography and a universal map. In these, he displayed some curiosity, whereupon his kinsman began to instruct his ignorance by explaining to him the divisions of the earth according to the old account and the new learning. With a wand, Richard Hakluyt pointed out to the youth all the known seas, gulfs, bays, straits, capes, rivers, empires, kingdoms, dukedoms and territories. He spoke also of their commodities and their particular wants, which, by the benefits of traffic and the intercourse of merchants, were plentifully supplied. Then he touched the boy's imagination by taking down the Bible, and, turning to the 107th *Psalm*, directed him to read in the 23rd and 24th verses that "they which go downe to the sea in ships and occupy the great waters, they see the works of the Lord, and his wonders in the deep." These words of the psalmist, together with his cousin's discourse, were, says

Hakluyt, things of high and rare delight to his young nature, and made upon him so deep an impression that he resolved that if ever he were preferred to the university, where he might have a more convenient place and better time for such studies, he would, by God's assistance, prosecute the knowledge of this kind of literature, the doors whereof, he says, after a sort, were so happily opened before him.

He was elected, in 1570, to Christ Church, Oxford, where he did not forget the resolution he had made, and fell to the course he had intended; so that by degrees he read whatever he could find of printed voyages in all languages. He lectured, but where is not definitely known, upon subjects relating to navigation, and became familiar, by reading, with the personalities of sea captains, and the enterprises of great merchants. He was incessantly employed in the examination of collections, and transcription of accounts of voyages and travels, and of all things bearing on the subject, and, in his later years, he was engrossed in this work, and in correspondence with all who could impart information.

His first published work was *Divers Voyages touching the Discoverie of America & the Islands adjacent unto the same*, issued in 1582, and dedicated to Sir Philip Sidney. This book, which is of extreme rarity, but has been republished by the Hakluyt society, 1850, had the direct and practical object of increasing the knowledge of navigation, and spreading abroad the fast growing impulse towards the colonising of newly discovered lands. In Paris, as chaplain to the ambassador, Hakluyt discovered a manuscript account of Florida, which was published at his expense in a French edition at Paris, in 1586, dedicated to Sir Walter Ralegh as the discoverer of Virginia. This volume was afterwards published in an English version in London, in 1587, under the title *A Notable Historie containing foure voyages made by certayne French Captains unto Florida*, the object being to promote the colonisation of Virginia. In 1587, Hakluyt published in Paris a revised edition of Peter Martyr of Anghiera's *De Orbe Novo*, which, also, was dedicated to Ralegh, and was intended further to extend the knowledge of discovery, seamanship and nautical astronomy among English mariners. With the age of Columbus and his successors the necessity of astronomical study had been realised, and improved methods of navigation grew with the thirst for maritime enterprise. This knowledge came originally from the continent, in its scientific form, and Johann Müller of Königsberg, known as Regiomontanus, compiled the *Ephe‑ merides*, from 1475 to 1506, which were used by Columbus and da Gama, while Martin Behaim, of Nürnberg, invented an improved application of the astrolabe to navigation, and con‑ structed the earliest globe now extant. Spanish students continued to work upon the exposition of these teachers for the next two hundred years. The best English work upon the subject was William Bourne's *Regiment of the Sea*, 1573. Hakluyt's edition of Peter Martyr, subsequently translated into English at his suggestion by Michael Lok, was an im‑ portant addition to scientific knowledge, and was followed, in 1594, by *The Seaman's Secrets* of John Davys, to which ref‑ erence has already been made. Hakluyt had been profoundly interested in the scientific aspect of navigation, and in "the means of bringing up skilful seamen and mariners in this realm," and had laid before Charles Howard, earl of Effingham, lord high admiral, in the dedication of the second edition of the *Principall Navigations*, the importance of establishing a lec‑ tureship in navigation for seamen in London, having in view the many noble ships that had been lost, the many worthy persons "drenched in the sea," and how the realm had been impoverished by loss of great ordnance and other rich com‑ modities through the ignorance of seamen.

We have been led to speak of this aspect of Hakluyt's literary work and his practical purposes by his publication of the revised edition of Peter Martyr's book at Paris in 1587. During many years previous to this date, he had been amassing materials for his great work, *The Principall Navigations, Voiages and Discoveries of the English Nation, made by sea or over land to the most remote and farthest distant quarters of the earth at any time within the compasse of these* 1500 *yeeres*, of which the first edition appeared in one volume folio published by George Bishop and Ralph Newbery in 1589. It was dedicated to Sir Francis Walsingham, while the second edition, containing the navigations *within the compasse of these* 1600 *yeeres*, in three volumes, dated 1598, 1599 and 1600, was dedicated, the first volume to Charles Howard, earl of Nottingham, and the others to Sir Robert Cecil, "whose earnest desires to do him [Hakluyt] good, lately broke out into most bountiful and acceptable effects."

It has already been shown that Hakluyt was a pioneer in the literature of English maritime discovery. He remarks, in an epistle dedicatory to an English translation of Galvano's *Discoveries of the World*, that, if any man should marvel that, in these discoveries, for the space of almost 4000 years, the British nation was scarcely four times mentioned, he was to understand that when Galvano completed his task about the year 1556, "there was little extant of men's travailes," and that, for aught he, Hakluyt, could see, no great matter would have come to light if he had not undertaken the "heavy burden." In the dedication of the first edition of his great book, he speaks of it as a burden, because these works lay so dispersed, scattered and "hidden in several hucksters' hands" that he wondered at himself to see how he was able to endure the delays, the curiosity and the backwardness of many from whom he was to receive his originals. Again, in the dedication of the first volume of the second edition to the lord high admiral, he says that "after great charges and infinite care, after many watchings, toils and travels and wearying out of my weake bodie," he had at length collected the materials for his volumes, and had

brought to light many rare and worthy monuments which long have lien miserably scattered in mustie corners, and retchlessly hidden in mistie darknesse, and were very like for the greatest part to have been buried in perpetuall oblivion.

There is surely a note of disappointment where he says, in another place in the dedication of the first volume of the second edition to the lord high admiral:

For the bringing of which into this homely and rough-hewen shape which here thou seest; what restlesse nights, what painefull dayes, what heat, what cold I have endured; how many long, and chargeable journeys I have travailed; how many famous libraries have I searched into; what varietie of ancient and moderne writers I have perused; what a number of old records, patents, privileges, letters, etc., I have redeemed from obscuritie and perishing; into how many manifold acquaintance I have entered, what expences I have not spared; and yet what faire opportunities of private gaine, preferment, and ease I have neglected, albeit thyself canst hardly imagine, yet I by daily experience do finde and feele and some of my entire friends can sufficiently testifie.

The gratitude he expresses to Cecil in the later introductions encourages the belief that his plaint did not go unheard. Though Hakluyt had to deplore the scarcity of his materials, and to labour under the multitude of his enquiries and the magnitude of his task, he was sustained until the end and spurred to boundless enthusiasm by the subject which he had made his own. He was full of pride in the deeds of Englishmen in former ages, but declared that in Elizabeth's time, they had excelled all the nations and people of the earth. Their half-concealed achievements were at last embodied in his own pages. Which of English kings, he said, before her Majesty, had seen their banners in the Caspian sea? which of them had ever dealt with the emperor of Persia, obtaining large privileges for merchants? whoever saw, "before this regiment, an English Ligier in the stately porch of the Grand Signor at Constantinople?" Who, he asks, had ever found English consuls and agents before at Tripolis in Syria, at Aleppo, at Babylon and at Balsara, and, what was more, who had ever heard of Englishmen at Goa before that time?

What English shippes did heretofore ever anker in the mighty river of Plate? passe and repasse the impassable (in former opinion) straight of Magellan, range along the coast of Chili, Peru, and all the backside of Nova Hispania, further than any Christian ever passed, traverse the mighty bredth of the South Seas, land upon the Luzones in despight of the enemy, enter into alliance, amity, and traffike with the princes of the Molluccas and the Isle of Java, double the famous Cape of Bona Speranza, arrive at the Isle of Santa Helena, and last of al returne home most richly laden with the commodities of China, as the subjects of this now flourishing monarchy have done?

Hakluyt ransacked chroniclers for such records of voyages as he could find. He investigated the papers of the merchant companies and, as he tells us, he travelled far in order to interview travellers and examine records of exploration. He gives the state of the ships of the Cinque Ports from Lambarde's *Perambulation of Kent*. He also included that remarkable essay *The Libel of English Policy*.[1]   The voyages to the north-east are mostly taken from the documents of the Muscovy company and include the navigations of Willoughby, Chancellor, Stephen Burrough and others.   The volumes also include some records of the naval fighting of the time, including *The Miraculous Victory atchieved by the English flete under the discreet and happy conduct of the right honourable, right prudent and valiant Lord, the lord Charles Howard, lord high admiral of England*.   The voyages to the south and south-east are taken largely from records of the Levant traders, and include the explorations of Challoner and Lok, Jenkinson, John Foxe and others.   Some papers relating to these voyages appear to have been taken from the records of Hakluyt's uncle, Richard Hakluyt, who was interested in these ventures. There are James Lancaster's expedition to the Cape of Good Hope, Zanzibar and Malacca, and Drake's expedition to Cadiz. In relation to the voyages to the north-west there are scanty accounts of the expeditions of the Cabots, and fine descriptive narratives of the voyages of Hawkins.   These, and the expeditions of Gilbert and Frobisher, have already been alluded to.   The expeditions of Philip Amada and Arthur Barlow, and various accounts of the enterprises of Drake, Ralegh and others also hold a notable place in the volumes.

There is no purpose in cataloguing the contents of Hakluyt's volumes here, nor in offering more than a general comment upon them.   The object has been to indicate their place and significance in national literature and to describe their origin and character.   Hakluyt was no doubt the editor as well as the collector of these records.   Amid all their variety and diversity of qualities and merits, it is possible to discern a certain unity and the influence of an individuality.   Much excellent prose, strong and vigorous in character, often dignified and persuasive, is to be found in the book.   Lucid and careful description, often lighted up by imagination and literary power, distinguishes many of these relations of voyages. They constitute a body of narrative literature which is of

---

[1] See Vol. II of the present work, p. 480 ff.

the highest value for an understanding of the spirit and tendency of the time, and, together with the later collection of Purchas, who brought together some things which had escaped the vigilance of Hakluyt, they are the basis of our knowledge of the part which Englishmen played in enlarging the boundaries of the known world in the great age of exploration and discovery.

CHAPTER V

Seafaring and Travel

The Growth of Professional Text-Books and Geographical Literature

THE preceding chapter has shown how the great race of the Tudor seamen left their mark on the literature of the country of their birth. In a survey of the written record of the seafaring of the sixteenth and seventeenth centuries, we are necessarily attracted more to its subject than to its manner. We cannot judge it by such standards as are applied to the poetry, the drama, or the historical literature of the time. Ralegh and Lodge, as men of literary study and training, stand almost alone among navigators. Most of their contemporaries and successors were men who fought the tempest and the enemy and knew little of the wielding of the pen. Rarely did they sit down to write anything more ambitious than a letter or a rough journal without making profuse apologies for their lack of literary experience. They were men, nevertheless, who dreamed dreams and saw visions: not always, indeed, dreams like those of Columbus, who thought that to add a realm to Christendom was object and reward enough, but dreams more often like those of the later Spaniards, who laid heavy burdens on the backs of treasure mules and filled caravels with silver. Explorers went in quest of the gold and spicery of the mysterious lands of Zipangu and Cathay, and the "commodities" of the new world fell into their hands in the search.

They were confronted from the beginning with the monopolies of Portugal and Spain. The Spaniards were firmly seated in central America and Peru. Vasco da Gama and his successors had made their own the route by the cape of Bôa Esperança to the treasures beyond. Magellan had gone to the south-west by the strait that bears his name, and Drake had followed him; but the Pacific coast of southern America had become the monopoly of Spain. If Englishmen, also, were to have monopoly and sway, that they might gather unimpeded the treasures of the unknown and half-fabulous lands of the Pacific, they must penetrate by the sea route of the north-west; and Gilbert and a hundred other seamen persuaded themselves and the merchants, by every argument to be found in heaven or earth, that through the icy passages there was an open way to the west. The temper in which navigators wrestled with the elements was exemplified by the remark of Robert Thorne, the Bristol seaman, who said: "There is no land unhabitable, no sea innavigable." Failure to pierce icy barriers was the root of all the expansion and rivalry that followed, both in the east and in the west. A hundred projects for penetrating the great Pacific were in the air. The Dutch were grasping at the spoil of the Portuguese, and, in England, men of commerce became men of war, merchant and mariner alike being resolute to snatch the sceptre of the sea from the weakening grasp of Spain. Thus, as Drayton says:

> A thousand kingdoms will we seek from far,
> As many nations waste in civil war;
> Where the dishevelled ghastly sea-nymph sings,
> Our well-rigged ships shall stretch their swelling wings,
> And drag their anchors through the sandy foam.
> About the world in every clime to roam;
> And there unchristened countries call our own
> Where scarce the name of England hath been known.

Hakluyt is the recorder of these deeds in queen Elizabeth's day—not of quite all of them, indeed, for he pays scanty heed to the earlier exploits of Drake, and, in his preface of 1589, excuses himself "to the favourable reader" for so doing. Perhaps he had in mind the comments which a complete narration might have aroused abroad. Navigators were men of action and not of words. Drake, on the famous occasion when he took upon himself to preach in place of Master Fletcher, the chaplain—"Francis Fletcher, the falsest knave that liveth"—

declared that he was a very bad orator, "for my bringing up hath not been in learning." Bacon, in his *Considerations Touching the War with Spain*, explains the underlying theory and object of their actions:

For money, no doubt it is the principal part of the greatness of Spain; for by that they maintain their veteran army; and Spain is the only state of Europe which is a money grower. But in this part, of all others, is most to be considered the ticklish and brittle state of the greatness of Spain. Their greatness consisteth in their treasure, their treasure in the Indies, and their Indies (if it be well weighed) are indeed but an accession to such as are masters of the sea. So as this axle-tree, whereupon their greatness turneth, is soon cut in two by any that shall be stronger than they by sea.

The strategical theories of Bacon, translated into action by navigators and recorded by Hakluyt, filling many adventurers with a new spirit of conquest and achievement in the years that followed, could not fail to move the imagination of poets and dramatists. We have seen how Spenser set forth the argument and inward character of these voyages; how they had their influence upon Shakespeare, and, we might have added, upon Marlowe and other dramatists. William Warner, in *Albion's England* (1602), sings of Willoughby, Chancellor, Jenkinson, Jackman and Pet, of Hawkins, Drake, Gilbert, Frobisher and others, advising resort to the recent pages of the *Principall Navigations*.

Samuel Daniel, in his *Musophilus, or Defence of all Learning* (1603), extols the new spirit in a colloquy with Philocosmus:

> Whenas our accent, equal to the best
> Is able greater wonders to bring forth;
> When all that ever hotter springs expresst,
> Comes bettered by the patience of the North.
> And who, in time, knows whither we may vent
> The treasure of our tongue, to what strange shores
> This gain of our best glory shall be sent,
> T' enrich unknowing nations with our stores?
> What worlds in th' yet unformed Occident
> May come refin'd with th' accents that are ours?
> Or, who can tell for what great worke in hand
> The greatness of our style is now ordain'd?

Ralegh's discovery and proposed colonisation of Guiana[1]
was the subject of George Chapman's *De Guiana Carmen* (1596).

> Guiana—whose rich feet are mines of gold,
> Whose forehead knocks against the roof of stars,
> Stands on her tip-toes at fair England looking,
> Kissing her hand, bowing her mighty breasts,
> And every sign of all submission making
> To be her sister, and the daughter both
> Of our most sacred maid.

It was an age of universal curiosity, and Englishmen were
seeking a wider knowledge of the world. The bibliography
will show that a copious volume of literature, descriptive or
otherwise, relating to history, discovery and navigation, issued
from the press at this time. Among writers who contributed
the fruit of much solid research to the knowledge then possessed of foreign countries and their history was Richard Knolles,
whose *General Historie of the Turkes from the first beginning
of that Nation to the rising of the Othoman Familie* was published
in 1603, and long continued to hold a high repute, by reason
of the fact that it was written in excellent prose and opened
a new field to the English student. A second edition appeared
in 1610, in which year Knolles died; and there were later
editions in 1621, 1631 and 1638. Johnson thought highly
of Knolles's style; and, though he found it sometimes vitiated
by false wit, considered it "pure, nervous, elevated and clear."
To Horace Walpole, Knolles was tiresome, but Southey admired him, and Byron, writing shortly before his death at
Missolonghi, said,

Old Knolles was one of the first books that gave me pleasure
when I was a child; and I believe it had much influence on my
future wishes to visit the Levant, and gave perhaps the Oriental
colouring which is observed in my poetry.

Some books issued at the time, like Robert Johnson's
translation, *The Traveller's Breviat, or an historicall description
of the most famous Kingdomes in the World* (1601), were merely
accounts from many sources of the character and peoples of
various countries. These were volumes intended for the enter-

[1] See *ante*, Chap. III, pp. 65, 66.

tainment of such as remained at home, and the instruction of those who desired to widen their experience by travel. Peter Heylyn's *Microcosmus: a little Description of the Great World*, which appeared augmented and revised in 1625, was of the same character. After going through several editions, it was published in an enlarged form in 1652 under the title *Cosmographie, in Four Bookes; containing the Chronographie and Historie of the whole World*, and, in that form, was several times reprinted. It is an illustration of the avidity with which descriptions of foreign countries were welcomed by English people. Heylyn was no more than an industrious compiler, who surveyed the world at large, its diversities, countries, cities, peoples, customs and resources, with encyclopædic interest and general intelligence. A serious volume much worthy of note is George Sandys's *A Relation of a Journey begun An. Dom. 1610*, which is descriptive of Turkey, Egypt, the Holy Land, Italy and other places. Narratives of land travel began to increase in number, to satisfy the universal curiosity, which craved a knowledge of the peoples of foreign lands, thereby leading also to the publication, in Italy and elsewhere, of volumes illustrative of the costumes of various countries.

To another class of books belongs the volume entitled *Coryats Crudities, Hastilie gobled up in five moneths travells in France, Savoy, Italy, Rhetia, commonly called the Grisons country, Helvetia alias Switzerland, some parts of high Germany and the Netherlands; newly digested in the hungrie aire of Odcombe in the County of Somerset*, 1611. Coryate was a literary oddity, and his book is a curiosity. The son of George Coryate, rector of Odcombe, and born in 1577, he was educated at Oxford, and entered the household of Henry, prince of Wales, by whose favour, together with the assistance of certain "panygericke verses upon the authour and his booke," which Coryate procured to be written by his friends, the volume of travels was published. It has two supplements or appendixes, both issued in 1611, entitled *Coryats Cramb, or his Colwort twise sodden, and now served with other Macaronicke dishes as the second course to his Crudities*, and *The Odcombian Banquet, dished foorth by T. the Coriat, in praise of his Crudities and Cramb too*.

Coryate's writings belong rather to the literature of travel than to that of discovery. In his *Crudities*, and in various letters written to his friends—the latter printed by Purchas and in the curious compilation entitled *Thomas Coriate Traveller for the English Wits: Greeting*—he displays acute observation and a lively understanding and appreciation of much that he saw. The oddity and extravagance of his manner are seen in the volume called *Coryats Cramb*, which consists mostly of encomiastic verses on his former *Crudities*, with addresses to great personages. There is a petition to Henry, prince of Wales, to "cherish and maintaine the scintillant embers of my diminutive lampe by infusing into them the quickening oyle of your gracious indulgence." The king is addressed as "Most scintillant Phosphorus of our British Trinacria," and the queen as "Most resplendant Gem and radiant Aurora of Great Brittaines spacious Hemisphere."

After his continental journey, Coryate visited Odcombe, to hang up, in the parish church there, the shoes in which he had walked from Venice. In the next year, he set out on his journey overland to India, which was his most remarkable achievement, and he died at Surat. He visited Constantinople, Aleppo and Jerusalem, crossed the Euphrates into Mesopotamia and waded the Tigris, which was very shallow at the time, joined a caravan and, ultimately, reached Lahore, Agra, and the Mogul's court at Ajmere. Sir Thomas Roe, ambassador to the Mogul, whose observations are in the collection of Purchas, says that he met Coryate in 1615. Purchas also prints a letter written by Coryate from the court of the great Mogul in the same year to L. Whitaker, *animae dimidium meae*, in which he describes his journey, and says that he enjoyed "as pancraticall and athleticall a health as ever I did in my life." There is also a letter addressed to his friends who were accustomed to meet at the Mermaid in Bread street, "Right Generous, Joviall, and Mercuriall Sirenaickes"—and subscribed, "the Hierosolymitan-Syrian-Mesopotamian-Armenian-Median-Parthian-Indian Legge-stretcher of Odcombe in Somerset, Thomas Coryate." In exaggerated language, he relates his experiences, and says he sends the letter by a reverend gentleman, whom he beseeches his friends to exhilarate "with the purest quintessence of the Spanish,

French and Rhenish grape which the Mermaid yieldeth." Both these letters are contained in the *Traveller for the English Wits*, in which Coryate says,

> Erasmus did in praise of folly write;
> And Coryate doth in his self-praise indite.

Coryate also sent commendations to his friends by name, including Purchas, "the great collector of the lucubrations of sundry classic authors." Purchas likewise prints a letter addressed by Coryate to his mother, with an address in Persian which the Odcombian had delivered to the great Mogul, with sundry other observations.

The mantle of Richard Hakluyt fell upon the shoulders of Samuel Purchas, a great editor of narratives of travel and a man of many words but of less modesty than his predecessor. *Hakluytus Posthumus, or Purchas His Pilgrimes, contayning a History of the World, in Sea Voyages, and Lande Travells by Englishmen and others*, was published in 1625. Purchas, who was born at Thaxted, in Essex, in or about the year 1577, was educated at St. John's college, Cambridge, where he took the degree of M.A. in 1600, afterwards proceeding to that of B.D. He was vicar of Eastwood from 1604 to 1614. Leigh on the Thames is within two miles of Eastwood, and was then a great resort of shipping, many voyagers on the return from their explorations sojourning there. Purchas, doubtless, began his own collections at this time, and took down some narratives from the lips of those who had travelled far. He was an untiring worker, and could never maintain a "vicarian or subordinate scribe" to help him. In 1614, he was preferred by John King, bishop of London, to whom he expresses unbounded gratitude, to the rectory of St. Martin's, Ludgate. He died in 1626. Prior to the publication of his *Pilgrimes*, he had written *Purchas His Pilgrimage, or Relations of the World and the Religions observed in all ages and places discovered from the Creation unto this Present* (1613), with new editions in 1614, 1617, and 1626. He had also written a volume called *Purchas his Pilgrim; Microcosmus, or the Historie of Man* (1619).

It is clear from a remark made by Purchas—"I was therein a labourer also"—that he assisted Hakluyt to arrange papers which were unpublished at Hakluyt's death in 1616, and, hence, his collection is called *Hakluytus Posthumus*. "Having out of a chaos of confused intelligences framed this historical world," Purchas was emboldened to dedicate it to Charles, prince of Wales. He explains to the reader that he had received "Master Hakluyt's many years' collections," and that "Purchas and his Pilgrimes" were as a bricklayer providing materials "to those universal speculators for their theorical structures." Purchas never travelled more than two hundred miles from his birthplace, but he says that bishop King gave him one wing, hoping some blessed hand would add the other, and, not finding this to be the case, the bishop "promised to right me himself (these were his syllables) but death righted him, and I am forced to wrong the world." What Purchas lacked in experience of travel, he made up by his indefatigable industry, in which he rivalled Hakluyt himself. Knowing that comparatively few of his countrymen could themselves see the world, he offered to them, "at no great charge,"

a world of travellers to their domestic entertainment, easy to be spared from their smoke, cup, or butterfly vanities and superfluities, and fit mutually to entertaine them in a better school to better purposes.

The design of the book separates the subjects into two main divisions, one dealing with the old world and the other with the new, each being further divided into ten books. The first book is an introduction to the rest, being concerned with Biblical history and travel, man's life as a pilgrimage, the journeys of Christ and the apostles, classic journeyings and other matters. Then he reaches improvements in navigation, recalls the voyages of Columbus and Magellan, gives narratives of Drake's, Cavendish's and later circumnavigations, and of early voyages to the east—Lancaster's, Middleton's and others. The first half of the book is devoted to a long array of narratives and statements regarding trading and voyages to India, China and Japan, Africa and the Mediterranean, including a mass of information concerning our dealings with the Dutch and the Portuguese. In the same way, the second division of the *Pilgrimes* is devoted to narratives of the Muscovy voyages, efforts to discover the north-west passage, explorations in the West Indies and Nova Scotia, including narratives of most of the great expeditions, and much information concerning our dealings with the Spaniards, as well as observations of foreign explorers.

Purchas was not the equal of Hakluyt, but he was his worthy successor, his collaborator in his later life and the depository of some of his collections. Possessed of the same valiant, untiring spirit, the vast volume of his researches, brought together with indefatigable exertion and invincible zeal, was, though in a much less degree than Hakluyt's collection, an inspiration and an encouragement to the men who came after. All that Purchas has amassed of the narratives of the explorations of Englishmen breathes the strong spirit of nationality. There is ample room in these accounts for the display of various talents and different temperaments, but there is scarcely one that does not have in it some pride of England. When Robert Fotherby, in 1615, cruised on behalf of the Muscovy company in a pinnace of 20 tons for the discovery of land to the north-east, he was questioned by a Danish admiral as to the right by which English merchants resorted to waters claimed for Denmark, and he replied, "By the king of England's right." There was courtesy, also, to the nation that was a greater rival. Thus, James Beversham, writing in July, 1618, from Fairhaven, refers to the insolence of the Dutch, which, however, he overlooked, advising his countrymen

not to impute to that nation what some frothy spirit vomits from amidst his drinke, but to honour the Hollanders' worth, and to acknowledge the glory of the Confederate Provinces; howsoever they also have their sinks and stinking sewers (too officious mouths such as some in this business of Greenland, beyond all names of impudence against his Majestie and liege people, as others elsewhere have demeaned themselves) whose loathsomeness is not to be cast as an aspersion to that industrious and illustrious nation.

When Purchas opens the glowing story of the western exploration, he has a fruitful field of interesting record and description, and here, in the sharp rivalry of interests which had brought us to war with Spain, the spirit of nationality glows still more brightly, not seldom marred by the bitterness of religious hate and intolerant invective. With the practical purpose of encouraging and assisting navigators and planters, he has given summaries of the writings of Spanish and Portuguese discoverers, coloured, sometimes, by his lively imagination, and descriptive of the curiosities and resources of the western lands. He has gathered with a rather indiscriminate hand, but ever with the purpose of adding new lustre to England's fame. The narrative of Peter Carder, who is said to have set out with Drake on his circumnavigation, to have separated from the company and, after many marvellous adventures, to have returned home nine years later, reads more like fiction than fact, and makes one think of the later writings of Defoe. Like most writers of his time, Purchas loves to note the freaks and peculiarities of nature, and revels in the wonderful. When he introduces a tragic narrative, like that of the unfortunate Cavendish, on his last journey, he improves the occasion. Cavendish's last letter to his friend and executor, Sir Tristram Gorges, is a pathetic page in our literature; for the dying man, with enfeebled hand, pours forth therein the utter depth of his misfortune. He speaks of tempest, cold, famine, cowardice, mutiny and the ill-fortune of war, saying:

And now by this, what with grief for him [his kinsman, John Locke] and the continual trouble I endured among such hell-hounds, my spirits were clean spent; wishing myself upon any desert place in the world, there to die, rather than thus basely to returne home again. . . . And now consider whether a heart made of flesh, be able to endure so many misfortunes, all falling upon me without intermission. I thank God that in ending of me, he hath pleased to rid me of all further trouble and mishaps.

But this poignant narrative does not escape the somewhat "precious" pen of Purchas, who had drunk at the Euphuistic spring. He likens the life of the navigator to the change from sunshine to shadow; from day to night, from summer to winter:

And if the elements, seasons, and heaven's two eyes, be subject to such vicissitudes, what is this little molehill of earth, this model of clay, this moveable circumference of constant inconstancy, immutable mutability, this vanishing centre of diversified vanity, which we call man; that herein also he should not resemble this sampler of the universe, as becometh a little map to be like that larger prototype.

And he goes on to express the glow of his pride in the deeds of English seamen:

This we see all, and feel daily in ourselves; this in Master Candish here, in Sir Francis Drake before, the sea's two darlings, there, and thence both living and dying; if dissolution of the body may be called a death, where the soul arriveth in heaven, the name fills the earth, the deeds are precedents to posterity, and England their country hath the glory alone that she hath brought forth two illustrious captains and generals, which have fortunately embraced the round waist of their vast mother, without waste of life, reputation and substance; yea victorious over elemental enemies, illustrious in wealth and honour, they have come home, like the sun in a summer's day, seeming greatest nearest his evening home, the whole sky entertaining and welcoming him in festival scarlets and displayed colours of triumph.

Among the most interesting pages in the travel-literature of the time are those which relate to the colony of Virginia. Hakluyt had a proprietary right in the colony; its exploration occupies a large place in his *Navigations;* and his last work was *Virginia Richly Valued* (1609), being a translation from the Portuguese of de Soto's narrative. "I shall yet live to see Virginia an English Nation," wrote Ralegh to Sir Robert Cecil, shortly before Elizabeth's death. His own efforts had left a shadowed memory. Purchas has preserved two narratives of the voyage of Gosnold to northern Virginia in 1602, as well as his account of the fertility of its soil, together with narratives of Pring's voyage from Bristol in 1603 and others. James's charter for the colonising of Virginia was the signal for great enterprise, which was urged by Hakluyt and his friends, and cheered on by Michael Drayton:

Britons, you stay too long;
Quickly aboard bestow you,
And with a merry gale
Swell your stretch't sail,
With vows as strong
As the winds that blow you.

The name of captain John Smith will ever be associated with the foundation of Virginia. Purchas has preserved some extracts from descriptions of his enterprises, but Smith's own account is contained in his book, *The General History of Virginia, New England, and the Summer Isles, with the names of the Adventurers, Planters, and Governors from their first beginning in Anno 1584 to this present 1624.* Of this famous book, there were other editions in 1626, 1627 and 1632. Smith's whole being had been mastered by the enthusiasm for planting new states in America, and, in the early days of Virginia, that colony depended for its life and preservation on his firmness and courage. The *History* is a freely written and very remarkable, but apparently straightforward, direct and forcible, narrative and record, and its author deserves a place in the literature of the sea above most men. Not only was he, in his own person, an adventurer, explorer and settler, as well as a writer and recorder, but he had an intense belief in the necessity to this country of possessing a powerful navy. He quotes with approval what Master Dee had said in his *British Monarchy*, concerning the creation of a fleet of sixty sail—a " little Navy Royall "—in queen Elizabeth's reign:

> To get money to build this navy, he saith, who would not spare the one hundredth penny of his rents, and the five hundredth penny of his goods; each servant that taketh forty shillings wages, four pence; and every foreigner of seven years of age, four pence, for seven years; not any of these but they will spend three times so much in pride, wantonness or some superfluities.

This, he would have them do by way of benevolence, and he proceeds to say how vast would be the advantage in spreading terror among pirates and amazement among enemies, while giving assistance to friends, security to merchants, and a great increase to navigation. Smith has also a title to our admiration as the author of a *Sea Grammar* for young seamen, of which some account will be given later.

In the history of the several plantations and settlements in the new world, Virginia, the New England colonies and Pennsylvania have literatures of their own. The prosperity of Virginia was retarded by many untoward circumstances, and, in a pamphlet issued in 1649, entitled *Virginia Impartially examined, and left to publick view, to be considered by all judicious and honest men*, William Bullock endeavours to discover the

reason of this slow progress. He had known the pioneers
and captains in the trade, his father had lived in the colony
twelve years and he himself had had extensive commerce
with it. Accordingly, he offers his little book as

no other than the adventurer's and planter's faithful steward,
disposing the adventure for the best advantage, advising people
of all degrees, from the highest master to the meanest servant,
how suddenly to raise their fortunes.

There is a study of the food and sport of the country, its
economic necessities, how it might be recovered, how money
might be disposed to advantage there, and how the plantation
might be reached, with advice to the adventurer, to the planter
and to servants. Edward Williams's *Virgo Triumphans; or
Virginia Really and truly valued* (1650), was written with the
same purpose.

The book named *Sir Francis Drake Reviv'd, calling upon
this Dull and Effeminate age to follow his noble steps for gold
and silver*, 1626, published by Sir Francis Drake the younger,
is the source of most of our knowledge of Drake's exploits
in Central America, though Froude, without much reason, has
thrown doubt upon its authenticity. It is mentioned here as
suggesting, by its title, the motive with which the navigators of
that age entered upon their enterprises. There was the double
incitement of adventure and spoil, and the honour of England
was an added reason for successive navigations to the west.
Both Hakluyt and Purchas wrote in the same spirit. So, also,
the Tudor poets and balladists gave expression to the imperial-
ism born of the increasing influence of England's naval power,
the widely-spread knowledge of the seamen's explorations and
the ever-growing impulse towards colonisation. The verses
entitled *Neptune to England*, printed in Halliwell's *Early Naval
Ballads*, sound this note:

> Goe on, great state, and make it knowne,
> Thou never wilt forsake thine owne,
>   Nor from thy purpose start:
> But that thou wilt thy power dilate,
> Since narrow seas are found too straight
>   For thy capacious heart.

So shall thy rule, and mine, have large extent:
Yet not so large, as just and permanent.

How, too, the sea life, with its wider outlook, attracted the more daring spirits of the nation is indicated in a ballad *In Prais of Seafaringe Men, in Hope of Good Fortune* (Sloane MSS.):

Too pas the seaes som thinkes a toille,
Sum thinkes it strange abrod to rome,
Sum thinkes it a grefe to leave their soylle,
Their parents, cynfolke, and their whome.
Thinke soe who list, I like it nott;
I must abrod to trie my lott.

In *The Relation of a Voyage to Guiana . . . Performed by Robert Harcourt* (1609), given by Purchas, and issued independently in an enlarged form in 1626, the objects are set forth in order. First comes the "glory of God, for the conversion of the heathen"; secondly, "the honour of our Sovereign"—"the obtaining and gaining the sovereignty of so many great, spacious, and goodly countries and territories"; and, thirdly, "the profit of our country," by the enrichment of the many commodities "in those parts daily found and easily obtained." Harcourt says that

all young gentlemen, soldiers, and others that live at home in idleness and want employment, may there find means to abandon and expel their slothful humours, and cast off their fruitless and pernicious designs, and may worthily exercise their generous spirits in honourable travels and famous discoveries of many goodly and rich territories, strange and unknown nations, and a multitude of other rarities, hitherto unseen, and unheard of in these northern parts of the world; which may be thought incredible, but that our own experience (besides the general and constant report and affirmation of the Indians) doth assure us thereof.

Another volume, devoted to westward expansion, with an analogous purpose, is *A New Survey of the West Indies, or the English American, his Travail by Sea and Land*, by Thomas Gage, published originally in 1648, and issued in several subsequent editions. By this time, Hakluyt and Purchas had many followers, who, though not in collected narratives, were de-

scribing the new places of the world, and, in a versified introduction to Gage's book, Thomas Chaloner thus speaks of the
author:

> Reader, behold presented to thine eye
> What us Columbus off'red long ago,
> Of the New World a new discovery,
> Which here our author does so clearly show;
> That he the state which of these parts would know,
> Need not hereafter search the plenteous store
> Of Hakluyt, Purchas and Ramusio,
> Or learn'd Acosta's writings to look o'er;
> Or what Herrera hath us told before,
> Which merit not the credit due from hence,
> Those being but reckonings of another score,
> But these the fruits of self experience.

So far we have dealt only with western explorations, but
the literature of the seventeenth century is rich in narratives
of travel and settlement in both hemispheres. The project
of reaching China, the Spice islands and farther India by the
north-west passage was destined to disappoint those who fixed
their hopes upon it. Nor did much success attend the efforts
to carry trade overland from the Levant, which was one of
the objects of the Turkey company, established in 1581. The
early efforts to wrest the monopoly from the Portuguese by
the long sea route also met with disaster. Raymond's expedition of 1591 suffered from sickness, tempest and mutiny,
and its misfortunes made failure inevitable from the beginning.
Still more disastrous was Benjamin Wood's navigation of 1596,
from which not one man of the company returned to tell the
tale. Purchas deplores the double disaster of the loss of the
ships, and of the record and history of the tragedy, upon which
light is thrown by a Spanish letter found among the papers
of Hakluyt. The Netherlanders were more successful than
Englishmen in 1597 in their effort to break down the supremacy
of the Portuguese; but quarrels among themselves deprived
their expedition of commercial success, and the consequent
rise in the price of pepper on the London market caused merchants to meet in 1599, thereby leading to the foundation
of the East India company. The first enterprise was Lan-

caster's famous expedition of 1600–2, which was equipped
with every necessity of war, and carried greetings from Elizabeth "to the great and mightie King of Achem, etc., in the
Island of Sumatra, our loving Brother." Purchas has preserved
a full narrative of the circumstances and events, with a copy
of Elizabeth's letter. Whatever is preserved of Lancaster's
writing shows him to have possessed in a marked degree the
forcible style of the seaman. His brief letter to the proprietors
of the East India company deserves to be quoted:

Right Worshipful, what hath passed in this voyage, and what
trades I have settled for this company, and what other events have
befallen us, you shall understand by the bearers hereof, to whom
(as occasion hath fallen) I must refer you. I will strive with
all diligence to save my ship, and her goods, as you may perceive,
by the course I take in venturing my own life, and those that are
with me. I cannot tell where you should look for me, if you send
any pinnace to seek me, because I live at the devotion of the wind
and the seas. And thus fare you well, desiring God to send us a
merry meeting in this world, if it be his good will and pleasure.

The first real discouragement to those who looked for the
success of the north-west route was Lancaster's triumph, combined with Waymouth's ignominious failure to find a way
to "Cataya or China or ye backside of America" which became
known before Lancaster returned. Hudson, Button, Baffin and
a score of other hardy navigators followed Waymouth's course,
but merchants recognised that, long and perilous as was the
route by the cape of Good Hope, it was preferable to the
doubts and dangers of the north-west.

The Dutch captured Amboina from the Portuguese in
1605, and burned their fleet at the Moluccas in the following
year, and it was the strong trade rivalry between the English
and the Dutch, leading to the massacre at Amboina, that ultimately caused our merchants to relinquish partially their
attempts to establish themselves in the islands, and to devote
their efforts to developing trade with India. Not, however,
until the third East India voyage, in 1607, was any attempt
made to establish trading ports on the Indian mainland.
Purchas includes in his *Pilgrimes* a brief narrative of Middleton's—the second—voyage to the east (1604–6), and a some-

what longer account of that of Keeling, which was the third
(1607–10), as well as an extremely interesting narrative
written by captain William Hawkins of his landing at Surat
and his visit to the court of the great Mogul at Agra, with
observations on life at the Mogul's court, the custom of *sati*
and many other matters. The *Pilgrimes* includes narratives
of all later expeditions to the east, and a full account of our
relations with the Dutch and the Portuguese up to the year
1613.

One of the most interesting narratives included in the collection is that of William Adams, descriptive of his voyage to
Japan and his long sojourn there (for he never returned),
written in the form of two letters, addressed severally to his
"unknown friends and countrymen" and to his wife. These,
Purchas has placed with his accounts of voyages to the east,
although Adams reached Japan by way of the strait of Magellan.
He was born at Gillingham in Kent, and, having been an apprentice at Limehouse, became pilot in the queen's ships and
served twelve years with the Barbary merchants. Being
desirous of gaining greater experience, he took service in 1598
as pilot of a fleet of five sail for the Dutch India company.
They entered the strait of Magellan on 6 April, 1599, and,
suffering much from cold and sickness, remained in the strait
until September, when they proceeded to the coast of Peru.
In February, 1600, the expedition reached a port in northern
Japan, which Adams names Bingo. The chief there showed
them great friendship, giving them a house on shore and all
needful refreshment, Jesuits and Japanese Christians being
their interpreters. The emperor of Japan, hearing of their
arrival, sent for Adams, apparently having had news that
he was a man of skill; and he was conveyed to Osaka, accompanied by a seaman. The emperor asked him many questions
—"there was nothing that he demanded not, both concerning
war and peace between country and country." Adams was
held in captivity, but was "well used." On a second occasion,
the emperor interrogated him, asking him why foreign ships
came so far.

I answered, We were a people that sought all friendship with
all nations and to have trade of merchandise in all countries,

bringing such merchandises as our country had, and buying such merchandises in strange countries as our country desired; through which our countries on both sides were enriched.

The Portuguese endeavoured to prejudice these strangers in the minds of the Japanese; but the emperor answered that, as yet, they had not done any damage to him or his land.

Adams was allowed to rejoin his ship, and she went round to Yeddo, where the emperor then was; and there she was detained, her company being dispersed in Japan. When Adams had lived four or five years in the country, the emperor asked him to build a small ship for him, to which Adams pleaded that he was no carpenter: "Well do it as well as you can, saith he; if it be not good, it is no matter." The vessel was built, with a burden of 80 tons, and was well liked, so that Adams was received into greater favour, and put on a good allowance. He often saw the emperor and even taught his majesty "some points of geometry and mathematics." So influential did he become that his former enemies asked him to befriend them in their business through the emperor, and both Spaniards and Portuguese received more friendly treatment in consequence.

Five years elapsed, and Adams besought his imperial patron to allow him to return to his own country; but this request was not granted, and he remained, apparently acting as nautical adviser to the emperor. He was presently building a vessel of 120 tons for imperial use, which, however, was lent in 1609 to enable the governor of Manila to proceed to Acapulco, the governor's own ship having been cast away and completely wrecked on the coast of Japan. For this service Adams had what he likened to a lordship, with eighty or ninety husbandmen, "who are as my servants and slaves." Of the Japanese, Adams said that they were

good of nature, courteous above measure, and valiant in war; their justice is severely executed without any partiality upon transgressors of the law. They are governed with great civility—I think no land better governed in the world by civil policy.

This letter, addressed to Adams's unknown friends and countrymen, was dated 11 October, 1611. The second letter, to his wife, is also a recital of his experiences, but is not complete. Adams died in 1620.

Much more might be written about the eastern navigations of the century; but perhaps enough has been said to enable the reader to understand what was the character of the literature of the sea so far as it dealt with exploration and discovery. Before leaving the subject, however, two other volumes may be referred to, which are concerned with the discovery of two great islands in the south and east—one of them a continent— namely, Australia and Madagascar. In the exploration of the eastern hemisphere, as of the western, much was brought to knowledge by the printing of translations or summaries of foreign books and letters. The collections of Peter Martyr, Oviedo and Ramusio had been a revelation to Englishmen of the great work done by foreign seamen, and Eden, Hakluyt and Purchas worked industriously in the field of their researches Others followed in their footsteps. Thus, a pamphlet printed in 1617 for John Hodgetts was a translation of a Spanish letter under the title *Terra Australis incognita, or A new Southerne Discoverie, containing a fifth part of the World, lately found out by Ferdinand de Quir* [Pedro Fernandez de Quiros] *a Spanish captaine; never before published.* It is in the form of a humble petition to the Spanish king not to neglect a golden opportunity, revealed by one who had devoted fourteen years to the discovery and had wasted fourteen months at the Spanish court in vain.

De Quiros says that this new discovery is of the fifth part of the terrestrial globe, and "in all probability is twice greater in Kingdoms and seignories than all that which at this day doth acknowledge subjection and obedience to your Majesty." De Quiros denominated his land "*Austrialia del Espiritu Santo*,"[1] but Wytfliet had indicated the continent as "*Terra Australis*" in 1598. The publication of de Quiros's account in an English form caused some stir in this country; but the Dutch were before us in exploring the continent, and it was

[1] De Quiros's "*Austrialia*" was, apparently, the New Hebrides and not the actual mainland. The legend of a great southern land had been current for some years, and the connection of de Quiros's name with Australia may be compared with that of Columbus's with America.

not until 1770 that an Englishman, the great circumnavigator captain Cook, examined the east coast.

The other volume referred to is that of a merchant who had been concerned in the East India trade, and had suffered much in his efforts to draw the attention of his countrymen to the resources of some countries little known to them. This merchant is Richard Boothby, whose *Briefe Discovery or Description of the most famous Island of Madagascar or St. Laurence in Asia near unto East India* was published in 1646, having been delayed two years by the hindrance of a "captious licenser," who blamed the rudeness of the author's style, and would place the island in Africa, whereas Boothby insisted that it belonged to Asia. The pamphlet is dedicated to the king, the author saying that his estate has been ruined through envy, malice and revenge in India, and oppressed by deep ingratitude, partiality and injustice at home, and imploring his majesty to support the plan of effecting an English plantation in Madagascar, for, "he that is Lord and King of Madagascar may easily in good time be Emperor of all India." The richness of the island and its resources are extolled as of great promise to the mercantile community.

We now may turn to another important class of literature concerning the sea, namely that which tells how seamen regarded their own profession and its duties, and in which they gave the fruit of their professional knowledge and skill for the advantage of their comrades and those who were to come after them. The sea service was becoming more highly organised and more scientific, and the distinction between war and merchant vessels, which before had been scarcely noticeable, began to be more clearly marked. Serious writers, like Henry Maydman, Robert Crosfeild, captain St. Lo and William Hodges, towards the end of the seventeenth century, began to concern themselves with the provision of men for the fleet, and the health and treatment of the seamen were much discussed. The seaman himself appeared earlier in the *Whimzies* of Richard Brathwaite (1631) and in the *Characters* attributed to Sir Thomas Overbury. The rise of a school of professional seamen was a marked feature of the age. There was a long-standing difference between hard, practical seamen and gentlemen captains, and, as we shall presently see, a controversy arose between the former and men of more scientific training. Drake, certainly, had the root of the matter in him when he said, on that memorable occasion during his voyage of circumnavigation when he enforced the need of union in the fleet and of hard, honest work in the sea service:

Here is such controversy between the sailors and the gentlemen and such stomaching between the gentlemen and the sailors that it doth even make me mad to hear it. But, my masters, I must have it left. For I must have the gentleman to haul and draw with the mariner, and the mariner with the gentleman.

The literary remains of Sir William Monson—his *Naval Tracts* —enable us to appreciate the outlook of an officer who was a contemporary of Drake, but who lived until after the outbreak of the civil war. Monson was a sea officer of some distinction and strong character, and also a critic of naval affairs. His literary memorials and tracts, originally brought to notice in the Churchill collection of voyages, 1732, are now being made known both to history and to literature in the publications of the Navy Records Society. Monson became a student at Balliol college in 1581, and ran away to sea. He rose rapidly, was Essex's flag captain at Cadiz and accompanied him in the Islands voyage of 1597. He was not concerned in any great events, but was imprisoned in the Tower in relation to the Overbury case. His writings are divided into six books, and he states that it is his purpose to describe the acts and enterprises of Englishmen at sea, in the first two books; to deal with the office of lord high admiral and other officers, and the duties of seamen, in the third; to touch upon the voyages and conquests of the Spaniards and Portuguese, in the fourth; to handle certain projects, in the fifth; and to discover the benefits of fishing on the coasts, in the sixth. He borrowed largely from Hakluyt and Purchas, but had no intention of dealing with history or narrative. His object was to apply lessons to be learned from certain facts in the past as warnings for the future, and he appears to have been the first English seaman to make a critical examination of the work of seamen afloat in his own time, as well as of that of some of his predecessors and successors at sea. As a strategical writer, he cannot rank with Ralegh or Essex, but his opinions have value as embodying the views of a vigilant, sagacious and thinking officer; and, in the dedication of two books to his two sons, he seems, almost, to anticipate Chesterfield. There was nothing in him of high imagination, little of generous sympathy or enthusiasm and, apparently, not much of the hard, fighting quality. The old writer who introduces Monson in a preface states that, with respect to the roughness which characterises his language, it should be remembered that Monson had "spent most of his time at sea," and that his language had been formed, as it were, in Elizabeth's day, and not in the refinement "of our time," *i.e.* of the Stewarts. In the dedication of the first book to his eldest son, the young man is counselled to seek the ways of peace and not to be deceived by the glamour of the soldier's glory. Wars by land and sea, says Monson, are always accompanied by everlasting danger and disasters, and are seldom times rewarded.

For one soldier that liveth to enjoy that preferment which becomes his right by antiquity of service, ten thousand fall by the sword or other casualties; and if you compare that computation with any other calling or profession, you will find much difference and the danger not so great.

Moreover, though arms have always been esteemed, they have in part been subject to jealousies and envy.

Compare the estate and advancement of soldiers of our time but with the mean and mercenary lawyer, and you shall find so great a difference that I had rather you should become prentice to the one than make profession of the other.

There is also an epistle dedicatory to the gentlemen who were the author's intimate friends, and a farewell to the same. In the latter, Monson again utters a warning "that you beware of adventuring yourself and estates upon sea journeys." They might perceive by his observations what peril such journeys brought without profit, and what pains without preferment:

For there are few, if you will enter into particulars, whose employment has gained them advantage; as to the contrary many are brought to want and misery by them. . . . The miserable **gentlemen** that undertook such enterprises for gain, to recover their spent and consumed estates, were Cavendish, Chidley, Manby, Cocke, with many others I could name, whose funerals were all made in the bottomless sea, and their lands turned into the element of water.

These, perhaps, were Monson's later reflections, or not, at least, his general and customary ideas. Certainly, elsewhere, he glories in our conquests and victories, both on sea and on land.

Books had begun to issue from the press in Elizabeth's reign which showed the larger place that science was taking in the work of the seaman. In the seventeenth century, the volume of this literature grew larger, and several writers followed in the footsteps of Eden, who translated the *Compendium* of Cortes in 1561, of Bourne, who published the *Regiment of the Sea* in 1573, and of Davys, whose *Seaman's Secrets* appeared in 1594. One of the earliest of these was captain John Smith, the first governor of Virginia, who wrote a sea manual which passed through several editions. This was his *Accidence, or the Path-way to Experience, necessary for all young Sea-men, or those that are desirous to goe to Sea,* 1626. The volume differed in some respects from its predecessors, and the author says it is upon a subject he "never see writ before." It is dedicated to the reader, and to "all generous and noble adventurers by sea, and well-wishers to navigation, especially to the Masters, Wardens, and Assistance of the Trinity House." Smith declared that he had never kept anything to himself, and that he knew he had been blamed for so doing. He describes the duties of all the officers of the ship, as well as her timbers and sails, and adds many quaint illustrations of the use of sea terms, and the manner of working the ship and giving battle.

Right your helme a loufe, keepe your loufe, come no neere, keepe full, stidy, so you goe well, port, warre, no more; beare up the helme, goe roumy, beyare at the helme, a fresh man at the helme. . . . Boy fetch my celler of bottles, a health to you all fore and afte, courage my hearts for a fresh charge; Maister lay him a bord loufe for loufe; Midships men see the tops and yeards well maned with stones and brasse bals, to enter them in the shrouds, and every squadron else at the best advantage; sound Drums and Trumpets, and St. George for England.

Smith goes on to describe the ordnance of the ship, with reference to gunnery treatises, saying, "any of these will give you the Theorike; but to be a good Gunner, you must learne it by practise." The excellence of his maxims caused a demand for his book: enlarged editions of the *Accidence* appeared under the title *The Sea-Man's Grammar; containing most plain and easie directions how to Build, Rigge, Yard and Mast any Ship whatever*, and it was still being republished in 1691.

Smith represented both the scientific and practical sides of his profession; but a conflict was growing up between theory and practice which was not without influence on the literature of the sea at this time. The new-born science of the sea was inclined to despise the rough methods and, perhaps, the rude manners, of the men who had attained their objects and had fought tempests and the dangers of rocks and lee shores in gales, with only the knowledge born of hard experience; while those of the older school regarded with contempt the new-fangled theories and scientific appliances of the modern seaman, which they did not understand, and his love for comforts which some of them scorned.

We find the literary expression of this controversy in two volumes, which are almost, if not quite, the earliest separately published English narratives of voyages in search of a north-west passage. These are *The Strange and Dangerous Voyage of Captain Thomas James in his Intended Discovery of the North-West Passage into the South Sea* (1633), and the whimsically named *North-West Fox; or Fox from the North-West Passage*, of captain Luke Fox of Hull (1635). These explorers were both engaged in their work in 1631, and met in the icy regions, their work, apparently, being inspired by the healthful rivalry of the Bristol and London merchants. James, who was furnished with a ship by the merchants of Bristol, and is said to have belonged to a good family, was a man of education, and a scientific seaman, who, while knowing the importance of setting sail in a well-found vessel with a trained company, was sensible of the necessity of a proper knowledge of navigation, and of being supplied with proper instruments. Accordingly, before putting to sea, he endeavoured to extend his former studies by obtaining journals, plots (or charts), descriptions, or whatever would assist him, and set skilful craftsmen to make quadrants, staves, semicircles and compass-needles. The narrative of his voyage is very interesting as a picture of the life of the explorer in those times, and of professional seamen at work. Fox, on the other hand, belonged to the old school. He had spent his whole life in the practical business of the sea.

"Gentle Reader," he says, "expect not heere florishing Phrases or Eloquent tearmes; for this child of mine, begot in the North-West's cold Clime (where they breed no Schollers), is not able to digest the sweet milke of Rhethorick, that's food for them."

He goes on to deride the "mathematicall sea-man," who, he avers, would fail in contest with the "ruffe and boisterous ocean." He proceeds:

Being deprived of sun, moon and stars for long season, they will then think that they only dreamed before; when they imagined of the course of the seas, and that their books were but weak schoolmasters; that the talk of art were far short of the practice, when, at beholding the stars, which they thought to have used as guides and directions, seem now as they threatened their ruin and destruction; nay, when they shall look forth and tremble at the rising of every wave, and shall be aghast with fear to refrain those rocks and dangers which lie hid within the sea's fairest bosom, together with the greatness of the ocean, and smallness of their ship; for want of experience to handle, not knowing how to shun, they will then think that the least gale is of force to overthrow them, and know that art must be taught to practice by long and industrious use. For it is not enough to be a seaman, but it is necessary to be a painful seaman; for a seabred man of reasonable capacity may attain to so much art as may serve to circle the earth's globe about; but the other, wanting the experimental part, cannot; for I do not allow any to be a good seaman that hath not undergone the most offices about a ship, and that hath not in his youth been both taught and inured to all labours; for to keep a warm cabin and lie in sheets is the most ignoble part of a seaman; but to endure and suffer, as a hard cabin, cold and salt meat, broken sleeps, mouldy bread, dead beer, wet clothes, want of fire, all these are within board; besides boat, lead, top-yarder, anchor-moorings and the like.

But Fox was not so insensible of the value of written experience as his words might imply, for he, like Eden, Hakluyt and Purchas, was a collector of voyages, and he deserves an honourable place here because his volume includes an account of expeditions from early times down to Baffin and some later discoverers. The narratives of James and Fox have been reprinted in a single volume by the Hakluyt society. They did not explore beyond the bay which takes its name, to use Purchas's expression, from "that worthy irrecoverable discoverer," Hudson.

The controversy of those times has had its echoes in later days. Fox was a representative seaman of an old school, but he and those who thought with him could not stay the advance of science into the seaman's domain. A truer understanding of the relative positions of theory and practice presently arose, and a considerable literature indicated the advances that were being made in the seaman's art. Sir Henry Manwayring, who was captain of the *Unicorn* in the Ship Money fleet of 1636, was an officer who helped to spread a knowledge of the practical things that concerned the sea profession, and he did so for the assistance of the gentlemen captains of the time, which was one of naval decay—the fleet of Charles I being greatly disorganised, ineptly commanded and much demoralised and mutinous. Manwayring's *The Sea-Man's Dictionary, or an Exposition and Demonstration of all the parts and things belonging to a ship*, was first published in 1644, a second edition appearing after the Restoration, in 1670. The author's object was to instruct those gentlemen who, "though they be called seamen," did not "fully understand what belongs to their profession," and to give them some knowledge of the names of parts of ships and the manner of doing things at sea. The information was intended to instruct those "whose quality, attendance, indisposition of body, or the like" prevented them from gaining a proper knowledge of these things. The significance, therefore, of Manwayring's book is that it throws a side-light upon the well-known shortcomings of some of the cavalier officers. The form of the book is alphabetical, in the manner of a glossary or dictionary.

The last writer we need mention in illustrating this aspect of the literature of the sea is captain Nathaniel Boteler, an officer of whom very little is known, but who was evidently an experienced student of his profession, and who had considerable knowledge of the internal economy of ships of war. His work, *Six Dialogues about Sea Services between an High Admiral and a Captain at Sea*, was published in 1685, but had evidently been written some years earlier. It deals with the commander-in-chief, officers and men, victualling, the names of the several parts of a ship, the choice of the best ships and the signals, sailing, chasing and fighting of ships of war. The admiral and the captain discourse on these and many related questions, such as punishments, sometimes by way of catechism, but, generally, by instructive comment and criticism. Boteler was a writer with a sense of humour, and some of his remarks are very incisive and instructive. He had a very exalted idea of the position and duties of a captain, and says that his charge was as high as that of any colonel on land, "and for the point of honour, what greater honour hath our nation in martial matters than in his Majesty's Navy?" He would have the lieutenant admonished "that he be not too fierce in his way at first (which is an humour whereto young men are much addicted), but to carry himself with moderation." So does Boteler discourse upon the character and duties of the purser, the boatswain and the other "standing officers," as also upon the men, for whom he had a good deal of sympathy, while never overlooking the necessities of discipline. Taken as a whole, Boteler's *Dialogues* is one of the most interesting volumes dealing with the sea service that appeared within the century.

If the subject treated in these chapters be pursued in regard to later times, it will be found to embrace many new features and, in some respects, to have a less specialised character. Records of travel begin to take the place of narratives of discovery, and the literature of the sea and of land journeys widens into channels of many varied interests. The literature of piracy occupies a position of its own, to which reference will be made later when the writings of Defoe are under consideration. The growing volume of the literature of the sea has many ramifications, and it includes purely technical treatises, historical narratives, controversial pamphlets, theatrical productions, broadsheets of song and many other things indicative of the channels through which the national interest in the sea and national love for the sea service manifest themselves.

CHAPTER VI
The Song-Books and Miscellanies

IN an earlier chapter of this work[1] was described the revival
of English poetry under the influence of Italy and France,
and the progress of the school of Wyatt and Surrey to its
decay. The impulse was worn out; the chivalric ideal had
ceased to be a genuine source of inspiration, and there was
need of new ideals, new blood and new literary methods. We
have now to consider the later and more national poetry which
the labours of Sidney and Spenser called into being.

It is impossible, of course, to name a date as that at which
new methods were employed and new themes sung. Before
the school of Wyatt and Surrey had fallen into decay, the
Elizabethan outburst of song had begun, and the writers to
be considered in this chapter will be found to cover a period
of nearly thirty years, during which the full chorus sang from
sunrise to high noon.

If this was a period, to a great extent, of poets by profession,
it was, also, to a degree never since equalled, a period when
every man was a poet not only in spirit but in practice. The
accomplishment which had belonged to a few courtiers in the
days of Henry VIII had spread to every man of education;
every one with an emotion to express may be said to have
expressed it naturally in poetry. And some of the sweetest
lyrics in Elizabethan poetry were the work of men whose very
names are to this day unknown. They were passed round in
manuscript, to be read aloud or sung to the lute and viol in
private houses, and have survived in manuscript collections,
in the song-books of the day, or, occasionally, in printed
miscellanies. When a song was popular, it was repeated

[1] See Vol. III, Chap. VIII.

in various publications; take, as an instance, the dialogue, possibly written by Sir Walter Ralegh, between Meliboeus and Faustus, beginning "Shepherd, what 's Love, I pray thee tell?" which appears in *The Phoenix Nest* (1593), *England's Helicon* (1600) and Davison's *Poetical Rapsody* (1602) and is set to music in Robert Jones's *Second Book of Songs and Airs* (1601).

The poetry now to be considered falls, in the main, into two divisions: there is the lyric of pure joy or grief, and there is the longer, graver, reflective lyric, revealing an attitude towards life which is, perhaps, more characteristically English. Poetry of the former kind is rarer in our language than poetry of the latter, and it is found at its best in the compositions of the days of Elizabeth. For its forms—the pastoral, the sonnet, the canzone and the madrigal—it is still dependent, no doubt, as was the poetry of Wyatt and Surrey, on foreign models; but the models have now been perfectly assimilated. The voice is pure English, and English of its day. The machinery of the Middle Ages—courts of love, allegorical visions and so forth—has passed out of use, and the feeling of the present moment is naturally, simply and sweetly expressed. It would, perhaps, be truer to say that the voice is not so much English as universal. There is so much in it of the paganism which is of the essence of the natural man that it can dispense with the particular. There is practically no reference to events or tendencies of the time. There is no sense of responsibility, no afterthought. To watch its growth is like watching primroses break into bloom, or like listening to the chorus of birds growing fuller in the woods as the dawn grows towards morning; so spontaneous, so much the effect of purely natural causes, does this poetry appear. The imagery, where imagery is employed, is almost always pastoral. We have seen a very early pastoral in *Tottel's Miscellany*, and have noticed in Googe the use of pastoral in the conventional classical manner. In the lyrists of the latter age its use is quite unconventional and brings with it no sense of artificiality. "Shepherd," as we read, means "man," and "shepherdess" mere "woman"; the use of these words and the talk about flocks, pipes and so forth, do nothing to cloak the sincerity of the outburst of feeling.

The mass of this poetry that has survived remains still unmeasured, though the labours of Arber, Bullen and others have done something to explore and map the large and intricate field. These poems, it must be noticed, were copied again and again for the purpose of singing. The practice of solo and part singing was more general in Elizabeth's days than in our own. "There is not any music of instruments whatsoever," wrote William Byrd, "comparable to that which is made of the voices of men." The lute, the viol and the virginals[1] were in every household for accompaniment, as a piano is to-day, and were put to a better use; and there can be no doubt that music had a great influence on the quantity, and no small influence on the quality, of the lyric poetry which was being produced with no thought, in many cases, beyond that of putting the song (as we saw in the case of *The Handefull of pleasant delites*) to a tune already known or of having it set to a new one.

"Poetry makes melody, not melody poetry," wrote Richard Garnett, and he implied that the only thing music can do for poetry is to increase the quantity of it. Certainly, in our own day, we have a terrible example of the amount of "poetry" which "music" can produce; and, in the days of Elizabeth, music was equally fruitful in this way. But a wide difference must be noted. To-day, feeble and slipshod music produces still more feeble and washy poetry; in those days, music that was still in the very salutary "bondage" of a pretty severe formalism co-operated with a lyric poetry of natural and sincere sweetness to produce perfect song.

Elizabethan composers for the voice made use of two distinct styles: the madrigal and the ayre. Of these, the madrigal was a piece of continuous music, not broken into stanzas, but woven from start to finish without break and without repetition. Further, it was written in the "polyphonic" style, in which four, five or six voices sang, at the same time, independent melodies, which had no necessary likeness in pitch or in rhythm. Different words were often sung simultaneously, or the same words to different rhythms, so that if each singer was made to accent his words with the greatest care, the impression on the hearer was general. This accounts, to some ex-

---

[1] For the musical instruments of the period see Grove's *Dictionary of Music*, and Furnivall's *Laneham's Letters* (1908), pp. 65–68.

tent, for the brevity, directness and simplicity of the madrigal form of poem. The ayre, on the other hand, was composed stanza by stanza, often repeating the same music to different stanzas. The musical idea, whether the ayre were composed for one or for several voices, was generally a single idea, and the parts were made to conform more or less to a single rhythm, which corresponded to the metre of the verse. Writers of ayres, who threw their words into prominence and kept the stanzas entire, necessarily had a much greater effect upon the lyric than madrigalists, especially those who wrote for a single voice with instrumental (usually lute) accompaniment.[1]

It is impossible to determine the shares accurately. The best lyric poetry of the age "sings itself": it suggests its own tune irresistibly, and is, in a sense, complete without the written music; and there can be no doubt that the demands of increasing variety and range in poetry spurred music on to greater freedom in the effort to cope with it. On the other hand, the freest music of the day was more rigid and more formal than the strictest poetry; and it would not be rash to state that music directly affected the quality of the poetry in two ways: first, by putting a check on all temptation to neglect conciseness of expression and strictness of form; and, secondly, by keeping it simple and sensuous, as lyric poetry should be. The standing danger to which music exposes poetry—that the rhythm of the poetry may be sacrificed to that of the music— is very rarely incurred in the Elizabethan ayres. Those who have had the privilege of reading the book of words of a modern musical comedy will know how the "lyrics" are, of themselves, for the most part, absolutely shapeless and rhythm- less. They only take shape when it is supplied by the rhythm or melody of the music; and this is rarely the case. An Eliza- bethan poet—amateur or professional—writing a lyric to mu- sic of his own or another's had a different task. The tune was, in itself, a little rigid in shape; his lyric could not, therefore, be shapeless. And, conversely, a composer putting a tune to a lyric had before him something with a structure of its own which he could not help respecting. In this connection, Thomas

[1] Thanks are due to H. C. Colles for much assistance in the passages in this chapter relating to Elizabethan music.

Campion, whose work, as a whole, is considered elsewhere in this volume, is a composer of especial interest. He wrote his words in order to set them himself; his ayres are melodies extending over a single stanza, and the contour of each melody is carefully devised, both in pitch and rhythm, to express the sense, throwing the important words into relief. He takes care, therefore, to bring the important words in each stanza into the same position in the line; and, as in Burns, each stanza corresponds not only in metrical rhythm, but in inner sense-rhythm, to all the rest. At the opposite extreme, as composers have found, stands Tennyson, who can only be set to music on the *durch-componirt* principle. And, as time went on, not only did the composer come to respect the structure of the lyric more and more, but it became more possible for him to respect it as the lyric became more perfectly shaped.

The earliest and most famous of composers of music for songs and part songs (for Thomas Whythorne, who published sets in 1571 and 1590, need not be considered) was William Byrd, composer of the famous masses, and "one of the gentlemen of the Queen's Majesty's honorable Chapel." He published three song-books, and contributed to several others. Nicholas Yonge did good service in circulating Italian madrigals in the two parts of *Musica Transalpina* (1588 and 1597). Next came John Dowland, a great traveller, who, at one time, was lutenist to the king of Denmark. Dowland, who is celebrated by Richard Barnfield in the sonnet sometimes ascribed to Shakespeare, "If Musique and Sweet Poetrie agree," made a distinct advance beyond Byrd in consulting the form of the poem when setting it to music: witness his setting of the poem, probably by Peele, "His golden locks time hath to silver turned," which was spoken before Elizabeth by Sir Henry Lee, when he resigned the office of champion in 1590, and is quoted by Thackeray in *The Newcomes*. By 1612, however, when Dowland published his last collection, *A Pilgrim's Solace*, we learn from his letter to the reader that the old musician was already considered as composing "after the old manner." Other composers and collectors of music who fall within our period are Thomas Morley, John Mundy, Thomas Campion, Philip Rosseter, William Barley, Thomas Weelkes, George Kirbye, Gyles Farnaby, John Wilbye, John Farmer, Robert Jones and Richard

Carlton; while Thomas Ravenscroft, Michael Este, Thomas Greaves, Thomas Bateson, Frances Pilkington, captain Tobias Hume, John Coperario, John Bartlet, John Danyel, Richard Alison, Thomas Ford, Alphonso Ferrabosco, William Corkine, Robert Dowland, Orlando Gibbons and others carried on the work well unto Jacobean times. Of these, Byrd, Weelkes, Kirbye, Wilbye, Este, Bateson and Gibbons wrote in the madrigal or polyphonic form, while Dowland, Morley, Campion, Jones and Ravenscroft were chiefly writers of ayres for one or more voices. The song-books of all these and other collections in print and manuscript have been searched by Bullen, whose editions of Elizabethan lyrics brought to light long unsuspected treasures.

To examine the whole list would take too long. William Byrd, who composed before the type of poem written for the madrigal had become popular in England, drew partly on writers who belong to the previous age—Oxford, Kinwelmersh, Churchyard, Sir Edward Dyer and, perhaps, Henry VIII. Dyer, the friend of Sidney (who left Dyer half his books), was ambassador to Denmark and elsewhere for Elizabeth and chancellor of the Garter; some of his work appears, also, in *The Phoenix Nest*, in *England's Helicon* and in *The Paradyse of Daynty Devises*, and he was justly praised as "sweete, solempne and of high conceit" by Puttenham in his *Arte of English Poesie* (1589). Younger men, however, like Ralegh and Thomas Watson the sonneteer, also appear in Byrd's song-books. The bulk of the poems he sets to music are anonymous; but his predilection for didactic and religious verse gives an air as of the previous age to his collection. Yet the voice of the new poetry is clear in some of the pastorals. The influence of foreign poets is only seldom directly apparent; but two, at least, of the poems appear again—one of them word for word— in the *Musica Transalpina* of Nicholas Yonge, which is entirely composed of translations from French and Italian authors made, in 1583, by "a Gentleman for his private delight." The authors at present identified in Dowland's song-books are Fulke Greville, George Peele, the earl of Essex (or his chaplain Henry Cuff), Sir Edward Dyer and Nicholas Breton. Among the other song-books, the scanty number of names that can be mentioned is a testimony to the extent to which the habit

of writing lyrics prevailed among others than professed poets. And study of these songs, composed for home use
or the convenience of a small circle of friends, with no more
serious import than the verses of Sir Benjamin Backbite or
the acrostics of our grandfathers, leads only to deeper wonder
at their perfection of form. In them, the mood and the manner
go hand in hand, as if inevitably. There is no sense of strain,
no artificial poetising, no bombast and, in the best cases, no
feebleness. There is, besides, a quality of sweetness which
is not a property of the words alone, nor of the sense alone,
and which, seeming even to be something other than the perfect
union of sound and sense, remains, in the last resort, beyond
analysis. It may, perhaps, be a quality of the time, an essential sweetness in a class educated and civilised, but full of
the frank gaiety, the ebullience, the pagan innocence and even
the quick and stormy temper, of children. The England
of the day was full of renascence learning, and its singers
swept as much of it as they could master into their songs;
but the spirit of the land was still the spirit of childhood,
frank in its loves and hates, unsophisticated and eager for
feeling and experience. The whole beauty of the world which
lay about them, spring and summer, the flowers, morning and
evening, running water, the song of birds and the beauty of
women, expresses itself in their songs; and, with the increase
of national prosperity and the freedom from the danger of a
dominion they had always dreaded, came an almost complete
loss of that cringing sense of sin and responsibility which the
reformation and the political dangers it had introduced had
imposed upon earlier generations. England, in fact, to a great
degree, was pagan, if we may use the word in the sense that
modern usage seems determined to establish. It was bent
upon enjoying its life in a very pleasant world. If a mistress
were kind, her kindness moved the swain to songs of joy; if
she were unkind, he turned on her with a pretty flouting that
is hardly less enjoyable than his praise. He did not fawn,
nor mope, nor serve, in the old, unhealthy, pseudo-chivalric
fashion of his fathers. If he were unhealthy, as, unquestion-
ably, was Barnabe Barnes, for instance, the fault was due to a
different cause.

Another valuable field for the lyric poetry of the time was

afforded by the drama; and, in considering this, it is necessary to bear in mind the important part played in the Elizabethan drama by the children of the queen's chapel and other companies of boy-actors, who were trained musicians and made music a prominent feature of their performances. Lyly, Marston, Jonson and others who wrote for these companies would regard songs as an essential feature of the book of the play, though, in certain cases, the play was printed without them. Again, in masques, acted by amateurs at court or in the houses of noblemen, music played a large part, and Jonson, Daniel and other authors of masques were careful to provide songs. Music was less cultivated in the public theatre, but it was far from being unknown there; and the number of songs to be found in Shakespeare's plays would of itself be sufficient proof that men-actors found it expedient to consult the contemporary passion for music.

So early as the middle of the sixteenth century, we find, in *Ralph Roister Doister*, a rollicking song from the hero of the comedy; but the drama first became a fit field for the lyric with John Lyly. His *Alexander and Campaspe* contains the beautiful and familiar poem, "Cupid and my Campaspe played"; his *Midas* is the source of a lyric almost equally well known, "Sing to Apollo, god of day." Lyly's example was followed, in particular, in the plays of the university wits; and the practice became general. Greene, Peele, Nashe, Dekker, Beaumont and Fletcher, Massinger, Ford, Heywood and many others incorporated songs with their dramas; and the custom continued till the closing of the theatres in 1642, to be resumed at their reopening. Indeed, it was, to some extent, under the pretext of music that Sir William D'Avenant was able to revive the drama under the protectorate.

The practice of compiling miscellanies was continued, and the first to show the influence of the new life and vigour was *The Phoenix Nest*, "set foorth" by "R. S. of the Inner Temple Gentleman," in 1593. *The Phoenix Nest* is dedicated, as it were, to the memory of the earl of Leicester, and opens with three elegies upon Astrophel (*i.e* Sidney). The volume contains poems by certain anonymous writers who clearly belong to the old, rather than to the new, school of poets. And, in the main, N. B. Gent, as Nicholas Breton is here written, belongs to that school too. A voluminous writer in verse and prose, Nicholas Breton, who was born about 1542 and was probably in the service of Sidney, or of his sister the countess of Pembroke, or of both, belongs in spirit, by his protestantism no less than by his poetical usage, to the school of Wyatt and Surrey. Many of his longer works are written in the fourteen-syllable lines and the "poulter's measure" beloved of the poets of that school; and his use of stanzas of six and eight lines, or of rime royal, does little to link him with the new writers. In *The Phoenix Nest*, too, he indulges very freely in the old allegory, a heritage from medieval times which was soon to fall out of use. *A strange description of a rare garden plot* is an allegorical poem in "poulter's measure." *An excellent dreame of ladies, and their riddles* and *The Chesse Play* are, also, allegorical. In the next anthology which we have to consider, we shall find Breton in a different guise; but, in *The Phoenix Nest*, the new note is struck most forcibly by Thomas Lodge. The fifteen poems by that author which the volume includes are the best of its treasures. Three of them are from his *Phillis* (1593), a volume of eclogues, sonnets, elegies and other lyrical pieces; the rest appear first in *The Phoenix Nest*, though one, "Like desart woods," is published in *England's Helicon*, where it is given either to Sir Edward Dyer, or to "Ignoto." It is worth noticing that Lodge, in one song, "The fatall starre that at my birthday shined," makes use of a metre which might be scanned as, and is clearly modelled upon, alcaics, but is, in practice, composed of iambic feet. The earl of Oxford has a charming lyric, "What cunning can expresse," and it is possible that the longest poem in the volume, *A most rare and excellent dreame*, is the work of Greene. The dream is the favourite one of the visit of a lady to her sleeping lover. Her beauties are described and his parlous state explained. Then follows a long argument on love, of the kind that had not yet passed out of fashion; and, on the relenting of his mistress, the lover wakes. There is much of the old school in the matter, but little in the manner. The stanzas in rime royal move freely and strongly, and the whole is a good specimen of the poetry of the time. It needs, however, only to place it side by side with such a lyric as Lodge's "My bonnie Lasse thine eie," in the same volume, to realise the immensely enlarged field in which the poet had to work. "Sweete Violets (Loves paradice) that spred" is a good example of the long stanza of complicated structure and involved rime-sequence which the poets of the day used with rare skill, and which led the way in time to the formal ode.

The next miscellany to be published has been generally found the most interesting and beautiful of all. The first edition of *England's Helicon* was published in 1600; it appears to have been projected by John Bodenham, and, possibly, collected by him, the editorial work being carried out by a certain "A. B.," who has not been identified. A second edition appeared in 1614 with a few additional poems.

In *England's Helicon*, we find the best of the pastoral and lyric poetry of the age. The only blot on the collection is the excessive space allotted to Bartholomew Young, or Yong, whose poems, taken from his translation of Montemayor's *Diana*, are not on a level with those of the other contributors. A list of the poets drawn upon for the collection will give some idea of its value. Sir Philip Sidney, Edmund Spenser, E[dmund] B[olton], Michael Drayton, Robert Greene, Thomas Lodge, Nicholas Breton, Shepherd Tony, George Peele, John Dickenson, Henry Howard earl of Surrey, Thomas Watson, John Wotton, Shakespeare(?), Richard Barnfield, the earl of Oxford, Sir Edward Dyer, Sir Walter Ralegh, H[enry] C[onstable], Bartholomew Yong, W[illiam] S[mith], Fulke Greville(?), Christopher Marlowe, William Browne and Christopher Brooke. The large number of poems subscribed "Ignoto" are also unusually interesting. Of these, three were attributed in the first edition to W[alter] R[alegh]; but, in later copies of that issue, a slip of paper bearing the word "Ignoto" has been pasted over the initials, though a manuscript list of poems made by Francis Davison (editor of *A Poetical Rapsody*) and now in the British Museum[1] ascribes them to Ralegh. The same signature "Ignoto" stands, in several cases, as Bullen has pointed out, for a mysterious poet, "A. W.," of whom nothing but his work is known, and that mainly through *A Poetical Rapsody*.

The poems by Sidney in *England's Helicon* are taken from *Astrophel and Stella, Arcadia, The Lady of the May* and *A*

---

[1] MS. Harl. 280.

Poetical Rapsody, while one, *An Excellent sonnet of a nymph*, appears in *England's Helicon*, probably for the first time.

The three poems by Spenser are taken from *The Shepheards Calender* and his *Astrophel*, the elegy on the death of Sidney. Edmund Bolton, the author, probably, of the four poems signed "E. B.," which include a particularly beautiful carol, was a retainer of George Villiers duke of Buckingham, and belongs, properly, to the Jacobean age. The poems of Drayton in *England's Helicon* are taken from his *Eclogues*, in *Poems Lyric and Pastoral*, and his *Idea*, while two appear for the first time in this volume. Greene's are taken from *Menaphon* and *Francesco's Fortunes;* Peele's from *The Hunting of Cupid* and *The Arraignment of Paris;* Lodge's from *Rosalind*, *A Margarite of America* and *Phillis*, while two appear here for the first time; and Watson's mainly from his *ΕΚΑΤΟΜΠΑΘΙΑ*, while one appeared first in *The Phoenix Nest* and another is not known before its appearance here.

Nicholas Breton, as we have said, appears here at his best. There are eight of his poems in the book, six of which do not appear elsewhere, and, of these six, one is in the old "poulter's measure," and three in the once popular fourteen-syllable line. But Breton's use of these almost discarded metres differs greatly from that of the lesser followers of Wyatt and Surrey. By dividing the long lines into two and giving them rimes at each pause—a practice that had been followed before—he breaks the monotony; and in his hands these measures no longer "jog," but flow. There is a buoyancy and a liveliness in his verse which is the very spirit of the lyrics of his age; and, though he never tries the elaborate harmonies of some of the writers in this miscellany, his note is clear and perfect in the short lyric outbursts which he too seldom attempted. His longer narrative, religious and allegorical poems, *The Pilgrimage to Paradise*, *The Countesse of Penbrooke's love*, *The Soules immortall Crowne* and others, which are written, some in fourteeners, some in rime royal, or stanzas of six or eight decasyllables, lack variety, and cannot stand by the side of Samuel Daniel's for dignity or depth. Nicholas Breton's best work is to be found in the short lyrics, and in the delightful *Passionate Shepheard*, a volume containing pastorals, many of which are written in the trochaic measure of four feet.

the lightness and grace of which was then becoming fully recognised.

It seems probable, though it is strange, that Shepherd Tony, the sweet singer of *England's Helicon*, is no other than "the Grub Street patriarch," the translator and playwright, Anthony Munday. The evidence [1] rests mainly on the charming song, "Beauty sat bathing by a spring," which occurs both in *England's Helicon* and in Munday's translation of *Primaleon*. His work in this miscellany is far superior to that in his *Banquet of Dainty Conceits* (1588). He replies to the old pastoral, "Phylida was a fayer mayde," which, as we have seen, *England's Helicon* ascribes to Surrey, and makes a lovelier melody by his mixed use of iambics and trochaics. In *The Woodman's Walk*, he carries us back, both by his use of the divided four-teener and the old subject of the failings of court and city life, to an earlier day; in "Fair nymphes, sit ye here by me," he is well abreast of his age in the long stanzas of short lines with interwoven rimes, which discuss pleasantly and sweetly the pleasures and pains of love—only to break at the close into a hymn in its praise.

John Dickenson, the author of three very dainty little songs, is a little known poet, whose *Shepheardes Complaint*, in which all three occur, was published in 1594. John Wotton, who, possibly, was the half-brother of Sir Henry Wotton mentioned by Izaak Walton, is the author of one very famous and delightful poem, *Damaetas' Jig in praise of his love*, beginning "Jolly shepherd, shepherd on a hill," in which is concentrated the whole quality of the collection of pastorals and the very breath of this springtime of poetry. The song ascribed to Shakespeare is the "On a day (alack the day!)" which appeared in the first edition of *Love's Labour's Lost*, and, again, in the *Sonnets to Sundry notes of Music* appended to *The Passionate Pilgrim* (1599). Both in that volume and in *England's Helicon* the songs immediately following are "My flocks feede not," and "As it fell upon a day." Of these two,

---

[1] See Bullen, *Lyrics from Romances and Prose-Tracts of the Elizabethan Age* (1890), pp. xviii, 77. His edition of *England's Helicon*, in which (p. xvii) he scouts the notion that Munday and Shepherd Tony could be one, was published in 1887. The notion that Shepherd Tony was a pseudonym of Anthony Copley was never tenable.

the latter had already appeared in the *Poems in divers Humors* attached to *The Encomion of Lady Pecunia*, by Richard Barnfield, published in 1598, together with the sonnet, "If Musique and sweet Poetrie agree," which also forms part of *The Passionate Pilgrim*. This is not the place to examine the ascription of particular songs: the best opinion determines for Barnfield's authorship of the sonnet; that of the "ode" "As it fell upon a day" is more doubtful.[1] The fact that, in *England's Helicon*, it follows immediately upon "My flocks feede not," and is entitled *Another of the same shepherd's*, is part of the evidence for his authorship of that poem also. Barnfield, who was born in 1574, in Shropshire, was educated at Oxford and died in 1627, was not a professional writer. His three volumes: *The Affectionate Shepheard* (1594), *Cynthia* (1595) and the *Encomion of Lady Pecunia* (1598), were all published before he was twenty-five, and bear evidence of being not so much the result of any strong impulse to poetry as the elegant amusement of a young scholar. All reveal a love of strangeness in subject, of conceit and far-fetched imagery. The *Affectionate Shepheard* begins by elaborating the second *Eclogue* of Vergil into a passionate address by an aged man to a youth named Ganymede (to whom, also, a number of sonnets in *Cynthia* are composed in the same vein), and passes on to give a great deal of good, if ill-arranged, advice on the same moral level as that of Polonius. For *Cynthia*, he claims that it is the first imitation of the verse of *The Faerie Queene*: its subject is a classical allegory, leading to a panegyric on queen Elizabeth, and the volume contains also a narrative "tragedy" on Cassandra, and an "ode," in which a lying shepherd is heard to complain that his love for Ganymede has been ousted by the greater beauty of a lass, whose name we learn to be Eliza. In the introductory letter to *The Encomion of Lady Pecunia*, Barnfield openly admits his search for an uncommon, novel subject. The poem is a satire on the power of wealth: it is followed by *The Complainte of Poetrie for the Death of Liberalitie*, a topic to which he refers more than once in his other works; and by an *estrif* between Conscience and Covetousness.

---

[1] See Grosart's and Arber's reprints of Barnfield's poems and **Henneman** in *An English Miscellany* (Oxford, 1901), p. 158.

Then follow those *Poems in divers Humors*, to which reference was made above. The traces of the poetic exercise are clear in all Barnfield's work. It is at its best and its pleasantest in the moments when, forgetting his intellectual foppery and affectation, he sings naturally and sweetly about the country. His descriptions of country scenes are sometimes admirable, and he has a quaint and pleasing way of dropping simple country similes into the most elaborate of his fancies. His favourite metre is the decasyllabic line, which he manages with dignity and variety in stanzas of a quatrain and a couplet, or of rime royal; and there are some good hexameters, as there are certainly some extremely bad ones, in an extraordinarily "conceited" poem called *Hellens Rape, or a light Lanthorne for light Ladies*. His vocabulary is rich and often strange; though not so much with the archaism of his "king of poets," Spenser, as with the homelier usages of his own day. Another prominent feature in Barnfield's work is his ardent and outspoken admiration for Spenser, his friend Watson, Sidney, Drayton and other contemporary poets. Bartholomew Yong we have mentioned already, and somewhat in disparagement. In him stands out prominently the affectation of the time, to which we shall return, and neither in spirit nor in melody is he worthy of the important place assigned to him in the volume. William Smith, a rather pedantic writer, was the author of *Chloris* (1596), and Christopher Brooke, whose spirited, if conventional, *Epithalamium* closes the volume, is known as the collaborator with Browne and Wither in *The Shepheards Pipe* (1614), and belongs, with Browne himself, to the generation following. To this list must be added a number of anonymous authors, of whom "W. H.," the author of two very graceful and charming songs, may, possibly, be William Hunnis, whom we met in *The Paradyse of Daynty Devises*.

It is clear, then, that the compiler of the book looked far and wide through the literature of the day for the pastorals to form his collection. Plays, romances, sonnet-sequences, song-books (for many of the poems in *England's Helicon* are taken from Byrd's or Morley's books), all were laid under contribution and he must be allowed to have been a man of fine taste. It is difficult to refer to these poems without using expressions of admiration that must seem excessive; but to open any page (unless, indeed, one hits on the laborious Bartholomew Yong) is to meet with something of great beauty. The book contains the best of the lyrics with which Lodge, that various master of light music, dotted his romances. Peele wrote but few lyrics, but the best of them are here; and Greene seems to give voice not only to the spirit of the renascence with its gay appetites, its rich fancies and its humanism, but to the graver spirit which is held to be characteristically English, and is frequent in the lyric poetry of his day, rarely as it appears in the book under notice.

Pastoral, as has often been pointed out, is always more or less an affectation. It is "the townsman's dream of country life."[1] It has always been written in stages of high civilisation, by Theocritus, Vergil, or Mantuan. It lends itself freely to allegorical use; the comparison of country innocence with the venality and falsehood of city and court life leads, naturally, to moralising, and that strain runs through pastoral in England from Barnabe Googe to *Lycidas*. In *England's Helicon*, and in much of the pastoral poetry of Elizabethan days, it is another aspect that we find. The convention is adopted, but for a different purpose; and, in the end, it amounts to no more than the nomenclature. A man is not less a man for calling himself a shepherd, and, to the Elizabethan courtier, flocks and herds, thrushes and nightingales, brooks and trees, must have been objects at least as familiar as streets and houses. For it is noticeable that, in spite of much classical imagery and talk of Phoebus, Diana and the rest, and many new versions of classical stories, it is English country of which the pastoral poets chiefly sing in this volume. We are to imagine a better climate than we have; but that is usually the greatest demand which the convention makes. It is not the poetry of nature, for nature is not studied as a source of consolation or strength or for any interest in itself: it remains the background of the loves of the shepherd; but, in dramatising himself against a background which he knew (though he chose to call it by strange names), the poet gains a good opportunity of expressing his feelings with more freedom than direct speech would allow. A shepherd is a simple and downright person; to pose as a

---

[1] Chambers's *English Pastorals*, p. xxxix.

shepherd is to have the advantages enjoyed by simple and downright persons. And, since the single subject of the poems in *England's Helicon* is love, that advantage is valuable.

The result is a strange but delightful mixture of simplicity and affectation. There is all the colour of association with classical poetry, the eager absorption of classical imagery characteristic of the renascence, combined with the naked feelings of the actual man. On the language of the poets, the combination could not fail to have the important effect of lending it richness and colour; but, through the pleasant tinsel, the native quality shows clearly. The affectation only becomes oppressive in the case of writers like Bartholomew Yong, whose feeling was insufficiently ardent to endow the borrowed form with life. His Arsilius, Melisea, Alanius and the rest strike the reader as pieces of pedantry, while Lodge's Montanus (we are speaking only of the lyrics), or some unknown poet's Philistus, or Daphne, or Phyllida, are men and women.

The contrast between the technical accomplishment of these poets and of those of the earlier school is very great. In place of the few, repeated measures, the often cramped movement and the halting progress of the early poetry, we find ease, grace, swiftness and freedom in metres of all kinds. The long fourteener and "poulter's measure" have been divided, and flow like rippling streams; the decasyllable has gained strength, dignity and variety, and great dexterity has been attained in the use of short lines. There is no end to the ingenuity of these poets in the arrangement of long, trilling stanzas, in which closely wrought rime-construction keeps the melody from feebleness. The way in which subtlety and ingenuity are combined with simplicity is one of the most remarkable qualities of the Elizabethan lyric. That the poem is a work of delicate and conscious art is plain; the devices of echo, refrain and repetition are freely used, and long and difficult schemes of rime and metre are sustained throughout. It was this age, moreover, that saw the introduction into English poetry of the "shaped verses" already common in Italy and France. The writer's object was to make his verse, when printed, take the shape of an egg, a pillar, a triangle, or one of many other shapes mentioned by Puttenham in his *Arte of English Poesie*.

It seems probable that the learned Thomas Watson, author of *The ΕΚΑΤΟΜΠΑΘΙΑ*, was the first to introduce the practice into England; his example takes the form of "a Pasquin Pillar." A classical origin was claimed for the idea of the shaped verse, the names of Anacreon and Simmias of Rhodes being cited; and the fashion, which did little more than take root in Elizabethan days, grew under the reigns of her successors into great popularity, issuing not only in the pleasing and appropriate shaped verses of Herbert, but into most fantastic absurdities in less poetical hands. In spite, however, of occasional instances of such misdirected ingenuity, the Elizabethan lyric remains a bird-song in sweetness and spontaneity, and the result is one which can only be attained in the rare moments when accomplishment and inspiration are on a level.

The last of the Elizabethan anthologies which need be seriously considered is *A Poetical Rapsody* issued by two brothers, Francis and Walter Davison, in 1602. Francis Davison was the eldest son of the secretary Davison who was Elizabeth's scapegoat in the matter of the execution of Mary queen of Scots. In his youth, Francis was sent to travel with his tutor, and it was while abroad that he wrote a prose work, the *Relation of Saxony*, which was highly praised by Anthony Bacon, and also (according to his letter to the reader) the poems which are collected in the *Rapsody*. Walter, his younger brother, became, it appears, a soldier in the Low Countries and died young.

The volume opens with a dedicatory sonnet to William Herbert earl of Pembroke; and the first contributor is Sir John Davies, whose work is considered in another chapter of this volume. Then comes the poem called *The Lie*, which is commonly, but erroneously, supposed to have been written by Ralegh on the eve of his execution; and then two pastorals by Sidney. Soon after these follows a *Dialogue between two shepheards, Thenot and Piers in praise of Astrea*, which was written by Mary countess of Pembroke, patron and friend of all the poets of the day, the "Sidney's sister, Pembroke's mother" of William Browne's immortal epitaph. It is possible that this dialogue was written for one of queen Elizabeth's visits to Wilton. Francis and Walter Davison themselves contribute a large number of poems: eclogues, "sonnets," odes, elegies, madrigals and epigrams, translations from Horace, Martial, Petrarch, Jodelle and others—the work, mainly, of persons of taste and education rather than of poets born, though one song, *In praise of a beggar's life*, has become familiar to many through its quotation by Izaak Walton in *The Compleat Angler*, as "Frank Davison's song, which he made forty years ago." One of Francis Davison's eclogues— written in a form of the long and elaborate stanza over which the poets of the day had great mastery—is a specially good example of the ease with which they moved amid the conventions of pastoralism. The shepherd Eubulus is no other than Elizabeth's late counsellor, secretary Davison, and his cruel mistress is the queen. It is a touching and manly plea for the poet's own disgraced father, written in a form which could deceive nobody. A specimen of unusual ingenuity is the long poem called *Complaint*, ascribed, in the *Rapsody*, to Francis Davison, and, in Davison's own manuscript,[1] to "A. W." Not only the eight rime-endings, but the actual words that compose them, are the same in each of the eight stanzas. The age delighted in echoes, and was constantly experimenting in metre and rime, but, usually, with more artistic purpose than in this instance. The madrigals of the brothers were very popular and are found in many of the song-books.

The miscellaneous contributors to *A Poetical Rapsody* include Greene (with a translation of Anacreon, from *Orpharion*) Campion, Henry Wotton, T[homas] S[pilman] or Spelman (a kinsman of the Davisons, who also translated Anacreon), Spenser, Constable and Charles Best, with, possibly, Joshua Sylvester and Ralegh (to the dialogue, "Shepherd, what's Love, I pray thee tell," we have referred before, and the volume contains another of the many poems which the opinion of the time was ready to attribute to Ralegh). But the largest and the most remarkable contributor is the mysterious "A. W.," whom all efforts have failed to identify, but whose songs worthily found place in many anthologies and song-books of the age. The earlier part of the volume contains a number of eclogues, the name of the shepherd being Cuddy. In these, the author shows himself a close student and follower of

---

[1] See above, p. 136.

Spenser. Rustic or antique phraseology is almost unknown in *England's Helicon*. Of the thirty-five words and phrases given by Bullen in the glossarial index to his edition of that book, four, at the most, were not in common use in the educated speech of the time. "A. W." delights in flavouring his eclogues, like Spenser, with words that shall be racy of the soil. Later in the volume we find a number of anonymous poems, heralded by three admirable Petrarchian sonnets, all of which are attributed to "A. W." in the manuscript list compiled by Francis Davison. There is a wide difference between these poems. It is difficult to believe that the three sets of hexameters on the death of Sidney are the work of the same author as *The Tomb of Dead Desire* or the madrigal, 'Thine eyes so bright"; and it is not impossible that the "A. W." of Francis Davison's list stands, not for the initials of a single poet, but for the words, "anonymous writers." A curious fact is that the poem mentioned above, which Izaak Walton ascribes to Davison himself, is initialled "A. W." by Davison in his list, and appears among the group in the *Rapsody* ascribed to that author. If these poems were, indeed, the work of a single author, he is sufficiently interesting to demand further research. His range is wide—from the solemn measures of a poem to Time, which, with others, recalls strongly the antithetical, paradoxical work of years before, to the sweetest of little madrigals, that sing themselves irresistibly. He indulges, too, in some use of classical metres. To his hexameters we have referred. He uses, also, a metre which he calls the Phaleuciack:

Time nor place did I want, what held me tongue-tied?

and, on one occasion, he rimes the lines of this structure, prefixing an apology to his lady for "so strange a metre." A set of sapphics upon the passion of Christ shows, also, that he was affected by the movement which started with Spenser and Gabriel Harvey and led even Campion astray for a while. His translations from Anacreon can hardly be set beside Thomas Stanley's.

In treating the lyrics of the song-books and miscellanies we have dealt almost exclusively with what may be called the renascence elements in them, the gaiety, the paganism, the use of mythology and classical allusion. It must not be supposed, however, that the more peculiarly English note, as it is commonly considered—the reflective, religious and didactic note—is absent. It is frequent even in the song-books, William Byrd in particular having, clearly, a fondness for sad subjects as vehicles for his music. In his *First Book* we find the famous poem by Sir Edward Dyer, "My mind to me a kingdom is," a perfect type of the moral poetry— the poetry of independence of character and sobriety of life—which was common at the time, and of which Samuel Daniel's poem *To the Lady Margaret Countess of Cumberland*, beginning "He that of such a height hath built his mind," Campion's *The man of Life upright*, Sir Henry Wotton's "How happy is he born and taught," are other notable instances. Byrd's *Second Book* is largely composed of short moral and didactic poems; and it is plain that this reflective vein ran as steadily in the heyday of Elizabethan glory as in earlier years. Barnfield's Ganymede is treated in *The Affectionate Shepheard* to a discourse on morality in the second day's lament which gives, perhaps, a truer picture of the genuine sentiments and character of that respectable man and good poet than the remainder of the poem. And, as the heyday passed towards sunset, as the ebullient joy in life and love died down, and the glory of the reign was clouded by troubles and shadows of coming evils, this note is heard more clearly. The last decade of Elizabeth's reign was a time of thought and reflection, even of apprehension; and instead of, or side by side with, the notes of apparently "careless rapture," we find the graver poetry of men of piety and philosophy.

CHAPTER VII

Robert Southwell.   Samuel Daniel

REFERENCE was made at the close of the previous chapter to the poetry of piety and philosophy which became prominent in the last decade of Elizabeth's reign.   Such poetry falls, roughly, into two classes, of which the two poets whose names give the title to this chapter are representative: Southwell of the purely religious poetry, Daniel of the humanistic and historical.

In purely religious poetry, the period was not rich.   There were few poets who did not, at one time or another, write a religious poem; on the other hand, the whole body of religious verse, if collected, would not amount to a large total, and only one important poet of the age is, specifically, a religious poet. Round Robert Southwell, the Jesuit, in late Elizabethan days no less than in our own, floated a glamour due to the story of his life and death.   Born in 1561, of an illegitimate branch of the old Catholic family of Southwell, probably at his father's estate of Horsham St. Faith near Norwich, he is said to have been stolen from his cradle by a gypsy who was tempted by his uncommon beauty.   At an early age, he came under the influence of the Jesuits, being sent to the college at Douay, and thence transferred to Paris.   Thomas Darbyshire, his chief guide in Paris, had resigned, on Elizabeth's accession, the archdeaconry of Essex which he had held under Mary.   South-well early showed an intense desire to belong to the Society of Jesus, and, after a period of probation which he found almost intolerably long, succeeded in making his own way to Rome, where he was admitted to the novitiate at the age of seventeen. At the end of his novitiate, he was appointed prefect of studies at the English college in Rome, a position which he held until, in 1586, he was selected to accompany Henry Garnett into England on the work of the English mission inaugurated by Parsons, and Edmund Campion in 1580.   The call appeared to him to be an almost certain promise of the martyrdom on which his desires had long been set.   Nevertheless, he carried on his perilous work in England for six years, before he was decoyed, in 1592, into the hands of the informer Topcliffe and imprisoned in Topcliffe's house in Westminster.   After thirteen applications of the torture and two years and a half of imprisonment, Southwell was executed at Tyburn, in February 1594/5.

It was in prison that his poems were mainly written. When poets sing of the shortness and the deceptive character of life, one is often tempted to wonder whether the sentiments are not the purely conventional utterances of men sitting at ease in comfortable homes, or merely signs of reaction from an excess of pleasure.   From Southwell's own statements, we know that his body never recovered from the tortures it had suffered, and, from his letters and journals, that such a death as he expected had long been his highest ambition.   This certificate of sincerity, combined with a vivid imagination and an epigrammatic keenness of expression, imparts to his poems a brilliance only tempered by the sweetness of nature to which they, with everything we know of the poet, bear witness.

In writing his poetry, Southwell may be said to have had before him three motives: the expression of his own thoughts and feelings, to which life in prison gave no other outlet; the comfort and edification of his fellow Catholics; and a third, which gives them a peculiar literary interest.   His poems were not published in his lifetime; but that he contemplated publication is clear from the letter to his cousin which prefaces *Saint Peters Complaint*.   His object, like Milton's in the following century, was to rescue the art of poetry from the worldly uses to which it had been almost solely devoted.

"Most poets," he writes, "now busie themselves in expressing such passions as onely serve for testimonies to howe unworthy affections they have wedded their wills.   And, because the best course to let them see the errour of their works is to weave a new webbe in their owne loome, I have here laide a few course threds together."

There can be no doubt that Southwell had read Shakespeare's *Venus and Adonis*, which was published in 1593 and at once became the most popular poem of the day. He seems, indeed, to have regarded it as the capital instance of the poetry he wished to supplant. His *Saint Peters Complaint*, published in 1595, soon after his death, is written in the metre of Shakespeare's poem, and the preliminary address from the author to the reader contains a line, "Stil finest wits are stilling Venus' rose," which may be a direct reference to it, and certainly would be considered so by Southwell's readers. And, if Southwell had read Shakespeare, it is clear, from a number of interesting correspondences to be found in their works, that Shakespeare had read Southwell. At any rate, the attempt to give to sacred poetry the merit and charm of profane did not pass unnoticed. *Saint Peters Complaint* was attacked by Joseph Hall in his eighth satire in the line: "Now good St. Peter weeps pure Helicon."

Saint Peters Complaint is a long poem describing the incidents of the last days of the life of Christ, seen in the light of the remorse of the saint for having denied his Master; and its theme is chiefly remarkable for the great number and ingenuity of the "conceits" which it embodies. Comparisons, which must seem extravagant and far-fetched were they applied to any subject but the Redeemer, paradoxes and antitheses, which must seem affected were they not the only means of expressing the illimitable in terms of the finite, and, therefore, inevitable in dealing with the Incarnation, are heaped one upon another until the poem becomes a leading example of the poetical "wit" of the age. The paradox is inherent in the subject, being almost entirely theological and embodying the Catholic view of the nature of Christ and the eternal contrast between the reality of things spiritual and the unreality of the things of this world.[1] Southwell, almost certainly, was a student at first hand of the Italian poetry which had been the origin of the "conceits" then common in English poetry; and the effort to express the eternal through the imagery of the temporal was one which his church, even in her liturgies, has always

---

[1] Cf. the poem written by another Catholic, Chidiock Tichborne, on the eve of his execution in 1586; published in Hannah: *Poems by Sir Henry Wootton, Sir Walter Raleigh and others*, p. 69.

sanctioned. The first line of a famous stanza in *Saint Peters Complaint*, for instance, in which the bloody sweat of Christ is compared to "Fat soil, full spring, sweet olive, grape of bliss," has its theological origin in the litany of Loreto, while the remainder of the stanza, which works out the comparisons, could be paralleled in a hundred poems of the time. Another form of contrast beloved by Southwell is that between the old dispensation and the new; the idea, for instance, expressed in the hymn, *Ave maris Stella*, finds its counterpart in one of his poems dealing with the change of "Eva" to "Ave."

To modern readers, however, and, especially, to modern readers other than Catholics, who may find these constant antithetical and paradoxical flights a little strange, Southwell's shorter poems will appeal more strongly. Some of them are to be found at the end of *Saint Peters Complaint;* others were collected a few months later and published under the title *Maeoniae* (1595). These, too are paradoxical: poems that deal with the nativity and the life on earth of Christ could hardly be anything else; but the shorter flight and the greater prominence of the poet's lyrical power render the antitheses less noticeable. And one or two of them, when the chance occurs, are free from antithesis, and are content with a simple, but profound, symbolism. Such are the poems called *New Prince, New Pompe; New Heaven, New Warre;* or the finely imaginative and glowing little poem, *The Burning Babe*, of which Ben Jonson said to Drummond of Hawthornden that "so he had written that piece of his, *The Burning Babe*, he would have been content to destroy many of his." Southwell is one of our few religious poets who have preferred the lyrical to the didactic manner, or, in being indirectly didactic (for *Saint Peters Complaint* draws a moral from every incident of the crucifixion), have maintained the lyric note. In a poem called *Foure-fould Meditation, of the foure last things*, published eleven years after his death and attributed on the title-page to 'R. S. The author of S. Peters complaint,' the meditation on the joys of heaven is not unworthy of Southwell; but, though Southwell may have revised the poem, the author of it was more probably his friend and fellow prisoner, Philip Howard, earl of Arundel, a grandson of the poet Henry Howard, earl of Surrey.[1]

As a metrist, Southwell's range is not wide. For his longer poems, he employs exclusively the decasyllabic line, arranged in stanzas of four or six. The metre of *Saint Peters Complaint*, admirably adapted for narrative or exposition, is one in which it is not easy to preserve the lyric exaltation; and Southwell's power as a poet may be gauged by his success in this respect. In *The Burning Babe*, he uses the old fourteener line, and indulges in a good deal of alliteration; but it is almost surprising to observe how, in such hands as his, this much abused metre is capable of a force and sweetness which its earlier practitioners had very rarely achieved. His language is simple and easy, though he has an affection for one or two archaic words; and he makes sparing use of words derived from Latin.

A good way of learning to appreciate Southwell's poetry is to compare it with that of another religious poet, John Davies of Hereford. Davies was born in Hereford, about 1565, and settled at Oxford as a writing-master, living, as it appears, an easy and prosperous life. The principal model of his uninspired verse was Joshua Sylvester, the translator of Du Bartas's *Semaines*, on which he founded his long poem, *Microcosmos* (1603); but he owed something, also, to his namesake, Sir John Davies, whose *Nosce Teipsum* formed the basis of *Mirum in Modum* (1602) and *Summa Totalis* (1607). Davies of Hereford is no lyric poet. He writes long philosophical and theological treatises in rime, modelling his stanzas on Spenser; and neither his imagination nor his reasoning power is sufficient to make him more than mildly interesting. The antithesis and paradox prominent in Southwell may be found also in Davies, but wearing the air rather of scholastic pedantry than of living and effectual truth. Davies borrows from Sylvester the practice of playing upon words, and carries it to tedious lengths. In spite of the work of Sir John Davies, it may be fairly said that the art of reasoning in verse was not mastered till Dryden's day; and John Davies of Hereford is chiefly valuable as illustrating by contrast the genius of Southwell, who dealt with the same theological truth, and from much the same intellectual standpoint, in an entirely different manner.

---

[1] *The Month*, vol. LXXXVI, Jan.–April, 1896, pp. 32 *et seq.*

The same might fairly be said of Abraham Fraunce's *The Countesse of Pembrokes Emanuell*, which appeared three years before *Saint Peters Complaint*. Fraunce, who was a fellow of Saint John's college, Cambridge, and a distinguished lawyer, is of interest in the story of English prosody, since he belonged to the Cambridge group, including Gabriel Harvey and others, which attempted to force upon English poetry the classical metres. All his poems are in hexameters. In *The Countesse of Pembrokes Emanuell*, the poem on *The Nativity* is in what he calls riming hexameters; but as this means that the last syllable only of the lines is rimed in couplets, the effect is scarcely different from that of the unrimed hexameters, especially as in both cases he avails himself to excess of the convenience of participles ending in *-ing*. Like many poets of his and the succeeding age, he paraphrased some of the *Psalms*. A learned and laborious person rather than a poet, he freely translated Thomas Watson's Latin poem *Amyntas*, and part of Tasso's *Amintà*, and published the two in *The Countesse of Pembrokes Yvychurch* in 1591.

In Samuel Daniel, we reach the leading example of the graver, reflective poetry of the later years of Elizabeth's reign. Daniel is not a religious nor a theological poet in the sense in which the words may be used of Southwell and John Davies; and, if he is called a philosophical poet, it is not in the sense in which the term is applied to such writers as Fulke Greville. There is no dialectic in his poems, and no system is advanced; they are philosophical in the sense that their author was a man with a wide and grave outlook upon life, in whom (though he sang exquisitely of love) judgment was stronger than passion, who moralised sincerely and sanely over his own and other people's feelings and who, in his culture, his synthetic mind and his belief in the importance of humanism, stands much nearer to later poets, "critics of life" as they have been called, than to the singers of the dawn. In his "vast philosophic gravity and stateliness of sentiment," to use Hazlitt's phrase about him, he resembles Wordsworth, to whom he has also other points of likeness to be mentioned later; in other respects, when allowance has been made for all differences of time and opportunity, it may not be fanciful to see in him the Matthew Arnold of his age.

Samuel Daniel, the son of a music master, was born, probably near Taunton in Somerset, in 1562, and went to Magdalen hall (now Hertford college), Oxford, where, however, he did not take a degree. In 1585, we find him in London, appearing as the translator of Paolo Giovio's book on *impresas*, to which he wrote a preface. He may, perhaps, have been in the service of lord Stafford. In 1586, he visited Italy, and, on his return, became tutor, at Wilton, to Shakespeare's friend and patron William Herbert, to whom he dedicated his *Defence of Ryme;* and here he made the acquaintance of Herbert's mother, Mary countess of Pembroke. Another of his friends was lord Mountjoy, afterwards earl of Devonshire, whom Daniel visited at Wanstead; and, in 1595, he was appointed tutor to Anne Clifford, daughter of Margaret countess of Cumberland, with whose family he remained on terms of intimate friendship, though he seems to have found the work of tutor a bar to his poetical progress. In 1603, after greeting James I with a *Panegyrike Congratulatorie*, he was appointed inspector of Kirkham's children of the queen's revels. Here he remained, living a prosperous and easy life, which was only once threatened by a slight incident. So far back as 1595, in the second book of his epic, *The Civil Wars*, he had eulogised Robert Devereux, second earl of Essex; and, on the publication of his play *Philotas*, in 1605, the character of Philotas was supposed to stand for that of Essex, and the author of the play to be in sympathy with that noble's rebellion. On being summoned before the lords in council, he was able to prove that the first three acts of the play had been read by the master of the revels before 1600. This, however, could not save him from a reprimand from Essex's old friend, Devonshire. Of his life, there is nothing more to chronicle except that he spent his later years on his farm at Beckington, in Somerset, where he died in 1619. His office passed to his brother John Daniel, author of *Songs for the Lute, Viol and Voice* (1606).

Samuel Daniel began his literary career with a set of sonnets entitled *Delia*. Twenty-seven sonnets by him had been appended to the 1591 edition of Sidney's *Astrophel and Stella*, without, as he declared, his authorisation, and, probably, through the action of Nashe. In the following year, appeared the first edition of *Delia*, containing fifty sonnets, and including revised versions of eighteen of those that had appeared in *Astrophel and Stella*.   In 1592, came the second edition of *Delia*, with four new sonnets, and *The Complaynt of Rosamond*. The third edition, published in 1594, includes twenty-three new stanzas to *Rosamond*, and *Cleopatra*, a tragedy.   In this third edition, the prose epistolary dedication to the countess of Pembroke, which had appeared in the previous editions, has given place to a sonnet addressed to her; while *Cleopatra* is also dedicated to the same lady, the poet stating that he wrote it at her command as a companion to her own tragedy of *Antonie* (1592).   In 1595, came the first four books of *The Civil Wars between the two Houses of Lancaster and York*, the fifth book being published the same year; and it was mainly the desire to go on with his epic that made his duty as tutor to lady Anne Clifford seem tedious to him.   During the next four years, he published nothing.   In 1599, *Musophilus, or a General Defence of Learning* was issued, dedicated to Fulke Greville, and, in the same volume, was included the first of the poetical epistles, that from Octavia to Marcus Antonius, which was dedicated to the countess of Cumberland.   In the same year, appeared the first collected edition of his works, the *Poeticall Essayes*; and, two years later, an augmented collection was published, including the sixth book of *The Civil Wars*, and showing much revision of the text of other poems. In 1602, he replied to Campion's *Observations in the Art of English Poesie* with his prose *Defence of Ryme*,[1] a curious and admirable work which was the last serious blow dealt to the Latinisers, whom old Gabriel Harvey, then still living, had advanced into estimation, until the movement was checked by the ridicule of Nashe and his fellows.   In the same year, came the *Panegyrike Congratulatorie*, on the accession of James I, and then followed a few years in which Daniel's attention was very largely occupied by the composition of the masques in which the queen, Anne of Denmark, delighted.   *The Vision of* 12 *Goddesses* (published 1604); *The Queenes Arcadia* (published 1606), adapted from Guarini's *Pastor Fido; Tethys Festival: or the Queenes Wake* (published 1610) and *Hymens' Triumph* (published 1615) all belong to this period, during which, also, Daniel became one of the grooms of the queen's privy chamber.

---

[1] See Vol. III of the present work, Chap. XIV.

In 1605, he published *Certaine Small Poems*, which included *Philotas* and one of his best known lyrics, *Ulisses and the Syren*, and, in 1609, a new edition of *The Civil Wars*, now comprising eight books. In 1623, his brother John issued his "whole works." It will be seen that Daniel's activity was wide; and it should be mentioned that his prose works included, also, a history of England (1612). He began, in the usual way, as a translator and a sonneteer; his scope increased until he embraced tragedy, masque and epic. And, his natural bent being set strongly towards history, it was to epic that he attached the greatest importance. He believed that men were more influenced by it than by any other form of literature.

Daniel's sonnets have been discussed elsewhere,[1] and no further mention need be made of them here, while his Senecan tragedies and his masques also belong to another section of this work.[2] With *The Complaynt of Rosamond*, we come into touch with Daniel in his most characteristic mood. The honour had been accorded to him of mention by name in Spenser's *Colin Clout*. The "new shepherd late up sprong" is bidden to "rouse thy feathers quickly, Daniell"; and Spenser goes on to say that "most, me seemes, thy accent will excell In tragick plaints and passionate mischance." In *Rosamond*, we have the tragic plaint, combined with the interest in English history, the "philosophic gravity," the pre-occupation with morals, which are all characteristic of Daniel. Rosamond describes and laments her sin with the king much in the manner of the stories in *A Mirror for Magistrates*, but with more flexibility, more sweetness and more smoothness. Churchyard's tale of *Shore's Wife*, doubtless, was his model; but the difference between the two poems is instructive as to the advance that the intervening years had brought about in the use of language, the form of English poetry and urbanity of judgment. *Musophilus* shows another side of Daniel's mind—the importance he attached to literature and "culture" as refining and enlarging elements of life. The poem is a dialogue between Philocosmus, a courtier, and Musophilus, a man of letters, in whom speaks Daniel himself. From the days of Daniel to those of Matthew Arnold there has been in English literature no

---

[1] See Vol. III, Chap. XII.   [2] See Volumes V and VI.

such important pleading for the influence of letters.   In Castiglione's view of a courtier, letters had played a part: Daniel soars far above the chivalric view of the subject; and one of the most eloquent and lofty passages of his poetry—an apostrophe to the English language as a force that is to spread civilisation over the world—includes a remarkable piece of prophecy. The "worlds in the yet unformëd Occident" are to "come refined with accents that are ours."   "O who," he cries, "can tell for what great work in hand The greatness of our style is now ordained?"

His immense faith in his native tongue unites in him the man of letters with the patriot and the statesman: a combination that may be seen also in his prose *Defence of Ryme*.   Secure of some niche in the temple of fame ("Something I shall be," he writes to the countess of Pembroke, "though not the best"), he values his immortality not so much for himself as for the English language; and the English language is to attain a beauty and an influence worthy of the English constitution. Frequently in the poems of Daniel there sounds a note of sadness, the regret, of a man who feels himself born too late, for great days that are gone.   It is heard in the epistle to prince Henry which introduces *Philotas*, and very clearly again in the *Panegyrike Congratulatorie*.   There must have been many thoughtful men and good patriots whose minds were similarly affected by the troubles of the later years of the reign of Elizabeth; and, whatever may have been Daniel's actual relation to the plot of Essex, there can be little question that though, like Essex, he was a protestant, he had, like Essex, sympathies with the Catholics, and must have been for some reasons inclined to wish that Essex could have become king.   At any rate, he addresses to James what is at once a glowing patriotic poem and a shrewd warning that the state of the times needs firm handling from the monarch. He looks back to the despotism of the Tudors with longing, and sees in a strong monarchy the promise of a return of the old order, decency and security—the "ancient native modesty" which had never existed in his lifetime, but was the dream of a patriotic poet.

This regret it was doubtless, which spurred him to the composition of his great epic, *The Civil Wars*.   An interest in

English history, manifested even more clearly in the dramatic *Chronicles* than in the printed poetry, was characteristic of the time. Even before the loss of the Spanish Armada, William Warner, sometime a student at Oxford and then an attorney, had published in 1586 a part of his long historical poem, *Albion's England*, which began with the Flood, passed through Grecian mythology to the Trojan war, and so, by means of Brute, to England, the history of which he carried down to his own period, including even the execution of Mary queen of Scots. Warner's poem is written in the old "fourteens," rimed in couplets, which Drayton was afterwards to adopt for his *Poly-Olbion*. *Albion's England* was very successful; and, as new editions were called for, the author continued to revise it, and to add recent events, including the loss of the Spanish Armada, to his story. Before his death in 1609, he had added three more books, in which he embarked on the history of Scotland and Wales. Often clumsy and sometimes dull, the poem contains a number of good stories, like that of the wooing of Argentile, daughter of Adelbright, king of Diria, and Curan, son of a Danish prince, or that of the murder of Turgesius the Norwegian conqueror of Ireland, by youths disguised as girls, all told with a brave simplicity. It delights in legend as much as does *Poly-Olbion;* but it lacks both the haunting regret which often inspires that protest against the inroads of time, and lacks, also, in its superficial, sturdy patriotism, the philosophic and humane intention of Daniel's *Civil Wars*.

In a less marked degree, Daniel took the Miltonic view of the poet's office. The poet was not only to delight, but to instruct and fortify; and, perhaps unwisely, Daniel regarded epic as the best form of poetry for the purpose. Guided always by principle rather than by passion, he adopted the poetic theory followed two centuries later by Wordsworth, and worked something on Wordsworth's lines, believing in the will and the message rather than in the inspiration. It is a tribute to the force of his mind and the fineness of his taste that *The Civil Wars* is as interesting as an unprejudiced reader must find it. At the worst, it can only be regarded as a mistake, in that it occupied time which the poet might have devoted to other kinds of poetry. There are, no doubt, long stretches of dulness in the eight books; there is too much chronicle and too little

drama; but the subject, though of little importance to the world
outside England, was, in Daniel's view, of immense importance
to the Englishmen through whom the world was to be civilised.
The whole poem is grave, dignified and wise; it never falls below
a very creditable level of matter and execution.   It stands to
Daniel's best poetry in much the same relation as *The Excursion*
stands to Wordsworth's best.   Daniel's example, indeed, may
have supported Wordsworth through the labour of writing *The
Excursion*, into which he wove,[1] with perfect propriety, a stanza
from Daniel's poem, *To the Lady Margaret, countesse of Cumberland*, ending with the well known lines:

> And that unless above himself he can
> Erect himself, how poor a thing is Man![2]

The eight books of *The Civil Wars* contain nearly 900 stanzas
of eight lines each.   The first book tells the story of England
from the Conquest to the return of Hereford against Richard
II; the other seven describe the wars of the Roses down to the
accession of Edward IV and his marriage to Elizabeth Grey.
The poet does not hesitate to draw the moral from these
events, as from the story of Rosamond or of Octavia, and
the poem becomes particularly interesting in book VI, where
Daniel ascribes Cade's rebellion to the spread of knowledge
and the invention of artillery.   In his desire to prove himself
"the remnant of another time" and to celebrate the good days
that are gone, Daniel seems here almost to contradict his own
views on the importance of culture and letters; but in his day
the ideals of Thomas Love Peacock's "learned friend" were
unknown.   Democracy was not even a name, and discontent
was not yet called "divine."   "Swelling sciences" were "the
gifts of griefe," and the political absolutist who told James I
that "the weight of all seems to rely Wholly upon thine own
discretion" put the spread of knowledge and the increase of
discontent together as unqualified evils.   Indeed, like all the
writers of his day in whom the spirit of the age of chivalry still
lingered —like Shakespeare himself—Daniel had no sympathy
with "the mob."   Yet the patriotism which his epic was written
to inspire was none the less lofty and sincere because he regarded

---

[1] *The Excursion*, IV, 324-331.   [2] *The Excursion*, book IV.

it, with knowledge and culture, as the province of the knight and the noble only.

Ben Jonson, who (for a reason that will probably never be discovered now, but may have been not unconnected with Daniel's opposition to the Latinists) never appreciated his work, not only parodied Daniel's verses in *Everyman in his Humour* (act v) and *The Staple of News* (act v, sc. i), but said bitter things about him to Drummond of Hawthornden. "An honest man, but no poet," was his phrase. "He wrote Civil Wars and yet had not one battle in all his book." "Too much historian in verse," said Drayton in his epistle to Henry Reynolds *Of Poets and Poesy*, and added that "his manner better fitted prose." Both Jonson and Drayton hit upon weak spots in Daniel's *Civil Wars*, regarded as an epic: neither, perhaps, took sufficiently into account the ethical purpose with which Daniel wrote. Daniel's model, undoubtedly, was the *Pharsalia* of Lucan; and Guilpin, in his *Skialetheia*, states that he was called by some "a Lucanist." It may be allowable, perhaps, to find him nearer to Vergil than Lucan. Admitting that the work has little of Vergil's dramatic power, its sweetness and the simplicity and purity of its style resemble rather the Augustan poet than the Neronian. Daniel's object was not so much to interest and excite his readers as to rouse in them, by presenting their national history in a moral and philosophic light, a spirit of wise patriotism; and the wisdom, gravity and sincerity of his epic atone for its lack of vivid incident and dramatic force. If, like his masques, it is "too serious," the fault was deliberately committed.

In some ways, the epic is Daniel's most characteristic work: as poetry, it falls short of such poems as his *Epistles* (to Sir Thomas Egerton, lord Henry Howard, lady Anne Clifford and others), his letter from Octavia to Marcus Antonius, the charming little lyrics in *Hymens' Triumph*, or the two which later taste has selected as the best of his shorter poems, the *Epistle to the Lady Margaret, countesse of Cumberland*, and the "ballad" —or, rather, the discussion upon honour—called *Ulisses and the Syren*. If the sonnets, beautiful as they are, savour a little of an exercise in poetry, if the masques are "too serious" and the epic shows him "too much historian in verse," in these two poems he completely proves his title to the "something . . . though not the best" he modestly claimed, and almost to the eulogies accorded to him by others of his contemporaries besides Spenser.

The most glowing tribute of all came from Francis Davison, who said in the *Poetical Rapsody* that Daniel's "Muse hath surpassed Spenser" and headed his poem: "To Samuel Daniel Prince of English poets, upon his three several sorts of poesie. Lyrical, in his Sonnets. Tragical, in Rosamond and Cleopatra. Heroicall, in his Civill Warres." The last verse of the poem states that as Alexander conquered Greece, Asia and Egypt, so Daniel conquered all poets in these fields. "Thou alone," says Davison, "art matchlesse in them all." From praise so extravagant as this, it is pleasant to turn to the comments of the author of *The Returne from Parnassus*, part II (acted 1601–2) who speaks (act 1, sc. 2) of "sweet honey-dropping D[aniel.]" The remainder of Judicio's remarks on this poet seem to imply that he knew little or nothing of Daniel's work besides the sonnets to Delia; for, after stating that he

> doth wage
> War with the proudest big Italian,
> That melts his heart in sugared sonneting,

he goes on to warn him that he should

> more sparingly make use
> Of other's wit, and use his own the more;
> That well may scorn base imitation.

We know from the dedication to *Cleopatra* that one of Daniel's wishes was to break free from Italian influence. He aspires to make

> the melody of our sweet isle
> . . . heard to Tyber, Arne and Po,
> That they might know how far Thames doth outgo
> The music of declinëd Italy.

Still, the criticism is not uninstructive. It shows that the sweetness and purity of Daniel's language, which won the praise of Meres, Lodge, Drummond, Carew and others, was fully recognised in his own day; and it hints at a timidity in the poet which may account for the comparative lack in his work of pure lyrical outburst. His was a mind of fine taste rather than of powerful creative genius. He was eminent as a poet, as Matthew Arnold was eminent, because he was first of all a critic of life and letters.

Coleridge bears a remarkable tribute to the purity of language which is not the least important of Daniel's characteristics. "The style and language," he wrote in *Table Talk* of the epic, "are just such as any very pure and manly writer of the present day—Wordsworth, for example—would use; it seems quite modern in comparison with the style of Shakespeare." Like Southwell's, the English of Daniel is notably free from words of Latin origin; and the constant labour he devoted to the revision of his text, as it passed through new editions, all tended towards greater simplicity and purity. Yet he was no archaist, as Coleridge saw. He had no taste for what in one of his sonnets he calls the "aged accents and untimely words" of Spenser. He regarded the English of his own era as a sufficient and living tongue, and, by his use of it, did more to establish it also as a classical and polite tongue than has, perhaps, been commonly recognised. As a metrist, he was no innovator. By his nature and the nature of his material, he was inclined, like Southwell, again, to the decasyllabic line. His *Civil Wars* are written in eight-lined stanzas riming *ababababcc; Musophilus* is in lines of the same length riming *ababab*, or, occasionally, *ababcc; Rosamond* is in rime royal; the letter from Octavia and the *Panegyrike Congratulatorie* are in the same metre as the epic. Only rarely, as in the lyrics in *Hymens' Triumph*, does he use anything like a complicated structure; and he invests the eights and sixes of *Ulisses and the Syren* with something of the grave dignity of the decasyllable. His technical triumph is the investment of the decasyllabic line with the utmost sweetness and smoothness, while yet contriving to evade monotony; and the skilful use of an occasional rugged line, such as "Melancholies opinion, Customs relation," or "Impietie of times, Chastities abator" (both from *Rosamond*), helps to prove him a finished artist in poetic structure.

For a reason which is not very easy to discover, Samuel Daniel has not been appreciated by ages subsequent to his own as he should have been. As a thinker, in his regret for the great days that had just passed, his hopes of a strong monarchy, his gravity, his culture and his philosophical outlook, he is fully representative of the best minds of a society already tottering to a fall. As a writer, he achieved a great advance towards clarity and fixity of style. It is difficult to avoid thinking that, if Dryden and his age had known and appreciated him better, Daniel could have been of considerable service to the men of letters of the Restoration, in their work of reducing the English language to accuracy and order.

CHAPTER VIII

Thomas Campion

THOMAS CAMPION, who was born on Ash Wednesday, 12 February, 1566/7, was the son of well-to-do middle-class parents. His father, John Campion, was a member of the Middle Temple, and, by profession, one of the cursitors of the chancery court, the clerks "of course" (who made out the writs *de cursu* according to the procedure requisite in the various districts).

John Campion was buried at St. Andrew's, Holborn, on 8 October, 1576, and, about a year later, his relict Lucy, who was the daughter of Laurence Searle, one of the queen's ser-jeants-at-arms, married Augustine Steward, of a family which was of some importance in the north-easterly home counties, and from which, through his mother, Oliver Cromwell was descended. There were no children of this marriage, which Lucy did not long survive, for she died in 1580, leaving her children, Thomas and his sister Rose, in the care of Steward. In 1581, Steward married Anne, daughter of Thomas Argall, and relict of Clement Sisley of Barking, who brought him a second stepson, Thomas Sisley, a lad of about the same age as Campion.

During their minority, both lads were under Steward's tute-lage; and, in 1581, they were entered as gentlemen pensioners at Peterhouse, Cambridge, then under the mastership of Andrew Perne, with whom, in his capacity as dean of Ely, Steward had business relations. Neither of the boys matriculated or pro ceeded to a degree. After four years of study, they left the university, and, on 27 April, 1586, Campion was entered at Gray's inn, possibly with a view to his pursuing a legal pro-fession. It is clear, however, from his works, that he had

163

little sympathy with, or respect for, legal studies; and he does not appear to have been called to the bar.

His later movements cannot be ascertained with certainty, though he appears to have kept up his connection with Gray's inn for some years. In 1591, a set of five of his poems appeared anonymously among the *Songs of Divers Noblemen and Gentlemen*, appended to Newman's surreptitious edition of Sidney's *Astrophel and Stella*. These, possibly, were pirated by the enterprising publisher from MS. copies in circulation after the fashion of those times, or lent by Nashe, who was a friend of Campion and who contributed the introduction: for not only are they full of obvious misprints, but there is an accumulated weight of internal evidence to show that the poet took part in the earl of Essex's expedition, for the succour of Henry IV, against the League, which reached Dieppe in August, 1591, and laid siege to Rouen.

The first published work bearing Campion's name is his volume of Latin *Poemata*, which appeared in 1595. This little book, which is extremely rare at the present day, contains panegyrics of Elizabeth and of the earl of Essex, a poem of rejoicing on the defeat of the Armada, and so forth, followed by a collection of elegies and a series of epigrams chiefly addressed to his own friends and contemporaries by name. It was not until 1601 that Campion's first collection of English poems, *A Booke of Ayres*, was given to the world in the form of one of the song-books to which reference has been made in a previous chapter. It was divided into two parts, the first set to airs composed by Campion himself, who thus made his first appearance as a musician, and the second to the airs of Philip Rosseter, musician and theatrical manager and Campion's lifelong friend.

In the following year, 1602, Campion published his *Observations in the Art of English Poesie*[1] "against the vulgar and unartificial custom of riming"; and, some time between 1602 and 1606, when he first signed himself "Doctor in Physic," he must have taken up the study of medicine and proceeded to the degree of M.D. We have already seen that this degree was not conferred on him at Cambridge, neither, so far as can be ascertained, was it conferred at Oxford or at Dublin. It

[1] See Vol. III of the present work, Chap. XIV.

only remains to assume that the poet studied at some continental university, and, while nothing certain has at present been ascertained as to this, it is interesting to note that the study of medicine and the practice of foreign travel were both sedulously fostered at Peterhouse, which not only possessed one of the finest early collections of books upon medicine, but frequently granted dispensations to its fellows to pursue some approved course of study *in partibus transmarinis*. In 1607, he wrote and published a masque for the occasion of the marriage of lord Hayes, and, in 1613, appeared a volume of *Songs of Mourning*, in which, in common with many other famous poets, he expressed the grief evoked in Britain by the untimely death of prince Henry. In the same year, he wrote and arranged three masques, the *Lords' Maske*, for the occasion of princess Elizabeth's marriage to the elector palatine, a masque entertainment for the amusement of queen Anne, during her visit at Caversham house, and a third for the occasion of the earl of Somerset's marriage to the notorious Frances Howard. To this last masque, some personal interest attaches, by reason of its connection with the Overbury poisoning case, in which Campion was slightly involved. He had performed some trifling duties for his patron, Sir Thomas Monson, which afterwards became of importance in the history of the trial. Monson himself was thrown into the Tower, upon suspicion of complicity, where the poet attended him in his professional capacity as physician; after some delay, during which the poet's evidence was heard, Monson received the royal pardon in circumstances and conditions which made it tantamount to a complete acquittal. If this verdict be accepted—and there is no reason for rejecting it—*a fortiori* Campion could not have been privy to the conspiracy.

In 1612, appeared *Two Bookes of Ayres*, followed, in 1617, by the *Third and Fourth Booke of Ayres*. To 1617, also, probably belongs his *New Way of Making Fowre Parts in Counter-point*, a technical treatise which, for many years, was the standard text-book on the subject. In 1618 was published *Ayres that were sung and played at Brougham Castle*, which were almost certainly written by Campion for the occasion of the king's entertainment on his return from Scotland; and, in 1619, he published a second edition of his Latin poems in two books, the latter of which was a reprint, with considerable alterations, omissions and additions, of the 1595 collection of epigrams, followed by a similar *réchauffé* of the elegies contained in that volume. He died on 1 March, 1619/20, and was buried at St. Dunstan's in the West, having, by his will, a nuncupatory one made *in extremis*, left the whole of his estate to his old collaborator, Philip Rosseter. From this circumstance, it may fairly be inferred that he left behind him neither wife nor issue.

As to the poet's religious views, divers opinions have been expressed. It has been thought by some that, in view of the fact that a large number of Campion's best friends were adherents to the older faith, and that he did not dissemble a distaste for puritans and puritanism, he was himself a Catholic. But it is not likely that any devout Catholic, howsoever loyal, could have alluded to Elizabeth as "Faith's Pure Shield, the Christian Diana," and the conclusion at which we must arrive is that Campion, though probably nominally a protestant, was not seriously concerned with dogma of any sort. However, his devotional poetry contains some of the finest things he has written. "Never weather-beaten Saile more willing bent to shore," "Awake, awake, thou heavy spright" and some others exhibit the union, all too rare in the annals of hymnology, of genuine spiritual exaltation with the true lyrical note.

He was thoroughly steeped in classical studies, as his *Observations in the Art of English Poesie* indicates. Hence, his Latin verses, of which he wrote a great number, show considerable familiarity with the Latin poets. They are, of course, mainly imitative: the epigrams are sometimes lacking in decisive point, and frequently express mere vituperation in place of wit—a valid substitute in the opinion of those times—while many of them, especially those in the earlier edition, are obscene. All, however, are graceful and easy, and exhibit dexterity in the handling of the various metres. They won him a great reputation among his contemporaries.

Of the musical work, *A New Way of Making Fowre Parts in Counter-point*, it will not be necessary to say much; its interest is entirely technical. The "new way" itself, the sole contribution of the book to the sum of contemporary musical knowledge, is a rule of thumb for the harmonisation of a continuous piece of vocal or instrumental music, given the bass and the first chord. But, apart from the value, such as it is, of this discovery, no doubt the book served as a useful compendium for the musical student, and it was very popular, being several times reprinted in Playford's *Introduction to the Skill of Musicke*.

As a masque writer, he was not pre-eminently successful. He had served no apprenticeship in the art of dramatic composition, and in dramatic invention and contrivance his powers were not remarkable. The construction of a masque should strike the happy mean between too great complexity and too great looseness, and Campion usually errs upon the side of unsuitable complication of incident. In this respect, his first masque, that written for the marriage of lord Hayes, is the best, and the dramatic part, as distinguished from the purely lyrical, though showing signs of the undeveloped character of the author's style (witness the larger proportion of end-stopped lines and couplets over those in the other masques), is exceedingly fresh, graceful and full of charming fancy. His other two masques proper, those written for the respective marriages of princess Elizabeth (the *Lords' Maske*) and the countess of Essex, are less direct, and have little dramatic merit. But no one can deny the superlative quality of the lyrical element in all these masques, admirably adapted as it is to the necessities of music and action, and comprising in "Now hath Flora rob'd her bowers," "So be it ever, joy and peace," and other short pieces, some of the most beautiful songs in the language.

The truth is that Campion's muse is chiefly lyrical, and to the song-books must we go for the more abundant field of his genius. As regards his place in English poetry, he constitutes a link between the Elizabethans and the Jacobeans, for he was contemporary with both Sidney and Jonson, Sackville and Donne. It is worthy of notice, too, that he shows no sign in his later period of the influence of the last-named, which, at that time, was becoming the predominant tendency of English poetry. This is probably due to the circumstance that Campion's style was based upon the earlier traditions of the time when he first began to write. Moreover, the style which he struck out for himself in his first essays was complete, and he adhered to it with little variation throughout his life. In the *Songs of Divers Noblemen and Gentlemen* above cited, appears in its perfect form one of his most perfect lyrics, "Harke, al you ladies that do sleep," in which fairylike imagination is combined with the most unshackled and musical expression. The appearance of this poem at such a time, written when the author was but twenty-four years of age is most remarkable, and indicates the possession of an ear keenly sensitive to music, and a predisposition to musical effect.

Campion has been called a Euphuist by a contemporary as well as by a recent critic; but his Euphuism is a refined and sublimated variety, the highest form of which it was capable. The characteristics of Euphuism were narrowed in him to the frequent use of balanced phrase and antithesis, and of moral reflections, with an occasional parallel from natural objects. It is not unusual to meet with poems such as "Harke, al you ladies," "There is a Garden in her face" (which, possibly, suggested Herrick's *Cherry Ripe*), "Young and simple though I am," and others, in which little taint of Euphuism can be observed. But the large majority of his poems are infused with it, tempered, however, by his admiration of the classics. Courthope describes Campion's development as a progress from romantic to classical Euphuism, instancing the lyrics from the *Lords' Maske;* but it should be remembered that masques, in consequence of an accepted tradition, were almost invariably classical, at least in subject-matter; while the songs of the third and fourth books, published some five years after the masques are not less romantic than those of *A Booke.*

Another, and a most important aspect of Campion's lyrics is the metrical. He has been truly called "a curious metrist"; and few can fail to be struck with the infinite variety of his cadences and rhythms. He not only rings every possible change upon the usual stanza measures of the period, but frequently introduces subtle changes, shifting from line to line in a single poem. The clue to this, as well as to any complete appreciation of this poetry, is the fact of the mutual interdependence of words and musical setting, and that, too, the setting of the poet, who emphasises his own conscious aims in this respect in the preface to the reader (*Two Bookes*):—"In these English ayres I have chiefly aymed to couple my Words and Notes lovingly together, which will be much for him to doe that hath not power over both." It seldom happens that poet and composer are one; but when, as in this case, the combination does occur, it is easy to see that there is likely to be a close connection between the twin offspring of the single brain. As one can readily understand, in many cases the words framed themselves to an air in composition, or an air suggested its suitable lyric. These verses were not intended to be read, or even printed alone; their sole function was to be sung, and adaptability, therefore, was an important requirement. Campion's success in this respect is testified to by his contemporaries, one of whom, John Davies, writes:

> Never did lyrics' more than happy strains,
> Strained out of Art by Nature, so with ease
> So purely hit the moods and various veins
> Of Music and her hearers as do these.

And, though this success is immaterial for the point of view of permanent literary criticism, it has left its trace in the absence of metrical uniformity, in the novelty of some of the forms and rhythms and especially in variable and shifting cadences, full of musical suggestion. Of this lack of uniformity, this liquid character in his rhythms, there are many instances, but a few will suffice from part II of *A Booke of Ayres*. "When Laura smiles, her sight revives both night and day," the first line of no. IX, is itself slightly peculiar in its freedom from any marked caesura, a feature reproduced in the first lines of stanzas 3 and 4. But hardly any two corresponding lines in the rest of the poem are metrically similar. No. XV, again, contains some curious rhythms: "If I hope, I pine; if I feare, I faint and die." No. XII, "Shall I come, if I swim? wide are the waves,you see," exhibits a lack of uniformity similar to that of no. IX. In this piece, too, we become aware of a feature which will frequently assert itself, a certain ambiguity as to the correct prosodic rendering. The two lines "Shall I come, if I flie, my deare love, to thee?" and "She a priest, yet the heate of love truly felt" correspond in their respective stanzas. But to get actual metrical correspondence, it would be necessary to read "my deáre love"; whereas the accent falls more naturally on "my." Which rhythm expresses the poet's intention? To this and similar queries there is no authoritative reply, because the poems were written for singing, not for reading; and such ambiguities only arise when they are read. It is, of course, of trifling importance which phrasing is upheld; but the point is that, unless the purpose of the poem had been chiefly musical, if, in fact, Campion had paid even a hasty regard to its reading quality, his accurate ear would not have tolerated the existence of such ambiguities. The poems which contain such doubtful passages are not the best, and we may conclude that he regarded these as mere lay-figures to be garbed in musical raiment. But in his finer pieces, those on which the hand of the lyrist lavished its craft, this instability and ambiguity are absent; and, though there is abundance of prosodic interest, it is chiefly due to other reasons. For there was a further cause which contributed in no less measure to this metrical variety. The period covered by Campion's lifetime, the period of transition from the infancy of prosodic control to complete mastery, was, *inprimis*, an age of experiment, on the triumphs and failures of which the fabric of English versification was securely established. While Campion was transitional in chronology only, in an age of experiment he was an arch-experimentalist. He was not only led into the false ways of more grievous experiment in quantitative verse and adapted classical measures, but he affords clear evidence of having given careful consideration to the analysis of metrical effect. It is impossible not to infer both from his work and his own admissions, that his metrical variety was, in great part, the fruit of conscious experiment, the deliberate assay of novel combinations, controlled and guided by an exquisite ear. Take, for example, "Harke, al you ladies that do sleep," already cited. Apart from the daring experiment of a refrain in the second line, there can be little doubt that the poem is an attempt to naturalise classical feet; for the lines of the last quatrain in each stanza scan, respectively: anapaestic, anapaestic, dactylic and adonic. The result is most charming. Take, again, the rhythms of "Follow your Saint; follow with accents sweet," with its echo in "Love me or not, love her I must or dye." These are novel cadences, and their success is as great as their novelty. And, even in the pieces of less metrical originality, there is much subtle handling of caesura to prove what an adept Campion was in fingering all the varied stops of his verse instrument.

We may take it, therefore, that there were two main influences working upon Campion's prosody. When the lyric was a mere puppet to dance to music, when the composer took precedence of the poet, the musical interest affected the prosody; but, when the composer was lost in the lyrist, his prosodic mastery had a clear field. In relation to the metrical progress that distinguished his age, he was an original force; an active, and not merely a passive, element; he must have contributed far more to that progress than he benefited by the example of others.

Tribute has been paid to the freshness and spontaneous charm of Campion's lyrics, concealing, as they do, beneath their seemingly artless ease, a subtle mastery of syllabic tones and values. In a few instances he goes beyond even this, and attains to that completeness and finality, that consummate roundness of expression which betokens close kinship with great poetry.

CHAPTER IX

The Successors of Spenser

IT will be remembered that John Pietro Pugliano commended the art of horsemanship to Sir Philip Sidney with such warmth that, "If I had not beene a piece of a Logician before I came to him, I think he would have persuaded me to have wished my selfe a horse." In like manner, Sidney's famous apology for poetry and the English language worked upon his successors so greatly that they one and all wished themselves poets; and a surprising number were poets. Influence cannot be confined to one man or two men, still less to a pamphlet. But there can be no doubt that the pamphlet of Sidney, and the poetry of Sidney and Spenser, gave impetus and direction to the work of succeeding poets. For through all the work of these men, varied as it is in subject and in value, runs the golden thread of sincerity. Each wrote about that which interested him most deeply, and, considering the manifold affectations of speech that were the fashion, wrote with remarkable directness. There was little affectation of language and manner; and no affectation in the actual choice of subject. The personality of each poet makes itself clearly felt in his work. Spenser and Sidney did much to remove the misconceptions which were beginning to throw out their life-killing feelers—that poetry must be kept apart from life, that poetry must borrow dignity for its subject from what was called learning, instead of lending dignity to any subject by its own graciousness, that things could exist which were too sacred or too commonplace to be treated in poetry. "Foole, said my Muse to me, looke in thy heart and write," might have been the "word" of each of these poets. It is the keynote of all their work. Even in adulatory addresses to king James, there is sincerity, because, in those addresses, the personal character of the king (where it was known) was easily lost in the love of the place which he held at the head of the country the writers loved. So they wrote and no subject was considered unfit for poetry. Fulke Greville, lord Brooke, was inspired by statecraft; George Wither by the puritan spirit; Browne and Basse celebrated the joys of country life; Sir John Davies and Drummond of Hawthornden explored the realm of the spirit; Phineas Fletcher took for his subject the whole construction of man; his brother Giles, the Christian faith.

Certain literary forms or conventions were prevalent at the time, especially the sonnet sequence, the pastoral and the allegory, which Sidney and Spenser had taken from French and from Italian models and by their superb use had established in English. But these forms were not dominant. The poets who used them inspired them with life, and in their hands, the forms are as fresh as the love of the country side or of their mistress, or the beliefs in the possibilities of life, which were expressed in them. At no other time, perhaps, was poetry so little an exercise of imitative wit, and so much and so generally an honest expression of personality.

William Drummond of Hawthornden was born on 13 December, 1585. His father, Sir John Drummond, was of a good Scots family. He was educated at the academy and the university of Edinburgh. In comparison with the lives of other poets of his day, his life was unremarkable. The spirit of adventure and exploration was not alien to him, but the world into which he was constrained to adventure was not the material, but, as was beginning to be more generally the case, the spiritual, world, into which he journeyed further than his contemporaries, and from which he brought back richer results of thought. He realised at an early age the scope of his possible kingdom and, unlike his many-sided contemporaries, was steadfast and undistracted in the pursuit of his object. Circumstances doubtless furthered, so far as circumstances may, the metaphysical bent of his disposition. In the year 1610, when William Drummond was twenty-five years of age, his father died, and the only reason for the continuance of his studies in law was, by this event, removed. He returned to

Scotland immediately, and lived the remainder of his life in quiet seclusion at the place which lent its gracious peace to his retirement, and which is indissolubly connected with his name.

His life, though not eventful, was not without event, and its records are pleasantly detailed and full.   The death of Elizabeth in the year 1603 interrupted his studies at Edinburgh, for Sir John Drummond accompanied James VI of Scotland on his royal progress to ascend the throne of England and, three years later, William Drummond journeyed south to join his father in London on his way to France to study jurisprudence.   He had taken his degree at Edinburgh, and his intelligence was alive to absorb in its own way the sights which awaited him in London.   The early years of king James's reign were days of pageant, and they stirred the boy's imagination.   The descriptions which he wrote to his friend of the festivities in honour of the queen's brother, king Christian of Denmark, read like passages from a medieval romance. These letters, six in number, the first of which is dated 1 June and the last 12 August, are printed in bishop Sage's folio of Drummond's works, published in 1711.

Drummond appears to have remained two or three years in France, and, according to bishop Sage, worked diligently.   But the list of books which he read during those years, a list which is extant in his own handwriting, is that of a literary epicure, and contains but one work of jurisprudence, namely the *Institutes of Justinian*.   A valuable letter which he wrote to Sir George Keith of Cowburn gives an account of his life abroad, and of the vivid impression which the beauty of certain pictures made upon his mind.   "A stately diction, recalling the language of his favourite romances; a love of beauty . . . a fanciful vein of moralising: these are the marked features of the young student's letters, and not less of the maturer writings of the poet."[1]

He returned in 1609 to Scotland, and, in the following year, he again came to London.   His father died in London the same year.   William Drummond returned at the age of twenty-five to Hawthornden and, as has been said, did not henceforth swerve from his resolution to adventure into the unknown kingdom of thought.

[1] Ward, introduction to his edition of Drummond's works.

The circumstances of his life brought him into singular touch with the shape of death, and the great mystery of death seems to have inspired his early life with a strange attractiveness. His first published poems were written to commemorate the death of prince Henry, who had died on 6 November, 1612. In 1613, appeared Drummond's pastoral elegy *Tears on the Death of Moeliades*, with a sonnet and two epitaphs. The poem was published by Andro Hart, and a second edition was printed in the following year.

Of all the elegances which were the fashion of his day, he makes use, and, though they cannot but seem artificial to a modern ear, they came so naturally to Drummond that they do not for a moment obscure the deep sincerity of the poem. Especially was he pleased at such play on words, as "O hyacinths, for aye your AI keeps still" or "Raise whom they list to thrones, enthron'd dethrone," and subtle illustrations drawn from the classics. Sir William Alexander, a Scots poet of some distinction, wrote a complimentary sonnet to the poem. He was some seventeen years senior to Drummond, and a friendship, which had lately begun by a chance visit, lasted between the two until Sir William's death.

In 1616, the *Tears on the Death of Moeliades* was reprinted, but the chief place in the volume was given to a sequence of sonnets, songs and madrigals in which the poet sings the praises of his lady and mourns her untimely death. For again and most darkly had the shadow of death fallen across his path. Just before his intended marriage with Mary Cunningham in 1615, the lady died. He had sought seclusion when worldly honours lay within his grasp, and the disaster did not send him to the world for distraction: it helped him to become more deeply contemplative. A continued consciousness of the end of things, noticeable in all his works, did not afflict him, but, rather, lifted him gently a little above the quiet world in which he chose to live, and filled his songs and poems with that sad sweetness to which they owe their peculiar charm. The lines which end with "Death since grown sweet, begins to be desir'd," seem to have a faint foreshadowing of the idea which turned Shelley's *Adonais* into a triumph song. There is no bitterness in the moods to which these poems give expression. His large nature was too enamoured of death's scope and mystery to feel small bitterness. But, for him, the quiet beauty of the country possessed a deeper meaning, of memory and, in some sort, of anticipation.

> . . . . . . and she is gone, O woe!
> Woods cut again do grow,
> Bud doth the rose and daisy, winter done,
> But we, once dead, no more do see the sun.

The elegances of his manner, which were so part of him that they never left him, put into abrupt relief the simplicity of such lines as these; and it is this sudden simplicity which shows that, in mind, Drummond was more akin to Sidney, whose very phrases he weaves into his verse, than to any other English poet.

His next published work was a poem of very different calibre and of small value. Its elegance is unalloyed, and, as an exercise in verse, it is almost perfect. In May, 1617, king James visited Scotland, and *Forth Feasting* is the felicitous title of the verses which Drummond's courtly instinct bade him compose to celebrate the king's visit. The verses are not memorable. But in the following year an incident both memorable and characteristic occurred. Joseph Davis arrived at Hawthornden bearing an introduction from Michael Drayton, for whose work Drummond cared greatly. He wrote to Drayton and, though the two poets never met, they began a correspondence which continued to the year of Michael Drayton's death in 1631. This was a kind of friendship which would appeal strongly to Drummond and to which his nature responded. Ben Jonson, who, on his northern tour, visited Hawthornden the same year, would have had greater sympathy with Drummond, if Drummond had not been disturbed by the man's vigorous actual presence. The world of letters, however, is the richer for their meeting, although many of their arguments must have been distasteful to Drummond's sensitive nature. "He dissuaded me from poetry, for that she beggared him when he might have been a rich lawyer, physician or merchant," writes Drummond, whose own opinion of riches is beautifully put in *The Cypress Grove*—"They are like to thorns which, laid on an open hand, are easily blown away and wound the closing and hard-gripping." The two men were at fundamental odds. Ben Jonson was a great poet almost in spite of himself: Drummond used all the forces at the command of his exquisite nature to become a better poet than he ever could be.

Flowers of Sion appeared in 1623, and to the poems was appended a prose essay on death, *The Cypress Grove*, in which Drummond reaches his highest sustained level. The poems are religious in the widest and best meaning of that word. Like Shelley, Drummond, beyond all the narrow limits of dogma, gave voice to the spirit of Christ's teaching, the ultimate spirit of all religion, namely, that God is love. He saw and sang the truth less clearly, and, therefore, less beautifully, than Shelley, but there is much in them of surprising similarity. In Drummond's poems, witness especially the *Hymn of the Fairest Fair*, the idea remained a beautiful theory, whereas Shelley applied the idea to human life and worked it out in amazing detail, helped by his profound knowledge of human nature. Drummond is a link, as it were, between Spenser's great conception of Beauty, as the informing spirit of life, and Shelley's greater application of that idea to human affairs. To have reached such a point of view amid the fierce religious quarrels of that day shows the strong independence of Drummond's mind. But he was inspired by his personal griefs, by his personal difficulties in finding an answer to great problems; he was not at all a reformer; he had no passionate wish to alleviate the sorrow of humanity. Therein lies at once his strength and his limitation.

He found at length a personal answer; and, having created his faith and won through to a certain tranquillity, he no longer wrote poetry, except as an occasional exercise, or to lament a friend's death. He lived twenty-six years after the appearance of *Flowers of Sion* and, from one point of view, his life in that year began. He took interest in the stirring events that followed the death of James I; he wrote a history of Scotland; he married and had many children; he wrote topical prose pamphlets; he travelled; he rebuilt his house.

Just as the solemn mystery of death fashioned Drummond into a poet, so the joy of life inspired George Wither his contemporary. There is no hesitation and little deep thought in his poetry.   But for him all the common things of life were decked with the grace of poetry.   "Before Wither," writes Charles Lamb, "no one ever celebrated its power *at home*, the wealth and the strength which this divine gift confers upon its possessor . . . it seems to have been left to Wither to discover that poetry was a present possession as well as a rich reversion."   Nor was his life passed, as was Drummond's, in seclusion: it was caught up in the fury of his times.   He was born in 1588 at Bentworth, near Alton, Hampshire.   John Greaves, the neighbouring vicar, taught him his rudiments, and, from the vicar's care, he went in 1604 to Magdalen college, Oxford, where he spent two years only before he was recalled by his father to the farm.   A country life, however, did not satisfy his nature.   He went to London in 1610, to try his fortune as a writer.   Little is known of his early doings—except that he made the acquaintance of William Browne—until, in 1612, his elegy on the death of prince Henry, dedicated to Sir Robert Sidney, was published.   The book contained elegies on the prince and a dialogue between the prince's ghost and Great Britain.   Among the mass of verse which prince Henry's death occasioned, Wither's effort attracted small notice. The subject was not so congenial to him as it was to William Drummond, though the dialogue gave some scope to his vein of unpedantic moralising.   But, in the following year, the marriage of princess Elizabeth with the elector palatine offered him a more suitable subject, and the princess was so pleased by his book of *Nuptial Poems* that she became his best patron. Though flattery meant favour, he, in that age of flatterers, was too honest to be servile, and his next book *Abuses stript and whipt or Satiricall Poems* had an original and a characteristic dedication which ran "to Himselfe G. W. wisheth all happiness."   The satire was popular, but displeasing to the authorities, and all the immediate happiness the book obtained for Wither was imprisonment in the Marshalsea.   The reason why the book should have brought such summary injustice upon its author is difficult to understand, for, unlike later satirists, he made no personal attacks, but tilted in a genial and not a very original manner against the general vices of human nature.   However, in the Marshalsea he was confined for some months and, during his confinement, wrote pastorals, which were published in 1615 under the title *The Shepherd's Hunting*. In the fourth eclogue, in praising the poetry of "my Willie," by whom he meant his friend William Browne, he extolled the power of poetry in general and wrote his most beautiful, if not his best known, lines. They are written in the measure to which

the wits of Queen Anne's days contemptuously gave the name of Namby-Pamby, in ridicule of Ambrose Philips . . . but Wither, whose darling measure it seems to have been, may shew, that in skilful hands it is capable of expressing the subtilest movements of passion.[1]

Of the same pastoral description were the poems that he next published: *Fidelia*, privately printed in 1617, and *Faire Virtue, the Mistresse of Phil'Arete*, the revision, probably, of earlier work, in 1622. The pastoral in Wither's hands was not a town convention; however conventional the shepherds may be, the freshness of the fields breathes in his poems, and an intimate knowledge of country lore is manifested on every page. The hounds of Philarete the Hunter are named after human virtues and human vices, but they have the character and bearing of real dogs; and they show, pleasantly enough, that George Wither, whatever may be the value of his judgment of men and their ways, knew and loved the ways of his pack with discriminating insight. But, between 1617 and 1622, he also wrote two works of a singularly diverse nature: *Hymnes and Songs of the Church*—of which king James approved, but of which his clergy disapproved—and Wither's *Motto*. The motto was *Nec habeo, nec careo, nec curo;* it is partly a satire and chiefly an extolling of the possibilities of his own personality:

My intent was to draw the picture of mine own heart. . . . But my principal intention was, by recording those thoughts, to confirm my own resolution and to prevent such alterations, as time and infirmities may work upon me.

Though the verses are as genial and harmless as is the intention, they gave offence to those in authority, and, again, Wither was shut up in the Marshalsea.

And here his first poetic period ends. He wrote countless topical pamphlets in prose and verse, which have been collected and printed by the Spenser Society, but nothing of literary note

[1] Charles Lamb.

except *The Scholars Purgatory* (c. 1625), in which, with his customary frankness, he defends himself against those stationers who "unchristianly vilify and scandalize alsoe" his hymns and songs, and passes from personal defence and his usual attractive self-revelation to an interesting dissertation on the subject of "divine" poems in general.

When the Civil war broke out, Wither joined the parliamentarians. In 1639, he was a captain of horse in the expedition against the Scots, was soon raised to the rank of major and, in 1642, commanded the garrison of Farnham castle in Surrey. The royalists took him prisoner soon afterwards, and he only escaped hanging by a jest of the gallant Denham, who declared that, as long as Wither lived, he, Denham, could not be accounted the worst poet in England. Wither survived the jest to become major-general of all Cromwell's horse and foot in the county of Surrey. At the restoration, he lost the considerable fortune which he had made from royalist sequestrations and, in 1660, was imprisoned in Newgate for three years. Four years after his release, he died (2 May, 1667), and was buried in the Savoy church in the Strand.

Such were the events of his second period. The poetry of that period was not pastoral, and is not so well known as his pastoral verse. It is, however, intensely characteristic, and deserves to survive not only for its continual quaintness but for its occasional beauty: *Haleluiah or Britain's Second Remembrancer* is the unpromising title, and stern puritan faith is the unpromising subject. But the poems, composed in a threefold volume, are instinct with his personality and vigorous charm. *Hymns Occasional, Hymns Temporary, Hymns Personall* are the names of the three parts; they are written "that all Persons, according to their Degrees and qualities, may at all times . . . be remembered to praise GOD; and to be mindful of their duties." There is no occasion too homely to be improved; and each hymn is prefaced by a short note of explanation as to the exact circumstances under which it should be sung. Such poems as *A Rocking Hymn* (exquisite in the simplicity of its beauty) show Wither at his best. They have a clear sincerity; and they express a joy in the possibilities of life which is remarkable and very different from what is usually understood by the puritan spirit. They are written in various metres, with the spontaneous ease which was part of Wither's very being, and in which he resembles his friend William Browne.

William Browne also shared Wither's joy in life, though the circumstances of his career formed a strong antithesis to those of his friend's stormy life. For Browne seems to have lived as peacefully and gracefully as he wrote. He was born at Tavistock not later than 1591 of a good Devon family. About 1603, he went from the grammar school of Tavistock to Exeter college, Oxford, and, leaving the university without taking a degree, he came to Clifford's inn and then settled at the Inner Temple (November, 1611). Little is known of his life, which was without great incident. Browne was twice married. Of his first wife, no record remains. In 1628, he married Tymothy Eversfield, daughter of Sir Thomas Eversfield, after a courtship of some thirteen years. He owed his position chiefly to the patronage of the Herberts and to the fact that he coached Robert Dormer, the future earl of Carnarvon. He died about the year 1645.

Browne's first printed poem, like that of Wither and of Drummond, was concerned with the death of prince Henry. It appeared in 1613, with an elegy by Christopher Brooke. In the same year was published the first book of *Britannia's Pastorals*, his longest and most famous work. It tells the story of the loves of Marina and Redmond and Celand. The story is elusive and unimportant, and serves chiefly as a means of singing the praises of England and of his own Devon. The charm of the poem lies in its simplicity of thought and diction. No rural incident is too trivial to be recorded, and, though this triviality, especially in metaphor, is sometimes a little far-fetched, the metaphors are often most effective, and give an atmoshpere of delicacy which is real and refreshing. For simple beauty, there are few passages to equal that which describes how Marina, trapped in a cave, was fed on strawberries and cherries by a robin redbreast; and it is impossible to forget the two little brothers who were scared by the angry bull, or the little lad who,

> gotten new
> to play his part amongst a skilful crew
> of choice musicians,

was obliged to emphasise his presence by a loud and sudden noise. His poems show a capacity for warm affection; and he had many friends among the many poets of his day. With Drayton, Wither, Christopher Brooke, Davies, Ben Jonson, he was on terms of intimacy; and the fact that they were his friends did not prevent him from celebrating in verse their achievements, for which he had great and discerning admiration. But Spenser was his master, as he is proud to avow, and, in a less degree, Sidney. That is to say, in the great view of life which is expressed in Spenser's poetry, the homeliest affairs of everyday existence have their place as surely as the heights of life's imagined possibilities; and Browne was strengthened in his love of these everyday affairs by Spenser's treatment of them. If the nature of influence be pressed too closely, a false conception is quickly produced. For the influence lies in the time in which the men lived: the time inspired each man according to his capacity, though the smaller men were strengthened by the utterance of the bigger man.

Browne ends the first song of the second book of *Britannia's Pastorals* with a eulogy of Spenser. He never missed an occasion for giving voice to his love and admiration of Spenser, but this is the most notable passage, and it seems to imply that a plan for erecting a monument in honour of Spenser was thwarted by "suborn'd, curs'd Avarice." This slight wrought upon Browne to compose lines almost unrecognisably fierce in denunciation of "that gulf-devouring offspring of a devil"— "my busied pen Shall jerk to death this infamy of men." But he returns at the beginning of the second song to his gentle vein, and passes in review the English poets. In his praises of them, he shows his discernment. He writes of "all-loved" Drayton, "a genuine note of all the nymphish trains began to tune"; of Ben Jonson, "One so judicious, so well knowing and A man whose least worth is to understand"; of "well-languag'd" Daniel; and of Brooke, "whose polish'd lines Are fittest to accomplish high designs."

For Browne was a scholar and could discriminate. He was interested in old MSS. and printed a poem of Occleve with his *Shepherd's Pipe* (1614); "as this shall please," he wrote, "I may be drawn to publish the rest of his works."

However, it did not please, and others of Occleve's works remained in Browne's possession. This trait probably accounts for the small care he took about the publishing of his own works. The first book of *Britannia's Pastorals* was published, as has been said, in 1613, the second in 1616, and the two were reissued together in 1625; but the third book remained during his lifetime in manuscript, and was not published till 1852. The same is true of the *Inner Temple Masque* which was performed on 13 January, 1614/15, and which was not printed till 1772, from a manuscript in the library of Emmanuel college, Cambridge.

Fulke Greville, lord Brooke, belonged to an elder generation than that of the other poets in this chapter, and was an exact contemporary of Sir Philip Sidney, whose life he wrote. Unlike Browne or Drummond, he was not primarily a poet; he belonged rather to the older school of men, who, like Castiglione's courtier, cultivated the germ of poetry as a faculty which should belong to every properly constituted man. Wither was a poet masquerading as a man of arms. His soldierly achievements cannot be taken with perfect seriousness. Fulke Greville, primarily, was a statesman and man of affairs. In 1598, he became treasurer of the navy and, in 1614, chancellor of the exchequer. Born at Beauchamp court, Warwickshire, in 1554, Fulke Greville entered Shrewsbury school on the very same day as Philip Sidney, 17 October, 1564, and, from Shrewsbury, he went to Jesus college, Cambridge, four years later. With Sidney, he came to the court in 1577, and travelled to Heidelberg with him in the same year. Like Sidney, he was rapidly taken into the queen's favour, and him, too, the queen forbade to go far from her presence. The secretaryship to the principality of Wales was given him before the age of thirty.

Fulke Greville was a great patron of letters. Camden was appointed Clarencieux through his influence. He freed John Speed's "hand from the daily employment of a manual trade." He endowed a history chair at Cambridge into which he put the renowned Dorislaus of Holland; Samuel Daniel, Henry Lok, John Davies, William D'Avenant were glad to acknowledge their indebtedness to him.

Except for an elegy on Sidney, which appeared in the miscellany *The Phoenix Nest* (1593), two poems in the first edition of *England's Helicon* (1600) and the tragedy of *Mustapha* (1609), the work of lord Brooke remained unpublished during his lifetime. In 1633, five years after his death, appeared a volume containing, as the title-page recounts, *Certaine learned and elegant workes written in his Youth and familiar exercise with Sir Philip Sidney*. They include *A Treatise of Humane Learning*, *An Inquisition upon Fame and Honour*, *A Treatie of Warres*, his tragedies *Mustapha* and *Alaham* and a set of poems which, according to the fashion of the time, are named sonnets, called *Caelica*.[1] In 1652, appeared his life of Sir Philip Sidney, and, in 1670, the *Remains of Sir Fulke Greville, Lord Brooke, being poems of Monarchy and Religion, never before printed*.

The reason which prevented the publication of his poems is, probably, the same as that which restrained him from publishing his life of Sidney and from writing his history of queen Elizabeth. With the exception of some of the poems in *Caelica*, they deal with subjects of statecraft which might have been easily misinterpreted by enemies. As Elizabeth grew old, the question of her successor and of the best form of government in general for the country troubled all the finest minds in England. Her death was not only a personal grief to such men as Greville and Ralegh; it foreshadowed to them the eventual death of monarchy. "Their author," writes Charles Lamb of his two tragedies, "has strangely contrived to make passion, character and interest, of the highest order subservient to the expression of state dogmas." Fulke Greville was forty-nine years old when the queen died. To his feeling for her he gives beautiful expression in his digression in the life of Sidney in which he recounts the features of her reign and policy, and this feeling merged into his conception of the place which, to his thinking, she filled admirably, that is to say, into his conception of monarchy. This is why, through the cold, intellectual force of his treatment and reasoning, there shines the living glow of personal passion. Nor is it necessary to search for the original of *Caelica;* internal evidence strongly points to the

[1] See Vol. III of the present work, p. 304.

fact that these poems afford one more proof of the power of Elizabeth.

Most of the "sonnets" in *Caelica*, and the whole of the poems *Of Humane Learning*, *Of Fame and Honour*, *Of Warres* and on *Monarchy and Religion* are written in a six-lined stanza, riming *ababcc*. The versification of the tragedies is of peculiar interest, for, although the choruses, for the most part, are written in riming couplets, in the speeches great care has been taken to obtain the effect of the couplet without its monotony. Consecutive couplets rarely occur; most speeches of any length conclude with a couplet: there are many instances of unriming lines, and many rimes run in quatrains *abab*.

Brooke's death was sudden and tragic. He was murdered in 1628 by his servant Haywood, who thought he had been omitted from his master's will. He wrote the epitaph which was cut on his tombstone. It amply epitomises his life: "Fulke Grevil—Servant to Queene Elizabeth—Councellor to King James —and Frend to Sir Philip Sydney. *Trophaeum Peccati*."

Sir John Davies (not to be confused with John Davies of Hereford) was a man of the same pattern, though without lord Brooke's memory of "the spacious days" and without his deep austerity. He, too, was a man of affairs, and rose to a high position in the state. His life, however, had not the same great beginning, and his was no smooth passage to fame. Born in 1569, at Tisbury in Wiltshire, he went to Winchester and Oxford (partly, it appears, resident at New college, partly at Queen's college), and, like the majority of young men of the time, came, in 1587, to study law in London. But he quarrelled with the friend to whom he had dedicated his *Orchestra*, Richard Martin, and, entering the hall, armed with a dagger, he broke his cudgel over Martin's head, who was eating dinner at the barristers' table. In consequence of this outrage on the benchers, he was disbarred. For an orphan, with his way to make, the calamity was heavy. He returned to Oxford in 1598, three years after he had been called, and wrote his great poem *Nosce Teipsum*. Lord Mountjoy, afterwards earl of Devonshire, approved of it so highly that he advised Davies to publish it, with a dedicatory poem to the queen. This, Davies was not slow to do. The poem appeared the year after his expulsion from the bar, and added largely to his growing reputation as a poet. The *Hymns to Astroea* appeared in the same year, and Davies's services were in request to write words for "entertainments" offered to her majesty. *A Dialogue between a Gentleman Usher and a Poet, A contention betwixt a Wife, a Widdow and a Maide* and *A Lottery*, are the names of those that are extant. *A Lottery* gained the queen's acknowledgment, and, through the influence of lord Ellesmere, Davies, after a formal apology to the benchers and to Richard Martin, was reinstated at the bar in 1601. His career now began. He was among those who went with lord Hunsdon to escort king James to the English throne, and James was sufficiently impressed with him to appoint him solicitor-general for Ireland, under lord Mountjoy, then lord deputy. In December, 1603, on his arrival in Dublin, he was knighted, and, some years later, he married the daughter of lord Audley. One of his children was the famous countess of Huntingdon. His work in Ireland, where he remained until 1619, was distinguished, and how deeply he was interested in Irish affairs may be gathered from his *Discourse of the true reasons why Ireland has never been intirely subdued till the beginning of His Majesty's reign.* In 1619, he resumed his seat in the House of Commons as member for Newcastle under Lyme, to which he had been elected in 1614, and, just before he could assume the office of chief justice, to which he had been appointed in 1626, he died suddenly of an apoplexy.

Orchestra or a Poeme on Dauncing was written before June, 1594, although it was not published until 1596. The poem is in the form of a dialogue between Penelope and one of her suitors, and consists of 131 stanzas of seven lines, each riming *ababbcc.* In the dedicatory sonnet to "his very friend M.A. Richard Martin," which, in spite of the reconciliation, was omitted from the edition of 1622, Davies describes the poem as "this suddaine, rash half-capreol of my wit," and reminds Martin how it was written in fifteen days. The fact is worthy of attention because it shows the writer's ability and mastery over his material. The poem bears no sign of haste in the making. Gallant and gay, it flows with transparent clearness to its conclusion, and the verse has the happy ease which marks all the work of Davies, and makes it comparable with the music of Mozart.

His next work *Nosce Teipsum* possesses the same fluidity of thought and diction, which is the more remarkable as the poem is deeply philosophical. The sub-title explains the subject: "This oracle expounded in two elegies. 1. Of Humane knowledge. 2. Of the Soule of Man and the immortalitie thereof." The first edition was published in 1599, the second, "newly corrected and amended," in 1602, the third in 1608, and, of course, the poem was included in the collected edition which Davies himself made of his poems in 1622.

"Wouldst thou be crowned the Monarch of a little world? command thyself," wrote Francis Quarles, who was certainly well-acquainted with *Nosce Teipsum*, in the second century of his *Enchiridion*, and that sentence gives the gist of the first part of the poem on *Humane Knowledge*. Davies then passes on to examine the nature of the soul, its attributes and its connection with the body; and, having defined with exactness what he means by the soul, proceeds to prove its immortality by means of arguments for and against his proposition. Proof in such a matter is not possible; but a personal answer to the great question, so sincerely thought and so lucidly expressed as is this answer of Davies, will always have its value. Nor is *Nosce Teipsum* a treatise which ingenuity has fashioned into verse and which more properly would be expressed in plain prose. Davies does not, as it were, embroider his theme with verse, but uses verse, and its beauties of line and metaphor, to make his meaning more clear, and, thereby, gallantly justifies the employment of his medium. This mastery of his is enviously complete; but, perhaps, it is most conspicuous in the *Hymns to Astroea* which were first published in 1599. As the title-page announces, they are written "in Acrosticke verse." They are twenty-six in number: each poem is of three stanzas (two of five lines, one of six lines), and each line begins with a different letter of the name Elizabetha Regina. Yet, in spite of this fantastic formality, not a line is forced, and one or two of the poems, notably hymn v, *To the Lark*,

> Earley, cheerfule, mounting Larke,
> Light's gentle usher, Morning's clark,

are exquisite songs.

Sir Henry Wotton owes his literary fame to one poem of memorable beauty, to his friendship with Sir Edward Dyer and John Donne, and to the twofold fact that an elegy on his death was composed by Abraham Cowley and that his life was written by his illustrious fellow-angler, Izaak Walton. The author of "You meaner beauties of the night" deserves immortality, though many authors of songs as beautiful remain unknown. He was born at Boughton hall, in the parish of Boughton Malherbe, Kent, in 1568, and was educated at Winchester and New college, which he entered on 5 June, 1584. His father's death left him in a position to travel, of which he availed himself to the full. He visited Linz, Vienna, Naples, Venice, Florence, and stayed with the scholar Casaubon at Geneva. Few provosts have had a career so chequered and adventurous as Sir Henry Wotton. For he sent news to the earl of Essex from abroad, and, being at home in the capacity of secretary to Essex at the time of his patron's disaster, was obliged to flee the country. He returned to Florence, and duke Ferdinand, hearing of a plot to assassinate king James of Scotland, sent him to warn the king. Wotton, taking up "the name and language," as Walton recounts, "of an Italian," travelled to Scotland from Florence by way of Norway, and arrived, as Octavio Baldi, at Stirling, where king James was. Three months he stayed at the court, disguised as Baldi, and the king alone knew the secret of his identity. Then he returned to Italy. When king James ascended the throne of England, Wotton was received into favour. He was three times sent as ambassador to Venice and, eventually, was made provost of Eton—a post which he retained until his death in 1639.

Sufficient of his poems have survived to make some wish that the number were less scanty. His play *Tancredo* and, doubtless, many poems are lost. His writings were collected and published in 1651 under the title *Reliquiae Wottonianae*. His character is typical of the days in which he lived. The power to write verse was considered an indispensable attribute of a courtier. Sir Edward Dyer, the earl of Essex and his great rival, Sir Walter Ralegh, afford eminent examples, and there are many more whose names are known by a song or two more generally than by other weightier though less important achievements. A gradual and indefinable change, however, was evolving; and poetry, leaving the court and the circle of those in authority, took, as it were, its own place in the country, and that place seems at first to have been the church. The two brothers Giles and Phineas Fletcher head the line of poets who were divines of the English church.

Giles Fletcher, the younger brother, was born in London about 1588, and went from Westminster school to Trinity college, Cambridge, in the spring of the year 1603. In 1618, he became reader in Greek, and, having taken holy orders, was appointed vicar of Alderton in Suffolk, where he died in 1623. Although he was some six years younger than his brother, his poem *Christs Victorie, and Triumph in Heaven, and Earth, over and after death* was published many years before his brother's poem *The Purple Island*, namely, in 1610, by C. Legge at Cambridge. *Christs Victorie and Triumph* is his principal work, but he also wrote a *Canto upon the Death of Eliza*, an *Elegy upon Prince Henry's Death* and a short poem in riming couplets, to which Boas has given the name *A Description of Encolpius*. *Christs Victorie*, written in 265 eight-lined stanzas (riming *ababbccc*) is divided into four parts. In the first part, he describes Christ's victory in Heaven through the intercession of Mercy against the indictment of man by Justice; in the second, His victory on earth where He overcomes Satan, who, in the guise of a reverend palmer, tempts Him to Desperation, to Presumption and to Vainglory; in the third, he describes Christ's triumph over death, "in generall by his joy to undergo it . . . by his passion itself," and the particular effects of the triumph throughout the universe; and, in the last part, Christ's triumph after death is narrated, as manifested in the resurrection and the effects of the resurrection on all living things. There is no doubt that, as a whole, the poem is hampered by the very quality which gave it birth—the author's devoutness. He is unable to weave his own fancy and the accepted traditions into a composite pattern; and the effort to make his verse worthy of its subject often produces the effect of constraint or of exaggeration. There are, however, many passages of individual beauty, such as the description of Mercy, and some of great dramatic power, notably the passage in which the effect of Christ's triumph upon Judas is told. The vigour of his phrase and the loftiness of his aim combine to make him a worthy link in the chain which connects his great master and his great successor—Spenser and Milton.

His elder brother, Phineas Fletcher, was born in 1582, and went from Eton to King's college, Cambridge, in the Commons book of which college his name first appears in 1600. A contribution of his appeared in *Sorrowes Joy*, a poetical miscellany, compiled at the university in 1603, in which his younger brother's *Canto upon Eliza* gained a place and which mourned Elizabeth's death at the same time as it welcomed the arrival of king James. The resemblance in the lives of the brothers is as marked as the resemblance in their work. The chief legacy which their father left them was a good education. Both lived at Cambridge for some years until Giles Fletcher became vicar of Alderton in Suffolk, and Phineas Fletcher, after being for five years chaplain to Sir Henry Willoughby, became rector of Hilgay in Norfolk, in 1621, two years before his brother's death in 1623. Phineas Fletcher wrote far more than Giles, and was possessed of a light manner as well as of the more deeply serious manner which characterises the extant work of his brother. *Brittain's Ida*, first published in 1628, *Sicelides* and *Piscatorie Eclogues* are the most notable examples of this lighter manner. *Brittain's Ida* is a pretty, amatory poem in six cantos on the subject of Shakespeare's *Venus and Adonis*. The stanzas are of eight lines and rime *ababbccc*. The long success of the publisher's ruse which attributed the poem to Spenser and which remained undiscovered until Grosart proved the authorship [1] shows how nicely Fletcher hit the manner of Spenser. *Sicelides*, a piscatory, is a fisher-play of spirited wit and fancy, which was acted at King's college, Cambridge on 13 March, 1614/15, and printed, also without the author's consent in 1631. No grave divine, such as Fletcher had then become, would have been pleased to own offspring so flippant and indecorous as these works of his youth. His immense poem *The Purple Island*, as well-known as it is little read, he did not, however, thus view askance. Its scope is colossal, for the purple island is the little isle of man, a

[1] See also Boas's preface to poetical works of Giles and Phineas Fletcher, vol. ii, Cambridge, 1909.

country which, be it observed, Davies, Wither and Drummond
had each in his own way explored.   For the secret realm of a
man's own nature had, for these poets, as great an attraction as
unknown lands had for the previous generation of pioneers in
exploration.   Though the intention is interesting, the setting—
the daily conversations of shepherds—is laboured, and the
allegory troublesome to follow.   He does not aid his minute
description of the body and its functions by his continual geographical analogies; indeed, many passages would be completely meaningless without his own explanatory notes.   But
his enthusiasm for the delicate mechanism of the body is none
the less remarkable that his expression of it is often amusing.
After a detailed description of man's anatomy, he turns his
attention to qualities of man's mind, and passes in review all
the virtues and vices.   Here, in small allegorical pictures, he
is more successful; many of them are happy in idea and beautiful
in execution, especially his pictures of ignorance, of Andreos
or fortitude, of Androphilus or gentleness.

His two best poems are *The Apollyonists* and *Elisa, an
Elegie*.   *The Locusts or Apollyonists* was published in 1627
with a poem *Locustae* on the same subject, in Latin hexameters,
and is written in five cantos of forty stanzas each.   The stanza
is of nine lines, riming *ababcccc*, and affords another variant
of the Spenserian stanza from the seven-lined stanza, riming
ababbcc in the *Elegy* and *ababccc* in *The Purple Island*.   In
this poem, he uses the fall of Lucifer as a device to explain the
strength of the church of Rome, whose machinations are made
to culminate in the Gunpowder plot.   He writes with the
bitterness that might be expected from an English clergyman
of the time; but this bitterness narrows the scope of the poem
to an expression of party-hatred—a function ill-suited to
poetry.   Many lines, however, especially at the outset, where
he deals with evil in general, are vigorous, and, at times, so
forcible and spacious as to justify the epithet Miltonic.   *Elisa*
is an elegy, published in the 1633 quarto, upon the death of
Sir Antony Irby, composed, as its separate title-page announces,
at the request, and for a monument, of his surviving lady.   The
poem is in two parts of fifty stanzas each, and maintains a high
level of sustained feeling.   It shows Phineas Fletcher at his
simplest and at his best.   He creates with striking power the

illusion of reality in a dialogue between the dying husband and his wife, which is singularly original and reaches its climax of pathetic beauty in the last eighteen stanzas of the first part, in which he begs her gladly to continue with the burden of life for the sake of their children—"this little nation to thy care commend them."

Both the Fletchers were steeped in Spenser's poetry, and carried on the Spenserian tradition. In their work is to be found Spenser's diffuseness, his use of allegory, many variants of his stanza and the echo, often a beautiful echo, of his music. Moreover, Milton knew the work of the Fletchers as intimately as he, or the Fletchers, knew the work of Spenser. And so one of the prettiest and most intricate problems that is to be found in literature arises on the question of what is known as influence. The best example of the affinity between the work of Milton and the work of Phineas Fletcher is to be found in a comparison between the way in which Milton treats that stock episode of the miracle play, the fall of Lucifer, and the way in which Fletcher treats it. In *The Apollyonists*, the fall of Lucifer is a prelude to an onslaught upon the Jesuits: the great opening is narrowed to the confines of religious hatred. But the sympathy which Milton could not but feel for the rebel transformed the figure of Satan from a fine conception to one of immortal grandeur. Milton humanised the devil, Fletcher diabolised the priest. Their meeting-point is found in Fletcher's lines

> To be in heaven the second he disdaines:
> So now the first in hell and flames he raignes,
> Crown'd once with joy and light: crown'd now with fire and paines,

and in the Miltonic

> Better to reign in hell then serve in Heav'n.

CHAPTER X

Michael Drayton

THE poet of whom this chapter treats was much admired by his contemporaries. The title "golden-mouthed," first given him by Fitzgeffry, clung to him, and Meres praises him for "the purity and preciousness of his style and phrase." After more than a century of neglect, he was reprinted and read in the middle of the eighteenth century; but, though he again acquired some vogue in the Elizabethan revival of the early part of the nineteenth century, it is only in recent years that his poetry has begun to receive the recognition it deserves.[1]

Michael Drayton, as we learn from the portrait by William Hole which forms the frontispiece to the *Poems* of 1619,[2] was born at Hartshill, in the county of Warwick, in 1563. He died, probably in London, near the end of 1631. Born within a year before Shakespeare, and dying when Milton was already twenty-three, he worked hard at poetry during nearly sixty years of his long life, and was successful in keeping in touch with the poetical progress of a crowded and swiftly-moving period. His earliest published work tastes of *Tottel's Miscellany:* before he dies, he suggests Carew and Suckling, and even anticipates Dryden. This quality of forming, as it were, a map or mirror of his age gives him a special interest to the student of poetry, which is quite distinct from his peculiar merits as a poet.

[1] The advance in Drayton's just reputation is brought into prominence by Elton, O.: *Michael Drayton: A Critical Study* (1895 and 1905). No modern student of Drayton can escape his obligations to this scholarly and stimulating work.

[2] Reproduced, Elton (1905), p. 107. All subsequent references are to this edition.

Drayton himself has left us, besides other scraps of autobiography scattered among his works, an account of the genesis of the great passion of his life. His family appears to have been of the same grade as Shakespeare's, that of well-to-do tradespeople;[1] and, in early boyhood, Michael Drayton, one of a large family, was taken to be page, or something of the kind—at any rate, to occupy a position of confidence and intimacy—in the family of Sir Henry Goodere of Powlsworth (now Polesworth), on the river Ancor, not far from Tamworth. His gratitude to Sir Henry Goodere, "the first cherisher of his muse," he expressed more than once: in the dedications of the *Heroicall Epistles* (1597) of queen Isabel to king Richard II, of lady Jane Grey to lord Guilford Dudley and of queen Margaret to the duke of Suffolk. And, in his sixty-fourth year, Drayton looked back and gave his friend Henry Reynolds, in a letter in verse, an account of his education at Polesworth, and the birth in him of the desire to be a poet.

> For from my cradle, (you must know that) I,
> Was still inclin'd to noble Poesie,
> And when that once *Pueriles* I had read,
> And newly had my *Cato* construed,
> In my small selfe I greatly marveil'd then,
> Amongst all other, what strange kinde of men
> These Poets were; And pleased with the name,
> To my milde Tutor merrily I came,
> (For I was then a proper goodly page,
> Much like a Pigmy, scarse ten yeares of age)
> Clasping my slender armes about his thigh.
> O my deare master! cannot you (quoth I)
> Make me a Poet, doe it if you can,
> And you shall see, Ile quickly bee a man,
> Who me thus answered smiling, boy quoth he,
> If you'le not play the wag, but I may see
> You ply your learning, I will shortly read
> Some Poets to you; *Phœbus* be my speed,
> Too't hard went I, when shortly he began,
> And first read to me honest *Mantuan*,
> Then *Virgils Eglogues*, being entred thus,
> Me thought I straight had mounted *Pegasus*,

---

[1] For some details and a pedigree see Elton, pp. 2–4.

> And in his full Careere could make him stop,
> And bound upon *Parnassus'* by-clift top.
> I scornd your ballet then though it were done
> And had for Finis, *William Elderton*. [1]

The account forms an interesting comment on Drayton's muse, which was always sensitive to the influence of other poets, and was largely inspired from without.

However he may have "scornd your ballet" and William Elderton, there was another influence, and one less pedantic than Mantuan or Vergil, at work upon him during those boyish years at Polesworth. In 1619, when dedicating his *Odes* to Donne's friend, Sir Henry Goodere the younger, he recalled to the memory of his old playmate

> John Hewes his lyre
> Which oft at Powlsworth by the fire
> Hath made us gravely merry.

John Hewes, presumably, was the minstrel attached to the Goodere household, and, from his name, presumably also Welsh; and it has been suggested [2] that on Hewes's lips the boy may have heard "those rough dactyls of the old folk-ballad *Agincourt, Agincourt*, which gallop through Drayton's own monumental war-chant," the *Ballad of Agincourt*, dedicated "To the Cambro-Britans and their Harpe."

It is not known whether Drayton went to a university. Our first news of him is that in February, 1591, he was in London. The sixth eclogue in the 1606 edition of his *Idea, the Shepheard's Garland*, contains a passage which, perhaps, may obscurely hint at some irregularity of life after he had left his native county; but nothing can be built upon it, and any supposition of debauchery would be contrary to other evidence of Drayton's character. [3]

On 1 February, 1591, his earliest extant work was entered at Stationers' Hall; and the dedication to the lady Jane Devereux of Merivale, sister-in-law of the earl of Essex, is dated the tenth of the same month. How Drayton came to enjoy the patronage of this lady is not known. *The Harmonie of the*

---

[1] Text from Brett, pp. 108–9. Elderton (*ob.* 1592?) was a ballad-writer.
[2] By Elton, p. 8.
[3] See Meres, *Palladis Tamia;* Fuller, *Worthies;* and *The Returne from Parnassus*, act 1, sc. 2.

Church, as has been said above, has a flavour of *Tottel's Miscellany*. The author, clearly, was well read in his Old Testament and Apocrypha; for the matter of his book is the versification of nineteen prayers and songs of thanksgiving from these sources, including *The Song of Songs*. The song of Moses, from the thirty-second chapter of *Deuteronomy*, the song of Deborah and Barak from *Judges*, the prayer and song of Judith and the joyful thanksgiving of the faithful from the twelfth chapter of *Isaiah* are among the passages paraphrased. There is nothing in all this painstaking 'prentice work that foreshadows the poet who was to be; and it is hard to believe that this was really the best that Drayton could do at the age of twenty-eight. Though quatrains and stanzas of six decasyllabic lines occur, the principal metre is that of the old "fourteeners," or twelves and fourteeners mixed, common in the earlier Elizabethan poetry. Drayton uses it without spirit or novelty, and it may not be unfair to regard *The Harmonie of the Church* as intended merely to acquire for the author a very respectable introduction to the public of his day. Were this his object it appears to have failed. For some cause still unexplained, the book was confiscated in the year of its publication,[1] forty copies only (which have all disappeared) being reserved for the library of the archbishop of Canterbury. It can hardly be that orthodoxy was offended, or that the paraphrase of *The Song of Songs* was considered as licentious; and perhaps the suggestion[2] of some irregularity in publishing is the most reasonable. Drayton reprinted the work under another title in 1610.

For something over two years, Drayton was silent. Then, in April, 1593, there was entered at Stationers' Hall a book which showed a different influence from that revealed in *The Harmonie of the Church*, and one which proved its author's title to the name of poet. Throughout his life, Drayton maintained a fervent admiration for Spenser, and Spenser was the model whom he followed in his second publication. In 1579, the voice of what was then the new poetry had spoken for the first time in Spenser's *Shepheards Calender*. In 1593, Drayton's *Idea, the Shepheard's Garland*, carried on the same form, though not entirely with the same end in view. In 1619,

---

[1] Collier, *Poems*, 1856, pp. xi *et seq.*
[2] Made by Courthope, *Hist. Eng. Poetry*, III, p. 28.

when he issued a third edition of *Idea* under a new title, Drayton prefixed to it a brief discourse on pastoral in general, which contains this characteristically ungrammatical sentence:

> The subject of Pastorals, as the language of it ought to be poor, silly, and of the coarsest woof in appearance; nevertheless, the most high, and most noble matters of the world may be shadowed in them, and for certain sometimes are.

Notably so, of course, in Spenser's *Shepheards Calender*. But Drayton, much as he owes to his great forerunner's work, shows two points of difference. His language is not "poor, silly, and of the coarsest woof." It almost entirely avoids the archaisms in which Spenser rejoiced, and it rises, when occasion demands, to a nobility which makes these eclogues one of his finest achievements. Secondly, he almost entirely discards the tradition which, starting in England, perhaps, from the study of Mantuan, had forcibly affected all the writers of pastoral from Googe to Watson, and was to reappear in *Lycidas*. *Idea* moralises but little, and includes few complaints of the decay of nobility, misgovernment in church and state and so forth. There is, in other words, little trace upon the work of that change from the decayed order of chivalry to a newly organised social scheme, which is the real topic of much previous pastoral. The "high and noble matters" of which it treats comprise only love, panegyric and poetry. In these eclogues as they first appeared, there is, it must be admitted, a good deal that is old-fashioned. In the first, Drayton, under his pastoral name Rowland, laments his sins and his misery; and there is small promise of a new poet in such lines as:

> My sorrowes waxe, my joyes are in the wayning,
> My hope decayes, and my despayre is springing,
> My love hath losse, and my disgrace hath gayning,
> Wrong rules, desert with teares her hands sits wringing:
> Sorrow, despayre, disgrace, and wrong, doe thwart
> My Joy, my love, my hope, and my desert.

The second eclogue gives us a debate between age and youth—in the persons of Wynken and Motto—about love; the third is in praise of Beta—that is, queen Elizabeth; the fourth is a lament for Elphin, Sir Philip Sidney; and the fifth sings the praises of Idea. Of the identity of the person intended by this name more must be said later. In the sixth eclogue, the departed worthies of England are touched upon; but the main theme of the poem is the panegyric of Pandora, who, probably, stands for the countess of Pembroke. In the seventh, we have another contest between an old man and a young about love; the eighth describes the pastoral golden age; and the ninth and last is another lament from Rowland, this time for unrequited love.

In 1606, Drayton, who spent much labour in the revision of his previously published poems, issued a new edition of *Idea, the Shepheard's Garland*, in his volume of *Poemes Lyrick and Pastoral*. The differences from the first edition are many. The title is changed to *Eglogs*, the dedication to Robert Dudley is omitted, a new eclogue is added, the order is rearranged and the text is much altered and much improved. The few archaisms have disappeared, and so have all such outworn tricks as that exemplified in the stanza quoted above. We find a fresher, sweeter and stronger music, a rejection of the conventional in image and scenery, and a greater freedom from that clumsiness of grammar and construction which was Drayton's besetting poetical sin all his life.

To the modern reader, nothing is more enjoyable in the *Idea* of 1593 than the songs introduced into the dialogue. In the *Eglogs* of 1606, these are even better; of the old songs, five have disappeared, four of them to be replaced by others much less "conceited," much fresher and more purely lyrical and showing something of the light and dainty music, the secret of which Drayton was to master later in life. The two which remain are polished, to their great benefit. One of these is the peculiarly brave and swinging song in praise of Beta, which uses the old "sixes and eights" (with shorter lines between each pair) with a skill and movement of which the author of *The Harmonie of the Church* would never be supposed capable; the other is a delightful ballad, in the metre of Chaucer's *Sir Thopas*, concerning Dowsabell and her shepherd boy, in which archaic terms are introduced to the best and quaintest effect. The new eclogue, the ninth, contains three songs, all among Drayton's best. It may be noted, too, that, in these pastorals, Drayton first makes the high claim for poets and poetry which he had learned from Spenser, and which he maintained throughout his life.

The pastorals of 1606 are of considerable interest on the biographical side. In the first place, the poet speaks more directly from the heart and more particularly of himself. It is only necessary to compare the two versions of the last eclogue (IX in 1593, X in 1606), to see the difference. The one is a vague, purely poetical and conventional complaint; the other, the very voice of the man who had passed through disappointment and sorrow. The references to other persons need further examination. [1] A few, about which there is no difficulty, have been mentioned above; and to these may be added the reference in eclogue VIII to a certain Sylvia, who may well be supposed to be a lady of the family of Sir William Aston, by 1606 Drayton's patron. But who is Idea, who Panape, who the "great Olcon," that has deserted Rowland and the sheepfold, and who Selena, who is roundly cursed by the poet for jilting Rowland in favour of "deceitful Cerberon"?

The questions are of importance in the biography of Drayton, since they affect his honour as a man. Now, for the first time in his writings, he gives, in his eclogue VIII of 1606, unmistakable evidence of the identity of Idea. A previous mention (in *Endimion and Phœbe*, ?1595) had supplied the fact that she was then an unmarried woman, living by the river Ancor. In the eclogue, we are told that she is the youngest sister of Panape, who still lives by the Ancor, and that she has lately moved to another part of England.

> The younger then, her sister not less good,
> Bred where the other lastly doth abide,
> Modest Idea, flower of womanhood,
> That Rowland hath so highly deified;
> Whom Phoebus' daughters worthily prefer,
> And give their gifts abundantly to her.

> Driving her flocks up to the fruitful Meene,
> Which daily looks upon the lovely Stowre,
> Near to that vale, which of all vales is queen,
> Lastly, forsaking of her former bow'r:

[1] In Fleay, *Biog. Chronicle of the Eng. Drama*, I, pp. 143–5 there is a list of interesting, if not always secure, identifications of Drayton's pastoral characters with actual persons.

> And of all places holdeth Cotswold dear,
> Which now is proud, because she lives it near.

Of the two daughters of Sir Henry Goodere, the patron of Drayton's boyhood, the elder, Frances, had married her cousin and lived on at Polesworth; the younger, Anne, had married, in 1595 or 1596, Sir Henry Rainsford of Clifford Chambers, "in Evesham vale, on the Stour, and north of Meon Hill, an outlying spur of Cotswold."[1] There can be little doubt that, by 1606, at any rate, Idea was Anne Rainsford, neé Goodere. Further evidence comes from *The Barrons Wars* (1603):

> My lays had been still to Idea's bower,
> Of my dear Ancor, or her lovèd Stour;

and from the thirteenth song of *Poly-Olbion* (1613), where Drayton, singing of Coventry and Godiva, has these lines:

> The first part of whose name, Godiva, doth fore-reed
> Th' first syllable of hers, and Goodere half doth sound;

and states that "her being here was by this name fore-shown," while

> as the first did tell
> Her sir-name, so again doth Ancor lively spell
> Her christen'd title Anne.

The passage ends by informing us that Coventry was Anne Goodere's birth-place.   Once more, in the *Hymn to his Ladies Birth-Place*, among the *Odes* of 1619, he states that Godiva was the type of Idea, and that Idea was born in "happy Mich-Parke," the "best and most frequent" street of Coventry.

There seems here ample evidence that, from 1595 to 1619— from Drayton's thirty-second to his fifty-sixth year—Idea was Anne Goodere; and his long friendship with lady Rainsford and her husband is, also, well attested.   Was Idea always Anne Goodere?   And is the Idea of the eclogues of 1593, and of the sonnets of 1594 and later years, which offer no evidence, the same person?   It would be natural to suppose that they were, and that Drayton was faithful throughout to his "lady." As we have seen, he distinctly states in eclogue VIII of 1606

[1] Elton, p. 20.

that the Idea of that eclogue was the lady "whom Rowland hath so highly deified"—that is, to whom Drayton had addressed the sonnets. But it has been suggested[1] that there was a change, and a very violent change, in Drayton's allegiance, and that the attack on Selena in eclogue VIII of 1606 is intimately connected with this change.[2] *Endimion and Phœbe* (?1595) was ushered in by a glowing sonnet addressed to Lucy countess of Bedford, the famous daughter of lord Harington, whose seat was at Combe Abbey on the banks of the Ancor. The sonnet thanks her for her bounty, and vows the poet's devotion; it is, in fact, the stock tribute of client to patron. The last twenty-two lines of *Endimion and Phœbe* form an address to a "sweet mayd," the "purest spark of Vesta's kindled fire," the "sweet Nymph of Ancor, crowne of my desire." It has been argued that the sonnet to the patroness and the closing lines of the poem must refer to the same person; to which it may be objected that the two tributes are quite different in tone, and that the phrases quoted above are very inaptly applied to a married woman, and very aptly to one who was still unmarried and who seems to have been the object of the poet's love, rather than of his reverence or gratitude. If, however, the Idea of *Endimion and Phœbe* be the countess of Bedford, it is fair to conclude that so is the Idea of the eclogues of 1593 and the sonnets of 1594. In 1596, Drayton dedicated to the countess of Bedford his *Mortimeriados;* in the same year, his legend of *Robert Duke of Normandy;* and, in 1597, his *England's Heroicall Epistles.* Then, in 1603, in issuing his *Mortimeriados* in a new form, he dedicated it, not to lady Bedford but to Sir William Aston, and omitted all the references to that lady. Finally, in eclogue VIII of 1606, comes the attack on Selena. It has been supposed that the countess of Bedford had withdrawn her patronage; that Drayton, in revenge, took

---

[1] By Courthope, III, pp. 29 *et seq*.

[2] There is a puzzle in eclogue IV of 1593. What is meant by saying of the unfaithful nymph that

> Her lippes prophane Ideas sacred name,
> And sdayne to read the annals of her fame?

The obvious explanation is that Anne Goodere had seen the sonnets to Idea in manuscript (cf. the introductory sonnet to Anthony Cooke), and made light of them; but this seems hardly satisfactory.

from her the dedication of the new form of *Mortimeriados;* and that, in the *Idea* of 1606, taking advantage of the fact that both ladies had dwelt by the Ancor, he turned Idea into Anne Goodere and made the countess of Bedford the hated and perfidious Selena. Unless it can be proved that the Idea of *Endimion and Phœbe* was the countess of Bedford, the accusation seems to break down; and it must be remembered that, though the new form of *Mortimeriados* was dedicated to Sir William Aston, the sonnet to the countess of Bedford was reprinted in the same volume, and continued to be reprinted with the other sonnets till Drayton's death. It seems possible, therefore, that Drayton effected the change of patron without grossly insulting his former benefactress or even quarrelling with her, and that he remained faithful in love throughout to a single lady, to whom he consistently gave the title of Idea. Who Selena was, who Cerberon and who Olcon, must remain uncertain. In a later and revised edition of these pastorals, published in 1619, the lines on Selena are omitted. [1]

In 1594, still following the poetical fashion, Drayton published a historical "legend." Readers of Elizabethan literature have no need to be reminded how ardently, in the last twenty years of Elizabeth's reign, the newly awakened patriotism of England turned to the history of past achievements. The form which Drayton chose for the expression of this sentiment was still the popular form, although it dated from the days of *A Mirror for Magistrates* [2] and was beginning to be shaken from its hold on the public by the success of the chronicle play. Perhaps a discerning admiration for Samuel Daniel's *Complaynt of Rosamond*, published in 1592, may have helped to incline Drayton towards this form, for Daniel was one of his three chief poetical masters.

The legend of *Peirs Gaveston Earle of Cornwall* was followed, in 1594, by that of *Matilda, the faire and chaste daughter of the Lord Robert Fitzwater;* in 1596, both were revised and issued together with a third, *The Tragicall Legend of Robert Duke of Normandy;* and, in 1607, Drayton, for some reason, turned back to the old form, and published *The Legend of Great Cromwel.* On these legends, there is little need to dwell. They

---

[1] On the whole question, see Courthope, *ut supra;* Elton, pp. 14–23.
[2] See Vol. III of the present work, Chap. IX; and, for Drayton, p. 223.

suffer from the faults common to all their kind: monotony, and an incomplete assimilation of the historical and poetical matter, whereby the facts, as they occur in the careful record, let the poetry down with a thud. One or two points, however, may be noticed. Perhaps the best passage in any of the four legends is the charming description of the poet's betaking himself on a summer morning to the banks of Thames, there to fall asleep and dream the quaint, old-fashioned *estrif* between Fortune and Fame over Robert of Normandy. It gives a foretaste of that love for the glory and beauty of his own land which was later to inspire and enrich *Poly-Olbion*. The legend of *Matilda* shows a warm humanity and some real pathos; and it is not too much to say that, when all allowance is made for Drayton's incorrigible clumsiness in grammar and construction, certain passages in *Great Cromwel* are the most remarkable example of the use of poetry for reasoning that occurs before Dryden. The versification is seldom attractive. *Robert, Duke of Normandy* and *Matilda* are in rime royal; *Peirs Gaveston* in stanzas of six; and *Great Cromwel* in stanzas of eight; but in none does Drayton use the decasyllabic line with much individuality or beauty.

His next work, in its first form, showed once more the influence of Daniel. In 1594, sonnet sequences were in the height of fashion. *Astrophel and Stella* had found its way into print in 1591; but it was not till some years later that Drayton's sonnets were to show the influence of Sidney. When he published *Ideas Mirrour*, in 1594, his model was rather Daniel, of whose *Delia* three editions had appeared in 1592. In 1594, *Ideas Mirrour* consisted of fifty-one sonnets, which, as we learn from the additional dedicatory sonnet to Anthony Cooke, had "long slept in sable night." The form of sonnet which Drayton principally affects is the typically Elizabethan form of three quatrains and a final couplet, not the strict Petrarchian form. Of these fifty-one sonnets, however, two consist of four quatrains with a final couplet, two are written mainly in alexandrines, which are also scattered through certain other sonnets, and, in eighteen, each quatrain is rimed not *abab*, but on the rarer principle of *abba*.

Any independence which these and a few other variations may be thought to show can find little counterpart in the

material of the sonnets of *Ideas Mirrour*. In this earliest edi·
tion, it is very seldom that the poet shakes himself free of the
conventions of the day, or so uses them as to convey an impression of the sincerity with which, of course, their use is
never incompatible. Of two sonnets which connect Idea with
the river Ancor, the first (Amour XIII) has a personal touch,
the second (Amour XXIV) displays the knowledge of the
streams of England which was to stand Drayton in good stead
in the future; but Amour XXXVIII is alone among these early
efforts in its simple, convincing force and directness.

> If chaste and pure devotion of my youth,
> Or glorie of my Aprill-springing yeares,
> Unfained love in naked simple truth,
> A thousand vowes, a thousand sighes and teares;
> Or if a world of faithful service done,
> Words, thoughts, and deeds devoted to her honor,
> Or eyes that have beheld her as theyr sunne,
> With admiration ever looking on her:
> A lyfe that never joyed but in her love,
> A soule that ever hath ador'd her name,
> A fayth that time nor fortune could not move,
> A Muse that unto heaven hath raised her fame.
>> Though these, nor these deserve to be imbraced,
>> Yet faire unkinde, too good to be disgraced.

The fact that the couplet shows Drayton's weakness in grammar
cannot undo the effect of the quatrains. It is, however, in
scattered lines and passages rather than in any complete
sonnet that the value of the earliest *Amours* will be found to lie.
Into the vexed question of the genuineness of the sentiments
expressed in these and other Elizabethan sonnets, this is not
the place to enter. It is, perhaps, generally recognised that
the adoption of a poetic convention does not necessarily denote
insincerity in the poet; and the question is not whether or
whence he borrowed his conventions, but whether he has
subdued them to his own genius. The fact that Drayton borrowed, as it appears, the title of Idea (and, as it also appears,
little, if anything, else) from a French poet,[1] and his material

---

[1] Claude de Pontoux, author of *L'Idée*, 1579. See Vol. III of the present
work, p. 300; and, on the Elizabethan use of the Platonic "idea," see Elton,
p. 47 and references.

and machinery from the poetical stores of his day, does not prove that these *Amours* of 1594 are a mere literary exercise. Nor does the mention of the river Ancor in two of the sonnets prove them sincere outpourings of his heart. The workmanship proves that Drayton was not yet poet enough to subdue the conventions of form to the matter of his own thoughts and emotions; and it is therefore that his earliest sonnets stumble and leave us cold.

Ideas Mirrour was much admired. Eleven new issues were called for between its first publication and the author's death in 1631. On none of his productions did Drayton spend so much care in revision. The issues of 1599, 1600,[1] 1602, 1605 and 1619, are all new editions, in which new sonnets are constantly included and old ones rearranged, omitted altogether, or polished, sometimes almost beyond recognition.[2] It is not always possible to agree with Drayton's own ideas of improvement; but the general result of all this care is that, as time goes on, the character of the collection changes. The rather heavy, elaborate model provided by Daniel gives place to the simpler and more direct style of Sidney. Conventions disappear, or are turned to good account; and, though there is, in the general opinion, only one masterpiece among all Drayton's sonnets, the edition of 1619 includes few sonnets that have not something masterly in them. The masterpiece referred to is the well-known sonnet: "Since there's no helpe, Come let us kisse and part." It suggests, irresistibly, a record of a definite moment in the actual relations between the poet and some woman; and, in general, it may be said that the sonnets, as time goes on, bear less and less the mark of the literary exercise and more and more that of the expression of geniune feeling. It is true that, in the editions of 1599, 1602 and 1605, Drayton introduced two sonnets: "Into these loves who but for passion looks," and "Many there be excelling in this kind," in which the reader is warned that

---

[1] See *Daniel's Delia and Drayton's Idea*; ed. Esdaile, A., p. 149.
[2] Elton, pp. 207–9, gives a table of one hundred and seven sonnets in the five editions. Brett, pp. 1–55, prints one hundred and eight (the extra sonnet being that to Sir Walter Aston, 1605) in their earliest forms, without variants; and, in an appendix, pp. 250, 251, gives three complimentary sonnets prefixed to works of other authors.

> My verse is the true image of my mind,
> Ever in motion, still desiring change,
> To choyce of all varietie inclin'd,
> And in all humours sportively I range;

and that

> My wanton verse nere keepes one certain stay,
> But now, at hand; then, seekes invention far,
> And with each little motion runnes astray,
> Wilde, madding, jocond, and irreguler;

but such statements, it may be submitted, mean nothing more than that love is not the only subject of which he intends to treat; while such sonnets as "Since there's no helpe"; "How many paltry, foolish, painted things"; "An evill spirit your beauty haunts me still"; "Whilst thus my pen strives to eternize thee," compel a belief in their sincerity.

Much has been written, and much more, doubtless, will be written, on the relation of Drayton's sonnets to Shakespeare's. It has been well said that

the question which of the two was the lender is insoluble, so long as we only know that some of Shakespeare's sonnets were in private circulation in 1598, while two were printed by Jaggard in 1599, and the rest not till ten years later.[1]

After the first edition of the sonnets, Drayton's next publication was *Endimion and Phœbe*, entered at Stationers' Hall in April, 1595, and, presumably, published in the same year. This is one of the most beautiful and interesting of Drayton's poems. In it the sweetness and simplicity of pastoral are exalted by the touch of the heroic; and the occasional display of philosophy and quaint learning, astronomical, medical and what not, though it sometimes brings the poetry perilously near to doggerel, is not without its historical interest or its charm. At the close of the poem, Drayton commends it, humbly, to three other poets, Spenser (Collin), Daniel (Musaeus) and Lodge (Goldey). The influence of the first two is plain in the poem, but a stronger influence still is that of Marlowe,

---

[1] Elton, p. 56. See the whole passage, which inclines slightly to the view that Drayton was the borrower. See also Beeching, *Sonnets of Shakespeare*, pp. 132–140.

whose *Hero and Leander* (published in 1598) Drayton must have seen in manuscript. *Endimion and Phœbe* has not the passion of Marlowe's work; or of *Venus and Adonis*, which, no doubt, Drayton had also seen. His are cool, moonlight loves; but the exquisite delicacy of rather fantastic ornament, combined with a freshness of atmosphere in the narrative and descriptive passages, shows a lighter touch and a suppler mind than anything the poet had yet produced. The poem recalls irresistibly some Italian painting of the renascence, where nymphs and satyrs occupy a quiet, spacious and purely decorative world. *Endimion and Phœbe* has its claims, moreover, on the side of poetical craftsmanship. However he may stumble in his "learned nines and threes" (as Lodge called his description of the celestial orders),[1] in his narrative, Drayton's movement is swift and graceful. The poem is written in rimed decasyllabic couplets, which, at their best, are not echoes of Marlowe, Spenser or Daniel, but Drayton's own, with a distinctive cadence, and not a little of that ease which he was by time and labour to acquire.

The couplets avoid both the wearisome, epigrammatic certainty of pause which this form acquired in the eighteenth century, and the straggling looseness with which it has been used since. Without jerkiness or shapelessness, they flow as brightly and smoothly along as any of the streams of Latmus.

For some reason, Drayton never reissued *Endimion and Phœbe*. Years later, he returned to the idea, and incorporated parts of his beautiful early poem in an uninteresting work, *The Man in the Moone*, 1606, which has a body of crabbed learning with a head and tail of satire.

For the next few years, Drayton devoted himself to historical poetry, and, in the course of them, hit upon what his contemporaries and the two following centuries considered his best production. With his ardour for Daniel still unabated, he published, in 1596, the *Mortimeriados*, of which mention has been made above. It is not among his most successful efforts. The story of the wars between Edward II and the barons, down to the capture of Mortimer at Nottingham castle by Edward III, is told in rime royal, and at great length. Drayton's

---

[1] In *A Fig for Momus* (1595). For "nines and threes," see also the eighth Amour of *Ideas Mirrour*, 1594.

struggles with history induce the faults observable, also, in Daniel.　The narrative of events is not clear, and it is continually standing in the way of the dramatic interest in the characters.　Nevertheless, there are admirable passages in this long and comprehensive epic, every line of which shows Drayton hard at work in his dogged, persevering way; determined to hammer out the best poetry he can, seldom slovenly, though often crabbed, and now and then meeting with the reward of his conscientious labours.　Mortimer's escape from the Tower, his meeting with queen Isabella in France, the unhappy state of England, the scene of Edward's deposition at Kenilworth and his lament at Berkeley, are at least vigorously told; while the description of the queen's bower at Nottingham gives Drayton an opportunity for letting his fancy run free in renascence ornament.　Seven years later, Drayton rewrote the whole poem, under the new title *The Barrons Wars*, and in a new metre, expanding his seven-lined stanza into an eight-lined stanza.　The reason for this change is set out in a preface which is interesting, not only for the excellence of its matter, but for its testimony to the conscientiousness and to the sound knowledge of poetry on which Drayton based his prolonged and determined efforts to be a poet.　In the stanza of seven lines, in which there are two couplets,

the often harmony thereof soften'd the verse more than the majesty of the subject would permit, unless they had all been geminals, or couplets. . . . The Quadrin doth never double, or to use a word of Heraldry, never bringeth forth gemells: The Quinzain too soon.　The Sestin hath twins in the base, but they detain not the musick nor the close, as Musicians term it, long enough for an Epic Poem. . . . This of eight both holds the time clean through to the base of the column, which is the couplet at the foot or bottom, and closeth not but with a full satisfaction to the ear for so long detention.　Briefly, this sort of stanza hath in it majesty, perfection, and solidity, resembling the pillar which in Architecture is called the Tuscan, whose shaft is of six diameters, and base of two.

In spite of this, *The Barrons Wars* is free from none of the essential faults of *Mortimeriados*, and even discards some of its fresher beauties, though the careful revision of diction was not without its good effect.

Drayton discovered the means of dispensing with those essential faults in 1597, when (having meanwhile published the *Legends* of *Robert*, *Matilda* and *Gaveston* referred to above) he produced the famous *Englands Heroicall Epistles*. These are a series of letters from heroic lovers, with, in every case, the answer. The amount of history is reduced to a minimum; yet Drayton is enabled to celebrate the great men and women of his country, and to fan in others that flame of patriotism which burned steadily in himself. The first edition of these *Epistles* was evidently soon exhausted; in 1598, they were reissued with additions; the number was again enlarged in 1599 and 1602; and, altogether, between the first issue and the poet's death, the *Heroicall Epistles* were issued thirteen, possibly fourteen, times. They have been reprinted since more often than any other of Drayton's works. Twelve couples exchange letters. Henry II and Fair Rosamond; king John and Matilda Fitzwater; queen Isabel and Mortimer; the Black Prince and the countess of Salisbury; Richard II and his wife Isabel; queen Catherine and Owen Tudor; Eleanor Cobham and her husband, Humphrey of Gloucester; William de la Pole duke of Suffolk and queen Margaret; Edward IV and Jane Shore; the queen of France and Charles Brandon, duke of Suffolk; Surrey and Geraldine; lady Jane Grey and lord Guilford Dudley. Two of these pairs, Drayton had already treated in other poems; to all, he gives a life and vigour for which we may look in vain in his more strictly historical poems. It cannot be said that he has a keen sense of character; but he has at least enough to avoid sameness in a work where sameness would have been easy. There is no confusing, for instance, the letter of Jane Shore with that of lady Jane Grey; and, in each case, Drayton bears carefully in mind the character as well as the circumstances. And the poems abound in pleasant features. The appeal of Mary to Suffolk is charming, for all the peculiarity of the conditions under which it was made. Geraldine describes delightfully her life in the country grange where she will await Surrey's return; and Matilda Fitzwater's reply to John is a noble piece of eloquence.

The form of these letters was due, it appears, to Ovid's *Heroides;* and, with the form, Drayton took something, also, of his model's versification. In *Englands Heroicall Epistles*,

14

we find completed the improvement of the rimed couplet which
was begun in *Endimion and Phœbe*. Nowhere is it better used
during the Elizabethan epoch. To the smoothness and the
crispness (always stopping short of epigram), which remind us
of Ovid's elegiacs, there are added other good qualities. Drayton's years of hard work were having their effect. When not
overburdened with his subject (and he was too ready to undertake subjects that would have overburdened greater poets), he
moves more easily and yet more strongly than any except
the supreme pair of his age, Spenser and Shakespeare. And
in the work under notice he did, in 1597, what Edmund Waller
has gained all the credit of doing nearly thirty years later,
in the "smoothening" of English verse. Further, to this
"smoothness" he adds a skill in the choice and placing of
words for the effect of sonority and point which is not found
again till Dryden.

After this achievement, Drayton might have been expected
to forge ahead and make profitable use of the years of his prime.
He was now famous and should have been prosperous; but
his output for the next few years consisted only of revisions of,
and additions to, his *Heroicall Epistles* and sonnets. He was
turning his energy into other channels. For one thing, as
Meres states in *Palladis Tamia*, 1598, he had already embarked upon that huge undertaking, *Poly-Olbion;* for another,
he had been drawn into the net of the theatre. It may not be
permissible to declare him unwise; but his work for the theatre
brought him no enduring fame (and, as it appears, but little
immediate reward), while *Poly-Olbion* was to embitter him with
disappointment and vexation while he lived, and leave an easy
mark for the scorn of impatient judges for centuries after his
death. [1]

It must not be supposed that the years 1598–1604 were
barren. Besides so much of *Poly-Olbion* as they may have
seen completed, they produced some of Drayton's best sonnets
and several new and good *Heroicall Epistles*. But they do not
show the marked advance that might have been expected

---

[1] Drayton's work for the theatre will be discussed elsewhere in this work.
Reference may here be made to Elton, pp. 83–93; Greg's *Henslowe's Diary*
and *Henslowe Papers;* Fleay, *Biog. Chron. s.v.* "Drayton"; and the article by
Whitaker discussed by Elton, pp. 91–93.

from a man in his prime, with such a *point d'appui* as he had
made for himself in those *Epistles*.

In 1603, came "the quiet end of that long-living Queene,"
Elizabeth. Drayton owed her nothing, though she owed to
him one of the sweetest songs ever sung in her praise, the song
to "Beta" in *Idea*. Within the year before her death, in the
sonnets of 1602, he had already celebrated James VI of Scotland as prince and poet; and, when Elizabeth died, he turned
immediately, without a word of regret for the star that had
sunk, to hymn the star that was rising. His haste was considered indecent;[1] his gratulatory poem, *To the Majestie of King
James*, received no attention either from the public or the
prince. A little later, he wrote a *Paean Triumphall* for the
society of the Goldsmiths of London; but there can be no doubt
that his disappointment was keen. Fortunately for himself, he found, about this time, a new patron, Walter Aston, of
Tixall, who, on receiving knighthood from James I, made
Drayton one of his esquires, an honour which the poet was careful to claim on his future title-pages.

It appears significant that the first of Drayton's satires
should have been published in 1604; but, while it doubtless
implies a mood of disappointment and depression, it cannot
be taken for certain to refer to the king's neglect of his advances. In the preface, Drayton states that *The Owle*, entered at
Stationers' Hall in February, 1604, had been "lastly finished"
almost a year before; and, therefore, it is unsafe to find in it
any autobiographical references. Nevertheless, the mere fact
that Drayton should have included satire at all in the list of
the then common forms of poetry which he seems to have
considered it his duty as a poet to practise is some indication
that he was not happy or content. The owl, in his satire, is
the keen-eyed, disinterested observer. Nagged at by little
birds, and attacked by the fear and jealousy of crows, kites,
ravens and other marauders, he is rescued by the kingly eagle,
to whom he describes the abuses he has seen carried on by
evil birds who prey on the commonwealth of fowls. The
poem is inspired, doubtless, by *The Parlement of Foules;* but

---

[1] See Chettle, *Englandes Mourning Garment* (1603), D. 3, and Drayton,
Epistle to George Sandys (1627), ll. 11, 19–26.

it imitates neither the metre nor the good qualities of that work. More than once in his works, Drayton makes use of birds, of which, however, he betrays no more than common knowledge; and the opening of *The Owle* contains a pretty enough description of the surroundings in which the poet fell asleep to dream his satire. In the satire itself, there is not sufficient trenchancy, originality, or humour to make the poem interesting, and the rimed couplets run sluggish and dull. *The Man in the Moone* has already been mentioned, and it may be convenient to dismiss the subject of Drayton's satires by saying here that, in 1627, at the age of sixty-three, he published, in a volume containing better things, *The Moone-Calfe*. It is pleasantest to think of this as inspired by his conscientious wish to leave no poetical stone unturned; and yet it was so long since Marston had published a satire that the attempt to follow in his steps was belated. *The Moone-Calfe* is a coarse, clumsy and brutal piece of work, redeemed only by the vigour of its sketches of contemporary manners.

In the same year as *The Owle* (1604), appeared *Moyses in a Map of his Miracles*, to be revised and published twenty-six years later, as *Moses, his Birth and Miracles*. Here Drayton once more makes a high claim for poetry,

> That from full Jove takes her celestial birth,
> And quick as fire, her glorious self can raise
> Above this base abominable earth;

and, in the days before the *Authorised Version*, he may be pardoned for thinking that he could do something for the story of Moses greater than had been done for it by "that sacred and canonic writ." He had before him, also, the example of Du Bartas and Sylvester, to whom he renders generous tribute. Unfortunately, his treatment of the story does not raise it in the eyes of modern readers; the poem throughout lacks exaltation and grandeur, and its chief interest lies in certain human moments, where the drama of the episodes is happily amplified by the poet's sturdy humanity. But *Moses* is not a negligible poem in any study of Drayton. It shows here and there his progress in the management of the decasyllabic line, and now and then strangely anticipates later workmanship. Of such a line as the second of these:

> Muse, I invoke the utmost of thy might,
> That with an armed and auspicious wing,

Drayton is not the poet who would be guessed as the author by one unacquainted with its *provenance*.

Of the importance of a publication of two years later, however, there can be no question. The *Odes* of 1606 were Drayton's second striking effort to plough a field untilled by his contemporaries. The Pindaric ode had already been imitated by Jonson: it went on being imitated with an irregularity that Congreve was the earliest author to reprehend. Drayton's model is the Anacreontic or Horatian ode. With these odes as with most, indeed, of the works of so stern a critic of himself and so slowly developed a genius as Drayton, we have to wait for the final edition before we can see them at their best. The *Odes* of 1606 were revised and issued with additions and omissions in 1619; and in that edition they are best studied.

It was Drayton's endeavour to revive "Th' old Lyrick kind"—the kind, perhaps, that was sung to the harp by Hewes at Polesworth, fortified and polished by the influence of Horace and Anacreon. His odes are nearly all composed in short, decisive lines, a medium that English poetry has always found difficult. If the charge against Drayton of being merely a laborious, imitative bungler were ever revived, a sufficient answer would be a few selections, showing how unusually sensitive he was to the faults and merits of his medium. The faults of a long line are monotony and unwieldiness. Drayton is often monotonous and unwieldy. The faults of a short line are jerkiness and excessive compression. Drayton is guilty of both. But in all cases he succeeds, when he is at his best, in bringing out the possible merits of his metre, the smoothness and progression of the long line, the delicate, involved patterns and the range of tones, from the trumpet to the flute, that are possible with the short line. In the *Odes*, there is plenty of compression and some jerkiness; but they cannot be regarded as otherwise than a remarkable achievement in the creation of a new music in English poetry. Their range, in their final

form, is extraordinary; and, in nearly every case, their music
is an anticipation of something that was to be more perfectly
achieved later.

> As those Prophetike strings
> Whose sounds with fiery Wings
> Drave Feinds from their abode,
> Touch'd by the best of Kings,
> That sang the Holy Ode.

Is there any sound like that between Drayton and Milton?[1]
The ode *To His Rivall* contains these stanzas :

> Therefore boast not
> Your happy lot,
> Be silent now you have her;
> The time I knew
> She slighted you,
> When I was in her favour.

> None stands so fast,
> But may be cast
> By Fortune, and disgraced:
> Once did I weare
> Her Garter there,
> Where you her Glove have placed;

stanzas brave and playful which anticipate Suckling. And
the exquisite *canzonet*, *To His Coy Love*, which begins as
follows:

> I pray thee leave, love me no more,
> Call home the Heart you gave me,
> I but in vain that Saint adore,
> That can but will not save me:
> These poor halfe Kisses kill me quite;
> Was ever man thus served?
> Amid an Ocean of Delight,
> For Pleasure to be sterved:

have the true cavalier ring. In these later *Odes*, too, Drayton
sometimes touches the "metaphysical" poetry of Donne and
Cowley, a kind which he did not often affect.

[1] Elton, p. 101, notes a curiously prophetic "Swinburnian" stanza in
the ode *To The New Yeere*.

Two of the odes have won more fame than the others; and both reveal that sturdy Elizabethan patriotism which, in Drayton, was to be proof against the solvent influence of the reign of James I. A long and interesting essay might be founded upon the contrast between the tone of Drayton's ode *To the Virginian Voyage* and Marvell's "Where the remote Bermudas ride." In the former, we have all the bravery of the golden days of the adventurers.

> Britans, you stay too long,
> Quickly aboard bestow you,
>   And with a merry Gale
>   Swell your stretch'd Sayle,
> With Vowes as strong,
> As the Winds that blow you.
>
>   . . . .
>
> And cheerfully at Sea,
> Successe you still intice,
>   To get the Pearle and Gold,
>   And ours to hold,
> Virginia,
> Earth's onely Paradise.
>
>   . . . .
>
> And as there Plenty growes
> Of Lawrell every where,
>   Apollo's Sacred tree,
>   You may it see,
> A Poets Browes
> To crowne, that may sing there.

The other of the two odes referred to is the most famous of Drayton's poems, the swinging *Ballad of Agincourt*, dedicated "to the Cambro-Britans and their Harpe." Here, more than anywhere, is heard the echo of Hewes and his like. Drayton worked upon the text of it to good purpose between 1606 and 1619, removing snags and obstructions in the course of its rhythm, and making clearer and clearer the ringing tramp of the marching army.[1] With his stanzas of eight short, crisp lines, riming *aaabcccb*, it is the model for a war-poem; and the brave old song has as much power to-day to quicken the heart-

[1] Cf. Elton, pp. 104–5.

beats as has the *Henry V* of Shakespeare, the success of which, doubtless, helped to inspire its composition.

To *The Legend of Great Cromwel*, Drayton's solitary publication in 1607, reference has been made above. During the next six years he published nothing but two reprints, with slight changes, of a collected edition of his poems which he had brought out in 1605. There was a reason for this. He was now steadily engaged on what he hoped was to be his real title to fame, his *Poly-Olbion*. Of this "Herculean labour," the first eighteen "Songs" were published in 1613.[1] The necessary leisure had been secured to Drayton partly by the patronage of Sir William Aston, partly by a pension of £10 a year paid him by prince Henry, and continued, for a period not yet determined, after the death of that prince in November, 1612.

The *magnum opus* fell flat. In his preface, the author complains that,

Verses are wholly deduced to chambers, and nothing esteemed in this lunatic age, but what is kept in cabinets and must pass only by transcription. . . . The idle humorous world must hear of nothing that either savours of antiquity, or may awake it to seek after more than dull and slothful ignorance may easily reach unto: these, I say, make much against me.

This, doubtless, was true, in part; nevertheless, it was not wise of the poet to fling his work at the head of the public in so contemptuous a fashion, with such outspoken remarks on the prevalent "stupidity and dulness." But Drayton had not yet recovered the serenity which he had lost by reason of his "distressed fortunes" and his disappointment of instant recognition by James at his accession, to which he refers in the same preface. The public, partly, no doubt, through its "stupidity and dulness," and partly, perhaps, frightened away by this mode of introduction, paid little heed to the book. The author's grief, however stoutly he may have prepared himself for failure, must have been great. This was the work upon which he had been engaged since his thirty-fifth year at the latest. He was now fifty, overtaken by times which

---

[1] There appears to have been an earlier edition of 1612(?). See Elton, p. 192.

he, with all other Elizabethans, felt and knew to be evil; and, therefore, he was all the more anxious, like a true Elizabethan, to rescue from oblivion the glories of his beloved country by the only means which he recognised as secure, that is by poetry. Into *Poly-Olbion*, he poured all his not inconsiderable learning and observation, all his patriotism and his fancy. The poem was his darling, his

Tempe and fields of the Muses, where, through most delightful groves, the angelic harmony of birds shall steal thee to the top of an easy hill, where in artificial caves, cut out of the most natural rock, thou shalt see the ancient people of this isle delivered thee in their lively images; from whose height thou may'st behold both the old and later times, as in thy prospect, lying far under thee; then conveying thee down by a soul-pleasing descent through delicate embroidered meadows, often veined with gentle-gliding brooks, in which thou may'st fully view the dainty nymphs in their simple naked beauties, bathing them in crystalline streams; which shall lead thee to most pleasant downs, where harmless shepherds are, some exercising their pipes, some singing roundelays to their gazing flocks.[1]

Thus, with a voice as of an earlier age, he spake to the age of James, which would not hear him. Worse than that: it seems to have scoffed.

Some of our outlandish, unnatural, English, (I know not how otherwise to express them) stick not to say that there is nothing in this Island worth studying for, and take a great pride to be ignorant in anything thereof; for these, since they delight in their folly, I wish it may be hereditary from them to their posterity, that their children may be begg'd for fools to the fifth generation until it may be beyond the memory of man to know that there was ever other of their families.[2]

He wishes them oblivion—the heaviest lot that a man of his time and temper could imagine. And so, with a round curse on the degenerate age, the sturdy old pilgrim grasps his staff, and sets out again on his high mission. The reception of the first eighteen "Songs" could not deter him from carrying on what he held to be his duty to his country and his great calling.

[1] "Epistle to the Generall Reader," *Poly-Olbion*, 1613.
[2] Preface to Second Part, 1622.

In spite of all odds, including the very serious difficulty of finding a publisher,[1] he brought out twelve more "Songs" in 1622, with a reprint of the first eighteen, and the statement that the public's neglect and folly could not "deter me from going on with Scotland, if means and time do not hinder me, to perform as much as I have promised in my First Song." Means and time were not forthcoming, and *Poly-Olbion* "stumbles to rest" with its thirtieth "Song."

The course of the itinerary, on the whole, is fairly regular. From the Channel islands, the pilgrim comes to Cornwall, and thence, by Devon and part of Somerset, down through the New Forest to Southampton and Wight. Thence, he goes north-west to Salisbury, and more or less straight on to the Avon and the Severn. Round the Severn and in Wales—a country whose inhabitants he always regarded kindly as the remains of the original Britons—he lingers long, with a little excursion to Hereford and Malvern; gradually working his way north to Chester, where he turns south-east past the Wrekin to the midlands, to celebrate Warwick, Coventry and his beloved Ancor. With a circuit through the vale of Evesham and the Cotswolds, hallowed to him, as were the spots he had just left, by their association with Anne Goodere, he follows the river from Oxford to London. Thence, he starts afresh southeast, down the Medway, through Surrey and Sussex into Kent, there to turn and work by degrees up the eastern counties, through Cambridge and Ely, to Lincolnshire and the fens, Trent and the forest of Sherwood. From there, he crosses England to Lancashire and Man, thence to work back to Yorkshire, and so to Northumberland, to end his pilgrimage in Westmoreland.

He has covered practically the whole of England, and little has escaped him on the way. Perfunctorily, but conscientiously, he has described the fauna, and especially the flora, the river-systems and mountain-ranges, making free use of the then old-fashioned device of personification in order to beguile and lure on his reader. But the present interests him little compared with the past. His real object is to preserve whatever history or legend (both are of equal importance

---

[1] See his letters to William Drummond of Hawthornden, with whom he corresponded between 1618 and 1631.

in his eyes, and he draws no clear distinction between the two) has recorded of great deeds, and great men, be they heroes of myth like Guy of Warwick, Corineus of Cornwall, or Elidure the Just, saints like those in the roll he celebrates at Ely, or historic kings and captains. Leaning chiefly on Camden's *Britannia*, he has ransacked also the chroniclers and poets, the songs of the harpers and minstrels, every source that he knew of information on that precious past which must be preserved against time's proud hand. And, to fortify what he records in rime, he has secured from the learned John Selden a set of notes or "illustrations" to each song, in which, though the antiquary's science sometimes smiles at the poet's faith, the general tenor of the poem is buttressed by a brave show of erudition and authority.

How much of the ground Drayton had covered in person, it is impossible to tell from the poem itself. Of the places which it is certain that he knew, he sings no otherwise than of some which it is very unlikely that he had ever seen. And, in fact, the point is unimportant. The purpose of his narrative was not, as was that of the narratives collected by the "industrious Hackluit" whom he celebrates in one of his odes, to make known the unknown present, but to eternise the known past; and vividness and authenticity of description are not among the essentials of such a work as his. Industry was the chief requisite, and of industry Drayton had as much as Hakluyt himself.

More industry, it must be admitted, than inspiration went to the making of *Poly-Olbion*. Drayton must have worked, like Wordsworth on *The Excursion*, in season and out of season, trusting to the importance of what he had to say to make his verses worthy of his subject. But *Poly-Olbion* is at least no nearer to being dull than is *The Excursion*. Drayton, in fact, took more pains than Wordsworth to diversify his poem. His rivers dispute, relate, or wed; his mountains and plains take on character and personality; criticism, as of the poetry of the Welsh bards; argument, as in the spirited and remarkably philosophic protest against historical scepticism in song VI; description, which, if sometimes lifeless, is sometimes bravely vivid, as in the view from his boat as it drops down from Windsor to London in song XVII; and admi-

rable story-telling, as in the account of Guy of Warwick in song
XIII; all take their turn in variegating the prospect. There are
stretches, it must be confessed, of dulness—long catalogues of
princes and events where the desire to record has clearly been
stronger than the power to sing; but the "historian in verse"
(to use Drayton's own words of Daniel) seldom leaves us
long without the reward of the "dainty nymphs in their simple
naked beauties" or some other of the delights promised in his
first epistle of 1613.

Drayton, whom we have seen from the preface to *The
Barrons Wars* to have had a philosophy of metre, doubtless
chose the metre of *Poly-Olbion* with care. It is written in
riming couplets of twelve-syllabled lines: a sober, jogging
motion, as easy to maintain and as comfortable as the canter
of a quiet hack. But it is not exciting; it has no surprises;
and the inevitable beat on the sixth and twelfth syllable,
which Drayton spares us scarcely twice in a "Song," is apt
to become soporific. Yet it may well be doubted whether
Poly-Olbion would not have been far less readable than it is
had Drayton adopted the rimed couplet of decasyllabic lines,
or taken a hint from the dramatists and employed blank
verse. No known form of stanza certainly could have carried
the reader on as does this amiable ambling pace, never very
fast, but never very slow. To quote a delightful phrase, "it
has a kind of heavy dignity like a Lord Mayor's coach."[1] At
its best, it is livelier than that; at its worst, it covers the
ground without jolting.

The modern reader with a taste for the antique will constantly meet little touches to interest and charm him. "The
wayless woods of Cardiff"—a phrase chosen at random as we
turn the pages—is eloquent, especially when taken in conjunction with the poet's repeated complaint that the iron works
(the very symbol to an Elizabethan of the passing of that
golden age when metals were unknown, and men rifled not the
womb of their mother Earth) were leading to the destruction
of all the forests which had been England's pride. The very
importance given to the river-systems is a reminder that the
poem was written in an England that was all but roadless.
But, as the book is laid down, its chief attraction, after all,

[1] Elton, p. 119.

is seen to be the pathetic bravery of the whole scheme—the voice of the dogged old Elizabethan raised amid an alien world, to sing the old song in the old way, to proclaim and preserve the glories of his beloved country in the face of a frivolous, forgetful age.

While *Poly-Olbion* was being completed, Drayton did little else. In 1618, a volume of collected *Elegies* was published, two of them being the work of Drayton; but, when the weight of his "Herculean labour" was lifted from his shoulders, he revealed, in the poetry of his old age, a playfulness, a lightness and delicacy, which are as charming as they are surprising. This comment does not apply to all the contents of the new volume of 1627. That volume opened with one of Drayton's mistakes—a translation into epic form of the brave *Ballad of Agincourt*. The new version of the story, called *The Battaile of Agincourt*, is written in the metre which the preface to *The Barrons Wars* had justified for poems of this kind. Its faithfulness to Holinshed brings it frequently into touch with Shakespeare's *King Henry V;* and the comparison is all to Drayton's disadvantage. The work lacks genuine fire and eloquence, and belongs to that part of Drayton's labours in which conscience was stronger than inspiration. The same metre and the same characteristics are found in the last of his historical poems, *The Miseries of Queene Margarite*, wife of Henry VI.

In *Nimphidia*, we find a new Drayton, and one not foreshadowed even by *Idea* or the *Odes*. Some time, as it seems, between his fifty-ninth and his sixty-fourth year, we hear the sound of his laughter, and find him playing, and playing lightly and gaily, with a literary toy. *Nimphidia* is a mock heroic poem relating the adventures of jealous Oberon, faithless Titania and her lover Pigwiggen. The parody of the old heroic ballads is carried out with the nicest particularity, and with a playful ingenuity which is surprising in a poet advanced in years and of a grave and laborious complexion. The lack of the higher imagination, which Drayton could not take over, with his characters and scene, from Shakespeare, is atoned for by the consistent humour of the finely polished verse, the very movement of which is a subtle and elaborate joke. In these tripping, dancing lines—the metre of the heroic ballads wonderfully transformed—we are far from the high heroic note of Elizabeth's days; we have reached the poetical land of Herrick and of the great Margaret, duchess of Newcastle, who both borrowed from Drayton's minute lore of fairyland.

Equally dainty and graceful, if not equally humorous, are other poems in this volume of 1627: *The Quest of Cynthia*, and *The Shepheards Sirena*, pastorals both. There is a marked difference between Drayton's earlier Spenserian pastorals *Idea* (though these were not, as we have seen, an extreme example of their form), and these later essays in the same field. In the two poems of 1627, there is an airy grace, a frank unreality that makes no attempt either to approximate to the real world of the country from which it draws its symbols, or to proclaim its difference from the world of town and court, the thought of which used to weigh heavily on earlier singers of the golden age. What applies to *The Quest of Cynthia* and *The Shepheards Sirena* applies also, in the main, to *The Muses Elizium*, divided into ten *Nymphalls*, which form the chief part of Drayton's last volume, published in 1630, and dedicated, part to the earl of Dorset, and part to his countess, who were the patrons of Drayton's last years. There is a little, but a very little, sad or satirical reflection here. Throwing back in the songs, with their lightness and spontaneity and the elaborate structure of their long stanzas of short lines, to the dewy lyrics of the later Eliazbethan song-books, they look forward, also, to a melody that was to be perfected later in the days of the cavaliers. Gallantry and grace have succeeded the swelling, heroic tones of the poet's youth. But in nothing does Drayton show himself so fine a master of words and rhythm as in these late pastorals; and some of the *Nymphalls* of *The Muses Elizium*, especially the second, the seventh and the eighth, should alone have sufficed to preserve his fame more steadily than has been the case.

To return to the volume of 1627: it contained, besides the pastorals mentioned and *The Moone-Calfe* discussed above, some excellent work in the form of *Elegies upon sundry occasions*. These have an obvious interest in the biographical information they provide. The first, entitled *Of his Ladies not Comming to London*, is a gallant but sincere compliment to a lady living in the west, in whom it is probably permissible to find his former love and present friend, Anne Goodere, now lady Rainsford. In another, he outpours a glowing tribute of affectionate regret at the death of her husband. From another, we learn of his friendship with William Browne, the poet, of Tavistock; and lady Aston, the wife of his patron is the recipient of another. Of these *Elegies*, some are complimentary and sometimes show a touch of the "conceited" or metaphysical; others, like that to Browne, are satirical. All show once more Drayton's skill in the management of the couplet. But the most interesting of all, perhaps, is the well known letter in verse *To Henery Reynolds*, in which Drayton tells the story of his boyish resolve to be a poet, and goes on to give an account of the development of English poetry from Chaucer to his own friends, John and Francis Beaumont and William Browne. It is full of sound sense and just criticism; and, if any of Drayton's verdicts—his harsh judgment on the Euphuists, for instance, or his idea of the language at Chaucer's command— have been upset, it has been by the growth of learning and the change of perspective, and not by any inherent fault.

The only works of Drayton which remain to be considered are the three "divine" poems which formed part of the volume of 1630. *Moses, his Birth and Miracles*, the revised version of *Moyses in a Map of his Miracles*, of 1604, has been mentioned above. The other two were *Noahs Floud* and *David and Goliah*, both written in the rimed couplets of decasyllables which Drayton had done much to beat into shape. It is notable that, in these last of Drayton's poems, we catch once more the Elizabethan note. The description of David carries us back to the Adonis of Shakespeare's poem, and there are passages of the same elaborate ornament that is found in *Endimion and Phœbe*. It has been noticed, also,[1] that, in the grand invocation at the beginning of *Noahs Floud*, there is "the presentiment of a greater sacred diction"—that of Milton.

Drayton's long and busy life closed at the end of 1631, and his body was buried in Westminster Abbey, under the north wall of the nave, and not in Poet's Corner where his bust may be seen.[2] His right to the honour will possibly be more fully

---

[1] By Elton, p. 134.   [2] For the evidence, see Elton, pp. 145, 146.

conceded by present and future ages than it has been at any
other time since his own day.   We see in him now, not, indeed,
a poet of supreme imagination, nor one who worked a revolution or founded a school, but a poet with a remarkably
varied claim on our attention and respect.   Drayton was not
a leader.   For the most part he was a follower, quick to catch,
and industrious to reproduce, the feeling and mode of the
moment.   So great, however, was his vitality and so fully
was he a master of his craft that, living from the reign of
Elizabeth into that of Charles I, he was able to keep abreast
of his swiftly moving times, and, by reason of his very powers
of labour, to bring something out of the themes and measures
he employed which his predecessors and contemporaries failed
to secure, but which after years owed to his efforts.   This
is especially the case, as we have seen, with his management of
the rimed couplet and the shortlined lyric.   Sluggish, perhaps,
of temper, and very variably sensitive to inspiration, he lacked
the touchstone of perfect poetical taste, and, like Wordsworth,
lacked also the finer virtues of omission.   Yet everything that
he wrote has its loftier moments; he is often "golden-mouthed,"
indeed, in his felicity of diction, whether in the brave style
of his youth or in the daintier manner of his age; and just
as, in his attitude to life, "out of the strong came forth sweetness," so, in his poetry, out of his dogged labour came forth
sweetness of many kinds.   In the long period which his work
covered, the many subjects and styles it embraced, the beauty
of its results and its value as a kind of epitome of an important era, there are few more interesting figures in English literature than Michael Drayton.

CHAPTER XI

John Donne

FROM the time of Wyatt, Surrey and their contemporaries of the court of Henry VIII, English lyrical and amatory poetry flowed continuously in the Petrarchian channel. The tradition which these "novices newly crept out of the schools of Dante, Ariosto and Petrarch" brought from Italy, after languishing for some years, was revived and reinvigorated by the influence of Ronsard and Desportes. Spenser in *The Shepheards Calender*, Watson with his pedantic *ΕΚΑΤΟΜΠΑΘΙΑ* and Sidney with the gallant and passionate sonnets to Stella, led the way; and thereafter, till the publication of Davison's *Poetical Rapsody*, in 1602, and, subsequently, in the work of such continuers of an older tradition as Drummond, the poets, in sonnet sequence or pastoral eclogue and lyric, told the same tale, set to the same tune. Of the joy of love, the deep contentment of mutual passion, they have little to say (except in some of the finest of Shakespeare's sonnets to his unknown friend), but much of its pains and sorrows—the sorrow of absence, the pain of rejection, the incomparable beauty of the lady and her unwavering cruelty. And they say it in a series of constantly recurring images: of rain and wind, of fire and ice, of storm and warfare; comparisons

> With sun and moon, and earth and sea's rich gems,
> With April's first born flowers and all things rare,
> That heaven's air in this huge rondure hems;

allusions to Venus and Cupid, Cynthia and Apollo, Diana and Actaeon; Alexander weeping that he had no more worlds to conquer, Caesar shedding tears over the head of Pompey; abstractions, such as Love and Fortune, Beauty and Disdain; monsters, like the Phoenix and the Basilisk. Here and there lingers a trace of the metaphysical strain which, taking its rise in the poetry of the troubadours, had been most fully elaborated by Guinicelli and Dante and Cavalcanti, the analysis of love in relation to, and its effect on, the heart of man and its capacity for virtue:

> The sovereign beauty which I do admire,
> Witness the world how worthy to be praised!
> The light whereof hath kindled heavenly fire
> In my frail spirit by her from baseness raised.

But the most prevalent reflective note derives not from Petrarch and Dante, but, through Ronsard and his fellow-poets of *La Pléiade*, from Catullus and the Latin lyrists: the pagan lament for the flectingness of beauty and love—Ronsard's

> Ah, love me love! we may be happy yet,
> And gather roses while 't is called to-day,

Shakespeare's

> Since brass, nor stone, nor earth, nor boundless sea,
> But sad mortality o'er-sways their power,
> How with this rage shall beauty hold a plea,
> Whose action is no stronger than a flower?

The poet who challenged and broke the supremacy of the Petrarchian tradition was John Donne. Occasionally, when writing a purely complimentary lyric to Mrs. Herbert or lady Bedford, Donne can adopt the Petrarchian pose; but the tone and temper, the imagery and rhythm, the texture and colour, of the bulk of his love songs and love elegies are altogether different from those of the fashionable love poetry of the sixteenth century, from Wyatt and Surrey to Shakespeare and Drummond. With Donne, begins a new era in the history of the English love lyric, the full importance of which is not exhausted when one recognises in Donne the source of the "metaphysical" lyric as it flourished from Carew to Rochester.

Nor was this Donne's only contribution to the history of English poetry. The spirit of his best love poetry passed into the most interesting of his elegies and his religious verses, the influence of which was not less, in the earlier seventeenth century perhaps even greater, than that of his songs. Of our regular, classically inspired satirists, he is, whether actually the first in time or not, the first who deserves attention, the first whose work is in the line of later development, the only one of the sixteenth century satirists whose influence is still traceable in Dryden and Pope. *Religio Laici* is indebted for some of its most characteristic arguments to Donne's "Kind pity checks my spleen"; and Pope found in Donne a satirist whose style and temper were closer in essential respects to his own than those of the suave and urbane Horace. For evil and for good, Donne is the most shaping and determining influence that meets us in passing from the sixteenth to the seventeenth century. In certain aspects of mind and training the most medieval, in temper the most modern, of his contemporaries, he is, with the radically more pedantic and neo-classical Jonson, at once the chief inspirer of his younger contemporaries and successors, and the most potent herald and pioneer of the school of poetic argument and eloquence.

The life of Donne—especially that part of it which concerns the student of his poetry—as well as the canon and text of his poems presents problems which are only in process of solution: some of them probably never will be solved. A full but concise statement of all that we know regarding his *Lehr-* and *Wander-jahre* is necessary both for the sake of what it contains, and because of the clearness with which it defines the questions that await further investigation.

John Donne (the name was pronounced so as to rime with "done" and was frequently spelt "Dun" or "Dunne") was the eldest son of a London ironmonger—probably of Welsh extraction—and of Elizabeth, the third (not, as hitherto believed, the only[1]) daughter of John Heywood, the famous dramatist of queen Mary's reign, by his wife Elizabeth Rastell. This Elizabeth was herself the daughter of John Rastell and Elizabeth the sister of Sir Thomas More. Donne thus, on his

[1] See Bang's article in *Englische Studien;* Acta Anglo-Lovanensia; "John Heywood und sein Kreis."

mother's side at any rate, came of a line of distinguished and devoted adherents of the old faith. He himself was bred in that faith, and, despite his conversion and later polemical writing and preaching, his most intimate religious poems indicate very clearly that he never ceased to feel the influence of his Catholic upbringing.

According to Walton and Anthony à Wood, Donne proceeded to Oxford in 1584 at the early age of eleven. Here, he formed a friendship with Henry Wotton, a friendship which counted for something in Donne's later life. From Oxford, he passed to Cambridge, where, Walton tells us, he studied diligently till the age of seventeen, but, neither here nor at Oxford, endeavoured after a degree on account of the "averseness of his friends to some parts of the oath that is always tendered at those times." Nevertheless, in 1610 he was entered in the Oxford registers as already an M.A. of Cambridge. Of these college years, no contemporary documentary evidence is extant.

Our first scrap of such evidence dates from 1592, the year of the first unmistakable reference to Shakespeare as a London actor and playwright. On the 6th of May in that year, Donne was entered at Lincoln's inn, having been already, the document testifies, admitted at Thavies's inn. Of his life between that year and his marriage in 1601, we have very few particulars, but these appear to indicate a life spent in England; a life similar to that led by many young members of the inns of court as Donne describes them,

Of study and play made strange hermaphrodites;

a life, too, of gradually broadening activity, which led him to the doorway of a public and political career.

In Donne's case, both the study and the play of these years were more than ordinarily intense. The record of the latter is his songs and elegies and earliest satires, the greater number of which were written, Donne told Jonson, before his twenty-fifth year. That he did not neglect law entirely for poetry, we know from his own statement, and this is corroborated by the poems themselves, in which legal metaphors abound. But the years 1593 and 1594 were also given to a serious and careful survey "of the body of divinity as it was then controverted betwixt the Reformed and the Roman Church." "About his twentieth year," Walton says, that is, apparently, in his twenty-first, he showed, to the then dean of Gloucester, all the works of Bellarmine, "marked with many weighty observations under his own hand." Bellarmine's *Disputationes*, indeed, were not published until 1593, and Rudde, who is the dean in question, ceased to hold that office in 1594, which gives but a short time for the study of such an important issue. But it is quite possible that Bellarmine's work, in which Donne found the best defence of the Roman cause, may have fallen into his hands at the end, not (as Walton implies) at the beginning, of a course of theological and controversial reading. To a mind that worked with the rapidity of Donne's, the analysis and digestion of an elaborate argument would not prove a lengthy task. Nor was his active adherence to the Anglican church precipitate. All that we can say with confidence is that when he entered the service of Sir Thomas Egerton, in 1597, he cannot have been a professed Romanist, and, in 1601, he disclaimed indignantly "love of a corrupt religion."

Donne's first approach to a public career was made by service as a volunteer in two combined military and naval expeditions. In 1595, Henry Wotton returned from a prolonged residence in Germany and Italy, to become at once an adherent of Essex, whom he had already served by his correspondence while abroad. The letters in verse and prose which passed between Donne and Wotton during the next few years (some of them yet unpublished) show that the intimacy begun at Oxford was renewed with ardour; and it is a fair conjecture, though only a conjecture, that it was Wotton's influence which brought Donne into contact with Essex, and induced him to join his friend as a volunteer in the expedition to Cadiz in 1596, and to the Azores in 1597. One of the letters referred to was written from Plymouth when the fleet, on the second of these expeditions, was driven back by press of weather; and Donne's verse epistles to Christopher Brooke, a Cambridge friend, *The Storm* and *The Calm*, describe, with extraordinary vividness and characteristic extravagance of "wit," the experiences of his voyage. They were the first of his poems, apparently, to attract attention outside the circle of his friends. Another verse epistle, dated 20 July, 1598, to Wotton, refers to their common adventure:

Here's no more newes than vertue,

he cries, writing "At Court,"

I may as well
Tell you Cales[1] or St. Michaels tales for newes, as tell
That vice doth heere habitually dwell.

On the second of these expeditions, Donne and Wotton were accompanied by another young volunteer, Thomas, eldest son of Sir Thomas Egerton, lord keeper of the great seal. By this young man, who was among those knighted for gallantry after the expedition, Donne was recommended to the lord keeper towards the close of 1597, and for four years was secretary to that influential statesman. The door which was thus opened to Donne leading to preferment, it might be even to wealth and station, was abruptly closed by his own rash action, a runaway marriage with Anne More, daughter of Sir George More of Losely and niece of the lord keeper's second wife. It may be that, in Donne's complex nature, love was blended with ambitious hopes of securing his position and strengthening his claims on Sir Thomas Egerton. If so, he was grievously disappointed. At the instance of Sir George More, he and his friends Christopher and Samuel Brooke, who assisted at the marriage, were thrown into prison; and, although Donne was soon released, and his father-in-law by degrees and perforce reconciled to the marriage, the poet's hopes of preferment were blasted by his dismissal from the service of the lord keeper.

This sketch of Donne's earlier years would be incomplete without a reference to the problem of his residence abroad, a residence the effect of which on his work is palpable. Through Walton, we have Donne's own authority for the statement that he visited Italy with the intention of proceeding to the east to

---

[1] Modern editors have disguised the reference in these lines, by translating the "Calis" of the printed edition into "Calais," and confounding "St. Michaels" with the "guarded Mount" of Cornwall. But some manuscripts read "Cales," and there can be no doubt that the allusion is to the storming of Cadiz, and to the "Islands expedition," when Essex's hope of capturing the Plate fleet was disappointed in consequence of his unseasonable attack on the island of St. Michael. "I might as well tell you what we both witnessed."

view the Holy Sepulchre; that, prevented from doing so, he passed over into Spain; that he "made many useful observations of those countries, their laws and manners of government, and returned perfect in their languages." Walton assigns this episode to the years following the "Islands expedition"; but this is manifestly erroneous, for, during these years, Donne was actively employed as Egerton's secretary. It is almost equally difficult to find a place for it in the years from 1592 to 1596, when he was studying law, theology and life in London. It is noteworthy that the earliest portrait of Donne, dated 1591, shows him in military dress and bears a Spanish motto. Again, in one of the three earlier satires, which Harleian MS. 5110 assigns to 1593, Donne describes his library as already lined with

> Giddie fantastique poets of each land,

and, long afterwards, he declared that it contained more Spanish authors than of any other nation, "and that in any profession from the mistress of my youth, Poetry, to the wife of mine age, Divinity." The books in a man's library would not, to-day, be a safe index to his travels, but, in the sixteenth and seventeenth centuries, it was not usual for a young man to have a considerable collection of foreign books unless, like Drummond and Milton, he had himself brought them home.

It is difficult to avoid the conclusion that the time which Donne spent abroad must have been in the last years of his earlier education, when he was still a Catholic and under Catholic direction. If this were so, it would explain his silence about the exact circumstances of a voyage probably undertaken without the permission of the government, and, possibly, with the intention on the part of his guardians that he should enter a seminary, despite the law of 1585, or take service under a foreign ruler.[1] With more light on this point, we might be able to see in the singularly emancipated moral tone of Donne's mind and its complete openness on religious questions during the early years in London something of a reaction in his nature against a bent which others would have imposed upon it.

[1] Donne's mother seems to have lived abroad most of her life. In 1602, Donne mentions service abroad in a way that shows it had been presented to his mind as a possibility: "From seeking preferments abroad my love and conscience restrains me."

Lastly, an early date fits best the evidence in the poems of foreign influence, which is not to be found specially in Donne's "wit," but in the spirit of Italian literature and life reflected in the frank sensuality of some, the virulent satire of others, of his elegies and songs. The spirit of the renascence in Latin countries, and a wide acquaintance with Spanish casuists and other religious writers, are the most palpable indications of foreign influence in Donne's work. His direct indebtedness to any particular poet, Italian or Spanish, has not been established. Of all Elizabethan poets, he is, for good or evil, the most independent.

From 1601 to 1615, Donne's life was one of dependence on, and humiliating adulation of, actual or possible patrons. He lived at Pyrford on the charity of his wife's cousin Francis Wooley; at Mitcham or in the Strand, on his wife's allowance from her father; at the town house of Sir Robert Drury, whose patronage he had gained by writing on the death of Elizabeth Drury, a girl of sixteen whom he had never seen, the most elaborate and exalted of his *Funerall Elegies*. He twice went abroad, on the second occasion accompanying Sir Robert Drury to France and Spa. He assisted Thomas Morton, afterwards dean of Gloucester and bishop of Durham, in his controversies with Roman Catholics, for, though by no means yet a devoted adherent of the Anglican church, he heartily detested the Jesuits. He wrote courtly letters in verse and prose to the countess of Bedford and other great ladies, or elegies on the death of their friends and relatives. He found one patron in the person of lord Hay, later earl of Doncaster, and he courted another in the king's favourite, Robert Carr, earl of Somerset, for whose marriage with the divorced countess of Essex he wrote a splendid epithalamium. Of his writings of this period, some are in the brilliant, but often coarse, satiric vein of his earlier satires and satiric elegies; one, *ΒΙΑΘΑΝΑΤΟΣ*, is an erudite, subtle and strangely mooded excursus into the field of casuistry; and one, *Pseudo-Martyr*, published in 1610, is a more restrained and official contribution to the controversies of the day, a defence of the oath of allegiance, Donne's first public appearance on the Anglican side, in which, however, he does not wander far from the single point at issue, and writes, not to convert Catholics, but to persuade them that they may take the oath.

Such were Donne's "steps to the altar." As early as 1607, Morton, on being appointed dean of Gloucester, had urged upon his collaborator the advisability of taking orders. But Donne did not feel that the author of the popular and widely circulated *Satyres* and *Elegies*, the *Paradoxes* and *Problems* and *The Progresse of the Soule*, could become a "priest to the temple" without some scandal to the friends and admirers of the brilliant and irregular "Jack Donne," not yet quite buried in the sage and serious husband and father, the controversialist and the courtly friend of Mrs. Herbert and lady Bedford. *Ignatius his Conclave* was written about this very year, the witty verses prefixed to *Coryats Crudities* in 1611, and he was yet to write the *Epithalamium* for Somerset. It is easier to respect, than to wonder at, such a decision, whether in 1607 or 1610. Moreover, it is doubtful, as Gosse has insisted, if, in his heart of hearts, Donne, by 1607 or 1610, was a convinced Anglican. As late as 1617, when he had been nearly three years in orders, he could write:

> Show me, dear Christ, Thy Spouse so bright and clear.
> What? Is it she who on the other shore
> Goes richly painted? or who robb'd and tore
> Laments and mourns in Germany and here?
> Sleeps she a thousand, then peeps up one year?

This is not the language of one who is walking in the *Via Media* with the intellectually untroubled confidence of Herbert.

When Donne at length became a priest in Anglican orders, it was as one convinced that, for him, every other path to preferment was closed, not to be opened even by the influence of Somerset. The king had resolved that Donne should enter the church, and, on 25 January, 1615, he was ordained by bishop King of London. The period of privation and suitorship was over. In 1616, he became divinity reader at Lincoln's inn, where many of his sermons were preached. In 1619 and 1620, he was in Germany as chaplain to his friend the earl of Doncaster, and preached before the unfortunate queen of Bohemia one of the noblest and most illuminating of his sermons. In 1621, king James appointed him dean of St. Paul's, where his fame as a preacher attracted large audiences and rose to its height about the beginning of Charles's reign. For a moment he fell under suspicion with the pedantic and imperious Laud. But the cloud soon passed and, had Donne lived, he would have been made a bishop. But, often ailing, he was stricken down at his daughter's house in the late summer of 1630. The strange and characteristic monument which stands in St. Paul's was prepared by his own directions while he lay ill. Some of the most intense and striking of his hymns were written at the same time. Once, he rose from his bed to preach the sermon entitled *Death's Duel*. Six weeks later, on 31 March, 1631, he died.

However blended the motives may have been which carried Donne into holy orders, he gave to the ministry a single-hearted and strenuous devotion. Whatever doubts may, at times, have agitated his secret thoughts, or found expression in an unpublished sonnet, they left no reflection in his sermons. He adopted and defended the doctrines of the church of England, and the policy in church and state of her rulers, in their entirety and without demur. His was a nature in which the will commanded, but was always able to enlist in the service of its final choice a swift and subtle intellect, an intense and vivid imagination and a vast store of varied erudition. And, while he made amends for his Catholic upbringing, and for a middle period of mental detachment, by the orthodoxy of his Anglicanism, the memory of the licence of his earlier life and wit was forgotten in his later asceticism and in the spiritual exaltation of the *Sermons*, the *Devotions* and the *Divine Poems*.

Reference is made elsewhere to Donne as a preacher.[1] Here, we are concerned with him as poet and prose artist. The history of his poems is involved in the difficulties and obscurities of his biography. Only three were published in his life time, *The Anatomy of the World* (1611, 1612); the satirical lines *Upon Mr. Thomas Coryat's Crudities* (1611); and the *Elegie on Prince Henry* (1613). In 1614, when about to cross the Rubicon, Donne thought of hurriedly collecting and publishing his poems before the doing so could be deemed an actual scandal to his office. He had, apparently, no autograph copies, at least of many of them, but was driven to apply to his friends, and especially to Sir Henry Goodere, the Warwickshire friend to whom the larger number of his letters are addressed.

[1] See Chap. XII.

"This made me ask to borrow that old book of you." The
edition in question never appeared, but when, in 1633, the first
collection was issued posthumously, the source was very probably this same "old book" (though Goodere had died before
Donne), for, along with the poems, were printed eight letters addressed to Goodere and one to the common friend of Goodere
and Donne, the countess of Bedford. In this edition, the poems
were arranged in a rather chaotic sequence of groups. The
volume opened with *The Progresse of the Soule* and closed
with the paraphrased *Lamentations of Jeremy* and the *Satyres*,
the latter edited with a good many cautious dashes. There are
obvious errors in the printing, but the text of such poems as this
edition contains is more correct than in any subsequent one.
In 1635, a second edition was issued, in which many fresh
poems were added, and the grouping of the poems was carried
out more systematically, the arrangement being adopted
which has been generally adhered to since, and is useful for
reference—*Songs and Sonets, Epigrams, Elegies, Epithala-
miums, Satyres, Letters to Severall Personages, Funerall Elegies,
The Progresse of the Soule, Divine Poems.* The editions which
followed that of 1635 added individual poems from various
sources, sometimes rightly, sometimes wrongly; and made
alterations from time to time in the text, conjecturally, or
with the help of MS. copies, which are sometimes emendations,
more often further corruptions. Modern editors have followed
in their wake, printing more carefully, correcting many errors,
but creating not a few fresh ones. The canon of Donne's poems
is far from being settled. Modern editions contain poems which
are demonstrably not his, while there are genuine poems still
unpublished. The text of many of his finest poems is disfigured by errors and misprints.

The order of the groups in the edition of 1635 corresponds,
roughly, to the order of composition. Donne's earliest works
were love songs or sonnets (using the word in the wider, freer
sense of the Elizabethans) and elegies (after the manner of the
Latin poets), through many of which runs a vein of pungent and
personal satire, and regular verse satires. Of these last the
editions since 1669 contain seven. We have, however, the explicit testimony of Sir William Drummond that Donne wrote
only five. It is clear, from MSS. such as Harleian 5110 and

others which have survived in whole or in part, that the first five, or some of them, were copied and circulated by themselves. These alone were included in the edition of 1633. The so-called sixth, which was added in 1635, if it be Donne's, is much more in the manner of the satirical elegies than of the regular satires; while the seventh, addressed *To Sir Nicholas Smith*, which was first inserted in the edition of 1669, an edition the text of which abounds in conjectural emendations, differs radically in style and tone from all the others, and there can be little doubt that it is the work of Sir John Roe, to whom it is assigned in more than one MS.

Donne's satires have features in common with the other imitations of Juvenal, Persius and Horace which were produced in the last decade of the sixteenth century, notably a heightened emphasis of style and a corresponding vehemence and harshness of versification. But, in verse and style and thought, Donne's satires are superior to either Hall's "dashing, smirking, fluent imitations of the ancients" or Marston's tedious and tumid absurdities. The verse of these poets is much less irregular than Donne's. It approximates more closely to the balanced couplet movement of Drayton's *Heroicall Epistles*. Hall's couplets are neat and pointed, Marston's more irregular and *enjambed*. But Donne's satiric verse shows something like a consistent effort to eschew a couplet structure, and to give to his verse the freedom and swiftness of movement to which, when he wrote, even dramatic blank verse had hardly yet attained. He uses all the devices—the main pause in the middle of the line, weak and light endings (he even divides one word between two lines)—by which Shakespeare secured the abrupt, rapid effects of the verse of *Macbeth* and the later plays:

> Gracchus loves all [*i.e.* religions] as one, and thinks that so
> As women do in divers countries go
> So doth, so is Religion; and this blind-
> Ness too much light breeds; but unmoved thou
> Of force must one, and forc'd but one allow;
> And the right? ask thy father which is she,
> Let him ask his; though truth and falsehood be
> Near twins yet truth a little elder is;
> Be busy to seek her. Believe me this,
> He's not of none, nor worst, that seeks the best.

Such verse is certainly not smooth or melodious. Yet the effect is studied and is not inappropriate to the theme and spirit of the poem. Donne's verse resembles Jonson's much more closely than either Hall's or Marston's. He had certainly classical models in view—Martial and Persius and Horace. But imitation alone will not account for Donne's peculiarities. Of the minor καλλωπίσματα of verse, he is always a little careless; but if there is one thing more distinctive than another of Donne's best work it is the closeness with which the verse echoes the sense and soul of the poem. And so it is in the satires. Their abrupt, harsh verse reflects the spirit in which they are written. Horace, quite as much as Persius, is Donne's teacher in satire ; and it is Horace he believes himself to be following in adopting a verse in harmony with the unpoetic temper of his work:

> And this unpolish'd rugged verse I chose,
> As fittest for discourse and nearest prose.

The urbane spirit of Horace was not caught at once by those who, like Donne and Jonson, believed themselves to be following in his footsteps.

The style of Donne's satires has neither the intentional obscurity of Hall's more ambitious imitations of Juvenal, nor the vague bluster of Marston's onslaughts upon vice. If we allow for corruptions of the text, one might say that Donne is never obscure. His wit is a succession of disconcerting surprises; his thought original and often profound; his expression, though condensed and harsh, is always perfectly precise. His out-of-the-way learning, too, which supplies puzzles for modern readers, is used with a pedantic precision, even when fantastically applied, to which his editors have not always done justice.

In substance, Donne's satires are not only wittier than those of his contemporaries, but weightier in their serious criticism of life, and happier in their portrayal of manners and types. In this respect, some of them are an interesting pendant to Jonson's comedies. The first describes a walk through London with a giddy ape of fashion, who is limned with a lightness and vivacity wanting to Jonson's more laboured studies of Fastidous Brisk and his fellows. The second, opening with a skit on the lawyer turned poet, passes into a trenchant onslaught—obscured by some corruptions of the text—upon the greedy and unprincipled exacter of fines from recusant Catholics, and "purchasour" of men's lands:

> Shortly (as the sea) he 'll compass all the land;
> From Scots to Wight; from Mount to Dover strand.

He is the lineal descendant of Chaucer's Man of Law, to whom all was fee-simple in effect, drawn in more angry colours. The third stands by itself, being a grave and eloquent plea for the serious pursuit of religious truth, as opposed to capricious or indolent acquiescence, on the one hand, and contemptuous indifference on the other. The lines which are quoted above in illustration of Donne's verse, and, indeed, the whole poem, were probably in Dryden's mind when he wrote his first plea for the careful quest of religious truth, and concluded that,

> 't is the safest way
> To learn what unsuspected ancients say.

These three satires are ascribed in a note on one manuscript collection to the year 1593. Whether this be strictly correct or not, they seem to reflect what we may take to have been the mind of Donne during his early years in London, at the inns of court, when he was familiar with the life of the town, but not yet an *habitué* of the court, and in a state of intellectual detachment as regards religion, with a lingering prejudice in favour of the faith of his fathers. The last two satires were written in 1597, or the years immediately following, when Donne was in the service of the lord keeper, and they bear the mark of the budding statesman. The first is a long and somewhat over-elaborated satire on the fashions and follies of court-life at the end of queen Elizabeth's reign. The picture of the bore was doubtless suggested by Horace's *Ibam forte via sacra*, but, like all Donne's types, is drawn from the life, and with the same amplification of detail and satiric point which are to be found in Pope's renderings from Horace. The last of Donne's genuine satires is a descant on the familiar theme of Spenser's laments, the miseries of suitors.

Donne's satires were very popular, and, to judge from the extant copies or fragments of copies, as well as from contemporary allusions, appear to have circulated more freely than the songs and elegies, which were doubtless confined so far as possible, like the *Paradoxes* and *ΒΙΑΘΑΝΑΤΟΣ*, to the circle of the poet's private friends. A Roman Catholic controversialist, replying to *Pseudo-Martyr*, expresses his regret that Donne has "passed beyond his old occupation of making Satires, wherein he hath some talent and may play the fool without controll." Such a writer, had he known them, could hardly have failed to make polemical use of the more daring and outrageous *Elegies* and those songs which strike a similar note. But, though less widely known, the *Songs and Sonets* and the *Elegies* contain the most intimate and vivid record of his inner soul in these ardent years, as the religious sonnets and hymns do of his later life. And the influence of these on English poetry was deeper, and, despite the temporary eclipse of metaphysical poetry, more enduring, than that of his pungent satires, or of his witty but often laboured and extravagant eulogies in verse letter and funeral elegy.

Of the *Songs and Sonets*, not one is a sonnet in the regular sense of the word. Neither in form nor spirit was Donne a Petrarchian poet. Some were written to previously existing airs; all, probably, with a more or less definite musical intention. The greater number of them would seem to have been preserved and may be found in the first section of Chambers's edition. He has rightly excluded the song, "Dear Love, continue nice and chaste," which was included in the edition of 1635, but was written by Sir John Roe. A fresh editor would have to exclude, also, the song "Soul's joy now I am gone" and the *Dialogue* beginning "If her disdain least change in you can move," which, if the collective evidence of MSS. be worth anything, were written by the earl of Pembroke, collaborating, in the last, with Sir Benjamin Ruddier. The Burley MS. contains a few songs, as well as longer pieces which, from their accompanying indubitable poems and letters of Donne, are, presumably, given as his. None of them is specially characteristic or adds anything of great intrinsic value. It has been not unusual, since its first publication as by Donne in *The Grove* (1721), to ascribe to him the charming song "Absence, hear thou my protestation." But, in Drummond's copy of a collection of verses made by Donne himself, of which only a few are his own composition, this particular song is ascribed to

J. H., *i.e.* (as another MS. proves), John Hoskins.   The touch is a shade lighter, the feeling a shade less intense, than in Donne's most characteristic work.

Of the *Elegies*, the canon is more difficult to ascertain exactly. Some of the most audacious, but not least characteristic, were excluded by the first editor, but crept into subsequent issues.   Of the twenty given in Chambers's edition, all are Donne's, with the possible exception of the twelfth, "Come, Fates, I fear you not"; and to these should be added that entitled *Love's War*, in the appendix, which was first printed by Sir John Simeon.   But the sixteenth, "To make the doubt clear that no woman's true," was included in Ben Jonson's posthumous *Underwoods*, and it is not impossible that the three which there accompany it are also Donne's. As Swinburne has pointed out, they are more in his style than in that of Jonson.   On the other hand, no MS. collection of Donne's poems includes them, whereas their companion appears in more than one.

It is not difficult to distinguish three strains in Donne's love poetry, including both the powerful and enigmatical elegies and the strange and fascinating songs.   The one prevails in all the elegies (except the famous *Autumnal* dedicated to Mrs. Herbert, and the seventeenth, the subject of which may have been his wife) and in the larger number of the lyrical pieces, in songs like "Go and catch a falling star," "Send home my long stray'd eyes to me," or such lyrics as *Woman's Constancy*, *The Indifferent*, *Aire and Angels*, *The Dreame*, *The Apparition*, and many others.   This is the most distinctive strain in Donne's early poetry, and that which contrasts it markedly with the love poetry of his contemporaries, the sonneteers.   There is no echo of Petrarch's woes in Donne's passionate and insolent, rapturous and angry, songs and elegies.   The love which he portrays is not the impassioned yet intellectual idealism of Dante, nor the refined and adoring sentiment of Petrarch, nor the epicurean but courtly love of Ronsard, nor the passionate, chivalrous gallantry of Sidney. It is the love of the Latin lyrists and elegiasts, a feeling which is half rapture and half rage, for one who is never conceived of for a moment as standing to the poet in the ideal relationship of Beatrice to Dante or of Laura to Petrarch.   *Das ewig*

Weibliche zieht uns hinan is not Donne's sentiment in these poems, but rather

> Hope not for mind in women; at their best
> Sweetness and wit, they 're but mummy possest.

But if Donne's sentiment is derived rather from Latin than from Italian and courtly poetry, it was reinforced by his experience, and it is expressed with a wit and erudition that are all his own. And, in reading some, both of the elegies and the songs, one must not forget to make full allowance for the poet's inexhaustible and astounding wit and fancy. "I did best," he said later, "when I had least truth for my subject." Realistic, Donne's love poetry may be; it is not safe to accept it as a history of his experiences.

The *Elegies* are the fullest record of Donne's more cynical frame of mind and the conflicting moods which it generated. Some, and not the least brilliant in wit and execution, are frankly sensual, the model of poems such as Carew's *The Rapture;* others, fiercely, almost brutally, cynical and satirical; others, as *The Chain* and *The Perfume*, more simply witty; a few, as *The Picture*, strike a purer note. A strain of impassioned paradox runs through them; they are charged with wit; the verse, though harsh at times, has more of the couplet cadence than the satires; the phrasing is full of startling felicities:

> I taught my silks their rustlings to forbear,
> Even my oppress'd shoes dumb and silent were;

and there are not wanting passages of pure and beautiful poetry:

> I will not look upon the quickening sun
> But straight her beauty to my sense shall run;
> The air shall note her soft, the fire most pure,
> Waters suggest her clear, and the earth sure.

This turbid, passionate yet cynical, vein is not the only one in Donne's love poetry. Two others are readily distinguishable, and include some of his finest lyrics. In one, which is probably the latest, as that described is the earliest, Donne returns a little towards the sonneteers, especially the more Platonising among them. Poems like *Twickenham Garden, The Funerall, The Blossom, The Primrose*, were probably addressed neither to the mistresses of his youth, nor to the wife of his later years, but to the high-born lady friends, Mrs. Herbert and the countess of Bedford, for whom he composed the ingenious and erudite compliments of his verse letters. Towards them, he adopts the hopeless and adoring pose of Petrarchian flirtation (of Spenser towards lady Carew or Drayton towards mistress Anne Goodere) and, in high Platonic vein, boasts that,

> Difference of sex no more we knew
> Than our guardian angels do;
> Coming and going we
> Perchance might kiss, but not between those meals;
> Our hands ne'er touched the seals
> Which nature, injured by late law, sets free;
> These miracles we did; but now alas!
> All measure and all language I should pass,
> Should I tell what a miracle she was.

Less artificial than this last strain, purer than the first, and simpler, though not less intense, than either, is the feeling of those lyrics which, in all probability, were addressed to his wife. To this class belongs the exquisite song:

> Sweetest Love, I do not go
> For weariness of thee,
> Nor in hope the world can show
> A fitter love for me.

In the same vein, and on the same theme, are the *Valediction: of Weeping:*

> O more than moon,
> Draw not up seas to drown me in thy sphere;
> Weep me not dead in thine arms, but forbear
> To teach the sea what it may do too soon;

and the more famous *Valediction: forbidding Mourning*, with its characteristic, fantastical yet felicitous, conceit of the compasses:

> Such wilt thou be to me who must,
> Like the other foot, obliquely run;
> Thy firmness makes my circle just,
> And makes me end where I begun.

The seventeenth elegy, "By our first strange and fatal interview," may belong to the same group, and so, one would conjecture, do *The Canonization*, "For Godsake hold your tongue and let me love" and *The Anniversary*. In these, at any rate, Donne expresses a purer and more elevated strain of the same feeling as animates *The Dream*, *The Sun-Rising* and *The Break of Day;* and one not a whit less remote from the tenor of Petrarchian poetry. At first sight, there is not much in common between the erudite, dialectical Donne and the peasant-poet Burns, yet it is of Burns one is reminded rather than of the average Elizabethan by the truth and intensity with which Donne sings, in a more ingenious and closely woven strain than the Scottish poet's, the joy of mutual and contented love:

> All other things to their destruction draw,
> Only our love hath no decay;
> This no to-morrow hath nor yesterday.
> Running it never runs from us away,
> But truly keeps his first, last, everlasting day.

Of the shadow of this joy, the pain of parting, Donne writes also with the intensity, if never with the simplicity, of Burns. The piercing simplicity of

> Had we never loved sae kindly

was impossible to Donne's temperament, in which feeling and intellect were inextricably blended, but the passion of *The Expiration* is the same in kind and in degree, however elaborately and quaintly it may be phrased:

> So, so, break off this last lamenting kiss,
> Which sucks two souls, and vapours both away.
> Turn thou ghost that way, and let me turn this,
> And let ourselves benight our happiest day;
> We ask'd none leave to love, nor will we owe
> Any so cheap a death as saying "Go."

The Ecstacy blends, and strives to reconcile, the material and the spiritual elements of his realistic and his Platonic strains. But, subtly and highly wrought as that poem is, its reconciliation is more metaphysical than satisfying. It is in the simpler poems from which quotations have been given that the diverse elements find their most natural and perfect union.

If Donne's sincere and intense, though sometimes perverse and petulant, moods are a protest against the languid conventionality of Petrarchian sentiment, his celebrated "wit" is no less a corrective to the lazy thinking of the sonneteers, their fashioning and refashioning of the same outworn conceits.

> The Muses' garden, with pedantic weeds
> O'er-spread, was purged by thee: the lazy seeds
> Of servile imitation thrown away,
> And fresh invention planted.

This is Carew's estimate of what Donne achieved for English poetry. He would say what he felt and would say it in imagery of his own fashioning. He owes, probably, no more to Marino or Gongora than to Petrarch. "Metaphysical wit," like *secentismo* or "Gongorism," is, doubtless, a symptom of the decadence of renascence poetry which, with all its beauty and freshness, carried seeds of decay in its bosom from the beginning. But the form which this dissolution took in the poetry of Donne is the expression of a unique and intense individuality; a complex, imaginative temperament; a swift and subtle intellect; a mind stored with the minutiae of medieval theology, science and jurisprudence. The result is often bizarre, at times even repulsive. When the fashion in wit had changed, Addison and Johnson could not see anything in Donne's poetry but far-sought ingenuity and extravagant hyperbole. His poetry has never, or never for long, the harmonious simplicity of perfect beauty; but, at its best, it has both sincerity and strength, and these are also constituents of beauty.

The intensity of Donne's feeling and the swiftness of his thought are reflected in his verse. It would not be true to say that there is nothing of the harshness of the satires in the elegies and songs. In riming couplets, Donne was always endeavouring after a fulness of thought, a freedom and swiftness of movement, which were not to be attained at once without some harshness of transition and displacement of accent, though a steady movement towards a greater degree of ease and balance can be traced from the *Satyres* and *Elegies* to the *Anniversaries* and later *Funerall Elegies*. Even in the lyrics, there are harsh lines. In verse, as in figure, Donne is careless of the minor beauties. But it is in his lyrics that he has achieved his most felicitous effects, and succeeded in making the stanza, long or short, simple or elaborate, the harmonious echo of that intimate wedding of passion and argument which is the essential quality of the "metaphysical" lyric. If we owe to the influence of Donne in English poetry some deplorable aberrations of taste, we owe to it, also, both the splendid cadences, the *élan*, of the finest seventeenth century lyrics from Jonson and Carew to Marvell and Rochester and, at a lower imaginative level, the blend of passion and argument in Dryden's ringing verse rhetoric.

During the last year of his residence in the household of Sir Thomas Egerton, Donne began the composition of a longer and more elaborate satirical poem than anything he had yet attempted, a poem the personal and historical significance of which has received somewhat scant attention from his biographers. *The Progresse of the Soule. Infinitati Sacrum.* 16 *Augusti* 1601. *Metempsycosis. Poema Satyricon* was published for the first time in 1633, but manuscript copies of the poem, by itself and in collections of Donne's poems, are extant. That he never contemplated publication is clear from the fact that he adopted the same title, *The Progresse of the Soule*, for the very different *Anniversaries* on the death of Elizabeth Drury.

Starting from the Pythagorean doctrine of metempsychosis, it was Donne's intention, in this poem, to trace the migrations of the soul of that apple which Eve plucked, conducting it, when it reached the human plane, through the bodies of all the great heretics. It was to have rested at last, Jonson told Drummond, in the body of Calvin; but the grave and dignified stanzas with which the poem opens show clearly that queen Elizabeth herself was to have closed the line of heretics whose descent was traced to the soul of Cain, or of Cain's wife:

> This soul to whom Luther and Mahomet were
> Prisons of flesh; this soul which oft did tear,
> And mend the wracks of the Empire and late Rome,
> And lived when every great change did come.

Writing to Sir Thomas Egerton in the following February, Donne disclaims all "love of a corrupt religion." Yet, during the preceding year, he had been busy on an elaborate satire, delineating, from a Catholic standpoint, the descent and history of the great heretics from Arius and Mahomet to Calvin and Elizabeth. There can be little doubt that the mood of mind which found expression in this sombre poem was occasioned by the execution of Essex in the preceding February. Nothing, for a time, so clouded Elizabeth's popularity as the death of her rash favourite. Up to the time of the outbreak, Egerton himself had been reckoned of Essex's party; and Wotton, through whom Donne had first, probably, been brought within the circle of Essex's influence, was one of those who went into exile after the earl's death.

It would have been interesting to read Donne's history of heresy, and characters of Mahomet and Luther, great, bad men as he apparently intended to delineate them; but the poem never got so far. After tracing through some tedious, not to say disgusting, episodes the life of the soul in vegetable and animal form, Donne leaves it just arrived in Themech,

Sister and wife to Cain, Cain that first did plough.

The mood in which the poem was conceived had passed, or the poet felt his inventive power unequal to the task, and he closed the second canto abruptly with a stanza of more than Byronic scepticism and scorn:

Whoe'ere thou beest that readest this sullen writ,
Which just so much courts thee as thou dost it,
Let me arrest thy thoughts; wonder with me
Why ploughing, building, ruling and the rest,
Or most of those arts whence our lives are blest,
By cursed Cains race invented be,
And bless'd Seth vex'd us with astronomy.
There's nothing simply good nor ill alone;
Of every quality comparison
The only measure is, and judge opinion.

The more normal and courtly moods of Donne's mind in these central years of his life are reflected in the *Letters* and *Funerall Elegies*. Of the former, the earliest, probably, were

The Storm and The Calm, whose vivid and witty realism first set Donne's "name afloat." When Jonson visited Edinburgh, he entertained Drummond by reciting the witty paradoxes of The Chain and the vivid descriptions of The Calm:

> No use of lanthorns: and in one place lay
> Feathers and dust, today and yesterday.

The two epistles to Sir Henry Wotton beginning "Sir, more than kisses letters mingle souls" and the above mentioned "Here's no more news than virtue," were, probably, both written in the same year, 1598. An interesting and characteristic reply to the first by Wotton is preserved in one or two manuscripts, but has never been published. The Burley MS. contains another to Wotton in Hibernia belligeranti, written, therefore, in 1599. That on Wotton's appointment as ambassador to Venice was composed five years later. To Goodere and to the Woodwards and Brookes, he wrote quite a number, in the same last years of the sixteenth century, not all of which are yet published. Those to more noble patrons, generally ladies, were the work of Donne's years of suitorship. He seems to have written none after he took orders. The long letter to the countess of Huntingdon, beginning "That unripe side of earth, that heavy clime" is assigned to Sir Walter Aston in two manuscripts; and the three short letters, to Ben Jonson and to Sir Thomas Roe, first printed in 1635, are pretty certainly not Donne's at all but Sir John Roe's.

The moral reflections in these letters are elevated, and are developed with characteristic ingenuity. The brilliance with which a train of metaphysical compliments is elaborated in such a letter as that to the countess of Bedford beginning "Madam—you have refined me" is dazzling. But neither Donne's art nor taste—to say nothing of his character—is seen to best advantage in the abstract, extravagant and frigid conceits of these epistles and of such elegies as those on prince Henry and lord Harington. The strain of eulogy to which Donne suffers himself to rise in these last passes all limits of decency and reverence. To two feelings, Donne was profoundly susceptible, and he has expressed both with wonderful eloquence in verse and prose. He has all the renascence sense of the pomp and the horror of death, the leveller of all earthly distinctions; and he can rise, like Sir Thomas Browne, to a rapt appreciation of the Christian vision of death as the portal to a better life. But his expression of both moods, when he is writing to order, is apt to degenerate into an accumulation of "gross and disgusting hyperboles." In an elegy on Mrs. Bulstred, which is divided into two separately printed poems, *Death I recant* and *Death be not proud*, these moods are combined in a sonorous and dignified strain.[1]

But the finest of Donne's funeral elegies is the second of the *Anniversaries*, which he composed on the death of Elizabeth Drury. The extravagance of his praise, indeed, offended even Jacobean readers, and the poem was declared by Jonson to be "profane and full of blasphemies." It is clear, however, that Donne intended Elizabeth Drury to be taken as a symbol of Christian and womanly virtue. He may have known something of the Tuscan poets' metaphysic of love, for Donne is one of the few poets of the day who had read "Dant." It cannot be said that he succeeded in investing his subject with the ideal atmosphere in which Beatrice moves. *The First Anniversary* is little more than a tissue of frigid, metaphysical hyberboles, relieved by occasional felicities, as the famous

> Doth not a Teneriffe or higher hill
> Rise so high like a rock, that one might think
> The floating moon would shipwreck there and sink?

The *Second*, however, is not only richer in such occasional jewels but is a finer poem. With the eulogy, which is itself managed with no small art, if in a vein of extravagance jarring to our taste, the poet has interwoven a *meditatio mortis*, developed with the serried eloquence, the intense, dull glow of feeling and the sonorous cadences which we find again in the prose of the sermons.

Of Donne's religious verses other than the funeral elegies, the earliest, *On the Annunciation and Passion falling in the same year*, was written, according to the title given in more

[1] In a manuscript collection made between 1619 and 1623, the two are given as one continuous poem. Further evidence, however, points to the conclusion that the two are distinct poems, the second, which replies to the first, being not by Donne, but, possibly, by the countess of Bedford

than one manuscript, in 1608. *The Litany* was composed in the same year as *Pseudo-Martyr;* and it is interesting to note that, though the Trinity is followed, in Catholic sequence, by the Virgin, the Angels, the patriarchs and so forth, there is no invocation of any of these, but only commemoration. The two sequences of sonnets, *La Corona* and *Holy Sonnets*, belong, the first to 1608-9, the second to the years of his ministry. One of the latter, first published by Gosse from the Westminster MS., refers to the recent death of his wife in 1617; and *The Lamentations of Jeremy* would appear to be a task which he set himself at the same juncture. The hymns *To Christ, at the Authors last going into Germany, To God, my God in my Sickness* and *To God the Father* were written in 1619, 1623-4 and either the same date or 1631.

There is a striking difference of theme and spirit between the "love-song weeds and satiric thorns" of Donne's brilliant and daring youth and the hymns and sonnets of his closing years; but the fundamental resemblance is closer. All that Donne wrote, whether in verse or prose, is of a piece. The same intense and subtle spirit which, in the songs and elegies, analysed the experiences of passion is at work in the latter on a different experience. To be didactic is never the first intention of Donne's religious poems, but, rather, to express himself, to analyse and lay bare his own moods of agitation, of aspiration and of humiliation in the quest of God, and the surrender of his soul to Him. The same erudite and surprising imagery, the same passionate, reasoning strain, meets us in both.

> Is the Pacific sea my home? Or are
> The Eastern riches? Is Jersualem?
> Anyan, and Magellan, and Gibraltar,
> All straits (and none but straits) are ways to them
> Whether where Japhet dwelt, or Ham, or Shem.

The poet who, in the sincerities of a sick-bed confession, can spin such ingenious webs for his thought is one of those who, like Baudelaire, are "naturally artificial; for them simplicity would be affectation." And as Donne is the first of the "metaphysical" love poets, he is, likewise, the first of the introspective, Anglican, religious poets of the seventeenth century. Elizabethan, and a good deal of Jacobean, religious poetry is didactic in tone and intention, and, when not, like

Southwell's, Romanist, is protestant and Calvinist but not distinctively Anglican. With Donne, appears for the first time in poetry a passionate attachment to those Catholic elements in Anglicanism which, repressed and neglected, had never entirely disappeared; and, from Donne, Herbert and his disciples inherited the intensely personal and introspective tone to which the didactic is subordinated, which makes a lyric in *The Temple*, even if it be a sermon, also, and primarily, a confession or a prayer; a tone which reached its highest lyrical level in the ecstatic outpourings of Crashaw.

Donne's earliest prose writings were, probably, the *Paradoxes* and *Problems* which he circulated privately among his friends. The Burley MS. contains a selection from them, sent to Sir Henry Wotton with an apologetic letter, in which Donne pleads that they were made "rather to deceive time than her daughter truth, having this advantage to escape from being called ill things that they are nothings," but, at the same time, adjures Wotton "that no copy shall be taken, for any respect, of these or any other my compositions sent to you." It was Donne's son who first issued them in 1633, printed so carelessly as, at times, to be unintelligible. Like everything that Donne wrote, they are brilliant, witty and daring, but, on the whole, represent the more perverse and unpleasant side of his genius. His other prose works are: a tract on the Jesuits, very similar in tone and temper to the *Paradoxes*, entitled *Ignatius his Conclave: or, His Inthronisation in a late Election in Hell*, which was published anonymously, the Latin version about 1610, the English in 1611; the serious and business-like *Pseudo-Martyr*, issued with the author's name in; 1610; *ΒΙΑΘΑΝΑΤΟΣ A Declaration of that Paradoxe or Thesis that Self-Homicide is not so Naturally Sinne that it may never be otherwise;* the *Devotions upon Emergent Occasions*, and *Several Steps in my Sickness, digested into Meditations, Expostulations and Prayers*, published in 1624; the *Essays in Divinity*, printed by his son in 1651; and the sermons.

All Donne's minor or occasional writings, except the rather perfunctory *Essays in Divinity*, partake of the nature of paradoxes more or less elaborately developed. Even *Pseudo-Martyr* irritated the Roman Catholic controversialist who replied to it by its "fantastic conceits." Of them all, the most interesting, because bearing the deepest impress of the author's individuality, his strange moods, his subtle reasoning, his clear good sense, is *ΒΙΑΘΑΝΑΤΟΣ*. It is not rightly described as a defence of suicide, but is what the title indicates, a serious and thoughtful discussion of a fine point in casuistry. Seeing that a man may rightly, commendably, even as a duty, do many things which promote or hasten his death, may he ever rightly, and as his bounden duty, consummate that process— may he ever, as Christ did upon the cross (to this Donne recurs more than once in the sermons), of his own free will render up his life to God?

But Donne's fame as a prose writer rests not on these occasional and paradoxical pieces, but on his sermons. His reputation as a preacher was, probably, wider than as a poet, and both contributed to his most distinctive and generally admitted title to fame as the greatest wit of his age, in the fullest sense of the word. Of the many sermons he preached, at Whitehall, at St. Paul's as prebend and as dean, at Linocln's inn, at St. Dunstan's church, at noblemen's houses, on embassies and other special occasions, some five were issued in his lifetime; and, after his death, three large folios were published by his son containing eighty (1640), fifty (1649) and twenty-five (1660/1) sermons respectively. Some are still in manuscript.

In Donne's sermons, all the qualities of his poems are present in a different medium; the swift and subtle reasoning, the powerful yet often quaint imagery; the intense feeling; and, lastly, the wonderful music of the style, which is inseparable from the music of the thought. The general character of the sermon in the seventeenth century was such as to evoke all Donne's strength, and to intensify some of his weaknesses. The minute analysis of the text with a view to educing from it what the preacher believed to be the doctrine it taught or the practical lessons it inculcated, by legitimate inference, by far-fetched analogy, or by quaint metaphor, was a task for which Donne's intellect, imagination and wide range of multifarious learning were well adapted. The fathers, the schoolmen and "our great protestant divines" (notably Calvin, to whom, in subtlety of exposition, he reckons even Augustine second) are his guides in the interpretation and application of his text;

and, for purposes of illustration, his range is much wider—classical poets, history sacred and secular, saints' legendaries, popular Spanish devotional writers, Jesuit controversialists and casuists, natural science, the discoveries of voyagers and, of course, the whole range of Scripture, canonical and apocryphal. It is strange to find, at times, a conceit or allusion which had done service in the love poems reappearing in the texture of a pious and exalted meditation. In the sermons, as in the poems (where it has led to occasional corruptions of the text), he uses words that, if not obsolete, were growing rare—"bezar," "defaulk," "triacle," "lation"—but, more often, he coins or adopts already coined "inkhorn" terms—"omni-sufficiency," "nullifidians," "longanimity," "exinanition."

Breadth and unity of treatment in seventeenth century oratory are apt to be sacrificed to the minute elaboration of each head, and their ingenious, rather than luminous and convincing, interconnection. But Donne's ingenuity is inexhaustible, and, through every subtlety and bizarre interpretation, the hearer was (and, even to-day, the reader is) carried forward by the weight and force of the preacher's fervid reasoning. Much of the Scriptural exegesis is fanciful or out of date. The controversial exposure of what were held to be Roman corruptions and separatist heresies has an interest mainly for the historian. In Donne's scholastic, ultra-logical treatment, the rigid skeleton of seventeenth century theology is, at times, presented in all its sternness and unattractiveness. From the extremest deductions, he is saved by the moderation which was the key-note of his church, and by his own good sense and deep sympathy with human nature. But Donne is most eloquent when, escaping from dogmatic minutiae and controversial "points," he appeals directly to the heart and conscience. A reader may care little for the details of seventeenth century theology and yet enjoy without qualification Donne's fervid and original thinking, and the figurative richness and splendid harmonies of his prose in passages of argument, of exhortation and of exalted meditation. It is Donne the poet who transcends every disadvantage of theme and method, and an outworn fashion in wit and learning. There are sentences in the sermons which, in beauty of imagery and cadence, are not surpassed by anything he wrote in verse, or by any prose of the century from Hooker's to Sir Thomas Browne's:

> The soul that is accustomed to direct herself to God upon every occasion; that, as a flower at sun-rising, conceives a sense of God in every beam of his, and spreads and dilates itself towards him in a thankfulness in every small blessing that he sheds upon her; that soul that as a flower at the sun's declining contracts, and gathers in and shuts up herself, as though she had received a blow, whensoever she hears her Saviour wounded by an oath, or blasphemy, or execration; that soul who, whatsoever string be strucken in her, base or treble, her high or her low estate, is ever tun'd towards God, that soul prays sometimes when it does not know that it prays.

The passage on occasional mercies (LXXX. 2); the peroration of the sermon on "a better resurrection" (LXXX. 22); the meditations on death, as the leveller of earthly distinctions, or the portal to a better life; the description of the death "of rapture and ecstasy" (LXXX. 27) are other passages which illustrate the unique quality, the weight, fervour and wealth, of Donne's eloquence.

Donne's letters to his friends and patrons were as much admired in and after his life-time as everything else he wrote. A few of them were issued in the first editions of the poems; a larger collection, carelessly edited and in no order, was published by his son in 1651; the interesting letters written to Sir George More and Sir Thomas Egerton were first published in Kempe's *Losely Manuscripts;* the Burley MS. contains one or two of an earlier date. Thus, they cover, though much more lightly at some parts than at others, the whole of his life from the Cadiz expedition to the year of his death. Like his poems, they paint the brilliant and insolent young man; the erudite and witty, but troubled and melancholy, suitor for court favour and office; the ascetic and fervent saint and preacher. And this is their chief interest. For some time, Donne held the position, almost, of the English *épistolier,* collections of the "choicest conceits" being made, in commonplace books, from his letters as well as his poems. But they were not well fitted to teach, like Balzac's, the beauty of a balanced and orderly prose, though they far surpass the latter in wit, wisdom and erudition. Their chief interest is the man whom they reveal, the characteristically renascence "melancholy temperament," now deep in despondence and meditating on the problem of suicide, now, in his own words, kindling squibs about himself and flying into sportfulness; elaborating erudite compliments, or talking to Goodere with the utmost simplicity and good feeling; worldly and time-serving, noble and devout—all these things, and all with equal sincerity.

The relation of Donne to Elizabethan poetry might, with some justice, be compared with that of Michael Angelo to earlier Florentine sculpture, admitting that, both as man and artist, he falls far short of the great Italian. Just as the grace and harmony of earlier sculpture were dissolved by the intense individuality of an artist intent only on the expression in marble of his own emotions, so the clear beauty, the rich ornament, the diffuse harmonies of Elizabethan courtly poetry, as we can study them in *The Faerie Queene*, *Hero and Leander*, *Venus and Adonis*, *Astrophel and Stella* or *England's Helicon*, disappear in the songs and satires and elegies of a poet who will not accept Elizabethan conventions, or do homage to Elizabethan models, Italian and French; but puts out to discover a north-west passage of his own, determined to make his poetry the vivid reflection of his own intense, subtle, perverse moods, his paradoxical reasonings and curious learning, his sceptical philosophy of love and life. It cannot be said of Donne, as of Milton, that everything, even what is evil, turns to beauty in his hands. Beauty, with him, is never the paramount consideration. If beauty comes to Donne, it comes as to the alchemist who

> glorifies his pregnant pot,
> If by the way to him befall
> Some odoriferous thing, or medicinal.

From the flow of impassioned, paradoxical argument, there will suddenly flower an image or a line of the rarest and most entrancing beauty. But the tenor of his poetry is witty, passionate, weighty and moving; never, for long, simply beautiful; not infrequently bizarre; at times even repellent.

And so, just as Michael Angelo was a bad model for those who came after him and had not his strength and originality, Donne, more than any other single individual, is responsible for the worst aberrations of seventeenth century poetry, especially in eulogy and elegy. The "metaphysical" lyrists learned most from him—the conquering, insolent tone of their love songs and their splendid cadences. In happy conceit and movement, they sometimes excelled him, though it is only in an occasional lyric by Marvell or Rochester that one detects the same weight of passion behind the fantastic conceit and paradoxical reasoning. But it is in the complimentary verses and the funeral elegies of the early and middle century (as well as in some of the religious poetry and in the frigid love poems of Cowley) that one sees the worst effects of Donne's endeavour to wed passion and imagination to erudition and reasoning.

And yet it would be a mistaken estimate of the history of English poetry which either ignored the unique quality of Donne's poetry or regarded its influence as purely maleficent. The influence of both Donne and Jonson acted beneficially in counteracting the tendency of Elizabethan poetry towards fluency and facility. If Donne somewhat lowered the ethical and ideal tone of love poetry, and blighted the delicate bloom of Elizabethan song, he gave it a sincerer and more passionate quality. He made love poetry less of a musical echo of Desportes. In his hands, English poetry became less Italian-ate, more sincere, more condensed and pregnant in thought and feeling. The greatest of seventeenth century poets, despite his contempt for "our late fantastics," and his affinities with the moral Spenserians and the classical Jonson, has all Donne's intense individuality, his complete independence, in the handling of his subjects, of the forms he adopts, even of his borrowings. He has all his "frequency and fulness" of thought. He is not much less averse to the display of erudition, though he managed it more artfully, or to the interweaving of argument with poetry. But Milton had a far less keen and restless intellect than Donne; his central convictions were more firmly held; he was less conscious of the elements of contradiction which they contained; his life moved forward on simpler and more consistent lines. With powers thus better harmon-ised; with a more controlling sense of beauty; with a fuller comprehension of "the science of his art," Milton, rather than Donne, is, in achievement, the Michael Angelo of English poetry. Yet there are subtle qualities of vision, rare intensities of feeling, surprising felicities of expression, in the troubled poetry of Donne that one would not part with altogether even for the majestic strain of his great successor.

CHAPTER XII

The English Pulpit from Fisher to Donne

THE reformation, like every other popular religious movement—the crusades, lollardy, the rise of nonconformity or the methodist revival—owed much to preachers and preaching. But it cannot be said that, in England, any more than in Germany, preachers originated the reformation, or that the reformation originated popular preaching. A new day had dawned for preaching, before Luther's influence was felt. The reproach of the neglect of preaching, which, in spite of some exaggerations, must still rest upon the fifteenth century in England, was already being rolled away in the opening years of the sixteenth, and the instigation came from orthodox quarters. For instance, in 1504, the king's mother, the lady Margaret, countess of Richmond, doubtless upon the advice of her confessor, John Fisher, established by charter a preachership. The preacher was to be a resident Cambridge fellow, with no cure of souls, and his duty was to preach once every two years in each of twelve different parishes in the dioceses of London, Ely and Lincoln. Fisher himself signalised his elevation to the see of Rochester in this same year by preaching a course of sermons upon the penitential psalms. While some of his colleagues were seldom or never heard, bishop Fisher continued to preach unremittingly, till old age obliged him to "have a chair and so to teach sitting." When he was vice-chancellor of Cambridge, he obtained a bull, allowing the university to appoint twelve doctors or masters to preach in all parts of the kingdom, "notwithstanding any ordinance or constitution to the contrary." It was Fisher, too, who advised that the Lady Margaret's Readers should give attention to preaching, and who urged Erasmus to write his treatise *Ecclesiastes, sive concionator Evangelicus.*

The renascence, also, with the marked religious character which it bore in England, could not fail to rouse interest in the pulpit. If Colet could hold the attention of doctors and students, as he expounded the Pauline epistles in an Oxford lecture-room, he might dream of a future for expository preaching from the church pulpit. His opportunity came in 1504, when Henry VII called him "to preside over the cathedral of that apostle, whose epistles he loved so much." As Erasmus tells us, Colet set about restoring the decayed discipline of the cathedral body of St. Paul's, "and—what was a novelty there —began preaching at every festival in his cathedral." Among the many statutory duties of the dean, there was none obliging him to take any part in preaching. Colet pursued his Oxford plan of delivering courses on some connected subject, instead of taking isolated texts; and what Colet did at St. Paul's perhaps inspired another dean to do the like at Lichfield. Ralph Collingwood, who may have known Colet at Oxford and must certainly have known of his doings, instituted a weekly sermon in his cathedral.

The practice of set preaching, as distinguished from the informal instruction which was the duty of every parish priest, had, therefore, received some impetus before the reformation. Yet that movement was to affect the pulpit more profoundly than the renascence and Catholic reformers were able to do. It was impatient of the "unpreaching prelates" who had not followed bishop Fisher's lead, and it afforded the preacher an audience greedy to hear him: the more controversial he was, the better they liked him. In an age when men read few books and had no newspapers, the sermon at Paul's cross or the Spital was the most exciting event of the week. Authority, whether ecclesiastical or civil, could not afford to ignore the power of the pulpit, and, therefore, sought to control it by a rigorous system of licensing. At every political crisis, general preaching was silenced and the few privileged pulpits were closely supervised by the government. At Mary's accession, her chaplain preached at Paul's cross with a guard of two hundred halberdiers; upon the very day of Mary's death, Cecil was taking steps to ensure that the next Sunday's preacher should not "stir any dispute touching the governance of the realm." The result of this strict supervision was that, in the country at large, the pulpit was often reduced to silence or to the dull fare of homilies. "A thousand pulpets in England are covered with dust," said Bernard Gilpin in a court sermon of 1552, "some have not had four sermons these fifteen or sixteen years, since friars left their limitations, and a fewe of those were worthie the name of sermons." In London, however, there was throughout the century an abundance of preaching, and it is London preaching which, almost alone, finds any place in literature.

From Fisher to Donne, almost all great preachers preached without book. William Perkins, in his *Art of Prophesying*, first published in 1592, can still speak of "the received custom for preachers to speak by heart (*memoriter*) before the people." To print a sermon gave it a second life, but it commonly entailed all the pangs of a new birth. Donne speaks of his spending eight hours over writing out a sermon which he had already preached. It was at the lady Margaret's request that Fisher's *Penitential Psalms* and his sermon preached at king Henry's lying in state were printed. Appropriately enough, the patroness of Wynkyn de Worde helped to establish the custom of committing sermons to print. The prejudice against publishing theological writings of any pretension in English had diminished since Pecock's day, but was not to disappear till Hooker's great work made a precedent. Even sermons originally delivered in English, like bishop Longland's *Tres Conciones*, were translated into Latin for publication. For another half century, divines would have to experiment with the English language before they found it a more natural medium for theological thought than the traditional Latin, with its stock of technical terms. It is, therefore, a real gain to English literature that Fisher did not count it below his dignity to issue some treatises in the vernacular, while he continued to use Latin for his larger efforts.

Fisher's literary skill is visible in his many comparisons and imageries. At times, they are homely and almost humorous, as when he recommends that men should become as familiar with death as with "these grete mastyves that be tyed in

chaynes," which "unto suche as often vysyte theym be more
gentyll and easy."   At times, the comparisons are far fetched
and over elaborated, as when he compares the Crucified to a
parchment which is stretched and set up to dry; the scourging
has left ruled lines across and the five wounds are illuminated
capitals.   The actual technique of sentence construction still
causes him some difficulty.   Long sentences do not always
come out straight.   The paragraph is neglected, and, owing to
defective punctuation, sentences are sometimes wrongly divided
and the connection in thought between one sentence and another is obscured.   Again, he cannot be acquitted of over-
working the words "so" and "such" till they give a feminine
tenderness to his writings.   Defects of this rudimentary type
are least frequent in the two funeral sermons upon Henry VII
and his mother.   Here, Fisher is at his best, and displays a
noble and sonorous rhetoric with all the charms of rhythm
and cadence.   It is impossible to doubt that, even better
than Malory, he knew what he was doing and delighted in it.
Perhaps to him first among English prose-writers it was given
to have a conscious pleasure in style.   Here is something more
than the naïve charm of the old-world story-teller; here is the
practised hand of the artist.   It is no chance that arranged
the order of words in the inventory of the dead king's treasures;

al his goodly horses so rychely dekte and appareyled, his walles
and galaryes of grete pleasure, his gradyns large and wyde with
knottes curyously wrought, his orcheyards set with vines and
trees moost delicate.

And in his description of the weeping of the countess of
Richmond's household at her death, Fisher makes as varied
and skilful use of inversion, as any writer has ever made.
Her most loyal admirer could wish the lady Margaret no fitter
commemoration than the sculpture of Torrigiano, the prose
of Fisher and the founts of Wynkyn de Worde.

In formal arrangement, as in subject-matter, Fisher belongs
to the old school of preachers.   Colet already suggests the
type of the future.   In his fondness for critical exposition of the
Scriptures, he is more modern than Fisher with his allegorical
interpretations; in his unsparing exposure of abuses, he sets
the tone to later preachers.   Colet has not Latimer's liveliness,

but he has the same courage and directness. The man who could preach humility to Wolsey at his installation as cardinal, and the injustice of war to Henry VIII and his soldiers, just setting out for the French campaign, had, at any rate, the first essential of the preacher, conviction. His very earnestness is so conspicuous that it has led some critics to think that it alone gave power to his preaching. But there was probably more art in his method than has been commonly allowed. According to Erasmus, Colet had been long preparing himself for preaching, especially by reading the English poets: "by the study of their writings he perfected his style." Some grace of expression might reasonably be expected from the man who could write the "lytelle proheme" to the grammar-book. The convocation sermon of 1512, which is the only complete specimen of Colet's preaching, was delivered, according to custom, in Latin, but there appeared almost at once an English translation, which has been assigned with some confidence to Colet himself. Its theme—the reform of moral abuses in the church—does not lend itself to imaginative or poetical treatment, but Colet shows that he quite understands how to secure variety by an inversion, and to use an effective refrain. His final appeal to his hearers, that they shall not let this convocation depart in vain, like many of its predecessors, is dignified and yet touched with feeling. Few sermons of the sixteenth century are more famous or have had a more interesting history. Thomas Smith, university librarian at Cambridge, reprinted it at the Restoration with an eye to his own times, and added notes and extracts from Andrewes and Hammond. Further reprints followed in 1701 and 1708. Burnet thought of prefacing his *History of the Reformation* by a reprint of the sermon, "as a piece that might serve to open the scene." No doubt, the theme, in all these cases, counted for more than any literary charm, but a merely bald and uninspired sermon could never have enjoyed so long a life.

When Colet died, Erasmus lamented "in the public interest the loss of so unique a preacher." At the court, Colet had already before his death made way for John Longland, dean of Salisbury, afterwards bishop of Lincoln and chancellor of Oxford university. Sir Thomas More spoke of him as "a second Colet, if I may sum up his praises in a single word."

He had considerable reputation as a preacher, but it hardly outlived his day, or the day of the unreformed faith, and his printed sermons have long been very scarce. His sermons at court were delivered in English, but they were rendered into Latin before publication. The only works printed in English were two Good Friday sermons preached before the court in 1536 and 1538. There is much which recalls Fisher in their style. It is evident that Longland, too, takes pleasure in his English writing, and can make skilful use of repetition, cumulative effects, interrogations and strings of sounding words.

Where are your taberettes, your drunslades and dowcymets? where are your vialles, your rebeckes, your shakebushes; and your sweet softe pleasaunt pypes?

Nor can he resist the charm of alliteration, when he speaks of Christ's "mooste pityous paynefull Passyon" and commends his hearers' "submysse softe and sobre mournynge voyces." Sometimes, he falls a victim to such a jangling trio as "multiloquie, stultiloquie, scurrilytye." But, if Longland has much in common with Fisher, he also anticipates Hugh Latimer in his raciness, his use of colloquial terms and his spirited indictment of the fashions in dress. Who, he asks, are they who mourn and lament in this tabernacle of the body? "The jolye huffaas and ruffelers of this wolde? the yonge galandes of the courte? . . . noo, noo, noo." Why, they study to make this body better in shape than God made it, "now with this fashion of apparel, now with that; now with this cutte and that garde. I cannot descrybe the thynge, nor I will doo." The very serving-man must spend upon one pair of hose as much as his half year's wages. "It is farre wyde and out of the nocke." If an orthodox bishop could preach before the king on a Good Friday in this free strain, the way is already prepared for Latimer's "merry toys" eleven years later.

No complete sermons of Latimer's Cambridge days have survived. In the *Sermons on the Card* we have only "the tenor and effect of certain sermons made by Master Latimer in Cambridge about the year of our Lord 1529." They are justly famous for their originality and promise and for their outspoken denunciation. But they do not compare, at least in the form in which they have come down to us, with the sermons which

he delivered before king Edward VI twenty years later. Of the
intervening period, there remain only two sermons: a short one
preached at the time of the insurrection of the north, and the
convocation sermon delivered in 1536, just after he had become
bishop of Worcester. The latter shows a great advance on
the Card sermons, and, in consideration of the occasion, was
probably composed with greater care than any other sermon
which we have. It contains the fine contrast between dead
images, covered with gold and clad with silk garments, and
"Christ's faithful and lively images . . . an hungred, a-thirst,
a-cold." The rest of Latimer's surviving sermons, thirty-
eight in number, those upon which his true fame depends,
belong to his old age. In them, he describes himself as "thor-
oughe age, boethe weake in body and oblivious." Yet this
"sore brused man," as if to make up for the years of enforced
idleness, since the Six Articles had driven him out of active
ministry, devoted the remaining years entirely to the pulpit;
he was happier there than in the bishop's throne, and "he
continued all Kyng Edwardes tyme, preaching for the most
part every Sunday two Sermons." He was a preacher first
and last, and he achieved such popular success as came to
no other English preacher till Whitefield and Wesley. Here,
at least, was a ploughman who set forward his plough, and
ploughed manfully with all his strength.

It is characteristic of his entire absorption in his pulpit
work that even the business of publishing his sermons does
not seem to have concerned him directly. Latimer's sermons
have a place in literature, but few books have had a less literary
origin. These free and easy discourses, good talking rather
than set speeches, have been written down by other hands,
probably without revision by their author. We recognise
unmistakably the ready speech of a debater, who can turn
interruptions or unforeseen accidents to account. "I came
hither to day from Lambeth in a whirry," and what the
wherryman said serves for an argument. If, in the course
of a sermon, which he has threatened to continue for three
or four hours, his hearers grow impatient and try to cough
him down, he can make a joke of it at their expense. He goes
backward and forward with his subject, and does not hesitate
to be discursive ("I will tell you now a pretty story of a friar

to refresh you withal"), or to say a good thing while he can remember it; "peradventure it myght come here after in better place, but yet I wyll take it, whiles it commeth to my mind." Even when he has worked up to a formal peroration, and ended with a text, he breaks in with "There was another suit, and I had almost forgotten it." There are repetitions, sometimes of great length, which must have been tedious even to hear. If he is pleased with a word, he will work it to death; in a Good Friday sermon he uses the word "ugsome" eight times. He can be plain, even to coarseness. Martin Marprelate might take a lesson from him in calling names: "those flattering clawbacks," "pot-gospellers," "these bladder-puffed up wily men," "flibberjibs," "upskips," "ye brain-sick fools, ye hoddy-pecks, ye doddy-pols, ye huddes." The Pharisees are represented as saying to Christ, "Master, we know that thou art Tom Truth." The Father did not intervene to save the Son but "suffred him to bite upon the brydle a whyle." No word or illustration is too homely for him to use. Latimer needed to have no thought for the dignity of literature or the conventions of reverence. He was not writing a book, but trying to keep the attention of a boy of eleven and a crowd of idle courtiers. Latimer the preacher cared for "no great curiousness, no great clerkliness, no great affectation of words, nor of painted eloquence"; he aimed only at "a nipping sermon, a rough sermon, and a sharp biting sermon."

These conditions were hardly favourable to the production of literature, but Latimer did valuable service in testing the possibilities of the language. None of his predecessors ever carried the art of story-telling to a higher point. He can take the most familiar narrative in the Bible and retell it with pointed allusions to current events. During the weeks that Latimer preached first before Edward VI, the lord high admiral, lord Seymour of Sudeley, lay in the Tower under sentence of death. Latimer hated the man and did not spare him. His hearers must have recognised in an instant what was his purpose when he began telling the story of Adonijah, "a man full of ambition, desirous of honour, always climbing, climbing." This "stout-stomached child" had Joab to help him, "a by-walker, that would not walk the king's highway." And so he went on climbing till, after David's death, he aspired to marry queen Abishag. The story, as told by Latimer, fills several pages, and yet the interest is throughout intense and dramatic, without ever a direct mention of Seymour and queen Catherine Parr.

Latimer reveals very little of the poetry and imaginative feeling which are conspicuous in Fisher's writing. There is seldom any illustration from nature, or any flights of what can be called eloquence. The personification which he makes of Faith—"a noble duchess with her gentleman usher going before her, and a train after her"—is not a characteristic feature of his style; but he is seemingly pleased with it, and uses it again a few weeks later to the same audience. The allegories which had been the stock-in-trade of earlier preachers he explicitly rejects; if he wants illustration, he draws from his experience of the market-place and the court. He prefers the wherryman's "good natural reason" to the arguments of the whole college of cardinals. Ever since his conversation with little Bilney, he "forsook the school-doctors and such fooleries." At the end of his great Lenten course, he claims that he has walked "in the brode filde of scripture and used my libertie." He has no taste for theological subtleties; "as for curiouse braynes nothinge can content them." There is some rough sledge-hammer controversy with papists and ana-baptists, but his real bent is towards practical questions; and that is one reason why he continues to interest readers of a later day. No one to-day stands where Latimer did in doctrinal theology but bribery is still bribery. One cannot imagine a more telling point in a discourse on bribery than when the preacher said, "He that took the silver basin and ewer for a bribe, thinketh that it will never come out; but he may now know that I know it."

It is his passionate desire to right social wrongs which gives Latimer his highest claim to be called a great preacher. He is never belabouring sin in the abstract but accurately diagnoses and fearlessly exposes the injustices of his time. The decay of discipline and reverence, and the wholesale spirit of greed, which accompanied the breaking up of the old order, are faithfully dealt with by the prophet of the new order. The lay landlords who have supplanted monastic landowners he calls step-lords; rent-raising, enclosures, idleness, covetousness and

all the other faults of the rich are denounced to their faces:
" be you never so great lords and ladies," the preacher " will
rub you on the gall." The impoverishment of schools and
universities, the corruption of judges, and the tricks of the
trades are unsparingly treated, and Latimer has the preacher's
best reward of seeing some wrongs redressed as a result of his
agitation. The poor and the oppressed have had no truer
friend at court than Latimer preaching before Edward VI.

Bishop Hooper, who succeeded Latimer as court preacher,
had equal courage, but less human sympathy. For his Lenten
course in 1550, he chose " a very suitable subject, namely the
prophet Jonas, which will enable me freely to touch upon the
duties of individuals." His chief aim was to urge the king
to use the arm of the law against unpreaching clergy, covetous
lawyers, thieves, adulterers, swearers and other offenders.
The king must show no "preposterous pity." The ship of
the commonwealth cannot sail in quiet waters, until the
mariners cast out all Jonases. "Into the sea with them,"
cries this vehement orator. There is a native vigour about
his denunciations, but he takes no pains to make his message
attractive. His grammar is often faulty and his illustrations
are trite: he uses the stock story of Cambyses and the judge's
skin, which Latimer used to the same audience the previous
Lent, and which Fisher used before either of them. His
humour, when he shows any, is of the broadest kind; if the
newly-ordained priest according to the first reformed ordinal
is to be given the chalice to hold, why do they not as well give
him the font?

The older generation of reformers was soon finding valuable
recruits for the work of preaching. Bishop Ridley had particular success in discovering able men and promoting them. In
1550, he ordained two Lancashire and Cambridge men—John
Bradford of Pembroke, the converted lawyer, whom he made
his chaplain and a prebendary of St. Paul's, and Thomas Lever,
fellow and, afterwards, master of St. John's college. Ridley
grouped Bradford and Lever with Latimer and Knox as the
most incisive preachers of the age. Bradford's short career was
ended by his imprisonment and martyrdom in 1555. Lever
lived on far into Elizabeth's reign, and was among the most
distinguished of the first nonconformists. Three fruitful ser-

mons of the year 1550 remain **to vindicate** his right to be
remembered as a preacher to Edward VI. The "yonge simple scholar," as he describes himself, shows remarkable self-
confidence, and is prepared to be thought "sumwhat saucye"
for his hitting out freely. "Thus hath God by Esaye in his
tyme, and by me at this tyme, described Rulers Faultes, with
a way how to amend them." Parsons who do not reside on
their cures, covetous landlords who let their labourers'
cottages go into decay and "turn all to pasture," "covitous
carles" who "forstall the markettes and bye corn at all tymes,
to begynne and encrease a dearth," judges who take bribes
and give wrong judgments, all come under Lever's lash, especially when he is preaching before the king. It is particularly
to his credit that he does not blink his eyes to the evils which
have grown up out of the reformation. If the abolition of ab-
beys, chantries and guilds has only enriched covetous men,
and actually set back the condition of schools and universities,
then it is time to look to these Judases which have the bag.
Lever does not resemble Latimer only in his fiery denunciation
of social wrongs, but has also something of his rough humour
and racy vernacular. In such a passage as the following,
where he attacks those lay-rectors who put in an incompetent
and underpaid curate to serve the parish, we might believe
ourselves to be reading Latimer himself.

Yes, forsoth, he ministreth Gods sacramentes, he sayeth his
servyce, and he readeth the homilies as you fyne flatring courtiers,
which speake by imagination, tearme it: But the rude lobbes of the
countrey, whiche be to symple to paynte a lye, speake foule and
truly as they fynde it, and saye: He ministreth Gods sacraments,
he slubbers up his service, and he cannot reade the humbles.

But Lever does not maintain our interest like his predecessor,
and he has some irritating affectations. Few writers before or
since can have abused more completely the habit of grouping
words in triplets. He will pursue this same trick through
clause after clause:

From whence shal we that be governors, kepers, and feders, bye
and provide with our own costes, labor and diligence, bread, foode
and necessaryes, etc.?

John Bradford's preaching is represented by two sermons, which afford an interesting contrast to one another. The first, on repentance, unlike most of the other extant sermons of that period, was not a London sermon, but was delivered "as I was abroad preaching in the country." He was with much difficulty persuaded to print it. Once before, when he had been diffident about his preaching, Bucer had counselled him, "If thou have not fine manchet bread, give the pore people barley bread." He had considerable learning, but he was probably not a practised writer, and he certainly gets into difficulties with long sentences. He tries to satisfy the prevailing taste for alliteration, and produces astounding examples with as many as eight words in sequence. The most interesting literary feature is his free use of colloquial and provincial words. More than any preacher of his age, he requires a glossary for the modern reader. He has a plentiful supply of similes and metaphors, but they are often tasteless and undignified. Still, he is always forcible and, upon fitting occasion, can be eloquent.

This death of Christ therefore look on as the very pledge of God's love toward thee, whosoever thou art, how deep soever thou hast sinned. See, God's hands are nailed, they cannot strike thee: his feet also, he cannot run from thee; his arms are wide open to embrace thee: his head hangs down to kiss thee: his very heart is open.

Bradford's other sermon was not published till nearly twenty years after his death. It was, perhaps, preached to his fellow-prisoners in queen Mary's reign before they took the Sacrament together, as their gaolers suffered them to do. It was, at any rate, written where he had no access to books, as he expressly says. The sermon was sent in manuscript, with other of Bradford's writings, to his friend Ridley for corrections. Whether the older writer pruned away any extravagances of style, or whether Bradford had himself learnt better, there are few traces left of the tricks and provincialisms which had disfigured his first sermon. His theme, the Lord's Supper, almost necessitated controversial treatment, but he sets out his argument with clearness and learning and religious feeling.

Another famous preacher made a single appearance at

king Edward's court, and, like many of his immediate predecessors, found empty benches. Yet no one had arisen since
Latimer who deserved a hearing better than Bernard Gilpin.
If the courtiers had attended, they would have heard a sermon
as free from literary affectations and almost as entertaining
as the sermon on the Plough.

In the more settled times of Elizabeth's reign, there begin
to appear sermons of a different order. Hitherto, the typical
vernacular sermon has been a popular harangue. If it is to
make a hit, it must aim low. A sermon at Paul's cross before
a demonstrative crowd must use the methods of the hustings
rather than of the lecture-room. But, since the reformation
began, a generation had grown up which was habituated to
theological controversy, and was interested in its technicalities.
Such men as Jewel, Hooker, Perkins and Rainolds address
their appeal, with what success they may, to the best intelligence in the country. Tirades and appeals to prejudice must
make way for arguments and appeals to antiquity. The
fathers and doctors are cited, and doctrinal statements are
minutely analysed and discussed. The effects of this change
on literature are both favourable and unfavourable. Undoubtedly, the progress of controversy taught men to express themselves clearly upon difficult topics. It may occasion surprise
that men like Jewel and Sandys should have so soon acquired
facility of expression. Their style may lack distinction or
charm, but at least it is adequate. Latimer can keep straight
with his short sentences and concrete themes. Elizabethan
preachers have to grapple with deep points of theology, and
yet can present them lucidly and methodically, without losing
their way in their more involved sentences. On the other hand,
the very weight of the matter, its technical character and its
array of authorities, are unfavourable to the production of an
attractive prose-style. There is little room for grace or fancy
in these learned and scholastic performances. Still, it is
much that they should have worked out for themselves the
means of expressing their thought in perfectly clear and un-
mannered English. It is a pleasure, for instance, to read
anything which says what it means so exactly and so easily
as does Jewel's famous Challenge sermon. Sandys was induced
at the close of his life to write out for publication twenty-two

of his sermons. The literary ability which distinguished his sons is not absent from the father's writing. His sentences are well-built, with a strict avoidance of any mannerism or exaggeration. There is never any excess of ornament, nor any lapse from good taste, except when the Roman controversy proves too much for him. His frequent quotations from St. Bernard and St. Chrysostom, from Horace and Terence, indicate the newer style of literary preaching.

The friendship of Sandys and Jewel, who were once "companions at bed and board in Germany," had important consequences for a greater than either, Richard Hooker. Jewel, himself a Devonshire man, befriended the promising Exeter boy, and sent him to his old college of Corpus Christi at Oxford, where another Devonian and famous preacher, John Rainolds, was his tutor. Jewel died when Hooker was in his nineteenth year, but he had already commended him to the notice of bishop Sandys, who sent his son Edwin to be under Hooker's tuition, and, afterwards, furthered his promotion to the mastership of the Temple. There is no need to deal in detail with Hooker's sermons, because they reflect the same great qualities, both in thought and expression, which have been already discussed in another volume of the present work.[1] But no account of Elizabethan preachers would be complete without some mention of the only name among them which has an assured place in the first rank   Hooker published none of his sermons; as Izaak Walton says, it was only the *felix error* of Travers's opposition which caused him to write out for private circulation some of the sermons to which the Reader had taken exception. Though Hooker's fame depends chiefly on his *Ecclesiastical Polity*, we should have been immeasurably the poorer for the loss of his sermons on the certainty of faith, justification and the nature of pride, which have more permanent value than any sermons of the reign. Samuel Taylor Coleridge wrote of the first:

I can remember no other discourse, that sinks into and draws up comfort from the depths of our being below our own distinct consciousness, with the clearness and godly loving-kindness of this truly evangelica and God-to-be-thanked-for sermon;

[1] See Vol. III., pp. 460 ff.

and he declared that one paragraph should be written in letters of gold. This testimony is valuable as showing that, in his sermons, Hooker could appeal to the feeling and the conscience, as successfully as in his book he appealed to the reason.

There is yet a further service which Hooker rendered to the contemporary pulpit. Here, as in his book, he set the tone of a controversialist who was not content to be barely just to an opponent but sought to find common ground with him. Jewel, for instance, though he abandons the scurrility of earlier protestant champions, fights hard to maintain the scandal of pope Joan and even takes as an axiom, "Let us remember to do the contrary" of what those before the reformation had done. The puritan divine Edward Dering could say outright, "Now we know the Pope to be anti-christ, and his prayers to be evill"; and similar bitterness mars the sermons of Rainolds. While such language was still prevalent, Hooker had the courage and the breadth of mind to assert that "the Church of Rome is a true Church of Christ, and a sanctified Church." He reverenced truth, as he conceived it, wherever he found it. This attitude in itself could not fail to affect the methods of the pulpit. When Hooker set himself to persuade, and not to denounce or "frighten men into piety," it led him, as his biographer acutely observed, to use another kind of rhetoric.

Probably Henry Smith, alone among Elizabethan preachers, shares with Hooker the distinction of finding modern readers. Hooker's sermons were as well suited to the learned auditory of the Temple as Smith's were to the popular congregation of St. Clement Danes. But "the silver-tongued preacher" knew that "to preach simply is not to preach rudely, nor unlearnedly, nor confusedly." He had no patience with the drones who "by their slubbering of the word (for want of study and meditation) do make men think that there is no more wisdom in the word of God than they shew out of it." We find ourselves in a different atmosphere from that of the controversial sermon, and hear instead plain moral duties set out with homely illustrations and playful turns: "The devil is afraid that one sermon will convert us, and we are not moved with twenty; so the devil thinketh better of us than we are." Some of his sermons, printed during his life-time, are described on the title-page as "taken by characterie and after examined." Whether in separate or in collected form, no sermons of the age were more frequently printed.

The strict enforcement of the penal laws, and the limited and furtive nature of their opportunities of church worship, prevented Roman Catholics in England from contributing to the general store of printed sermons.   Controversial and devotional writings exist in sufficient quantity to show that there were men who might have made good use of happier times.   Edmund Campion's letters are attractive, Parsons's *Christian Directory* received the compliment of many protestant editions, and the rich fancy of Robert Southwell's tracts won the praise of Francis Bacon.

The puritan tendency to exalt the sermon was not without its dangers to religious life, and had not an altogether wholesome influence on the sermon itself.   In the times when religion flourished most, said Hooker, men "in the practice of their religion wearied chiefly their knees and hands, we especially our ears and tongues."   Bishop Andrewes, in an earnest sermon on the text, "Be ye doers of the word and not hearers only," urged that St. James's teaching was specially needed in an age " when hearing of the word is growen into such request, that it hath got the start of all the rest of the parts of God's service"; "sermon-hearing is the *Consummatum est* of all Christianitie."   It affected the preaching of Andrewes himself adversely, when the pedantic king James I and his courtiers crowded to hear a sermon as an intellectual entertainment. Andrewes spoke out of bitter experience when he said of Ezekiel's contemporaries,

they reemed to reckon of sermons no otherwise than of songs: to give them the hearing, to commend the aire of them, and so let them goe.   The Musike of a song, and the Rhetorique of a sermon, all is one.

If this common attitude towards the sermon encouraged the preacher to spend pains upon the literary workmanship of his sermon, it also robbed him of that which gives wings to his rhetoric and can alone make it tolerable, namely, the force of conviction.   Ingenious types and metaphors, paradoxical illustrations, verbal conceits, grammatical subtleties, may be useful allies; but, in the sermons of the period, they were apt to be valued for themselves. Exquisite pains were lavished upon the exposition, but the application was not pressed home.

Happily, there can be no question of bishop Andrewes's personal piety and earnestness. The witness of his contemporaries agrees with the witness of his *Private Devotions*. In his preaching, he gave in too much to the mannerisms of the day and the taste of his audience, but the holiness of his inner life and the sincerity of his aims were not doubted by the most frivolous, or without influence upon a corrupt court. His life forms a link between several ages. He was born in the year that Latimer was burnt, he lived to see Charles I crowned and Milton wrote a Latin elegy upon his death. Few men have owed more to their schoolmasters and few have acknowledged their debt more handsomely. Samuel Ward of Ratcliffe, to whom he afterwards gave the rectory of Waltham, discovered his merit, and prevented his parents from making a 'prentice of him. Richard Mulcaster, the first headmaster of Merchant Taylors' school, secured him for the new school. Andrewes "ever loved and honoured his Master Mulcaster . . . and placed his picture over the doore of his Studie; whereas in all the rest of the house, you could scantly see a picture." At Pembroke hall, Cambridge, he became, in succession, scholar, fellow and master. He was always "a singular lover and encourager of learning and learned men," and his friendship with Casaubon and their enthusiastic studies at Ely form one of the most attractive pictures in the history of scholarship. His stores of erudition and his knowledge of many languages were fitly employed in the translation of the *Pentateuch* for the *Authorised Version;* they were less felicitously used in his sermons, where they sometimes cumber the ground. His knowledge of the fathers was wider than his knowledge of men, and his one intrusion into secular life, in the matter of the Essex divorce, was disastrous and bitterly repented.

His sermons were collected for publication by the command of Charles I, who was "graciously pleased to thinke a paper-life better than none," though the editors, Laud and Buckeridge, were well aware that the printed sermons "could not live with all that elegancie which they had upon his tongue." His preaching owed as much to his perfect delivery as Hooker's lost by his diffidence. After-ages will always find the contemporary opinion of Andrewes's sermons extravagant, but, in spite of the most exasperating faults of style, there is much to praise. He prefers to tread the well-worn highway of common Christianity, and will not easily be drawn either into the Roman controversy or into the insoluble "deep points" of predestination and the like, in which puritan preachers often lost themselves. The determination to extract the most possible from the sacred text leads him into over-nice distinctions, till he can only express himself with the help of brackets, and even of brackets within brackets. Yet, notwithstanding his clumsy apparatus, finicking exegesis and tortuous language, he commonly rewards the reader's patience. The remark of the presbyterian lord to James I at Holyrood, "No doubt your Majesty's bishop is a learned man, but he cannot preach. He rather plays with his text than preaches on it," is not the whole truth. The texts which Andrewes took for his great series of Christmas and Good Friday sermons are permanently enriched by the musings of his devout mind.

It is unfortunately easy to trace the influence of Andrewes upon the younger preachers of his times. The Andrewes tradition lasted far on into the century, and, in the hands of lesser men, it lost the life which the genius of Andrewes had been able to infuse into it. When, at last, it was superseded by preaching of a plainer and sincerer style, bishop Burnet wrote its epitaph:

The impertinent way of dividing texts is laid aside; the needless setting out of the originals and the vulgar version is worn out. The trifling shews of learning, in many quotations of passages, that very few can understand, do no more flat the auditory.

John Donne, although eighteen years younger than Andrewes, survived him only six years. While Laud, Montagu, Ussher and Hall were destined to preach to another age, Donne preached only to the age which knew Andrewes. From the first, it must have been inevitable to compare the two most famous preachers of James I's reign. Both are deeply read in the fathers and love to quote them in their original languages. Neither can resist the fanciful imagery and verbal conceits that their age loved. Yet, though they work with the same clay, the one achieves a success in spite of his clumsiness, the other is a finished artist. Andrewes is read with difficulty for the sake of his matter; Donne is read by many who care little for his theology. Yet Donne was not simply a man of letters caring more for his style than for his matter. He impressed his own age, as he impresses the reader of to-day, with his tremendous earnestness. Whether the reasons which brought him to enter the ministry in his forty-second year were adequate or not, he gave himself to his new calling with an evergrowing sense of his responsibility. He took the most exacting view of the preacher's office, and would excuse "no man's laziness, that will not employ his whole time upon his calling." In one of his Candlemas sermons, he discusses the preacher's business and maintains the need of preaching to the educated and the court in a different style from that which will suit the simple. It was Donne's *métier*, more than that of any man then alive, to preach to "the learneder and more capable auditories" that the times had produced. The honourable society of Lincoln's inn got the preacher they wanted, and parted from him with regrets and fervent gratitude. At St. Paul's, he gave himself more preaching duties than had fallen to previous deans, and a sermon from him was an occasion of which fashionable London took advantage.

It is a little surprising that a man of his literary experience published only a few occasional sermons, such as the first sermon preached to king Charles, printed by royal command, or the sermon in commemoration of George Herbert's mother, lady Danvers. A partial explanation is that his sermons, for the most part, were not ready for the press. It was not till the plague of 1625 drove him out of London and gave him some months' leisure, that he set to work upon them. In a letter of this year (25 November) he wrote:

I have revised as many of my sermons as I have kept any note of and I have written out a great many, and hope to do more. I am already come to the number of 80, of which my son, who, I hope will take the same profession, or some other in the world of understanding, may hereafter make some use.

Again, in 1630, he utilised a time of sickness at Abrey Hatch in "revising my short notes." Doubtless this free revision enabled the author to write at greater length than he had preached. Nine years after his father's death, John Donne the younger published *Eighty Sermons;* but they cannot be identical (as Gosse suggests) with the eighty mentioned by Donne in 1625, since many of this first folio belong to a later date. A second volume and a third appeared later, forming together a larger library of sermons than Andrewes or any other divine had yet furnished.

"There is some degree of eloquence required in the delivery of God's messages," wrote Donne, and he intended to use all the literary craft he had learnt to give life to his sermons. Sometimes, his rich fancy leads him into sheer extravagance or paradox. Sometimes, his delight in assonant words will make him speak of "a comminatory or commonitory cross," or he will end a paragraph with portentous sesquipedalians, "irreparably, irrevocably, irrecoverably, irremediably." Coleridge disliked "a patristic leaven" in him, and Hallam said roundly that he had perverted his learning "to cull every impertinence of the fathers and schoolmen." Yet few readers would willingly spare the penitent's fond references to "that blessed and sober father," St. Augustine. His wit, his learning and his poetic feeling are far more often turned to profit than used for display. The old wit has still its use when he can write, "The devil is no recusant; he will come to church, and he will lay his snares there." And his poetic fancy can take unceasing delight in the metaphors of the Bible and marshal his rhythmical periods.

The obscurity of Donne's sermons has been often exaggerated. No doubt they would be difficult to follow with the ear only, but we have no means of knowing how closely the printed sermon recalls the preacher's words. In spite of his profusion of metaphors and similes, he seldom leaves us in any doubt of his meaning, and he can be as simple as any man without being ordinary. It is less easy to say that we always know whither he is taking us. Every reader must be conscious of a certain arbitrariness in his treatment. And we must particularly notice how his sombre cast of thought, and his severe view of his own past failings, are apt to assert themselves in unexpected quarters. Andrewes and he begin a Christmas sermon on the same text, but Donne soon loses the Christmas feeling and brings us face to face with death and judgment to

come. Death has been called the preacher's great commonplace. Donne repeatedly comes back to this topic, but,
with him, it is never commonplace. Never does he hold us
more in thrall than when he warns in solemn, measured and
impassioned tones of that which " comes equally to us all, and
makes us all equal when it comes."

CHAPTER XIII

Robert Burton, John Barclay and John Owen

IT has been rightly observed that the first half of the seventeenth century may be reckoned eminently the learned age, and the authors who form the subject of the present chapter carry, each in his own way, this mark of the period.   Two of these, the epigrammatist Owen and Barclay the writer of satire and romance, delivered themselves in Latin, one producing the best known body of Latin epigrams since Martial, the other the most famous work in Latin prose fiction since Apuleius.   From Burton, we have his own confession that it was not his original intention to "prostitute his muse in English," but, could a printer have been found, to publish his huge medical and moral treatise in Latin.   Yet, while the frame of the book is in his native English, Latin is never far away.   We find it in phrases interwoven with the text, in formal citation on page or margent, visible through the paraphrase of the sources from which he drew.   Composition in Latin, at a time when that language was still international, was, in itself, no special sign of learning, but Barclay and Owen give proof of wide and apt knowledge, and possess an individual style and flavour.   In their day, they are remarkable instances of men of real literary inspiration, who chose to speak in a past tongue. For width of reading, rather than precise scholarship, Burton may count among the most learned of English men of letters. The study of all three was Man.   To a modern mind, the way in which tradition and direct experience often lie side by side unblended in seventeenth century literature is strange.   An eager interest in human character and activity consorted with something that is hard to distinguish from pedantry.   But the

impulse of the classics was then stronger if less delicate, and
the relation between life and books has been variously apprehended at various epochs.

The three differ in their lives, literary performance and
subsequent fate. Owen, a Welshman, educated at Winchester
and Oxford, showed, while devoid of the higher qualities of
a poet, a surprising readiness and dexterity in sallies of verbal
wit. Barclay, courtier and cosmopolitan, born in Lorraine of a
Scottish father, spending his manhood in London and Rome,
after writing a satirical fiction in his youth, combined, later, in
a romance of elevated and serious tone, imaginative power
with an acute judgment in the treatment of political questions.
Burton the Englishman, an Oxford resident and priest in the
Anglican church, "by profession a divine, by inclination a
physician," devoted his large leisure to the elaboration of a
work which, while technical in its immediate aim, became, because of its author's vast reading, a storehouse of multifarious
learning; because of his disposition, a book of satirical though
kindly humour; and, because of the subject itself, a panorama
and criticism of human life.

The success achieved by each was remarkable. Owen's
first volume was reprinted within the month. Six editions of
Burton's voluminous treatise appeared within thirty years.
Barclay's chief work, which was posthumous, was reissued on
an average once a year during the half century that followed
the author's death. The sphere and period of their popularity
were not the same. Owen and Barclay, composing in Latin,
quickly attained a continental reputation, and were translated
into the principal languages of Europe; Burton, writing in
English, was practically unknown across the Channel. The
fame of all suffered eclipse, at one time, through changes of
literary fashion. Owen, though his production is less bulky
and his merit more on the surface, is still strangely neglected.
Barclay, since 1674, has been the subject of many learned
monographs. *The Anatomy of Melancholy*, revived by men
of genius in the early years of the nineteenth century, the
haunt of the literary, rather than the province of professed
students, alone continues to be reprinted. It is Burton,
beyond doubt, who, of the three, has best preserved his
vitality.

Robert Burton is ften spoken of as though his personality were quite exceptiona., his book an unparalleled piece of eccentricity.   But much which might seem peculiar to him is, in reality, shared with other writers of his time.   It is no paradox to assert that Burton is representative of the nation and period to which he belongs.   He was of English ancestry in the fullest sense, a native of that midland district which has given us his great contemporary, Shakespeare.   His family had been settled there for many generations, and an ancestor in the fifth degree had borne king Henry VI's standard in France. Burton's own career was normal and uneventful.   He was a permanent resident in Oxford at a time when the number of students at our English universities bore a higher proportion to the population of the country than at any subsequent period.[1]   In his large interest in life, his humorous, half-ironical sympathy with his fellow men and his shrewd commonsense, he was a typical Englishman; English, also, in his tendency to overflow the channels of his thought, in his want of that delicate sense of measure more commonly associated with the Latin races.

Before entering Oxford, Burton had acquired the usual grammar school training of his day, which did not include a belief in a rigid canon of Latin authors.   While ability to read and write Latin was a chief aim of school education, the classics were regarded as sources of wisdom and not merely as models of literary form, and writers of the renascence were even admitted to a place beside those of the Roman republic and empire.

As a student of Christ Church and keeper of his college library, enjoying, too, the advantages of the newly founded Bodleian, Burton had ample opportunity for study.   He held some small ecclesiastical preferments, and there are indications that he would have been glad to obtain more substantial promotion. Anecdotes about him must be received with caution. His book became so much better known than himself that there was probably a tendency to draw inferences from his work to his person, and to emphasise such details of his life as seemed most in keeping with his character as an author.

[1] Venn, *Biographical History of Gonville and Caius College*, vol. 1, pp. xx, xxi.

The whisper of suicide which Anthony à Wood mentions was, presumably, based on the last lines of the "Abstract of Melancholy" prefixed to the third and later editions of *The Anatomy*, or on a phrase on his monument in Christ Church. Burton, who was "by profession a divine," declared that he might, had he chosen, have published sermons, but he had "ever been desirous to suppress his labours in this kind." The nature of his sermons may fairly be inferred from the section on "Religious Melancholy." His extant minor works consist of his academic Latin play *Philosophaster* and occasional Latin verse—elegies, epithalamia and the like—scattered through university collections. His Latin comedy, the theme of which is the trickery and exposure of pretenders to learning in a Spanish university, the arch-villain being a Jesuit, is ingenious and diverting and of special interest as containing, in many places, thoughts and expressions that can be paralleled in *The Anatomy*. The lyrics, few but effective, are in rime. The metre of the dialogue, even after allowance has been made for inevitable ignorance of Plautine and Terentian prosody, is rough.

The first edition of *The Anatomy of Melancholy* appeared in 1621, in the same year as Barclay's *Argenis*. In modern days, at least, *The Anatomy* has been read rather in parts than as a whole, and some misunderstanding has prevailed as to its purpose. It has been regarded as a mere conglomerate of miscellaneous excerpts, as a colossal jest, and the synopsis prefixed to each of the three parts as nothing but a parody. A study of the work in its entirety should convince a reader that, however curious in some of its developments, Burton's main object was the practical one that he himself proclaimed. The present Regius professor of medicine at Oxford, while speaking with keen appreciation of its literary qualities, has pronounced *The Anatomy* "a great medical treatise, orderly in arrangement, serious in purpose." [1]

The introduction, "Democritus Junior to the Reader," after justifying the assumed name, the title, the choice of subject and the method, shows, by "a brief survey of the world," that melancholy is "an inbred malady in every one of us." The first partition deals with the definition, causes, symptoms

---

[1] Unpublished lecture on Robert Burton by W. Osler.

and properties of melancholy; the second (and shortest) with the cure; the third, in its final form by far the longest, with the definition, symptoms and cure of the two distinct species, love melancholy and religious melancholy. "The Conclusion of the Author to the Reader," with which the first edition ends, did not appear again; but it has not always been observed that a large proportion was incorporated in the introduction.

Though the book is primarily a treatise on melancholy, the elasticity of the term, the universality of the disease and the elaboration with which Burton tracks its several phases, extend the subject to the life of man. The writer's temperament, matched with his theme, exhibits him not merely as the physician of body and soul, but as a satirist, a humorist and a social and political reformer, in which last character he constructs the ideal Utopia of his introduction. The general literary aspect of *The Anatomy* has so far overpowered the medical, that Fuller could speak of it as a "book of philology."

Burton's is one of those minds whose interest in human emotion, conduct and character expresses itself in a meditative, rather than in a dramatic, form. But he is not confined to man's nature in the abstract. *The Anatomy* is peopled with men and women. Many a great name from history is there; and instances, various and picturesque, of affliction and healing, gathered by Burton from physicians' records—the young maid in *Amatus Lusitanus* that would wash her hair in the heat of the day; the strange malady of Katherine Gualter, a cooper's daughter; the country fellow that had four knives in his belly, with other baggage; the merchant from Nordeling that fancied he had lost his money at the fair; the painful preacher at Alkmaar in Holland and countless other cases.

Panoramic effects are frequent, arising from the author's fertility and readiness in enumeration. In this impression of multitudinousness, he recalls in different ways both Rabelais and Whitman. A most characteristic example of the torrential manner in which Burton's memories are poured forth is his rhapsody of the world of books in the member on "Exercise rectified."

Burton's humour is pervasive and inseparably intertwined with his irony and the kindly commonsense of his attitude to life. Comparisons are dangerous, but it may safely be said that in Burton there are touches of Montaigne, and contact in his character with the most English of our writers, Chaucer and Fielding. Jusserand points to his kinship with Izaak Walton in his susceptibility to the charm of country life.

Neither in thought nor in style can he rival the subtlety of Sir Thomas Browne, to whom he has been compared and with whom he certainly has this in common that the same readers seem drawn to both. Though he cannot pretend to the serene impartiality of *Religio Medici*, Burton, in his theological views, shows a widely tolerant spirit. We see him at his highest in "Religious Melancholy," especially in "The cure of despair," though this is not the only place in which his grave pathos is felt, and his tenderness for the "fear and sorrow" of others that he must have known himself.

The extent to which the words and names of other authors appear in *The Anatomy of Melancholy* is, undoubtedly, its most striking external feature. But the practice of profuse quotation was not peculiar to Burton. It was an age when appeal lay to tradition and authority, and the tendency was fostered by the formation of libraries. The attitude of a typical scholar of the day has been summed up by his modern biographer, "If a great writer has said a thing, it is so."[1] It was the fashion of the time to quote by way of proof or illustration, in talk, in writing, from the pulpit. No exposition or argument could be conducted "without refreshment on the road from Jerome or from Athanasius." In enforcing the most familiar of truisms, men appealed to the classics without fear of consequences. The pretender to learning had perforce "his sentences for Company, some scatterings of *Seneca* and *Tacitus*."[2] The difference between Burton and his contemporaries is one of degree:

No man in his time did surpass him for his ready and dexterous interlarding his common discourses among them with verses from the Poets, or sentences from classic authors: which being then all the fashion in the University made his company the more acceptable.[3]

[1] Pattison, *Isaac Casaubon*, p. 442.
[2] Earle, *Micro-Cosmographie*, character 31.
[3] Anthony à Wood.

Indeed, if the occasion be considered, the wealth of ancient instances, of Greek and Latin in Taylor's sermon, "The House of
Feasting," is as surprising a phenomenon as anything in Burton.
Taine, "superseding the facts by a statement of his own subjective consciousness," has spoken of Burton's casting on paper
"a folio column of heraldry" and "the history of the particle
que," but, though Burton modestly spoke of his work as a
"cento" that he had "collected out of divers writers," there
is always reason and method in his borrowings. He never
flung his commonplace book in the face of the public.

Undoubtedly, Burton possessed an inordinate appetite for
books, a *cacoethes legendi*. He confesses to a "want of art" and
"order" in his reading; "I have confusedly tumbled over divers
authors in our libraries," "rambling amongst authors (as often
I do)." So Boswell wrote of Johnson in his youth, "He read
a great deal in a desultory manner, without any scheme of study,
as chance threw books in his way and inclination directed him
through them."

But Burton in his ramblings must have been ready to suck
melancholy out of all that he met. For all his omnivorous
reading, he was no bookworm. It was the human interest in
the printed page for which his eye was open. Modern critics,
unversed in a literature familiar to Burton's day, have dwelt
pleasantly on dusty folios, and made merry over the names
of authors of whose works they were ignorant, as though what
is obsolete for us was already rare and far-fetched in the seventeenth century. Taine pictured Burton sporting with ante-
diluvian monsters, the first being Besler of Nürnberg! and an
English writer seems to imagine that Codronchus was a special
find for him. There was little remoteness in the newly printed
text-books of medicine and botany.

In the case of a reader so all engulfing as Burton, it is not
easy to sum up his sources with precision, but the following
heads will afford a rough notion of the field covered: medical
writers of all periods, and scientific works; the Bible, the fathers,
theologians; Greek and Latin classics (the former "cited out
of their interpreters") : some few are largely or wholly neglected,
such as Aeschylus: to others, such as Horace, he has frequent
recourse; historians and chroniclers; travels, descriptions of
cities and countries (Burton was "ever addicted to the study

of cosmography"); treatises on government and politics; the *miscellanea* of scholars and Latin *belles lettres* from the revival of learning: poems, orations, epistles, satires, *facetiae* and the like; English poetry: Chaucer, Spenser, Marlowe, Shakespeare, Jonson, Daniel, Drayton; Harington's *Ariosto*, Florio's *Montaigne*, Rabelais and others. Interesting light is thrown on Burton's reading by the list of the books given to the Bodleian in accordance with his will, which includes a large number of pamphlets and controversial tracts.

Burton was anxious on principle to indicate his obligations. "I have wronged no Authors," he protested from the first; "I cite and quote mine Authors," he adds, in the third edition, continuing, in the fourth, "which howsoever some illiterate scriblers accompt pedanticall as a cloake of ignorance, and opposite to their affected fine stile, I must and will use." Burton, it would seem, is here glancing at writers such as Owen Felltham, who, in the second edition of *Resolves* (1628), wrote "I am to answer two Objections, One, that I have made use of Story yet not quoted my Authorities, and this I have purposely done." Yet, while Burton renders to his medical writers what is theirs, to a great number of the illustrative and literary quotations in *The Anatomy*, as is only natural, no name is attached; to pause at the end of each borrowed phrase to interject a "Shakespeare, ahem!" was clearly impossible. But there is unconscious humour when, in the famous passage conveyed by Sterne, Burton declares that "as Apothecaries we make new mixtures every day, pour out of one vessel into another"; and forgets to refer his readers to Andreae's *Menippus*. In many instances, the quotations embedded in Burton's text have not been drawn directly from their original sources. Not that Burton had any need to fall back on *florilegia*, a practice that he expressly disclaims; but it often happens that what in itself is a quotation, especially if it be an island of verse in the midst of prose, has caught his eye as it faced him on the page of another writer and found its way to his own. Lines that stand out in Xylander's Latin version of Plutarch's *Moralia*, in Lilius Gyraldus, in Cornelius Agrippa, in Cardan, in Lipsius, have thus recruited his ranks; English writers, too, are made to pay tribute of their spoil. At times, we may track him down a whole page of a predecessor. The pro-

test, in the preface to Love-Melancholy, against forbidding
the reading of the *Canticles*, the *Ballade of Ballades*, as
'too light and amorous a tract,' has been borrowed from an
oration of Beroaldus. Elsewhere, successive quotations from
Aulus Gellius, Pliny the elder and the philosopher Seneca
hail from a controversial piece by Justus Baronius, and Burton commits a curious error through misreading his original.
When he protests in his preface that his collection has been
sine injuria, that he has given every man his own, it can be
shown, from passages he refers to, that he is recalling Camera-
rius's emblem under that motto. The insertion of supplementary matter in later editions has here, by separating these
quotations, helped to conceal their *provenance*. Burton's
reading was so wide and devious, his paths of association so
unexpected, that it is rarely safe to assume by what road a
quotation has reached him. One more example must suffice.
It might be supposed that the two lines

> *Virgines nondum thalamis jugatae*
> *Et comis nondum positis ephoebi*

came directly from Seneca's *Hercules Furens*. This is not so.
Burton took them from Gaulmin's Latin translation of the
Greek romance of Theodorus Prodromus.[1] The ways in
which he interlaces the words of others into his own fabric
are very various. Sometimes, a quotation stands in his text,
sometimes, in the margin; at times, through inadvertence,
in both. The margin, again, may supply the original of the
rendering that figures on the page. His translations often are
"paraphrases rather than interpretations." Burton's racy re-
statements by the side of the Latin have, at times, a humorous
effect akin to that of the advocates' speeches in *The Ring and
the Book*—or in Calverley's parody.

Burton exercises an author's privilege in taking only what
is to his purpose and in combining separate excerpts into one
period. Naturally, among the thousands of passages that
he has occasion to quote, he has not been able to avoid errors.
His memory plays him false. He slips in a rendering, assigns
words of Silius to Statius, is led astray by his authorities.
If Lipsius refers a sentence of Plato to the wrong dialogue,

---

[1] *N. and Q.* 10 S. XI, 101.

Burton takes it on trust. Lipsius says "Horace" when he should have said "Ovid," Burton copies his mistake. The number of reference marks in the text and margin become a source of error when complicated by fresh insertions in successive issues. Although each edition has a list of errata, these bear but an insignificant proportion to what may be detected. It is obvious that Burton's *modus operandi* was not always the same. He often quotes from memory; there are places, apparently, where the book from which he cites lay open before him; at times, he made use of memoranda. In his introduction, he represents himself as writing "out of a confused company of notes." Several books containing his autograph show strokes of the pen against words or passages utilised in *The Anatomy.*

Everywhere there is evidence that Burton's brain was soaked in literature. In his elegiacs *ad librum suum*, echoes are to be heard from Nicholas Gerbelius, Palingenius, Claudian, Ausonius, Juvenal, Martial, Ovid, Vergil. Elia's "I cannot sit and think. Books think for me," can be applied to Burton. His constant habit was to express himself in terms of quotation. But in this method lies dizziness for the reader and a danger, at times, that the real strength and individuality of the author's own thoughts may be overlooked.

Burton himself describes his style when he confesses that his book was "writ with as small deliberation as I do usually speak." What we are listening to is the intimate persuasive ring of vigorous and unaffected talk. He never shrinks from homely metaphors:

> The whole world belike should be new-moulded when it seemed good to those all-commanding Powers, and turned inside out as we do haycocks in harvest . . ., or as we turn apples to the fire, move the world upon his centre.

"The world is tossed in a blanket amongst them." "As common as a barber's chair." "As a tinker stops one hole and makes two." It was because of his expressing himself in such terms as these that, two generations later, the Christ Church men complained of Bentley's "low and mean ways of speech." It would be an error to suppose that Burton was not consciously concerned for his vocabulary and the rhythmical movement of his English. Comparing his book to a bear's whelp, he laments that he has no time to lick it into form, but the changes introduced in each new edition prove his anxiety on re-reading to prune away pleonasms, to escape awkward repetitions and, by numerous slight touches, to ease the running of his sentences. When further additions have affected what was previously in place, he is at pains to alter it. Only a complete collation could exhibit the amount of care that Burton bestowed on revision.

The success of his *Melancholy*, instead of prompting Burton to the production of any new work, caused him to concentrate his energy on improving what he had already printed. Additional references or the names of other authors were adduced to support or illustrate statements already made. The insertion of entirely new matter is frequent. In more than one edition, he records a resolve to make no further change, but the method of the book invited fresh touches and Burton found it hard to abstain. He pleads in excuse that "many good authors in all kinds are come to my hands since," and his treatise is continually being made new by contributions that had been published since the last edition, while he explains of certain earlier books that they had not been seen by him till now.

From the first, *The Anatomy of Melancholy* found a ready audience, and its vogue, to judge from the number of editions absorbed, lasted for half a century. As its success was due to its having suited, rather than originated, the taste of the time, it is not always easy to trace its direct influence. Resemblances have often been pointed out between Milton's *L'Allegro* and *Il Penseroso* and "The Author's Abstract of Melancholy," verses which Burton prefixed to his third and following editions. John Rous, the Bodleian librarian, was a friend of Burton as well as of Milton. It has been suggested that the song in Fletcher's *Nice Valour* was Milton's immediate source and that Fletcher owed hints to Burton. The authorship of the play is matter of controversy, and Fletcher himself died three years before Burton's verses were printed. The anonymous *Vulgar Errors in Practice Censured* (1659) shows extensive borrowings. The author copies without much intelligence and goes astray through mechanically repeating Burton's

references. Greenwood's *Philalethes,* that appeared in 1657,
makes considerable use of *The Anatomy*, but the extent of his
acknowledgment is greater than Anthony à Wood's statement
implies.   At the close of the century, the passion for accumulating authorities was growing fainter, and Burton's book was less
in touch with the prevailing literary tone.   Indebtedness to
The Anatomy was now less likely to be detected.   Archbishop
Herring, in an often-repeated passage, asserted that the wits of
queen Anne's reign and the beginning of George I's were not
a little beholden to Burton.   Swift, it would seem, had some
acquaintance with him.   However little in accordance with
literary fashion, *The Anatomy* could hardly fail, if only by
reason of its title, and the more obvious peculiarities of its
contents, to attract the attention of any curious reader who
encountered it; and, in the middle of the century, two athuors
of importance fell under its fascination.   Samuel Johnson,
whose wide reading and hypochondriacal taint instinctively
drew him to *The Anatomy*, was emphatic in its praise, and
affords another instance of admiration extended at the same
time to Browne and Burton.   The influence of *The Anatomy* is
apparent in several passages of Johnson's talk and writing, although Burton was not among the English authors from whom
the examples for his dictionary were selected.   His definition
of oats, his conversational comparison of a ship to a prison and
the Vergilian quotation by which he points the miseries of
a literary life, are all reminiscent of Burton.

But one name in eighteenth century literature is inseperably
linked with his.   Sterne's cast of mind inclined him to reading
that which was curious and away from the common track,
and he turned over *The Anatomy* with a special gusto.   To
the literary taste of the day, Burton was obsolete, and Sterne
freely transferred his thoughts and phrases to *Tristram Shandy*.
Ferriar's list of passages is far from exhaustive.   At the end
of the century, the real revival of Burton began.   He was a
favourite with Coleridge, Lamb and Southey.   Coleridge
annotated his friend's copy of *The Anatomy*.   Lamb, besides
producing an imitation which has deceived some readers,
though with less excuse than was the case with Crossley's
imitation of Sir Thomas Browne, gives frequent tokens of
his fondness for Burton, with whose thought and expression,

as with those of many seventeenth century writers, he was in close sympathy. Southey was a diligent reader of *The Anatomy* and noted many passages from it in his commonplace book. The year 1800 saw the first reprint of *The Anatomy* since 1676, and the book thus became more accessible. Keats, with his *Lamia*, gave the passage of Burton that suggested the poem, and a volume of the edition which he used, containing notes from his hand, has been preserved. Byron praised it as the most entertaining of literary miscellanies. But criticisms on Burton are too often evidence that the book has been thought of as an amusing collection of isolated anecdotes, a vast quarry for quaint phrases and quotations, and seldom viewed in its purpose and entirety.

Thackeray, who, in *Pendennis*, had represented captain Shandon as putting *The Anatomy* to base uses of journalism, made it the favourite reading of Martin Lambert in *The Virginians*—a book over a great part of which the spirit of Burton is felt to brood. But the second volume of *The Virginians* is largely made up of essays, and it is in the essay of to-day, if anywhere, that the influence of Burton yet lingers.

The Scot abroad, winning success in arms or commerce, has long been a familiar figure. In the sixteenth and seventeenth centuries, the countrymen of Buchanan and Dempster are often found in foreign lands as scholars of fortune. William Barclay, of an old Aberdeenshire family, a Catholic and an adherent of queen Mary, after some years' legal study in France, accepted a chair at Pont-à-Mousson in the territory of the duke of Lorraine, and married a lady of that country. Their son, John Barclay, born in 1582, counted himself a subject of king James, though circumstances gave a cosmopolitan tinge to his character. Himself married to a Frenchwoman, a resident successively in England and Italy, suing for the patronage of the sovereigns of different realms, Barclay nowhere achieved the position his powers might have won. Too little is known of his life in London and his eleven years' connection with the English court. That he was employed on important missions is certainly an exaggeration, though passages in his work appear to indicate some official errand.

To the modern reader, Barclay's yearning for the favour

of the great is, doubtless, distasteful. Each royal personage in turn is posed as the noblest and pleasantest prince of his acquaintance; but, in his days, to touch without adorning was unpardonable, and we have the testimony of such men as Casaubon and Peiresc and Thorie to the real charm of his character. Intellectually, Barclay was a compound of the student, the man of letters and the curious observer of affairs, and his highest work combines "the scholar's learning with the courtier's ease."

His first performance, at the age of eighteen, was in the character of a scholar, a commentary on four books of Statius's *Thebais*, with notes on the four following. It has been asserted that subsequent editors have neglected this book: but Barth refers to it frequently, and, while criticising it severely at times, styles the author *vir doctissimus*, and applauds several of his suggestions.[1] Barclay was a fluent and pleasing master of Latin verse, and some lines of his were published as early as 1599.[2] His collected poems contain matter of autobiographical interest, and also much adulation of James and others, with an occasional touch of grotesqueness. In his hexameters on the Gunpowder plot, the poet expresses his horror that men should have proposed to send the king piecemeal to the skies, when his own soaring virtues would more rightly bear him thither.

The first part of *Euphormionis Satyricon* was published when Barclay was only one-and-twenty. Before considering this, it is convenient to note briefly some other productions. His short account of the 1605 plot was written in the November of that year, but its appearance was postponed because of James's own manifesto. The king's sagacity is, of course, applauded; at the end are placed the lines already referred to.

In 1609, Barclay introduced a posthumous work of his father, *De Potestate Papae*, in which William Barclay, already known as the champion of the rights of monarchy against Buchanan, was now seen as the opponent of the papal court in its claims to overrule the secular power. In reply to the attacks provoked by the work, Barclay wrote his *Pietas, sive publicae pro regibus ac principibus et privatae, pro G. Barclaio*

---

[1] Barth's *Statius* (1664), tom. iii, p. 514. See Barth's indexes.
[2] In the *Tacitus* edited by William Barclay, M.D.

contra Bellarminum Vindiciae. In 1614 appeared *Icon Animorum*, Englished by Thomas May in 1631 as *The Mirrour of Mindes.* In this, he treats of the principal nations of Europe and their characteristics, beginning with the French, the various dispositions of mankind and the qualities peculiar to times of life, station and profession. It shows Barclay's alertness of observation, soundness of judgment and happiness in expression, and has caused him to be compared with Montaigne. Merits and failings are skilfully presented, habits of thought as well as of demeanour. Of the English, he writes: *se ipsos, et suae gentis mores, ingenia, animos, eximie mirantur.* The practice of the *duello* in France here condemned was glanced at in *Euphormio*, and its discouragement by Louis XIII made a merit of that king in the dedication to *Argenis.* The criticisms are in no unkindly spirit, but, some thirty years later, a Pole was moved to protest against Barclay's account of his country.[1]

Much in Barclay's writings had been eagerly welcomed by the opponents of Catholicism, but his *Paraenesis ad sectarios*, written soon after his settlement at Rome in 1617, served to justify his attitude in the eyes of the Catholic church.

Barclay's main importance, however, for the history of literature rests on his two adventures in fiction, *Euphormionis Satyricon* and *Argenis*, the one a contribution to the development of the picaresque novel of real life, the other a finished example of a type of ideal romance. The first part of *Euphormio* is said to have appeared in London in 1603, but no copy is forthcoming. The 1605 edition (Paris) of this part is described on the title as *Nunc primum recognitum, emendatum, et variis in locis auctum.* Until the earlier edition is found, the extent of the changes must remain unknown. In his *Apologia Euphormionis pro se*, Barclay has ingenuously confessed his reasons for choosing satire: youth and desire for fame. "I decided," he says, "to accuse the whole world with guiltless violence, more in the hope of winning praise for myself than of bringing shame on others." In plot, Barclay's satirical novel is a string of adventures. In the first part, the narrator Euphormio becomes, in a foreign land, the slave of an ennobled parvenu,

---

[1] *Polonia Defensa contra Joan: Barclaium* etc. (Dantzig, 1648, anon [by L. Opalinsky]).

Callio. He is persecuted, feigns insanity, and wins his master's favour. Sent on journeys with a fellow slave, he undergoes a variety of experiences, is flogged and branded and escapes. The narrative breaks off on a sudden. Interspersed are an account of a lecture on Roman law, details of supernatural phenomena, ghost stories and witchcraft, a play acted in a Jesuit college, an attack on physicians (whose pretensions Barclay was as ready to satirise as Fielding) and a long dissertation on the present state of learning, on the faults of verbal and antiquarian scholarship, and the extremists in Latin style, whether erring through obscurity or ultra-Ciceronianism, on mistakes in systems of education; in which last there is excellent good sense. Besides unworthy nobles, there are many other objects of the author's satire; and we have in especial an account of the eager and intrusive ambition of the followers of Acignius, who typifies the Society of Jesus. With much that is vigorous and interesting, there is a lack of connection. An elaborate episode in the earlier pages, which shows promise of continuance, is abruptly dropped, and we miss sureness in tone and touch. The *saeva indignatio* of the opening is not sustained, and one can understand, without accepting, Scaliger's criticism: *il y a un pédant à Angers qui a fait un Satyricon qui au commencement semble estre quelque chose mais puis n'est rien du tout.*

Through the second part of *Euphormio* (1607), there runs a more distinct clue. We have Euphormio's first impulse to follow the life of the philosophers (enter a religious order), his recognition of his mistake, his pursuit of fortune and pleasure, his fresh attraction to "philosophy" and the wiles by which Acignius attempts to secure him for his Society. From these, he frees himself with difficulty, and, finally, reaches the court of Tessaranactus (James), who admits his service. The scene is laid in Delphium (Pont-à-Mousson), Marcia (Venice), Ilium (Paris), Boeotia (Germany) and Scolimorrhodia (England). The atmosphere is more spacious and the interest wider than in part I. There are again many episodes—a long dramatic performance, a literary display at a Jesuit college, an account of the habits of the emperor Rudolf and a puritan household in England. *Euphormio* was placed on the Index; the latter part gave especial offence, and, in reply to attacks, Barclay wrote his *Apologia*. He justifies his satire, never scurrilous, on the Jesuits, and adheres to the view he had given of the dispute between Venice and the papal court. On the charge of libelling individuals, he tries to show the absurdity of some identifications; in other cases, he maintains that the praise outweighs the blame, but, at times, his defence is disingenuous. Hoping for the favour of princes, he felt bound to explain away what might prejudice his career. How far was fact blended with fiction? According to one view, part I closely follows the elder Barclay's experiences, part II the son's, the characters being largely based on originals. This is supported by Père Abram's *Histoire de l'université et du collège de Pont-à-Mousson*.[1] A recent critic has endeavoured to minimise the element of exact imitation. Certain characters (for example, Protagon-Henri IV) and incidents are, undoubtedly, real, and, without following any "headstrong allegory," the safer course is not to assign too important a share to imagination pure and simple. Barclay's habit was to build fiction on fact.

It is a separate task to trace the indebtedness of *Euphormio* to preceding writers and its influence in subsequent literature. In the mixture of verse with prose, and in style and expression, Barclay betrays frequent reminiscences of Petronius, while adhering to his own standard of decency. Echoes of other writers are frequent and two most prominent qualities are a display of erudition and a taste for rhetoric. His annotator of 1674 was ludicrously unable to cope with his references to Greek history. There is a general resemblance between *Euphormio* and the picaresque novels of Spain, but the chief of these were later than Barclay's satire, and, as yet, few had appeared in a French form. Some effects of *Euphormio* may be felt not only in subsequent Latin writings, but in the vernacular literature of France and Germany, for example in Grimmelshausen's *Simplicissimus*. It is a curious fact that those who have written on *Euphormio* in recent times have often failed to read it through. Körting, in describing the first part, believed that he was giving an account of the whole, and Dukas, in his useful contribution to the bibliography, confessed he had left some pages unread.

---

[1] In MS. See Collignon, *Notes sur l' "Ephormion,"* pp. 9-21.

Apologia Euphormionis pro se was printed later as a third part of *Euphormio;* to this was added, as a fourth, *Icon Animorum*, though it had no connection with the other three. After Barclay's death, the publishers included as part V *Alitophili Veritatis Lachrymae*, nominally a continuation of *Euphormio*, though the connection is of the slightest. Claude Morisot was the author of this indifferent piece, which Robert Burton quoted several times without naming the source. A sixth part, *Alitophilus castigatus*, appeared in the 1674 annotated edition of *Euphormio*. It is a slight production, giving the stories and discussions of a group of friends who meet at one another's houses during a three days' vacation. Dukas, who refrained from reading it, gives a completely erroneous account, and, in dealing with the question of the authorship, attributed to L. G. Bugnot, overlooks the most important pieces of evidence.

Argenis is a far more mature work than *Euphormio;* its author's intention is clearer, it has a carefully constructed plot, and, in style too, a distinct advance is perceptible. The work was written at Rome where Barclay had settled in 1617, and Rome is recalled by some of the details in description. Light is thrown on the composition of *Argenis* by Barclay's own letters and by those of Peiresc and others. They show us quite plainly that *Argenis* must not be regarded as a purely artistic work of imagination, but, at least in part, as inspired by political motives. In a letter to de Puysieu, dated Rome, 12 July, 1620, Barclay writes:

> *Le suiet du liure ou je pretends faire entrer au bon escient Monseigneur le Chancellier et vous aussy, est une inuention assés gaye comprise en cinq liures ou se traitte de la pluspart des affaires de nostre temps. J'y adiousteray cette preface de laquelle je vous ay parlé si le Roy accepte mon seruice et tournoray aisement le stile de tous les cinq liures à l'honneur de la France.*

In a letter which Barclay sent to Louis XIII with a copy of *Argenis* a few days before his death, he says of his book:

> *son principal but est de traicter des guerres et des amours d'un jeune et chaste Prince qui semblent estre tirees sur le modelle de vostre courage et genie.*

This time, Barclay was anxious to avoid giving offence, and specimens of what he had written were submitted to the judgment of others. In his dedication to Louis XIII, he speaks of his work as a new kind of writing and, in the course of the book, expounds its principles in the person of Nicopompus. The poet describes how he proposes to write a story in the style of a history. The fictitious element, the exciting and unexpected incidents, are to attract readers: the pictures of virtues and vices with their appropriate rewards are to compel men to self-criticism and self-condemnation. He is careful to add that no persons will be portrayed to the exact life, but that disguise will be secured by fictitious details; consequently, to take offence will be a confession of the reader's own guilt. It will be an equal error to assume that everything or that nothing corresponds to real fact. As, in *Euphormio*, the satirical element was dominant, in the later fiction it is the didactic.

There is no need to repeat the details of the story. Argenis, daughter and heir presumptive of Meleander, king of Sicily, has four aspirants to her hand: Lycogenes, the rebel whose attempt to carry her off is frustrated by Poliarchus, disguised as a girl; Radirobanes, king of Sardinia, her father's ally against the rebels, who fails in an attempt to seize Argenis and is afterwards slain in single combat by Poliarchus; Archombrotus, a prince who arrives in Sicily incognito, but proves to be Meleander's son by a secret marriage; and the hero Poliarchus, a Gallic king, whose union with Argenis is celebrated at the conclusion.

According to one view, *Argenis* is simply a political treatise cast in the form of a novel. According to another, it is a perpetual historical allegory; while a third would make it, in all that is essential, a romance. That there is really a fusion of romantic, political and historical motives is proved, if proof be needed, by the author's own words.

Like his father, Barclay was a strong but not unreasoning supporter of the power of the crown. The abuses of monarchy are debated, but he is careful not to let the Whig dogs have the best of the argument. His was evidently that acute and cautious type of mind that sides with authority and shows resourcefulness in opposing the advocates of less arbitrary rule. In the remedies suggested for strengthening the crown against two powerful nobles, there is a curious anticipation of Richelieu's measures.

The political questions are those of the day, but how far are the principal characters and situations historical? The detail and order of the action is imaginary and a precise allegory is out of the question, but it would certainly seem that, in describing the condition and relation of various countries, Barclay had in mind the recent history of Europe. The troubles of Sicily, it is reasonable to suppose, were at least suggested by those of France during the wars of the League. To give an exact picture was no part of Barclay's intention; but Sardinia, under the ambitious and encroaching Radirobanes, recalls Spain, while Mauretania, which repels Radirobanes's attack and is governed by a queen unable to take her subjects' money without their consent, has its analogue in England. The chief characters are no portraits. Lycogenes may correspond to the duke of Guise, but Henri III would be flattered in Meleander. Argenis, in a sense, typifies the succession to the crown, and Barclay may have thought of Marguerite of Valois, the subject of his touching verses in *Euphormio*. Poliarchus has usually been taken to represent Henry of Navarre; that Archombrotus is his understudy illustrates the danger of demanding an exact resemblance. Barclay's claim that his hero is meant for Louis XIII is not inconsistent, as he elsewhere attributes the father's merits to the son. Certain minor characters are easily recognised—Ibburranes and Dunalbius are the cardinals Barberini and Ubaldini; Hieroleander is Hieronymus Aleander; Antenorius, Antonio Querenghi. Nicopompus, ever ready with occasional verse, is Barclay's self. One of Barclay's letters gives his intention of introducing Sillery, who may be Cleobulus. There are undisputed references to historical incidents—the story of Concini, of Somerset and lady Essex; the dispute between the emperor Ferdinand and the Pfalzgraf Friedrich. The narrative, though never lost sight of, is relieved by poems, by discussions, in which the parts maintained are in skilful keeping with the characters, by descriptions of scenery, works of art and pageants, in which, perhaps, we may see recollections of the masques at James's court. There are lighter passages and some attempts at mirth, but the prevailing tone is elevated and serious, at times approaching the epic. Consistency is maintained in the characters, with little development. Of Barclay's reading, there is continual evidence. We are reminded of the Greek novelists with whom the pirate is often the *diabolus ex machina;* of Polybius, to whom the description of Epeircte is due; of Xenophon's *Cyropaedia* (the name Gobrias, however, may be taken from Theodorus Prodromus, the Vatican MS. of which writer Barclay examined for Gaulmin's edition[1]). But a list of authors who colour his poetry and prose would be endless.

Barclay's Latin style has been lauded without limit by Grotius and Coleridge, and severely dealt with by Scaliger, the author of *Censura Euphormionis*, Scioppius and others. If we judge by a classical standard, it is easy to "smell false Latin." The vocabulary is not pure. There are lapses in usage. Among his merits can scarcely be counted "a witty and dexterous use of the subjunctive mood." But, as an example of the application of Latin to modern use, Barclay's language deserves high praise. While no Ciceronian, he has not affiliated "Lipsius his hopping style." His own is ready, flexible and expressive, and has the inestimable merit of conveying the author's meaning.

To whatever degree the belief in a *clavis* may have contributed to the success of *Argenis*, its literary merits are beyond question. Sorel criticised it with some animosity in his *Remarques sur le Berger extravagant*, but its popularity is proved by translations into ten languages and more than one continuation.[2]

While there is little direct imitation of *Argenis*, it was among the influences that passed into the heroic novel, and separate signs of it are frequent in the literature of the seventeenth century. We may trace them in other Latin works of fiction, in Erythraeus's *Eudemia* and in *Nova Solyma*. The story yielded material for dramas, in French, Spanish, Italian and German. Fénelon's indebtedness has been doubted. Burton quotes from *Argenis*, as well as from *Euphormio* and *Icon Animorum*. Crashaw translated verses from *Argenis*. There are touches of it in Boyle's *Parthenissa*. Katherine Philips addresses a friend as Poliarchus.

[1] *N. and Q.* 10 S. XI, 101.   [2] See the bibliography.

Barclay's works were even employed for purposes of instruction. A selection was made of his political aphorisms. In Earle's *Micro-Cosmographie*, a college tutor sets his pupil an extract from *Euphormio*, and the suitability of Barclay as a Latin author for boys' reading was discussed in a school programme of Schulpforte (1729). It has been often repeated that *Argenis* appealed to Richelieu and Leibniz: we know that Rousseau read it. Cowper's praise and Coleridge's are familiar.

Before the close of the seventeenth century, the Latin text of *Argenis* was reprinted between forty and fifty times. The demand during the next hundred years was satisfied with half-a-dozen editions, all proceeding from Nürnberg, since the last of which no publisher has thought it worth his while to issue it. Recently, several monographs dealing with Barclay's life, bibliography and chief works have appeared in France and Germany. But published statements in the bibliographies still require some corrections; there are important particulars in his life which have not been exhaustively investigated; and the full influence of his works on subsequent literature still requires to be traced in detail.

The bulk of medieval and modern Latin verse is enormously greater than the whole of extant classical poetry. In England, during the past century, while the art has been greatly exercised and has formed a prominent item in higher education, the usual aim of its adepts has been to display their ingenuity and scholarship in devising the most appropriate equivalents by which to give a Latin metrical dress to the thoughts and expressions of English poets. As a rule, the renderings are of short poems or isolated extracts. Widely different from this was the method in vogue at the time of the renascence, when, while translation from the Greek was not unknown, most Latin verse was an attempt on the part of scholars and men of letters to express their own thoughts and feelings. Some, like Petrarch, Vida, Fracastorius and Sannazarius, aspired to produce works of permanent value; in the case of others, such as J. C. Scaliger, verse was a conscious relaxation from severer labours. Too often, instead of careful finish, we find fluent inprovisation. For a century and a half, Italy,

France, Germany and the Netherlands lisped in Latin numbers. In our own country, where the effect of the renascence was less and later, the amount of Latin verse was inferior. Still, during the sixteenth and seventeenth centuries, there is a succession of Latin versifiers from Sir Thomas More to Abraham Cowley. Nor is production confined to lighter and more occasional pieces: poems of more ambitious scope were attempted, such as the *De Re Publica Anglorum instauranda* of Sir Thomas Chaloner the elder (1521–62), some lines of which are familiar through Burton's quotation.

In the north, the art was cultivated with success; Buchanan won the highest praise from J. J. Scaliger; and Arthur Jonston, himself a Latin poet of merit, edited *Delitiae Poetarum Scotorum* under the patronage of Scot of Scotstarvet, as a pendant to Gruter's collections.

The making of Latin verses was an essential part of the curriculum of a good English grammar school in the sixteenth century. John Owen, both as boy and as master, must have had plenty of experience in "longs and shorts." Leach has pointed out, in his *History of Warwick School*, that the education at Winchester when Owen was a scholar was largely devoted to the production of Latin epigrams, and the lines on Drake, composed while their author was yet a schoolboy, had the honour of a place in Camden's *Annales*.

The date conventionally assigned to Owen's birth is *c.* 1560, but Leach has shown from the evidence of his age when admitted a scholar at Winchester that the right year is 1563 or 1564. This inference is supported by the pedigree supplied by H. R. Hughes of Kinmel,[1] according to which Owen had three elder brothers, the first born in 1560. Another account makes him the third son. His father, Thomas Owen of Plas dû, was sheriff of Carnarvonshire in 1569, and it seems certain that Hugh Owen, the conspirator, who died at Rome in 1618, was his uncle. Whatever the truth of the story that the poet was disinherited by an uncle because of an epigram reflecting on the church of Rome, we learn from Hugh Owen's monument,[2] that his heir was his sister's son, a Gwynne.

Although several of his epigrams are earlier, Owen's

---

[1] *Y Cymmrodor*, xvi, 177.
[2] *Archaeologia Cambrensis*, vol. iv (second series), pp. 130, 131.

first volume did not appear till 1606, three other volumes following within the next six years. His success was immediate and
extraordinary; his admirers hailed him as the equal, if not
the superior, of Martial; and the comparison, though too
often repeated in an uncritical fashion, undoubtedly contains
some slight element of truth. It must be confessed at once
that, in Owen, one looks in vain for the poetic side of Martial,
for his pathos and tenderness. One misses, too, the variety of
metre, above all the hendecasyllables in which Martial's hand
is exceedingly light, the great majority of Owen's epigrams
consisting of a single elegiac distich. Wherein, then, lies his
merit? He is the very embodiment of that "quick venew of wit:
snip, snap, quick and home," which finds its fittest expression
in the brief compass of two Latin lines, as Latin, too, has no
rival as the language for terse inscription. If, without pro-
fanity, Owen's name may be set by Martial's, it is because he
has caught something of the spirit of one class of Martial's
epigrams—the couplets which are all point with no room
for poetry. If we apply the familiar precept, Owen's performances possess the *aculeus* and are *corporis exigui*, but
the honey is to seek.

It was the point and brevity which captivated his auditors;
the tastes of that audience are seen in Manningham's *Diary*.
The *Epigrammata* would especially be welcomed by members of
the universities and inns of court, daily conversant with Latin,
enamoured of verbal quips, impresses and anagrams. They
would find Owen singularly free from the two faults which rendered much modern Latin verse intolerable, namely, insipidity
and tediousness. In a quatrain prefixed to Owen's second
volume (1607), Sir John Harington pays his friend the curious
compliment of saying that his verses do not make the reader
sick.[1] This is no faint praise. Owen is eminently readable;
his very faults are rarely associated with ineffectiveness. They
are, for the most part, due to devices for arresting the reader's
attention. Among the least satisfactory is the selection of
words of similar sound, where, without point enough for a pun,
the result is a jingle—*Mars* and *mors; audiret* and *auderet;
Venetiae* and *divitiae; A summo sumo Principe principium.*

---

[1] *Provenit ex versu nausea nulla tuo.*

But there are times when his mere dexterity in playing with the letter compels admiration, as in the line describing the care of physicians and lawyers for their clients:

Dant patienter opem, dum potiuntur opum.

We have in him a concise Latin counterpart of the punning and alliterative titles of contemporary controversial tracts. Owen abounds in the tricks by which a word is written backwards or stripped of a syllable or letter. His alertness in detecting his opportunity is only paralleled by De Morgan's prompt discovery, when Burgon had repudiated an invitation to a public dinner, that curt refusal was spelt by the reversal of the dean's name. In keeping with the fashion of his age, Owen is great in anagrams, ringing the changes to the fifth degree.[1] There is juggling with figures, as when he shows that the digits of prince Henry's birth year, when added together, make up the golden number, nineteen.[2] In the higher *paronomasia*, Owen is supreme; his happiest efforts have all the shock and the inevitableness of the famous *neque* bene*fecit neque* male*fecit, sed* inter*fecit.*[3] Hood's inexhaustible fertility would have found in him a rival. Akin to this is the readiness with ingenious comparisons, and the skill by which a new and unexpected turn is given to familiar proverbs and quotations, or new light shed on a familiar truth, as in the epigram *Ad Juvenem:*

Quisque senectutem, mortem tibi nemo precatur;
Optatur morbus, non medicina tibi.

It was hardly to be expected that, in his criticisms of social life, Owen would refrain from claiming the licence traditionally enjoyed by the epigrammatist, and he has Sterne's unedifying trick of making a sentence in itself innocent the vehicle of an unseemly meaning. Whatever the method employed, Owen's perpetual aim is to startle the reader by the flash of his wit, whether the result be reached by the soaring of a rocket or the splutter of a squib. As befits a schoolmaster, he affords

---

[1] *Epigrammata*, lib. VI, 12. (The books are numbered consecutively, as in Renouard's edition.)

[2] V, 51.

[3] Attributed to Porson in *Facetiae Cantabrigienses* (1825), p. 134.

us scraps from the feast of languages; besides Latin and English, Greek, Welsh, Hebrew, French and Italian all have a part in his jests. Nor is learning absent; to a hasty reader, satisfied with seeing that a point is complete in itself, the echoes from the classics may remain unheard. It is not always recognised that his praise of Thomas Neville, his patroness's son,

Qui puerum laudat, spem, non rem, laudat in illo,
Non spes, ingenium res probat ispa tuum

is based on a saying of Cicero, quoted in Servius's commentary to Vergil. The words *Semper in incerta re tu mihi certus amicus* are suggested by a line of Ennius, quoted in *De Amicitia.* The epigram on Sir Philip Sidney has been cited as an example of Owen's power; it is really the versification of the younger Pliny's panegyric on his uncle. Owen takes his profit where he finds it. An etymology of Varro, a line of Persius, a hexameter proverb, and an aphorism of Matthaeus Borbonius, are alike pressed into his service. It is not always easy to distinguish between imitation and coincidence nor to decide whether indebtedness is unconscious or intentional. The remark on Nicholas Borbonius's *Nugae*[1] has a parallel in Joachim du Bellay: elsewhere, we meet with an apparent reminiscence of Johannes Secundus. The distich obnoxious to quotation on Peter and Simon at Rome embodies a jest presumably ancient. It may be seen in Euricius Cordus. Another epigram of Cordus on our attitude to a physician closely resembles one of Owen's.[2] There are many such parallels in the vast literature of modern Latin. The remarkable instance of the lines of Hieronimo Amalteo and Passerat is given in Hallam.[3] Similarity of theme must often have involved similarity of treatment.

Owen's epigrams are no mere imitative exercises in Latin style. He must pack his meaning in a small space and he feels the difficulty of his task. *Crede mihi, labor est non levis esse brevem.*[4] He is bent on making his point and makes it often at the cost of correctness. He is not infallible in the order of his words and the modern schoolmaster would be aghast at some of his irregularities in syntax. His prosody

[1] I, 42.
[2] *N. and Q.* 10 S. XI, 21.
[3] *Lit. of Europe*, part II, chap. 5.
[4] I, 168.

is scarcely that of the Augustan age and he is even guilty of
false quantities. In some points, however, modern scholarship is apt to misjudge the practice of earlier verse writers.
A critic of archbishop William's epitaph on the poet in old
St. Paul's has objected to *parva statura* on the ground that
Owen would not have tolerated this from a fourth form boy.
If so, to be consistent, Owen ought himself to have submitted
to the rod.   The rule that a short vowel should not be retained
before *sc-*, *sp-*, or *st-* was no matter of common notoriety
in his day.   It was left for Richard Dawes,[1] in 1745, to point
out the general neglect of the principle, and to ask schoolmasters to urge it on their pupils.

Owen exercises his wit on many subjects. We meet the
familiar figures of the poor author, the degenerate noble,
the courtier, the lawyer, the physician, the atheist, the hypocrite, the miser, January and May, the uxorious husband, the
cuckold. We have a host of imaginary personages—Aulus,
Cotta, Harpalus, Marcus, Quintus, Camilla and Flora, Gellia,
Pontia and Phyllis and many another. It was the succession
of general and unconnected ideas which caused Lessing to
declare that it made him dizzy to read a book of Owen through.
There are epigrams on Winchester college, the university of
Oxford, Christ Church, the Bodleian library, Saville's edition
of Chrysostom, Holland's translation of Pliny, Sidney's
Arcadia, Overbury's *Perfect Wife*, Joseph Hall's *Meditations*
and other literary topics. Many are addressed to Welsh
kinsfolk, to personal friends, to patrons actual or prospective,
to prominent people of the day. Among others, are bishop
Bilson, his former headmaster at Winchester, archbishop
Abbot, archbishop Williams, Vaughan, bishop of London,
Burleigh and Salisbury, lord chancellor Ellesmere, Coke, lord
Dorset, Lucy, countess of Bedford, the earl of Pembroke,
Sir Edward Herbert, Sir Henry Wotton, Sir Henry Goodyer,
Sir Henry Fanshawe, Daniel the poet, Sir John Harington, Sir
Thomas Overbury. His first three books were dedicated to
lady Mary Neville, daughter of the earl of Dorset; his second
volume, a single book, to Arabella Stuart; the third volume
to Henry prince of Wales and his brother Charles; and   the

---

[1] Notes on Terentianus Maurus in his *Miscellanea Critica*.

last volume to his three "Maecenates" Sir Edward Noel, Sir William Sidley and Sir Roger Owen.   There are touches of sincere emotion, as in his lines to his friend, John Hoskins; but Owen's habitual style is hardly adapted for the finer shades of personal feeling, nor, in an age of fulsome dedications, did he possess the art of flattering with delicacy.   James I and his family are naturally the recipients of the grossest adulation, witness the epigram in which the prayer is offered that the king may live nineteen hundred years.   Owen, as he reminds us, was of the order of *Fratres Minores;* he makes no secret of his eagerness to be patronised and is outspoken in his desire to receive pecuniary help, a weakness which he shared with Martial.   After ceasing to be master at Warwick, he seems to have been in difficulties, and it has been stated that, in the latter part of his life, he owed his support to the kindness of his kinsman archbishop Williams.   About ten years elapsed between his last volume and the death of "little Owen, the epigrammaker"; but so little is known of his career that it is impossible to say whether his silence was due to the consciousness that he had exhausted a particular vein or whether other causes were at work.   There are signs of falling off in his later productions, and he seems to have been aware of this.

Of the favourable impression which Owen made upon his contemporaries, there can be no doubt.   His first volume was reissued within a month, and, during the seventeenth century, his epigrams were frequently reprinted in England, Holland and Germany.   Camden, in his *Remains*, when speaking of the poets of his day couples Owen's name with those of Sidney, Spenser, Daniel, Holland, Ben Jonson, Campion, Drayton, Chapman, Marston, Shakespeare, "and other most pregnant wits of these our times whom succeeding ages may justly admire."   Five English translations of the whole or part of his epigrams appeared before 1678, the earliest by John Vicars in 1619.   The clumsiness of much in these translations makes the merit of the original Latin more evident.   The best known of the half-dozen French versions (the latest of which appeared in 1818, that by N. Le Brun (1709), is entirely wanting in point and concentration.   Many attempts to interpret him were made in Germany, the most conspicuous of which is by Valentin Löber (1653).   He has also been translated into Spanish.

Any effect of Owen on subsequent Latin verse was, naturally, confined to the epigrammatists. Caspar Barth, whose own extemporaneous style was ill-calculated to reproduce Owen's neatness, frequently addresses him in his work *Scioppius excellens*, and in his *Amphitheatrum Seriorum Jocorum* (thirty books of epigrams). Barth, it may be noted, resents Owen's imputation of drinking habits to the Germans. Bauhusius of Antwerp and Cabillavus, though their style and subject matter are far other than Owen's, show, in a few epigrams, distinct traces of indebtedness to him. To take another example, Ninian Paterson, a Scotch minister whose *Epigrammaton libri octo* was published at Edinburgh in 1678, shows, amid much flatness, strong evidence of his study of Owen. But the author whose obligations are most marked is H. Harder, whose epigrams are included in the second volume of Rostgaard's *Deliciae Quorundam Poetarum Danorum* (Lugd. Bat. 1693). In his second and third books in especial, Owen is echoed again and again. We find the same themes, the same points and the same play upon words. Harder shows considerable skill in this style, and, in many cases, if epigrams of his were inserted among Owen's, it would require a close acquaintance with the latter's writings to detect the imposition.

There are many references to Owen and some imitations of his epigrams in the English literature of the century. Robert Burton quotes him several times without acknowledgment, and there are traces of indebtedness in such widely different authors as Sir John Harington and "the matchless Orinda." But the strangest phenomenon about Owen's influence is to be found in the German literature of the seventeenth century. At a time when artificiality and pedantry were rampant, a whole school of writers arose who devoted themselves to epigram, after the manner of Owen. This singular and interesting episode of literary history has been treated by Erich Urban, in his *Owenus und die deutschen Epigrammatiker des* XVII *Jahrhunderts*. In the eighteenth century, Owen's work was still alive. Lessing criticised him with severity but paid him the sincerest form of flattery. Cowper translated some of his epigrams. In the second year of the French republic, one of the very first books issued from the press of Didot, when the scarcity of compositors due to the recent troubles came to an end, was the epigrams of Owen, edited by Renouard. Southey's omnivorous taste did not neglect Owen.

The last edition of the epigrams appeared at Leipzig in 1824. Collected editions published after his death contain a few posthumous epigrams, but, by a curious fate, many moral and political distiches of Michael Verinus and an epigram of Ausonius came also to be included, and a great number of inaccuracies crept into the text. It is not possible that Owen should ever again be so highly valued as in the past, but it is equally certain that his present neglect is undeserved. It is strange that he should be so little read at a time when some knowledge of Latin is still an essential part of literary training.

CHAPTER XIV

The Beginnings of English Philosophy

THE English language may be said to have become for the first time the vehicle of philosophical literature by the publication of Bacon's *Advancement of Learning*, in 1605. Hooker's *Ecclesiastical Polity*, which preceded it by eleven years, belongs to theology rather than to philosophy; and the little-known treatise of Sir Richard Barckley, entitled *A Discourse of the felicitie of man: or his Summum bonum* (1598), consists mainly of amusing or improving anecdotes, and contains nothing of the nature of a moral philosophy. Bacon's predecessors, whether in science or in philosophy, used the common language of learned men. He was the first to write an important treatise on science or philosophy in English; and even he had no faith in the future of the English language. In the *Advancement*, he had a special purpose in view: he wished to obtain help and co-operation in carrying out his plans; and he regarded the book as only preparatory to a larger scheme. The works intended to form part of his great design for the renewal of the sciences were written in Latin. National characteristics are never so strongly marked in science and philosophy as in other branches of literature, and their influence takes longer in making itself felt. The English birth or residence of a medieval philosopher is of little more than biographical interest: it would be vain to trace its influence on the ideas or style of his work. With the Latin language went community of audience, of culture and of topics. This traditional commonwealth of thought was weakened by the forces which issued in the renascence; and, among these forces, the increased consciousness of nationality led, gradually, to greater differentiation in national types of culture and to the use of the national language even for subjects which appealed chiefly, or only, to the community of learned men. However much he may have preferred the Latin tongue as the vehicle of his philosophy, Bacon's own action made him a leader of this movement; and it so happened that the type of thought which he expounded had affinities with the practical and positive achievements of the English mind. In this way, Bacon has come to be regarded, not altogether correctly, as not only the beginner of English philosophy, but also representative of the special characteristics of the English philosophical genius.

From the end of the eighth century, when Alcuin of York was summoned to the court of Charles the Great, down to the middle of the fourteenth century, there was an almost constant succession of scholars of British birth among the writers who contributed to the development of philosophy in Europe. The most important names in the succession are Johannes Scotus Erigena, John of Salisbury, Alexander of Hales, Robert Grosseteste, Roger Bacon, Johannes Duns Scotus, William of Ockham and Thomas Bradwardine. An account of the English scholastics has been given in the first volume of this work. Here it must suffice to characterise in general terms the movement of which they formed part, and some of the directions in which their ideas exercised an influence on later science and speculation.

The philosophy of the Middle Ages was, above all things, an attempt at the systematisation of knowledge. The instrument for this synthesis was found in the logical conceptions and method of Aristotle. Its material consisted of the existing records of ancient philosophy and science, what was learned from contemporary experience and the teachings of the church. In the heterogeneous mass of material thus brought together, a pre-eminent position was assigned to religious doctrine. Philosophy came to be regarded as ancillary to theology; and the claims of theology were based upon ecclesiastical authority. This feature became characteristic of the scholastic method, and a frequent ground of objection to it in its decline. Connected with this was another and a more favourable feature. In accepting and interpreting theological doctrine, the thought

of the period recognised the independent value of the facts
of the spiritual life. What the Scriptures and the fathers
taught was confirmed by inner experience. In the laborious
erudition and dialectical subtleties of the schoolmen, there is
seldom wanting a strain of this deeper thought, which attains
its full development in medieval mysticism. Thus, in the
words of a recent historian,

it dawned upon men that the spiritual world is just as much a
reality as the material world, and that in the former is man's true
home. The way was prepared for a more thorough investigation
of spirit and matter than was possible to antiquity. Above all
things, however, a sphere of experience was won for human life
which was, in the strictest sense, its own property, into which no
external powers could penetrate.[1]

To Erigena, may be traced both medieval mysticism and the
scholastic method. He seems to have been born in Ireland
about 810, and to have proceeded to France some thirty
years later. Charles the Bald appointed him to the *schola
palatina* at Paris. He appears to have had no further connection with Ireland or with England, and to have died in France
about 87   It was probably owing to the protection of the
king that he escaped the graver results which usually followed
a suspicion of heresy. His works were officially condemned by
papal authority in 1050 and 1255. Erigena was the predecessor of scholasticism but not himself one of the schoolmen.
His anticipation of them consists not only in his dialectical
method, but, also, in his recognition of the authority of the
Bible and of the fathers of the church as final. But this recognition is guarded by the assertion that it is impossible for
true authority and true reason really to conflict; and he deals
quite freely with the letter of a doctrine, while he interprets
its spirit in his own way. On the development of mystical
thought, he exercised an even greater influence. The fundamental conceptions and final outcome of his great work, *De
Divisione Naturae*, are essentially mystical in tone; and, by his
translation of the pseudo-Dionysian writings, he made accessible the storehouse from which medieval mystics derived
many of their ideas. These writings are first heard of dis-

---

[1] Höffding, *History of Modern Philosophy*, Eng. tr. 1, 6.

tinctly in the early part of the sixth century; even in that uncritical age they were not received without question; but they soon gained general acceptance as the geniune work of Dionysius the Areopagite who "clave unto" St. Paul after the address on Mars' hill and who was supposed to have become bishop of Athens. The work attributed to him contains an interpretation of Christian doctrine by means of Neoplatonic ideas. It exercised a strong influence upon Erigena himself and upon subsequent medieval thought; and this influence was powerfully reinforced long afterwards by the study of Plato and the Neoplatonists at the time of the revival of learning.

Erigena's work opens with a division of the whole of reality into four classes—that which creates and is not created, that which is both created and creates, that which is created but does not create and that which neither creates nor is created. The last class is not mere non-existence. In general, it may be said to signify the potential as distinguished from the actual; in ultimate analysis, it is the goal or end towards which all things strive that in it they may find rest. It is, therefore, God, as final cause, just as the first class in the division—the uncreate creator—is God, as efficient cause. God is thus at once the beginning and end of all things, from which they proceed and to which they return. From the uncreate creator proceed the prototypes or ideas which contain the immutable reasons or grounds of all that is to be made. The world of ideas is created and yet eternal, and from it follows the creation of individual things. Their primordial causes are contained in the divine Logos (or Son of God), and from these, by the power of the divine Love (or Holy Spirit), is produced the realm of created things that cannot themselves create. God created the world out of nothing, that is to say, out of His ineffable divine nature, which is incomprehensible to men and angels. And the process is eternal: in God, vision does not precede operation. Nor can anything subsist outside God:

the creature subsists in God, and God is created in the creature in a wonderful and ineffable manner, manifesting himself, the invisible making himself visible, and the incomprehensible comprehensible, and the hidden plain, and the unknown known.[1]

[1] *De divisione naturæ*, III, 18, ed. Schlüter, 1838, p. 238.

Thus, while God, as creator and as final cause, transcends all things, He is also in all things. He is their beginning, middle and end. And His essence is incomprehensible; nay, "God Himself knows not what He is, for He is not a 'what.'" Hence, all expressions used of God are symbolical only. Strictly speaking, we cannot even ascribe essence to Him: He is super-essential; nor goodness: He is beyond good ($\dot{v}\pi\epsilon\rho\dot{a}\gamma a\theta os$).

Erigena was more influenced by Plato than by Aristotle. His acquaintance with the latter's works was restricted to certain of the logical treatises. The greater part of the Aristotelian writings became known to the schoolmen at a later date and mainly by means of Latin translations of a Syriac version. The new Aristotelian influence began to make itself distinctly felt about three centuries after Erigena's time. Alexander of Hales is said to have been the first schoolman who knew the whole philosophy of Aristotle and used it in the service of Christian theology. The metaphysical and physical writings of Aristotle were at first viewed with suspicion by the church, but afterwards definitely adopted, and his authority in philosophy became an article of scholastic orthodoxy. The great systems of the thirteenth century—especially the most lasting monument of scholastic thought, the *Summa* of St. Thomas Aquinas—are founded on his teaching.

But uniformity of opinion was not maintained completely or for long, and three English schoolmen are to be reckoned among the most (if not the most) important opponents of St. Thomas. These are Roger Bacon, Duns Scotus and William of Ockham. "Scotism" became the rival of "Thomism" in the schools. The effect of Duns Scotus's work was to break up the harmony of faith and reason which had been asserted by St. Thomas, and which was of the essence of orthodox scholasticism. Scotus was not himself heretical in religious belief, nor did he assert an antagonism between faith and reason; but he was critical of all intellectual arguments in the domain of theology. The leading school had not attempted a justification by reason of such specifically Christian doctrines as those of the Trinity or the Incarnation (as Erigena, for instance, had done). These were accepted as mysteries of the faith, known by revelation only. But certain doctrines—such as the being of God, the immortality of the soul and the creation of the world out of nothing—were held to admit of rational proof, and thus to belong to "natural theology." The arguments for the latter doctrines are subjected to criticism by Scotus. He denied the validity of natural theology—except in so far as he recognised that a certain vision of God may be reached by reason, although it needs to be reinforced by revelation. In restricting the power of intellect, Scotus exalted the significance of will. Faith is a voluntary submission to authority, and its objective ground is the unconditional will of God.

At the hands of Ockham, who was a pupil of Duns Scotus, the separation between theology and philosophy, faith and reason, was made complete. He admitted that there are probable arguments for the existence of God, but maintained the general thesis that whatever transcends experience belongs to faith. In this way, he broke with Scotism as well as with Thomism on a fundamental question. He denied the real existence of ideas or universals and reverted to the doctrine known as nominalism, of which he became the greatest exponent. Entities are not to be postulated without necessity shown. The universal exists only as a conception in the individual mind; though it signifies, without change of meaning, any one of a number of things. The only reality is the individual, and all knowledge is derived from experience. Ockham, further, is remarkable for his political writings, in which he defended the independent power of the temporal sovereign against the claims of the pope. His philosophical doctrines had many followers and opponents; but he is the last of the great scholastics, for his criticisms struck at the root of the scholastic presuppositions.

Roger Bacon, the earliest in time of the three named, was also the greatest and the most unfortunate. He lived and wrote under the shadow of an uncongenial system then at the height of its power. He suffered persecution and long imprisonments; his popular fame was that of an alchemist and a wizard; his works were allowed to lie unprinted for centuries; and only later scholars have been able to appreciate his significance. His learning seems to have been unique; he read Aristotle in Greek, and expressed unmeasured contempt for the Latin translations then in vogue; he was acquainted with the writings of the Arab men of science, whose views were far in advance of all other contemporary knowledge. He does not appear himself to have made the original scientific discoveries with which he used to be credited, but he had thoroughly mastered the best of the science and philosophy of his day. There is, of course, much in his writings that may be called scholasticism, but his views on the method of science are markedly modern. His doctrine of method has been compared with that of his more famous namesake Francis Bacon. He was as decided as the latter was in rejecting all authority in matters of science; like him, he took a comprehensive view of knowledge and attempted a classification of the sciences; like him, also, he regarded natural philosophy as the chief of the sciences. The differences between the two are equally remarkable and serve to bring out the merits of the older philosopher. He was a mathematician; and, indeed, he looked upon mathematical proof as the sole type of demonstration. Further, he saw the importance in scientific method of two steps that were inadequately recognised by Francis Bacon—the deductive application of elementary laws to the facts observed, followed by the experimental verification of the results. "Roger Bacon," it has been said, "has come very near, nearer certainly than any preceding and than any succeeding writer until quite recent times, to a satisfactory theory of scientific method."[1]

For more than two centuries after Ockham's death, only one writer of importance can be reckoned among English philosophers. That writer was John Wyclif, in whose case a period of philosophical authorship — on scholastic lines — preceded his theological and religious activity, and to whose writings reference has been made in a previous volume. After him comes a blank of long duration. The leaders of the renascence, both in philosophy and in science, belonged to the continent; and, although their ideas affected English scholarship and English literature, philosophical writings were slow to follow. And the theological controversies of the reformation led to no new enquiry into the grounds of knowledge and belief. On the universities, the teaching of Aristotle retained its hold, at least as regards logic, even after the introduction

---

[1] R. Adamson, *Roger Bacon: the Philosophy of Science in the Middle Ages* (1876), p. 33.

of the new "humanistic" studies. In the latter part of the sixteenth century, Aristotelianism experienced an academic revival, though its supporters, in all cases, were suspected of papistical leanings. John Case of St. John's college, Oxford (B.A. 1568), gave up his fellowship on this ground (it is said), married and was allowed by the university to give lectures on logic and philosophy in his house. In 1589, he took the M.D. degree and, in the same year, became a canon of Salisbury. He died in 1600. Between 1584 and 1599, he published seven books—text-books of Aristotelianism—dealing with logic, ethics, politics and economics. His *Speculum moralium questionum in universam ethicen Aristotelis* (1585) was the first book printed at Oxford at the new press presented by the earl of Leicester, chancellor of the university. John Sanderson, fellow of Trinity college, Cambridge (B.A. 1558), was appointed logic reader in the university in 1562, but, in the same year, was expelled from his fellowship for suspicious doctrine. He became a student at Douay in 1570, was ordained priest in the Roman Catholic church and was appointed divinity professor in the English college at Rheims. He died in 1602. The only work of his that is known is *Institutionum Dialecticarum libri quatuor*, printed at Antwerp in 1589, and at Oxford in 1594. About the year 1580, a vigorous controversy regarding the merits of the old logic and the new was carried on between two fellows of Cambridge colleges, Everard Digby and William Temple. They were both younger in academic standing than Sanderson or Case, but they published earlier. Digby took his B.A. in the beginning of 1571, and became fellow of St. John's early in 1573, shortly before Francis Bacon entered Trinity college as an undergraduate. He began to give public lectures on logic soon after this date. It is possible — we have no evidence on the point — that Bacon attended these lectures. If he did, they may have been the means of arousing his interest in the question of method, and they may also, at the same time, have awakened the spirit of criticism in him and led to that discontent with the philosophy of Aristotle which, according to his own account, he first acquired at Cambridge.

Digby's career was chequered. He was suspected of "corrupt religion," and he made enemies in his own society by his contempt for the authorities. In the end of December, 1587, on the nominal ground of an irregularity in his payments for commons, he was deprived of his fellowship by Whitaker, master of the college and a stern puritan. But Digby seems to have had friends in high place. He appealed to Burghley the chancellor and to archbishop Whitgift. By their order a commission was appointed to enquire into the grounds of his dismissal, and, as a result, Digby was restored 28 May, 1588. But, by the end of the same year, he seems to have been got rid of—how, we do not know.[1] Probably, the real ground of objection to him—his lukewarm protestantism—made it prudent for him to leave the university. Digby was famous in his day for his eloquence as a lecturer, his skill in the disputations of the schools and his learning. His learning, however, is much less than appears from the mere array of authorities which he cites. These are often taken from Reuchlin's *De arte cabbalistica* (1517), the fictitious personages of this work being sometimes referred to as actual authors. Digby wrote in the true scholastic spirit; for him, Aristotle's doctrines were authoritative, and to disagree with them was heresy. At the same time, his own Aristotelianism was coloured by a mystical theology for which he was largely indebted to Reuchlin. Digby's chief work, *Theoria analytica, viam ad monarchiam scientiarum demonstrans*, was published in 1579. This was followed next year by two books—a criticism of Ramus entitled *De duplici methodo*, and a reply to Temple's defence of the Ramist method. He was also the author of a small treatise *De arte natandi* (1587), and of an English *Dissuasive from taking away the lyvings and goods of the Church* (1589).

William Temple passed from Eton to King's college, Cambridge, in 1573; in due course, he became a fellow of the latter society, and was soon engaged in teaching logic. From about 1582 till about 1585, he was master of Lincoln grammar school. He then became secretary to Sir Philip Sidney (to whom his edition of the *Dialectica* of Ramus had been dedicated. After the latter's death, he occupied various secretarial posts, and was in the service of the earl of Essex when he was obliged

---

[1] All the ascertainable facts were for the first time brought together by R. F. Scott in *The Eagle* (St. John's college magazine), October term, 1906, pp. 1–24.

by the favourite's fall to leave England. He does not seem
to have returned till after the accession of king James. In
1609, he was made provost of Trinity college, Dublin, and,
a few months later, master of chancery in Ireland. He was
knighted in 1622, and died in January, 1627.

Temple's important philosophical writings belong to the
early part of his career. He was a pupil of Digby at Cambridge,
and wrote in terms of warm appreciation of his master's abil-
ities and fame and of the new life that he had put into philosophical study in England. But he had himself found a more
excellent way of reasoning in the logical method of Ramus,
then coming to be known in this country. When scarcely
twenty years of age, Ramus had startled the university of
Paris by his strenuous opposition to the doctrines of Aristotle;
he had allied himself to the Calvinists; and he ended his life as
a victim of St. Bartholomew's eve. The protestant schools,
accordingly, tended to favour his system, in which logic, as the
art of discourse, was assimilated to rhetoric and given a practical character. Ascham, indeed, in a letter of 1552, and, again,
in his *Scholemaster* (1570), expressed his disapproval of it.
But, as early as 1573, we hear of its being defended in Cambridge.[1] And, in 1574, when Andrew Melville returned from
Geneva and was appointed principal of the university of
Glasgow, he "set him wholly to teach things not heard in this
country of before,"[2] and the *Dialectica* of Ramus took the place
of Aristotle's *Organon* or the scholastic manual elsewhere
current in the universities of Great Britain. By his published
works, Temple became celebrated on the continent as well as at
home as an expositor and defender of Ramist doctrine; and,
doubtless, it is owing to his activity that Cambridge acquired a
reputation in the early part of the seventeenth century as the
leading school of Ramist philosophy.[3] Temple began authorship in 1580, under the pseudonym of Franciscus Mildapettus
Navarrenus,[4] with an *Admonitio* to Digby in defence of the

[1] Mullinger, *History of the University of Cambridge*, II, p. 411.

[2] James Melvill's *Diary* (Edinburgh, Wodrow Society, 1842), p. 49; cf.
Sir A. Grant, *Story of the University of Edinburgh*, I, p. 80.

[3] See Mullinger, *op. cit.* II, p. 412.

[4] "Navarrenus" proclaims the author's allegiance to Ramus, who was
educated at the Parisian collège de Navarre; "Franciscus" may indicate
nothing more than the French origin of the doctrine. The explanation of
"Mildapettus" is obscure.

single method of Ramus. Other controversial writings on the
same text, against Digby and Piscator of Strassburg, followed in 1581 and 1582. In 1584, he published an annotated
edition of Ramus's *Dialectica*, and, in the same year, he
issued, with a preface by himself, a disputation against Aristotle's doctrine concerning the generation of simple and
complex bodies, written by James Martin of Dunkeld, then a
professor at Turin. These two books must have been among
the first published by the university press, after the restoration
of its licence by Burghley, the chancellor, in this year.[1]

In clearness of thought and argumentative skill, Temple
was far superior to Digby. On the more special point in
dispute between them—whether the method of knowledge
is twofold, from particulars to universals and from universals
to particulars, or whether there is only one method of reasoning,
that from universals—the truth was not entirely on Temple's
side. Nor had his method anything in common with the induction used in the physical sciences. But the new logic he
recommended had the advantage of clearness and practicality,
and was free from the complicated subtleties of the traditional
systems. That Bacon was acquainted with the works of
Digby and Temple is highly probable, though it cannot be
conclusively established. Their influence upon him, however,
must have consisted mainly in stimulating his interest in the
question of method: they did not anticipate his theory of
induction.

While these questions occupied the schools, William Gilbert, fellow of St. John's college, Cambridge, 1561, president
of the royal college of physicians, 1600, was engaged in
the laborious and systematic pursuit of experiments on
magnetism which resulted in the publication of the first
great English work of physical science, *De Magnete, magneticisque corporibus* (1600). Gilbert expressed himself as decidedly
as did Bacon afterwards on the futility of expecting to arrive
at knowledge of nature by mere speculation or by a few vague
experiments. He had, indeed, no theory of induction; but he
was conscious that he was introducing a "new style of philoso-
phising." His work contains a series of carefully graduated
experiments, each one of which is devised so as to answer a par-

---

[1] See Mullinger, *op. cit.* II, pp. 297, 405.

ticular question, while the simpler and more obvious facts set
forth and their investigation led by orderly stages to that of the
more complex and subtle. It is unfortunate that Bacon was
so little appreciative of Gilbert's book, as a careful analysis of
the method actually employed in it might have guarded him
from some errors. Gilbert has been called "the first real
physicist and the first trustworthy methodical experimenter." [1]
He was also the founder of the theory of magnetism and
electricity; and he gave the latter its name, *vis electrica*. He
explained the inclination of the magnetic needle by his conception of the earth as a magnet with two poles; he defended
the Copernican theory; and, in his discussion of the attraction
of bodies, there is a suggestion of the doctrine of universal
gravitation. He had also reached a correct view of the atmosphere as extending only a few miles from the surface of the
earth, with nothing but empty space beyond.

On an altogether different plane from Gilbert were two
younger contemporaries of Bacon. Robert Fludd, a graduate
of Oxford, was a man of fame in his day. He followed Par-
acelsus, defended the Rosicrucians and attacked Copernicus,
Gilbert, Kepler and Galileo. His works are distinguished by
fantastic speculation rather than by scientific method. Na-
thanael Carpenter, a fellow of Exeter college, Oxford, attacked
the physical theory of Aristotle in his *Philosophia libera* (1621).
The works of William Harvey belong to the period following
Bacon's death, although he had announced his discovery of the
circulation of the blood in 1616.

Francis Bacon was the younger of the two sons of Sir
Nicholas Bacon, lord keeper of the great seal, by his second
wife Anne, daughter of Sir Anthony Cooke and sister-in-law
of lord Burghley. He was born at York house, London, on
22 January, 1561. In April, 1573, he was sent, along with his
brother Anthony, to Trinity college, Cambridge, where he
remained (except for an absence of about six months when
the plague raged there) till Christmas, 1575. Of his studies in
Cambridge, we know little or nothing; and it would be easy
to lay too great stress on the statement long afterwards made
to Rawley, his first biographer, that, before he left the univer-

---

[1] K. Lasswitz, *Geschichte der Atomistik* (1890), I, p. 315.

sity, he "fell into the dislike of the philosophy of Aristotle; not for the worthlessness of the author, to whom he would ever ascribe all high attributes, but for the unfruitfulness of the way." In 1576, he was sent by his father to France with Sir Amyas Paulet, the ambassador, and in his suite he remained until recalled home by Sir Nicholas's sudden death in February, 1579. This event had an unfortunate effect upon his career. A sum of money which his father had set apart to purchase an estate for him had not been invested and he inherited a fifth part of it only. He had, therefore, to look to the bar for an income and to the grudging favour of the Cecils for promotion. He was called to the bar in 1582, and entered parliament in 1584: sitting in each successive House of Commons until he became lord keeper. But office was long in coming to him. The queen had been affronted by an early speech of his in parliament in which he had criticised the proposals of the court; and the Cecils always proved more kin than kind. The objects which he sought were never unworthy nor beyond his merits; but he sought them in ways not always dignified. He pleaded his cause in many letters to Burghley and Salisbury and Buckingham; and the style of his supplications can hardly be accounted for altogether by the epistolary manners of the period. In 1589, Burghley got him the reversion of an office in the Star chamber, worth about £1600 a year; but to this he did not succeed till 1608. From about 1597, he had come to be employed regularly as one of the queen's learned counsel. In 1604, he was made one of his ordinary counsel by king James, with a salary of £40; and this, Bacon reckoned as his first preferment. He was made solicitor-general in 1607, attorney-general in 1613, privy councillor in 1616, lord keeper in 1617, lord-chancellor in 1618. He was knighted in 1603, but, to his chagrin, along with a crowd of three hundred others; he was created baron Verulam in 1618, and viscount St. Albans in 1621. A few weeks later, charges of having received bribes from suitors in his court were brought against him in the newly-summoned House of Commons; these were remitted to the House of Lords for trial; he was convicted on his own confession, and sentenced to deprivation of all his offices, to imprisonment in the tower during the king's pleasure, to a fine of £40,000, to exclusion from the verge of the court and to incapacity from sitting in parliament. The imprisonment lasted a few days only; the fine was made over to trustees for Bacon's benefit; the exclusion from the verge was soon removed; but, in spite of many entreaties, he was never allowed to sit in parliament again.

In the midst of the legal and political work which crowded these years, Bacon never lost sight of his larger ambitions. He published the first edition of his *Essays* in 1597, the second (enlarged) edition appearing in 1612 and the third (completed) edition in 1625. The *Advancement of Learning* was published in 1605, addressed to king James, *De Sapientia Veterum* in 1609, *Novum Organum* in 1620. After his disgrace, he lived at Gorhambury, the paternal estate to which he had succeeded on the death of his brother Anthony in 1601, and there he devoted himself to writing. The *History of Henry VII* appeared in 1622, and *De Augmentis Scientiarum* in 1623; the *New Atlantis* was written in 1624; at his death, he was at work on *Sylva Sylvarum*, and he left behind him many sketches and detached portions of his great but incomplete design. Bacon had been married in 1616 to Alice Barnham, the daughter of an alderman. He died on 9 April, 1626, from the effects of a chill caught by moving out of his carriage in order to try an experiment on the antiseptic properties of snow.

Bacon's plan for the renewal of the sciences was never fully elaborated by himself, and it has never been deliberately followed by others. In his personal career, too, there are some events that still remain obscure. But material is not lacking for forming a judgment on his philosophy and on his life. We cannot expect to remove either from the range of controversy. But the life-long devotion of Spedding may be said with confidence to have made one thing clear. Pope's famous epigram—"the wisest, brightest, meanest of mankind" —and the brilliant elaboration of the same in Macaulay's essay are false, and cannot be made to fit the facts. We can understand Bacon aright only if we do not assume any such absurd antithesis, but remember that life and philosophy are revelations of the same mind, and allow for one shedding light on the other. It is on this account that it is necessary to attempt an estimate of Bacon's character and to touch upon the disputed events in his career, although the questions cannot be discussed at length, and little more can be done than to indicate results.

In a fragment[1] written about 1603, and, apparently, intended as a preface to his great work, Bacon set forth the ambitions which guided his life; and there is no reason for doubting the substantial accuracy of his account. Believing (he begins) that he was born for the service of mankind, he set himself to consider for what service nature had fitted him best. He saw that the good effects wrought by practical statesmen

extend over narrow spaces and last but for short times; whereas the work of the Inventor, though a thing of less pomp and shew, is felt everywhere and lasts for ever.

And for this end he thought nature had destined him.

I found that I was fitted for nothing so well as for the study of Truth; as having a mind nimble and versatile enough to catch the resemblances of things (which is the chief point), and at the same time steady enough to fix and distinguish their subtler differences; as being gifted by nature with desire to seek, patience to doubt, fondness to meditate, slowness to assert, readiness to consider, carefulness to dispose and set in order; and as being a man that neither affects what is new nor admires what is old, and that hates every kind of imposture. So I thought my nature had a kind of familiarity and relationship with Truth.

His first object, therefore, was the knowledge that would extend and establish the empire of man over nature. But birth and education had introduced him to the service of the state; and "a man's own country has some special claims upon him." For these reasons, he sought civil employment: the service of the state may be said to have been his second object in life. Finally, he adds:

I was not without hope (the condition of Religion being at that time not very prosperous) that if I came to hold office in the state, I might get something done too for the good of men's souls.

According to Bacon's own account, therefore, the service of mankind to which he held himself born was to be carried out

---

[1] *De interpretatione naturæ proœmium*, *Works*, III, pp. 518–520. In this and other quotations from the Latin works the translations contained in Ellis and Spedding's edition have been used.

by devotion to three objects: the discovery of truth, the welfare of his country and the reform of religion. And of these three objects the first always held the highest place in his thoughts. "I confess" he wrote to Burghley about 1592, "that I have as vast contemplative ends as I have moderate civil ends: for I have taken all knowledge to be my province."

This greatness of design was characteristic of the mind of the period as well as of Bacon personally. But it was accompanied by inadequate preparation in the methods and principles of the exact sciences as understood at the time, and often by an imperfect grasp of details. If the latter defect may be traced in his intellectual work, it is still more apparent in his practical activity. It is not fanciful to connect with this characteristic some of the actions for which he has been most censured. Throughout his career he was never free from financial difficulties; and, when he had obtained high preferment, he maintained a magnificent style of living without exercising any effective control over the expenditure of his household. When the charge of taking bribes was made against him he was much surprised, but he had no defence. It may be true, as he asserted, that he never allowed a present from a suitor to influence his decision; nor do any of his judgments appear to have been reversed on this ground. It may be true, also, that Bacon only followed the custom of his time; though, on this point, it is difficult to get evidence. But he himself saw the impropriety of a judge being "twice paid"—to quote the mild term of censure used in his *New Atlantis*. And he took no care to guard against the impropriety in his own conduct. In the main, he was probably a just, as well as an efficient, judge. But he was too tenacious of his office as he had been too eager to obtain it; and it is hardly possible to resist the evidence for the conclusion that, on one occasion at least,[1] he allowed the court favourite Buckingham to influence his decision. In another matter—that of the trial of the earl of Essex—Bacon's conduct has been unjustly blamed. The benefits which he had received at the hands of Essex would not have been a sufficient reason for his standing aside when the need arose for his taking part in the prosecution.

[1] See the letter of D. D. Heath (one of the editors of the *Works*) in *Bacon's Letters and Life*, VII, pp. 579–588.

The rebellion of Essex had been a real danger to the state and not merely an explosion of bad temper. It was essential that the prosecution should not fail through the case being badly presented; and Bacon's intervention was not merely excusable: it was his duty to safeguard the interests of the state, and to subordinate to them the claims of private friendship and gratitude in spite of the tragedy of the personal situation. At the same time, it has to be said that the record of the trial does not suggest that he felt the tragedy. Judging from the manner in which he pressed home the charge, the personal factor seems to have touched him but slightly. And this, perhaps, is characteristic. He was capable of high enthusiasm for ideas and for causes. His philosophical works are inspired by the former; and his writings on public affairs show a spirit of devotion to the common weal as well as political wisdom. But, on the side of personal sentiment, his nature seems to have been not easily stirred to the love or hate which unite and divide mankind.

Bacon intended that his Great Instauration or Renewal of the Sciences should be set forth in six parts. These, he enumerated as follows: (1) The Division of the Sciences; (2) The New Organon, or Directions concerning the Interpretation of Nature; (3) The Phenomena of the Universe, or a Natural and Experimental History for the foundation of Philosophy; (4) The Ladder of the Intellect; (5) The Forerunners, or Anticipations of the New Philosophy; (6) The New Philosophy, or Active Science. Of these parts, the last was to be the work of future ages; for the fourth and fifth only prefaces were written; the first three are represented by considerable works, although in none of them is the original design carried out with completeness. Latin was to be the language of them all. The *Advancement of Learning*, which, in great part, covers the ground of the first division, was not written as part of the plan; but *De Augmentis*, which takes its place in the scheme, is little more than an extended Latin translation of the *Advancement*. Bacon's last work, *Sylva Sylvarum*, which belongs to the third part, was written in English.

Bacon, as he said himself, took all knowledge as his province; his concern was not so much with particular branches of science as with principles, method and system. For this purpose, he sets out by reviewing the existing state of knowledge, dwelling on its defects and pointing out remedies for them. This is the burden of the first book of the *Advancement* and of *De Augmentis*.   In the second book, he proceeds to expound his division of the sciences. The principle with which he starts in his classification is psychological:

The parts of human learning have reference to the three parts of man's understanding, which is the seat of learning: history to his memory, poesy to his imagination, and philosophy to his reason.

The subdivisions of these, however, are based on differences in the objects, not in the mental faculty employed. History is divided into natural and civil. To the latter of these, ecclesiastical and literary history are regarded as subordinate (although made co-ordinate in the *Advancement*). Poetry is held to be "nothing else but feigned history," and is subdivided into narrative, representative and allusive or parabolical. But it is with the last of the three main divisions of learning that Bacon is chiefly concerned.

In Philosophy the contemplations of man do either penetrate unto God, or are circumferred to nature, or are reflected or reverted upon himself. Out of which several enquiries there do arise three knowledges, Divine philosophy, Natural philosophy, and Human philosophy or Humanity. For all things are marked and stamped with this triple character, of the power of God, the difference of nature, and the use of man.

But, as the three divisions all spring from a common root, and certain observations and axioms are common to all, the receptacle for these must constitute "one universal science, by the name of *Philosophia Prima*, Primitive or Summary Philosophy." Among the three divisions of philosophy, Bacon's most important thoughts concern natural philosophy. One of his fundamental ideas is expressed by its distinction into two parts— "the inquisition of causes, and the production of effects; Speculative, and Operative; Natural Science, and Natural Prudence." More subtle is the distinction of natural science into physic and metaphysic. The latter term is not used in its traditional sense, nor is it synonymous with what Bacon calls summary philosophy, which deals with axioms common to several sciences. Both physic and metaphysic deal with natural objects: physic with their material and efficient causes, metaphysic with their formal and final causes. Thus,

> Physic is situate in a middle term or distance between Natural History and Metaphysic. For Natural History describeth the variety of things; Physic, the causes, but variable and respective causes; and Metaphysic, the fixed and constant causes.

In elaborating this view, Bacon covers ground traversed again in *Novum Organum.*

Both for its style and for the importance of the ideas which it conveys, *Novum Organum* ranks as Bacon's greatest work. To its composition he devoted the most minute care. Rawley tells us that he had seen no less than twelve drafts of it in Bacon's own handwriting, re-written from year to year. As it was at last published, its stately diction is a fit vehicle for the prophetic message it contains. The aphorisms into which the matter is thrown add impressiveness to the leading ideas, without seriously interfering with the sequence of the argument.

It is chiefly to *Novum Organum* that we must go if we would understand the message and the influence of Bacon. And this understanding will be facilitated if we distinguish, as he himself never did, between certain leading ideas which he, more than anyone else, impressed upon the mind of succeeding ages, and his own more special conception of nature and of the true method for its investigation.

Of those leading and general ideas, two have been already indicated. One of these is the belief in the unity of science. His classification of the sciences had in view not only their differences but, also, their essential oneness. "The divisions of knowledge," he says, "are like branches of a tree that meet in one stem (which stem grows for some distance entire and continuous, before it divide itself into arms and boughs)." They are to be accepted "rather for lines and veins, than for sections and separations."

The second of these leading ideas is the practical aim of knowledge. This is a constantly recurring thought, and is, in his own mind, the most fundamental; it is the first distinction which he draws between his own new logic and the old, and it was meant to characterise the new philosophy of which he claims to have made only the beginning.

The matter in hand is no mere felicity of speculation, but the real business and fortunes of the human race, and all power of operation. For man is but the servant and interpreter of nature; what he does and what he knows is only what he has observed of nature's order in fact or in thought; beyond this he knows nothing and can do nothing. For the chain of causes cannot by any force be loosed or broken, nor can nature be commanded except by being obeyed. And so those twin objects, human knowledge and human power, do really meet in one; and it is from ignorance of causes that operation fails.

Bacon's object was to establish or restore the empire of man over nature. This empire depends upon knowledge; but, in the mind of man, there are certain obstacles to knowledge which predispose it to ignorance and error. The doctrine of the tendencies to error inherent in the human mind is another of his fundamental thoughts. These tendencies to error he called *idola mentis*—images or phantoms by which the mind is misled. The name is taken from Plato and contrasted with the Platonic "idea"; and emphasis is laid on the difference between the idols of the human mind, which are abstractions that distort and misrepresent reality, and the ideas of the divine mind, which are "the Creator's own stamp upon reality, impressed and defined in matter by true and exquisite lines." This doctrine had long occupied Bacon's thought; it was stated in the *Advancement*, where, however, the last of the four classes of idols is wanting; and it was completely set forth for the first time in *Novum Organum*. In the latter work, four classes of idols are distinguished: idols of the tribe, idols of the cave, idols of the market-place and idols of the theatre. Under these graphic titles, Bacon works out a doctrine which shows both originality and insight. The originality is conspicuous in what he says concerning the idols of the tribe. They are deceptive tendencies which are inherent in the mind of man as such and belong to the whole human race. The understanding, he says, is like a false mirror that distorts and discolours the nature of things. Thus, it supposes more order and regularity in the world than it finds, as when it assigns circular motion to the celestial bodies; it is more

moved and excited by instances that agree with its preconceptions than by those that differ from them; it is unquiet, and
cannot rest in a limit without seeking to press beyond it, or in an
ultimate principle without asking for a cause; it "is no dry
light, but receives an infusion from the will and affections";
it depends on the senses, and they are "dull, incompetent and
deceptive"; and it is "prone to abstractions and gives a
substance and reality to things which are fleeting." The idols
of the cave belong not to the race but to the individual. They
take their rise in his peculiar constitution, and are modified
by education, habit and accident. Thus some minds are apt
to mark differences, others resemblances, and both tend to
err in opposite ways; or, again, devotion to a particular science
or speculation may so colour a man's thoughts that everything
is interpreted by its light. The idols of the market-place are
those due to the use of language, and they are the most troublesome of all.

For men believe that their reason governs words; but it is also
true that words react on the understanding; and this it is that has
rendered philosophy and the sciences sophistical and inactive.

Finally, the idols of the theatre are due to "philosophical
systems and the perverted rules of demonstration." In this
connection, Bacon classifies "false philosophies" as sophistical,
empirical and superstitious. In his amplification of this
division, his adverse judgment upon Aristotle may be dis-
counted; his want of appreciation of Gilbert is a more reasonable
matter of regret; but, at bottom, his view is sound that it is
an error either to "fashion the world out of categories" or to
base a system on "the narrowness and darkness of a few
experiments."

This criticism of the sources and kinds of error leads directly
to an explanation of that "just and methodical process" of
arriving at truth, which Bacon calls the interpretation of nature.
The process is elaborate and precisely defined; and it rests on a
special view of the constitution of nature. Neither this view
nor the details of the method have exerted much influence upon
the progress of science. But underlying them both was the
more general idea of the importance of an objective attitude
to nature and of the need of systematic experiment; and of

this general idea Bacon was not indeed the originator, but the most brilliant and influential exponent. In the study of nature, all preconceptions must be set aside; we must be on our guard against the tendency to premature "anticipations" of nature; "the subtlety of nature is greater many times over than the subtlety of argument"; men must be led back to the particular facts of experience, and pass from them to general truths by gradual and unbroken ascent; "we must begin anew from the very foundation," for "into the kingdom of nature as into the kingdom of grace entrance can be only obtained *sub persona infantis.*"

These general but fruitful ideas do not exhaust Bacon's teaching. He looked forward to the speedy establishment of a new philosophy which should be distinguished from the old by the completeness of its account of reality and by the certainty of its results. His new method seemed to give him a key to the subtlety of nature; and this method would have the incidental result of levelling intellectual capacities so that all minds who followed it with care and patience would be able to find truth and use it for fruitful works.

"It is a correct position," says Bacon, "that true knowledge is knowledge by causes." But the way in which he understands this position is significant. He adopts the Aristotelian division of causes into four kinds: material, formal, efficient and final. Physic deals with the efficient and material; but these, apart from their relation to the formal cause, "are but slight and superficial, and contribute little, if anything, to true and active science." The enquiry into the other two belongs to that branch of natural philosophy which he calls metaphysic. "But of these the final cause rather corrupts than advances the sciences, except such as have to do with human action," and "the discovery of the formal is dispaired of." Yet forms must be investigated if nature is to be understood and controlled. Thus, the second book of *Novum Organum* opens with the aphorism

On a given body to generate and superinduce a new nature is the work and aim of human power. Of a given nature to discover the form . . . is the work and aim of human knowledge.

What, then, does Bacon mean by "form"? He gives many

answers to this question, and yet the meaning is not altogether easy to grasp. Form is not something mental; it is not an idea, nor is it a mere abstraction; it is itself physical. According to Bacon, nothing really exists in nature except individual bodies. But a body has several qualities perceptible by our senses (these qualities he calls "natures"); the form is the condition or cause of these natures; its presence determines the presence of the relative nature; with its absence the nature vanishes. Again, a thing acts by certain fixed laws: these laws are forms.

"When I speak of forms," he says, "I mean nothing more than those laws and determinations of absolute actuality which govern and constitute any simple nature, as heat, light, weight, in every kind of matter and subject that is susceptible of them. Thus the form of heat or the form of light is the same thing as the law of heat or the law of light."

And, again,

the form of a thing is the very thing itself, and the thing differs from the form no otherwise than as the apparent differs from the real, or the external from the internal, or the thing in reference to man from the thing in reference to the universe.

Further, the form is itself a manifestation of a still more general property which is inherent in a still greater number of objects.

The complexity of the physical universe is thus due to the combination, in varied ways, of a limited number of forms which are manifested to us in sensible qualities. If we know the form, we know what must be done to superinduce the quality upon a given body. Hence, the practical character of Bacon's theory. Here, also, is brought out an idea that lies at the basis of his speculative doctrine—the idea that the forms are limited in number. They are, as it were, the alphabet of nature; when they are understood, the whole language will be clear. Philosophy is not an indefinite striving after an ever-receding goal. Its completion may be expected in the near future, if only the appropriate method is followed.

The new method leads to certainty. Bacon is almost as contemptuous of the old induction, which proceeded from a few experiments to general laws, as he is of the syllogism. His new induction is to advance by gradual stages of increasing generality, and it is to be based on an exhaustive collection of instances. This collection of instances is the work of what Bacon called natural history, and he laboured to give specimens of the collections required. He always recognised that the collaboration of other workers was needed for their completion and that the work would take time. His sense of its magnitude seems to have deepened as it progressed; but he never realised that the constant process of development in nature made an exhaustive collection of instances a thing impossible.

Given the requisite collection of instances, the inductive method may be employed without risk of error. For the form is always present where the nature (or sensible quality) is present, absent where it is absent and increases or decreases with it. The first list of instances will consist of cases in which the nature is present: this is called the table of essence and presence. Next come the instances most akin to these, in which, nevertheless, the nature is absent: this is called the table of absence in proximity. Thirdly, a list is made of instances in which the nature is found in different degrees, and this is the table of degrees or comparison. True induction begins here, and consists in a "rejection or exclusion" of the several natures which do not agree in these respects with the nature under investigation. The non-essential are eliminated; and, provided our instances are complete and our notions of the different natures adequate, the elimination will proceed with mechanical precision. Bacon saw, however, that the way was more intricate than this statement suggests—especially owing to the initial difficulty of getting sound and true notions of simple natures. Aids, therefore, must be provided. In the first place, he will allow the understanding to essay the interpretation of nature on the strength of the instances given. This "commencement of interpretation," which, to some extent, plays the part of hypothesis (otherwise absent from his method), receives the quaint designation of First Vintage. Other helps are then enumerated which Bacon proposes to treat under nine heads: prerogative instances; supports of induction; rectification of induction; varying the investigation according to the nature of the subject; prerogative natures (or what should be enquired first and what last); limits of investigation (or a synopsis of all natures in the universe); application to practice; preparations for investigation; ascending and descending scale of axioms. Only as regards the first of these is the plan carried out. The remainder of *Novum Organum* is taken up with the discussion of twenty-seven kinds of prerogative instances; and here are to be found many of his most valuable suggestions, such as his discussion of solitary instances and of crucial instances.

Although the new method was never expounded in its completeness, it is possible to form a judgment on its value. In spite of the importance and truth of the general ideas on which it rests, it has two serious defects, of which Bacon himself was not unaware. It gives no security for the validity and accuracy of the conceptions with which the investigator works, and it requires a complete collection of instances, which, in the nature of things, is impossible. Coupled with these defects, and resulting from them, are Bacon's misunderstanding of the true nature and function of hypothesis, upon which all scientific advances depend, and his condemnation of the deductive method, which is an essential instrument in experimental verification. The method of scientific discovery and proof cannot be reduced to the formulae of the second book of *Novum Organum*.

In spite of the width of his interests, especially in the domain of science, Bacon himself did not contribute any new discovery. His suggestions sometimes show insight, but also a certain crudity of conception which is connected with his inadequate general view of nature. The exposition of his method in the second book of *Novum Organum* is illustrated throughout by an investigation into the form or cause of heat. The result to which he permits himself to arrive as the "first vintage" of the enquiry exhibits this combination of insight and crudity. He reaches the conclusion that heat is a particular case of motion. The specific differences which distinguish it from its genus are that it is an expansive motion; that its direction is towards the circumference of the body, provided the body itself has a motion upwards; that it is a motion in the smaller parts of the body; and that this motion is a rapid motion of fine (but not the finest) particles of the body.

This and other investigations of his own were abandoned without reaching a clear result. His knowledge of science was also deficient, especially in the region of the exact sciences. He looked for an increase of astronomical knowledge from Galileo's telescope, but he appears to have been ignorant of the work of Kepler; he ignored Napier's invention of logarithms and Galileo's advances in mechanical theory; and his judgment on the Copernican theory became more adverse at the very time when that theory was being confirmed by Galileo and Kepler.[1] These defects in his own scientific equipment were closely connected with some of the peculiarities in detail of the method he recommended. And the two things to-gether may explain the sneer of his contemporary Harvey, that he wrote philosophy like a lord chancellor. Nor is it very difficult to understand the attitude of most subsequent men of science, who have honoured him as the originator of the experimental method, but silently ignored his special precepts. His method was not the method of the laboratory. When the objects investigated can be observed only directly as they occur in nature, greater importance must be assigned to the exhaustive enumeration of facts upon which Bacon insisted. Darwin, for example, has recorded that, in starting his enquiry, he "worked on true Baconian principles, and, without any theory, collected facts on a wholesale scale." But Bacon did not recognise that, in investigations of this sort also, the enumeration must be guided by an idea or hypothesis, the validity of which is capable of being tested by the facts. He overlooked the function of the scientific imagi-nation—a power with which he himself was richly endowed.

According to Bacon, "human knowledge and human power meet in one"; and the stress which he laid upon this doctrine lends interest to his discussions on practical principles. His views on ethical and political theory, however, were never set forth systematically or with completeness. They are to be found in the second book of the *Advancement* and in the seventh and eighth books of *De Augmentis*, as well as in the *Essays* and in some of his occasional writings. His observa-tions on private and public affairs are full of practical wisdom, for the most part of the kind commonly called "worldly." He

---

[1] Compare Spedding, in Bacon's *Works*, III, pp. 511, 725.

was under no illusions about the ordinary motives of men, and he thought that "we are much beholden to Machiavel and others, that write what men do and not what they ought to do." Fundamental principles are dealt with less frequently, but they are not altogether neglected. A preference is expressed for the active over the contemplative life, for "men must know that in this theatre of man's life it is reserved only for God and angels to be lookers on." Aristotle's reasons for preferring the contemplative life have respect to private good only. But the "exemplar or platform of good" discloses a double nature "the one, as everything is a total or substantive in itself; the other, as it is a part or member of a greater body; whereof the latter is in degree the greater and the worthier." In this way, Bacon introduced into English ethics the distinction, on which many controversies have turned, between private and public good. But the nature of this good is not subjected to philosophical analysis. A similar remark has to be made regarding Bacon's contributions to political theory. There is much discussion of matters of detail, but first principles are barely mentioned. The "arts of government" are said to contain three duties: the preservation, the happiness and prosperity and the extension, of empire; but only the last is discussed. Bacon maintained the independence of the civil power, and, at the same time, defended the royal prerogative; nevertheless, his ideal of the state was not arbitrary government, but the rule of law. In the *Advancement*, he had noted that

all those which have written of laws have written either as philosophers or as lawyers, and none as statesmen. As for the philosophers, they make imaginary laws for imaginary commonwealths; and their discourses are as the stars, which give little light because they are so high. For the lawyers, they write according to the states where they live, what is received law, and not what ought to be law.

And he goes on to say that "there are in nature certain fountains of justice, whence all civil laws are derived but as streams." To this subject he returns in the eighth book of *De Augmentis*, which closes with a series of aphorisms on universal justice. In these aphorisms, all civil authority is made to depend on "the sovereign power of the government, the structure of the constitution, and the fundamental laws"; law does not merely protect private rights; it extends to "everything that regards the well-being of the state"; its end is or should be the happiness of the citizen: and that "law may be set down as good which is certain in meaning, just in precept, convenient in execution, agreeable to the form of government, and productive of virtue in those that live under it."

Bacon's contributions to "human philosophy" do not rank in importance with his reforming work in natural philosophy; and his influence on the moral sciences was later in making itself felt, though it was similar in character to his influence on natural science. He often appealed for help in carrying out his new philosophy; but, neither in natural science, nor in moral science, nor in philosophy generally, did he found a school. Harvey's unfavourable judgment has been already quoted. Hobbes, who acted for a time as his secretary, does not seem to have been influenced by him in any important manner. And yet it is the leading thinkers—men such as Leibniz and Hume and Kant—who acknowledge most fully the greatness of Bacon. His real contribution to intellectual progress does not consist in scientific discoveries or in philosophical system; nor does it depend on the value of all the details of his method. But he had the insight to discover, the varied learning to illustrate and the eloquence to enforce, certain principles, regulative of the mind's attitude to the world, which, once grasped, became a permanent possession. He did more than anyone else to help to free the intellect from preconceived notions and to direct it to the unbiassed study of facts, whether of nature, of mind, or of society; he vindicated an independent position for the positive sciences; and to this, in the main, he owes his position in the history of modern thought.

While Bacon was engaged upon his plan for the renewal of the sciences, his younger contemporary Edward Herbert was at work upon a similar problem. But the two men had little in common except their vaunted independence of tradition and their interest in the question of method. And their thinking diverged in result. Bacon is claimed as the father of empirical or realistic philosophy; Herbert influenced, and, to some extent, anticipated, the characteristic doctrines of the rationalist or intellectualist school of thought.

Edward Herbert, the representative of a branch of the noble Welsh family of that name, and elder brother of George Herbert the poet, was born at Eyton in Shropshire on 3 March, 1583, matriculated at University college, Oxford, in 1595, married in 1599 and continued to reside at Oxford till about 1600, when he removed to London. He was made a knight of the Bath soon after the accession of king James. From 1608 to 1618, he spent most of his time on the continent, as a soldier of fortune; seeking, occasionally, the society of scholars in the intervals of the campaign, the chase, or the duel. In 1619, he was appointed ambassador at Paris; after his recall, in 1624, king James rewarded him with an Irish peerage. He was created an English peer as baron Herbert of Cherbury in 1629. The civil war found him unprepared for decision; but he ultimately saved his property by siding with the parliament. He died in London on 20 August, 1648.

His works were historical, literary and philosophical. His account of the duke of Buckingham's expedition to Rhé and his history of Henry VIII were written with a view to royal favour. The latter was published in 1649; a Latin version of the former appeared in 1658, the English orginal not till 1860. His literary works—poems and autobiography—are of much higher merit. The former were published by his son in 1665; the latter was first printed by Horace Walpole in 1764. His philosophical works give him a distinct and interesting place in the history of thought. His greatest work, *De Veritate*, was, he tells us, begun in England and "formed there in all its principal parts." Hugo Grotius, to whom he submitted the manuscript, advised its publication; but it was not till this advice had been sanctioned (as he thought), by a sign from heaven that he had the work printed (Paris, 1624). To the third edition (London, 1645) he added a short treatise *De Causis Errorum*, a dissertation entitled *Religio Laici* and an *Appendix ad Sacerdotes*. In 1663 appeared his *De Religione Gentilium*—a treatise on what is now called comparative religion. A popular account of his views on religion was published in 1768 under the title *A Dialogue between a Tutor and His Pupil, by Edward Lord Herbert of Chirbury;* and, although the external evidence is incomplete, it may have been from his pen.

Herbert does not stand in the front rank of speculative thinkers; but his claims as a philosopher are worthy of note. In the first place, he attempted a far deeper investigation of the nature of truth than Bacon had given; for he based it on an enquiry into the conditions of knowledge. Here, his fundamental thought is that of a harmony between faculty and object. Mind corresponds with things not only in their general nature but in all their differences of kind. The root of all error is in confusion—in the inappropriate connection of faculty and object. Underlying all experience and belonging to the nature of intelligence itself are certain common notions. In the second place, Herbert's treatment of these common notions made him the precursor of the philosophy of common sense afterwards elaborated by Reid and the Scottish school. Some of his tests of common notions are logical: knowledge of particulars depends upon them. But others of them are psychological: they are prior in time, and all sane minds possess them. And it is this last test—that of universality— that he uses most frequently. "What is in all men's ears," he says, "that we accept as true"; and he adds that this universal consent is the highest philosophy and theology. In the third place, the common notions which he discovered in all minds determined the scope and character of English Deism. He attempted no complete account of them, except in the sphere of religion. These common notions of religion are: (1) that there is a supreme Deity; (2) that this Deity ought to be worshipped; (3) that virtue combined with piety is the chief part of divine worship; (4) that men should repent of their sins and turn from them; (5) that reward and punishment follow from the goodness and justice of God, both in this life and after it. These five articles contain the whole doctrine of the true catholic church, that is to say, of the religion of reason. They also formed the primitive religion before the people "gave ear to the covetous and crafty sacerdotal order." In the fourth place, Herbert was one of the first—if not the first—to make a systematic effort after a comparative study of religions; but he had no idea of the historical development of belief, and he looked upon all actual religions—in so far as they went beyond his five articles—as simply corruptions of the pure and primitive rational worship.

CHAPTER XV

Early Writings on Politics and Economics

THE political and economic life of England has had an enormous effect on the whole modern world; her constitutional monarchy and her parliamentary government have been consciously imitated by one nation after another, since the time when Montesquieu held them up to admiration. The political ideas which have had such far-reaching influence were taking definite shape in our own country in the Elizabethan and Jacobean periods. They have left their mark on our literature in many ways; but, in attempting to survey these early writings on politics and economics, and to group them conveniently, it is important to remember that the views they embodied were finding their fullest expression in political action and fiery debate, rather than in graceful literary form. The first essays in English political and economic literature can be best appreciated when they are viewed in connection with contemporary struggles and experience.

In the sixteenth and seventeenth centuries, England was really anticipating the movement which occurred in many continental countries at a subsequent time; she was taking the lead in the rise of nationalities, and her literature, at that era, illustrates the various phases of conscious life which this revolution seems to involve wherever it occurs. In the first place, there was an intense patriotic sentiment, and a keen interest in national history and traditional custom. Secondly, with the aim of advocating increased opportunity for popular self-government, reflection was directed to the basis on which existing authority rested and the limits within which it should be exercised. Lastly, much consideration was given to the material means of gratifying national ambitions for such political objects as the maintaining of English independence and the expansion of English influence.

Taking these three divisions, we may say that the literary expression of patriotic sentiment and the discussions as to natural resources and the means of developing them were intensely, though not exclusively, insular; while the discussions on the power of the prince and the nature of sovereignty were much more easily applicable to the circumstances of other countries, and were relatively cosmopolitan. England was working out her own destiny; and the form of democratic doctrine which was eventually popularised in this country attracted attention both in the old world and in the new. But history has repeated itself in regard to the other elements of national consciousness. Similar patriotic sentiment, which may be stigmatised as narrow, and jealous care for material resources, have been developed, in one country after another, among the rising nationalities. The special importance of our literature lies in the fact that it not only reflects the first emergence of this modern type of community, but that this early example had a complexity of its own; Great Britain was the scene of the simultaneous rise of two nationalities. Throughout the seventeenth century, with the exception of the years of the protectorate, this island was governed as a dual monarchy. England and Scotland were each prepared in turn to expand and to assimilate her neighbour, and each has exercised an important influence on the political development of the other. The reaction of these two nationalities upon one another, during the Elizabethan and Jacobean periods, is a political feature that can be best brought into full light by the study of the literature of the day.

It might seem to follow that this political and economic writing, as a direct expression of actual political experience, would be little affected by foreign influence; but this is only true with considerable qualifications. Even as regards the expression of patriotic sentiment, the influence of foreign models may be seen in the form that was adopted, as in the case of the *Debate Betwene the Heraldes*. Further, England was a backward country, both commercially and industrially, in Tudor times; and the economic literature of the day is full of suggestions for copying expedients that had been devised in Holland or in France. It is also noticeable that the reflection on the problem of sovereignty, though the forms in which it was raised were dictated by English experience, was yet concerned with issues that had been defined by Jesuits and Calvinists in France. Still, when all this is admitted, it is true to say that English thought seems to have been but little affected by the writers who were chiefly making their mark in Italy and France. Bodin's great work had, indeed, been translated and was used as a text-book at Oxford, but it does not appear to have had more than academic influence. *The Prince* of Machiavelli may, possibly, have influenced the careers of particular men such as Edmund Dudley or Thomas Cromwell; but, for the most part, the great Florentine lay outside the circle of English thought. He was very frequently alluded to as though he had been the evil genius of political life; but, even as a bugbear, he did not obtain such a tribute of antagonism as was paid in the latter part of the seventeenth century to the commanding figure of Hobbes.

The early writers on political and economic subjects did not confine themselves to formal treatises; of these, there were very few. The thought of the day found incidental expression in literature of every sort: in plays and sermons, as well as in essays, satires and pamphlets. There can be no attempt to deal exhaustively with all the references in contemporary English literature to political and economic topics. On the other hand, some question may be raised as to how far all the fugitive pieces dealing with political and economical subjects which have survived attained to the dignity of literature. It certainly is difficult to find any criterion, and to say with confidence what should be dismissed as merely technical; but it is at least to be remembered that Malynes and Misselden and other writers on such highly technical subjects as foreign exchanges were anxious to obtain attention for their writings in polite and courtly circles; they attempted to deck their argument with literary graces in the fashion of the day. It would be churlish to refuse them a place among English authors.

Students of political science in recent times have been inclined to classify and compare different types of polity, with the view of elucidating the strong points of each and of noting their various contributions to the sum of political wisdom; but the early writers in England on political subjects seem to have felt no need of adopting this method. They concentrated their attention on England, almost as if it were the only type of polity worthy of consideration, and they discussed its characteristics. The example was set by Fortescue in his *De Laudibus Legum Angliae*,[1] but the same tone prevailed among Elizabethan and Jacobean writers. Sir Thomas Smith, who, like Sir Henry Wotton after him, had seen much of foreign lands, does, indeed, in his *Discourse on the Commonwealth of England* recognise a more general study of politics and alludes to other states, ancient and modern; he has some difficulty in classifying the realm of England under any of the Aristotelian divisions; but, while he assigns a very high place to regal power, he does not, like Bodin, treat England as an example of monarchy, but includes it among the democracies. On the whole, he is prepared to justify the institutions of his country as superior to those of any other land, and to regard it as a well organised commonwealth, in which the crown, the nobility and gentry, the burgesses and yeomen, have each their part to play. The free co-operation of distinct classes for the good of the community is a characteristic feature on which he insists; and a similar political ideal appears to have been in Shakespeare's mind. There is a striking speech in *Troilus and Cressida*, act i, sc. 3, in which Ulysses insists on the importance of degree, and its necessity in well ordered society.

> Degrees in schools and brotherhoods in cities,
> Peaceful commerce from dividable shores,
> The primogenitive and due of birth,
> Prerogative of age, crowns, sceptres, laurels,
> But by degree, stand in authentic place?
> Take but degree away, untune that string,
> And, hark, what discord follows! each thing meets
> In mere oppugnancy: the bounded waters
> Should lift their bosoms higher than the shores
> And make a sop of all this solid globe:
> Strength should be lord of imbecility,
> And the rude son should strike his father dead:
> Force should be right: or rather, right and wrong,

[1] See Vol. II of the present work, p. 338

> Between whose endless jar justice resides,
> Should lose their names, and so should justice too.
> Then every thing includes itself in power,
> Power into will, will into appetite;
> And appetite, an universal wolf,
> So doubly seconded with will and power,
> Must make perforce an universal prey,
> And last eat up himself.

Shakespeare, too, seems to recognise the supreme importance of the kingly office in a well-ordered community. The conversation between king Henry and his soldiers on the eve of Agincourt is very instructive on this point; and it is clear that his political ideals were closely connected with his conception of the English constitution. The glory and greatness of the English monarchy, as a controlling power in the English realm, is eloquently set forth in the speech assigned to Cranmer at the baptism of queen Elizabeth. A similar conception runs through Bacon's writings; and he also calls attention to the importance of the personal qualities of the prince, since, "in the great frame of kingdoms and commonwealth, it is in the power of princes or estates to add amplitude and greatness to their kingdoms." Selden, who was by no means inclined to exalt the kingly office unduly, yet recognises it as the source from which the various titles of honour and grades in the higher ranks of society spring. This well-ordered community, with a monarch at the head, was habitually spoken of as the *respublica* or commonwealth; and this last was a current term for the English realm long before it was officially adopted under the Long parliament. The importance of a strong personality at the head of a state was apparent in the reigns of Henry VIII and his children; the personality of Elizabeth, in particular, and her success in rallying round her the loyalty of her subjects and in guiding the affairs of state, continued to give actual shape to the vague political ideas of cultivated Englishmen, so that Massinger, in *The Maid of Honour*, pointed to the English monarchy as a model for less fortunate peoples.

This view as to the exceptional merit of the English *régime* was strengthened by the religious sentiment, and the belief that England was called by God to a high destiny. In looking out on the nations of the world, and on the tyrannies and internecine struggles in Spain and in France, Englishmen of the Elizabethan and Jacobean periods felt as if there had been direct divine intervention on behalf of England and, hence, divine approval of the English type of polity. The success of England, in holding her own against the power of Spain and against the dangers which beset the realm from foreign plots, was referred to by archbishop Sandys and others as a token that the course which England had pursued was divinely sanctioned. Such historical writings as Camden's *Annales* are full of patriotic sentiment; and this faith also inspired many of the efforts for expansion which were made by Sir Francis Drake and Sir Walter Ralegh. In reading the journal in which the first of these empire builders recorded his adventures in sailing round the world, we see how keenly he felt that it would be a crime against God and man to leave the newly discovered lands to be dominated by Spanish influence, and that there was a positive duty in striving to bring about the expansion of England.

So far as internal political problems are concerned, discussion in Tudor times turned almost exclusively on the conflict between public and private interests. The doctrines of Mandeville, that private vices were public virtues, and of Bastiat, that private interests necessarily co-operated for public good, were unknown, and would have been wholly repugnant, to Elizabethan writers. Private interest appeared to be diametrically opposed to patriotic sentiment. The writers of the first half of the sixteenth century who describe the social evils of that period of rapid economic transition are constantly inveighing against the mischief wrought by private men who disregarded public welfare. They had little sympathy with the spirit of competition, since the efforts of individuals to get on in the world might easily come to be inconsistent with the maintenance of each man's proper degree, and of the whole social order. This idea appears to have taken hold of the mind of Edward VI; it found expression in the prologue of Fitzherbert's *Husbandry* and in Caxton's *Game and playe of the Chesse* as well as in Starkey's *Dialogue between Cardinal Pole and Thomas Lupset* and in More's *Utopia*. The anarchy which Shakespeare describes as arising from Cade's rebellion is a

picture of the disorder which ensues when private interest
has free play and the maintenance of social order is neglected.

In the latter part of the sixteenth century, there was
increasing difficulty in seeing what classes or persons were
to be trusted to act for the public good in the present and in
the future, and as willing to leave in the background private
tastes and personal interests which conflicted with public
duty. There are frequent complaints as to the neglect of
country gentlemen to play their part in the work of local
government; the new type of non-resident proprietors was regarded with special suspicion, and depopulating and enclosing,
which continued to be denounced from time to time, seemed
to be a survival of the ruthless evictions which had moved
the indignation of bishop Latimer, and of John Hales in his
Discourse of the Commonweal. While the gentry were thus
negligent, the mercantile classes and the burghers in the
towns appeared to need direction and guidance, if the reputation of our manufactures was to be maintained and the commerce of the country to develop. So far as old traditions
survived among the industrial classes, they favoured a narrow
civic patriotism rather than the good of the realm; while the
merchants concentrated in London were affected by the
new commercial morality, and inclined to commercial enterprises, from which political trouble might easily ensue.
Every class needed to be kept up to the sense of public duty;
the clergy and ecclesiastical corporations were not above
diminishing the future value of their livings with a view to immediate gain. The council, inspired by the ceaseless activity
of Burghley, was continually engaged in putting down abuses
at which men, who ought to have been public-spirited citizens,
were accustomed to connive. Under these circumstances, it was
plausible to look to the crown as the one hope of public-
spirited conduct throughout the realm, and to regard the
king as being not only the source of honour, the fount of justice
and the arm of military power, but as supreme trustee for the
public good in all the affairs of life. This, in substance, is the
claim which was put forward by king James in *The True Law of
Free Monarchies*, and it would probably have been admitted as
sound by men who were repelled by the arguments with which
his adherents endeavoured to support it. The real refutation

was a practical one; and it was the misfortune of James and Charles that many of the undertakings in which they endeavoured to execute this trusteeship miscarried disastrously, and not only interfered with private interests, but proved detrimental to the realm as a whole.

As a consequence, under the early Stewarts, the legitimacy of giving free play to private interests was advocated in a way in which it had never been done before; and an attempt was made to treat as merely private many matters which had hitherto been regarded as of public concern. It is, of course, true that, in a body politic, no action can be exclusively private; the interconnection between individuals in the body politic is so close that wrong done by an individual may be at least a bad example and injurious to the community. Religion, which many to-day regard as a merely personal affair, was generally thought of in the Elizabethan and Jacobean periods as of supreme importance to the state. Christianity, as understood and practised by Englishmen, was held to be the foundation of Christian morality; and, hence, was a matter of public concern in which the king might be bound to interfere. The extreme Erastianism of men like Cranmer, or, for that matter, of Luther, is a surprise to many in the present day; but among Englishmen generally in Elizabeth's time, there was little sympathy with the scruples of a private conscience which set itself up against the established order, though sympathy was growing. While freedom, within limits, for conscientious conviction was coming to be regarded as not unreasonable, the freedom of the individual to carry on his business as he liked, and where he liked, apart from all moral restrictions or considerations of what was expedient for the public good, asserted itself more and more. Under Elizabeth and Burghley, it had been taken as an axiom that the direction of commercial intercourse between this country and foreign nations was a matter of public concern, and that even the internal trade of the country, so far as regards the necessaries of life, ought to be a matter of public regulation. It may be doubted whether the Elizabethan monarchy, as organised by Burghley, could have maintained itself in all its activities against the invading agitations for freedom of conscience and freedom of enterprise; but king James and king Charles completely failed to justify their position as trustees for the public welfare. Under the Council of State, the machinery for control fell into desuetude; and individual freedom, both as regards conviction and enterprise, asserted itself as it had never done before. In this era, there was a new type of patriotic sentiment, which contained no element of loyalty to the crown.

Whether they proceeded from a religious or an economic motive, the attempts to evade interference on the part of the crown with the consciences or enterprise of individuals demanded some justification. The writers of the day did not attack the fundamental question in regard to the meaning and ground of sovereignty as a mere philosophical problem: the issue was raised by practical experience and took different forms in England and in Scotland; and the efforts to organise popular self-government were very distinct in the two countries.

In England, throughout the reign of Elizabeth, popular opinion, on the whole, sympathised with the royal claims to very extensive authority in matters ecclesiastical and in foreign and commercial policy. The bull of Pius V, which was issued in 1570, had excommunicated Elizabeth and released her Roman Catholic subjects from the obligations of allegiance; it roused fierce indignation among her subjects, who felt that the maintenance of all they held dear in church and state depended on the preservation of the queen's person; and it opened the way for a rigorous persecution, as the Roman priests, and those who harboured them, were under suspicion of being traitors. Just, however, because feeling ran high, there does not seem to have been much printed discussion of the validity of the pope's claim to release subjects from their allegiance to the crown. Parsons, the Jesuit, was content to argue against the claims of the English crown to inherent authority; and Sir John Hayward, in his answer, insisted on the right of hereditary succession to the regal power of England. The underlying difficulty was scarcely dealt with by English writers of the period; if the authority of the crown was not derived from the papal authority, it would seem that it must either be directly conferred by God, inherent in the princely stock or derived from the subjects. Hooker and other writers who defended the existing order failed to make their position clear as regards these various alternatives; expressions might easily be quoted which would go to show that they did not always maintain the same standpoint.

In Scotland, during the last half of the sixteenth century, issues of fundamental principle were raised more definitely. The reformation, in that country, had been thoroughly Calvinistic; and the doctrine of Calvin was inconsistent with any claims to inherent authority on the part of a hereditary monarchy. Calvin and his followers were keenly alive to the supremacy of the Divine Will, and they believed that this Will was fully set forth in the pages of the Bible. The ministers and stewards of God's Holy Word professed to be in a position to interpret that Will from day to day and hour to hour. The conception of a mundane authority which claims to exercise any control in matters of religion seemed to be blasphemous; and the part which was left for civil officials to play in the management of public affairs was very restricted. In the free cities, like Geneva, in which Calvinism had established its hold at first, magistrates were not in a position, even if they had desired it, to contest these claims; but, when Calvinism crossed the channel from Switzerland and France to Great Britain, its pretensions came into conflict with those of the monarchy. The first notes of defiance had been sounded by Goodman, and by John Knox in his *Monstruous Regiment of Women*; and the line of argument by which he attacked the claims of queen Mary to the throne of England showed that he was out of sympathy with those who exalted the power of the prince. But the full consequences of the Calvinistic doctrines only came into light north of the Tweed. George Buchanan put forward a Calvinistic theory of national government in 1579; his *De Jure Regni* insists that the monarch is elected by the people, that he is responsible to the people and that he may be judged by the people. Though Buchanan's doctrine was not accepted by constitutional authority, it found congenial soil in Scotland. In that kingdom, the monarchy had hardly ever enjoyed a position of independence from the attacks of a turbulent nobility, and there was little difficulty in supporting the principle of the responsibility of the crown by illustrations drawn from Scottish history. The reception of civil law in the northern kingdom rendered it less possible to regard the crown as the supreme source of

right. While the prerogatives of the crown were thus mini-
mised, the claim to self-government was being effectively
pushed forward. The Scottish parliament had not, indeed,
been an important popular power, and, therefore, there was a
field left in which the self-government of the Scottish people
could be organised afresh on new lines. Despite the opposition
of the regent and the antagonism of the nobility, Andrew
Melville succeeded in completely recasting the ecclesiastical
system in 1580, and in creating a series of representative
assemblies, local, provincial and national, throughout the
country. Popular opinion was able to take complete possession
of the national ecclesiastical system; the new scheme of government professed to be strictly scriptural, and it treated the king
as an official who was bound to be subservient to this ecclesiastical democracy.

The form which national self-government attempted to
assume north of the Tweed was a direct challenge to the constitutional authorities: it raised the whole question as to the
duty of civil obedience. An attempt to counteract Buchanan's influence was made in *The True Lawe of Free Monarchies*, which was attributed to king James. The defenders of Scottish monarchy were forced to take very high
ground in order to meet their assailants, and it was under
these circumstances that the Stewart doctrine of the divine
right of kings was formulated. Similar principles had, indeed, been widely disseminated in England by the *Homily*
published in 1547, as well as by that in 1570; but the English
puritans did not, by their refusal to submit to the ecclesiastical
authorities, directly raise the issue as to the duty of obedience
to the king. The struggle was with ecclesiastical administrators
and the question as to the nature of civil authority was hardly
raised. The high doctrine of monarchy does not seem to have
received much attention or roused much antagonism until it
re-entered England from the north along with the Stewarts.
The doctrine of divine right, as fully formulated, had two aspects; on the one hand it maintained that the monarchy was
not elective, but that the occupant of the throne had an inherent hereditary right; on the other hand, it asserted that the
king was a trustee who was not responsible in any way to
his subjects, but to God Himself. Hence, it appeared that, if

there had been any contract between the king and his people, the people could never be justified in claiming to judge of a breach of contract or to take the law into their own hands. It was their duty to obey God's minister, the king; or, if he commanded them to do anything directly contrary to God's word, they might, indeed, refuse to carry out his wishes actively, but were yet bound to show their respect by submission to the punishment he might impose for their refusal. Archbishop Ussher and others, who viewed civil authority in this religious aspect, would not admit for a moment that they were giving any apology for arbitrary or tyrannical government, while they insisted on a duty of passive obedience. At all events, the doctrine is self-consistent; and those who reject it, and try to formulate principles which shall justify resistance in emergencies, have always found difficulty in explaining any rational grounds for obedience at all, except in so far as the dictates of self-interest render it expedient at the moment.

The question between popular self-government and the interference of the crown was raised in another form and debated on other grounds in England, where the parliamentary system had long been in vogue. In Elizabeth's time, the puritans had endeavoured to bring ecclesiastical grievances before the House of Commons; this, the queen resented, as it seemed that the commons were endeavouring to go outside their province and legislate on matters which could only be constitutionally dealt with by the clergy in convocation and by the crown. In this way, the religious question assumed a constitutional form. There were, indeed, many abuses in the church, both as regards ceremonial and the enforcement of discipline; and, among many Englishmen, there was little confidence in either the desire or the power of the bishops to carry out what they regarded as necessary reforms. There was, besides, widespread dissatisfaction, among the public and among lawyers, in regard to both the pretensions and the practice of the ecclesiastical courts. When the House of Commons insisted on dealing with these matters, the question came to be one of constitutional right. Hence, the party who desired an extension of popular self-government over ecclesiastical as well as civil affairs devoted their attention to the search for precedents rather than to the laying down of principles. The struggle for ecclesiastical democracy had led to the creation of a new system of popular assemblies in Scotland; in England, it took the shape of the demand for increased power on the part of one estate of the realm as against the other elements in the constitution.

At the accession of James I, the struggle was both confused and embittered by the misunderstandings which arose through identifying the corresponding movements in England and Scotland. The puritans in England doubtless expected that a Scottish king might be willing to have the church of England reformed on the lines of the Scottish church, which they regarded as scriptural. They could hardly have been aware of the horror with which he regarded this presbyterian organisation, as inconsistent with effective control of public affairs by the civil power, and incompatible with the good government of the realm. On the other hand, James was probably unaware of the importance of the House of Commons as an organ through which popular self-government might be exercised. He assumed that it might be induced to play the *rôle* with which the Scottish parliament had been content. He regarded the popular assembly as an excellent place in which to bring private grievances to the knowledge of the sovereign, but he held that it was for the sovereign, as trustee of the common weal and directly responsible to God, to shape the policy of the country for the public good.

Whether the new claims of the House of Commons called forth the assertion of higher privileges by the crown, or the manner in which the prerogative of the crown was put forward roused the antagonism of the commons, the old balance between the different elements in the life of the state was upset. The well-ordered community, as vaguely conceived in Elizabethan times, had been a body in which the nobles and gentry, and the burgesses and yeomen, co-operated for the common weal. But, in view of the need of finding a basis for insisting on the duty of civil obedience, this whole conception of the realm was modified. The supporters of the crown regarded England as a monarchy in which the king was personally responsible to God, and to God only, for all public affairs, while it was desirable that he should get such assistance from his subjects, by counsel and advice, as seemed to him to be required.   This new view of the English realm failed to commend itself to moderate churchmen; while much of the secular learning and sentiment of England, which, under other circumstances, might have been conservative, was thrown into opposition to the crown.   Those who were aggrieved by the advancement of Williams and Juxon, or irritated by the reforms of Laud, threw the weight of their influence into opposition to the crown. The controversialists were somewhat at cross-purposes; on the royalist side, there was an assertion of principles, while Prynne and his associates were engaged in accumulating precedents and attacking persons.

Both in England and in Scotland, the determination not to brook royal interference in matters of religion was momentous; but, while the presbyterians in England were willing to accede to the claims of the House of Commons the presbyterians in Scotland were more thorough-going in their insistence on spiritual independence, and had far greater difficulty in coming into line with any form of civil government.   For our immediate purpose, it may suffice to note that each movement made its own contribution to the criticism of the Stewart *régime* and proved to be a step in the progress of democratic ideas.

The century is remarkable in the history of economic thought, since the close connection between political well-being and economic activities was more generally recognised than had ever been the case before.   So soon as the king came to be dependent for a substantial part of his income not on his own estates, but on the money regularly raised by taxation, it was obviously important to him that the sources from which taxation was drawn—whether landed property or commercial profit—should be well supplied.   Hence, in the writings of the sixteenth and seventeenth centuries, there was a new concern for the material resources of the realm as contributing not merely to the wealth of private persons, but, indirectly, to the power and dignity of the realm as a whole. The few medieval treatises which have survived may be regarded as prudent maxims about private affairs—such are Robert Grosseteste's rules for the management of a household, Walter of Henley's paternal advice on the management of an estate and the ancient treatises on the duties of a seneschal. Even Fitzherbert and Tusser, in the sixteenth century, hardly pass beyond this point of view. A new note is set in John Hales's *Discourse of the commonweal of this realm in England*, which was written in 1549 and published in 1581. In no previous work had the interconnection of private business concerns and the public weal been so clearly recognised, and no writer has put more forcibly the fact that the pursuit of private interest is not necessarily inimical to, but may often be for the good of, the state. In modern times, when the government has been largely dependent for its revenue upon taxation, the promotion of the harmony between public and private interests became more apparent. Unless subjects were prosperous, there was no fund from which revenue could be drawn, and, hence, it came to be a matter of definite importance to develop the resources of the realm and to give private enterprise free play, or to guide it into those directions in which it could contribute most effectively to the maintenance of the power of the realm. This doctrine was clearly grasped by Burghley, who set himself to build up the industrial and maritime greatness of England as the foundation of her power. As the Elizabethan monarchy presented the type of polity which was accepted as normal in English literature, so the Elizabethan organisation gave a concrete economic system, which the economic writers of the period accepted as typical, and in regard to which they endeavoured to suggest improvements.

A great deal of the literature of the period is concerned with the description of the realm and its actual resources. Very interesting, in this connection, is the *Itinerary* of John Leland; a more complete account of England as a whole was issued in 1578 by Harrison in his *Description of England*.[1] Additional information, from a later date, occurs in the admirable descriptions of each county in turn which are to be found in Fuller's *Worthies;* there are also accounts of particular counties such as Westcote's *Devonshire* and John Aubrey's *Surrey* and *Wilts*, which give vivid descriptions of the conditions of large areas of the country. Very special attention, also, was turned to the condition of the Fens. The rivers which ran through these districts served as convenient channels

[1] See Vol. III of the present work, Chap. xv.

for navigation; but, at time of high tide or of heavy rain in the midlands, they were apt to flood the adjoining country. During the latter part of the sixteenth and the seventeenth century, great efforts were made to recover the land thus inundated for purposes of pasturage during the summer, if not for tillage. Dugdale's *History of Imbanking* gives a clear account of the steps which were being taken for reclaiming fen-land in this and other parts of England, while *The Anti-projector* puts in an interesting plea for the maintenance of the old conditions and the value of the products which could be obtained in the Fens by those who were acclimatised to life there. It was in these regions that the work of agricultural improvement was most obviously a matter of public concern, to which the private interests both of the fen men and of all those who were busied with internal navigation were opposed. The story of the successive attempts to deal with this problem, through different bodies of undertakers, and under the personal direction of the crown, illustrates not only the physical obstacles which had to be encountered, but the difficulty of reconciling conflicting interests and the public good. Improvement in the practice of tillage was also urged, not merely as a means of successful estate management, but because of its bearing on the prosperity of the realm. It was in this spirit that Gervase Markham and others directed attention to the agriculture of the Dutch, and indicated that, in regard to the conditions of tenure, the treating of the soil and the crops which it was well to cultivate, England would profit by studying Dutch experience. Much was to be learned from the Low Countries in regard to the development of English resources, both by sea and by land. The success of the Dutch in fishing off the English coasts roused a patriotic sense of the expediency of ousting them from this encroachment by copying their methods. Lord Burghley had been particularly keen in regard to the importance of encouraging the fishing trades as a school for seamanship. With his enormous grasp of detail, he set himself, both by precept and by example, to increase the consumption of fish; and numerous writers—Jeninges, Keymor, Hitchcock and others—insisted on the advantages which would accrue to the wealth of the realm from attention to the harvest of the sea.

Another large section of the economic writing of the

period was undertaken by men who were concerned in the official administration of national or local affairs. Such handbooks had existed from time immemorial; a great example of this kind of writing was set by bishop Richard of London, in the *Dialogus de Scaccario*, and a similar treatise on the business of the mint was probably compiled by Walter de Bardes; but, in subsequent times, there had been an enormous expansion of the administrative duties undertaken by local officials on behalf of the crown. Fitzherbert's book on the justice of the peace was the recognised manual for those who were increasingly employed in economic duties connected with apprenticeship, the conditions and remuneration of labour and the employment of the poor. The book of John Fisher, of Warwick, gives a vivid picture of the duties which fell to the clerk of the market at the time. The regulation of the prices of the necessaries of life was a constant subject of public care. No part of the economic activities of the crown was more necessary, and none presented greater difficulties in practice, than that of authoritatively maintaining the qualities of wares presented for sale in the markets. Much may be gathered on this topic, so far as the reputation of our chief English export was concerned, from the writings of Thomas Milles, a collector of customs, and of John May, who held the office of "aulnager" and was responsible that the pieces of cloth exported should be of full length. A considerable portion of the writing of the period takes the form of complaint as to the want of regulation, and the desirability of bringing some new department under the direct control of government, or of reviving the care which had been formerly bestowed. It is in this way that Malynes, in a work which has considerable pretensions to literary grace, argues against the malpractices of dealers in coin and in favour of more stringent regulation in regard to currency and exchange.

The needs of the time called forth a form of business management which was generally regarded as almost peculiar to England. In no other country did company trading proceed on quite the same lines. The great commercial companies of the seventeenth century were, historically, an offshoot of older civic institutions; for the most part, they had the character of associations where each member traded independently, but with the use of common facilities and under the acceptance of common rules. The Merchant Adventurers' was by far the most celebrated of these companies; its affairs were managed in a residency beyond the sea, and it had a large membership not only in London but in Newcastle, York and Hull. Along with the Eastland company, which traded to the Baltic, it had been the chief organ through which the successful rivalry of Englishmen with the Hanse league had been carried on. There were many complaints, however, that this company did not show an enterprising spirit and had failed to develop the market for English cloth abroad as it might have done. Its privileges were suspended, for a time, by James I, and were the subject of constant debate. Two of the secretaries of the company, John Wheeler and Henry Parker, wrote effectively in its defence, and the policy for which they argued may be said to have triumphed. The Adventurers entered on a new lease of life before the restoration, and maintained an important position in the commercial world till the Hamburg residency was suppressed by Napoleon in 1806.

The great company which was formed to compete with the Dutch and Spaniards, and to obtain direct access to the markets of the east, was organised on somewhat different lines, as it was soon found convenient that such distant adventures should be carried out on the basis of a joint stock. The advantages and disadvantages of this new trade gave rise to much criticism and discussion. The critics argued that it diverted capital from home, and denied the expediency of allowing bullion to be exported from the country. The answers were given by Sir Dudley Digges, by Robinson and, especially, by Sir Thomas Mun, whose *Discourse of Trade to the East Indies* and *England's Treasure by Foreign Trade* put the case extremely forcibly; and this company also was reinstated under Cromwell and entered on a career of commercial greatness and political power, such as its first advocates could never have foreseen.

The company form was also employed successfully for purposes of colonisation. The Virginia company has the credit of overcoming the difficulties which had rendered the first experiments of English plantation on the American continent disastrous failures. It was under the wing of a Plymouth company that the Pilgrim Fathers settled in the New world, and the settlers who were sent out by the company of Massachusetts bay developed powers not only of self-government but of federation which have done much to determine the character of the polity of the United States.   The possibilities and methods of plantation called forth a large amount of pamphlet literature, and the writings of captain John Smith, Sir William Alexander and many others, show, not only the extraordinary risks which had to be run by the pioneers, but the forethought and enthusiasm by which they were inspired to surmount them.

The risk of distant colonisation threw the adventurers back upon considering more closely the possibilities of plantation in Ireland.   Indeed, it was generally recognised that, while it might be desirable for England to obtain a footing in the New world, it was essential that Ireland should be so developed as to become a source of strength rather than of weakness to the crown.   The problem why Ireland had not been brought into line with the English model of well-ordered society was discussed by Edmund Spenser and by Sir John Davies.   Efforts continued to be made to introduce such elements from England and from Scotland that portions of the country might be successfully Anglicised; and, in some cases, this work was facilitated by the deportation of the older inhabitants, for which political unrest had given an excuse.   The most completely organised and interesting of the settlements was that which was carried out in the county of Derry with the help of the great London companies; in it we see most clearly what was the Stewart ideal of a well-organised territory, with a city and market towns and townships and estates.   The whole policy of these undertakings was bitterly criticised on the fall of Strafford, and James I cannot be said to have been very successful in inducing the citizens of London to enter heartily into this scheme of public welfare.

Another direction in which the development of public resources occupied the attention of the government was in regard to the introduction of new industries.   England, which has since become the workshop of the world, was then almost entirely destitute of skilled work in iron or steel, and was particularly badly equipped with guns and munition of war. From the beginning of the reign, lord Burghley set himself steadily and persistently to introduce new industries from abroad; but he was careful that they should not be injurious to existing trades, and that they should be really planted in the country, and not merely carried on by foreigners settled in England, who had no abiding interest in the realm. The same policy was pursued, though with less wisdom and caution by both James I and Charles I. On paper, their schemes for introducing the art of dyeing, the manufacture of alum, the development of a silk industry and the use of native materials in the manufacture of soap, appeared admirable; but the projects were not practically successful, and private interests were roused in opposition without the attainment of any real public good. Sometimes, these attempts were made by concessions granted for a period of years; sometimes, they were undertaken by the crown under official management. James and Charles could not but be inspired by the successes of Henri IV in dealing with similar problems in France; but they were unfortunate in not having advisers of the capacity of Sully and Olivier de Serres.

The attempts made under Elizabeth and the early Stewarts to control all the relations of economic life in the public interest gave a new character to the morality of industrial and commercial life. It ceased to be entirely concerned with a man's personal relations, and his personal connections, and came to be more a matter of loyal acceptance of the course projected in the public good. In its ultimate effect this change was wholly bad. The Stewarts failed to secure respect for their efforts to promote the public good; and, in the time of Adam Smith, the merchant who professed to trade in the public interest was, apparently, an object of some suspicion. When this new criterion of honourable dealing was entirely abandoned, there was neither tradition nor principle available for the maintenance of disinterested business morality, and the course of deliberately pursuing individual interest came to have defenders and, indeed, to be idealised. At least, we may see that the defenders of the old morality, who appeared to be mere pedants, were right in thinking that the new morality, which was coming in, was built on insecure foundations. The chief question of dispute was as to the terms on which capital might rightly be lent. According to the old ecclesiastical tradition, which is embodied in the 109th canon of 1604, it was wrong to bargain for any payment for certain for the use of a principal sum. The man who had borrowed it might fail to make money with it; and, therefore, though the lender was justified in requiring the return of the principal, and even in bargaining for a share of the profit if any accrued, he had no right to ask for a certain gain, or to put himself in the position of gaining at the expense of another. But in the conditions of extending business which were current in the latter part of the sixteenth, and the first half of the seventeenth, century, it was desirable, in the public interest, that hoards of money should be brought into play and used as capital in agriculture, industry or trade. In order that this might be done as easily as possible, the practice of lending money on moderate interest came into vogue, and it could be certainly argued that, in ninety-nine cases out of a hundred, or in nine hundred and ninety-nine cases out of a thousand, the merchant who borrowed at what was regarded as low interest, say, six per cent., was able to pay this interest easily and make a considerable gain for himself, while the lender got interest on money that would have been otherwise unremunerative. Henceforward, the term usury came to be applied to excessive interest, where an element of extortion might be supposed to come in; but city men generally had no scruple about the giving or taking of moderate interest as likely to land them in harsh or unneighbourly conduct. The purists, the most remarkable of whom was Thomas Wilson, whose treatise was published in 1576, and who was followed by Fenton and many of the clergy, condemned what we now call lending money on interest as a wrong bargain for a man to make, since it might render him subject to the temptation of extortion. Malynes, and the English public generally, insisted that moderate interest, which gave free play to capital, was for the public good, and that harm arose only when excessive rates were charged. This was the view which was adopted by parliament in 1624; the new commercial morality was accepted by the state, and the efforts of churchmen to maintain the old standard soon fell into abeyance.

In a somewhat similar fashion, the duty of paying a fair day's wage for a fair day's work had been, to a large extent a personal thing, though the obligation, doubtless, was limited by gild rules and manorial customs; but, after the statute of 1562, when an elaborate machinery was set up for regulating the proper rates of wages and providing for their necessary variation, the duty of considering what was fair and right almost ceased to be personal and became official, and the conscientious employer might be satisfied if he paid the rates as authoritatively fixed by statute. In that age, the personal kindness of an employer towards his hands took the form of continuing to give them employment at times when the markets were bad and work was unremunerative. It was to this course that clothiers, in times of interrupted trade, were urged by Wolsey, and by other statesmen who held that capitalists, since they carried on their business under the protection of the state and obtained a market through royal alliances, were not at liberty, in their own private interest, to dismiss their hands and thus to render their unemployed workmen desperate and liable to break out into riot.

In the Elizabethan period, attempts were also made to substitute public organisation for private benevolence in the relief of the poor. By seeking to take over the care of the poor, the state may be said to have condemned the spasmodic efforts of personal charity as insufficient, and to have attempted organised relief which rendered them unnecessary. The problem of pauperism had assumed enormous proportions both in town and country, in the early part of the sixteenth century; and the dissolution of the monasteries and the breaking up of religious houses had, at all events, helped to render the evil more patent. The *Supplication for the beggars* is an instructive picture of the variety of mendicants who were to be met with before affairs reached their worst.[1] The drastic measures of Edward VI were insufficient; but it appears that the administration of Elizabethan laws, coupled with the efforts that were made to introduce new industries, and especially with the wide diffusion of spinning as a domestic art, caused an enormous improvement in many parts of the country before the civil war broke out. There is much interesting writing in this period on the causes of poverty and on the best means of meeting it. We hear both from Devonshire and Wiltshire of fluctuations in the clothing trade as the main causes of distress,

---

[1] Cf. also Vol. III of the present work, Chap. v.

while there was also a tendency to attribute it to the introduction of pasture farming and the enclosure of commons; others urged that the squatters on the commons were the most usual source of mischief, and that greater stringency in dealing with them was essential if the problem was to be tackled. The charitable spirit, indeed, was not dead, and, during the early part of the seventeenth century, a very large number of parochial benefactions were founded for the teaching of children, for apprenticing boys or enabling them to start in business and for the care of the aged. But, on the whole, the relief of the poor was coming to be thought of more and more as a duty that was to be exercised through public channels and not by personal gifts. How far this machinery could have continued to serve its purpose may be doubtful; but, at all events, the disorder which was caused by the outbreak of the civil war put an end to the centralisation on which its efficiency depended; many years were to elapse, and many local abuses to arise, before the various factors could be once more co-ordinated in the pursuit of a common policy throughout the realm.

The early seventeenth century was a period of transition, when the power of capital was beginning to make itself felt in many directions. There was great difficulty in finding any practical reconciliation of the aims of maintaining the social stability on which comfort depends, and yet of giving sufficient scope for progress and change. The storm which broke out in the civil war was the most obvious result of the efforts of the Stewarts to exercise a mediating influence, and to organise a well-ordered system of industry and trade. Eventually, the interplay and conscious interdependence of interests in all parts of the country in carrying out the common object of building up a national mercantile marine gave cohesion to the economic activities of the realm, but this was effected by the parliaments of the Restoration period and of the Whig ascendency, not through the personal government of the crown. Patriotic sentiment found satisfaction in the success of the efforts to develop material resources of every kind, and to render them conducive to national power.

CHAPTER XVI

London and the Development of Popular Literature

CHARACTER WRITING. SATIRE. THE ESSAY

SINCE the collapse of feudalism, London had become the centre of political power in England, and the nobility tended more and more to abandon their estates and frequent the court, where preferment was to be won. But, since the fall of Antwerp (1576), London had also established its lf as the capital of European commerce, to which all nationalities crowded in search of wealth. Thus, the rich men of the upper, as well as the middle class were gradually being gathered into one city where, for want of other investments, their wealth was converted into gold plate, jewellery and rich apparel, till London became the city of fastastic costumes and extravagant ostentation. With its cosmopolitan population and foreign imports, London soon inspired the desire for travel; and Italy, the cradle of the renascence and the school of courtesy, became the goal of all voyagers. But Italy was also the home of immorality and intrigue, and northerners brought back to their own country the cynical curiosity and the ribald insincerity of the south. The centre of wealth and commerce is, also, the centre of civilisation, and the sons of rich men, whether nobles or farmers, came to London to avail themselves of its opportunities. These young men, though nominally students of law, attendants at court, or professional soldiers, formed a new and disturbing element in society. They affected a cult of modernity in which literary dilettantism and a false sense of honour combined with contempt for English traditions and indulgence in all forms of dissipation. These gilded vagabonds crowded places of public resort, introduced new fashions, cultivated foreign vices and even made their influence felt in current literature. But they achieved more lasting harm by calling into existence a class of unscrupulous tradesmen and insidious usurers, who grew rich by ministering to their capricious extravagance.

Such degeneracy, however, was not universal. Ever since Tudor times, the evils of progress had met with strong opposition from the steadier and sounder portion of the nation. Brinkelow, Bansley, Awdeley, Copland, Harman, Bullein, Gosson and a host of anonymous writers had lamented specific abuses of society,[1] and reflected the feeling of discontent which oppressed the people. But their work was not adjusted to the new conditions. In the last half of the century, London had grown to twice the size it had reached at the reformation,[2] and this vast concentration of human beings, together with new activities, luxuries and temptations, occasioned problems of existence which the Tudor pamphlets were powerless to solve. Besides, the number of educated men had increased enormously. Grammar schools had been multiplied;[3] the universities were in closer touch with the capital; a literary atmosphere was being created; intellectual interests were bringing men together. It became fashionable to read books, to criticise them and to introduce their phraseology into conversation. But the social writers of Tudor times had not that subtle persuasiveness which comes from style, and without which the man of taste can never be won. And it was this type, whether courtier, graduate, divine, soldier, lawyer, merchant, or 'prentice, who now formed the reading public. Among them arose a generation of brilliant, but mostly penurious, youths who, urged by the pinch of hunger or the spur of ambition, now came forward as authors. Their task was to interpret the features of London social life and, at the same time, to gratify the existing tendency towards literary style and conversational witticisms.[4] In their efforts to meet this double demand,

[1] *Ante*, Vol. III, Chap. v, bibl., pp. 558, 559.

[2] C. Creighton, in Traill's *Social England*, vol. III, p. 375.

[3] *Ante*, Vol. III, Chap. xix.

[4] Barnabe Rich catches the spirit of the times when he talks of "this quicke sprited age, when so many excellent wittes are endeavouring by

they created a literature of comment and observation which was, eventually, to evolve some of the best work in the language.

But the secret of realism was not discovered at once. Thomas Lodge made one of the first attempts in *An Alarum against Usurers containing tryed experiences against worldly abuses*[1] (1584). Money-lenders, with their devices for discovering the pecuniary embarrassments of young men, for gradually involving the spendthrift in debt and then using him as a decoy to enmesh others, were a theme of deadly interest to a large number of Londoners and offered endless opportunity for wit and narrative power. Although usurers had been an object of satire for more than a century, Lodge was the first systematically to expose their practices. But he still, in a style designed to appeal to the educated, relies for literary effect on the insincerities of the euphuistic novel, and presents a narrative full of apostrophes, harangues and reflections.

One of the next efforts was an examination of the age by Thomas Nashe, in *The Anatomie of Absurditie* (1588). The work is a prolix and erratic satire, coloured by touches of euphuism and confused by innumerable digressions. But, amongst an arraignment of feminine character, in the manner of *The Schole-howse of Women*, a defence of fabulists, an interpretation of Ovid's *Metamorphoses*, a discussion on diet, an invective against ballad-mongers and the customary defence of poetry, the writer vigorously criticises classical pedantry as one of the great errors of the age; while his thoughts on study and conduct, with the assertion that "the fruits of our private studie ought to appeare in our publique behaviour," and the warning to "think not common things unworthy of thy knowledge," foreshadow a literature of counsel and reflection which Bacon was to realise. But, for the moment, London was agitated by controversy, and the public looked for satire and invective only. So Nashe turned to the ruder and more profitable trade of lampoonist.

Four years later, Robert Greene changed the current of

---

their pennes to set upp lightes, and to give the world new eyes to see into deformitie." *The Honestie of this Age*, 1614.

[1] For the prose fiction of Lodge, Greene and Nashe, see Vol. III of the present work, Chap. xvi; for their plays, see Vol. V.

prose literature, discarding all the canons of euphuism by which he himself had made his reputation. But even Greene did not at once discover the want of his age. He began by appealing to the old English love of felonious ingenuity and humorous knavery in the coney-catching pamphlets already described.[1] He gives but few facts of thief life, and these are mostly drawn from the second part of Awdeley's *Fraternitye* and Parker's *Manifest Detection of Dice-Play*.[2] The bulk of his work is taken up with "pithy and pleasant" tales, which lack the picturesque touches and sociological interest of Harman's great work. But, at the same time, his pamphlets are most significant. To begin with, he is no longer writing of the organised vagrants who infested the country, but of the versatile London thief, a modern type, whose existence was bound up with the development of the capital. And, again, though this realistic interest in city life has compelled even a successful euphuist to denude his diction of all ornamentation, yet the framework of his pamphlets shows the skill of the professional author. His methods of presentation are well illustrated by *The Defence of Conny-catching*. The pamphlet claims to be a plea for the disreputable thief, and contends that worse cozenage was to be found among the respectable classes.[3] Yet this argument merely served as a pretext for exposing the dishonesty of usurers, millers, butchers, lawyers and tailors, and, still more, as an excuse for presenting the public with some admirable tales. Apparently, the success of these rather superficial pamphlets led him to widen his scope, and to include the practices of female criminals. This new material afforded an opening for novelty of form. Greene, always in search of variety, revived the medieval dialogue, presented the public

---

[1] *Ante*, Vol. III, Chap. XVI, pp. 410–412.

[2] *Ibid.*, Chap. V, pp. 110 and 115.

[3] The idea was quite in keeping with the spirit of the sixteenth century: see below, Nashe's *Lenten Stuffe*, and bibl. under Burlesque Encomia. Parson Hyberdine had delivered a sermon in praise of thievery. Many broadside ballads sang the joys of vagabondage. *The Defence of Conny-catching* claims to be a counterblast to Greene's preceding pamphlets, *A Notable Discovery* and the later parts of *Conny-catching*. But those booklets are gratuitously commended by their self-constituted antagonist, and our author is addressed with a respectful suavity, quite out of keeping with the sixteenth century spirit of controversy, but quite in keeping with Greene's methods of self-advertisement.

with *A Disputation betweene a Hee Conny-catcher and a Shee Conny-catcher*, in which the interlocutors discuss the comparative merits of male and female with a view to theft and blackmail. Though a burlesque debate, this tract really penetrates deeply into the sociology of crime, by considering the questions of sex and character which underlie the superficial dexterity of coney-catching.

This series of pamphlets marks Greene's apprenticeship in social literature. Having exhausted his material, he produced, in July, 1592, *A Quip for an Upstart Courtier*, in which he reaches his consummation. It has already been shown[1] how the greater part of the tract is taken up with a dispute between the courtier and the tradesman; and how the jury of tradesmen brought in to decide the case enables Greene to pass in review representatives of differing trades and pursuits.

The value of the pamphlet consists in the new life and meaning that Greene puts into old forms of thought. Tradesmen had been victims of caricature since the early Middle Ages.[2] The attack on the fashionable spendthrift, the central figure of *A Quip*, is part of the immemorial feud between men of wealth and men of learning, and had already found expression with Sir Thomas More and Roger Ascham. The idea of reviewing the representatives of each trade and profession had been used again and again by pamphleteers since *The Ship of Fools*, to go no further back.[3] Yet the pamphlet marks a fresh stage in the development of popular literature. The types of society are brought into immediate contact with the social controversy which culminated in the civil war. Moreover, their portraiture is new. Character sketches arise as soon as a writer has a point of view from which to contemplate a class or a type. In Bartholomaeus Anglicus,[4] the aim of the descriptions is sociological; in Higden[5] and, later, with Andrew Boorde,[6] the trend is ethnological and political. Awdeley and Harman use the character sketch to distinguish the different departments in the art of roguery, which at first

---

[1] *Ante*, Vol. III, Chap. XVI, p. 411. [2] *Ibid.*, Chap. V. p. 94.
[3] *Ante*, Vol. III, Chap. V, bibl., pp. 548–550.
[4] *De Proprietatibus Rerum* (first printed *c.* 1470).
[5] *Polychronicon*, ptd. by Caxton, 1482.
[6] *The fyrst boke of the Introduction of Knowledge*, pub. 1547.

sight appears homogeneous. But very few writers before Greene had embodied the moral or humorous aspect of a class in the individuality or mannerisms of its representatives. If we take the knight, the tailor, or the usurer, we recognise them at once as living personalities. And what draws or repels us is the man's occupation, or, rather, Greene's conception of his occupation. Henceforth, Londoners were to look for the glory or shame of their society in the description of familiar figures which thronged the street or St. Paul's.

But Greene's most profound commentary on his age is the *Groat'sworth of Wit*. The outline of the story is probably reminiscent of readings in Terence, and the main idea may well have been suggested by the Dutch Latin comedies of the Prodigal Son.[1] But autobiographical touches are unmistakable. We see there the evil effects of a boyhood spent in an unsympathetic home, hopelessly out of touch with the new movements of the time. Such an environment was not likely to prepare a sensitive, impulsive youth for the dissipations of the university or the storm and stress of Elizabethan London. Greene represented a fairly numerous class of men whom an undiscriminating study of Latin and Italian poetry led to the hiding of debauchery under an appearance of art and culture. The spectacle of the perfidious Lamilia, composing love ditties and accepting courtship couched in Ovidian[2] and Terentian preciousness, is an unconscious allegory on the fundamental imperfection of the renascence.

Greene had discovered the way to satisfy London's interest in itself. His mantle fell on Nashe, who, at the termination of the Marprelate controversy, was driven to look for other means of subsistence. He returned to the review of society with a keener and wider perception of life, a satirical vein not uncoloured by Juvenal and Rabelais and the mastery of an exuberant and torrential style, in which *argot* blends with Latinisms. Like Greene, he cast about for an attractive setting. The devil was still an object of ribald curiosity, so Nashe associated his satire with that suggestive personality, and, in *Pierce Penilesse, his Supplication to the Divell*, he

[1] For this influence on Greene's repentance-novels, see J. D. Wilson's article in *The Library*, Oct., 1909.

[2] *De Arte Amandi.*

represents the literary man as a proverbial lackpenny addressing a complaint to the devil, since appeals to the church are
useless. But, though the supplication contains contemporary
portraiture of life and character,[1] yet old forms of thought were
too deeply ingrained in popular sentiment to be eluded.
Nashe reverted to the conception of the seven deadly sins.
During the storm of the reformation, the "sins" were banished
from literature, but they reappear, towards the end of the
century, as a comic interlude in Marlowe's *Faustus*, and as
a vehicle for political invective and elaborate imagery in
Spenser's *Faerie Queene*.[2] Nashe presents all the humours
of the age and his own disillusionments and aspirations under
these "sins." In this expansive age, when love of travel
blended with national self-consciousness, Londoners took a
critical interest in foreign types. So Nashe vividly portrays
the pride peculiar to the Spaniard, the Italian and the Frenchman. Dutchmen, unwelcome in England because of their
commercial competition, are overwhelmed with invectives.
In due course, the writer passes on to Gluttony, and then to
Drunkenness, in which the Dutch are again satirised. "The
nurse of all this enormitie (as of all evils) is Idleness," the
type of which is the stationer who referred all would-be cus-
tomers to his shop-boy with a jerk of his thumb, but was full
of activity at meal-time. Covetousness is not treated; but
the supplication is followed by a disquisition on devilry and
spiritualism, at that moment one of the burning questions of
the day.[3]

But this brilliant and felicitous commentary on contemporary London was by no means uninfected by the contentious
spirit of the age. The city was still echoing with the Marprelate
controversy, which had been suppressed at the height of the
conflict. But the public had not lost their taste for vituperative literature, and Nashe, foreseeing opportunities for "copy,"
had advertised himself in *Pierce Penilesse* as a professional
controversialist. In this capacity, he undoubtedly aspired to
imitate Pietro Aretino, who held all Italy at bay from his one
refuge in Venice (1527–57). Nashe, in order to be sure of

[1] *Ante*, Vol. III, p. 412.
[2] F. Rogers, *The Seven Deadly Sins*, 1907, chap. VI.
[3] See bibl. under Witch-controversy.

rousing an antagonist, followed his challenge by a personal attack on the two Harveys,[1] who had already crossed swords with him, and a "flyting" at once began. In studying this controversy, it must be remembered that literary duels, quite apart from personal animosity, had been a quasi-academic tradition since the days of the medieval *Serventois* and *Jeu-partis*. Dunbar, Kennedy, Montgomerie, Churchyard, Skelton, Alexander Barclay, Lily the grammarian, James V, David Lyndsay and Stewart had taken part in "flytings."[2] But both Nashe and Harvey were probably more influenced by the classical scholars of the renascence. Beside Aretino, Poggio had given models of vituperative skill against Felix Anti-papa, Filelfo Valla[3] and Petrarch. Julius Caesar Scaliger and Étienne Dolet[4] had both attacked Erasmus with the vilest scurrility; and, lastly, Cicero, Harvey's supreme authority, had proved a past master in the art of invective against the living and had not spared the dead. Personal resentment was certainly a motive in the Harvey-Nashe controversy; but private animosity was merged in the class hatred which the university nourished against the literary adventurers of London.

Nashe's *Apologie of Pierce Pennylesse* marks a new stage in the art of personal abuse. Martin Marprelate had written in the style of a boisterous monologue, in which his arguments were enlivened by parentheses, ejaculations and puns.[5] Nashe, undoubtedly his imitator, cultivates the same torrential and eccentric eloquence, but hardly attempts to refute his adversary. He merely uses him as a canvas on which to display his brilliant ingenuity. He invents amazing terms of vituperation, whose force is to be found in their imagery rather than imputation. Harvey is a "mud-born bubble," a "bladder of pride newe blowne," a "cotquean and scrattop of scoldes," a "lumpish leaden-heeld letter-dauber," "a mote-catching carper." Sometimes, his antagonist becomes the occasion for notes and observations in which the original subject is

[1] See *ante*, Vol. III, pp. 449, 615.

[2] T. Schipper: *W. Dunbar*, Berlin, 1884. R. Brotanek: *Alex. Montgomerie*, Vienna and Leipzig, 1896.

[3] Voigt: *Die Wiederlebung des classischen Alterthums.* Körting: *Gesch. der Literatur Italiens im Zeitalter der Renaissance*, I, p. 388.

[4] R. C. Christie: *Étienne Dolet*, 2nd ed., 1899.

[5] *Ante*, Vol. III, Chap. XVII, pp. 435-437.

lost sight of, as in his digression on Roman satire, or on the adaptability of the hexameter to English. Such exuberant fertility of fancy and expression was primarily Nashe's innate gift. But his unceasing efforts at *paronomasia* betray the influence of such Italian Latinists as Guarino, and his affectation of figurative paraphrase is, in its essence of the kind which the Theophrastians made fashionable a few years later. But there are other passages in which his imaginative sarcasm overreaches itself and collapses in mere buffoonery.

Harvey retaliated with *Pierces Supererogation*. But the reply remained unanswered, since Nashe now came forward as a religious reformer in *Christs Teares over Jerusalem* (1593), to which he prefixed a declaration of peace and goodwill to all men. Such sudden conversions were not uncommon in an age of conflict between the traditions of medieval Christianity and the Graeco-Oriental morality advocated by the classics of the silver age. Gosson and Rankins both wrote plays before condemning the immorality of the stage; Anthony Munday is alleged to have written *A Ballad against Plays;* John Marston followed the production of an erotic poem with an attack on licentious verse; R. Brathwaite, after playing with the toys of fancy, published *The Prodigals Teares: or His fare-well to Vanity* (1614); and both Dekker and Rowlands unexpectedly appear in the guise of missionaries. As we have seen in the case of Greene, the ideals of ancient Rome and of renascent Italy were a treacherous guide among the temptations of London, and but a sorry consolation in times of poverty and pestilence. But the taste of the reading public must have chiefly weighed with these bread-winners. The lower classes loved the spectacle of a stricken conscience, even in their street ballads, and the ever-increasing sect of puritans must, by now, have formed a body of opinion difficult to resist. The booklet begins with a long paraphrase of Christ's prophecy of the fall of Jerusalem. Then follows an account of its fulfilment, drawn from Joseph Ben Gorion.[1] But it is easy to see that the narrative is coloured by a national sense of uneasiness. The signs and tokens which foreshadowed the

---

[1] *History of the Latter Times of the Jews' Commonweal.* *Vide* McKerrow, *Works of T. Nashe*, vol. IV, 1908, p. 212.

destruction of the holy city are like the broadside prodigies[1] which were circulating throughout England, and the horrors of the siege recalled the downfall of Antwerp, still fresh in men's minds.[2] Nashe pointed to the ruin of Jerusalem as an object-lesson for London, whose sins, he cried, were no less ripe for judgment. Thus he introduces an arraignment of city life.

The transformation of society from an aristocracy based on the subjection of the masses to a monarchy based on the balance of classes was being accompanied by the development of commerce and the diffusion of knowledge. The age offered many more prizes to wit, and life in London became a struggle for self-advancement. Such a period of transition inevitably bred abuses. Men and women did not scruple about the means they employed to push their fortunes. The successful spared no ostentation which might command the respect of their fellows, while the unsuccessful were filled with envy and dis-content. Immorality increased in imitation of Italy, or as a reaction from the restraints of the medieval church. Finally, in this expansion of the intellectual and social world, many found the faith of their ancestors insufficient, and turned to atheism. Such was the society which Nashe denounced in the last part of *Christs Teares*. The style is still vigorous, but it has lost its exuberant originality and, in places, approximates to pulpit oratory. There are a few touches of Nashe's irresistible satire and an exposure of London stews unparalleled in English literature. But his attitude is that of a Tudor church-man. Like Latimer, he anathematises pride as the fundamental vice of the strenuous, ambitious city life. Like Crowley, he designates all the necessary and accidental abuses of competi-tion as a violation of the Biblical law to love one another. But what the booklet loses in spirit, it gains in thoughtfulness. It is largely an attempt to examine the social sentiments. Avarice, extortion, vainglory, atheism, discontent, contention, disdain, love of "gorgeous attyre," delicacy (worldliness), lust

[1] *Ante*, Vol. III, Chap. v, p. 124 and Bibl., p. 561.
[2] Cf. *The Spoyle of Antwerpe, Faithfully reported by a true Englishman* (*i.e.* G. Gascoigne), Novem., 1576, London, 1577(?). *The Tragicall Historie of the citie of Antwerpe since the departure of King Phillip*, 1586. *A Looking Glasse for London and England* (by R. Greene and T. Lodge), 1594. *A Larum for London or the siedge of Antwerpe*, 1602. Dekker's (?) *Canaan's Calamitie*, 1598.

or luxury and sloth are all anatomised and all traced back
to pride. In this method of analysis and synthesis, Nashe
evolves a literary process hardly removed from the essay.
Each sin forms a theme of its own, introduced by a definition.
Thus,

> vaine glory is any excessive pride or delight which we take in things
> unnecessary; much of the nature is it of ambition but it is not so
> dangerous or conversant about so great matters as ambition. It
> is (as I may call it) the froth and seething up of ambition.

This play of thought and fancy on familiar ideas, already
noticeable in *The Anatomie of Absurditie*, illustrates a habit of
mind made familiar to us by Bacon and his school.

But Nashe was not destined to create the essay. He had,
indeed, the sympathy with daily life, the knowledge of character, and the familiarity with classical wisdom necessary to
cultivate this genre. But he had also to earn his bread and
pay his debts. He could not distil his philosophy into a volume
of detached counsels and reflections, which might slowly
win its way. So he continued to squander his wit, learning
and experience in pamphlets "botched up and compyled"
on the sensations of the moment.

Thus, in his next production, reflections on Turkey, Iceland,
physiognomy, consumption and Camden hurtle one another in
a counterblast to dream-superstitions. Europe, at this moment,
was agitated with the belief that the devil was regaining his
control over man. His handiwork was being discovered everywhere; old women were witches, cats were spirits or trans-
figured men, dreams were messages from hell. The report of a
gentleman, who died after experiencing seven fantastic visions,
had just reawakened Englishmen's alarm at the unseen perils
of sleep and darkness. Nashe seized this opportunity to
compose the *Terrors of the Night*. At this time, demonology
belonged to the realms of theological disquisition. Even R.
Scot had not escaped the academic atmosphere, and G. Gifford[1]
and H. Holland[2] had recently delivered themselves of treatises
unutterably scholastic. It is a striking illustration of the

---

[1] *Discourse of the subtile Practises of Devilles*, 1587.
[2] *A Treatise against Witchcraft*, 1590.

vitality of popular literature that Nashe discovered how to burst the bubble of these superstitions by sound common sense and sympathetic insight into human nature. He claims that one thought of faith will put to flight all the powers of evil, and answers with a volley of ridicule the dogma of St. Chrysostom that the devil can multiply himself indefinitely. He quotes history to prove that dreams seldom or never come true unless they are direct intimations from God; and he refutes the belief in astrologers from his own experience of their careers. Most of them, he declares, began as apothecaries' apprentices and dogleeches, who used to impose on rustics with ointments and syrups made of toasted cheese and candle ends. By and bye, some needy gallant hears of their practices and introduces them to a nobleman on condition of sharing the profits. Thus, they make their way through the world, sometimes rising by their counterfeit art to the position of privy councillor. He disposes of the mystery of dreams, explaining them as after-effects of the day's activity; "echoes of our conceipts," often coloured by sensations felt in sleep, so that the sound of a dog's bark suggests the "complaint of damned ghosts" in hell, and "he that is spiced wyth the gowte or the dropsie" dreams of fetters and manacles. This theory had already been outlined by Scot,[1] but Nashe surpasses the older controversialist when he describes the moral terrors of the night. Not only does a guilty conscience breed "superstitions as good as an hundred furies," but the sorrows and anxieties of life have special power, as Bullein had pointed out,[2] in the loneliness and gloom of sleep-time.

But Nashe was never again to approach so near the high level of a moralist. Some more skirmishing took place between him and Gabriel Harvey in the autumn of 1593 and in 1594.[3] And then, in 1596, he produced *Have with you to Saffron-Walden, or, Gabriell Harveys Hunt is up.*

This piece of invective is unique in English literature, and it exhausts the literary resources of the age. To multiply his ridicule and give scope to his digressions, he borrowed from comedy and cast the lampoon into the form of a tetralogue,

---

[1] *Discoverie of Witchcraft*, 1584, Bk. x.
[2] *Bulwarke of Defence: Booke of Compoundes*, fol. liiij.
[3] *Ante*, Vol. III, Ch. xvii, bibl., pp. 615, 616.

in which four speakers contribute to criticise Harvey's style and to make merry over his humble origin. Then ensues a burlesque biography of the doctor. His conception and birth are narrated in the manner of Rabelais, and his academic character is travestied on the model of *Pedantius*.[1] Nashe creates a truly infernal picture of the university scholar, absorbed in his own spite:

In the deadest season that might bee, hee lying in the ragingest furie of the last plague, when there dyde above 1600 a week in London, ink-squittering and printing against me at Wolfes in Powles churchyard.

Neither Nashe nor anyone else expected such accusations to be taken seriously. But the tract deserves a place in permanent literature. It is a saturnalia of invective such as only the age could produce. Nor must we regard this intellect and ingenuity as altogether wasted in a barren attempt to defame a fellow-creature. The impeachment was composed for a critical audience, and, in the effort to attain rhetorical effect, the art of expression was perceptibly enlarged. Among other features, there is a full-length portrait of Harvey, executed with a thoroughness of detail which Mme. de Scudéry might have envied, and the character of an intelligencer which the Overbury collection never surpassed.

Nashe passed through two years of adversity, and then reappeared in 1599 with *Lenten Stuffe*. This pamphlet is an ambitious attempt to "wring juice out of a flint": to heighten his humour by extracting it from unproductive material, and he succeeds in uniting many of the lighter types of prose literature in a single pamphlet. He begins by introducing a personal note telling the public of his literary difficulties and financial embarrassments. These led him to leave London. In return for the hospitality which he enjoyed at Yarmouth, he recounts the history of that town (drawn from Camden) in a fine spirit of pageantry, trumpeting its origin and development "as I have scrapped out of worm-eaten Parchments." He then treats his readers to a specimen of burlesque encomium, such as the Romans, Italians and especially the German anti-

---

[1] See ed. Moore Smith (Louvain, 1905) and *post*, Vol. V, the chapter on Academic Plays.

Grobianists, had made popular,[1] working up an eulogy on the herring fisheries, not forgetting their services to Lent (hence the title). *The Prayse of the Red Herring* soon develops into a kind of jest-book. But the tales and anecdotes no longer turn on the humiliation of monks or the "quicke answers" of wenches.[2] Nashe wittily parodies the legends of antiquity and adapts them to the glorification of this homely fish. How the fable of Midas, who turned everything to gold, originated from the fact that he ate a red herring. How Leander and Hero (after a burlesque account of their adventures, in Nashe's best manner) were converted into fish—the youth to a ling, the maiden to a Cadwallader herring and the old nurse, who had a sharp temper, into the mustard which always accompanies them at table. The curing of the herring was discovered in a manner suggestive of Charles Lamb's roast pig, and the first red herring was sold to the pope by methods reminiscent of the sibyl's sale of the prophetic books.

But, besides a sense of the romance of history, and an ingenious appropriation of classical lore, there is an unmistakable love for the sea and sympathy with the rough, simple, life of seamen. In one place, he tells how "boystrous woolpacks of ridged tides came rowling in." Again, he describes the cobbles which skim "flightswift thorow the glassy fieldes of Thetis as if it were the land of yce, and sliding over the boiling desert so earely and never bruise one bubble of it." And he talks of "these frostbitten crabtree faced lads, spunne out of the hards of the towe."

Yet, *Lenten Stuffe* never enjoyed the popularity of *Pierce Penilesse*. With all its cleverness and narrative power, the tract did not gratify the Londoner's interest in city life. This taste for realistic satire and humour continually increased and tended every year to number more educated men within its ranks. At the same time, court circles began to grow weary of Euphuism, and to prefer discussing their fellow-creatures rather than indulging in the apostrophes and soliloquies of

[1] *Vide* C. H. Herford, *The Literary Relations of England and Germany*, chap. VII, pp. 381–3. Also bibl. under Burlesque Encomia.

[2] Cf. *A C. Mery Talys, Merie Tales of Master Skelton, The Geystes of Skoggan*.

prose romances[1] or such poems as *Ovid's Elegies*[2] and *Venus and Adonis*. These two elements combined to form an upper stratum in the general reading public. "Select" persons lived in the same city as ordinary members of the middle classes, and were attracted by the same phenomena. But they were more fastidiously critical, and they looked more uncompromisingly for the stamp of classicism, in any publication of which they were to approve.[3]   Even Sir John Harington's Rabelaisian descents[4] into the secrets of cloacinean burlesque (1596) are illuminated with bookish allusions and classical quotations.   The school of pamphleteers who had formerly secured patronage with erotic poetry now followed, perforce, the new tendency.   Thomas Lodge set the example, in 1595, by producing a slim volume of verse eclogues and satires, and, with a show of self-assertion made fashionable by Nashe, he entitled the venture *A Fig for Momus.*

Verse satire had flourished throughout the sixteenth century, and, in many instances, developed individual portraiture under the guise of types.   Within the last fifty years, Crowley's *One and Thirty Epigrams* (1550), Bansley's *Pryde and Abuse of Women* (1550), Hake's *Newes out of Poules Churcheyarde* (1567) and Gosson's *Quippes for Upstart Gentlewomen* (1596) had covered the most prominent abuses of the time and kept pace with the growing spirit of puritan censoriousness. But Lodge ignored their example and revived the new genre which Wyatt[5] had introduced, almost unobserved, into English literature: the avowed imitation and occasional paraphrase of classical models.   He chose Horace[6] for his satirical prototype; but, attempting to copy the Roman's genial discursiveness, he merely gave the public ten dull, ill-constructed satires and epistles, mingled with a few Vergilian eclogues.   And yet *A Fig for Momus* is important.   Wyatt was before his time and, moreover, confined his animadversions to the court, in a

---

[1] *Ante*, Vol. III, Ch. XVI.   [2] Marlowe.

[3] Note the condescension of Peacham: *Compleat Gentleman*, "There is no book so bad, even Sir Bevis himselfe, Owleglasse, or Nashe's herring, but some commodity may be got out of it."

[4] See bibl. under Miscellaneous Burlesques.

[5] *Ante*, Vol. III, Chap. VIII.   For popular satirists, see *ibid.* Chap. v.

[6] Sat. v, however, is an imitation of Juvenal x, and a forerunner of *The Vanity of Human Wishes.*

difficult metre borrowed from the Italian. Lodge's production is as miscellaneous and bookish as a volume of essays. Moreover, he made current the use of pseudonymous allusion, and, while Gascoigne had rather unsuccessfully experimented in blank verse, he demonstrated that classical satire could be most effectively written in the decasyllabic couplet.

In 1597, Joseph Hall, then a young fellow of Emmanuel college, claimed the honour of being the first English satirist with *Virgidemiarum*. It is possible that Hall's satires existed in manuscript as early as 1591, and, again, it is just conceivable that he was unacquainted with the work of Wyatt, Gascoigne, Donne and Lodge.[1] But, in any case, the boast of originality was partly justified, inasmuch as Hall discovered Juvenal as the true model for Elizabethan and Jacobean satire. In the hands of Horace, the Roman *Satura* was little more than a series of desultory conversations, dominated by an unembittered scepticism of human activities. Juvenal, however, was a rhetorician, who devoted a life's training in oratory to the task of making out a case against society. As such, his satires have all the uncompromising sweep of an indictment and are enforced with every artifice of arrangement and expression. Both his systematic thoroughness and his aggressive indignation, though largely a pose, were adapted to this contentious age, and Hall may fairly claim to be the first who reproduced his method and spirit in English verse.[2]

But this originality of imitation did not fetter a very living interest in the questions of his own day. This was an age when all educated men discussed literary criticism,[3] and Hall devotes the first book of his satires to these debatable topics. He merely champions the poetic reaction of the "nineties," when he censures the insipidity of love poetry, declaring that Cupid has now made himself a place among the muses, who begin to tolerate "stories of the stews." Academic circles, however, must already have been preparing the way for the Augustan age, when Hall ridicules such poets as Spenser for compiling "worm-eaten stories of old time," full of invocations

---

[1] *Vide* A. B. Grosart, *Occasional Issues*, vol. ix, 1879; Bp. Hall's *Complete Poems*, intro., pp. vi–viii.

[2] *Vide* A. B. Grosart, *ibid.* pp. viii–xiv, for list of parallel passages between Hall and Horace, Juvenal and Persius.

[3] *Ante*, Vol. III, bibl. to Ch. xiv, p. 594.

and strange enchantments, and when, in a graphic description of a play-house, he represents "Turkish Tamberlaine" stalking across the stage, declaiming verses of half Italianised English, and followed by a "selfe misformed lout," who mimics his gestures, disgraces the tragic muse and sets all his spectators in a roar.[1] The second and third books deal with more general abuses. But the commonplaces of satire gain new force and directness from the spirit of cultured irony with which Hall invests them. The time-honoured accusation against the fee-serving physician[2] reappears in the form of a sarcastic commendation.[3] The impostures of astrology are ridiculed by a maliciously absurd calculation on the issue of a love affair.[4] We have the inevitable satire on the gallant, but the form is new. Ruffio is seen disporting himself in "Pawles," "picking his glutted teeth since late noontide." Yet, on closer inspection, we find that his face is pinched and his eye sunken, and we realise that the youth is starving himself to buy clothing, the fantastic embellishments of which give him the appearance of a scarecrow.[5] And Hall's most perfect piece of workmanship is a mock advertisement in which a "gentle squire" looks for a "trencher-chaplaine," and, in return for abject servility and unremitting toil, offers him "five markes and winter liverie."[6]

The first three books of *Virgidemiarum* are termed "toothless satires," because they aim at institutions, customs or conventionalities. The last three are styled "byting," since they attack individuals under pseudonyms which were probably no disguise to contemporaries. The composition is even more defective. Some pieces suggest the incoherences and obscurities of the rough copy. But the future bishop had studied human nature in the provinces, where a moralist may trace the ravages of a vicious propensity through all the actions of a man's life. And so, among the confusions and solecisms of his

---

[1] Sat. III. As Marlowe in his prologue deprecates the "conceits" of "clownage," Hall's tirade should be considered as an attack on the actors rather than on the author.

[2] Cf. Chaucer's *Canterbury Tales* and Bullein's *Dialogue against the Fever Pestilence*, 1584.

[3] Bk. II, Sat. IV.   [4] *Ibid.* Sat. VII
[5] Bk. III, Sat. VII.   [6] Bk. II, Sat. VI.

thought and diction, we find a few sketches of misspent lives fully charged with mordant irony. There is the story of old drivelling Lollio, toiling night and day in poverty and squalor, extracting every groat from the land, in order that his son may study at the inns of court and have means to cultivate the dissipated refinements of the cavalier. The son revels in the pleasures of the capital, where he is too proud to recognise his father's acquaintances. But, when visiting his home, he is an object of admiration to the simple rustics. That is his father's reward. By and bye, the old man dies, the son succeeds to the property and proves more grasping than his sire. Hall entitles this sketch *Arcades Ambo*.[1] Then there is Gallio, whose self-indulgence is regulated by an effeminate regard for his well-being. He is a glutton at heart, but considerations of health keep him from coarser food than plovers' wings. Others may turn soldier or pirate from lust for blood or hope of booty. Gallio must pick roses, play tennis and wed in early adolescence. What though his children be puny? Virginius delayed too long and now regrets that he cannot marry.[2] Lastly, there is the picture of the glittering hall along the roadside. You knock at the gates but, like Maevius's Italianate poetry, all is showy without but empty within. No smoke comes from the chimneys, the sign of old-fashioned hospitality. The truth is that hunger and death are now abroad, and the rich, who should make head against them, have fled, leaving the poor to bear the brunt.

Although Hall's moral earnestness found few imitators in verse satire, others[3] were not slow to recognise the possibilities of Juvenalian invective as a literary exercise. Edward Guilpin produced a volume entitled *Skialetheia or A Shadowe of Truth* (1598), possibly influenced by Du Bartas's *Semaines*,[4] in which he vigorously protested against the emasculated poetry of his age, and claimed that satires and epigrams were the only antidote. John Marston, in the same year, coupled a very erotic poem, *The Metamorphosis of Pygmalion's Image*, with *Certaine Satyres*, which were probably composed in haste to keep up with the new trend of literary taste. The work of

---

[1] Bk. IV, Sat. II.   [2] *Ibid*. Sat. IV.
[3] See bibl.   [4] Translated that year into English by Joshua Sylvester.

both writers bears the mark of academic fabrication. Yet both are unmistakably influenced by the London around them. These satires are not moral denunciations, but studies in hypocrisy, affectation and compromise — vices peculiar to urban society—which they illustrate with lifelike silhouettes culled from the court, the ordinary, the street and the aisle of St. Paul's. Marston adds zest to these character sketches by a literary controversy with Hall, who had satirised him as Labeo;[1] and, next year, abandoning love poetry once for all, he produced another volume of satires, *The Scourge of Villanie* (1599), in which the hypocrisy of the sensualist is exhibited in its most offensive forms. The tract is memorable for an "essay in criticism" and a "Dunciad" combined, in the sixth satire. After ingeniously accounting for *The Metamorphosis of Pygmalion* as an object-lesson against erotic verse, Marston turns on his literary *confrères*, ridiculing the invocations of some, the dreams and visions of others and the bathos to which the over-inspired descend. The critics are even more contemptible. When Capro approves, we know that he has found a line which "incends his lustful blood"; Muto, the fop, admires what he cannot understand; Friscus, in criticising a book, always pretends to recognise passages from Horace and Juvenal, though he has never read a line of either. In these and similar productions, scurrility was rapidly becoming an end and object in itself. The spirit of the Tudor "flytings," which had reappeared in the Marprelate controversy and the Harvey-Nashe feud, was now taking yet another lease of life under the stimulating influence of Roman satire. But the licensers became alarmed at this recrudescence of envy and hatred, and, before the end of 1599, an order was issued to suppress the offensive works of Nashe, Harvey, Hall, Guilpin, Marston and others.[2] However, the edict by no means brought peace and goodwill into literature. A "flyting" arose over *The Scourge of Villanie* within two years of its suppression, and gladiatorial combats continued, in the world of letters, to be the recognised resource of the intellectually unemployed.[3]

But, quite apart from personal animosity, formal satire was bound to thrive among the upper classes. As we have seen,

---

[1] Bk. III, Sat. x.   [2] See bibl. for particulars of the edict.
[3] See bibl. under Flytings.

this form of classical imitation originated in a reaction from love poetry, but its subsequent developments were due to a deeper movement. By the beginning of the seventeenth century, a sense of disillusionment was prevading the nation, caused, partly, by the corruption of the governing classes, and, even more, by the bitter social and religious antagonisms among the people themselves. They began to lose faith in high ideals and heroic sentiments, and, as the passions and deeds of men lost their hold on the imagination, the petty curiosities and materialised interests, inseparable from city life, came out of the shadow. Attention was drawn more and more to the commonplace side of human nature. This tendency is already noticeable in Nashe, and, by the death of Elizabeth, the moods and idiosyncrasies of people were becoming the commonest themes of creative literature. As the physicians had explained temperament to be dependent on the predominance of one of the four humours or moistures—phlegm, blood, choler and melancholy—which pervaded the physiology of man, it became fashionable to dignify any mental characteristic or even pose with the name of "humour," and to deem the most miserable affectations worthy of literary comment.[1]

The debasement of thought was accompanied by a growing preoccupation in form and style. Seneca's maxim *in hoc omnis hyperbole extenditur ut ad verum mendacio perveniat* began to be universally abused. It will be pointed out elsewhere how this decadence affected the theatre and caused the unsympathetic and exaggerated portrayal of types to take the place of the humour and pathos of incident. But it concerns us to notice here that this artificiality of sentiment and expression, which caused the decay of comedy, stimulated an enormous output of tractarian literature. A vast number of miscellaneous pamphlets began to appear. They treated the "humours" of men hardly less effectively than the theatre, and they offered endless opportunity for experiments in style and classical imitation, which the theatre did not offer.

[1] *Vide* Shadwell, *The Humourists*, Epilogue; Ben Jonson, *Every Man out of his Humour*, *The Induction* and *The Magnetic Lady*, introduction; John Marston, *Scourge of Villanie*, Sat. x; S. Rowlands, *The Letting of Humors Blood*, Epig. 27; Nym hopelessly misuses the word: *vide* H. B. Wheatley, intro. to *Merry Wives*, 1886. Also *N. & Q.* Ser. x, vol. XI, Feb. 20, 1909.

Juvenalian satire fell under this influence and became a fashion. A large number of writers wrote in this style with elaborate and suggestive titles.[1] Even R. C., author of *The Times Whistle*, chose the decasyllabic couplet as the vehicle for his homilies on such subjects as atheism, pride, avarice, gluttony and lasciviousness. His moralisations, like some of George Wither's, are unsuited to dramatic form, but so vitalising was the study of London "humours," that, while his denunciations of the more heinous vices are dull to the extreme, his character sketches of men's weaknesses and affectations are bright and vivid.[2]

At the end of the sixteenth century, it was discovered that the abnormalities and eccentricities of conduct about which men laughed and talked, rather than waxed indignant, could be best portrayed by some detached, fragmentary form of composition, and imitation of the Latin epigram became the rage. This interest in human peculiarities and oddities dates from the production of *Mery Tales and Quicke Answers*, and the new departure in classicism impoverished the development of the jest-books as well as of the drama. Even at that period, John Heywood had embodied this type of anecdote in fragments of rough verse which his publishers chose to call epigrams,[3] and Robert Crowley had issued sallies of moral and social satire under the same name.[4] But the progress of civilisation and the growth of London had made character far more complex, and the taste for literary form, coupled with increasing social intercourse, had prepared men of culture for the pointed Latin epigram which had already been refined into a subtle but formidable weapon by the Italians from the days of Pius II to Leo X (1458–1522). Sir John Harington and Sir John Davies were among the first who adapted this type to English uses, and they were followed by Thomas Bastard (1597), John Weever (1598) and Samuel Rowlands (1600). After the accession of James, Catullus and Martial were imitated as frequently as Juvenal, and were preferred by those who realised that "humours" were a theme for the witticisms of conversation rather than for the tirades of a moralist. John

---

[1] See bibl. under Satire.
[2] *Vide* satires "Against shams" and "Against pride."
[3] See bibl.   [4] *The One and Thirty Epigrams*, 1560.

Davies of Hereford was, perhaps, the most typical. In 1610 he brought out *The Scourge of Folly*, depicting such social offences as Fuscus's boorishness,[1] Gorgonius's slovenly appearance,[2] Brunnus's unctuous manners[3] and Classus's loquacity.[4] But the epigram, then as always an offspring of social intercourse, must culminate in a conceit, and Davies frequently relinquishes the scourging of folly merely to present a play of paradox or fancy.[5] In parting company with satire, the epigram came to rely more on the artifices of literary form, and its votaries, however frivolous their theme, helped to prepare the age of Addison and Pope by recognising the importance of workmanship and cultivating the niceties of expression.[6]

Bastard's work and that of Davies mark the stage when literature was being cultivated as a social art. The epigram has all the atmosphere of a coterie. It is conceived in a lighter vein, it is suited to the eccentricities, not the degradation, of character; it adorns everyday interests with the charm of literary form; it is a detached fragmentary production convenient for circulation. But, by the beginning of the seventeenth century, it was discovered that the Theophrastian character sketch fulfilled all these conditions, offered greater scope to the play of conversational idiom, gave the sanction of classical form to the age's love of portrait-writing and, in some measure, satisfied the interests which it was the function of the stage to gratify.

In order to understand the influence of Theophrastus, it must be remembered that his life falls into the period 373–284 B.C., when the Athenian commonwealth was a community of burghers, all educated in the same manner, dressed in the same style and occupied in the same pursuits. Their lives were not, apparently, much complicated by political strife, commercial expansion, or religious controversy. Hence, the moral and ethical differences of men were noticeable only in the common traffic of existence, and study of character became

---

[1] Epig. 8.   [2] Epig. 101.   [3] Epig. 1 or 2.   [4] Epig. 263.

[5] Cf. Epig. 176, comparing a gamester to the ivy which first loosens the masonry, grows over and then holds it together, as a gambler does his estate.

[6] Cf. Epig. 106, which is practically a paraphrase of one of Bastard's on the slowness of his composition.

a close attention to details of conduct. Theophrastus, probably under the inspiration of Aristotle,[1] discusses about thirty cases in which men vary from normal perfection. This variation he does not find in their appearance, dress or thoughts, but in one side of their habitual conduct. A sketch or description from this point of view requires a special technique. Theophrastus begins each essay by briefly defining the quality under discussion—be it irony, avarice, boorishness, or stupidity—and then illustrates the definition by a number of typical actions. As the actions have no necessary connection with each other, but are drawn from any kind of situation, in which the particular propensity will betray itself, the portraits may fairly claim to be generic. As the instances and anecdotes are within the range of everyone's daily experience, the portraits have a touch of reality. Now, character sketches, as we have seen, were already a common feature of English social literature. But they were accidental productions subordinated to the main interests of a connected work, produced without method, overladen with non-essentials, or disfigured by gross caricature. Theophrastus introduced three changes. He raised the character sketch to the dignity of an independent creation, containing its own interest within itself; he emphasised action as the essence of such description; he provided a stereotyped technique. This genre, the product of a simpler civilisation, but a more mature literary art, was quickly adopted by the writers of the age and transformed into a vehicle for ideas far beyond the dreams of the inventor.

The first printed adaptation came from the pen of Joseph Hall, who, after indulging his satirical vein, especially against Roman Catholics, in *Mundus alter et idem* (1605), had devoted himself to the production of moral and religious treatises. He published a third series of *Meditations and Vowes* in 1606, and then settled on the Theophrastian character sketch as a means of putting religious problems in a practical light. In 1608 appeared *Characters of Virtues and Vices*, an attempt to bring home to men's conviction the nobleness of virtue and the baseness of vice. Nothing illustrates more clearly how tentative was the progress of social literature. Theophrastus had aimed

[1] *Vide* "The Analyses of Character" in *Ethics*, bk. IV, and *Rhetoric*, bk. II.

at reproducing the humorous side [1] of social faults, Hall employs his method to expound the practice of a moral system. The first book of characters, *The Characterisms of Virtue*, all exemplify in different forms an ideal of spiritual aloofness and self-mastery amid the errors and turmoil of the age. This stoic doctrine in a Christian setting is seen not less clearly in "The Humble Man," who "can be more ashamed of honour than grieved with contempt, because he thinks that causeless, this deserved," than in "The Happy Man," who "knows the world and cares not for it; that, after many traverses of thought is grown to know what he may trust to and stands now equally armed for all events." [2] But the character sketch was intended to describe action, and Hall forces it to portray a state of mind. Thus, though there are passages of a noble and restrained eloquence, the general effect is wearisome and monotonous.

The second book, *The Characterisms of Vices*, has a no less didactic purpose. But its object is to render vice despicable, and Hall has, perforce, interwoven his descriptions with illustrations of the complex follies and errors of his time. Thus, the second series of characters, if less artistically perfect, serves a higher purpose and embraces a wider field than the work of Theophrastus. We read of frauds, superstitions, conspiracies, libels and lampoons, vain doctrines and reckless extravagance. Perhaps the best piece is the character of "The Ambitious Man," in which we have an arraignment of court life. The scornful irony of *Virgidemiarum* is revived in the portrait of the courtier, a slave to all those who can advance him, cleaving like a burr to a great man's coat, and, when accompanied by a friend from the country, crowding into "the awful presence," in order to be seen talking with the mightiest in the land.

But, in adapting Greek form to modern ideas, Hall has modified the technique. As his subject has grown more complex, the initial definition is refined into a conceit which implies more, though it says less. For instance, "The Patient

---

[1] *Vide* intro. to *The Characters of Theophrastus*, English translation and revised text, by Sir R. C. Jebb, re-edited by J. E. Sandys, 1909.

[2] The desire for stoic consistency was a feature of this unsettled age. Cf. Hamlet's "Give me the man that is not passion's slave," and Ben Jonson's *Discoveries, De sibi molestis.*

Man" "is made of metal not so hard as flexible," superstition
"is godless religion, devout impiety." The idea thus hinted
at in a paradox, after careful elaboration, is rounded off in an
epigrammatic summary, whereas each chapter in Theophrastus
terminated abruptly.

Another indication of the new tendency is found in *The
Man in the Moone*, a popular treatise on practical morality
composed by W. M. in 1609. A belated traveller is represented
as receiving hospitality one night from the typical wise man
of romance, a venerable hermit who has seen all the world and
condemns its vanity. Thirty years earlier, such a situation
would have developed into a dialogue full of confessions,
apostrophes and homilies. But, instead of a euphuistic disquisition, we learn that the wise man is regarded as a magician,
and that folks are coming to have their fortunes told. A
stripling opens the gate and describes the appearance of each
visitor—drunkard, glutton, usurer, lover, tobacconist (tobacco-
smoker) and parasite. An elder youth stands by the philosopher and delineates each character; the old man, as fortune
teller, predicts the consequences of the enquirer's way of living.
This triple method of portraiture betrays no direct imitation,
though some hints may have been drawn from the character
sketches in *Cynthia's Revels*. But so descriptive an examination of well-doing and ill-doing would hardly have been possible unless Hall had shown from Theophrastus how much
personal details signify in morality.

Meanwhile, the character sketch was assuming a new aspect in the aristocratic circles of London. The period had
come when a number of courtiers, who were also scholars and
men of the world, were using their position to introduce among
the ruling classes more "cultured" habits of thought and expression. A movement was on foot, similar to that which
Mme. de Rambouillet was soon to lead in France. English
humanists had no *salons* to which they could retreat from
friction with the outer world, and where intercourse with ladies
could change in one generation from insipid adulation to an
artistic accomplishment. They cherished a literary life of
their own, and they used the Theophrastian character sketch
to draw attention to what was sordid or material both within
the court and without. These compositions were an amuse-

ment, at first privately circulated. None the less, they encouraged and interested people in conversational style and, by emphasising the imperfections of others, raised their ideal for themselves.

Sir Thomas Overbury was a prominent figure in this society, and, after his death, twenty-one characters were added to the second edition of his poem *A Wife* (1614), some by himself and others by his friends, as the title admits. The collection, in its final form, must have been largely the work of amateurs who had come under Overbury's influence as a lover of culture. Their publications were a tribute to the name of the man who had practised and, perhaps, introduced the art, and the interest aroused in his death would ensure a good sale. The volume contains three distinct styles of character sketch: the eulogistic, the satirical and the humorous. But, among variations of detail, the whole series presents a unity not inconsistent with co-operation: the review of society from the experienced courtier's point of view. In the first place, we have a number of commendatory portraits, which, unlike Hall's, are not spiritual studies, but examples of how "a worthy commander in the warres" would act who knows the hazard of battle, never pardons a mistake in the field and despises calumny. Or, it is a model of "A noble and retired house-keeper" (landed gentleman), still cherishing a spirit of old-fashioned hospitality in a country seat whose Gothic architecture will "outlast much of our new fantasticall building." Or, best of all, a "franklin," who withstands the modern scramble for wealth, never goes to law, does not evict tenants to enclose pastures and, despite the puritans, would approve of king James's permission[1] for dancing in the churchyard after evensong. Or, lastly, "An excellent actor," one of the earliest and most successful attempts to place that profession among the fine arts, in the teeth of calumny.

But class spirit becomes more evident in the satirical portrait. A series of sketches expose, with the bitterest caricature, the shifts and antics of the upstart courtier: his meanness, servility and sordid materialism.[2] Even "The

---

[1] *The King's Majesties Declaration to his subjects concerning Lawful Sports to be used*, 1618; rptd. *Social England Illustrated*, intro. by A. Lang, 1903.

[2] *Vide* "A Courtier," "An Ignorant Glory-hunter," "A Timist," "An Intruder into favour."

Dissembler" is no longer a mere transgressor against good faith, but a diplomatist who "baits craft with humility . . . and of the humours of men weaves a net for occasion." When character beyond the pale of the court is studied, it is the obstinate narrowness, the hostility to the refinements of a liberal education, among the inns of court, the university or the country gentry, which are emphasised.[1] This bias is best illustrated by the character of "An hypocrite," which begins with an analysis of the type on broad lines, but soon narrows into a pamphleteering attack on the puritan, who condemns the culture of the age as "vaine ostentation," revolts against all authority of church or king and yet exacts not only maintenance and obedience but even admiration from the sect over which he tyrannises.

These sketches and descriptions follow the Theophrastian technique, but the style is highly coloured by a conversational element. Wit, as we have seen, consisted largely in extracting imagery or allusion out of the most prosaic or even sordid topics, and definitions of types offered an excellent field for elaborate comparisons and imaginative paraphrases. It is true that, in portraying the middle-class types who opposed their ideals, the display of wit was somewhat hampered by the bitterness of the satire. But courtiers and humanists found free scope for their fanciful cleverness in describing the humbler walks of life. We have a number of lighter pieces, which turn into merriment the most ordinary of occupations. Thus, we learn that a tinker's[2] "conversation is unreprovable for hee is ever mending"; and that a French cook, with his attractive dishes made out of slender materials, "is the last relic of popery, that makes men fast against their conscience." A humorous connection is also traced between a man's occupation and his habit of thought. "An Ingrosser of corn" hates tobacco (a supposed substitute for food), and a sexton cannot endure to be told that "we ought to live by the quick not the dead." Thus, we see that the humour of earlier and simpler generations still survived in conversational literature. These periphrases, double meanings and obliquities of expression

[1] *Vide* "A country gentleman," "An elder brother," "A meere common lawyer," "A meere scholar," "A meere fellow of an house."

[2] By J. Cocke, added to the 6th impression.

sometimes resemble the scholarly puns of the Italian Latinists;
but we must also remember that, in a more ingenuous form,
they were the essence of the Tudor books of riddles.[1]   Overbury's chapters on "A very Woman" and "Her next part"
read like a continuation of the medieval controversy on women
which the author of *The Schole-howse of Women* had revived.[2]
The character of "An ordinary Widdow" is one of the most
studied in the book, yet the witticisms are but brilliant variations on a standing joke which appears in *A C. Mery Talys*,
The Boke of Mayd Emlyn, and *The Wife of Bath's Prologue*.

Besides involved and artificial pleasantry, the Overbury
collection is already touched with an air of supercilious mock-
ery which, later, was to become the characteristic of court
life. A different line of development is traceable in another
miscellany published by a young lawyer, John Stephens, in
1615, together with prose and verse essays entitled *Satyrical
essayes, characters and others*, and followed, in the same year,
by a second series.[3] In these two collections, after conventional sets of commendatory portraits, and a number of
legal characters adorned with the usual style of conceit, we
find a few sketches inspired by a wider and more independent
curiosity in life. To begin with, some of the definitions show
a less affected interest in men and women. For instance,
Overbury had enlarged on "An Apparatour" as "A chicke of
the egge abuse, hatcht by the warmth of authority." Stephens
explains an informer as "A protected cheater or a knave in authority"; and there is insight as well as wit in his characterisa-
tion of a churl as "the superfluity of solemne behaviour." But
the chief importance of Stephens's work lies in the fact that,
now and then, he discovers the individual beneath the type.
His picture of "A Ranke Observer" is not a typical detractor,
but a man who mockingly cultivates the faults he notes in
his friends till they become second nature in himself. "A
Gossip" and "An Old Woman" are not invectives, but sketches,
full of personal observation as vivacious as Rowlands's *Tis
Merrie when Gossips meete*. His character of a page takes
us behind the scenes, and shows to what depravity lads were
exposed at court. In two sketches, he borders on the short

1 *Ante*, Vol. III, Chap. v, p. 106.
2 *Ibid.* pp. 100–102; bibl. 551–554.   3 *Vide* bibl.

story. One depicts "A Begging Schollar," who, while at college, was nicknamed the "Sharke," and, being expelled, wanders about the country consorting with vagrants, preaching if an opportunity occurs. When admitted to a few nights' hospitality, he steals the silver spoons. The other character is "A Sicke Machiavell Pollititian," that is to say, the insincere man who, after posing all his life, is now face to face with the reality of death.

But it was not in London that the character sketch reached its fullest development. A number of manuscript portraits had been in circulation for some years at Oxford, when Edward Blount printed them in 1628 under the title *Microcosmographie*. It was afterwards known that the collection was chiefly the work of John Earle. These productions are composed with a more chastened humour and in a more scholarly style than those of Hall, Overbury or Stephens. Conceits, of course, are not wanting, and many of the characters consist of jests and paradoxes invented out of such familiar figures as a trumpeter, a sergeant, a carrier, or a cook. Others, again, describe institutions, such as Wye Saltonstall was afterwards to portray.[1] And others have a satirical or controversial purpose, coloured by the university point of view.[2] But *Microcosmographie* contains something beyond wit, style and ephemeral satire. The other Theophrastians were exposing the absurdities which rival classes always discover in each other, or, at best, were analysing some type which creates interest because conspicuous. But Earle, under the guise of character sketches, enquires into the moral significance of the day's unrecorded words and actions. He was one of the first writers who showed how essential a part of the ordinary man's life is made up of trivial and familiar things, and, consequently, how carefully these trifles should be studied. Hence, he explains characters

---

[1] *Picturae loquentes or Pictures drawn forth in characters* (1630) (2nd ed. enlarged, 1635,) contains, among other sketches, "The World," "A Country Fair," "A country ale-house," "A horse-race," "A Gentleman's house in the country." Earle has "A taverne," "A bowle alley," "Paul's Walke," "A prison."

[2] Earle's "A Downe-right Schollar" and "A good old man" are answers to Overbury's "A meere Scholar" and "An olde man." Earle treats questions of university interest in "A raw young preacher," and his essay on "A Scepticke in Religion" deals with the difficulties of a student who hesitates between conflicting creeds.

which seem so colourless that they generally pass unnoticed. We have searching analyses of such commonplaces as a child, a weak man, a mere formal man, a plain country fellow, a modest man, a poor man and a coward. Earle shows how a lack of vigilance in the veriest routine of life ends in self-deception, error or discontent, and he constantly draws a comparison between the judgment of wise men and that passed by the common herd. His technique, roughly, is the same as that of his predecessors, but his initial definitions are sometimes more felicitous, and his conclusions sometimes break off with a studied heedlessness more contemptuous than any invective.[1]

Hall, Overbury, Stephens and Earle completed the nationalisation of the Theophrastian character sketch. They were followed by a host of imitators,[2] of whom John Cleveland, Samuel Butler and William Law were the greatest; and, from the time of the Civil War, this type of literature became a recognised weapon in party strife. Their work is important because it gave direction and method to the study of character, and introduced a crisp, concentrated style of description. They cannot be regarded as having materially influenced the novel, because the Theophrastian character sketch remained objective, but they supplemented, and, in some measure, supplanted the drama, which is always hampered in an age of class satire or political warfare. The beginning of a more subjective treatment is marked by the publication of *The Wandering Jew* (1649). This work is largely a reproduction of *The Man in the Moone*, with the important difference that the characters, besides being described, plead for themselves and thus enlist our sympathies.[3]

The character sketch was mostly an attempt to ventilate the newly roused interest in morals and manners. But, as we have seen, its association with conversational preciousness often lowered it to a mere triumph of paradox. Moreover, it did not fully meet the needs of the age. As men became conscious of the growing complexity of London life, they also

[1] West's edition of Earle's *Microcosmography*, 1897, intro. p. xxviii.
[2] See bibl.
[3] Cf. Raleigh's comparison between Overbury's Country Knight and Sir Roger de Coverley, *History of the English Novel*, 1891, chap. v.

grew conscious of a running commentary on similar problems to be found in classical literature. The humanists of court circles discovered lessons of statecraft and diplomacy in Machiavelli and Tacitus, examples of daring and fortitude in Plutarch, and hints for wit and courtesy in Castiglione, Cicero and Suetonius. Such reading started new trains of thought on topics too fleeting and miscellaneous to be classified in a methodical discourse. But, unsystematised reflection was not the creation of the Jacobean age. Caxton's prefaces have the qualifications of essays in criticism. While the form and style of the medieval *Exempla* were serving as models for Tudor jest-books, the apologue tended to expand into a discussion.[1] The writings of Andrew Boorde and William Bullein are full of digressions on the occasional interests of daily life, and Nashe's tracts were practically a patchwork of miscellaneous notes and observations. The character sketch was far too restricted and too polemical to gratify this aptitude for desultory comment; but men of a more contemplative and less satiric frame of mind[2] began to jot down their reflections and thoughts after the manner of religious meditations. This habit of thinking on paper rapidly assumed importance among the intellectual coteries of London; manuscripts were passed from hand to hand, and the more finished and methodical commonplace books even found their way into print,[3] following the example of Montaigne (1580), from whom they took the name of "essay." The new genre entered timidly on its career, the very title being an apology for its informality and incompleteness.[4] The first essayist who anonymously put forth *Remedies against Discontentment drawn into severall discourses from the writinges of auncient philosophers*, in 1596, explains, in an introductory address, that they were "onely framed for mine owne private use; and that is the reason I tooke no great paine, to set them foorth anye better"; and then, after speaking of the great moralists of the past, he excuses his own work

[1] *Vide* the concluding commentary attached to some of the anecdotes in *Mery Tales and Quicke Answers*.
[2] Cf. the Theophrastians' merciless caricature of the gallant with Cornwallis's essay on "Fantasticnesse."
[3] See bibl.
[4] *Essay* from low Latin *exagium*, a trial or testing, Italian *saggio*, Spanish *ensayo*, French *essai*.

by adding, "From these faire flowers, which their labours have afforded mee, I have as I passed by, gathered this small heape, and as my time and leasure served me, distilled them and kept them as precious." In the following year, Bacon produced his slim pamphlet of *Essayes. Religious Meditations. Places of perswasion and disswasion*, in which, among "*Meditationes sacrae*" and "The Coulers of good and evill," we have a number of maxims and directions jotted down under ten headings, possibly suggested by lord Burghley's *Precepts or Directions for the well ordering and carriage of a man's life.*[1] Bacon's essays have a narrow but practical scope. They virtually recognise the courtier's career as a profession, and show how health, wealth and even learning, must be directed to the development of the special qualities necessary for success. Nay, more, his reflections shed light on the management of men, and penetrate the cross purposes and conflicting judgments which make up the atmosphere of the court. This side of human nature was already familiar to statesmen, but it had never before been discussed in maxims and rules which, if terse to obscurity, nevertheless reveal the basis of egoism underlying a maze of intrigues and shifting reputations.

But the scope and range of the essay had not yet been discovered. Bacon's first series must have appealed to men as a manual of diplomacy, a kind of *Complete Courtier;* and, for this reason, Sir William Cornwallis's work has an importance which its literary merit would not have justified. He produced in 1600 and 1601 two sets of essays, with some of the diffuseness, but none of the charm, of Montaigne. He, too, discussed problems of high life, especially the means by which men rise to prominence or favour; and, in many places, he gives the same advice as his more illustrious predecessor. But he has introduced a personal touch (also a feature of Montaigne) which was afterwards to become a characteristic of the essay. His reflections are sometimes prefaced by curious confidences and self-revelations which give them the air of a diary. Again, his outlook is wider. The study of Plutarch's *Lives* had given him an admiration for manliness, wisdom and heroism, and he examines modern character and enterprise from this point of

[1] See bibl. The *Precepts* were not printed at this time, but Bacon may well have seen them in MS.

view; thus showing how to use the past as a commentary on the present. And, above all, he formulates the new ideal[1] of gentlemanly culture; the man of no special science but of liberal interests,[2] who can turn all kinds of books, even nursery rimes and street ballads, to his profit,[3] talk of horses and hawks to those who understand nothing deeper, and use all knowledge "to looke upon man."[4]

This conception of the *honnête homme*, formulated thirty years before Faret's *L'Art de plaire à la cour* (1630), is the centre of Robert Johnson's reflections, published as *Essaies or Rather Imperfect Offers*, in 1601. Education[5] is, for him, merely the training for action; affability,[6] the art of concealing offence; wisdom,[7] the secret of successful statesmanship. His work is more direct and educative than that of Cornwallis. Frequently, he gives rules for self-training in special excellence, notably in the essay on experience,[8] with its examination of the historical lessons to be learnt from Tacitus. But he never loses sight of the humanist's ideal of culture. He argues that learning is no inconvenience to the soldier,[9] but renders him more virtuous; and, while Ascham, Greene, Nashe and Hall [10] were anathematising foreign travel, Johnson advocates it in an essay from which Bacon was not ashamed to borrow.

The essay was rapidly becoming, instead of an established form of literature, a collection of notes and maxims. David Tuvill used it wherein to display amazing familiarity with anecdotes of Greek and Roman worthies in two garrulously discursive and unpractical volumes.[11] Before long, the practice of detached composition became the object of parody—the surest sign of recognition—in such productions as *The Penniless*

---

[1] This conception did not originate with Cornwallis, but is found underlying Lyly's *Euphues* and Ascham's definition of εὐφυὴς in the *Scholemaster*, 1570. *Vide Elis. Crit. Essays*, vol. 1, p. 1. Perhaps Cornwallis took the idea straight from Montaigne "*Or à cet apprentissage (= à bien juger et à bien parler) tout ce qui se presente à nos yeulx sert de livre suffisant; la malice d'un page, la sottise d'un valet, un propos de table ce sont autant de nouvelles matières.*" *Institution des Enfants.*

[2] "Of Discourse," pt. 1.

[3] "Of the Observation and Use of things," pt. 1.

[4] "Of knowledge," pt. 11.   [5] Ess. iii.   [6] Ess. x.   [7] Ess. xiv.

[8] Ess. v.   [9] Ess. viii, "Of Art Military."

[10] *Quo vadis? A Just Censure of Travell*, 1617.

[11] *Essaies politicke and morall*, by D. T. Gent, 1608; *Essayes morall and theologicall*, 1609.

Parliament of Threadbare Poets (1608). It blended with the collections of characters. In the fourth edition of Overbury's works (1614), a number of witty and humorous essays on countries, manners and customs were added in the form of "Newes." John Stephens, in 1516, coupled his *Characters*[1] with some verse essays more or less in the manner of Persius, and some serious prose reflections full of quaint illustrations of thought, in which he discusses the claims and responsibilities of high-birth, the need of paternal kindness, the sin of "disinheritance" and the lessons of sympathy and kindness to be learnt from others' sorrow. Geffray Mynshul employed both fashionable types, though both inadequately, to expose the rapacity of jailors in *Essayes and Characters of a Prison and Prisoners* (1618); Nicholas Breton endeavoured to fuse the two types into one in *Characters upon Essays* (1615). He chose the topics already discussed by the essayists—wisdom, knowledge, resolution, truth, death, fear—and, in each case, wove a few commonplace ideas into an embroidery of antithesis and metaphor. Each essay begins with a conceited definition, which is elaborated by every artifice of paraphrase, and then relinquished with an affectation of courtly indifference. Thus, the essay, which had originated as a record of informal meditation, would probably have degenerated, for several decades at least, into a mere literary toy, unless Bacon had shown its true scope and capacity.

Bacon's virtue consists in his style and sagacity, which is all the more penetrating because confined to a certain range of ideas. In the edition of 1597, he had refrained from the ornaments of diction to be found in his earlier works, apparently because the essays were intended only as private notes for the perusal of a few friends. But, by 1612, the popularity of the genre and his own reputation as the inventor[2] induced him to revise the first series and add twenty-eight new essays in a smoother, less jejune style. By 1625, his final edition was complete. This collection contains fifty-eight essays, written

---

[1] *Ante*, p. 389.

[2] "I have read of many essays and a kind of charactering of them, by such, as when I looked into the form and nature of their writing, I have been of the conceit that they were but imitators of your breaking the ice to their inventions." Nicholas Breton, dedication to Bacon in *Characters upon Essays*.

with a perfect mastery of language in a spirit of superb confidence.[1]

The true importance of his style is to be found in its pregnancy. In an age of complicated and superficial verbiage, he turns the licence of imaginative and allusive expression into an instrument of accurate and chastened thought. Character writers had introduced their portraits with a pointed or fanciful definition. Bacon does the same, but so as to express an abstract idea in the commonest objects of sight and experience. Thus, "Men in great place are thrice *servants*," "Fortune is like the *market*," "Virtue is like a *rich stone, best plain set*," "Praise is the *reflection of* virtue," "He that hath wife and children hath *given hostages* to fortune." These appeals for confirmation to everyday facts run all through his essays. Selfish statesmen are compared to ants in an orchard; men are bettered by believing in a God, as a dog when he owns a master. Again, though he never condescends to convince, his oracular utterances are the fruit of minute calculation; and this scientific process appears in the almost judicial balancing of pros and contras, as in the essay, "Of Usury," or in the methodical and detailed directions which he gives, as in the essay "Of Travel." His logical habit of mind has transformed even the materials of pedantry. The numerous quotations and illustrations drawn from the Bible, the classics and Machiavelli, seem necessary to his argument, and his unacknowledged appropriations from Montaigne strike one as mere coincidences of thought.[2] All forms of knowledge are subjected to the elucidation of his views on life. The *primum mobile* of astronomy illustrates "the motions of the greatest persons in a government," and the legend of Briareus is interpreted as an emblem of the people's power.

These excellencies were largely due to the fact that Bacon regarded the popularity of the *Essays* as ephemeral and was

[1] *Vide* S. H. Reynolds, intro. to *Essays or Counsels of Francis.*

[2] For list of plagiarisms *vide* F. A. F. Dieckow, *John Florio's Englische Uebersetzung der Essais Montaignes und Lord Bacon's, Ben Jonson's und Robert Burton's Verhältniss zu Montaigne.* It might be noticed, also, that the essay on death is largely coloured by Lucretius, bk. III, and Erasmus, *Colloquia Familiaria* (Funus), while that on youth and age is borrowed from Aristotle (*Rhetoric*, bk. II).

not posing for posterity.[1] He wrote down simply the things
which interested himself. This spontaneity carried its own
limitations. Many of the essays are made up of extracts,
compiled from his other works, and woven together into a new
whole. He frequently misquotes or misrepresents his quoted
authors; and, sometimes, he does not adhere closely to the title
of his essay.[2] Besides, Bacon led two lives, and in his views
on worldly matters we have only half the man: the side of him
engaged in a struggle for advancement.[3] Hence, he regards
life as a stage, and his meditations almost always recur to
the *rôle* which men play in the eyes of the world. Adversity
is discussed as a means of evoking the practice of virtue; friendship is viewed as a condition in which a man's judgment may
become clearer and his happiness more complete. Even love
and marriage are considered chiefly as an impediment to the
serious pursuits of life. But the greater number of his "Dispersed Meditations" deal with the immediate problem of
success; how far secrecy in dissembling will substitute an inborn
gift of discretion; whether boldness will counteract a reputation
for failure; in what way a knowledge of men rather than of
books can be turned to account in the intrigues of court life.
These speculations lead him into higher circles of government
and diplomacy, where, to penetrate the problems of statecraft,
he dispels the illusions of greatness. He fathoms the "in-
scrutable hearts of kings" and pictures their pitiable isolation
and toilsome existence. His book is destined for the commons
of the realm: so the advice which he professes to give their
rulers is really an exposure (perhaps not intentional) of the
machinery of government. We have glimpses of the monarch seated at the council-board, preparing his public utterances or choosing his favourites. The same interest leads him
to raise questions of public policy. In the essay "On Superstition," he marshals the chief accusations against the Roman
Catholic church; and, in treating of the greatness of kingdoms,
he does not ignore the bitter quarrel between the peasantry

---

[1] *Vide* quotations from Bacon's letters in "English Men of Letters"
Bacon, by R. W. Church, 1892, chap. IX.

[2] *Vide* S. H. Reynolds, *ibid.*

[3] J Boudoin, in translating the *Essays* in 1640, entitled them *L' Artisan de
la Fortune*.

and the gentry. Through every discussion, whether on death and religion, or on gardens and masques, there runs that subconscious ideal of versatile liberal culture out of which the essay sprang.

Bacon proved the possibilities of this type of literature as a repository of miscellaneous and desultory meditations. His influence is seen in such men as Owen Felltham, who, endowed with an interest in moral problems, and a certain mastery over reflective prose, published essays from time to time. These, apparently, were intended as exercises for confirming and strengthening the writer in his own opinions, and show only occasional efforts at an imitation of Bacon's gnomic style. And yet, Felltham's respectable, though commonplace, moralisations established the essay's right to embrace even sacred topics; especially are the virtuous deeds of the ancients selected with no little intuition to illustrate Christian ideals. Meanwhile, this art of extemporising modern ideas out of antiquity had reached its highest pitch in the desultory notes and reflections which Ben Jonson was making out of his vast reading. In 1641, these were published posthumously as *Timber or Discoveries made upon men and matter*. Practically, all the ideas contained in this miscellany, from aphoristic jottings to continuous discourses, have their origin in some other book. The influence of Velleius Paterculus, Euripides, Aulus Gellius, Quintilian and Seneca are particularly noticeable.[1] But *Timber* is not a mere work of paraphrase and transcription. Sometimes, several borrowed sentences are fused into one; sometimes, thoughts from different treatises are brought together or sentences of the same treatise are arranged in a different order. The passages on Shakespeare and Bacon were taken from what Seneca wrote of Haterius and Cassius Severus; in another place, Jonson condenses several pages of the *Advancement of Learning* into one short essay. A sense of manly integrity, and a keen eye to practical virtue and intelligence, guided this selection of the world's wisdom, and the style has an almost colloquial simplicity and directness far in advance of Bacon.

---

[1] *Vide* bibl. for authorities who have investigated sources of the *Discoveries*, and also cf. *Wits Commonwealth*.

We have seen how social literature, under the influence of classicism, grew into Juvenalian satire, character writing and essays, without losing sight of contemporary interests. But city life was too varied to find expression within the limits of any literary canon, and Londoners continued to welcome any type of tract which reflected their many-sided interests. No sooner had the fashion of tobacco-smoking become prominent, than it divided pamphleteers into two camps. Its supporters either founded their adhesion on its alleged medical properties,[1] or indulged their literary gift in burlesque encomia. Among others, an anonymous author, imitating Ovid, composed *The Metamorphosis of Tobacco*, in heroic couplets of pleasing and harmonious rhythm. He sings of the elements gathering in council to create a herb of almost Promethean virtue, which Jupiter, fearing for his sovereignty, banishes to an unknown land. But the graces discover the plant and remain so constant to its charms that mortals, who would win their favour, must follow their example. On the other hand, the growing insistence on good manners inspired scathing criticisms on smoking as it was then practised. "Tobacconists" were freely ridiculed by dramatists, character writers and puritans. King James issued in 1604 *A Counterblaste to Tobacco*, in which a sound if pedantic refutation of its alleged virtues is followed by quaint but vigorous descriptions of the smoker's disgusting habits. Among the many subsequent writers[2] who used this theme as a whetstone for their wits, the most noteworthy is, undoubtedly, Richard Brathwaite. Following the method of *The Metamorphosis*, he works up the contention that smokers waste their time into an allegorical romance, in which tobacco is traced back to its origin as a son of Pluto, god of the nether world. This phantasy is entitled, *The Smoking Age, or, the Man in the Mist* (1617).

These ephemeral pamphlets are worth quoting, in order to illustrate how varied, as well as elaborate, popular literature was becoming. Even rogue-books began to multiply the artifices of narration. E. S.[3] produced, in 1597, the *Discoverie*

---

[1] H. Buttes, *Dyets Dry Dinner*, 1599; E. Gardiner, *Triall of Tobacco*, 1610.
[2] *Vide* bibl.
[3] Supposed by G. C. Moore Smith to be Edward Sharpham; *N. & Q.* no. 257, 11 July, 1908.

of the Knights of the Poste. These gentry were professional bailees, utilising the name of some respectable citizen to stand surety for any criminal who would make it worth their while. As the average law-breaker was almost certain to be committed for another offence before the year was out, this form of livelihood could be made safe by ordinary precautions. Thus, the booklet is of very moderate interest. But the style is significant. The *Discoveries* is a connected story recounting a journey undertaken by the author on foot from London to Plymouth. He falls in with two fellow-travellers, and the trio beguile the tedium of the way with anecdotes and personal reminiscences of the knights of the post. The narrative has all the bye-play of a realistic novelette. Each of the author's companions has his own individuality. Goodcoll is almost destitute, but trusts to his witty tongue for escaping the dilemmas of impecuniosity. Freeman has store of gold, and is so fond of good fellowship, that he not only claims the right to finance the party, but deviates from his own course in order to enjoy their society. We visit the inns at which they lodged, are told of what they drank at night, how they slept and how they breakfasted. Freeman requests both Goodcoll and the author to disburse small sums, since his own wealth is in gold coin which he cannot realise till they come to Exeter. But, when that city is reached, Freeman finds that his store has vanished, and offers an explanation, which, apparently, satisfies the two travellers, but leaves the reader dubious.

Authors who had been through prison now began to clothe their experiences[1] in varied forms. Luke Hutton's *The Blacke Dogge of Newgate* (*c.* 1600) recounts the customs of that institution in a versified description of a vision, followed by a prose dialogue which tells of the amateur thieves to be found amongst the attendants of the prison. *The Compter's Commonwealth* (1617), by William Fennor, introduces the humours and tricks of the jest-books, into the usual exposures of roguery. Geffray Mynshul, who had left the debtor's prison with a lively recollection of its jangling keys, fawning yet tyrannical warders, and embittered or reckless inmates, actually endeavoured to give his friends an idea of these miseries by describing them

[1] For a fuller list see bibl.

in essays and character sketches. But the most important pamphleteer of Jacobean London is, undoubtedly, Thomas Dekker.

Apart from his dramatic work,[1] Dekker stands alone in this period. He is remarkable not as a satirist but as the first great literary artist of London street life. He discovered how to describe the city populace as a whole in its pursuits and agitations; but, as literature had not yet evolved a special medium[2] for this portraiture, his gift finds expression only in a number of erratic and ephemeral tracts. For instance, like other free lances,[3] he seized the obvious opportunity of producing a celebration of Elizabeth's death and James's accession. He entitled this tract *The Wonderfull Yeare* (1603). But the writer's thoughts are soon drawn from perfunctory adulation to the more suggestive theme of the plague which raged that year in London. We have a picture of Death encamped like an army in the sin-polluted suburbs. Its tents are winding-sheets, its field-marshal the plague, its officers burning fevers, boils, blains and carbuncles; the rank and file consist of mourners, "merrie sextons," hungry coffin-sellers and "nasty grave-makers"; the two catchpoles are fear and trembling. The invaders storm London, massacring men, women and children, breaking open coffers, rifling houses and ransacking streets. There are passages of almost unparalleled horror describing the rotten coffins filling the streets with stench, or the muck-pits full of putrid corpses, among which the worms writhe in swarms. There is originality in this conception of death, but much more in Dekker's description of the narrow London streets at night time, filled with the groans or raving of sick men, with glimpses of figures stealing out to fetch the sexton or sweating under the load of a corpse which they must hide before "the fatall hand writing of death should seale up their doores." Then, we watch the stampede into the country,

---

[1] He had already written eight plays single-handed and seven in collaboration, besides historical works in conjunction with Drayton.

[2] As we have seen, character writers sometimes described scenes and institutions. But, before Donald Lupton's *London and Country Carbonadoed* (1632), none, apparently, are touched with the fascination of London streets.

[3] Cf. Richard Johnson, *Anglorum Lachrymae*; H. Chettle, *Englande's Mourning Garment*; J. Hall, *The King's Prophecie or Weeping Joy*; Thomas Bing, *Sorrowes Joy*; S. Rowlands, *God save the King*.

and note the touches of meanness and heroism which a commotion always brings to the surface. The tract ends with the humorous side of the plague, discovered in some witty though rather grim anecdotes, one recounting how the death of a Londoner at a country inn threw the whole village into the most grotesque disorder, until a tinker consented, for a large sum, to bury the corpse.

One of Dekker's next productions[1] was an attempt—very common in this age—at appealing to the people by a denunciation of sin. He adopted one of their popular allegories[2] and, at the same time, gratified their love of pageantry, in *The Seven Deadly Sinnes of London* (1606), representing the triumphal entry of these into the capital, each drawn in a symbolic chariot and each welcomed by its special adherents. But all moral or theological sentiment is overshadowed by the fascination of city life. The sins are no longer those of the Roman Catholic church, but such as would strike an observer of street scenes. We have "Politick bankruptisme," the practice of merchants who pass through the court to avoid paying their debts; "Lying," which begets the minor cruelties and backslidings of life, notably oaths, which are "crutches upon which lyes go"; "Candle light," by which London streets are illuminated like a theatre, so that merchants and 'prentices alike are tempted to dissipation and thieving; "Sloth"; "Apishnesse" or dandyism; "Shaving," or the exaction of undue profits, and "Cruelty," which is rampant in extortionate prisons, among exorbitant creditors, merchants who take trade from their own 'prentices, relatives who abandon their own kith and kin in plague-time, and fathers who force their daughters to uncongenial marriages. While there is nothing profound or new in this view of London life, the booklet abounds in good humour and felicitous conceits. Above all, we have graphic views of the city, both in the hurry and rush of midday traffic, and glimmering with its taverns and gloaming alleys in the night-time.

The Seven Deadly Sinnes was a brilliant development of the theme revived by Nashe and the author of *Tom Tel-Troths Message and his pens Complaint* (1600). In the same year,

---

[1] See bibl. for a list of Dekker's works, with notes.
[2] *Ante*, p. 368.

Dekker borrowed another idea from *Pierce Penilesse*. Nashe, in his second edition, had promised to describe the return of the knight of the post from hell. The hint was taken by "an intimate and near companion," who produced an eminently insipid pamphlet[1] in 1606. Dekker followed this, in the same year, with *Newes from Hell, brought by the Divells Carrier*. Again we see the skilful adaptation of an ancient form of thought. Visions of heaven, purgatory and hell had originated in paganism, had flourished all through the Middle Ages in a Christian form[2] and still retained their popularity. Caxton had printed an English version of Deguileville's *Pilgrimage of the Soul* and Machlinia had revived the *Monk of Evesham*. The *Kalendrier des Bergers*, which contained a description of the punishments of the seven sins as revealed to Lazarus, was frequently translated during the sixteenth century. Ford, the dramatist, in one of his plays, introduces a friar who gives a gruesome account of the tortures of hell, and *The Dead Man's Song* treats the same subject in a broadside. "St. Patrick's Purgatory" was famous all through the sixteenth century, thanks to the disseminating influence of printing; and Calderon, in the seventeenth, made it the subject of one of his dramas. Burlesque versions of visions had existed since Old English times, and continued through popular literature from the Norman *fabliaux* to Rabelais.[3] After the reformation, these legends, like the sins, lost their theological significance, but the people were still medieval at heart, and literary free-lances were only too glad to avail themselves of the spell which visions still exercised over the popular imagination. Before 1590,[4] some nameless writer represented the famous Tarlton giving his impressions of purgatory, and, in this form, conveyed social satire as well as a collection of good stories. *Tom Tell-Trothe's New-yeares Gift* (1593) contains Robin Goodfellow's account of a visit to hell, and reproduces an oration against jealousy which he heard in those regions. In Dekker's *Newes from*

---

[1] *The Return of the Knight of the Post from Hell with the Divels answere to the Supplication of Pierce Penilesse, with some relation of the last Treasons*, printed by John Windet, 1606.

[2] *Vide* T. Wright, *St. Patrick's Purgatory, an essay on the legends of Purgatory, Hell and Paradise current during the Middle Ages*, 1844.

[3] *Pantagruel*, bk. II, chap. 30.

[4] See bibl. under Jest-books and Miscellaneous Tracts on London.

Hell, we have a booklet full of brilliant descriptions. The messenger starts for the nether world through France and Venice, stopping only in London, where dissipated youths call wildly to him through tavern windows, and he hears one spendthrift, in a fit of inebriated veracity, curse the wealthy merchant, his father, who left him money to waste. In hell, he finds the sessions in progress and dead souls being tried by a jury of their own sins. Before leaving, he catches sight of several familiar types of London street life; notably a hollow-eyed, wizened, old usurer, who offers to accept "any base drudgery" if he can create an opportunity for making money. The tract also illustrates the intellectual exuberance of the age, which, even in burlesque, assimilated the imagery and sentiment of different ages and civilisations. Lucian, in *Menippus*, had pictured a visit to the nether world, which Dekker had certainly read in John Rastell's translation and travestied in his own fashion.[1] But the place of torment—hideous, inaccessible, pestilential with "rotten vapors," crawling toads and sulphurous stench— is still medieval and the caricature of the devil reflects the ribaldry of the fifteenth century. In the following year, Dekker added a view of Elysium and the description of a thunderstorm, caused by the conjurations performed to summon up the knight of the post. On the strength of these additions, the pamphlet was issued as a new publication entitled *A Knight's Conjuring*.

It is not surprising that a pamphleteer, with Dekker's curiosity about life and his gift of realistic description should publish some tracts on roguery, and, in 1608, he produced *The Belman of London*, using the same material as his predecessors. In some respects, the pamphlet is disappointing; it lacks the type of anecdote which is attractive in Greene's work, and the character drawing which enlivens the *Knights of the Post*. But the setting has all Dekker's charm. The title suggests a picture of city life; but the scene opens in the country, where the author, after wandering among the serene pleasures of nature, finds himself in a disreputable farm-house, concealed in a gallery, watching a ragged gang of diseased and misshapen vagabonds devour like savages a steaming feast and initiate

---

[1] See bibl for visions in classical literature, including Lucian.

new members to their fraternity. The squalor and wretchedness of these outcasts being thus heightened by contrast, Dekker proceeds to tell us, as Harman had done, of their orders, classes and practices. But the account must be made attractive: so it is given by a "nymble-tongd beldam, who seemed to have command of the place," under the influence of a pot of ale. We then accompany the author back to London and, entering the city at midnight, at last encounter the bellman, whose bell and voice are heard echoing along the shadowy silent streets. This picturesque figure introduces an account of card-sharping, shop-lifting and pocket-picking. The exposure is straightforward and commonplace, but the style is embroidered with quaint and elaborate conceits. The pamphlet enjoyed immediate recognition and, according to Dekker, was plagiarised by *The Belman's Brother*. Probably to anticipate further imitation, Dekker produced in the same year a sequel: *Lanthorne and Candle-light or the Bell-Mans second Nights-walke*, in which, after a number of picturesque episodes, the devil decides to make a visit to London. We accompany him on his rounds and see how "Gul-gropers" cozen young heirs out of their acres by usury, cards and dice; how "Fawlconers" extract gratuities from country knights in return for a counterfeit dedication in a pamphlet; how "Ranckriders," posing as gentlemen, take up residence at an inn and, when a fictitious summons arrives from a nobleman, borrow one of the landlord's horses and do not return: how a "Jacke in a boxe" borrows silver on a money-box full of gold, for which is afterwards cleverly substituted one of similar exterior but very different contents. But these are no longer mysterious deceptions which only a specialist can detect. Exposures of villany were becoming more and more exposures of human nature; they appeal to a curiosity about life rather than to the instinct of self - defence. The best passage in the book reveals, not an elaborate fraud which only technical knowledge could unmask, but the picture of an ostler slinking half clothed at dead of night into the stable to steal a horse's provender.

It has already been shown how young men of wealth or birth were attracted to London by the hope of advancing their fortunes or of gaining experience. This class formed a new

order in society, without traditions, recognised status or code
of manners.   No aggregate of human beings, with the possible
exception of rogues and vagabonds, seems to have attracted
so much attention.   Sir Humphrey Gilbert[1] had suggested the
organisation of a gentleman's university, devoted to the cultivation of refined manners and courtly accomplishments; the
essayists had given much attention to the pursuits of monied
youth; Peacham wrote a whole book[2] on the subject; and, by
1633, Milton had constructed a complete scheme of education,
which should combine the soldier's, courtier's, and scholar's
training all in one.   But, at present, the playhouses, drinking
taverns and ordinaries of London were filled with inexperienced
boys, who had been taught something of their duty to their
king and country, but no other rules of deportment in these
novel situations than resenting an insult and holding their own
with their equals.   New conventionalities had not yet been
evolved to meet new conditions, and public opinion was content to condemn them as gulls, roaring boys, coxcombs, woodcocks, cockneys and popinjays.   Social pamphleteers had
satirised them again and again; and Dekker, while engaged on
a translation of Dedekind's *Grobianus*, conceived the idea of
turning the German's old-fashioned[3] satire on the boorishness
suggestive of an Eulenspiegel into a pasquil on the modern
English type.   Following his model, he produced an ironical
book of manners, entitled *The Guls Hornebooke* (1609), which
begins by closely following the original, but gradually develops
into an independent work.

The booklet surpasses other attacks on the gallants and
fops of the age, because Dekker has penetrated beneath their
conduct so as to satirise their motives.   We see that the Jacobean gull's irresponsible actions are entirely dominated by the
desire to assert his personality, and these efforts rendered
odious by lack of breeding and vulgarity of surroundings.
Dekker sarcastically explains to the gull how this ambition
can be realised by his making himself offensively conspicuous
at places of public resort.   Incidentally, we accompany the
young man of leisure through a typical day's occupations,

---

[1] *Queene Elizabethes Achademy.*
[2] See bibl.
[3] *Grobianus* was printed 1549.   See bibl.

from the business of dressing to the stroll in St. Paul's; thence to the "ordinary" for the midday meal; then to the play-house, followed by the tavern and the nocturnal prowl through the city. The book had no great sale, because the scenes were too familiar, and the invective too mild; but, for the modern student, no better picture can be found of Jacobean London, with its literary cliques, its publicity and the scope it gave to the free play of personality.

The public's insatiable demand for novelty reduced professional free-lances to the most amazing shifts to win popularity. In this respect, Dekker's *A strange Horse Race* (1613) is an almost unique production. He begins with an account of Roman "pageants" (that is, gladiatorial displays), dwelling particularly on the quips and jeers with which the populace greeted the hero of a triumph. These anecdotes introduce a popular encyclopaedia, in which the knowledge of the day is vulgarised under the attractive conceit of a race. Astronomy is taught under the guise of races of the heavenly bodies, and physiology as the races in a man's body, earth, water, air and fire all competing. Then there are races of minerals; lead striving to overtake tin, tin silver and silver gold, which is the victorious metal, "the eldest child of the sun." From the physical, he turns to the moral, world. Once more, we have a pageant of the vices and virtues, but still in the form of a race. The vices of an enriched *bourgeoisie* are pitted against the old-fashioned virtues of modesty and contentment. Among others, Blasphemous Insolency challenges Innocent Humility; the temperate Spaniard races the English drunkard; epicures run from a "cry of sergeants"; the lawyer from his own conscience; the vicar for four benefices, which he wants to enjoy at the same time; and the tailor vainly strives to keep up with Pride. As practically all the vices are beaten, the devil, out of chagrin, falls so sick that he makes a will after the manner of the sixteenth century mock Testaments.

Other writers were hardly less versatile than Dekker. Samuel Rowlands attempted every type of popular literature except essays and character sketches, which were no occupation for bread-winners. As Drayton,[2] Nashe[3] and

---

[1] *Ante*, Vol. III, Chap. v, pp. 95–98, and bibl., pp. 548–550.
[2] *Harmonie of the Church*, 1591.   [3] *Christs Teares*, 1593.

Lodge[1] had attracted attention by religious compositions, Rowlands began his career with *The Betraying of Christ* (1598). In this trifle, he produces fully-developed that polished flow of verse which is one of his contributions to the literature of his age. The other contribution, the witty portrayal of the "humours" of eccentricity and class spirit, is found in his next production, *The Letting of Humours Blood in the Head-Vaine*, which appeared in 1600. Latinised verse was now the fashion; so Rowlands gibbets the bad manners of Londoners under personalities: first, in classical epigrams, which give admirable glimpses of conduct, and then in satire of the school of Hall, in which we have more detailed portraits. Among others, we see the countryman filled with contempt for the citizen and led by his arrogance to commit absurd blunders; the censorious spirit, slovenly, poor and quarrelsome, pulling everyone's reputation to pieces; and the two drunkards who strengthen each other in their vice by enumerating the benefits of wine after the manner of burlesque encomiums.

In 1602, Rowlands reverted to an older type in *Tis Merrie when Gossips meete*. The gay gossip of the alehouse had been for centuries a commonplace of popular literature,[2] and Sir John Davies had brought something of that spirit into his "a wife widow and maid" in *A Poetical Rapsody* (1602). Rowlands's poem shows us a middle-aged widow who has gathered from life a store of worldly wisdom and a connoisseur's appreciation of burnt sack. She meets two acquaintances, a wife and a maiden, who are reluctantly induced to join her in the private room of a tavern. Claret is ordered, and the usual feminine conference on men begins. The value of the poem, however, does not consist in the egoistic views of these women, but in the dramatic development of their characters. The widow, a judge of ales and wine, is inclined to flaunt her independence; the wife is at first indifferent and preoccupied with domestic cares; the maid is timid and inclined to be shocked. But, as the wine percolates through their veins, they discuss old times and their present fortunes with the utmost freedom. When the conversation turns from dances to husbands, they talk faster and interrupt each other more frequently. Anon,

[1] *Prosopopeia*, 1596.
[2] *Ante*, Vol. II, p. 439; Vol. III, p. 98, and bibl., pp. 551–555.

sausages and sack are called for; even the maid begins to put in her say, while the widow talks so loudly that the eaves-dropping attendant bursts out laughing. The incensed lady delivers a voluble and incoherent reprimand, and they stagger down the stairs after a friendly competition as to who should pay the bill.

This brilliant sketch met with immediate popularity. Seven editions were called for during the century, and Row-lands now definitely abandoned standard literature. He turned his hand to coney-catching pamphlets and, trading on Greene's reputation, entitled his tract *Greenes Ghost haunting Coniecatchers*, in which he contributes a few new facts to the subject, but, for the most part, fills his pages with picaresque anecdotes of farcical encounters and triumphs of mother wit. Then he combined the old idea of the dance of death with the new taste for type satire in *Looke to it for Ile Stabbe ye* (1604). Death is represented as threatening a number of typical wrong-doers, each of whom has his malpractices briefly characterised in two six-lined stanzas. Rowlands still writes the same clear smooth verse; but most of the characters had been the veriest commonplaces for a century. Yet there are a few interesting figures grouped under the heading of death's vengeance, includ-ing the king who spills his subjects' blood to enhance his own glory;[1] the miser, now distinguished from the usurer; the husbandman who keeps almanacs to calculate the rainy weather and is never happy unless the price of grain is high;[2] and the spendthirft, blinded to the dangers of the future, who neglects his family but is always "a good fellow to his friend." In this poem, Death was employed merely as a figure-head; but, two years later, he produced a poem directly on that subject. For centuries, death, in popular imagination, had played a double part; on the one hand, as a gruesome monarch, on the other, as an antic or jester. Rowlands incorporates both these conceptions in the moral dialogue *A terrible Battell betweene the two consumers of the whole world: Time and Death*. Time and Death hold conference on the worldly-minded vic-tims whom they have struck down in their sins, and review the brevity and temptations of life. The beginning of the

---

[1] This idea is found in Erasmus: *Bellum Erasmi*, T. Berthelet, 1533.
[2] Ben Jonson's *Every Man out of his Humour:* the character of Sordido.

poem has an almost Miltonic[1] grandeur. Then, suddenly, the
tone changes. Time comically complains that he is credited
with many of Death's escapades, and a dispute follows. Each
claims to be the greater. Death scornfully insists that no man
fears Time, while Time accuses Death of stabbing like a coward,
and then compares his head to an oil-jar, his arms to a gardener's rake, his legs to a pair of crane stilts and his voice to the hiss-
ing of a snake. After an interchange of even more outrageous
insults, a reconciliation is effected.[2]

The literary resourcefulness of the age is also illustrated
by a number of pamphlets which ridicule romantic ballads.
The *Heroical adventures of the Knight of the Sea* (1600) was
followed by Beaumont and Fletcher's comedy *The Knight of
the Burning Pestle* in 1611 and by *Moriomachia* in 1613. In this
clever prose burlesque, interspersed with rimes, Robert Anton
tells how the queen of the fairies transforms a submissive and
apathetic cow into a knight errant to do her business in the
world. The knight's adventures are as futile as those of Sir
Thopas, but they serve the further purpose of satirising society.
The hero blunders into encounters which set off the bluff kindness of the common folk beside the arrogance and vanity of the
wealthy with their bought titles and pampered menials. At
Moropolis (London), the adventurer visits the frivolous shows
and sham prodigies of the city, and he catches some glimpses of
city vice which much amaze his ingenuous soul. The burlesque
ends in a mock-heroic contest. The Knight of the Sun enters
the lists against the Knight of the Moon, but is worsted, and
the earth is plunged in darkness. Amid the disorder which
ensues, "fogging solliciters," "extorting brokers," "peaking
pandars," tapsters and others appear in their true characters.
The tract has something in it suggestive of *Candide* as well as
of *Hudibras*. In 1615, Rowlands brought out *The Melancholic
Knight*, a verse monologue proceeding from a character dis-
gusted with the commercialism of his own age and ravished
by the enchanted world of medieval romance. He is a studious
reader of fly-sheets and broadsides which tell of dragons and
other monstrosities, and has himself composed "the rhyme of
Sir Eglamour." But this poem is really a burlesque imitated

[1] *Vide* E. Gosse, intro. to works of Rowlands, 1880 [Hunterian Club].
[2] See bibl. for list of Rowlands's works.

from *The Knight of the Sea* and its author proves to be a poltroon who despises money because he is in debt, refuses charity to beggars (the mark of the upstart nobleman of that age),
grinds his tenants to clothe his wife bravely and smokes and
spits all day long while nursing his melancholy. *Don Quixote*
had been published in 1605, and its popularity may have
stimulated this type of literature. But the real impulse came
from the reaction of the "nineties" against Elizabethan idealism. The love of mythical and heroic literature was not,
indeed, dead but was relegated to the uneducated and the old-
fashioned. Verse satirists had already inveighed against the
Spenserian school and the versified legends of old time. Now,
less academic writers, following the city love of cynicism and
ridicule, reproduced the same satire in a more humorous form.

The atmosphere of the capital made itself felt in many
ways, apart from experiments in style and the study of types.
There are constant allusions to noted and notorious characters
of the city, such as Lanum, Garret, Singer, Pope, Backstead,
Field and Hobson. Tarlton became so famous that Gabriel
Harvey was proud to have jested with him, and Fitzgeoffrey[1]
and Stradling[2] honoured him in Latin epigrams. Some of these
characters became the heroes of jest-books,[3] in which old
stories were told anew and associated with their names. Yet
even in this field, the popular interest in London gives a touch
of freshness. The compiler of the *Merrie Conceited Jests of
George Peele* has managed to centre all his detached anecdotes
round the attractive and novel personality of literary bohemians.[4] Koggan and Eulenspiegel were traditional figure-heads,
in which gipsy cunning blended with bucolic ineptitude. In
George Peele, however, we find a consistent character devoted
to pleasure and prodigality, who has discarded the inane antics
of earlier jest-books, and governs his vagaries by the desire
to escape a creditor or gain a dinner. But his frauds are still

---

[1] *Affaniae*, 1601.   [2] *Epigrammata*, 1607.
[3] *Vide* bibl. For origin of Jest-books *vide ante* Vol. III, Chap. v,
pp. 102–107.
[4] The book was probably compiled after the dramatist's death. One episode, at least, is taken from *A C. Mery Talys*, and the conception of the
character is similar to that of George Pyeboard in *The Puritan* (1607). As
the earliest known edition of the jests has the same date, the question of
imitation cannot be settled.

perpetrated with the heartlessness of an earlier age, and the book does not bear witness to the "civilitie" of London so convincingly as *John Taylor's Wit and Mirth* (1635), in which the current witticisms of taverns, ordinaries and bowling-greens are worked up into "yerks" and "clinches." Here we find the educated man's amusement at the clown's misuse[1] of new Latinised words such as Dogberry mutilated, and the Londoner's contempt for provincial arrogance.[2] The phantasy on a bowling-alley contains conceits as elaborate as those of Overbury and Breton, and other anecdotes[3] have touches of epigrammatic wisdom such as the essayists loved to record. The most noticeable feature is the predominance of the modern repartee—the flash of ridicule or humour struck out of a word taken in two senses—which is often associated with Sheridan.

So great was this interest in city personalities, that actors and public humourists would perform wagers in order to gain money by publishing accounts of them. Ferris's colourless report of *The Most dangerous and memorable Adventure* (1590) in a wherry boat was followed by *Kemp's nine days wonder* (1600), in which the actor vivaciously describes the episodes of his morris dance from London to Norwich. John Taylor, after an adventurous career in the navy and a few years' struggle to earn a living in the decaying profession of waterman, devoted himself to literary hackwork and undertook wagering journeys, which were afterwards turned into rollicking pamphlets. It was, perhaps, this fashion which induced Richard Brathwaite, after trying his hand at essays and characters, to devote his learning and Goliardic humour to the narration of a voyage. Adopting the name of a proverbial drunkard,[4] he described a pilgrimage through the towns and villages of England in *Barnabae Itinerarium or Barnabee's Journal*. Occasionally, he notes local peculiarities; but the story, mostly, is a record of the vagabond's escapades, which sometimes meet a vagabond's condign punishment. The booklet is a triumph of easy rhythmic verse.

[1] Cf. Rowlands's *Letting of Humours Blood*, 1600.
[2] *E.g.* Jest no. 100, "A toy to mocke an Ape." [3] *E.g.* no. 127.
[4] *Vide* Ben Jonson, *The Gipsies*, and also the introduction of Barnaby as a bibacious coachman in *The New Inn, or the light Heart*. See, also, *A*

The sentiments and ideas of former ages now began to reappear in connection with localities in and around London. Brainford, Hogsden (Hoxton), Southwarke, Eyebright and Queen-hive frequently figure in catch-pennies.   One publicist, under the name of "Kinde-Kit of Kingstone," borrowed tales from such sources as the *Decameron* and the *Romance of the Seven Sages*, and put them in the mouths of seven fishwives who take boat for the western suburbs after a good day's business in London.[1]   Each prose story is introduced by a verse description of the narrator, after the manner of Skelton, and is followed by the outspoken comments of the listeners. Another story book, composed in the same style and manner, represents a journey from Billingsgate to Gravesend.[2]   But the most remarkable pamphlet of this class is *Pimlyco*[3] *or, Runne Red Cap* (1609).   The poet describes himself lying in the grass amid the delights of spring, and watching lovers sport together, while, in the background, the towers and steeples of London

Lifted their proud heads above the skies,

gleaming like gold in the morning sunlight.   By chance, he finds Skelton's *Tunnyng of Elynour Rummyng;* and, while reading the satire, looks up and beholds a motley crowd of men and women surging towards Hogsden to consume its ale.   The contagious enthusiasm carries him along, and, with Skelton's poem in his hand, "with those mad times to weigh our times," he first breaks out into a burlesque eulogy on Pimlyco ale, and then wittily describes the insane rush for the pleasures of the resort.   Payment for alehouse fare was vulgarly known as "shot"; so he represents the place as a fort which an impetuous army is attacking with this artillery. In the ranks are all types of society who scramble for tankards,

---

Brown Dozen of Drunkards (ali-ass Drinkhards) whipt and shipt to the Isle of Gulls (1648), and memoir by J. Haslewood prefixed to ninth ed. of *Barnabee's Journal*, 1820.

[1] *Westward for Smelts.*   Steevens believes in an edition of 1603, but Collier thinks that of 1620 to be the first.

[2] *The Cobler of Canterburie*, 1608 (largely reprinted in *The Tincker of Turney*, 1630).

[3] Discussion on the origin of the word has been reopened in *N. & Q.* no. 256, 21 Nov., 1908.

calling "Fill, Fill, Fill." Poets seek inspiration; ballad singers exercise their "villanous yelping throats." Lawyers, usurers, courtiers, soldiers, "lads and greasie lownes," women of every age and figure, jostle one another in their eagerness to squander money on tippling. Such a production is far more than a topical effusion. *Pimlyco* is a satirical rhapsody on the age's animal spirits and headlong folly, a burlesque review in which the genius and method of *Cocke Lorell's bote*[1] are adapted to the interests of Jacobean London.

All this while, the exuberant national life continued to find yet another form of expression in the broadsides and street ballads which had grown out of the people's love of singing in early Tudor times.[2] Songs were sung and sold at every street corner and crossway, or outside the theatre doors, and so popular did some airs become that Guilpin reckoned the chanting of *Kemp's Jigge* and *The Burgonians Tragedy* among the nuisances of London. Cornwallis describes a crowd gathered round a city minstrel. He tells us "how thoroughly the standers by are affected, . . . what shift they make to stand to heare. Ballad-mongers, who were sometimes men of education,[3] represented the public opinion of the lower classes. News of foreign and political events was circulated this way; accounts of monstrosities, portents, prodigies and disasters were graphically reported. Prophecies were composed or revived. R. Waldegrave even published, in 1603, a whole volume of medieval oracles from Merlin, Eltraine, Beid, Thomas the Rimer and others. Murders and executions were described with appropriate apologues or, as in the case of Ravaillac's tortures,[4] with harrowing and imaginary details. Tales of love-making and domestic scenes are found, some in dialogue or a kind of rude four-act drama. There were other ditties, especially drinking songs, which were merely coarse, and "Nownow," in *Kinde Hart's Dreame*, complains that crowds gather to hear children

---

[1] *Ante*, Vol. III, Chap. v, pp. 93–95.

[2] *Ante*, Vol. III, Chap. v, p. 107, and bibl., p. 557.

[3] One of them, Thomas Spickernell, was first a ballad-monger and then a minister; and another, Richard Corbet, M.A., was first a doctor of divinity and then an itinerant musician. See A. Clark, *Shirburn Ballads*, 1907.

[4] *The terrible and deserved Death of Francis Ravilliack*, 1610. Rptd. *Harl. Misc.* vol. VI.

sing immoral lays.   The old heroic ballads were still favourites,[1] as, also, were naïve tales which bore mark of medieval origin. A large number were nothing else than church hymns, which a householder could buy on Saturday evening for Sunday use. A pronounced liking for repentances and confessions can also be traced.   Many broadsides represent a doomed man on the scaffold, addressing a farewell homily to the world, in which he confesses his crimes and warns others to shun his besetting sin. Some contain tragedies of love or jealousy; others touch on social and political grievances.

It will be noticed that these doggerel fragmentary verses deal with the very subjects which supplied material for the great pamphleteers and satirists of the age.   Nor can the work of Greene, Nashe, Dekker, Rowlands, Hall, Marston, Guilpin and their peers be really understood unless this vast background of varied plebeian sentiment be kept in view.   And yet the golden age of popular literature was past.   The sixteenth century had seen the rise of thoughtful humourists and investigators, whose first care had been to probe the errors and expose the frauds of the common people among whom they lived.   But, in the literary atmosphere of Jacobean London, this tractarian movement was gradually becoming a series of elaborate experiments.   The brilliant writers of the age were evolving complex organs of expression and, already, before the Civil War, had laid the foundations of eighteenth century prose literature.   But they lost touch with the deeper interests of the people.   Meanwhile, broadsides and flysheets continued to multiply; but it was not till the advent of the romantic movement that a school of writers again devoted their talents to the interpretation of social life.

[1] Cf. *The Knight of the Burning Pestle,* and Martin Parker's *Ballads.*

CHAPTER XVII

Writers on Country Pursuits and Pastimes

GERVASE MARKHAM

WHILE the great Elizabethan writers were producing poems, plays and other masterpieces destined to take an enduring place in English literature, there was another side of literary activity, which, though practically unrecognised as literature, yet had an important influence on a large body of readers for the majority of whom polite literature scarcely existed. The books that formed this by-stream appealed to the country squire and the yeoman, not, indeed, as literature, but as storehouses of facts—practical guides to their agricultural occupations, or instruction in their favourite pastimes of hunting and hawking, fishing and gardening.

Before this period, but few books dealing with these subjects had appeared in print. The first and most famous among them was *The Book of St. Albans*,[1] first printed about 1486, which stood practically alone until the appearance, early in the sixteenth century, of Walter of Henley's *Book of Husbandry* and Fitzherbert's treatise on the same subject. But it was not till the second half of the century that these subjects, in common with every other branch of literature, were fully developed in that productive age.

For the materials of this literature, there were two main sources: one, the stock of native lore, which was the outcome of the practical experience of generations, supplemented by an occasional dip at the well of superstition, and this was preserved to some extent in manuscript as well as handed down by oral tradition; the other, contemporary foreign literature, notably

[1] See Vol. II, p. 362.

that of Italy, which was freely drawn upon in the way of translation, these versions being often the work of the purely literary man or of the hack-writer who brought to the subject little or nothing of first-hand knowledge.

The outstanding name among the workers in this field is that of the prolific and versatile enthusiast Gervase Markham, whose activity extended from the last decade of the sixteenth century to his death in 1637. He was born about 1568, and, in his early years, spent at his Nottinghamshire home, he naturally became familiar with every aspect of country life. Like many other younger sons of the time, he took to a military career; but, after some years' experience in the wars of the Low Countries, he exchanged his sword for the pen.

The subjects with which he dealt included such matters as hunting, hawking, husbandry, gardening, housewifery and the military art, diversified by occasional excursions into polite literature in the shape of plays and poems. But, of the many sides of his literary activity, the most prominent, as well as most congenial, was, without doubt, that dealing with horsemanship and the veterinary art.

The first of the long series of his books on horses was issued in 1593 under the title *A Discource of Horsmanshippe*. In this same year, also, he made his first essay in *belles lettres*, by preparing for the press a poem entitled *Thyrsis and Daphne;* but no copy of this is known to have survived. After having reissued the *Discource* in a new and enlarged guise, under the title *How to chuse, ride, traine, and diet, both hunting-horses and running horses,* he followed it, in 1605, with a treatise on *How to trayne and teach horses to amble.* Two years later, Markham produced his chief work on his favourite theme, the horse, "with whose nature and use," he claims with some pride, "I have been exercised and acquainted from my Childhood, and I hope, without boast, need not yield to any in this Kingdome."

This book he entitled *Cavelarice, or the English Horseman.* But it was not in Markham's nature to be satisfied with so brief, though comprehensive, a title. Showman at heart as he was, the big drum must be beat, and the attention of the world called to the wonders to be found within. So, characteristically, and with a flourish, he sets forth his wares in detail, and acclaims their originality and his own altruism.   Here is the whole:

Cavelarice, or the English Horseman: contayning all the Arte of Horsemanship, as much as is necessary for any man to understand, whether he be Horse-breeder, horse-ryder, horse-hunter, horse-runner, horse-ambler, horse-farrier, horse-keeper, Coachman, Smith or Sadler. Together with the discovery of the subtill trade or mistery of horse-coursers, and an explanation of the excellency of a horses understanding, or how to teach them to doe trickes like Bankes his Curtall: And that horses may be made to drawe drie-foot like a Hound. Secrets before unpublished, and now carefully set down for the profit of this whole Nation.

But, if Markham was adept at displaying his wares, he was no less a master in the choice of appropriate patrons and in the writing of dedications—a practice reduced to a fine art in those days. It was a poor book which could not be made to carry two, if not three, of his dedicatory epistles, for each of which he doubtless looked for some remuneration. In *Cavelarice*, the division into books affords him opportunity for no less than eight dedications, leading off with prince Henry, to whom succeed noblemen of various titles duly graduated. In issuing a new edition, "corrected and augmented, with many worthy secrets not before known," ten years later, the name of Charles, prince of Wales, is quietly substituted for that of the late prince, without the slightest change in the terms of the address.

And, when we come to the text of the book itself, Markham is not wanting in this matter either. He is master of his subject; and, whether he calls upon the stores of his own experience, or, as was much the fashion in his time, uses material "drawen out of the most approved authors," he conveys the impression of writing with full knowledge, and inspires confidence as one who speaks with the unhesitating assurance of authority. His directions are full and clear, and his style is touched with an enthusiasm and an engaging familiarity which bring his reader into close contact and almost convey the illusion of oral instruction. Now and again, one comes across bits of that deep-rooted country tradition which has not even yet worn itself out, such as when he directs that "If your horse be shrewe-runne, you shall looke for a briere which growes at both endes, and draw your horse thorow it and he

will be well." But Markham is not much given to this kind
of thing, and, whether it was a concession to rural superstition
or a filching from one of his "approved authors," it is noticeable
that he neither gives the symptoms of being "shrew-runne" nor
describes the nature of the malady.

The mention, in the title-page, of "Bankes his Curtall," is a
reference to a celebrated performing horse, called "Marocco,"
which his owner, one Banks, a Scotsman, had taught to do
tricks so astonishing that both the "dancing horse" and its
trainer achieved a European reputation. Shakespeare, in
Love's Labour's Lost, makes reference to Marocco's power of
counting money, and many other allusions to his cleverness
may be found in contemporary literature. The most renowned exploit of this famous animal was the ascent of St.
Paul's Cathedral, which took place in 1600. He was afterwards exhibited in Paris, Frankfort and other places, and
the amazement which his performances created brought his
owner under the suspicion of employing magic. But Markham,
with his knowledge of horse training, calls Banks an "exceeding honest" man; and, since it would be impossible for
Markham to admit his inferiority to any one in any matter
relating to horsemanship, a chapter is, accordingly, devoted
to showing "How a horse may be taught to doe any tricke done
by Bankes his Curtall."

In one of his later books,[1] Markham complains that, by
reason of a too greedy and hasty bookseller, his *Cavelarice*
was not only exceedingly falsely printed, but, also, the most
part of the book of cures was left out. To supply this omission,
he brought out, in 1610, his *Maister-peece*, wherein, he says,
"I have set down every disease, and every medicine, so full and
so exactly that there is not a farrier in this kingdome, which
knowes a medicine for any disease, which is true and good
indeed, but I will finde the substance thereof in that booke."
Markham evidently prided himself on this work, in which he
describes himself to be amply and fully adorned with the best
of his own feathers; and his estimation of it as his master-piece
finds justification in the fact that it continued in use for
upwards of one hundred years.[2]

[1] *Markhams Method:* preface.
[2] The twenty-first edition appeared in 1734.

Not content with having produced these comprehensive works on his special subject, he sought to reach a still wider circle; and, in 1616, he brought out a popular little octavo called *Markhams Method: or Epitome*, which, with an innate knowledge of the essential elements of popularity, he further attractively described as containing "his approved remedies for all diseases whatsoever, incident to horses, and they are almost 300, all cured with twelve medicines onely, not of twelve pence cost and to be got commonly everywhere"; and he also includes remedies for the diseases of every description of domestic live stock, from oxen and sheep to hawks and singing birds. By this time, he is well aware that he has gained the reputation of being a book-maker, for, in the preface, he says,

me thinks I heare the world say: Sir, why load you thus both mens mindes and the Booke-sellers stalls with such change and variety of Bookes, all upon one subject, as if men were tyed to your readings?

and he then proceeds, in three pages, to justify the appearance of this epitome. But, however plausibly Markham might defend his book-making in print, the stationers concerned in his publications felt that this multiplying of treatises was becoming a serious matter, and, from the following entry in the register of the Stationers' company, it appears that they took steps to protect their interest in such of his books as were already in print.

Memorandum That I Gervase Markham of London gent Do promise hereafter Never to write any more book or bookes to be printed, of the Deseases or cures of any Cattle, as Horse, Oxe, Cowe, sheepe, Swine and Goates &c. In witnes whereof I have hereunto sett my hand the 14th Day of Julie. 1617.

Gervis Markham.

It is probably this memorandum which has led to Markham being often described as the first English "hackney writer," a phrase used by Harte; but he no more deserves this appellation than many another contemporary writer, and there is no evidence that he was employed by the booksellers to write any of his numerous books. How, or by whom, he was induced to sign the promise does not appear, but it was hardly to be expected that such an enthusiast could thus completely forswear his especial hobby.

For some years, he spent his energies upon other subjects, but, in his later days, he brought out yet two other small horse books, *The Complete Farriar, or the Kings High-way to Horsmanship* and *Markhams Faithfull Farrier*. In sending forth the latter, he utters a note suggestive of the weariness of age, but he shows no abatement of his claim to supremacy in veterinary lore, he has lost nothing of his valiant assurance, and he still does all "for the publick good."

Having [he says] gained experience all my life to these present dayes, wherein I am ready to creepe into the earth, willing now at the important request of my best friends, [I] have yeelded my selfe to lay the glory of my skill in Horsemanship, open to the World: and having kept secret in the Cabinet of my Brest, these Secrets, by which I have gained from many a Noble person, many a fayre pound, I now bestow it upon thee for the value of sixe pence. It may be; some will account me a Foole in Print, for disclosing my Secrets, but I ever regarded the life of the worthy Horse, before the word of a foole.

Among the modern writers on horses to whom Markham, in his *Maister-peece*, acknowledges his indebtedness, he especially esteemed Salomon de la Broue, "a man of exquisite practice and knowledge," whose work *Le cavalerice François* was printed at Paris in 1593–4. Of English authors, he names Clifford and Mascall, and also mentions among his authorities fifteen names which he terms private, meaning, it may be presumed, practitioners of the veterinary art who did not publish. Christopher Clifford was the author of *The Schoole of Horsemanship*, published in 1585; the works of Leonard Mascall are referred to below.

No other writer on this subject approached Markham, either in popularity or in knowledge and literary craft. His books were continually reprinted throughout the seventeenth century, and they were not entirely superseded even by the great horse-masters of the latter part of the century, the duke of Newcastle and Sir William Hope, translator of Solleysel.

Perhaps yet better known than his books on horses is the collection of treatises on country matters which he gathered into one volume, under the alluring title, *A Way to get Wealth*. This comprehensive work forms an encyclopaedia of rural occupations and recreations, in which Markham brought up to date the existing literature of the subject.

The earliest of his predecessors in this field was Walter of Henley, whose *Book of Husbandry*, originally written in the thirteenth century, circulated largely in manuscript,[1] being added to from time to time and amended as need arose. Its long continued popularity must have been due to the practical nature of the work; and the sphere of its usefulness was extended by a translation, out of the original Anglicised Norman French, into English, this version being attributed, on apparently insufficient grounds, to Robert Grosseteste, bishop of Lincoln. After having enjoyed popularity in manuscript for two hundred years, it was at length printed by Wynkyn de Worde early in the sixteenth century, only to be shortly afterwards superseded by Fitzherbert's *Book of Husbandry*, which made its appearance about 1523.

It is a question whether the authorship of this treatise, as well as of its companion volume, *The Book of Surveying*, should be rightly assigned to Sir Anthony Fitzherbert, justice of the common pleas, or to his elder brother John Fitzherbert, lord of the manor of Norbury in Derbyshire; but the balance of probability is in favour of the latter.[2] The squire, if he it be, tells us that the work was the outcome of more than forty years' experience, and that it was intended for the benefit of "poore fermers and tenauntes." The familiarity with detail, the minuteness of instruction and the care with which the author states his reasons, well bear out his claim to long experience. The whole course of farming operations is dealt with, including the management of horses, cattle and sheep; woodcraft finds a place, and there is likewise a chapter on bees, which are "lyttell charge but good attendaunce." And, country squire-like, caring for the welfare of his people, he concludes with some thirty admonitory essays suited to various occasions, from "the Occupation of a Wife" to "the Manner of Almsdeeds." *The Book of Surveying*, which had a forerunner in the rules drawn up by bishop Grosseteste for the countess of Lincoln, dealt with duties pertaining to the office of steward

---

[1] See Lamond and Cunningham's edition (1890) for a list of the twenty-one extant copies.

[2] See *English Historical Review*, XII, 255 ff. (1897).

or bailiff, and was, in effect, a hand-book of estate management, designed for "the profytte of all noble men and women."

For a considerable period, Fitzherbert's *Book of Husbandry* had no rival, and it was several times reprinted before the end of the century, when it finally gave way to the Elizabethan writers on the subject, to whom it had served as a useful quarry. Of these writers, the most notable, to name them in chronological order, were Thomas Tusser, Leonard Mascall, Barnabe Googe, Sir Hugh Plat and Markham.

Thomas Tusser, whose *Hundreth good pointes of Husbandrie* (1557), afterwards amplified into *Five Hundreth Pointes* (1573), was rather a collection of riming aphorisms than a regular treatise, is dealt with in another volume of the present work.[1]

Leonard Mascall, quoted by Markham as one of his authorities and, next to Markham, the best known writer of the time on husbandry, is said by Fuller to have introduced pippin apples and carp into England; but carp were already known in 1496,[2] and Mascall's statement in his *Book of Fishing* may have referred to one of his ancestors rather than to himself. Mascall's first book was *Of the arte and maner howe to plant and graffe all sortes of trees* (1572), and, for this, he drew upon French and Dutch sources, supplemented by his own observation. *The husbandlye ordring and governmente of Poultrie*, which he brought out in 1581, seems to be the earliest independent treatise which was printed on the subject. Mascall's chief work, *The government of cattell*, made its first appearance in 1587, and, though very largely a compilation, nevertheless represented the best practice of the day, and continued in vogue together with Markham's books until far into the succeeding century. This was followed in 1590 by *A booke of fishing with hooke and line . . . Sundrie engines and trappes to take polcats, buzards, rattes, mice, and all other kindes of vermine.*

Barnabe Googe takes his real place in literature in another department,[3] but his translation of the *Foure bookes of Husbandry, collected by M. Conradus Heresbachius* (1577) must be noted here. As Googe remarks in his preface, you have here set down before you "the rules and practices of the olde auncient husbands, as well Greekes as Latines whose very

---

[1] See Vol. III, Chap. VIII.   [2] See *Book of St. Albans.*
[3] See Vol. III, Chap. VIII.

orders, for the most, at this day wee observe"; and, though he professes to have increased the work both by his own reading and the experience of his friends, yet it represents precepts of the older writers rather than contemporary knowledge and practice, and the subject is treated from the standpoint of a man of letters rather than from that of a professed agriculturist. The authorities quoted in the preface include the names of several Englishmen, and he mentions in terms of respect "Master Fitzherbert and Master Tusser: whose workes may, in my fancie, without any presumption, compare with any, either Varro, Columella, or Palladius of Rome." Some fifty years later, the book was re-edited and enlarged by Markham.

Sir Hugh Plat, an interesting person whose activity extended to other matters besides agriculture, was known as the author of many curious inventions, a number of which are described in his *Jewell House of Art and Nature: conteining divers rare and profitable inventions, together with sundry new experimentes in the art of husbandry, distillation, and moulding* (1594). He applied himself more particularly to improvements in farming and gardening, his most useful contribution to the subject being a treatise on manures, which, under the title of *Diverse new sorts of soyle not yet brought into any publique use, for manuring both of pasture and arable ground*, formed the second part of the *Jewell House*. About 1596, he also issued an exposition of *The new and admirable arte of setting corne*. Harte, in his *Essays on Husbandry* (1764), speaks of him as the most ingenious husbandman of his times, and says that he corresponded with all the lovers of agriculture and gardening throughout England.

Here, again, as in the field of horsemanship, Markham holds the foremost place in his day. His books on husbandry are, perhaps, not written with so intimate a first-hand knowledge, but a faculty for minute observation and a long acquaintance with country matters in general enabled him to supplement his own knowledge by selecting and assimilating what was best and most advanced in existing literature; and his literary taste and skill enabled him to present it in a form at once attractive and practical. He is equally at home in expounding the best methods of tillage, the treatment of live stock, the subtleties of hawking, the secrets of angling, or the most approved recipes for the housewife; there is little, indeed, in the whole range of country pleasures and duties, upon which he did not discourse with ease, enthusiasm and authority, and, on all occasions, with that display of omniscience which is a mark of the true journalist.

All these characteristics are seen to advantage in that encyclopaedic and seductive volume, *A Way to get Wealth*. The first treatise in this collection, *Cheap and Good Husbandry*, deals with the management of domestic animals and fowls and the cure of their diseases. As in duty bound, he leads off with his favourite, the horse, and, in the directions for training, the gentleness of his methods is particularly noticeable. Correction, indeed, is to be given "soundly and sharply, as oft as just occasion shall require"; but there is much more of "cherishing" than chiding, and *suaviter in modo* is the key-note of all his instruction. No treatise on rural economy of this period seems to have been considered complete without its chapter on bees, and Markham duly devotes a section to these "gentle, loving and familiar creatures."

Having dealt with the duties of country life, Markham then proceeds in *Country Contentments* to set out the various recreations wherewith a husbandman may refresh himself after the toil of more serious business. Here he writes with accustomed ease, and in somewhat more leisurely manner, as befits the occasion. The singular rhythmical charm of his style is at its best; nothing is abrupt or unfinished; sentences are rounded off with a due regard to effect; and, in the direct simplicity of his diction, nothing of clearness is lost. What, for instance, could be better and more attuned to its subject than these instructions for the composition of a pack of hounds:

If you would have your Kennell for sweetnesse of cry, then you must compound it of some large dogges, that have deepe solemne mouthes, and are swift in spending, which must as it were beare the base in the consort; then a double number of roaring, and loud-ringing mouthes, which must beare the counter tenor; then some hollow plaine sweete mouthes, which must beare the meane or middle part: and soe with these three parts of musicke, you shall make your cry perfect. . . .

If you would have your Kennell for loudnes of mouth, you shall not then choose the hollow deepe mouth, but the loud clanging mouth, which spendeth freely and sharpley, and as it were redoubleth in the utterance: and if you mix with them the mouth that roareth, and the mouth that whineth, the crye will be both the louder and smarter; . . . and the more equally you compound these mouthes, having as many Roarers as Spenders, and as many whiners, as of either of the other, the louder and pleasanter your cry will be, especially if it be in sounding tall woods, or under the eccho of Rocks.

Hunting is followed by hawking, "a most princely and serious delight"; and shooting with long-bow and cross-bow, and the games of bowls, tennis and baloon are all included. The moralising chapter in which *The whole Art of Angling* is introduced is entirely in keeping with the spirit of "the contemplative man's recreation," and therein Markham shows himself a not unworthy precursor of Izaak Walton. After commendation of the gentle art, the making of rods, lines and other implements is described with a particular nicety, and other directions follow, all set forth with similar conciseness.

In the *English Huswife*, which forms the second part of *Country Contentments*, Markham, for once, does not claim originality, but describes it as being in great part from "a Manuscript, which many yeeres agon belonged to an Honourable Countesse." In it, the whole sphere of the housewife's domain is dealt with, household physic, cookery, distilling, dairying and brewing. Recipes are given for every domestic occasion, from a remedy for the Tysicke to the making of Ipocras, with many other conceited secrets. The cookery directions are characterised by lavishness, and some of the other recipes are, to say the least, somewhat curious. If Markham had been challenged as to the "halfe a bushell of the doune of Cats tailes" prescribed for the concoction to cure burning or scalding, he would, probably, have referred it to the countess's manuscript; but he might not have disowned the description of qualities which should be discernible in the good housewife, when he says

First, shee must bee cleanly both in body and garments, shee must have a quicke eye, a curious nose, a perfect taste, and ready eare; (shee must not be butter-fingred, sweete-toothed, nor faint-hearted) for, the first will let every thing fall, the second will consume what it should increase, and the last will loose time with too much nicenesse.

A Way to get Wealth also contains The Inrichment of the Weald of Kent and Markhams Farewell to Husbandry, both of which treat of the manuring and enrichment of poor soils; and it concludes with two or three horticultural treatises, the most important of which, A New Orchard and Garden, was the work of William Lawson. The collection was many times reprinted, the fifteenth edition making its appearance in 1695.

Markham wrote several other books on practical subjects, the titles of which, as well as of works by contemporary writers on country matters, will be found in the bibliography. Among the latter, may be specially noted Turbervile's Booke of faulconrie (1575), and The Noble arte of venerie or hunting, also attributed to Turbervile, and both compilations from foreign sources; Simon Latham's two books of Falconry (1615–8); and John Dennys's Secrets of angling (1613), from which Markham drew more than inspiration, and with which Walton was acquainted. Descriptive natural history makes a good beginning in Topsell's illustrated Historie of Fourefooted Beastes (1607), in which, as the author frankly and quaintly says,

I have followed D. Gesner as neer as I could, I do profess him my Author in most of my stories, yet I have gathred up that which he let fal, and added many pictures and stories as may apeare by conference of both together.

A companion volume, The historie of Serpents, or the second booke of living creatures, was published in the following year. Both these books were re-issued in 1658, together with the Theater of Insects, the latter being a translation of Thomas Moffett's Insectorum sive minimorum animalium theatrum, which, though written in 1590, first appeared in its Latin form in 1634. Moffett, who had studied medicine in Cambridge and Basle and travelled in Italy and Spain, was also the author of a descriptive and moralising poem on The silkewormes and their flies (1599). Silk culture was receiving some attention in England about this time, and other practical treatises on the subject were brought out. The newly imported accomplishment of smoking tobacco was also contributing its quota to literature.

The earliest of the numerous herbals which appeared in England, the *Grete Herball*, founded on the French *Grand Herbier*,.was printed by Peter Treveris at Southwark in 1526, and several times reprinted before the middle of the century. William Turner, the reformer, who had a garden at Kew, diversified his protestant polemics with botanical pursuits; and his *New herball* (1551–62) is considered a starting point in the scientific study of botany in England. Matthias de L'Obel, whose important works appeared only in Latin, was a resident in England and botanist to king James I. The *Niewe herball* (1578) of Rembert Dodoens, in its English dress by Henry Lyte, through the French version of L'Écluse (Clusius), was very popular, as was also the abridgment by William Ram, published in 1606 under the title *Rams little Dodeon*. It was also from Dodoens's *Pemptades* that John Gerard, through the manuscript of Priest's translation which came into his hands, derived and adapted, without acknowledgment, a great part of his celebrated *Herball or generall historie of Plantes* (1597). The majority of the numerous woodcuts used in this folio had previously appeared in the *Eicones plantarum* of Tabernaemontanus (1590). A revised and enlarged edition was brought out by Thomas Johnson in 1633.

These herbals, though not professedly horticultural works, give occasional glimpses into plant culture as practised at that time; and the art of gardening, which was then making considerable progress in this country at the hands of a number of enthusiastic devotees, also began to produce its own special literature. Dutch and other foreign sources provided ready material and inspiration for some of the earlier writers, among whom there is naturally a good deal of repetition; illustrations were also freely copied, especially designs for knots, or carpet beds, which seem to have been highly esteemed, but of which Bacon, in his magnificent plan of a princely garden, says contemptuously that "you may see as good sights, many times, in Tarts." Tusser has introduced a considerable amount of gardening detail into his *Pointes of good husbandrie;* but Thomas Hill, or "Didymus Mountain" as he sometimes facetiously styled himself, was one of the earliest to compile a book devoted exclusively to horticulture. This was printed in 1563 under the title *A most briefe and pleasaunt treatyse, teachynge howe to dress, sowe, and set a garden*, and afterwards enlarged as *The proffitable arte of gardening*. Markham's writings on the subject are to be found chiefly in his *English Husbandman, Country-mans Recreation*, and *Country Housewifes Garden*, the latter sometimes printed with Lawson's *New Orchard* mentioned above. In 1608, Sir Hugh Plat published his contribution to horticulture under the title *Floraes Paradise;* and, in 1629, the ardent botanist and lover of flowers, John Parkinson, king's herbarist, brought out his delightful *Paradisi in sole Paradisus terrestris, or a garden of all sorts of pleasant flowers which our English ayre will permitt to be noursed up: with a kitchen garden . . . and an orchard*, the woodcuts for which were specially done in England; this was followed in 1640 by his great herbal, *Theatrum botanicum*, with its description of nearly 3800 plants and its 2600 illustrations.

In his recension of the *Book of St. Albans*, issued in 1595 as the *Gentlemans Academie*, Markham came into touch with heraldry; but, as he merely modernised the diction without revision of the matter, he can scarcely be deemed a writer on this science. The section on coat-armour in the St. Albans book was the first English treatise on heraldry, and is not without some practical value; it was derived largely from Nicholas Upton's *De officio militari* (1441), first printed in 1654 by Sir Edward Bysshe. In 1562, Gerard Legh brought out his popular *Accedens of Armory*, and several other writers, such as John Bossewell, Sir John Ferne and William Wyrley, followed him; but most of these works were vitiated by flights of imagination and absurd legends about the antiquity of coat-armour, and it was left to John Guillim, whose *Display of Heraldrie*, first printed in 1610, is still a classic, to place the science on something approaching a sound basis.

According to Langbaine, Markham was esteemed a good scholar and an excellent linguist, understanding perfectly the French, Italian and Spanish languages. He was certainly well read in the subjects which he handled, and thoroughly conversant with the classical allusions with which it was the fashion in his day to overlay polite literature. In verse, however, his achievement does not reach a high order; his was not a lyric muse, and the long narrative poems which he attempted are dull conventional productions, lacking inspiration and spontaneity. Even his best opportunity, the thrilling story of the last fight of the *Revenge*,[1] fails to arouse him, and the poem, dragged out through 174 stanzas of eight lines each, is a tedious performance, clogged with laboured metaphor and classical simile. In other poems he deals with some of the sacred themes much affected at that time: the *Poem of poems, or Sions muse, contayning the divine Song of Salomon in eight eclogues*, the subject of one of bishop Hall's satires[2] and mentioned by Francis Meres in *Palladis Tamia*, made its appearance in 1595; and, in 1600, was printed *Teares of the Beloved: or, the lamentation of Saint John concerning the death and passion of Christ Jesus our Saviour*, a poem of 140 six-lined stanzas in heroic metre; *Marie Magdalens lamentations for the losse of her Master Jesus*, a similar poem of the following year, has also been attributed to him.

Besides these original exercises, Markham translated from the French of "Madam Genevefve Petau Maulette," *Devoreux, or vertues tears* (1597), a lament on the death of Henry III of France and of Walter Devereux, a brother of the earl of Essex. In 1609, he produced *The Famous Whore, or Noble Curtizan*, being the story of the career of "Paulina, the famous Roman curtizan, sometimes m[es] unto the great Cardinall Hypolito, of Est," a poem in riming couplets translated, it is said, from the Italian; but the original of this, as likewise of *Devoreux*, has not been traced. *Rodomonths Infernall, or the Divell conquered*, a spirited English rendering from the French of Desportes, also belongs to him; but the version of *Ariostos Satyres*, issued under Markham's name in 1608, was claimed by Robert Tofte. This ascription may have been an error, either accidental or intentional, on the part of the publisher; and a similar confusion seems to have occurred in the case of the *Pastoralls of Julietta*, which was entered by Thomas Creede in the Stationers' register in November, 1609, as "translated out of French by Jarvis Markam," but in the following year was published by him as the work of Tofte.

Seeing the freedom with which he "paraphrastically" used

---

[1] *The Most Honorable Tragedie of Sir Richard Grinvile, Knight*, 1595.
[2] Bk. I, Sat. VIII.

other writers' work, it is not surprising to find that Markham adventured the hazardous *rôle* of continuator. In 1607, he published *The English Arcadia, alluding his beginning from Sir Philip Sydnes ending*, and followed it, six years later, with *The second and last part of the first booke of the English Arcadia. Making a compleate end of the first history;* but neither of these attempts seems to have met with any marked success.

Markham is further known as collaborator in the production of two plays, but precisely what share belongs to him is not apparent. *The Dumbe Knight* (1608), founded on one of Bandello's Italian novels, was written in conjunction with Lewis Machin of whom nothing further is known. *The true tragedy of Herod and Antipater*, printed in 1622 but written some ten years earlier, was the joint work of Markham and William Sampson. Both plays belong to the older school of dramatic writing, and present no features of importance in either the progress of the drama or the development of literary art.

In appraising Markham as a writer, his efforts in poetry and drama may well be ignored. He is essentially an open-air man. Any rural occupation or manly sport is fit subject for his willing pen, and therein we find the true Markham. He is delightfully human, and everything upon which he touches is lighted up by his enthusiasm and made, for the moment, the most engrossing theme in the world.

CHAPTER XVIII

The Book-Trade, 1557-1625

THE outstanding feature in the history of English printing and bookselling in the second half of the sixteenth century is the incorporation of the Stationers' company. This organisation of the trade was the means whereby a strong dual control over the output of the press was acquired, in the first place by the state, for political and ecclesiastical reasons, and, secondly, by the company itself, for the domestic regulation of the trade.

The guild or fraternity of scriveners and others connected with the production and sale of books, which had been formed in 1403, had, with the increased trade in books and the introduction of printing, developed in course of time into the craft of Stationers; and, as all persons carrying on any business in the city of London connected with the book-trade were required to become members of the craft, this association had long exercised considerable influence in fixing and controlling trade customs. Prompted by the desire of increased power, the craft, in 1557,[1] procured a royal charter of incorporation which invested the fraternity not only with a more formal dignity, but, also, with a greater authority over the trade. The government of the new corporation was vested in a master and two wardens to be elected annually, and the list of original members of the company, as set forth in the charter, contains ninety-seven names. In 1560, the development of the association was completed by its admission as one of the liveried companies of the city.

Under the rules of the company, every member was required to enter in the register the name of any book or copy

---

[1] This, as has been pointed out by E. Gordon Duff, is the correct date, not 1556, as is usually stated.

which he claimed as his property and desired to print, paying at the same time, a fee for the entry. Besides these entries of books, the registers also contain records of the admission of freemen, the taking of apprentices, and other matters relating to the affairs of the company. The registers served, primarily, as an account of the fees received by the wardens; and the book entries were, doubtless, also intended to prevent disputes as to who might possess the right to print any particular work. It should be observed that the registers by no means include everything which appeared from the press. Those who held special privileges or monopolies for printing a certain book or, maybe, a whole class of books, were not, apparently, under obligation to enter such books, and the royal printers were also superior to the rule so far as the works included in their patent were concerned. But, notwithstanding these *lacunae*, the registers of the company form a marvellous storehouse of information concerning the productions of the press during the period which they cover.

As a direct consequence of the company's charter, no one, thenceforth, could print anything for sale within the kingdom unless he were a member of the Stationers' company, or held some privilege or patent entitling him to print some specified work or particular class of book. And even the members of the company who printed or published were subject to many limitations in the exercise of their calling. Royal proclamations and injunctions, and Star chamber decrees must not be ignored; the numerous printing monopolies granted to individuals must not be infringed; and, more important still, the strict trade regulations, as laid down and enforced by the Stationers' company, could not be disregarded with impunity.

The charter of incorporation was probably the more readily granted by the authorities of state, in that it provided an organisation for securing better supervision of the press, and furnished means of suppressing those seditious and heretical publications which haunted the authorities with a perpetual fear, and which were the subject of frequent prohibition. The extent to which this supervision was made effective may be gathered from the shifts to which the secret presses were put in order to carry on their hazardous work.[1]

---

[1] See the chapter on the Marprelate tracts in Vol. III of the present work.

The particular class of book to which the terms heretical, traitorous and seditious were applied varied, of course, with the form of religion professed by the reigning sovereign. Quite naturally, popish books were banned under Edward VI, but, in the reign of queen Mary, a great effort was made to stem the tide of protestant literature which the preceding reign had encouraged. In 1555, a stringent royal proclamation was issued prohibiting the printing or importation of the works of Luther, Calvin, Bullinger, Melanchthon, Latimer, Coverdale, Tindale, Cranmer, Becon, and other reformers; and, in 1558, another brief but peremptory proclamation was directed against heretical and treasonable books, including the service books of Edward VI.

By the death of queen Mary, these enactments were soon rendered null, but the accession of a protestant queen brought no real freedom, as, with the increase of printing, there also grew up an increasing desire on the part of both state and church to obtain complete control over the production and distribution of printed literature.

In the first year of her reign, Elizabeth confirmed the Stationers in their charter, and, in the same year, issued the *Injunctions geven by the Quenes Majestie*. One of these injunctions had an important bearing on book production in England, for it is the authority on which was based that licensing and censorship of books which was actively enforced by the dignitaries of the church during this and the next two reigns, and which enabled them to obtain and retain a tight hold on the output of the legitimate press. This injunction[1] ordained that no manner of book or paper should be printed unless the same

be first licenced by her maiestie by expresse wordes in writynge, or by .vi. of her privy counsel, or be perused and licensed by the archbyshops of Cantorbury, and yorke, the bishop of London, the chaunselours of both universities, the bishop being ordinary, and the Archdeacon also of the place where anye suche shalbe printed, or by two of them, whereof the ordinary of the place to be alwaies one. And that the names of such as shal allowe the same to be added in thende of every such worke, for a testymonye of the allowaunce thereof.

[1] No. 51: quoted from one of Jugge and Cawood's early undated editions.

Had this injunction been literally obeyed, the object of its promoters would have been at once secured. But the numerous proclamations which were issued against dangerous and obnoxious books attest both the determination to suppress them and the ineffectiveness of the means employed. In June, 1566, the Star chamber issued a decree against the printing, importing, or selling of prohibited books, threatening offenders with pains and penalties and authorising the Stationers' company to make search for such books in suspected places. The publication of one of William Elderton's ballads, entitled *Doctor Stories stumblinge into Englonde*, in 1570, was made the occasion for a further effort in the shape of a privy council order addressed to the master and wardens of the Stationers' company, commanding that they suffer neither book nor ballad nor any other matter to be published without being first seen and licensed. Admonition was backed up by example, and the severity with which offenders were occasionally treated served as a reminder of the risk involved in intermeddling with such matters. William Carter, a printer who had been imprisoned on divers occasions for printing "naughtye papysticall books," found that these were no empty threats, for, as Stow relates in his *Annales*, on 10 January, 1584, he was condemned for high treason as having printed a seditious book entitled, *A treatise of schisme*, and, on the morrow, he was drawn from Newgate to Tyburn and there hanged, bowelled and quartered.

A long-standing feud, between the printers who held monopolies and the unprivileged men who were continually infringing patents, resulted in appeals by both parties for state intervention, and the authorities were not slow to avail themselves of this opportunity for tightening their hold on the press. Accordingly, in June, 1586, the Star chamber enacted a most important decree for the regulation of printing, which was practically a consolidation and amplification of previous legislation, and was superseded only by the still more stringent but short-lived decree issued by the Star chamber of Charles I in 1637. By the ordinance of 1586, it was enacted that all presses at present set up, and any which might hereafter be set up, should be reported to the master and wardens of the company; that no press should be set up in any other place than London, except in the universities of Cambridge and Oxford, and only one press in each of these two places; that, in order to diminish "the excessive multytude of prynters havinge presses already sett up," no further press to be erected until such time as, by death or otherwise, they are reduced to the number which the archbishop of Canterbury and the bishop of London shall think requisite for the service of the realm; and, on the occurrence of vacancies, the company is to nominate free stationers to fill the vacancies and to present them to the ecclesiastical commissioners to be licensed. Severe penalties are threatened against those who shall print any books except such as have been allowed according to the order appointed by the queen's *Injunctions*.

The order in the injunction of 1559 that the names of the licensers should be added at the end of every book was practically a dead letter; but the "seen and allowed according to the order appointed," which appears on some title-pages soon after that date, shows that some degree of supervision was being exercised, and the form of the book entries in the Stationers' registers clearly indicates the gradually extending operation of the censorship. Previous to 1561, books are entered merely as licensed by the company, without any reference to censorship, but, from the March of that year, books are occasionally noted as authorised by the bishop of London, and, in a few cases, by the archbishop of Canterbury. Twenty years later, when John Aylmer had become bishop of London, and was taking a lively interest in the subjection of the press to authority, his name very frequently appears as licenser of all kinds of books, and even trifles like ballads receive his *imprimatur*. The elevation of the rigorous disciplinarian Whitgift to the see of Canterbury in 1583, and the promulgation of the Star chamber decree of 1586, mark further steps in the progress of control. By 1588, it had become the practice to enter the name of the licenser and that of one or both of the wardens of the company, and, in the same year, Whitgift, whose interest in the censorship was receiving a stimulus from the activity of his Marprelate opponents, appointed twelve persons to license books to be printed. The most active among these twelve were Abraham Hartwell, the younger, secretary to Whitgift, and Dr. Stallard. Another of them was Robert Crowley, author and formerly printer, from whose press came three editions of *Piers Plowman* in 1550. After sojourning abroad during queen Mary's reign, he renewed his connection with printing, being admitted a freeman of the Stationers' company in 1578. Among prominent censors in succeeding years were Richard Bancroft, chaplain to Whitgift and afterwards his successor, to whose activity was largely due the unearthing of the Marprelate press; William Barlow, also chaplain to Whitgift and, later, bishop of Lincoln; Richard Mocket, the reputed author of the tract *God and the King* (1615), which was ordered to be bought by every householder in England and Scotland; and Daniel Featley, controversialist and Westminster assembly divine.

Besides these censors by ecclesiastical warrant, various secular authorities sometimes authorised the printing of books, such as Sir Francis Walsingham, the lord treasurer's secretary, or even lord Burghley himself. Occasionally, the countenance of the privy council was obtained, and, at other times, a book is passed by the lord mayor or the city recorder. In certain cases, professional aid was invoked, as in 1589, when a medical book was entered under the hands of both the wardens "and three Chirurgyans appointed to peruse this boke." In the beginning of the seventeenth century, the drama received special attention, and plays were licensed by the master of the revels; an office filled by Sir George Buck from about 1608 to 1622, his immediate successors being Sir John Ashley, and Sir Henry Herbert, a brother of the poet. But all these, with the exception of the plays, were rather in the nature of occasional instances, and the vast majority of books were licensed either by the archbishop or bishop, or by his chaplain or secretary. Such was the narrow and hazardous channel through which the impetuous stream of English literature in Elizabethan days had to force its way before being allowed to reach the world of letters.

By their charter, the Stationers were empowered to search the premises of any printer or stationer to see that nothing was printed contrary to regulations, and, accordingly, searchers were appointed to make weekly visits to printing-houses, their instructions being to ascertain how many presses every printer possessed; what every printer printed, the number of each impression and for whom they were printed; how many workmen and apprentices every printer employed, and whether he had on his premises any unauthorised person. These inquisitorial visits resulted in frequent seizures of illegally printed books, and, in the records of the company, there are many instances of such books being brought into the hall and there either burned or damasked.

But the attentions of the company were not confined to illegal productions; the brethren themselves were well looked after, and the accounts of fines received for breaking of orders and other offences show that a rigorous supervision was maintained. In 1559, John King is fined two shillings and sixpence for printing *The Nutbrowne Mayde* without licence, and William Jones is mulcted in twenty pence "for that he solde a Communion boke of Kynge Edwardes for one of the newe." In 1595, Abel Jeffes, having printed "lewde ballades and thinges verye offensive," it was ordered by the court of the company that his press, type, and other printing stuff, which had been seized and brought into the hall, should be defaced and made unserviceable for printing. Penalties were also imposed for printing other men's copies, that is, infringing copyright, and for "disorderly" printing, which evidently included carelessly, as well as wrongfully, printed books. These are mostly individual cases, but, occasionally, a wholesale raid is made, as in 1562-3, when William Powell was fined for printing the prognostication of Nostradamus, and nineteen other booksellers were fined for selling the book. In 1594, several stationers were heavily penalised for selling "psalmes disorderly printed"; and, in 1603, thirteen booksellers got into trouble for being concerned in an unauthorised edition of *Basilicon doron*, which had been first printed at Edinburgh in 1599, in a private edition of only seven copies. This second edition was printed by Edward Allde, and a bookseller, Edward White, who had sold 500 copies which, therefore, could not be forfeited, was condemned to imprisonment but respited to the further order of the company. Cases are not wanting in which contumacious offenders were actually committed to prison. Even in those early days, the soul of the bookseller was vexed by the intrusion of other trades upon his domain, and Thomas Purfoot was fined for selling *Primers* to the haberdashers.

Fines for keeping open shop on Sundays and festival days are not infrequent in the sixteenth century, and the keeping of an apprentice without presenting him was a common offence.

A cause of much dissension and frequent dispute among the printers was the number of printing monopolies granted during the reign of Elizabeth. These privileges were not only for the exclusive right of printing a definite book, but frequently covered a whole class of books. Thus, in 1559, the printing of law books was confirmed to Richard Tottel, for his lifetime. William Seres, who, in queen Mary's reign, had been deprived of his privilege of printing *Primers* and books of private prayers and had suffered imprisonment, succeeded in recovering his patent with reversion to his son and the addition of *Psalters* to his monopoly. Christopher Baker, successor in 1577 of Richard Jugge in the office of queen's printer, had the privilege of printing Bibles, the *Book of Common Prayer*, statutes and proclamations. Through the influence of the earl of Leicester, John Day had been given the monopoly of printing the *Psalms in metre* and the *ABC and Catechism*. The printing of dictionaries and chronicles was granted to Henry Bynneman. Richard Watkins and James Roberts had a patent for twenty-one years for almanacs and prognostications, and in 1603 this valuable privilege was conferred by King James I upon the Stationers' company for ever. Thomas Marshe's patent included a number of the most usual school books in Latin. "Master Birde and Master Tallis of her Majesty's Chappel have all music books and also ruled paper for music." There are also instances of a monopoly being granted for a term of years for a specified book, a privilege which corresponds to our present copyright.

It will be noticed that these privileges were mainly for books of a stereotyped kind for which there was a constant demand, and the production of works of real literature was scarcely, if at all, affected by them. But this concentration of the best paying work in a few hands bred much discontent in the trade, and, together with scarcity of employment, led to frequent complaints by those who felt the pinch.

The forces thus brought into conflict were, on the one side, the possessors of profitable privileges or valuable copyrights which formed the backbone of their business; these were the leading members of the trade, men of influence in the affairs of the company. On the other side, forming a natural opposition, were ranged the unprivileged men, who, possessed of small means and being, to some extent, outsiders, were driven to a more speculative class of business, and picked up —no great matter how—copy which was likely to appeal to the popular taste, such as plays, poems, ballads, or any other unconsidered trifles out of which they might turn a penny. Notwithstanding the specious argument of the monopolists that

privileges are a means whereby many books are now printed which are more beneficial to the commonwealth than profitable to the printer, for the patentee being benefited by books of profitable sale is content to bestowe part of his gain in other books, which though very beneficial to the commonwealth will not repay the tenth part of his charge,

it is, as a matter of fact, to the unprivileged printers that we owe the preservation in print of the greater part of the poetical, dramatic and popular literature of the time. But, though the names of these men have become known to us mainly in connection with this literature, it is not necessary to credit them with either great literary taste or a consciousness of the part they were playing in this cause; it merely means that necessity and keen competition for business had given them a shrewd eye as to what was likely to find a good market.

This clashing of interests led to various efforts on the part of the lesser men to obtain redress of their grievances, and a few adventurous spirits took matters into their own hands and proceeded to pirate some of the smaller books for which there was a large and steady sale. Besides being quickly printed, these small publications possessed the advantage of being easily dispersed, and many of them were sent into the country, where, as imprints were also forged, there was little risk of their spurious origin being detected. Legal proceedings naturally followed, and, in 1582, John Day, one of the largest patentees, preferred a complaint to the Star chamber against Roger Ward for printing, and William Holmes for selling, pirated copies of the *ABC with the little catechism*, a publication for which Day held a patent of monopoly. In his answer to the charge, Ward makes a stout defence, eked out with convenient lapses of memory, and pleads that, a very small number of stationers having gotten all the best books to be printed by themselves by privilege, have left little or nothing for the rest of the printers to live upon. In the same year, William Seres appealed to lord Burghley against the infringement by certain stationers of his right of printing *Primers* and *Psalters*, and the form in which his complaint is stated indicates the existence of some more or less organised piracy by the younger men of the company.

The leader of this lawless band was John Wolfe, of the Fishmongers' company, a born agitator; he not only printed other men's copies, but incited others to defy the constituted authorities. A petition against him and his associates, addressed to the privy council by the Stationers' company in 1583, relates that, on being remonstrated with, Wolfe declared that he would print all their books if he lacked work. Being admonished that he, being but one so mean a man, should not presume to oppose her Highness's government, "Tush," said he, "Luther was but one man, and reformed all the world for religion, and I am that one man that must and will reforme the governement in this trade." However, efforts made to compose the differences between the disputants met with some success. The patentees surrendered a number of their copyrights for the use of the poor of the company; and Wolfe, it was reported, "acknowledged his error," and was admitted into the Stationers' company. It is amusing to discover Wolfe and Francis Adams, a year or so later, appearing in a Star chamber case righteously indignant at the lawless infringement of a printing patent in which they had acquired a share; and Wolfe is afterwards found taking an active part, as an official of the company, in the search for secret presses.

About the year 1577, the number of printers and stationers, journeymen and all, within the city of London was 175, besides a large number of apprentices; and in a report on the printing patents which he drew up in 1582, Christopher Barker, the queen's printer, stated that there were about threescore journeymen connected with the printing trade alone. He also says that there were twenty-two printing-houses in London, and expresses the opinion that "8 or 10 at the most would suffise for all England, yea and Scotland too." A not very liberal view, perhaps, but Barker was a patentee. In 1586, the number of master printers had risen to twenty-five, and they had among them a total of fifty-three presses; but, by the Star chamber decree of that year, no further increase in the number of master printers or presses was permitted, and there was little variation in this number, until, under the stress of public affairs in 1640, the restrictions on printing were relaxed, when there was a rapid increase, and, by 1649, there were in London upwards of sixty printing-houses.

But, though the amount of work that could be provided by the presses was thus strictly limited, there was no similar limit to the supply of workmen, and, owing to the masters having taken too many apprentices in past years, the number of journeymen so increased that there was lack of work for them all and consequent discontent and distress. Endeavours were made to remedy this state of matters by limiting the number of apprentices; but, as a more immediate step for relieving the lack of employment, the company, in 1587–8, made certain orders concerning printing, which provided that no apprentice should be employed in composing or working at the press if any competent journeyman wanted work, and that no forms of type should be kept standing to the prejudice of workmen. By these regulations, also, the number of copies of one impression of a book was limited, in ordinary cases, to 1250 or 1500 copies. The effect of this restriction was to supply more work for compositors, inasmuch as the type had to be reset for each impression. The operation of some similar earlier trade regulation may, possibly, explain the existence of such bibliographical puzzles as the appearance in duplicate of the second edition of *Tottel's Miscellany*, a book which achieved an immediate popularity. The first edition of this is dated 5 June, 1557, and the enlarged second edition, of which there are two very similar variants, appeared as early as 31 July in the same year. The fact that, in all probability, the second impression of a book would be set up from a copy of the first edition may account for a close typographical similarity of appearance between successive editions, which might easily cause copies of them to be taken for variations of the same edition.

The term of appenticeship varied from seven to eleven years, so arranged that the apprentice should reach at least the age

of twenty-four years before the expiration of his term. At
the end of his time, his master was bound to make him free
of the company "if he have well and truely served"; but,
as Arber has remarked, hardly more than one-half of the
apprentices ever attained to the freedom of the company.
On becoming a freeman, an ambitious young printer would
naturally turn his thoughts towards starting in business for
himself. As has been seen, the number of master printers
was, for a long period, limited to about 25, and the prospect of a young man gaining admission to this small company was very slender. The picturesque tradition of
the industrious apprentice marrying his master's daughter
suggests itself in this connection, but, as a matter of
fact, it was much more often his master's widow that
he married, and cases are not uncommon of the business and the widow being "taken over" by two printers in
succession.

To embark on his career as a bookseller and publisher
was a simpler, if more hazardous, undertaking. If possessed
of means, the young bookseller might purchase a stock of
saleable books, and at once open a shop in some busy thoroughfare or take up a point of vantage in one of the stalls or booths
which crowded round the walls of St. Paul's, and there expose
his wares for sale. But, supposing him to have nothing
save his native wit to aid him, there was still a way by which
he could set up for himself. If he could procure the copy
of some book, or pamphlet, or, may be, even a ballad, which
he could enter in the register as his property, and then get
printed by some friendly printer, he would have made a modest
beginning; and, if this first essay happened to promise a fair
sale, he might, by exchanging copies of it with other publishers
for their books, at once obtain a stock in trade. This system
of interchange seems to have been a common practice, and
books were sometimes entered in the register with the proviso
that the stationer "shall not refuse to exchange these bookes
with the company for other good wares." The custom continued in vogue throughout the seventeenth century, and it
was in this way that, in 1681, the celebrated John Dunton
began his career as a publisher; having ventured to print
Doolittle's *Sufferings of Christ*, he says, "by exchanging it

through the whole trade, it furnished my shop with all sorts of books saleable at that time."

Besides publishing books brought to them by authors, stationers often took the initiative and engaged writers to produce works for them. Thus, it was at the instance and expense of Christopher Barker that George Turbervile undertook the compilation of *The noble arte of venerie or hunting* (1575), the publisher himself seeking out and procuring works of foreign writers for the use of the compiler. When William Fulke was at work upon his *Confutation of the Rhemish Testament*, he and two of his men with their horses, were maintained in London for three-quarters of a year by the publisher of the book, George Bishop, who also supplied Fulke with such books as he required, and at the finish paid him forty pounds for his work. The six revisers who went up to London to make the final revision of the *Authorised Version* of the Bible, each received thirty shillings a week for the nine months during which they were engaged upon the task. For his *Survey of London*, John Stow had £3 and 40 copies; and, "for his pains in the *Brief Chronicle*," he received twenty shillings and 50 copies.

Correcting and editing for the press afforded occupation for a few scholars in the more important printing-houses, and it is probable that John Foxe, after his return from the continent, worked in some such capacity in the office of John Day, as he had previously done in the house of Oporinus at Basel. Christopher Barker, in 1582, mentions the payment of "learned correctours" as one of the expenses which printers had to bear; and, about 1630, the king's printing-house was employing four correctors, all of whom were masters of arts.

Translations, of which an extraordinary number were published during this period, formed a large part of the work which hack writers did for booksellers, and it was generally poorly paid work. For the writing of an ordinary pamphlet, two pounds seems to have been a customary payment, but oft-times, especially in the case of translation, the writer had to content himself with receiving a certain number of copies to dispose of for his own benefit. After 1622, when news sheets began to be issued, the translating of these from foreign *Corantos* offered another means of earning a pittance, and if there were dearth of news, or the supply of foreign print failed, the resourcefulness of writers was, doubtless, quite equal to that of Thomas Herbert and his companions who, some twenty years later, sat themselves down at the sign of the Antelope and there "composed" *Good Newes from Ireland, Bloudy Newes* and other equally reliable information, and then sold their fabrications to the stationers for half-a-crown apiece.

A humble form of literature, which provided occupation for inferior writers and work for smaller printers, was the ballad, which came forth from the press in thousands. Not the old narrative ballads of oral tradition, but their debased descendants, topical street ballads—sentimental ditties in amorous, moral, or satirical vein; story of horrid crime or monstrous birth; relation of disaster by fire or flood; or any other popular excitement of the hour: in short, any peg upon which could be hung a jingling rime or doleful ditty served for a ballad, and "scarce a cat can look out of a gutter," it was said, "but presently a proper new ballad of a strange sight is indited." Yet, in spite of the vast number which were printed, these ephemeral sheets have perished almost as completely as the names of their writers. Those who bought them cared as little to know who wrote them, as do the patrons of the popular songs of to-day. William Elderton was responsible for a large number in his time, Thomas Deloney had written some 50 by 1596, and Anthony Munday also contributed his quota; but, as is only natural, ballads, with few exceptions, are known only by their titles. Printers of them were as numerous as writers; one of the earliest, John Awdeley, wrote as well as printed them, as did also Thomas Nelson later in the sixteenth century. Among the most active producers of these sheets were Thomas Colwell of Fleet Street, Alexander Lacy of Little Britain, William Pickering of London Bridge, Richard Jones the publisher of several of Elderton's writing, who, in 1586, entered in the Stationers' register no fewer than 123 at one time, and Edward Allde and Henry Carr, who entered batches of 36 and 20 respectively in this same year.

To the professional writer, a patron, to whom he might dedicate his book, was almost as essential as a publisher; and the competition for the favour of distinguished persons who patronised literature was very keen. Prominent among these were the earl of Leicester, who befriended Spenser and Ascham; the earl of Southampton, the friend, as well as patron, of Shakespeare; Sir Philip Sidney and his sister the countess of Pembroke; and William Herbert, earl of Pembroke, the friend of Donne, who was accustomed, on the first day of each new year, to send to Ben Jonson a gift of £20 to buy books. No doubt it was an advantage to a book to be launched under the approbation of some person of mark, but the needy writer had also well in view the more substantial reward which was invariably expected in return for the flattering compliments or often fulsome eulogy, of the dedication. Occasionally, this desired recompense might be an appointment to some office or other similar recognition, but, more generally, it took the form of a gift of money, varying in amount with the generosity of the patron or the persuasive importunity of the author, though, sometimes, the mere acceptance of the dedication must have been the only *solatium*. In the record of his literary earnings which Richard Robinson, compiler and translator of a number of dull religious works between 1576 and 1598, has left in manuscript,[1] we get a glimpse of what the ordinary occasional dedication was worth. For a book dedicated to the master of the Leathersellers, of which company he was a member, he received 2s. 6d. from the master and 7s. 6d. more from the company. In 1579, Sir Philip Sidney, to whom he had "presented" a book, gave him four angels, increased by a gift of 10s. from Sir Henry Sidney. But, for the third series of his *Harmony of King Davids Harp* (1595), which he dedicated to queen Elizabeth and presented to her highness as she was "goyng to the Chappell in the morning," he received no gratification: in fact, the queen characteristically told him that she had quite enough to do in paying and relieving her needy soldiers, and that as she had not set him on the work she did not intend to pay him any wages.

The only form of copyright recognised at this time was the entry of a "copy" in the Stationers' register by a member of the company, and the right to print any work so entered became vested in the stationer in whose name it stood. So far as

[1] "Eupolemia" (British Museum, Royal MSS., 18 A. lxvi). See *Gentleman's Magazine*, April, 1906, pp. 277-284.

the author was concerned, no rights existed; in a few cases, it is true, a royal patent was granted to a particular individual giving him a monopoly of his work for a specified period, but these exceptions only serve to accentuate the general case. The author was thus at the mercy of the stationer. He could, no doubt, take his manuscript in his hand, and, making the round of the shops, conclude a bargain with some bookseller whom he found willing to undertake the publication of his work; but, except by agreement, he could retain no control over his book: it would be entered in the register in the stationer's name and become his property. As for the author who allowed his writings to be circulated in manuscript, as was often done in the case of poems and other forms of polite literature, he was in a still more defenceless state, for his manuscript was liable to be snapped up by any literary scout who might scent a paying venture; and the first stationer who could acquire it might forthwith proceed to Stationers' Hall and secure the copyright of the work, leaving the hapless author without recompense or redress, and without even the consolation of his literary pride of correcting the errors of copyist and printer. In such cases, the publisher frequently prefixed an address from his own pen, dedicating the work to whom he would, and taking credit to himself for presenting it to the reading public. It was in this way that Sidney's *Sonnets* in 1591, Shakespeare's *Sonnets* in 1609, and other worthy shelf-fellows first attained the dignity of print, if that description may be applied to such mean typographical productions.

John Minsheu, the lexicographer, indeed, took matters into his own hands, and, in 1617, printed "at his owne charge, for the publicke good," his polyglot dictionary, *Ductor in linguas;* but, as stationers boycotted the book, he was forced to seek subscribers for it himself, and the experiment does not seem to have been a success. John Taylor, the Thames waterman, also resorted to publication by subscription, and, in his case, his whimsical personality, added to the amusement afforded by the rough wit and boisterous humour of his effusions, secured a large number of patrons. Before starting on one of his eccentric journeys, he would circulate a quantity of prospectuses or "Taylor's bills," as he called them, with the object of securing subscribers for the account of his travels to be afterwards published. In this way, he obtained more than sixteen hundred subscribers to *The Pennyles Pilgrimage* (1618), a record of his journey on foot into Scotland. On the strength of this list, he had 4500 copies printed, but nearly half the subscribers refused to pay, and he castigated the defaulters in an amusing brochure entitled *A Kicksey Winsey, or, A Lerry Come-Twang*, which he issued in the following year. He also worked off copies of his publications by "presenting" them to various people, not forgetting to call on the morrow for "sweet remuneration." But, notwithstanding king James's dictum, as reported by Ben Jonson, that he did not "see ever any verses in England equal to the Sculler's," Taylor cannot be accounted as anything more than a voluminous scribbler, possessed of irrepressible assurance and facile wit of a coarse vein. He had, however, the saving grace of acute observation of men and manners, and this has given his productions a certain value for the student of social history. The term "literary bargee" befits him much better than his own self-styled title "the water-poet"; and his unrelenting satirical persecution of Thomas Coryate shows him in an unamiable light. In 1630, he gathered into one folio volume, which he called *All the Workes of John Taylor the Water-poet*, sixty-three of his pieces in prose and verse; but, before his death, in 1653, the number of his publications had exceeded one hundred and fifty.

It would appear that the dramatist was especially exposed to the predatory habits of the piratical publisher. The playhouse authorities, believing that the circulation of a play in print was likely to detract from its financial success on the stage, gave no encouragement to the publishing of plays. But a popular play was sure of finding a ready sale, and a stationer on the look-out for "vendible copy," if he could obtain an acting copy of a favourite play, or procure a shorthand writer to take notes during its performance, would have little regard to the wishes of either playwright or players.

The printers and publishers of the early Shakespeare quartos belonged almost entirely to the class of unprivileged men, and, though th y were otherwise quite unimportant as stationers, their association with the production of the plays makes them an interesting group. Of the thirty-six plays contained in the first folio (1623), sixteen had previously been issued in separate form. The earliest in date is the *Titus Andronicus* of 1594, which was printed by John Danter for Edward White and Thomas Millington. This Danter, who, three years later, issued the first edition of *Romeo and Juliet*, was one of the least reputable members of the trade, and was given to the printing of pirated works and scurrilous pamphlets. Millington also published *The First Part of the Contention* and *The True Tragedie of Richard the Third*, which appeared in 1594 and 1595 respectively. In 1600, jointly with John Busby, another publisher of plays, he issued the first edition of *Henry V;* and, on 15 October, 1595, he entered for his copy in the Stationers' register *The Norfolk gent his will and Testament and howe he Commytted the keepinge of his Children to his owne brother whoe delte moste wickedly with them and howe God plagued him for it*—a story which has since found a briefer and more poetical title in *The Babes in the Wood.*

Next comes Andrew Wise, a small stationer in St. Paul's churchyard, who, in 1597, brought out the first issues of *Richard II* and *Richard III*. The first two quartos (1598 and 1599) of 1 *Henry IV* were also published by him. It was in conjunction with Wise, that William Aspley, another stationer of St. Paul's churchyard, published the only known quartos of *Much Ado about Nothing* and 2 *Henry IV* in 1600. In addition to issuing several plays by Chapman, Dekker and other writers, Aspley was concerned in the publication of both the first and second Shakespeare folios, and his name also appears on some copies of the first edition of the *Sonnets*. Another Shakespeare publisher was Cuthbert Burby, who, in 1598, first issued *Love's Labour's Lost*. Among other plays which bear his name are John Lyly's *Mother Bombie* (1594 and 1598), the anonymous *Taming of a Shrew* (1594), and *The Raigne of King Edward the Third* (1596 and 1599). He is also known as the publisher of Francis Meres's *Palladis Tamia*, which appeared in 1598, and joint publisher of Robert Allot's *England's Parnassus* in 1600.

Among the plays associated with the press of James Roberts, the almanac patentee, are the two issues of the *Merchant of Venice* dated 1600, and one of *A Midsummer Night's Dream* also dated 1600, and the *Hamlet* of 1602 and 1605.[1] He succeeded John Charlwood as printer of "the players' bills," or theatre programmes, an office which passed to William Jaggard in 1615. Among other stationers connected with the plays are John Smethwick, who was one of the four at whose charges the first folio was printed; Thomas Pavier, who published as Shakespeare's the plays *Sir John Oldcastle* (1600) and the *Yorkshire Tragedy* (1608); and Nathaniel Butter, who published the two issues of *Lear* in 1608, and also Chapman's *Homer*, but who is even more interesting as a pioneer of newspaper publishers. He is said to have issued a *Courant, or Weekly Newes from Foreign Parts*, as early as October, 1621; but his first entry of *A Currant of Newes* in the registers is dated 7 June, 1622, and this publication must very shortly afterwards have assumed a regular periodical issue, for "Number 24" is entered on 26 March, 1623, and it seems thereafter to have made a habitual weekly appearance.

The first two of Shakespeare's poems which passed through the press, the *Venus and Adonis* of 1593 and the *Lucrece* of 1594, were printed by Richard Field, who was a native of Stratford-on-Avon and may, therefore, it is allowable to suppose, have been personally acquainted with the author.

In 1609, a manuscript of Shakespeare's *Sonnets* having fallen into the hands of Thomas Thorpe, a stationer who played the part of a literary agent by the picking up of this kind of floating "copy," he commissioned George Eld to print them for him, and, having apparently no shop of his own, he employed two other stationers, William Aspley and John Wright, to sell the book for him. One of Thorpe's earliest successes in this line was the publication in 1600 of Marlowe's translation of the first book of Lucan, and his subsequent achievements include Healey's translation of Saint Augustine's *Citie of God* (1610), three plays by Chapman and works by Ben Jonson and others.

In 1599, the unauthorised anthology entitled *The Passionate Pilgrime, by W. Shakespeare* was issued by William Jaggard, whose name is also well known as one of the publishers of the first collected edition of the plays, issued with the co-operation

---

[1] The genuineness of the imprints of some of these has recently been questioned. See *The Library*, 1908-9, and A. W. Pollard, *Shakespeare Folios and Quartos*, 1909.

of Shakespeare's friends in 1623. This monumental volume, which, though a large undertaking, is by no means a remarkable piece of printing, came from the press of Jaggard's son Isaac, and was printed at the charge of four stationers, William Jaggard, Edward Blount, John Smethwick and William Aspley. The chief share in the enterprise appears to have been taken by Edward Blount, who was something more than a mere trader in books and must have possessed a nice and discriminating literary judgment, fostered, doubtless, during his ten years' apprenticeship with William Ponsonby. To the 1598 edition of Marlowe's *Hero and Leander*, he wrote a preface, defending the dead poet against his detractors. To him we are indebted for Florio's Italian dictionary *A Worlde of Wordes*, which appeared in 1598, and for the same writer's translation of Montaigne's *Essays*, first published in 1603. From 1609, he was, for a time, in partnership with William Barret, and together they issued, in 1612, Shelton's translation of the first part of *Don Quixote*, notable as being the first translation of Cervantes's great novel into any language. In 1622, he brought out James Mabbe's rendering of Aleman's *The Rogue, or the life of Guzman de Alfarache;* and to Earle's *Microcosmographie*, which he published anonymously in 1628, he wrote a preface.

Booksellers seem to have got the upper hand of printers as well as of authors; and Christopher Barker, in his report of 1582, complains that booksellers were able to drive such good bargains that printers were mostly but small gainers and ofttimes losers. George Wither cannot be cited as an impartial witness, since his embittered controversy with the stationers, about the privilege which he obtained in 1623 ordering his *Hymns and Songs of the Church* to be appended to every copy of the *Psalms in metre*, no doubt surcharged his ink with gall. He himself says that he goes not about to lay a general imputation upon all stationers, but there is no reason to question the general truth of the statement which he makes in his *Schollers Purgatory*, when he says that

the Bookeseller hath not onely made the Printer, the Binder, and the Claspmaker a slave to him: but hath brought Authors, yea the whole Commonwealth, and all the liberall Sciences into bondage.

And in his description of "A meere Stationer" in tne same work, after castigating the printer and the bookbinder, he says of the publishing bookseller that

He makes no scruple to put out the right Authors Name, and insert another in the second edition of a Booke; And when the impression of some pamphlet lyes upon his hands, to imprint new Titles for yt, (and so take mens moneyes twice or thrice, for the same matter under diverse names) is no injury in his opinion. If he get any written Coppy into his powre, likely to be vendible; whether the Author be willing or no, he will publish it: And it shallbe contrived and named alsoe, according to his owne pleasure: which is the reason, so many good Bookes come forth imperfect, and with foolish titles—

with much more in the same vein.

But the publisher of that day was not necessarily a mere profit seeker, and many of the larger works published in the period between the incorporation of the company and the establishment of the Commonwealth must have involved substantial risk, and are evidence of public spirit and some taste for letters in those who undertook their production.

Among the earlier men, Richard Grafton holds a distinguished place. In conjunction with Edward Whitchurch, he was concerned in the publication of the English Bibles of 1537 and 1539, printed at Antwerp and Paris respectively, and afterwards began printing on his own account, his press being largely occupied with the production of service books, for the printing of which he and Whitchurch obtained an exclusive patent in 1544. In 1547, he was appointed printer to king Edward VI, and several of the issues of the *Book of Common Prayer* bear his imprint. On the death of the king, miscalculating the drift of political events, he printed the proclamation of lady Jane Grey and was deprived of his office by queen Mary. Besides issuing John Hardyng's *Chronicle* in 1543, and editions of Edward Hall's *Union of Lancaster and York* in 1548 and 1550, Grafton himself compiled an *Abridgement of the Chronicles of England*, which was published by his son-in-law Richard Tottel in 1562, and *A Chronicle at Large*, issued also by Tottel in 1569. Tottel's serious business in life was the printing of law books, for which he received a patent in 1552; but he is, perhaps, better known as the publisher of *Tottel's Miscellany.*

first issued in 1557, and of which there were at least seven other editions before the end of the century. He was also a partner with John Cawood, and John Walley in the publication of the folio edition of Sir Thomas More's *Works*, which bears the same date as the first edition of the *Miscellany*.

William Copland, probably a son of "old Robert Copland" printer and translator, was the printer of Gawin Douglas's translation of the *Aeneid*, which appeared in 1553, and of an undated edition of the same writer's *Palice of Honour*. Among other books which came from his press are editions of Caxton's *Recuyell of the Histories of Troy*, *The Four Sons of Aymon*, Malory's *King Arthur*, edited by the printer, and *A boke of the properties of Herbes*, the compilation of which is also attributed to him.

Among all the stationers and printers of this period the most prominent name is that of John Day, whose career, beginning in 1546, extended into four reigns. His important patent for printing the *Psalms in metre* and the *ABC and Catechism* has already been referred to; but, in addition to this advantage, he was fortunate in securing the support of those in authority and especially of archbishop Parker, in whom he found a generous patron. With Parker's encouragement, he did much to set a high standard of printing, and he had several new founts of type cut. About 1567, he published the first book (Aelfric's *Paschal Homily*) printed in Anglo-Saxon characters; and this Saxon type was also used in the archbishop's edition of Asser's *Aelfredi regis res gestae* of 1574, which is one of the finest specimens of Day's typographical art. The purely literary interest of Day's press is by no means commensurate with the important place which it holds in the history of English printing. Most of the books which bear his imprint are theological and ecclesiastical works of a strictly orthodox character, but among them there stands out the first English edition of Foxe's *Actes and Monuments* (1563). He also issued many of the works of Thomas Becon and, in 1570, the first authorised edition of *Gorboduc* and Ascham's *Scholemaster*. William Seres, who printed with Day in the years 1546 to 1550, produced some noteworthy translations, including Thomas Hoby's English version of Castiglione's *Il Cortegiano*, and Arthur Golding's *Caesar* and *Ovid*. In 1569, he published *An orthographie* by John Hart, Chester herald, which contains examples of phonetic spelling.

From a literary point of view, one of the most notable of the publishers was William Ponsonby, from whose house there issued between 1577 and 1603, the year of his death, a number of important books, among them being Sir Philip Sidney's *Arcadia* in 1590, and his works (*Arcadia*, etc.), 1598, Bedingfield's translation of Machiavelli's *Florentine Historie*, 1595, and Greene's *Mamillia* (1582–93). But it is as the publisher of Spenser's works that he is best known to fame. Beginning with *The Faerie Queene* (books 1–3) in 1590, he issued all Spenser's works, with the exception of the *Shepheards Calender*, which was published by Hugh Singleton in 1579. Simon Waterson, who, on Ponsonby's death, acquired some of his copyrights, published many of Samuel Daniel's works, and for some years acted as London bookseller for the university printers of Oxford and Cambridge. The most influential man in the trade, in the latter part of the sixteenth century, was Christopher Barker, the queen's printer, who has already been mentioned. His presses were largely occupied with the printing of Bibles and official work, and, on his death in 1599, he was succeeded in the office of royal printer by his son Robert, whose name is associated with the issue of the royal version (the *Authorised Version*) of the Bible in 1611. Among the other five hundred or more stationers who printed or published books during this period may be mentioned Thomas Marshe, who, between 1554 and 1587, issued many other books besides the school books for which he held a patent of monopoly; Henry Fetherstone, the publisher of *Purchas his Pilgrimes;* Ralph Newbery and George Bishop, two of the partners in the issue of Holinshed's *Chronicles* and Hakluyt's *Voyages;* and Nicholas Bourne, a prolific publisher of undistinguished books, who had an interest in the *Swedish Intelligencer* and other budgets of foreign news.

In London, the localities most favoured by the booksellers of the Elizabethan period were St. Paul's churchyard, Fleet street and, towards the end of the century, Paternoster row; but St. Paul's was quite clearly the focus of the trade. The business premises around the cathedral church were of two classes, the houses which bordered the churchyard, and the less substantial booths (or lock-up snops) and stalls which clustered round the walls and at the doors of the building itself. Those stationers who dwelt at any distance from St. Paul's evidently felt the need of getting into closer touch with this business centre, for some of them are found also occupying stalls at the doors. One of these was Henry Bynneman, a printer and stationer who lived at the Mermaid in Knight Rider street and had also a shop at the northwest door of Paul's. His publications include some of the Latin works of Gabriel Harvey, and he printed for Richard Smith the first acknowledged edition (1575) of Gascoigne's *Posies*, as well as the previous issue which appeared about 1573 under the title of *A Hundreth sundrie Flowres;* the 1577 edition of Holinshed's *Chronicles*, and Stanyhurst's translation of the first four books of the *Aeneid*, also came from his press, the latter in 1583, the year of his death. When John Day found that his printing house in Aldersgate was not well situated for the sale of his books, he, too, in 1572, secured a site in the churchyard as offering a better opportunity for the disposal of his large stock, and the description of the little structure which he put up gives us a good idea of the appearance of one of these churchyard shops.

He got framed a neat handsome shop. It was but little and low, and flat-roofed, and leaded like a terrace, railed and posted, fit for men to stand upon in any triumph or show.

And it cost him, we are told, forty or fifty pounds.

London Bridge did not attain its fame as a resort of booksellers until the second half of the seventeenth century; but, as early as 1557, William Pickering, a bookseller, whose publications consisted chiefly of ballads, and other trivial things, had a shop there. In the next year, he was "dwellyng at Saynt Magnus Corner," which, if not actually on the bridge, was at least hard by, and at this address the business continued for upwards of a century. As might be expected from its situation at the port of London, many nautical books were published here, and the seaman making his preparations for a voyage would step into the well known shop and purchase *The Art of Navigation*, or, perhaps, if he were thither bound, a *Card or rutter of the sea lyenge betwene Holland and Ffryseland*, and, were he so minded, he might fortify himself with *The seamans sacred safetye or a praier booke for seamen*.

English printing during the period under review cannot be said to be conspicuous for typographical excellence. The general conditions of the trade probably militated against any high standard being attained or even aimed at. Most of the prominent printers were those who possessed valuable monopolies, and, thus safeguarded from competition, there was little inducement to them to incur the expense of having new founts cut, or to bestow the pains required to ensure good workmanship. The less fortunate printers possessed neither the means, nor, perhaps, save in a few cases, the capacity, for turning out good work, and many of their productions are slovenly and illiterate to a degree surpassed only in the succeeding era, when the endeavour to make men bring forth good works completely obscured their ability to produce good work.

In the first part of this period, when some of the earlier traditions were retained, the artistic feeling shown in the arrangement of the page and the setting of the type gives to many of the books, in spite of the frequently worn condition of the type and cuts, a repose and dignity, which disappeared under the incursion of roman type, and which even recent efforts have not succeeded in recovering. Even down to 1580, or, perhaps, later, there is often a certain delicacy of perception and tasteful handling which gives the book an organic character and conveys a feeling of craftsmanship—qualities which are quite lacking in the later books in which effect is too often sought by the use of adventitious ornament or the display of an incongruous variety of types. It is a little difficult to draw a line between the good and the indifferent printers, but among the better craftsmen may be named Thomas Berthelet, printer to king Henry VIII, also noted as a bookbinder; Richard Grafton; Reyner Wolfe; John Day, whose pre-eminence has already been referred to; Richard Jugge, the printer of the *Bishops' Bible;* Henry Denham, who produced some tasteful work between 1564 and 1589; Thomas Vautrollier, the Huguenot printer, and his successor Richard Field; Thomas East, the printer of music books; William Stansby, who produced a very large number of books in workmanlike fashion; John Norton, who worked the Eton press; the two Barkers; and Felix Kingston.

The illustrations to be found in English books of the period are greatly inferior to contemporary continental work. The woodcuts, when not the worn-out blocks which had seen service since the days of Pynson and Wynkyn de Worde, were generally unskilful copies of foreign work, or, occasionally, still less successful original designs. Woodcut illustrations of a pictorial character are used in the *Bishops' Bible* (1568), Foxe's *Book of Martyrs*, Holinshed's *Chronicles* and a few other books. The edition of Barclay's *Ship of Fools*, printed by Cawood in 1570, was also illustrated by a series of woodcuts, but these were only a resuscitation of those which had appeared in Pynson's edition of 1509. Woodcuts are also to be found in many books on practical subjects, but the use of them for pictorial illustration of imaginative works was not common. To John Day is due some improvement in the art, and portraits of himself and of William Cunningham, the author of *The Cosmographical Glasse* (1559), are among his more notable examples.

The use of copperplate engravings, first introduced into this country in 1540 but not much employed until some years later, doubtless contributed to the disuse of woodcuts, and most of the more ambitious books relied on the new art for their adornment. The first edition of the *Bishops' Bible*, printed by Jugge in 1568, contains, besides woodcut illustrations, engraved portraits of the earl of Leicester and lord Burghley printed in the text, and an elaborate emblematic title-page which includes a portrait of the queen. Sir John Harington's *Orlando Furioso*, issued by Field in 1591, is illustrated with forty-six full-page engravings; Sir William Segar's *Honor Military and Civill* (1602) has eight engraved portraits; and Sandys's *Relation of a Journey*, which appeared in 1615, contains many engravings illustrative of scenes and costumes. This art was also used for topographical illustrations in such works as Camden's *Britannia* (1607), Drayton's *Poly-Olbion* (1613) and captain John Smith's *General History of Virginia* (1624).

For the decoration of their books, as apart from illustration, the earlier printers relied chiefly on ornamental initial letters. A border round the title-page was soon discovered to be an effective adornment to a book, and in a few instances every page of the book is thus treated. The designs of these borders took various forms, such as scroll work, arabesques, or architectural framework, and some contain the device of the printer. Occasionally, borders were emblematic of the subject of the book, and these were afterwards used quite indifferently for other works without relation to the subject. One of the best of these specially designed borders is that which is seen in the 1593 and 1598 editions of Sidney's *Arcadia*. Another form of border, both graceful and effective, which has been aptly called a lace border, is built up of small ornaments of homogeneous character. When copper engraving had come into use, a frequent form of embellishment was an engraved title-page of emblematic or symbolic design, such as those in Drayton's *Poly-Olbion* of 1613, and Bacon's *Instauratio magna* of 1620.

In the early days of printing in England, when the native press produced but a very small proportion of the books in demand, the foreign printer and stationer were so freely tolerated, if not actively encouraged, that a large part of the trade fell into the hands of strangers. But, by the beginning of the sixteenth century, the pinch of competition began to be severely felt by the native craftsmen, and, in the succeeding years, repeated efforts were made to eliminate the alien element and reduce the importation of foreign-printed books. By an act passed in 1523, aliens were forbidden to take any but English-born apprentices, and, in 1529, another act prohibited any foreigner, not already established, from setting up a house or shop for the exercise of any handicraft within the realm. These enactments aimed at squeezing out the foreigner from the home trade; and a further act in 1534, directed against competition from abroad, prohibited the importation for sale of books ready bound, and also provided that no undenizened alien should sell foreign-printed books within the kingdom except by wholesale. This act protected the native bookbinder and the retail bookseller, and, at the same time, helped to limit facilities for the dissemination of seditious literature.

These efforts ultimately rescued the home trade from the domination of the foreigner; but, since the demand for books

could not be limited to those produced in the country—
scholars, especially, being dependent on continental presses for
certain classes of literature—there was necessarily a large and
continuous business in the legitimate importation of foreign
books of various kinds. In the first half of the sixteenth
century, service books represented no inconsiderable part of
the books so brought into the country, and François Regnault,
who had shops both in Paris and London, was one of the leading men in this particular traffic. Other prominent foreigners
engaged in importation were the Birckmans, who had places
of business in Cologne, Antwerp and other towns, and whose
connection with London extended over the greater part of the
sixteenth century. The books of Plantin, the great printer-
publisher of Antwerp, must also have found their way here
in large numbers, for, in 1567, he was negotiating for the establishment of a branch in London, but the project fell through.

Of the many English books printed abroad from the middle
of the sixteenth century, by far the larger number were concerned with the acrimonious poltico-religious controversies
of the day, and were produced on foreign soil either because
their authors had sought safety there, or, possibly, because
there was less chance of the work being interrupted. Among
the chief places of their origin were Antwerp, Rouen, Louvain,
Leyden and Dort; Amsterdam, whence proceeded the "Family
of Love" books; Middleburg, chiefly from the press of Richard
Schilders; Geneva and Zurich, the protestant strongholds;
and Douay and St. Omer, the Roman Catholic fortresses.
Much interest centres round the early editions of the English
Bible, several of which were printed on the continent, the
first of them (Coverdale's version) at Zurich in 1535, and some
editions of the Genevan version which bear an English imprint
were actually printed at Amsterdam or Dort. The first (Latin)
issue of Foxe's *Book of Martyrs* was printed at Basel in 1559;
and the edition of William Turner's *New herball* printed by
Arnold Birckman at Cologne, in 1568, may be cited as an
example of a different class of English book for which we are
indebted to the foreign press.

The great international book exchange at this period was
the half-yearly fair, held at Frankfort. To this mart came representatives of the book-trade from all parts of the continent

—Froben of Basel, Estienne of Geneva, Plantin of Antwerp and other leading printers from the great centres, bringing supplies of their recent books and, perhaps, specimen sheets of important fresh undertakings; there, also, would be gathered booksellers from far and near, some having in view the selling of copies of their own ventures, but most of them eager to lay in a stock of the newest literature most likely to suit the tastes of their patrons. At this period, too, when catalogues were rare, and no journals existed as a medium of regular literary information, a visit to the fair afforded opportunity to writers, scholars, and keen book lovers to see and become acquainted with the new literature.

The important place which this fair held, even in the English book trade, is indicated by the agreement concluded between the Stationers' company and the university of Cambridge in 1591, that the Cambridge printers should, "for the space of one month after the return of every Frankfort mart," have the choice of printing any foreign books coming thence. Not many of the books printed in England were likely to find a sale on the continent, but several English booksellers either attended the mart or were represented there. Early in the seventeenth century, Henry Fetherstone, the stationer at the Rose in St. Paul's Churchyard, harvested still further afield, and his results are to be seen in the catalogue of books bought in Italy which he issued in 1628. Perhaps the most notable of the regular English visitors to the fair at this time was John Bill, the leading London stationer, who numbered among his distinguished clients king James and Sir Thomas Bodley. His business there and at other continental centres must have been fairly extensive, for, in 1617, he thought it worth while to begin the issue of a London edition of the half-yearly Frankfort *Mess-Katalog*, which he continued for about eleven years, and to which, from 1622 to 1626, was added a supplement of *Books printed in English*. This supplement was not the first attempt at a catalogue of English books. The credit for that enterprise is due to Andrew Maunsell, who, induced, one must believe, by a love of books, deserted the calling of a draper to become a bookseller and the earliest English bibliographer. He had already published a number of books before he brought out, in 1595, the first part of his *Catalogue of Eng-*

lish Printed Bookes, which comprised works on divinity. In the same year, he printed the second part of the catalogue, which deals with the writers on arithmetic, music, navigation, war, and physic, and contains some 320 titles. The completion of the last part was prevented by failing health, followed by his death in 1596. This third and last part was, said Maunsell, to be "of Humanity, wherin I shall have occasion to shew, what wee have in our owne tongue, of Gramer, Logick, Rethoricke, Lawe, Historie, Poetrie, Policie, &c. which will for the most part concerne matters of Delight and Pleasure." Maunsell's attempt to record the output of the English press found no successor till the appearance of John Bill's supplement in 1622; but from this time onwards several other lists were published which fairly well bridge the period to the beginning of the quarterly *Term Catalogues* in 1668.

The books which a stationer kept in stock for sale at his shop might be either in sheets, or stitched, or ready bound. A large number of books were sold in sheets, that is, merely folded, and the binding was a separate transaction carried out according to the taste and purse of the purchaser, either by the stationer who sold the book, or by any binder whom the purchaser might choose to employ. Pamphlets and books of an ephemeral nature were generally stitched, that is, stabbed through with a bodkin or awl and stitched with thread or a thin strip of leather, maybe with a paper wrapper to keep the outside leaves clean, or, sometimes, without any covering. By a regulation of the year 1586, it was ordered that no books so stitched should exceed forty sheets if in folio, twelve sheets in octavo, or six sheets in decimo sexto; any books consisting of more sheets than these were to be sewn in the regular manner upon a sewing press. The books kept in stock ready bound would be those for which there was a steady demand. These would be bound either in leather, sheep and calf being commonly used; or in vellum, finished off with two silk ties to keep the book closed; or they might be bound in paper boards.

In the first half of the sixteenth century, these commercial leather bindings were frequently ornamented with panel stamps, often of beautiful design, in which the royal arms and the Tudor rose frequently figured. The later panel stamps are much inferior in design and interest; and, in course of time, this form of decoration was to a large extent superseded by the roll, a tool which applied the ornament in the form of a ribbon on which the design was repeated. This method lent itself very readily to the decoration of either a folio or smaller cover; but the mechanical nature of the use of this tool soon extended to the ornamentation itself, which rapidly deteriorated both in the size of the roll and in the character of the design, and this was followed by the practical extinction of stamped work.

When books were bound in more luxurious fashion, they were usually executed for wealthy collectors or royal personages, and often represent the personal taste and predilection of the owner. The use of gold tooling on bindings, which originated in Italy towards the end of the fifteenth century, was introduced into England in the reign of Henry VIII, probably by Thomas Berthelet, printer and stationer to the king. In the bills for books bound for, and supplied to, the king by Berthelet, in the years 1541–3, are several instances of this new style of binding; some are described as "gorgiously gilted on the leather," or "bounde after the Venecian fascion," while others are "covered with purple velvet and written abowte with golde." The English gilt leather bindings of this time, and throughout the sixteenth century, are almost entirely imitations of foreign styles, in which French influence predominates. Not only were a large number of the binders actually foreigners, but even the English craftsmen did little more than copy foreign designs.

One of the favourite styles of design in the latter half of the century was an imitation of the Lyonese manner, in which the sides were decorated with heavy gold centre and corner pieces, enclosed within a plain or gilt border, the ground being either left plain or, more generally, powdered with small ornaments. This style continued in vogue into the reign of James I. Archbishop Parker, whose catholic tastes included bookbinding, employed a bookbinder in his own house, and the special copy of his *De antiquitate Britannicae ecclesiae*, which he presented to lord treasurer Burghley, and which was "bound by my Man," was done in this manner. On the other hand, the copy of this book which he presented to the queen was in an elaborate and beautiful embroidered binding, possibly in deference to the taste of Elizabeth, whose preference appears to have been for embroidered bindings and for books bound in velvet, especially red, with clasps of gold or silver. This taste was shared by her successor, for whom, in 1609, Robert Barker, at that time printer and binder to the king, bound books in "crymson, purple, and greene velvet," and "in taffity, with gold lace." James I, who was a lover of sumptuous bindings, also had many books finely bound in leather, and these usually bore the royal arms stamped in gold on the side, the ground being powdered with fleurs-de-lis or other small emblems. Another style which obtained in the sixteenth century was a plain binding of leather or velvet, decorated with corners and clasps of pierced silver work. The elaborate embroidered bindings in which coloured silks, gold and silver thread, and occasionally pearls were employed was an essentially English art.

Among the notable collectors who dressed their books in distinctive coverings were Thomas Wotton, who adopted the style and adapted the motto of Grolier, and Robert Dudley, earl of Leicester, whose most characteristic style was a plain binding having his well known badge, the bear and ragged staff, with his initials stamped on the side. But there were book lovers as well as book collectors, and one's heart warms much more towards the scholarly library of archbishop Parker, or the plain brown folios of Ben Jonson with their familiar inscription *Sum Ben: Jonsonij*, and his motto *Tanquam explorator*.

In the early seventeenth century, there worked at Eton a good binder, who commonly had "his hands full of worke, and his head full of drinck"; at Oxford, Pinart and Milles bound for Sir Thomas Bodley; and, from Cambridge, where good work was being carried on, Nicholas Ferrar obtained the craftswoman "that bound rarely," and the result of her instruction is seen in the bindings of that distinctive character which is associated with the settlement at Little Gidding and the name of Mary Collet.

Notwithstanding the keen competition in the book-trade and the great number of works which were issued from the press, books were by no means cheap. They were, it is true, no longer a luxury for the rich alone, and it is quite probable that the prices at which they were sold brought them fairly within the reach of most of those who were able to use them. The prices of those days multiplied by eight will, approximately, represent present day values, and it should be noted that the cost mentioned is often that of the book in sheets, the binding being an additional expense.

The prices of books published under official auspices were sometimes limited by a special regulation; thus, the first edition of the *Book of Common Prayer* (1549), as appears by the king's order printed at the end of the book, is not to be sold above the price of 2s. 2d. apiece, and bound in paste or boards not above 3s. 8d. Such a regulation was rendered the more necessary by the fact that the right to print such books was usually granted as a monopoly to some individual printer, and they were not therefore subject to the healthy influence of competition. A curious tract entitled *Scintilla, or a Light broken into darke Warehouses*, published anonymously in 1641, throws some interesting light on the doings of the monopolists and the way in which they had raised the prices of the books which they had gotten into their grasp. Church Bibles, which formerly cost thirty shillings, are now, it is said, raised to two pounds, and large folio Bibles in roman print, which used to sell at 12s. 6d., now cost twenty shillings. The prices of other editions, before being raised, were: the Cambridge quarto Bible, with Psalms, 7s., the London quarto Bible, with notes and concordance, also 7s., and Bibles in octavo, 3s. 4d. Testaments in octavo cost 10d., and in duodecimo, 7d.; the *Book of Common Prayer*, 3s. in folio, and 1s. 6d. in quarto. The *Grammar of Oxford and Cambridge* cost 5d., and Camden's *Greek Grammar*, 8d.; there was also an edition of the latter printed in France which was sold at 4½d.

In 1598, the Stationers' company, with a view to prevent the excessive prices of books, made a general order that no new copies without pictures should be sold at more than a penny for two sheets if in pica, roman and italic, or in english with roman and italic; and at a penny for one sheet and a half if in brevier or long primer letter. A quarto volume of 360 pages in small type might thus cost, in sheets, two shillings and sixpence, equal to about one pound at the present day. At this rate, the first folio Shakespeare, which contains nearly one thousand pages, should have cost about fourteen shillings; an oft quoted statement that the actual selling price was one pound appears to be based on the insufficient evidence of a manuscript note in a copy not now traceable.   For a copy of Shakespeare's *Sonnets*, Alleyn the actor paid fivepence in June, 1609.   Quarto plays and similar productions were mostly issued at sixpence, and ephemeral pamphlets were sold at two-pence, threepence, or fourpence.

In 1576, the hall Bible at King's college, Cambridge, to be read during meals, cost sixteen shillings; and, in 1585, New college, Oxford, paid ten shillings for a copy of Estienne's edition of Diodorus Siculus.   Corpus Christi college, Oxford, a frequent purchaser of books, in 1604 gave three shillings and sixpence for the *De idololatria ecclesiae Romanae* of John Rainolds.   The college also bought Bacon's *History of Henry VII* for seven shillings on its appearance in 1622, and paid £3. 8s. 6d. for *Purchas his Pilgrimes*, which appeared in four volumes in 1625.   In 1621, Dodoens's *Niewe herball* and Selden's *Titles of Honour* cost six shillings and five shillings respectively.   It is probable that, in all these instances, the price included the binding of the book.

The methods employed by the bookseller and publisher for advertising his books are mainly a matter of surmise.   Book buyers who lived in the metropolis would, no doubt, frequent the stationers' shops and there see and dip into new books; and the title-page of the latest pamphlet, stuck up on the door post of the shop or any other prominent place, would catch the eye of those eager to see and read some new thing.   Ballads may have been hawked in the streets and at busy corners, but books were certainly not allowed to be thus vended, for the Stationers' registers record the seizure of certain books which were "goynge hawkynge aboute the stretes which ys contrary to the orders of the Cytie of London."   Catalogues were not yet in fashion; occasionally, other works by the same author are mentioned in the preface of a book, but it is not till well into the seventeenth century that one now and again meets with a paragraph telling the "courteous reader" to expect shortly from the press some new work by the same writer; and it was still nearer the end of the century before the publisher hit upon the expedient of impressing a spare leaf at the end of a book into the service of announcing other books issued by him.

The provinces were supplied by stationers in the larger towns and by the great periodical fairs, while popular literature was carried into the remoter country districts in the pack of the travelling merchant or chapman. Stationers carried on business in most of the important towns, and sometimes published books, printed, of course, in London; or joined with a London stationer in a similar venture, the portion of the impression taken by the provincial bookseller generally bearing his name in the imprint. At York, there existed a company of stationers and bookbinders, who had a new code of laws confirmed by the corporation in 1554. In the east, Norwich, and, in the west, Chester and Exeter, were prominent centres of the trade; at Shrewsbury, Roger Ward, the pirate printer of London, kept a shop, and thither he despatched a large number of his illegally printed *ABC and Catechism* in 1582; and John Norton had a shop in charge of his servant Edmond Wats, as far away as Edinburgh. Among the principal provincial fairs were those of Oxford, Bristol, Salisbury, Nottingham, Ely, Coventry, and, chief of all, the renowned Sturbridge fair near Cambridge. These marts played an important part in the internal trade of the country, and were largely depended upon for the laying in of supplies for the year. Stationers, both from London and the provinces, attended them, and a large trade in books was one of the features of the multifarious business transacted there; indeed, so far as the provinces were concerned, new books were practically published at these fairs, and the issue of books was frequently timed with a view to the dates on which they were held.

In the first half of the sixteenth century, printing had been carried on in the provinces at Oxford, St. Albans, York, Cambridge, Tavistock, Abingdon, Ipswich, Worcester and Canterbury. The productions of these presses were mainly works of a theological, liturgical, or grammatical character, and contributed little or nothing to English literature, if we except a few books such as the translation of Boethius's *Boke of Comfort*, printed at Tavistock monastery in 1525, Lydgate's *Lyfe and Passion of Seint Albon*, attributed to John Herford's press at St. Albans in 1534, and the undated edition of the same author's *Churle and the Bird* which John Mychell may have printed at his Canterbury press.

By 1557, the year in which the Stationers' company was incorporated, all these presses had already ceased; and, until the revival of the Cambridge press in 1583, the only printing carried on in England, outside London, was that by Anthony de Solempne, who, from 1568 to 1580, was printing Dutch books in Norwich for the use of the refugees there, for which he seems to have obtained the queen's authority. Although the monopoly conferred upon the company did not contribute to the extinction of the provincial presses, the opposition to the re-establishment of the Cambridge press clearly indicates that any attempted revival would have been promptly strangled.

The right to elect "three stationers or printers or sellers of books" had been granted to the university of Cambridge by Henry VIII in 1534, but, though printers were regularly appointed under this grant, no actual printing was done in Cambridge from the cessation of John Siberch's press in 1522 until the appointment in 1582 of Thomas Thomas as university printer. The Stationers' company, having got wind of this intention to establish a university press, scented dangerous competition and infringement of their privileges, and the "presse and furniture" intended for Mr. Thomas's establishment, having been discovered by their searchers, were seized and detained. In this action, the company was supported by the bishop of London (John Aylmer), who, though professing great concern for the interests of printing, was, no doubt, alarmed at the power which this new press might place in the hands of the puritan party in Cambridge. The university appealed to their chancellor, lord Burghley, for the restoration of the press, and succeeded in vindicating their claim to the privileges of the patent; but a jealous struggle with the London company continued for many years, with varying successes and reprisals on both sides, the university, on the whole, steadily gaining ground and, in the end, completely establishing its right to print.

Besides his work as university printer, Thomas, who was a fellow of King's college, is known as the author of a Latin dictionary, of which eight editions had been issued from the

Cambridge press by 1610. Thomas was succeeded on his death in 1588 by John Legate, who, in 1609, removed to London, and was followed in the office by Cantrell Legge. Among the productions of this press, books in divinity and scholastic subjects naturally preponderate, and there is very little of literary interest. Certain things such as *The Returne from Parnassus* (1606), Tomkis's *Albumazar* (1615), and Ruggle's *Ignoramus* (entered 18 April, 1615), which, being university plays, one might very well expect to find with a Cambridge imprint, were, nevertheless, printed and published in London.

The revival of printing at Oxford, two years later, met with no such stormy reception, though the university possessed no printing patent similar to that of Cambridge. Its immunity from interference may have owed something to the protection of the earl of Leicester, chancellor of the university, under whose auspices the press was established. Anyhow, Joseph Barnes, the printer appointed by the university, at once carried the attack into the London camp, and, in the very year (1585) in which he began work, reprinted one of their "most vendible copies." John Wight, the bookseller to whom the book (Parsons's *Christian Exercise*) had been entered in the Stationers' register, on hearing of the piracy, sent his son to Oxford, who there bought the impression and paid Barnes ready money for it, Barnes making faithful promise that he would never reprint the book. But, notwithstanding this promise and Wight's "curteous dealinge" with him, Barnes, being thus furnished with money, forthwith prints two other impressions of the work; and, when the London printers in retaliation reprint Thomas Bilson's *Christian subjection and unchristian rebellion*, which Barnes had just published, they are stopped by the privy council, their printing tools seized, and one of their number thrown into prison. The Oxford press was officially recognised in 1586, by a Star chamber ordinance allowing one press and one apprentice.

In 1586, Barnes brought out Chrysostom's *Homilies* printed in Greek type, and, in 1595, his first Welsh book *Perl mewn adfyd*, a translation from Otto Wermueller. Before his resignation in 1617, Barnes had issued from his press a rendering into English verse of six poems of Theocritus (1588), Richard of Bury's *Philobiblon* (1599),—"the first English edition of the

first book on the love of books,''—two editions of John Davies's
Microcosmos, captain John Smith's *Map and description of
Virginia* (1612), and works by Nicholas Breton, Thomas
Churchyard and Richard Hooker.   Barnes was succeeded
by John Lichfield, who printed till 1635; the issue of the first
four editions (1621–32) of Burton's *Anatomy of Melancholy*
lends distinction to his press.   Archbishop Laud, when he
became chancellor of the university in 1630, bestowed much
care in forwarding the interests of printing at Oxford, and
one of his earliest actions in this direction was to procure from
king Charles I a charter which conferred upon the university
privileges equal to those possessed by Cambridge.

In 1610–13, an edition of Chrysostom's works in Greek,
in eight volumes folio, was printed at Sir Henry Savile's
press at Eton college by John Norton, the king's printer in
Latin, Greek, and Hebrew.   Five other books are known to
have issued from the Eton press before its cessation in 1615.
The celebrated Greek type, the "silver letter" as it was called,
was afterwards presented by Sir Henry Savile to the university
of Oxford.

The rigorous enforcement of the policy of regulating printing in the interests of church and state naturally drove the
opponents of the establishment, the papists on the one side
and the puritans on the other, to resort to secret printing, and
several illicit presses were at work during the latter part of
the sixteenth century.   At the secret press of Thomas Cartwright, the puritan opponent of Whitgift, was printed in 1572
An Admonition to the Parliament; and several other allied tracts
followed before the press was run down and seized at Hemp-
stead.   In 1580–1, a Jesuit press, with which Robert Parsons
and Edmund Campion were connected, was at work first at
Greenstreet House, East Ham, and afterwards, at Stonor
Park.   But the chief of these secret and fugitive sources of
contraband literature was that known as the Marprelate press,
of which an account has been given in a previous volume of
the present work.[1]

The art of printing was introduced into Scotland in 1508,
and the work of the Scottish press at once assumed that strongly
national character and detached attitude towards the outside

[1] See Vol. III, Chap. xvii.

world which continued to be its distinguishing feature until the eighteenth century brought with it the Union and other elements of a broadening influence. Its chief productions were official documents, such as statutes and proclamations, for the service of the state, native Latin works for the scholar, school books for youth, vernacular literature for the people, and theology for all.

As in the case of the first English press, Chepman and Myllar of Edinburgh made their first essay with a series of small tracts of a popular nature, and of these there have survived nine pieces, each extant in a single copy. There has also been recorded a fragment of an edition of Blind Harry's *Wallace*, printed in the same type. The *Aberdeen Breviary*, the real work for which the press had been imported, was printed by Chepman alone in 1509-10, and with it the work of this press came to an end.

John Davidson, who was printing in Edinburgh in 1541, issued shortly before that date a folio edition of Bellenden's translation of Boece's *History of Scotland*, which is one of the monuments of early Scottish printing. From a fragment of a single leaf, discovered by the late David Laing, it seems probable that an edition of Gawin Douglas's *Palice of Honour* was also printed by Davidson. John Scot, who printed at St. Andrews and afterwards at Edinburgh between 1552 and 1571, issued works by Sir David Lyndsay, Quintin Kennedy and Ninian Winzet. The earliest Scottish printer whose extant issues reach any considerable number is Robert Lekpreuik, who began printing in 1561; he is to be especially remembered for the numerous ballads by Robert Sempill and other reformation politicians, which in his broadsides have survived to the present day. The first Bible printed in Scotland, which, after some vicissitudes, made its appearance in 1579, was the work of Bassandyne and Arbuthnet, the latter of whom also published in 1582 the first and faulty edition of Buchanan's *Rerum Scoticarum Historia*.

The earliest known edition of the collected works of Sir David Lyndsay is that printed in Edinburgh in 1568, to which the publisher, Henry Charteris, who probably began his long career with the issue of this book, prefixed an introduction.

Charteris, who, in 1580, acquired John Ross's printing business, is the most notable figure among the Scottish booksellers of the sixteenth century. In addition to works by Barbour, Blind Harry, Henryson and others, he issued, before his death in 1599, at least six editions of the works of Sir David Lyndsay. The position occupied in Edinburgh by Henry Charteris in the sixteenth century was, for the first twenty years of the following century, held by Andro Hart, the bookseller, who took up printing in 1610 with the acquisition of the plant which had been used by Charteris. The first book known to have been issued from his press is a folio Bible (1610), which gained considerable reputation for its correctness; and among the large number of interesting books which he printed are first editions of works by Drummond of Hawthornden, Napier of Merchiston and Sir William Alexander, earl of Stirling, also several reprints of the older writers. John Wreittoun, who printed in Edinburgh from 1624 to 1638, issued in 1627 an edition of *Venus and Adonis*, the only work by Shakespeare known to have been printed in Scotland before the eighteenth century.

The strongly national character of the productions of the Scottish press has already been indicated; but it must not be forgotten that these by no means represent the whole literary output of the country. The close intellectual and commercial intercourse between Scotland and the continent, together with the restricted facilities at home, naturally resulted in many of the works of the more scholarly writers, who wrote almost entirely in Latin and appealed to a European audience, being published abroad, and scholars not unfrequently made the journey overseas for the purpose of seeing their work through the press.

There was in Scotland no trade combination corresponding to the London Stationers' company; indeed, the limited number of persons engaged in the trade rendered such an organisation unnecessary. Measures, however, were adopted from time to time by the state for preventing the printing or importation of undesirable books, and a more or less watchful eye was kept on the trade; but, on the whole, there was considerable liberty, and it was not until the latter half of the seventeenth century that the cramping effects of monopoly were experienced.

When Edinburgh booksellers felt themselves aggrieved by incursions of alien traders, they found means of protecting themselves by appeal to their town council, and Thomas Vautrollier, John Norton, and others were on various occasions proceeded against in this manner.

The inventories of property recorded with the wills in Scottish registers of testaments afford some extremely interesting glimpses of the stock-in-trade of the printer and bookseller of this period, and those of the printers indicate that the impressions of many of the popular works were surprisingly large. The list of the books in the inventory of Robert Gourlaw, bookbinder and bookseller of Edinburgh, who died in 1585, occupies no less than six pages as printed in the *Bannatyne Miscellany*, and, if it may be taken to represent the current demand, points to a wide and cultivated standard of reading. Most noticeable are school books, chiefly Latin, and small books of devotion, such as psalms and books of prayers. The classics are well represented in the *Iliad* and the *Odyssey*, Ovid's *Metamorphoses*, the *Ethics* of Aristotle, Virgil, Terence, Apuleius and Silius Italicus. Erasmus is much in evidence, probably in school editions. Theology, especially of a contemplative character, is the chief element; two copies of Bradford's *Meditations* are followed impartially by three copies of "ane lytill Fortoun buik." The immense popularity of Sir David Lyndsay is easily perceived, and lighter literature is well represented in ballads and other vernacular pieces. *Piers Plowman* and *Sir John Mandeville* appear, but contemporary English literature is practically absent, and there are no plays. There are also two copies of *Gargantua* and a Hebrew grammar.

The beginning of printing in Ireland is represented by the *Book of Common Prayer* which was printed in Dublin in 1551 by Humphrey Powell, who had migrated from London a year or so previously. The other extant productions of this press are two or three broadsides, and a theological tract which he issued in 1566. In 1571, a broadside poem on *Doomsday*, and John Kearney's *ABC and Catechism* (*Aibidil Gaoidheilge, agus Caiticiosma*) were printed in the first fount of Irish characters. John Franckton, who began printing in Dublin apparently in 1600, printed also, in Irish characters, archbishop

Daniel's Irish versions of the *New Testament* (1602) and *Book of Common Prayer* (1608). In 1618, Franckton's press was acquired by the Stationers' company of London, who continued it until about 1640, when it was taken over by William Bladen; but the only productions of any literary interest before the publication of Sir James Ware's *History of Ireland* in 1633, are editions of Sidney's *Arcadia* in 1621 and Sir Thomas Overbury's *Wife* in 1626.

CHAPTER XIX

The Foundation of Libraries

I N previous volumes of the present work, some account has been given of early monastic libraries, of collections of books made by such men as Richard of Bury, of the contents of a typical collegiate library as illustrating the reading of the medieval student and of the effect upon libraries of the dissolution of the monasteries. The work accomplished by Sir Thomas Bodley within the period covered by the present volume provides an occasion for a brief retrospect of the foundation of libraries generally, and for the presentation of certain details regarding monastic, cathedral and collegiate libraries, supplementary to the references which have been already made.

A recent publication[1] enables us to realise the conditions under which such collections were preserved and accumulated, from the days when the papyrus rolls began to multiply on the shelves in the archives of Assur down to those of dean Boys of Canterbury, who, to the day of his death, in 1625, still adhered to the practice of placing the volumes of his library on the shelf with their fore-edge outwards.

Beginning our retrospect, however, with the time when the roll, "book" or "volume," began to take shape as a series of leaves fastened together by the art of the binder, we find the movable press, with shelves and doors, and supported on legs, appearing as the most ancient form of the bookcase. As the press became larger and heavier, the legs were discarded, and in those cathedrals or convent churches in which there was a triple apse, one of these would be used for keeping the service books, while the *armarium* (or chest) would be sometimes

---

[1] *The Care of Books*, by J. W. Clark (2nd ed.), Cambridge, 1902.

represented by a recess in the wall closed by a door. The apse also, not unfrequently, served as the depository for the library of the choir school, and of this, together with the service books, the precentor would sometimes be the custodian; but, in larger cathedrals, the duty would be assigned to a second functionary, known as the *armarius*.

"An examination of the statutes affecting the library in the codes imposed upon the colleges of Oxford and Cambridge shows that their provisions were borrowed directly from the monastic customs."[1] But it is not less certain that the monastic rules themselves were partly derived from practice anterior to western monasticism itself. In Vitruvius (who wrote probably in the time of the emperor Augustus) it is laid down as a canon that "bed-rooms and libraries should face the East, their use requiring the morning light; while in libraries, books will be preserved from rotting."[2] But where the presses were movable, it was the practice to place them at right angles to the windows; and it was not until the accommodation thus afforded became insufficient, that shelves, resting against the wall, began to make their appearance, and, in many cases, ultimately superseded the movable press. In either case, the volumes on the shelves were generally placed with their edges outwards, and with their titles, or certain distinctive marks, inscribed on the same, the covers being compressed together, sometimes with massive clasps, sometimes with strings, and each volume secured in its place by a hanging chain which fastened on a rod passing along the transom of the bookcase. This rod was itself made fast by a vertical metal plate attached to the end of the case, and opened or closed by a lock. Underneath the lock, there would be a framed list of the contents of the shelves.[3]

In monasteries, and especially in those of the Benedictine order, libraries gradually assumed a more important character, and the practice of lending volumes began to come into vogue. A limited number would be distributed among the members of the house for temporary personal use, while the larger and more

[1] J. W. Clark, *The Care of Books* (2nd ed.), p. 126.

[2] *De Architectura*, lib. vi. c. 7; ed. Valentin Rose. Willis and Clark (*Architectural History of the University of Cambridge*, III, pp. 414–6) have given the orientation of the college libraries of both Oxford and Cambridge.

[3] See J. W. Clark's *Medieval and Renaissance Libraries*, pp. 43, 45 and 48.

valuable portion would be kept in safe custody in a separate chamber. Then it became not unusual for one house to lend a volume to another community, and, in this manner, volumes have occasionally been found among collections belonging to various houses, which, by the character of the ornamentation, or by the binding, could be shown to have originally belonged to another house, although it by no means follows that they had been purloined.

The library of the monastery at Durham, a Benedictine house, appears, from a catalogue drawn up in the twelfth century, to have possessed 366 volumes; that at Croyland, if any credit attaches to the fifteenth century writer who wrote under the name of Ingulphus, possessed, at the time of its destruction by fire (1091), 300 volumes and some 400 tracts; that of the neighbouring monastery of St. Peter at Peterborough (where the original library had been destroyed by the Danes in 870) received, through the good offices of abbot Benedict, secretary of Thomas Becket, some eighty different works especially transcribed for its enrichment. At Glastonbury, the collection, at first of but small importance, contained, in 1247, 500 works in 340 volumes.

The fact that abbot Benedict's gift to Peterborough consisted entirely of transcriptions, reminds us that another stage had been reached in the history of monastic libraries; and it is at about the same time that we find one Henry, a monk of the Benedictine abbey at Hyde, near Winchester, becoming known for his industry as a copyist—his transcripts including Terence, Boethius, Suetonius, Claudian and other classical authors. It is, indeed, to such labours, far more than to the growth of new literature, that we must attribute the great increase in the numbers of volumes, in the catalogues of monastic and cathedral libraries alike, which becomes observable throughout the fourteenth and fifteenth centuries; the transcriber's toil, from time to time, receiving an abnormal stimulus from some fire which may have resulted in the entire destruction of a library in a single night. At Canterbury, the catalogues of its two monasteries, that of Christ Church, compiled about the year 1300, and that of St. Augustine's, nearly two centuries later, afford valuable evidence: the former contains nearly 3000 titles (or about 1850 volumes), and, while abounding in patristic and scholastic literature, is characterised as also "respectable in science and rich in history";[1] the latter numbers over 1800 volumes, including a large collection of French, and more especially Romance, writers. Here the numerous duplicates are another noteworthy feature, attributable, doubtless, to the desire of enabling several members of the community to study the same author concurrently,[2] and also attesting the increasing activity of the copyists. The St. Augustine's catalogue, however, is obviously incomplete, and the same may be surmised to be the case with the catalogue at Peterborough, which, in 1380, contained no more than 300 volumes. The society at Worcester, although 280 volumes still remain, is conjectured to have lost more than double that number, and no contemporary catalogue exists. The Benedictines at Dover possessed in 1389 some 449 volumes; and their house at Bury St. Edmunds, at the close of the same century, as many as 2000. At Durham, to which, after the Danish invasions of the ninth century, the devastated monasteries of Wearmouth and Jarrow had become affiliated as "cells," the "reserved" library, by which we are to understand, probably, the collection kept under especial surveillance in the *spendimentum* (or bursary), contained, in 1416, 500 volumes.

A brief account may here be given of a library remarkable alike for its character and its history. The foundation known as Syon monastery,[3] some twelve miles from London, at Isleworth, was one of the Brigittine order, the only one of its kind in England, its rule being "planned to suit the needs of religious men and women serving God together in one church and dwelling in adjoining houses." There were, however, separate libraries for the two sexes, and the catalogue which has come down to us (now in the library of Corpus Christi College, Cambridge) appears, by internal evidence, to be that

---

[1] Edwards, I, 62; see, also, for an analysis of the contents of both libraries, the introduction to M. R. James, *The Ancient Libraries of Canterbury and Dover*, Cambridge, 1903.

[2] See Sir F. Madden, in *Notes and Queries* (2nd ser.), I, pp. 485–6.

[3] Neither Sion college (see *post*, p. 495), now on the Thames Embankment (formerly in London Wall), nor the Sion nunnery now existing at Chudleigh, in Devonshire, is in any way connected with the ancient institution at Isleworth.

of the library for men. The value attached to its maintenance and increase is indicated by the fact that there was a rule enjoining that masses should be said for the souls of all donors, even of a single book, and the librarian himself was charged with the duty of offering up such intercession or seeing that it was made. The extent to which the practice of lending books had, by this time, obtained among monasteries partially accounts for the numerous losses which the collection had sustained prior to the dissolution.[1] The binding appears to have been executed without regard to contents—a Horace, for example, being bound up with a life of Thomas of Canterbury, and a Rabanus Maurus with a Latin translation of Homer. No less than 1421 titles were duly entered in the catalogue, and, of the entire collection, only six volumes have as yet been traced.[2]

But all such collections, whether those of the monastery, the friary, or the cathedral, were exposed to special dangers. At monasteries, the traveller was wont to receive shelter and hospitality, and, if wealthy, would seek to make some return, his gratitude not unfrequently finding expression in the gift of an addition to the library. On the other hand, the opportunity thus afforded to the outer world of gaining access to the interior itself rendered the library liable to losses which not even the vigilance of the guardian of the *spendimentum* could always prevent. At friaries, whose members were in closer touch with the laity, owing to the fact that their houses were generally within the precincts of some city or large town, and sometimes in a main thoroughfare, the risk, probably, was still greater. Thomas Gascoigne describes the house of the Franciscans, as it existed in Oxford in the middle of the fifteenth century, in the following terms:

They had two libraries in the same house; the one called the convent library, the other the library of the schools; whereof the former was open only to graduates; the latter to the scholars they called seculars, who lived among those friars for the sake of learning.[3]

[1] Catalogue of the Library of Syon Monastery, Isleworth. Ed. M. Bateson, Cambridge, 1898, preface, p. x.
[2] *Ibid.*, pp. xvii, xviii.
[3] Dugdale, *Monasticon*, VI, p. 1527.

Gottlieb, in commenting on this passage, points out that such a division of libraries was, probably, a regular custom, and that it affords an obvious explanation of the fact that not a few of their catalogues, many of them very old, contain nothing but classical authors and manuals of instruction.[1] That, among the mendicant orders, Franciscans and Carmelites were especially distinguished by their zeal for learning and energy as book hunters, is well known; and, as early as 1381, we find them sharing with the university of Cambridge the dislike of the townsmen.[2] According to Mabillon, a like arrangement with respect to their libraries existed among the larger monasteries, especially those of the Cluniac order, on the continent, one library being that of the choir of the monastery church, the other that for the exclusive use of the monks—the *libri scientifici et ascetici;* and, in like manner, in the English cathedrals, the respective duties of the *armarius* and the *praecentor* (also *cantor*) point to the same distinction, although, at minor foundations, the duties of each were often discharged by the same individual. But, at all alike, there would generally be among the service books one or more beautiful antiphonals, richly illuminated and adorned with massively embossed covers; and an additional temptation was thus presented to the despoiler, when the dissolution came, besides that of the gold and silver chalices, censers, crosses, ewers and candlesticks which adorned the altar and the chapels. Such entries, again, as occur in the sales of the plunder which took place in 1548, of "fourteen great books in the quire, 14s.," "four prycksong mass books of paper," certainly bear out the view, that the love of choral song (noted by Erasmus as an interesting feature in the social life of the English), had been to a great extent fostered by those monastic or cathedral choirs of youths and boys, whom he described as "singing, to the accompaniment of the organ and with harmonious modulations of voice, their matin song in honour of the Virgin."

Generally speaking, however, accounts contemporary with the reformation are wanting, and we must rely on much earlier evidence, derived from inventories, for such information as the

---

[1] *Mittelalterliche Bibliotheken*, p. 305.
[2] Cooper, *Annals of Cambridge*, I, pp. 120–1.

following, which relates to the chapel of the collegiate church of Windsor, where,

in addition to the service books there were (*temp*. Richard II) 34 books on different subjects (*diversarum scientiarum*) chained in the church; among them a Bible and a concordance, and two books of French romance, one of which was the *Liber de Rose*.[1]

This, however, was an exceptionally wealthy foundation.

The work of destruction that went on at the dissolution of the monasteries has been dealt with in a previous chapter of this work. Well might Thomas Fuller, as he bemoaned the havoc, more than a century later, exclaim,

What beautiful Bibles, rare Fathers, subtile Schoolmen, useful Historians,—ancient, middle, modern; what painful Comments were here amongst them! What monuments of mathematics all massacred together—seeing every book with a cross was condemned for Popish,—with circles, for conjuring.[2] Yea, I may say that then holy Divinity was profaned, Physics hurt, and a trespass, yea a riot, committed on Law itself. And, more particularly, the History of former times then and there received a dangerous wound, where of it halts at this day, and, without hope of a perfect cure, must go a cripple to the grave.[3]

Cathedral libraries suffered far more serious losses during the civil war than at the reformation. They were less carefully guarded than those of the monasteries, there being no regulation requiring their annual inspection; partly owing to the fact that the collections were mostly small: it is rarely that, prior to the fifteenth century, we find evidences of their being catalogued; and, even where a catalogue existed, the entirety of the library which it represented was too often left unverified. The Restoration marks a third stage in their history, when churchmen made an effort to replace, to some extent, the vanished treasures; and collections, large or small, were brought in from localities where they were likely to be less serviceable,

---

[1] *Victoria County History of Berkshire*, II, p. 109.
[2] In allusion, perhaps, to the use of symbols, which mathematicians were beginning to resort to in their works. See W. W. R. Ball, *Short History of Mathematics*, pp. 211–215; also his *Hist. of Mathematics at Cambridge*, pp. 15, 16.
Church History of Britain (ed. Nicholls), II, pp. 248–9.

the newly-introduced volumes, as at York and Wimborne, requiring the practised eye of the expert to distinguish them from the remnants of the original collections.

In the early decades of the seventeenth century, the library of the minster at York still possessed the MSS. brought from the abbey at Rievaulx, and, in 1628, it received from the widow of its former archbishop, Tobias Matthew, his valuable collection of printed books; but the costly volumes relating to liturgic use and to ritual were not acquired until the eighteenth century. Llandaff, at this time, still possessed the library which it afterwards transferred to Cardiff castle for safety, but only to be destroyed by Cromwell's soldiery. Durham had suffered severely at the reformation, losing no inconsiderable portion of its fine illuminated manuscripts, but still owned St. Cuthbert's copy of the Gospels (now at the British Museum), and the *editio princeps* of Tacitus, by Vindelin de Spira. Here, the former refectory of the monastery (rebuilt in 1685) contains the chapter library, while the fine library presented by Cosin— a thoroughly representative collection of the Jacobean era, of which the catalogue, on vellum, still exists—has been transferred to the castle. Rochester has preserved but few manuscripts of any interest; but, among the printed books, there is a copy of the first printed English Bible of 1535, and a fine missal (Salisbury use) printed by Regnault in 1534. Lichfield possesses little that can be considered strictly monastic, its library dating from the benefaction of Frances, duchess of Somerset, in 1672. Ceadda's (St. Chad's) copy of the Gospels, however, found its way thither from Llandaff, and the collection also includes a fine MS. of the poems of Chaucer. Hereford, on the other hand, preserves (but in a special building) a library which presents, both in its literature and in its furniture, a singularly pleasing example of a medieval institution—the catalogue itself chained to the desk, the volumes arranged according to the then customary classification, while the *Mappa Mundi* is of world-wide fame. There is also a copy of Coverdale's Bible of 1535. None of the preceding, however, could compare in regard to literature with Salisbury, which can still show an array of MSS. filling one hundred and eighty-seven volumes, remained intact for a period of four hundred years and included productions ranging from the ninth to the fourteenth century, among them the Gallican *Psalter* of the ninth century, an English version of the *Gospel of Nicodemus*, Chaucer's translation of Boethius and a MS. of Geoffrey of Monmouth. The *Inventory of the Riches of the Cathedral Church of Sarum*, "made by Master Thomas Robertson, Treasurer of the same Church in 1536," contains a list of items which attest the wealth of the ancient foundation. Winchester, on the other hand, did not become possessed of its fine collection of Bibles, bequeathed by bishop Morley, until 1684. The collection also includes the early editions of Izaak Walton's works At Lincoln, many of the MSS. have suffered mutilation; while, about the middle of the seventeenth century, the ancient library was greatly injured by fire. There is still, however, to be seen a MS. of Old English romances, collected (*c.* 1430) by Robert de Thornton, archdeacon of Bedford. Exeter possesses no catalogue earlier than 1683. Out of the sixty volumes given by Leofric, its first bishop, the library can still show its *Liber Exoniensis*, to which reference has been made in Volume I of the present work. At Wells, there are the five volumes of the Aldine Aristotle, one of them with the autograph of Erasmus. Ely possesses no *editiones principes*, but there is a considerable number of tracts relating to the history of the Nonjurors. At Lambeth, the valuable collection (which may be said to have originated in the bequest of archbishop Bancroft) remained uncatalogued until the time of Edmund Gibson, bishop of London, who made a beginning, which was not carried to completion until the time of Ducarel, its librarian towards the end of the eighteenth century. At Chichester, the library possesses MSS. of the statutes of Peterhouse, Cambridge, and of an account of the foundation of Christchurch, Oxford. At Westminster, Hacket tells us that John Williams, when dean,

converted a waste room . . . into a goodly library, model'd it into decent shape, furnish'd it with desks and chairs, accoutred it with all utensils and stored it with a vast number of learned volumes. For which use he lighted most fortunately upon the study of that learned gentleman, Mr. Baker of Highgate, who in a long and industrious life had collected into his own possession the best authors in all sciences, in their best editions, which being bought at

500l. (a cheap pennyworth for such precious ware) were removed into this storehouse.[1]

The libraries in both universities sustained irreparable losses during the period of the reformation.

It is clear, from Leland's *Collectanea*, that Clare College possessed in his time a large number of books of which there is no trace now. We have in print catalogues of the old libraries at Corpus Christi, Trinity Hall, King's, Queens', St. Catherine's, and the University. At the present moment [1899] 19 of the University Library books are known to exist out of 330. At Corpus Christi, 3 out of 75; at Queens', I believe, none; at King's, 1 out of 176; at Trinity Hall, 1; at St. Catherine's none out of about 100.[2]

On the other hand, most of these libraries had also been receiving considerable accessions. Perne, who held the mastership of Peterhouse from 1553 to 1589, was distinguished by his efforts on behalf of the university library and also of the library of his own college. In relation to the former, Bradshaw says that "we may fairly look upon him as the principal agent in its restoration at this period." While, as regards the college, he not only provided for the erection of the present library, but "enriched it with a large share of his magnificent collections."[3] None of the colleges (with the exception of Corpus Christi) bestowed greater care than did Peterhouse on its books and on their preservation—a tradition, possibly, from those earlier days, when, as night came on, the town gates were closed, and the little society without was called upon to trust solely to its own vigilance, against the marauder and the purloiner. As early as 1472, the library had been further augmented by the bequest of the royal physician, Roger Marshall, and a portion of his bequest had, by his instructions, been placed *in apertiori libraria*, evidently with the design of rendering the volumes more generally accessible, without allowing them to be borrowed. Eight years later, however, during the mastership of John Warkworth (the reputed author

[1] *Life of Williams*, pt. I, p. 47.

[2] M. R. James, *The Sources of Archbishop Parker's Collection of MSS. at Corpus Christi College, Cambridge*, Camb. Ant. Soc., Octavo Publications, vol. XXXII; Willis and Clark, *Architectural History*, etc. III, p. 404.

[3] T. A. Walker. For an account of the original library, See Vol. II, Chap. XV, pp. 410–416.

of the *Chronicle*), further regulations were enacted, whereby it was made permissible to lend a volume to a member of the society for a term of two years, but with the precaution of first obtaining a valuation of the book so as, in the event of its not being returned, to mulct the borrower in its full value. At Corpus Christi college, at the time when archbishop Parker bequeathed his noble collection, the original library had almost disappeared.[1] He made it his first care, on succeeding to the mastership in 1544, and finding many volumes in the library "scattered about without any safe keeping," to take measures which involved a radical reform. The earliest catalogue—that compiled by John Botener in 1376—and other records, enable us to realise the serious losses which had been sustained and also to understand how such experiences may well have seemed to him to justify the almost unprecedented regulations wherewith he sought to guard against their recurrence. In 1578, the college chapel was rebuilt, and rooms were constructed over it; and, in a small chamber over the ante-chapel, the famous Parker MSS. were safely housed for some 250 years.

Parker stands at the head of the race of modern book collectors. As Archbishop of Canterbury during the early years of Queen Elizabeth's reign, he had the first pick of the whole of the plunder of the libraries and muniment-rooms of the dissolved religious houses; and his suffragans were only too ready to gain his favour by almost forcing upon him the treasures of the Cathedral libraries.[2]

A series of catalogues, from those compiled by Parker himself to that drawn up by M. R. James, give proof of what may be described as a continuously growing sense of the value of the entire collection. Among the chief treasures, the MS. of the four Gospels (no. 286) is asserted to have been one of the volumes that pope Gregory the Great sent from Rome for the use of St. Austin of Canterbury; two chronicles (nos. 16 and 26) are supposed to have been composed, written and illustrated by Matthew Paris, historiographer of St. Albans. The collection is also strong in liturgiology; but it is, perhaps, most

[1] See *A Catalogue of the Books bequeathed to C. C. College by Tho. Markaunt in* 1439, ed. J. O. Halliwell, Camb. Ant. Soc. Publ., vol. II, pp. 15–20.
[2] Bradshaw and Wordsworth, *Lincoln Cathedral Statutes*, pt. I, p. 184.

widely known by its wealth in Old English literature, of which there are five distinct classes: *Gospels*, *Annals of England*, *Glossaries*, *Homilies* (Aelfric's *Lives of the Saints*) and *Canons*. James has identified no less than 47 volumes as formerly belonging to Christ Church priory, and 26 to St. Augustine's abbey, both at Canterbury.

The losses against which Parker had sought to guard his bequeathed treasures either menaced, or actually overtook, other colleges, but not until long after his death, and then chiefly in connection with political events, of which the experience of Emmanuel college affords a singularly noteworthy but somewhat complicated illustration. Richard Bancroft, who had been educated at Christ's college and was, subsequently, a fellow of Jesus, becoming, finally, archbishop of Canterbury, died in 1610, bequeathing a valuable library to his successors in the see; but his bequest was accompanied with certain conditions which proved difficult to carry into effect. Those who were to inherit it were to give security for its due preservation in its entirety, a requirement which the enforcement of the covenant rendered impracticable. Failing this proviso, the collection was to become the property of Bancroft's projected foundation of Chelsea college, of which the scheme, however, altogether collapsed. And, finally, the donor, in anticipation of such miscarriage, had designated the university of Cambridge as the recipient. For thirty years, however, owing to certain obstacles, although the collection was augmented by considerable gifts from both archbishop Abbot and his rival Laud, it remained stowed away in "the study over the Cloisters at Lambeth," until parliament, on being formally petitioned, intervened, and order was given, in February 1645/6, that the entire collection, now unrivalled as a source of information with respect to church history in the Jacobean era, should be sent to Cambridge. It was not, even then, until after John Selden and others had used their influence that these instructions were carried into effect. On the arrival of the books, the imposing array was described by the academic authorities as evoking no little "exultation"; and parliament itself, on learning that the first result had been to render increased accommodation imperatively necessary, was induced to grant £2000 "for the building and finishing the Public

Library at Cambridge." The Lords, although unable to give their assent, concurred, notwithstanding, in a separate grant for the purchase from Thomason of a valuable collection of Hebrew books—noted by Henry Bradshaw as constituting the nucleus of the Hebrew library of the university. The volumes given by Abbot and other later donors had not been sent with Bancroft's, but in the following year (1649) these also arrived. It was at this junction that the death of Richard Holdsworth gave rise to unlooked for complications. Holdsworth was a distinguished scholar who had filled the office of public orator with marked ability, but, owing to his refusal to take the covenant, had been ejected, in 1644, from the mastership of Emmanuel and, subsequently, imprisoned in the Tower. He was well known, however, to Manchester, the puritan general, and had, consequently, been able to save his own valuable library from sequestration by declaring his intention of bequeathing it to his college; but, at his death, in 1649, it was found, on opening his will, that he had finally decided to leave the collection to the university library should the Bancroft collection ever be reclaimed for Lambeth. When the Restoration came, it was one of Juxon's first measures as primate to make that demand, as it was one of his last, to provide for the fit reception of the books by the erection of the noble building which bears his name. The university promptly complied; but, when it sought to obtain some compensation for its loss, by applying for the transfer of Holdsworth's library (then in London) to its own shelves, the authorities at Emmanuel contested their claim, and a suit was consequently begun in the court of Arches. Eventually, the matter was left to be dealt with by three adjudicators—the archbishop of York, the bishop of London and the bishop of Ely—who, in December 1664, gave a formal award on parchment to the following effect: (1) Holdsworth's printed books and MSS. were to come to the public library at Cambridge; (2) duplicates were to be disposed of, as Holdsworth had directed in his will; (3) Emmanuel college was to receive from the university £200 in settlement of its claim, and also to be repaid its costs, provided the said costs did not exceed £20.

To St. Catharine's belongs the credit of having been the first to print its entire catalogue, 1771; but that by Stanley, of the Parker MSS. at Corpus, had appeared in 1722; and, in 1827, Queens' college printed its catalogue, compiled by Thomas Hartwell Horne, in two large octavo volumes.

The library of St. John's college, Cambridge, affords an excellent example of both the literature and the architecture of the period, having been built in 1624, by John Williams, the lord keeper (whose arms are over the doorway), in the style known as Jacobean Gothic; the interior, with its white-washed walls, dark oak ceiling and presses, still presenting very much the same appearance that it must have done in 1654, when John Evelyn pronounced it "the fairest of that university." The presses, more particularly—each with its sloping top, designed, originally, to serve as a reading-desk, and list of contents at the end, enclosed under folding panels—are a good illustration of the medieval arrangements already described.[1] Among the contents to be noted are: the so-called Cromwell's Bible, printed (on vellum) partly in Paris and partly in London, and "finished in Aprill, A.D. 1539"—a vast folio, splendidly illuminated, bearing the arms of Thomas Cromwell; the service books used by Charles I and archbishop Laud at the coronation of the former, and that used by Sancroft at the coronation of James II; a curious Irish *Psalter* supposed to be of the ninth century, with grotesque drawings, and interlined throughout with Latin glosses written in Celtic minuscules;[2] and an illuminated book of Hours, an admirable specimen of Flemish art, containing the autograph of the foundress, the Lady Margaret.

Neither the statutes of Michael house nor those of King's hall (the two foundations subsequently absorbed in Trinity) contain any reference to books, and the erection of the magnificent library of Trinity, of which the plans were first begun by Sir Christopher Wren in 1676, belongs to a period beyond our present limits. Among the donors to the Trinity collection, Sir Edward Stanhope, a fellow of the society, bequeathed fifteen manuscripts and over 300 volumes, among them the Polyglot Bible, known as king Philip's Bible; and James Duport, vice-master of the society, and afterwards master of Magdalene, was a liberal donor of "English books," under

[1] See *ante*, p. 475.

[2] See M. R. James's introduction (p. xciii) to *The Ancient Libraries of Canterbury and Dover*.

which denomination the compiler of the catalogue includes not only works in the English language, whether printed in the country or abroad, but books which "though not in the English language, have a distinct connection with the English Church, history, or literature."[1]

The original catalogue of Magdalene college library is still preserved, "a volume with an illuminated heraldic frontispiece" bearing the arms of Thomas Howard, a distinguished benefactor to the society, whom king James had created first earl of Suffolk in 1603; while, on the opposite page, the names of the earliest donors to the library appear on the leaves of an olive-tree. The list begins with the name of Thomas Neville, of Pembroke college, whom the earl had appointed master in 1582. A Nuremberg Chronicon (folio, 1493); an Aesop (de Worde, 1503); a *Manuale ad usum Sarum* (Rouen, 1504); a Salisbury breviary (London, 1556), are among the chief rarities.[2]

At Oxford, college libraries had, in most instances, been unscrupulously plundered by the Edwardian commissioners, and little of value or importance remained at the beginning of the seventeenth century. At Balliol, the college of that great patron of learning, William Grey, bishop of Ely, the newly-built library possessed, in 1478, two hundred volumes (including a *printed* copy of Josephus), by virtue of his bequest; but, by Anthony à Wood's time, most of the miniatures in the volumes that remained had disappeared. At Merton, the library retained every structural feature of bishop Rede's original work, and continued, down to the year 1792, to afford, with its chained volumes, an excellent example of a medieval interior. Oriel still preserved its catalogue of 1375, comprising about 100 volumes arranged according to the traditional branches of study. Queens' still gave shelter to its modest

---

[1] See *Catalogue of the English Books printed before MDCI. now in the Library of Trinity College, Cambridge*, by Robert Sinker, Cambridge, 1885.

[2] A few words may here be added by way of anticipation respecting the Pepysian library, which, along with the MS. of the donor's diary (in cipher) he bequeathed to the college, although they were not actually received until 1724. By his directions they were placed in a separate chamber, the catalogue having been compiled by himself. Among the contents are six Caxtons, five folio volumes of old ballads, a splendid Sarum missal (1520) and a valuable collection of prints, chiefly portraits.

collection in the original building—the present fine library being an erection of the last decade of the seventeenth century. New college could still boast the possession of its MS. copy of the *Nicomachean Ethics* as, also, of the first printed edition (1495–8) of Aristotle's collected works; but Lincoln had been plundered of the greater part of the valuable collections given by Thomas Gascoigne and Robert Fleming. Its catalogue of 1474 shows the college to have been, at that time, in possession of 135 manuscripts, arranged in seven presses. Faithful to the traditions derived from Linacre, the shelves of All Souls were largely laden with that medical literature which continued to increase throughout the sixteenth and seventeenth centuries. It possessed, also, a few volumes of the collection (chiefly theological and of writers on civil and canon law) given, in 1440, by Henry VI; manuscripts and books given by cardinal Pole; and, a far more valuable gift, those bequeathed by his relative, David Pole.

Brasenose, where the library had twice changed its orientation, was not, as yet, in possession of the tenth century manuscript of Terence, which once belonged to cardinal Bembo. At Corpus Christi, the *trilinguis bibliotheca*, which Erasmus had prophesied would one day attract more scholars to Oxford than Rome, in his time, attracted to behold miracles, scarcely fulfilled his sanguine prediction, but it has been stated that the college possessed, at this period, the largest and best furnished college library then in Oxford.[1] Christ Church, in the room which had formerly been the refectory of St. Frideswide's convent, had stowed away some early MS. copies of Wyclif's Bible, and was possessed of one of the original transcripts of the life of her great founder by Cavendish, together with a service book which Wolsey had been wont to use. St. John's could already pride itself on a fine collection of rare books relating to English history and also on one of pre-reformation books of devotion, while its specimens of the Caxton press still outvie those possessed by any other college.

Although a regard for learning, and, especially, theological learning, was a marked characteristic of James I, he was by no means distinguished as a book collector; and, whatever was

---

[1] *Corpus Christi College* (Oxford), by Thomas Fowler, pp. 34, 255.

done during his reign towards carrying out the designs of his predecessors, in this direction, was chiefly owing to the short-lived influence of his son, prince Henry, and the mature energy of scholars like Sir Thomas Bodley and Sir Robert Cotton, whose names are associated with the great collections at Oxford, and in the British Museum. It was owing to the prince that the royal library was saved from spoliation, and to Bodley that the "Old library," in the university of Oxford, which had been completely dispersed, was re-established to such an extent as to lead convocation, in 1617, to greet the latter as *Publicae Bibliothecae Fundator*. His father, John Bodley, had been one of the exiles who fled from England during the Marian persecution. In Geneva, Thomas, the eldest son, read Homer with Constantine (author of the *Lexicon graecolatinum*), and attended the lectures of Chevallier in Hebrew, of Phil. Beroaldus in Greek and of Calvin and Beza in divinity. On his return to England, he was entered by his father at Magdalen college, Oxford, where Laurence Humphry, a scholar of repute, was president. Before long, Bodley was appointed to lecture on Greek in the college, and, subsequently, on natural philosophy in the schools. In 1576, he left Oxford to travel for four years on the continent, visiting, in turn, Italy, France and Germany, and, also, acquiring a good knowledge of Italian, French and Spanish. His autobiography leaves it doubtful how far he succeeded in gaining access to the libraries of these countries: but it may be well to recall that the Vatican library in Rome had not, as yet, been rebuilt by Sixtus V, nor the Ambrosian founded by cardinal Borromeo in Milan; that the Laurentian library in Florence had only recently been made accessible to the scholar, and had long before been despoiled of some of its greatest treasures; that Petrarch's choice collection at Arqua lay scattered far and wide, in Naples, in Pavia, or in Paris; that, in France, the royal library at Fontainebleau had not, as yet, acquired the valuable collection of Greek MSS. included in the library of Catherine de' Medici, and had only recently begun to profit by the enactment whereby all publishers were required to forward a copy of every work printed *cum privilegio;* that, in Germany, the library formed by the Jesuits at Trier had but just been opened, while that at Bamberg was not yet in existence. The great Fugger collection, on the other hand, had just been added to the ducal library at Munich, and made accessible, in the new buildings, to scholars; while, in the north, the ducal library at Wolfen-büttel, although jealously fenced in by special restrictions, was beginning to attract numerous visitors, and, at the beginning of the seventeenth century, numbered some five thousand volumes. But, generally speaking, the library at this period was an institution either guarded with a vigilance which made it difficult of access, or with a negligence that foreshadowed its ultimate dispersion.

After his return to England, Bodley, from 1588 to 1596, filled the post of English resident at the Hague. But, on coming back to England in the latter year, although repeatedly solicited to fill more than one important office under government, he decided to retire altogether from political life, and his remaining years may be said to have been almost exclusively devoted to the foundation of his great library at Oxford.

"I concluded," he said, "at the last, to set up my staff at the Library Door at Oxon; being thoroughly persuaded that in my solitude and surcease from publick affairs, I could not busy myself to better purpose than by reducing that place (which then in every part lay ruined and waste) to the publick use of students."[1]

The ancient chamber—originally assigned as the keeping-place of a lending library, for the use of poor students allowed to borrow volumes on giving pledges for their safe return—had been a room to the north of the chancel of St. Mary's church, built from moneys bequeathed by Thomas Cobham, bishop of Worcester, himself the donor of sundry books; but, in 1488, this chamber was discarded for the building erected by Humphrey, duke of Gloucester, over the noble divinity school, and the library named after him, pointing east and west, and accessible probably by only one staircase, was formally opened. The duke, at the same time, presented numerous books[2]—chiefly Latin classics and versions of Plato and Aristotle, the chief Italian poets and also a Greek vocabulary—the library, at his death, numbering, it is said, some 600 volumes.

[1] *Reliquiae Bodleianae*, p. 14.
[2] For a catalogue of the same, see Anstey's *Munimenta Academica*, pp. 158–772.

Only 62 years passed, and then the books so carefully and lovingly gathered together were destroyed or dispersed. In 1550, the Commissioners for the Reformation of the University appointed by Edward VI laid waste its contents. . . . So complete was the destruction that in 1556 the very bookshelves and desks were sold as things for which there was no longer any use.[1]

In the prosecution of his labours, Bodley himself tells us, he was encouraged by the consciousness that he possessed "four kinds of necessary aids—some knowledge of the learned and modern tongues and of the scholastical literature, ability and money, friends to further the design, and leisure to pursue it." As regards the second "aid," however, his generosity somewhat exceeded his resources, for we learn that, in 1611, he was fain to borrow upon bond and to pawn and sell his plate for a few hundred pounds, in order to complete his last building of the library, which cost him, in all, £1200.[2] On 8 November, 1602, that library, which now numbers fully three-quarters of a million volumes, had been formally opened with about 2,500. One of his earliest measures had been to cause a massive folio register to be prepared for entering the benefactions which he was able to place on the shelves in 1604, a record subsequently kept by John Hales of Eton; and, as time went on, some of the volumes of the original library were restored either as a donation or by purchase. The year 1605 saw the publication of the first catalogue, with a dedication to prince Henry, and a preface containing *memoranda* on the origin and growth of the whole collection. In 1609, Bodley executed conveyances of land in Berkshire and houses in London for the endowment; and, in 1610, the Stationers' company undertook to present to the library a copy of every book that they published.[3] This latter measure induced Godfrey Goodman, of Trinity college, Cambridge (afterwards bishop of Gloucester), to come forward in 1616 to urge upon the vice-chancellor of his own university the desirability

---

[1] *Pietas Oxoniensis in memory of Sir Thomas Bodley, Knt., and the Foundation of the Bodleian Library*, 1902. "Erasmus could hardly refrain from tears when he saw the scanty remains of this library, and, in Leland's day, scarcely a single volume survived," J. E. Sandys, *A History of Classical Scholarship*, vol. II., p. 221. As Erasmus died in 1536, this would seem to prove that the chief losses took place prior to the reformation.

[2] *Pietas Oxoniensis*, p. 12.   [3] Wood, *Annals*, II, pp. 306-7.

of procuring "the like privilege" for that body. "It might," he said, "be some occasion hereafter to move some good benefactors towards the building of a publick librarie."[1] In 1611, the statutes for the regulation of the library were approved in convocation. And now it was that Bodley's first librarian, Thomas James, could venture to affirm that "upon consideration of the number of volumes, their languages, subjects, condition, and their use for six hours daily (Sundays and Holy days excepted), we shall find that the like Librarie is no where to be found."

"He reckons up," continues the *Pietas*, "thirty foreign languages (including 'High-dutch, Lowe-dutch, Un-dutch,' and 'Scotish') in which books are to be found, and gives a list of the nations from which readers had frequented the place, 'French, Spanish, Italian, Dutch, Danes, Bohemians, Polonians, Jewes, Ethiopians, and others,' Germans, of course, being here included in 'Dutch.'"

In the course of the generation succeeding Bodley's death, a series of gifts further enriched the collection over which he had untiringly watched and in behalf of which he had disinterestedly laboured. Foremost among these were the Greek MSS. of Giacomo Barocci, in 242 volumes, presented, in 1629, by William Herbert, earl of Pembroke and chancellor of the university, whose munificence was largely owing to the good offices of Laud, his successor in that office. The archbishop himself gave some 1300 MSS. in eighteen different languages and also his fine collection of coins, carefully arranged with a view to their use in the study of history. Other donors were Sir Kenelm Digby, who gave 240 MSS., and Robert Burton, author of *The Anatomy of Melancholy*, who, dying in 1640, bequeathed a large miscellaneous collection of books. Oliver Cromwell, while chancellor of the university, sent 22 Greek and two Russian MSS., and the executors of John Selden presented the greater part of that distinguished scholar's library, numbering about 8000 volumes, and 350 MSS., chiefly Greek and Oriental.

The public library of the university of Cambridge dates, apparently, from the early decades of the fifteenth century; and

[1] *Communication* by J. E. B. Mayor in *Communications of Camb. Ant. Soc.*, II, pp. 123-4.

John Croucher, who gave a copy of Chaucer's translation of Boethius, was regarded by Bradshaw as the founder of our English library. The earliest catalogue contains 122 titles, and, later in the same century (1473), Ralph Songer's and Richard Cockeram's catalogue contains 330, classified and arranged. These books were kept in the First room. The library gained greatly through the generous benefactions of Thomas Rotheram, both in books and in buildings. Later benefactors were archbishop Parker and Andrew Perne, master of Peterhouse, who, at a time when the library (owing to successive losses) scarcely contained 180 volumes, worked jointly to increase its usefulness.

In July 1577, we find for the first time a member of the university appointed librarian, at an annual stipend of £10. The person chosen was William James, a Peterhouse man . . . [and in] the vice-chancellor's accounts for 1584–5 is a payment "for a carte to bring certayne written bookis from Peter howse to the schooles, gyven by Mr Dr Perne to the librarye," and also "for twoe that did helpe to lade and unlade the same."[1]

Among these, possibly, may be included the eighth century copy of the Latin gospels.

The erection and endowment of the Chetham library, by Humphrey Chetham, a wealthy Manchester tradesman, resulted in the formation of a collection which may compare, in both its origin and its design, with that of Bodley. In founding his library "within the town of Manchester for the use of scholars," and also directing that "none of the books be taken out of the Library at any time, but be fixed or chained, as well as may be," Chetham would seem to have profited by the experience of the friaries; while his puritan sympathies are shown in his bequest of a special fund of £200 for the purchase of the works of Calvin, and, also, of those of two eminent Cambridge divines, Preston and Perkins, which he directed should be affixed to the pillars in the churches of Manchester and the neighbouring localities. Chetham died in 1653, and his executors proceeded, forthwith, to carry out his instructions by purchasing, and placing in fine old shelves, a considerable collection of the chief English protestant di-

---

[1] Bradshaw, *Collected Papers*, pp. 191, 192.

vines, among whom were Baxter, Cartwright, Chillingworth, Foxe, Jewel, Joseph Mede and Ussher. In some of the parishes, however, the collections were allowed to fall into neglect and have altogether disappeared. In Manchester itself, the main library was stored in a fine old building known as the Baron's hall, and, before 1664, had acquired some 1450 volumes.

In 1630, Sion college was founded, as a corporation of all ministers and curates within London and its suburbs; and, during the Commonwealth, it gave shelter to the library of old St. Paul's when the latter was menaced with confiscation. With the Restoration, a portion of the collection went back to the cathedral, but only to be consumed in the Great Fire. Of the portion that remained in the college, not a few of the volumes are of great rarity; while, in the reign of queen Anne, the library was admitted to share in the privilege which had been granted in 1662–3, whereby every printer was required to

reserve three printed copies of the best and largest paper of every book new printed . . . and before any publick vending of the said book bring them to the Master of the Company of Stationers, and deliver them to him, one whereof shall be delivered to the Keeper of His Majesties library, and the other two to be sent to the vice-chancellors of the two universities respectively, for the use of the publick libraries of the said universities.[1]

In singular contrast to the numerous collections which have been dispersed by war, the library of Trinity college, Dublin, originated in a victory won by English arms. It was in the year 1601, after the rebellion in Munster had been crushed, that the conquerors at Kinsale subscribed the sum of £700 for the purchase of books to be presented to the college; and, in 1603, James Ussher and Luke Challoner were sent to London to expend the money. While thus employed, they fell in with Thomas Bodley, engaged in a like errand on behalf of the future Bodleian. The total fund at their disposal had been increased to £1800, which was soon invested in purchases; and, by 1610, the original forty volumes in the library had been increased to 4000.

Ussher's own library, however, the same that had very narrowly escaped dispersion after he left Oxford for Wales, and

[1] Pickering, *Statutes at Large* (ed. 1763), VIII, p. 147.

which he was designing to present to Dublin, had been confiscated by parliament as a mark of its displeasure at his refusal to recognise the authority of the Westminster assembly of divines; and it was only through the intercession of John Selden in his behalf, that he eventually succeeded in recovering the larger part of the collection; then it was, that, in order to make some provision for his daughter, lady Tyrrell, the primate was diverted from his original intention, and bequeathed the books to her. On his death, her ladyship received various offers for the same, the king of Denmark and cardinal Mazarin having been among the would-be purchasers; but Cromwell forbade the sale, and all that remained of the collection was ultimately purchased by the parliamentary army in Ireland for £2200.

"By the acquisition of Ussher's books," says Macneile Dixon, "the library of Trinity College was at once raised to high rank. Grants from the Irish House of Commons and the benefactions of many private persons added to its treasures in the seventeenth and eighteenth centuries. . . . During the nineteenth century, the chief increase in the number of volumes has been due to the act of parliament which, in 1801, gave to Trinity college library the right to a copy of every book published in the United Kingdom."[1]

In the same year that Holdsworth died, William Drummond, laird of Hawthornden, also passed away. He had already presented, in 1627, a collection of 500 volumes to the university of Edinburgh, which is still carefully preserved in the university library. Among them are early editions of some of the following writers: Bacon, Chapman, Churchyard, Daniel, Dekker, Donne, Drayton, Heywood, Ben Jonson, Marston, May, the countess of Pembroke, Quarles, Selden, Shakespeare (*Love's Labour's Lost*, 1598, *Romeo and Juliet*, 1599), Sidney, Spenser, Sylvester and George Wither. The Latin preface which Drummond himself wrote and prefixed to the catalogue is worthy of note as embodying a kind of philosophy of bibliography conceived in the spirit of an educated layman of the time.

"As good husbandmen," wrote the Scotch laird, "plant trees in their times, of which the after-age may reap the fruit, so should

[1] *Trinity College, Dublin*, by W. Macneile Dixon, p. 223.

we; and what antiquity hath done for us, that should we do for Posterity, so that letters and learning may not decay, but ever flourish to the honour of God, the public utility, and the conservation of human society."[1]

[1] See Drummond's *Works* (1711), p. 223; *Drummond of Hawthornden*, by David Masson, p. 169.   See also *ante*, Chap. ix.

BIBLIOGRAPHIES

CHAPTER I

TRANSLATORS

TRANSLATIONS FROM THE GREEK AND LATIN CLASSICS

Achilles Tatius. The most delectable and pleasant history of Clitophon and Lucippe, from the Greek of Achilles Tatius by W. B. 1597.

Aelian. Translated by Abraham Fleming. 1576.

—— The Tactiks of Aelian. . . . Englished by J. B(ingham). 1616.

Aesop. Æsop's Fabls in tru Ortography. Translated out of Latin into English by William Bullokar. 1585.

Appian. An auncient historie and exquisite chronicle of Roman warres . . . from the death of Sextus Pompeius till the overthrow of Antonie and Cleopatra. Translated out of divers languages by W. B. 1578.

Apuleius. The XI Bookes of The Golden Asse, containing the Metamorphosis of Lucius Apuleius. Translated into English by William Adlington. 1566. Rptd. in the Series of Tudor Translations, with Introduction by Whibley, C. 1892.

Aristotle. The Ethics. Translated out of the Italian by John Wylkin. 1547.

—— Politics. Translated out of Greek into French, by Loys le Roy, called Regius, and translated out of French into English, by J. D. 1597.

Aurelius, Marcus. Meditations. Translated out of French into English by John Bourchier, Knighte, Lorde Berners. Between 1534 and 1588 some ten editions. See Guevara, Antonio de.

Ausonius. Epigrams from Ausonius, translated by Timothie Kendall in his Floures of Epigrams. 1577.

—— Idylls. Translated by Sir John Beaumont in his Bosworth Field and other Poems and set forth by his son. 1620.

Caesar. The Eyght bookes of exploytes in Gallia and the Countries bordering. Translated out of Latine into English, by Arthur Golding. 1565.

—— Five books of his Wars in Gallia, by Clement Edmonds with observations, etc. on the five first books, and upon the sixth and seventh books. 1601.

—— De Bello Civili. Three books translated by Chapman. 1604.

Cicero. The thre bookes of Tullies Offices translated by R. Whyttington. 1533.

—— Three books of Dueties, to Marcus his Sonne. Tourned out of Latin into English, by Nicolas Grimalde. 1580.

—— The Booke of Marcus Tullius Cicero entituled Paradoxa Stoicorum. Translated by Thomas Newton. 1569.

Cicero.   Tusculan Questions which Marke Tullye Cicero disputed in his Manor
of Tusculanium, etc.   Englyshed by John Dolman.   1561.
—— The Familiar Epistles of M. T. Cicero Englished and conferred with the
French, Italian and other translations by J. Webbe.   n.d.
—— Select Epistles by Abr. Flemming, in his Panoplie of Epistles.   1576.
—— An Epistle to Quintus.   Translated by G. Gilby.   1561.
—— On Old Age.   Latin and English by R. Whyttington.
—— The worthie Booke of olde age, otherwise intitled the elder Cato, &c.
By Thos. Newton.   1569.
—— On Friendship.   Translated by John Harrington.   1550.
Claudian.   The Rape of Proserpine.   Translated by Leonard Digges
into English verse.   1617.   See also Sir John Beaumont's Bosworth
Field.
Curtius, Quintus.   The History, conteyning the Actes of the great Alexander.
Translated out of Latine into English by John Brende.   1553.
Demosthenes.   The three Orations in favour of the Olynthians, and his four
Orations against Philip, King of Macedon, translated by Dr. Thomas
Wylson, etc.   1570.
Diodorus Siculus.   The History of the successors of Alexander, etc. out of
Diodorus Siculus and Plutarch by Tho. Stocker.   1569.
Diogenes Laertius and others.   A Treatise of Morall Phylosophye, con-
tayning the sayinges of the wyse.   Gathered and Englyshed by Wylliam
Baldewyn.   1550.
Dionysius.   Dionysius' description of the Worlde.   Englyshed by Thomas
Twyne.   1572.
Epictetus.   The manuell of Epictetus, translated out of Greeke into French,
and now into English.   Also the Apothegmes, etc. by James Sandford.
1567.
—— Epictetus Manuall.   Cebes Table.   Theophrastus Characters by Jo.
Healey.   1616.
Euclid.   The Elements of Geometry, trans. Richard Candish (d. 1601?).
—— The Elements of Geometrie of the most auncient Philosopher Euclide of
Megara.   Faithfully (now first) translated into the Englishe toung, by H.
Billingsley, Citizen of London. . . . With a very fruitfull Preface
made by M(aster) J(ohn) Dee.   1570.
Eunapius Sardianus.   The Lyves of Phylosophers and Orators, from the
Greek of Eunapius.   1579.
Euripides.   Jocasta.   Written in Greeke by Euripides; translated and
digested into Acte by George Gascoigne and Francis Kinwelmarsh,
of Greie's Inn, and there by them presented.   1556.   (This version was
adapted from the Italian of Dolce.)
Eutropius.   A briefe Chronicle of the City of Rome.   Englished by Nicolas
Haward.   1564.
Florus, Lucius Annaeus.   The Roman Historie.   Translated by E. Bolton.
1618.
Heliodorus.   An Æthiopian Historie written in Greeke by . . . very wittie
and pleasaunt.   Englished by Thomas Underdoune.   1569(?).   Rptd. in
the Series of Tudor Translations, with Introduction by Whibley, C.
1895.
—— The Beginning of the Aethiopicall History in English Hexameters by
Abraham Fraunce.   1591.
Herodian.   Translated out of Latin into Englyshe, by Nicolas Smyth.   n.d.

Herodotus. The Famous Hystory of Herodotus Conteyning the Discourse of Dyvers Countrys, the succession of theyr Kyngs. . . . Devided into nine Bookes, entituled with the names of the nine Muses, by B. R. 1584. (It is unknown who B. R. is. Barnabe Rich has been suggested. Only books I and II translated. Euterpe rptd. in 1898 with preface by Lang, A.)

Hesiod. The Georgicks. Translated elaborately out of the Greek, by George Chapman. 1618.

Hippocrates. The Aphorismes of Hippocrates, redacted into a certaine Order, and translated by Humfrie Llwyd. 1585.

Homer. The Battel of the Frogges and Myce, and certain Orations of Isocrates by T. Purfoote. 1579.

—— Ten books of the Iliad, translated out of a translation in the French language by Arthur Hall, Esq., of Grantham, M.P. 1581.

—— The Strange Wonderfull and bloudy Battel between Frogs and Mise; paraphrastically done into English Heroycall Verse by W. F. (supposed to be William Fowles). 1603.

—— Seaven Bookes of the Iliades of Homer, Prince of Poets. Translated according to the Greeke in judgment of his best commentaries. 1598. (The books are 1, 2, 7 to 11. This is the first instalment of Chapman's Homer.)

—— Achilles Shield. Translated as the other seven Bookes of Homer, out of his eighteenth booke of Iliades by George Chapman. 1598.

—— Homer, Prince of Poets, translated according to the Greeke in twelve Bookes of his Iliads. George Chapman. 1609.

—— The Iliads of Homer, Prince of Poets. Never before in any language truely translated. With a comment on some of his chiefe places. 1611. (This is the first complete edition of Chapman's Iliad.)

—— Twenty-four Bookes of Homer's Odisses by George Chapman. Entered in the Stationers' register, 1614.

—— The Crowne of all Homer's Workes, Batrachomyomachia or the Battaile of Frogs and Mise. His Hymn's and Epigrams. Translated by George Chapman. 1624.

Horace. A Medicinable Morall, that is, the two Bookes of Horace his Satyres, Englyshed according to the prescription of Saint Hierome by T. Drant. 1566.

—— Arte of Poetrie, Pistles and Satyrs, Englished, and to the Earl of Ormounte by Th. Drant addressed 1567. (The Ars Poetica was translated also by Ben Jonson.)

Isocrates. The doctrinall of princes made by the noble oratour Isocrates, and translated out of Greke in to Englishe by syr Thomas Eliot, Knyght. 1534.

—— Isocrats paranesis or admonytion to Demonicus, translated into English. Printed by W. Copland. 1557.

—— Isocrates's sage Admonition, translated by R. Nuttall. 1557.

—— Epistles out of Isocrates, translated out of Latine into English by Abraham Flemming, in his Panoplie of Epistles. 1576.

—— A perfite Looking Glasse of all Estates: most excellently and eloquently set forth by the famous and learned Oratour Isocrates; as contained in three orations of Moral Instructions. Translated into Latine by that learned Clearke Hieronimus Wulfius. And now Englished. 1580. (The name of the translator, Thomas Forrest, is given in the Dedication.)

Isocrates. Isocrates's Oration, intitled Evagoras, by Jer. Wolfe. 1581.

—— The good Admonition of the sage Isocrates to young Demonicus, translated from Greek by R. Nuttall. 1585.

—— Archidamus, or the councell of warre. Translated by Thomas Barnes. 1624.

Josephus. The famous and memorable workes of Josephus. Translated out of the Latin and French by Thomas Lodge. 1602.

Justin. Thabridgemente of the Histories of Trogus Pompeius, gathered and written in the Laten tung, by the famous Historiographer Justin, and translated into Englishe by Arthur Goldinge: a worke conteyning brefly great plentye of moste delectable Historyes and notable examples, worthy not only to be read, but also to bee embraced and followed of al men. Newlie conferred with the Latin copye, and corrected by the translator. Anno Domini. 1563 and 1570.

—— The Hist. of Justine, translated into English, by Dr. Philemon Holland. 1606.

—— Translated by G. W. with an Epitomie of the Lives, etc. of the Roman Emperors, from Aurelius Victor. 1606.

Livy. The Historie of two of the most notable Captaines of the Worlde, Annibal and Scipio, of theyr dyvers Battailes and Victories, excedyng profytable to reade, gathered and translated into Englishe, out of Titus Livius, and other authoures, by Antonye Cope, esquier. 1544.

—— The Hystorie of P. Sulpicius Consulls, according to Titus Livius, by Thomas Wylson, Doctor of the Civill Lawes; prefixed to his Translation of the three Orations of Demosthenes in favour of the Olynthians, etc 1570.

—— The Orator: handling a hundred severall Discourses, in form of Declamations; some of the Arguments being drawne from Titus Livius and other ancient writers, the rest of the authour's owne invention: part of which are of matters happened in our Age. Written in French, by Alexander Silvayne, and Englished by L. P. (Lazarus Piot). 1596.

—— The Romane Historie, written in Latin by Titus Livius, translated by Philemon Holland. 1600.

Longus. Daphnis and Chloe, excellently describing the weight of affection, the simplicitie of love, the purport of honest meaning . . . by Angell Day, 1587. Rptd. with an Introduction by Jacobs, J. 1890.

Lucan. Lucan's Firste Booke translated line for line by Christopher Marlowe. 1593.

—— Lucan's Pharsalia. . . . Translated into English verse by Sir Arthur Gorges. 1614.

—— Lucan's Pharsalia. . . . Englished by Thomas May. 1627.

Lucian. Necromantia. A dialog of the Poet Lucyan, for his fantesye faynyd for a mery pastyme. And furst by hym compyled in the Greke tonge, and after translated owt of the Greke into Latyn, and now lately translatyd owt of Laten into Englissh for the erudicion of them, which be disposyd to lerne the tongis. Interlocuters Menippus and Philonides. n.d.

—— Toxaris, or the friendship of Lucian, translated out of Greke into English, With a dedication to his frende A. S. from A. O. 1565.

—— Orations and Dialogues. 1604.

—— Pleasant Dialogues and Drammas by T. Heywood. 1637.

Lucian. Certain select dialogues together with his True Historie. Translated by Mr. Francis Hickes, 1634. The True Historie, edited by Whibley, C. 1895.

Marcellinus, Ammianus. The Romane Historie. Translated by Dr. Philemon Holland. 1609.

Martial. Flowres of Epigrammes out of sundrie the most singular Authors, selected, etc. by Tim Kendall: annexed to which is Trifles by Timothy Kendall devised and written (for the most part) at sundrie tymes in his yong and tender age. 1575 and 1577.

Musæus. Translated by Christopher Marloe, left unfinished at his death, continued by one Henry Petowe in 1598.

—— Translated by George Chapman. 1606.

Ovid. The fable of Ovid treting of Narcissus, translated oute of Latin into English metre, with a moral thereunto, very pleasaunte to rede by Thomas Howell. 1560.

—— The pleasant fable of Hermaphroditus and Salmacis, translated by T. Underdowne. 1565.

—— The fyrst four Bookes of P. Ovidius Naso's Worke, intitled Metamorphosis, translated oute of Latin into Englishe meter by Arthur Golding. Gent. A woorke very pleasaunt and delectable. 1565.

—— The XV Bookes of P. Ovidius Naso, entytuled Metamorphosis, translated out of Latin into English meeter, by Arthur Golding. 1567. Rptd. in the King's Library series, ed. Rouse, W. H. D. 1904. [George Sandys published a verse trans. in 1621–6.]

—— The Heroycall Epistles of the learned Poet Publius Ovidius Naso, In Englishe Verse; set out and translated by George Turbervile, Gent., with Aulus Sabinus Aunsweres to certaine of the same. 1567.

—— Ovid his Invective against Ibis. Translated into English meeter. Wherunto is added by the Translator, a short draught of all stories and Tales contained therein, very pleasant to be read, by Thomas Underdoune. 1569.

—— The three first Bookes of Ovid de Tristibus, translated by Tho. Churchyard. 1578.

—— Ovid's Banquet of Sauce, a Coronet for his Mistress Philosophy, and his amorous Zodiac. Translated by G. Chapman. 1595.

—— The Remedie of Love. Translated and intituled to the Youth of England by F. L. 1600.

—— Salmacis and Hermaphroditus, translated by Fr. Beaumont. 1602.

Plato. Of the Knowledge which maketh a wise man. Translated by Sir Thomas Elyot; as appears by the proheme. 1533.

—— Axiochus, a Dialogue, attributed to Plato, translated by Edm. Spencer. Edinb., 1592. This was translated also by A. Munday.

Plautus. Menaechmi; a pleasaunt comoedie, taken oute of Plautus, by W. W. i.e. William Warner. 1595.

Pliny. Plinie's Natural Historie of the World translated into English by Dr. Philemon Holland. 1601.

Pliny the Younger. Certain selected Epistles oute of C. Plinius, translated oute of Latine into English, by Abraham Flemming: In his Panoplie of Epistles. 1576.

Plutarch. A righte noble and pleasant History of the Successors of Alexander surnamed the great, taken out of Diodorus Siculus: and some of their lives written by the wise Plutarch: translated out of French into Englysh by Thomas Stocker. 1568.

Plutarch. The Lives, translated from the French of Amyot, by Sir Tho. North. 1579. Rptd. in Tudor Translations with Introduction by Wyndham, G. 1895. Shakespeare's Plutarch, ed. Skeat, W. W. Oxford, 1875 ff.

—— The Philosophy, commonly called the Morals, translated into English, by Philemon Holland. 1603. Ed. Jacobs, Joseph, 1888; ed. Jevons, F. B., 1892.

Polybius. Hystories of the most famous worthy Cronographer, Polybius, translated by Christopher Watson. 1568.

Pomponius Mela. The Rare and Singuler worke. Translated by Arthur Golding. 1590.

Sallust. Here begynneth the famous Cronicle of warre, whyche the Romaynes hadde against Jugurth usurper of the Kyngedome of Numidie: whiche Cronicle is compiled in Latin by the renowned Romayne Saluste: and translated into Englyshe by syr Alexander Barklaye, prieste, and nowe perused and corrected by Thomas Paynell. 1557.

—— The Two most worthy and Notable Histories . . . viz. The Conspiracie of Cateline . . . and the Warre which Jugurth for many yeares maintained. . . . Translated by Thomas Heywood. 1608.

Seneca. A frutefull worke by L. A. Seneca, named the forme and rule of honest lyvynge, Latin and Englyshe. Lately translated, by Robert Whyttyngton, Poete laureate, and now newlye emprinted. 1546.

—— L. A. Senecæ ad Gallionem de remediis fortuitorum. The remedyes agaynst all casuall chaunces. Dialogus inter sensum & Rationem. A Dialogue between Sensualyte and Reason. Lately translated out of Latyn into Englyshe by Robert Whyttynton poet Laureate and nowe newely Imprynted. 1546.

—— Thyestes. Englished by Jasper Heywood. 1560.

—— Hercules Furens translated into English by Jasper Heywood. 1561.

—— Troas, translated by Jasper Heywood. 1561.

—— Oedipus translated by Alex. Nevyle. 1563.

—— The eyght Tragedie, entituled Agamemnon, translated out of Latin into English, by John Studley. 1566.

—— The Octavia, translated by Thomas Newce. 1581.

—— Thebais, translated by T. Newton. 1581.

—— The Woorke concerning Benefyting, that is to say the dooing, receyving, and requyting of good Turnes. Translated by A. Golding. 1558.

—— The Works of L. A. Seneca. Translated by Th. Lodge. 1614.

Suetonius. The Historie of Twelve Caesars, Emperours of Rome, written in Latine . . . and newly translated into English by Philemon Holland, togeather with a Marginall Glosse, and other briefe annotations thereupon. 1606. Rptd. in the series of Tudor Translations, with Introduction by Whibley, C. 1899.

Tacitus. The ende of Nero and beginning of Galba. Fower bookes of the Histories of C. Tacitus. The Life of Agricola, by H. Savile. 1598.

—— The Annals of C. Tacitus. The Description of Germany, by Richard Greneway. 1598.

Terence. Floures for Latine spekyng selected and gathered oute of Terence, and the same translated into Englysshe, etc. by Nicolas Udall. 1544.

—— Sentences of Terence. Printed in the house late Tho. Berthelettes. 1560.

—— Andria, carefully translated out of Latin, by Maurice Kyffin. 1582.

Terence. Terence in English. Fabulae comici facetissimi elegantissimi Poetae Terentii omnes Anglicae factae primumque hac nova forma nunc editae: opera ac industria R. B. in Axholmiensi insula Lincolnsherij Epivortheatis. R. B. is Richard Bernard. 1582.

Theocritus. Six Idillia, translated (anon.). Oxford, 1588. See Arber's English Garner, Some Longer Elizabethan Poems, ed. Bullen, A. H. 1903.

Theophrastus. See under Epictetus.

Thucydides. The hystory writtone by Thucidides the Athenyan . . . translated oute of the Frenche into the Englyshe language by Thomas Nicolls, Citezeine and Goldesmyth of London. 1550.

Vegetius. The Foure Bookes of Flavius Vegetius Renatus of Martiall policye. Translated by John Sadler. 1572.

Vergil. The First Foure Bookes of Virgils Aeneis. Translated into English Heroicall Verse, by Richard Stanyhurst: with other Poëticall devises thereto annexed. 1583.

—— The Seven first bookes of the Eneidos of Virgill, converted in Englishe meter by Thomas Phaer, Sollicitor to the King and Queenes majesties, attending their honourable counsaile in the Marches of Wales. 1558.

—— The Thirteene bookes of Aeneidos translated by Thomas Phaer. 1583. [Completed by Thomas Twyne, *i.e.* books XI–XIII.]

Xenophon. The Historie of Xenophon: containing the Ascent of Cyrus. Translated by J. Bingham. 1623.

—— Treatise of Householde. Translated by Gentian Hervet.

—— The VIII Books of Xenophon, containing the Institution of Cyrus. Translated by W. Bereker. 1567.

—— Cyropaedia. Translated by Philemon Holland. 1632. See also under Grisone.

TRANSLATIONS FROM MEDIEVAL AND CONTEMPORANEOUS AUTHORS

Alberti, L. B. Hecantonphila, The Art of Love or Love discovered in an hundred several kinds. 1598.

Aleman, Mathew. The Rogue: or the Life of Guzman de Alfarache. Translated by James Mabbe. 1623.

Alessio. A very excellent and profitable Booke conteining six hundred foure score and odde experienced Medicines. Translated out of Italian by Richard Androse. 1569.

Anglerius (Peter Martyr). The Decades of the New World or West India. Translated by Richard Eden. 1555.

—— Most learned and fruitfull Commentaries. Lately translated out of Latine into Englishe, by H. B. 1568.

Aretino. The Historie of Leonard Aretine, concerning the Warres betwene the Imperialles and the Gothes for the possession of Italy; a worke very pleasant and profitable; translated out of Latin into Englyshe by Arthur Goldyng. 1563.

Ariosto. Orlando Furioso in English Heroical Verse by Sir John Harington of Bathe, Knight. 1591.

—— Gli Soppositi. Translated by George Gascoigne with the title Supposes. 1556. Ed. by Cunliffe, J. W. Boston, 1906; Cambridge; 1907.

Augustine, St. A pretious booke of heavenlie meditations, called A Private Talke of the Soule with God. Translated by Thomas Rogers. 1581.

Augustine, St. Of the City of God. Translated by John Healey. 1610.
—— A Worke of the Predestination of Saints. Translated by N. Lesse.
     1550.
—— The Confessions. Translated by Sir Tobie Matthew. 1620.
Avila y Zuniga, Luis de, Comentaries of, which treateth of the great wars
     in Germany, made by Charles V. Translated by John Wilkinson. 1555.
B., F. N.   A Certain Tragedy written first in Italian by F. N. B. entitled
     Free Will, and translated into English by Henry Cheeke.   n.d.
Bandello.   Certaine Tragicall Discourses written oute of Frenche and Latin
     by Geffraie Fenton.   1567.   Rptd. in the series of Tudor Translations,
     with Introduction by Douglas, R. L.   1898.
        Broke, Arthur (d. 1563), translated his Romeus and Julieit from
     Bandello, through the French version of 1559.   1562.   [The source of
     Shakespeare's plot.]
Bartello.   The Pleasant Fable of Ferdinando Jeronimi and Leonora de
     Valasco translated out of the Italian riding tales by George Gascoigne,
     in his Posies.   1575.   Rptd. by Cunliffe, J. W.   1907.
Boccaccio.   A treatise excellent and compendious . . . the falles of sundry
     Princes Translated by Dan John Lidgate, newly imprynted and aug-
     mented.   1554.
—— Philocopo.   Translated by H. Grantham.   1566.
—— Amorous Frainmetta.   Translated by B. Yong.   1587.
—— The Modell of Wit, Mirth, Eloquence and Conversation framed in Ten
     Dayes. . . .   Preserved to Posterity by the Renowned John Boccaccio
     . . . and now translated into English.   1620.   This is the first complete
     translation.   Rptd. in the Series of Tudor Translations with Introduction
     by Hutton, E.   1909.
Boccaccio and Bandello.   Ten Tales, eight by Boccaccio, two by Bandello,
     with the title Tragical Tales, translated by Turbervile in time of his
     troubles out of sundry Italians, with the argument and lenvoye of eche
     tale.   1587.   Versions of Boccaccio's Tales may be found in other
     collections, such as Painter's Palace of Pleasure, and H. C.'s Forest of
     Fancy (1579).
Boehme, Johann.   The Fardle of Facions conteninge the aunciente maners
     of the partes of the earth, called Affricke and Asie.   Translated by
     W. Watreman.   1555.
—— The manners, lawes, and customs of all nations . . . newly translated
     into English by E. Aston.   1611.
Boethius.   Translated by George Colville, 1556.   Ed. Bax, E. Belford.   1897.
     See, also, Queen Elizabeth's Englishings of Boethius, Plutarch, etc., ed.
     Pemberton, C., 1899.
Boiardo, M.   Orlando Innamorato.   The first three Books . . . done into
     English Historical Verse by R(obert) T(ofte).   1598.
Botero, G.   The Traveller's Breviat.   Translated by Robert Johnson.   1601.
—— A Treatise concerning the Causes of the Magnificence and Greatness of
     Cities . . . done into English by Robert Peterson.   1606.
Braunschweig, H.   A most excellent apothecarye.   Translated by J. Holly-
     bush.   1561.
Brenz, J.   A verye fruitful exposicion upon the syxte Chapter of Saynte
     John . . . translated by Richard Shirrye.   1549.
Caius, J.   Of Englishe Dogges . . . drawne into Englishe by Abraham
     Fleming.   1576.

Calahorra, Diego Ortuñez de. The Mirrour of princely deedes and knighthood. Translated by Margaret Tiler. 1579.

Calvin, John. A Harmonie upon the three Evangelistes Matthewe, Marke, and Luke, with the commentarie of M. John Calvine. Faithfully translated into English by E. P. Whereunto is also added a Commentarie upon . . . Saint John, by the same Author. 1610.

—— A Commentarie of John Calvaine, upon the first booke of Moses called Genesis. Translated by Thomas Tymme, Minister. 1578.

—— The sermons of M. John Calvin upon the Epistle of S. Paule too the Ephesians. Translated by Arthur Golding. 1577.

—— The institution of Christian Religion. . . . Translated by T. Norton. 1561.

—— Commentaries upon the Prophet Daniell. Translated by Arthur Golding. 1570.

—— A Commentarie upon the Booke of Josue, finished a little before his death: translated out of Latine into Englishe by W. F. 1578.

—— A faythful and moste Godly Treatyse concernynge the sacrament. Translated into Englishe by M. Coverdale . . . whereunto is added the order that the Church in Denmarke doth use. 1546(?).

—— The Forme of Common Praiers. Translated by William Huyche. With Preface by T. Broke. 1550.

Camden, William. Britain, or a chorographicall description of the most flourishing Kingdomes, England, Scotland and Ireland. Translated from the Latin by Philemon Holland. 1610.

Cardano, Girolamo. Cardanus Comfort. Translated into English by T. Bedingfield. 1573.

Cartier, J. A Short and Briefe Narration of the Two Navigations and Discoveries to the North-weast Partes called New Fraunce. First translated out of French into Italian by that famous learned Man, Geo. Bapt. Ramutius, and now turned into English by John Florio. 1580.

Castanheda, Hernan Lopes de. Historie of the discoverie and conquest of the East Indias enterprised by the Portingales. Translated by Nicholas Lichfield. 1582.

Castiglione, Baldessar. The Courtyer, done into Englyshe by Thomas Hoby. 1561. Rptd. in series of Tudor Translations, with Introduction by Raleigh, W. 1899.

Cataneo, Girolamo. Most Briefe Tables to know readily how many ranks of footmen armed with corselets, as unarmed, go to the making of a just battle. Translated by H(enry?) G(rantham?). 1574.

Ceriol, Federico Furió. Treatise declaring howe many counsels and what manner of counselers a prince that will governe well ought to have. Translated by Thomas Blundeville. 1570.

Cervantes, Miguel de. The History of the Valorous and Wittie Knight-Errant Don Quixote of the Mancha. Translated by Thomas Shelton. 1612. 1620. Rptd. in the Series of Tudor Translations, with Introduction by Kelly, J. Fitzmaurice. 1896. [The Exemplary Novels were trans. by James Mabbe, 1640.]

Chartier, Alain. Delectable demandes and pleasaunt Questions, with their several aunswers in matters of Love, Naturall causes, morall and politique devises. Newly translated out of French. 1566.

Cinthio, Giraldi. Several of the stories in his Hecatommithi were trans. by George Whetstone under the title An Heptameron of Civill Discourses. 1582.

Coignet, Matthieu. Politique Discourses on trueth and lying. An instruction to Princes to keepe their faith and promise. . . . Translated out of French . . . by Sir E. Hoby. 1586.

Commines, Philippe de. The Historie. Translated by Thomas Danett. 1596. Rptd. in the series of Tudor Translations, with Introduction by Whibley, C. 1897.

Conestaggio, G. The History of the Uniting of the Kingdom of Portugall to the Crown of Castile. . . . Translated by Edward Blount. 1600.

Contarini, G. The Commonwealth and Government of Venice, written by the Cardinal Gaspar Contarin. Translated by Lewis Lewkenor. 1599.

Corte, Claudio. The Art of Riding. . . . Translated by Thomas Bedingfield. 1584.

Cortés, Martin. The Arte of navigation. Translated by Richard Eden. 1561.

Dedekind, Frederick. The Schoole of Slovenrie: or Cato turn'd wrong side outward, translated by R. F. from Grobianus. 1605.

Desportes, Philippe. Rodomanths Infernall, or the Devill conquered. Paraphrastically translated by G. M(arkham). 1607.

Doni. The Moral Philosophie: drawne out of the auncient writers. A work first compiled in the Indian tongue, and afterwardes reduced into divers other languages: and now lastly Englished out of the Italian by Thomas North. 1570. Ed. Jacobs, J. 1888.

Du Bartas. His Divine weekes and workes translated by Josuah Sylvester, Gent. 1605–6. [See also Thomas Hudson's Historie of Judith, 1584]

Du Bellay, G. Instructions for the Warres. Translated by Paul Ive. 1589.

Erasmus, Desiderius. The seconde tome or volume of the Paraphrase upon the newe testament. Translated by Myles Coverdale and J. Olde. 1549.

—— The Complaint of peace. Wryten in Latyn by the famous Clerke Erasmus. And truely translated into Englishe by Thomas Paynell. 1559.

—— Two dyalogues wryten in Latin by the famous Clerke D. Erasmus, one called Polyphemus . . . the other dysposyng of thinges and names, translated in the Englyshe by E. Becke. 1550.

—— The Apophthegmes of Erasmus, translated into English by Nicolas Udall. 1542.

—— The Praise of Folie. Translated by Sir T. Chaloner. 1549.

—— Proverbes or Adagies gathered out of the Chiliades of Erasmus by Richard Taverner, with newe addicions as well of Latin Proverbes as of Englishe. 1550.

—— The first Tome of the Paraphrase of Erasmus upon the newe Testamente. 1548. (The text is that of Taverner's Bible and the Paraphrase was translated for the most part by Nicolas Udall.)

Estienne, Henri. The Stage of Popish Toyes, Conteining both Magicall and Comicall partes. Collected out of H. Stephanus in his Apologie upon Herodot. Compiled by G(eorge) N(orth). 1581. [But as to the authorship, see Mark Pattison's essay The Stephenses.]

—— A mervaylous Discourse upon the Lyfe, deedes, and behaviour of Katherine de Medicis. 1578.

—— A World of Wonders. Translated by R. C. 1607.

Fernandez, Jerónimo. The Honour of chivalrie, set downe in the . . . historie of the magnanimous and heroike Don Bellianis. Translated by L. A. 1598.

Fonseca, Jeronymo Osorio da. The five Books of . . . Hieronims Osorius, contayning a discussion of civill and Christian nobilitie. Translated by William Blandy. 1576.

Galen, Claudius. Certaine Workes, . . . called Methodus Medendi. . . . Translated into English by Thomas Gale. 1586.

Galvão, Antonio de. The Discoveries of the world from their first original unto the yeere of our Lord 1555. Translated anonymously. 1601.

Gelli, Giovanni Battista. The Fearful Fancies of the Florentine Cooper. . . . Translated by W. Barker. 1568.

—— Circes. Translated by Henry Iden. 1557.

Gentillet, Innocent. A discourse upon the meanes of well governing and maintaining in good peace, a Kingdome, or other principalitie. Against Nicholas Machivell the Florentine. Translated into English by Simon Patericke. 1602.

Gesner, Conrad. The newe Jewell of Health . . . published in Englishe by G. Baker. 1576.

—— The Historie of the Foure-Footed Beastes. Describing the true and lively figure of every Beast, with a discourse of their severall Names, Conditions, Kindes, Vertues. Translated by Edward Topsell. 1607.

Giovio, Paolo. The worthy tract of Paulus Jovius, Containing a Discourse of rare inventions both military and amorous called Imprese. Translated by Samuel Daniel. 1585.

Giraldo, Baptista. A Discourse of Civill Life. Trans. Lodowick Bryskett. 1606. (Made some years before.)

Gómara, Francisco Lopez de. Historie of the conquest of the Weast India, now called Newe Spayne. Translated by Thomas Nicholas. 1578.

Granada, Luis de. A memoriall of a Christian life; wherein are treated all such thinges, as apperteyne unto a Christian to doe, from the beginninge of his conversion, until the ende of his perfection. Translated by Richard Hopkins. 1586.

—— Of Prayer and meditation; wherein is conteyned fowertien devoute meditations for the seven daies of the weeke, bothe for the morninges and eveninges. And in them is treyted of the consideration of the principall holie mysteries of our faithe. Translated by Richard Hopkins. 1582.

—— A Paradise of prayers gathered out of the works of L. de Granada. Translated by Thomas Lodge. 1601.

—— Devotion. Translated by Francis Meres. 1598.

Grisone. A new booke containing the art of riding and breaking great horses. . . . Translated by Thomas Blundeville. n.d.

—— The Art of Riding . . . out of Xenophon and Gryson Verie expert and excellent horsemen. Translated by John Astley. 1584.

Guarini, Battista. Il Pastor Fido or the faithful Shepherd. Translated by Edward Dymock. 1602

Guazzo, Stephen. The Civile Conversation . . . foure bookes, the first three translated out of French by G. Pettie. . . . In the fourth a Banquet translated by B. Young. 1586.

Guevara, Antonio de. Golden Epistles . . . gathered as well out of the remainder of Guevara's works as other authors, Latin, French and Italian. Translated by G. Fenton. 1575.

—— Golden Boke of Marcus Aurelius. Translated by J. Bourchier, Lord Berners. 1546.

—— Dispraise of the Life of a Courtier. Translated by Sir F. Bryan. 1541.

—— The Diall of princes. Translated by Sir Thomas North. 1557.

—— A Chronicle, conteyning the lives of tenne Emperours of Rome. . . . Translated out of Spanish into English by Edward Hellowes. 1577.

Guevara, Antonio de. A Booke of the invention of the arte of navigation.
  Translated by Edward Hellowes. 1578.
—— Familiar Epistles. Translated by Edward Hellowes. 1574.
Guicciardini, F. The History of Guicciardin, containing the Wars of Italy. . . .
  Translated by Geoffrey Fenton. 1579.
—— The Description of the Low Countries. Translated by Th. Danett. 1593.
Huarte, Juan. The Examination of men's wits. Translated by Richard
  Carew. 1594.
Hurault, Jaques. Politicke Moral and Martial Discourses translated by
  Arthur Golding. 1595.
Hurtado, Luis. Palmerin of England. Translated by Anthony Munday. 1581.
Hyspanus (Petrus). The Treasuri of Helth, contaynynge many profytable
  Medicines . . . translated into English by Humfre Lloyd. 1585(?).
La Noue, François de. The Declaration of the Lord de la Noue, upon his
  taking arms for the just defence of the Townes of Sedan and Jametz.
  Truely translated according to the French copie printed at Verdun
  by A. N. 1589.
—— The Politicke and militarie discourses of the Lord de la Noue. Where-
  unto are adjoined certaine observations of the same author, of things
  happened during the three late civill warres of France. All faithfully
  translated out of the French by E. A. (i.e. Edward Aggas). 1587.
La Primaudaye, Pierre de. The French Academie wherin is discussed the
  institution of manners, newly translated by T. B. 1586.
Leo Africanus. A Geographical Historie of Africa written in Arabicke and
  Italian by John Leo a More, borne in Granada and brought up in Bar-
  barie. Translated by John Pory. 1600.
Llwyd, H. The Breviary of Britayne . . . Englished by Thomas Twyne.
  1573.
Lobeira, Vasco de. The moste excellent and pleasant Booke, entituled the
  Treasurie of Amadis of Fraunce. Translated by Thomas Paynell. 1567.
Lomazzo, G. P. A Tracte Containing the Artes of Curious Painting, Carving,
  and Building. Englished by R(ichard) H(aydocke). 1598.
Lopes, Duarte. A Report of the Kingdome of Congo. Translated by Abra-
  ham Hartwell the younger. 1597.
Luther, Martin. Every-dayes sacrifice. Wherein are comprehended many
  comfortable Prayers and Meditations, very necessary for all Christians.
  . . . Written by D. M. Luther, a little before his end. Translated by
  W. R. S. 1624.
—— A Treatise Touching the Libertie of a Christian. . . . Translated
  by James Bell. 1579.
—— The chiefe and pryncypall Articles of the Christen faythe . . . with
  other thre very profitable . . . bokes. . . . (A singular . . . maner of
  prayeng.) 1548.
—— Special and chosen sermons. . . . Englished by W. G(ace). 1578.
—— A commentarie of doctor martin luther upon the epistle of S. Paul to
  the Galathians, first collected and gathered word by word out of his
  preaching, and now out of Latine faithfully translated into English for
  the unlearned. . . . 1575.
—— A commentarie upon the xv. psalmes, called Psalmi gradum, that is,
  psalmes of Degrees: Faithfully copied out of the lectures of D. Martin
  Luther, very fruitfull and comfortable for all Christian afflicted consciences to read. Translated by Henry Bull. 1537.

Machiavelli, Nicolo. The Florentine Historie, translated into English by Thomas Bedingfield. 1595.

—— The Arte of Warre, set forthe in Englishe by Peter Whitehorne, student at Graies Inne. 1560. Both rptd. in the series of Tudor Translations, with Introduction by Cust, H., 1905, together with The Prince, translated by Edward Dacres, 1661.

Mantuanus. The eclogues of the poet B. Mantuan. Translated by George Turbervile. 1597.

Maraffi, B. The pretie and wittie Historie of Arnalte and Lucenda. Translated by Claudius Hollyband from B. Maraffi's Italian version of a Greek original. 1575.

Marco Polo. Travels of Marcus Paulus. Translated by John Frampton. 1579.

Medina, Pedro de. The Arte of navigation. Translated by John Frampton. 1581.

Mediolano, Johannes de. Regimen Sanitatis Salerni. Translated into englyshe by Thomas Paynell. 1557. And by Philemon Holland. 1649.

Melanchthon, Philip. A Godly treatyse of Prayer. Translated by John Bradforde about 1551.

—— A waying and considering of the Interim. . . . Translated . . . by John Rogers. 1548.

—— A newe work cōcerning both partes of the sacrament to be receyved of the lay people as wel under the kind off wine as under the kind off bread with certan other articles cōcerning the masse and the auctorite off bisshops the chapters whereof are cōteined in the next leafe made by Philip Melancthon and newly translated out off latyn. 1543.

—— A very godly defense . . . defending the mariage of Preistes . . . sent unto the Kyng of England Henry the aight trāslated . . . by lewes beuchame. 1541.

Mendoza, Bernardino de. Theorique and practice of warre. Translated by Edward Hoby. 1597.

Mendoza, Diego Hurtado de [?]. The pleasant History of Lazarillo de Tormes. Translated by David Rowland. 1576.

Mexia, Pedro. The Historie of all the Romane Emperors. Translated by William Traperon. 1601.

—— Dialogue concerning phisicke and phisitions. Translated by Thomas Newton. 1580.

—— The Forest, or collection of historyes. Translated by Thomas Fortescue. 1571.

Minadoi, G. T. The History of the Warres between the Turkes and the Persians. Translated by Abraham Hartwell. 1595.

Monardes, Nicolas. Joyfull Newes out of the newe founde worlde. Translated by John Frampton. 1577.

Montaigne, Michel de. Essayes, done into English by John Florio. 1603. Ed. Saintsbury, G., Tudor Translations, 6 vols. 1892–3; ed. Waller, A. R. 6 vols. 1897.

Montalvo, García Ordoñez de. Amadis de Gaule. Translated by A. Munday. 1589.

—— The Treasurie of Amadis of Fraunce, translated by Thomas Paynel. 1568.

Montano, Reginaldo Gonzalez. A Discovery and playne declaration of sundry subtill practices of the Holy Inquisition of Spayne. Translated by Vincent Skinner. 1568.

Montemayor, Gorge de. Diana. Translated by Bartholomeu Yong. 1598.
[Also by Sir Thomas Wilson (1560?–1629) B. M. Addit. MSS., 18638.]
—— Eglogs, epytaphes, and Sonettes, translated by Barnaby Googe. 1563.
Mornay, Philippe de. The Defense of Death. Containing a most excellent
discourse of life and death. Doone into English by E(dward) A(ggas).
1577.
—— A Voluble Treatise of the Church, in which are handled all the principall
questions, that have been mooved in our time, concerning that matter.
Translated out of French into English by J. Fielde. 1580.
—— A Woorke Concerning the trewnesse of the Christian Religion, Begunne
to be translated into English by Sir P. Sidney, and finished by A. Golding.
1587.
—— Discourse of Life and Death. Antonius a Tragedie written also in
French by R. Garnier. Both done in English by the Countesse of Pem-
broke. 1592.
Nannini, Remigio. Civil Considerations upon Many and Sundry Histories
. . . containing rules and precepts for Princes, Commonwealths, . . .
Translated in English by W. T. from the French translation by Gabriel
Chappuys. 1601.
Ochino, B. Fourteen Sermons of Bernardine Ochyne concerning the
predestination and election of God. Translated by A(nne) C(ooke).
1550(?).
—— Sermons. Translated by R. Argentine. 1548.
—— A tragoedie or Dialoge of the unjuste usurped primacie of the Bishop of
Rome. Translated by John Ponet. 1549. Rptd. 1899, ed. Plumptre,
C. E.
—— Certain godly and very profitable Sermons of Faith, Hope, and Charity.
Translated by William Phiston. 1580.
Painter, William. The Palace of Pleasure. Beautified, adorned and well
furnished, with pleasaunt Histories and excellent Nouvelles, selected
out of divers good and commendable Authors. 1566–7, 1575 (authorised
ed.). Ed. Jacobs, J. 3 vols. 1890.
Paleario, Aonio. Of the Benefit that true Christians Receive by the Death of
Jesus Christ. Translated by Edward Courtenay, Earl of Devonshire.
1548.
Palingenius, Marcellus. The first six Books of the Most Christian Poet,
Marcellus Palingenius called the Zodiak of Lyfe. Translated by Barnaby
Googe. 1561.
Palmerin d'Oliva. Translated by Anthony Munday, from an unknown
Spaniard. 1588. [See D. of N. B. for a list of Anthony Munday's
further translations.]
Petrarch. Phisicke against Fortune. Translated by Thomas Twyne. 1579.
—— Trionfi. Translated by Henry Parker, lord Morley, c. 1553. Pub.
Roxburghe Club. 1887.
Philibert of Vienne. The Philosopher of the Court. . . . Englished by
George North, Gentleman. 1575.
Rogas, Fernando de. The Spanish Bawd represented in Celestina, or the
Tragicke-Comedy of Calisto and Melibea. Translated by James Mabbe.
1632. Rptd. in the Series of Tudor Translations, with Introduction by
Kelly, J. Fitzmaurice. 1894.
Romei, Annibale. The Courtier's Academie. Translated by John Kepers.
1598.

Sansovino, F. The Quintessence of Wit. Translated by Robert Hitchcock. 1590.

Sarpi, Paolo. The Cruell Subtilty of Ambitioin, discovered in a discourse concerning the King of Spaines Surprizing The Valteline. Translated by the Renowned Sir Thomas Roe. 1628–1650.

—— Historie of the Councel of Trent. Translated by N. Brent. 1620.

Serres, J. de. The Thre Parts of Commentaries of the Civill Warres of Fraunce. Translated by Thomas Timme. 1574. The fourth parte. 1576.

—— The Lyfe of the most godly Jasper Colignie Shatilion. Translated by Arthur Golding.

—— A general Inventorie of the History of France. Translated by Edward Grimeston. 1607. [See Boas, F. S., Modern Philology, vol. III, April, 1906.]

Silva, Juan de. The description of Portugall, of the East Indies, The isles of Terceses. 1600.

Silvaine, A. See under Livy.

Sleidanus, Johannes. A famouse Cronicle of oure Time. Translated by Jhon Daus. 1560.

Solinus, Julius. The excellent and pleasant worke. Translated by Arthur Golding. 1587.

Tartaglia, N. Three Books of Colloquies concerning the Art of Shooting in great and small pieces of Artillery. Translated by Cyprian Lucar. 1588.

Tasso. Godfrey of Bulloigne or the Recoverie of Hierusalem. An heroicall poeme translated into English by Richard Carew, Esquire. 1594.

—— Godfrey of Bulloigne or the Recoverie of Jerusalem. Done into English Heroicall verse by Edward Fairfax, gent. 1600.

Torquemada, Antonio de. The Spanish Mandevile of miracles. Translated by Ferdinand Walker. 1600.

Ulenspiegel. Howleglass. Here beginneth a merye jest of a man called Howleglass, and of many marvelous thinges and jestes that he did in his lyffe, etc. Translated by William Copland. 1560 (?).

Valdés, Francisco de. The Serjeant major. Translated by John Thorius. 1590.

Vasquez, Francisco. History of Palmendos. Translated by Anthony Munday. 1589.

—— Primaleon of Greece. Translated by Anthony Munday. 1589.

Vega, Luis Gutierres de la. De Re militari; containing principall orders to be observed in martiall affaires. Translated by Nicholas Lichfield. 1582.

Viret, P. A notable collection of . . . places of the Sacred Scriptures. Translated by Anthony Scoloker. 1548. Cf. also A. S.'s trans. from the German of A goodly Dysputation betwene a Christen Shomaker and a Popyshe Parson, 1548.

Vives, Juan Luis. Private Prayers and meditations, translated by John Bradford. 1559.

—— The office and duetie of an husband. Translated by Thomas Paynel. 1553.

—— Godly Meditations, translated by John Bradford. 1562.

Zárate, Augustin de. History of the discoverie and conquest of the provinces of Peru, in the South Sea. Translated by Thomas Nicholas. 1581.

Zwingli, Ulrich.   Certeyne Preceptes.   Translated by Richarde Argentine.
    1548.
    The following translators may also be mentioned:
Partridge, John (*fl.* 1566).   Translator of romances into verse.   See Collier's
    Illustrations of Old English Literature, 1866.
Robert Smith's Strange Lamentable and Tragical Histories.   Trans. from
    French.   1577.
Twyne, Lawrence (*fl.* 1576).   Patterne of Painefull Adventures.   1576,
    c. 1595, 1607.   [One of the sources of Pericles.]

AUTHORITIES

Ascham, Roger.   The Scholemaster.   1570.
Cunliffe, J. W.   The Influence of Seneca on Elizabethan Tragedy.   1893.
Einstein, Lewis.   The Italian Renaissance in England.   1902.
Farmer, Richard.   An Essay on the Learning of Shakespeare.   1767.
Hall, Bishop.   See bibliography to Chap. XVI.
Harris, W. J.   The First Printed Translations into English of the Great
    Foreign Classics.   n.d.   [1909.]
Harvey, Gabriel.   Correspondence with Spenser.   1579–80.
Herford, C. H.   Studies in the Literary Relations of England and Germany
    in the Sixteenth Century.   1886.
Elizabethan Sonnets, with an introduction by Sidney Lee.   1904.
Meres, Francis.   Palladis Tamia.   1598.
Moss, J. W.   A Manual of Classical Bibliography.   1824.
Nashe, Thomas, The Works of.   Ed. McKerrow, R. B.   1904 ff.
Puttenham, George [?].   The Arte of English Poesie.   1589.
Scott, M. A.   Elizabethan translations from the Italian: the titles of such
    works now first collected and arranged, with annotations.   Mod. Lang.
    Ass. of America, vols. X, XI, XIII, XIV.
Smith, G. Gregory (ed).   Elizabethan Critical Essays.   1904.
Snell, F. J.   The Age of Transition.   Vol. II.   1905.
Ancient Translations from Classic Authors.   Drawn up by Steevens and
    printed in Malone's Prolegomena to Shakespeare.   1790.
Tucker, T. G.   The Foreign Debt of English Literature.   1907.
Underhill, John Garrett.   Spanish Literature in the England of the Tudors.
    1899.
Upham, A. H.   The French Influence in English Literature from the Ac-
    cession of Elizabeth to the Restoration.   New York, 1909.
Webbe, William.   A discourse of English Poetrie.   1586.
Whibley, C.   Literary Portraits.   1904.   [Montaigne, etc.]

CHAPTER II

THE AUTHORISED VERSION AND ITS INFLUENCE

[See bibliographies to Volume II, Chapter II, and Volume III, Chapter III.
    The following works may, also, be mentioned here.]

Authorised Version.   The Translators' Preface.
Caxton, William.   The Golden Legend.   Ed. Ellis, F. S.   7 vols.   1900 ff.
Cheyne, T. K. and Black, J. S.   Encyclopaedia Biblica.   1899 ff.

Cook, A. S.   The Bible and English Prose Style.   Boston, 1892.
—— Biblical Quotations in Old English Prose Writers.   1898.
—— The Christ of Cynewulf.   Boston, 1900.   Albion Series.
Gardiner, J. H.   The Bible as English Literature.   1906.
Gasquet, F. A.   The Old English Bible and other Essays.   1897.
Halsey, L. J.   The Literary Attractions of the Bible.   1889.
Hastings, J.   Dictionary of the Bible.   Edinburgh, 1898 ff.
Konig, E.   Stilistik, Rhetorik, Poetik in Bezug auf die biblische Litteratur.
     Leipzig, 1900.
Lightfoot, J. B.   On a fresh Revision of the English New Testament.   1871.
     New York.   1873.
Loftie, W. J.   A Century of Bibles or the Authorised Version from 1611 to
     1711.   1872.
MacCulloch, J. M.   Literary Characteristics of the Holy Scriptures.   1845.
Marsh, G. P.   Lectures on the English Language.   New York, 1863.
Mombert, J. I.   English Versions of the Bible.   1907.
Moulton, R. G.   The Literary Study of the Bible.   1899.
—— The Modern Reader's Bible.   The books of the Bible with three books
     of the Apocrypha presented in modern literary form.   1907.
Petty, W. T.   An Essay upon the influence of the translation of the Bible
     upon English Literature.   1830.
Revised Version.   The Revisers' Preface.
Scrivener, F. H. A.   The Authorised Edition of the English Bible, 1611, its
     subsequent reprints and modern representatives.   Cambridge, 1884.
Westcott, B. F.   A General View of the History of the English Bible.   Rev.
     by Aldis Wright, W.   1905.
Wright, W. Aldis (ed.).   The Authorised Version of the English Bible,
     1611.   5 vols.   Cambridge English Classics.   1909.   [A literal reprint,
     with a list of variations between the two issues of 1611.]

CHAPTER III

SIR WALTER RALEGH

[Students should consult the second edition of Dr. Brushfield's admirable
bibliography (see below).   It is quite indispensable.   The writer of this
chapter and the editors of the History are much indebted to Dr. Brushfield for kindly placing his work at their disposal in respect of some
of the entries in the following brief list.]

Judicious and Select Essayes and Observations by . . . Sir Walter Raleigh
     upon
          (a)   The first Invention of Shipping.
          (b)   The Misery of Invasive Warre.
          (c)   The Navy Rouall and Sea-Service.
          (d)   Apologie for his voyage to Guiana.   Portrait.   1650, 1667.
Remains of Sir Walter Ralegh.   1651, 1656, 1657 ff.
     The title of the 1651 edition is Sir Walter Raleigh's Sceptick or Specula-
tions.   And Observations of the Magnificency and Opulency of Cities, his
Seat of Government And Letters to the King's Majestie, and others of
Qualitie.   Also his Demeanor before his Execution.
     The title of the 1656 edition is Maxims of State.   With instructions to
his Son, and the Son's advice to his aged Father.   Whereunto is added

Observations touching Trade and Commerce with the Hollander and other Nations, Proving that our Sea and Land Commodities inrich and strengthen other Countries against our own.

The Remains include the following articles, but some are omitted in certain editions:

> Maxims of State.
> Advice to his Son: his Son's advice to his Father.
> Observations concerning the magnificency and opulency of Cities.
> Seat of Government.
> Observations concerning Trade and Commerce with the Hollander.
> Poems.
> Speech immediately before he was beheaded.
> Letters to divers persons of quality (in all eds.).
> The Prerogative of Parliaments.

The edition of 1657 is the first that bears the title, Remains of Sir Walter Raleigh.

Three discourses of Sr. Walter Ralegh:

> I. Of a War with Spain and our Protecting the Netherlands.
> II. Of the Original and Fundamental Cause of . . . War.
> III. Of Ecclesiastical Power.
> Published by Phillip Ralegh, Esq., his only Grandson. 1702.

The Works of Sir Walter Raleigh, Kt., Political, Commercial, and Philosophical; together with his Letters and Poems. The whole never before collected together, and some never yet printed, to which is prefix'd a new account of his Life by Tho. Birch. 2 vols. Portrait. 1751.

The Works of Sir Walter Ralegh, Kt., now first collected; to which are prefixed the Lives of the Author, by Oldys and Birch. Oxford, 1829. 8 vols.

Apologie for his voyage to Guiana. 1650.

The Discoverie of the large, rich and bewtiful Empyre of Guiana, with a relation of the Great and Golden Citie of Manoa (which the Spanyards call El Dorado) And of the Provinces of Emeria, Arromaia, Amapaia, and other Countries, with their rivers adjoyning. 4to. 1596. Reprinted in Hakluyt's Voyages, III (1598). See also Voyages of the Elizabethan Seamen, ed. Payne, E. J., 1880. Ed. Schomburgk, Sir R. H. (Hakluyt Society, vol. for 1848), with copious notes, a life of Ralegh and some hitherto unpublished documents.

A Discourse of Sea Ports; principally of the Port and Haven of Dover. 1700. Reprinted in Harleian Miscellany, IV (1744), X (1810).

A Discourse of Tenures, which were before the Conquest. Gutch, J., Collectanea Curiosa. 1781.

An Essay on Ways and Means to maintain the Honour and Safety of England, to encrease Trade, etc. 1701.

The History of the World. In Five Bookes. 1614. Licensed to Walter Burre, 15 April, 1611. (For later editions see Brushfield.) The History of the World in five books. By Sir Walter Ralegh, Kt., printed from a copy revis'd by himself. To which is prefixed the Life of the Author, newly compil'd from Materials more ample and authentick than have yet been publish'd; by Mr. Oldys. Also his Trial, with some Additions: together with A new and more copious Index. 2 vols. Folio. 1736.

An Abridgment of Sir Walter Raleigh's History of the World. In five
books. To which is added

- (a) His Premonition to Princes.
- (b) Of the first invention of shipping.
- (c) A Relation of the Action at Cadiz.
- (d) A Dialogue between a Jesuite and a Recusant.
- (e) An Apology for his unlucky Voyage to Guiana.

Publish'd by Phillip Raleigh. 1698 ff.

The Interest of England with regard to foreign alliances, explained in two
Discourses. I. Concerning a Match propounded by the Savoyan be-
tween the Lady Elizabeth and the Prince of Piemont. II. Touching a
Marriage between Prince Henry of England and a Daughter of Savoy.
By Sir Walter Rawleigh, Knt. 1750.

An Introduction to a Breviary of the History of England, with the Reign of
King William the I entitled the Conqueror. 1693. (It is very uncertain
whether this is by Ralegh.)

Observations, touching Trade and Commerce with the Hollander, and other
Nations, as it was presented to K. James. 1653.

The Poems of Sir Walter Raleigh now first collected. With a Biographical and Critical Introduction: by Sir Egerton Brydges. 1813,
1814.

Poems by Sir Henry Wotton, Sir Walter Raleigh and others. Edited by
John Hannah. 1845, etc. See also Hannah's Courtly Poets, 1870, etc.

The Prerogative of Parliaments in England Proved in a Dialogue (pro and
contra) betweene a Councellour of State and a Justice of Peace. 4to.
Midelburge, 1628; Hamburgh, 1628. Reprinted in all editions of
the Remains from 1657.

The Prince, or Maxims of State. Written by Sir Walter Rawley, and presented to Prince Henry. 1672.

A Report of the truth of the fight about the Isles of Acores, this last Sommer.
Betwixt the Revenge, one of her Majesties Shippes, and an Armada of
the King of Spaine. 4to. 1591. Reprinted in Hakluyt's Voyages
(1598–60), Pinkerton's Voyages (1808), Somers's Collection of Tracts
(1809) and in English Reprints by Arber, E.

To-day a man, To-morrow none: or Sir Walter Rawleigh's Farewell to his
Lady, the night before hee was beheaded. Together with his advice con-
cerning Her and her Sonne. 1644. Reprinted in Ashbee's Occasional.
. . . Reprints (in facsimile), No. 26, 1872; in the Old Book Collector's
Miscellany, by Hindley, C. (1873), etc.

Brushfield, T. N. Bibliography of Sir Walter Ralegh. Exeter. Second
ed. with notes revised and enlarged. 1908.

Cayley, A. The Life of Sir Walter Ralegh. 2 vols. 1805.

Creighton, Louise. Life of Sir Walter Ralegh. 1877.

Edwards, Edward. The Life of Sir Walter Ralegh, together with his letters
now first collected. 2 vols. 1868.

Gosse, Edmund. Raleigh. 1886.

Hennessy, Sir John Pope. Sir Walter Ralegh in Ireland. 1883.

Kingsley, C. Sir Walter Raleigh and his Time. 1880.

St. John, James Augustus. Life of Sir Water Raleigh. 1868.

Selincourt, H. de. Great Ralegh. 1908.

Stebbing, William. Sir Walter Ralegh. Oxford, 1891.

Stephen, H. L.   State Trials.   Vol. 1.   1899.

[Cf., also, the political writings of Thomas Scott (1580?–1626), for list of
which see D. of N. B.; and Thomas Harriot's New-Found Land of Virginia.
1588.]

CHAPTERS IV AND V

THE LITERATURE OF THE SEA
AND
SEAFARING AND TRAVEL

Allison, Thomas.   An Account of a Voyage from Archangel in Russia in the
    year 1697.   Of the ship and company wintering near the North Cape,
    their manner of living, and what they suffered by the extreme cold.
    1699.   (Reprinted in Pinkerton's Voyages.)
Archdeacon, Daniel.   A True Discourse of the Armie which the King of
    Spaine Caused to bee assembled in the Haven of Lisbon, in the Kingdom
    of Portugall, in the Yeare 1588, against England.   Trans.   1588.
Ashe, Thomas.   Carolina; or a Description of the Present State of that
    Country, and the Natural Excellencies thereof.   1682.
Ashley, Anthony.   The Mariner's Mirrour.   An English translation of the
    Speculum Nauticum by Lucas Wagenaar (published in 1583).   1588.
Bedwell, William.   The Way to Geometry, being necessary and usefull for
    Astronomers, Geographers, Land-Meters, Sea-Men, Engineers, Archi-
    tecks, Carpenters, Paynters, Carvers, etc.   (Translated from the Latin
    of Peter Ramus.)   1636.
Best, George.   A true discourse of the late voyages of discoverie for the
    finding of a passage to Cathaya by the north-weast under the conduct
    of Martin Frobisher, Generall.   1578.
Bilberg, John.   A Voyage of the late King of Sweden, and another of the
    Mathematicians sent by him, in which are discovered the Refraction of
    the Sun, etc.   1698.
Billingsley, Sir Henry.   The Elements of Geometrie of the most ancient
    philosopher Euclide of Megara.   (Trans.)   With a preface by John Dee.
    1570.
Binning, Thomas.   A Light to the Art of Gunnery Wherein is laid down the
    True Weight of Powder both for Proof and Action, of all Sorts of Great
    Ordnance.   Also the True Ball, and Allowance for Wind, With the most
    necessary Conclusions for the Practice of Gunnery, either in the Sea or
    Land Service.   Likewise the Ingredients, and making of the most
    necessary Fire-Works.   1676.
Blagrave, John.   The Mathematical Jewel, shewing the making, and most
    excellent use of a singular Instrument so called: in that it performeth
    with wonderfull dexteritie, whatsoever is to be done, either by Quadrant,
    Ship, Circle, Cylinder, Ring, Dyall, Horoscope, Astrolabe, Sphere, Globe,
    or any such like heretofore devised: yea or by most tables commonly
    extant: and that generally to all places from Pole to Pole . . . by John
    Blagrave of Reading Gentleman, and well willer to Mathematicks, who
    hath cut all the prints or pictures of the whole worke with his owne
    hands.   1585.   Imprinted by Walter Venge, dwelling in Fleetelane over
    against the Maidenhead.   (One of the earliest English books on mathe-
    matics.)

Blount, Sir Henry. A Voyage into the Levant. 1636.

Blundevile, M. His Exercises, containing six treatises in Cosmographie, Astronomie, and Geographie, as also in the Art of Navigation. 1594, etc.

Bond, Henry. The Boatswain's Art. 1670.

Bonoeil, John. His Majesty's Gracious Letter to the Earle of Southampton, Treasurer, and to the Councell and Company of Virginia heere: commanding the present setting up of silk works, and planting of vines in Virginia. 1622.

Boothby, Richard. A Briefe Discovery or Description, Of the most Famous Island of Madagascar. 1646.

Boteler, Nathaniel. Six Dialogues about Sea-Services between an High Admiral and a Captain at Sea. 1685.

Bourne, William. A Regiment of the Sea. 1573.

—— Inventions and Devices. 1578.

—— The Arte of Shooting in Great Ordnaunce. 1587.

—— The Safeguard of Sailors: or, a Sure Guide for Coasters. Describing the Sea-Coasts of England, Scotland, Ireland, France, Flanders, Holland, Jutland and Norway. With Directions for bringing a Ship into the principal Harbours. 1677. (Possibly by a son of the elder Bourne.)

Browne, John. A Briefe Description of the whole world. 1599. Another ed. 1605. (Translated from the Italian of Giovanni Botero.)

Brugis, Thomas. Vade Mecum, or Companion for a Chirurgion fitted for Sea or Land, Peace or War, showing the use of Instruments and Virtues of Simples and Compounds. 1681.

Budd, Thomas. Good Order Established in Pennsylvania and New Jersey, in America. Being a true account of the Country; with its Produce and Commodities there made. . . . 1685.

Bullock, William. Virginia, Impartially examined, and left to publick view, to be considered by all Judicious and honest men. Under which Title, is comprehended the Degrees from 34 to 39, wherein lies the rich and healthful Countries of Roanock, the new Plantations of Virginia and Maryland. 1649.

Burrough, Sir John. The Sovereignty of the Seas. 1633.

Bushnell, Edmund. The Complete Shipwright. 1664.

Catameo, G. Most Briefe Tables to know readily how many rancks of Footemen armed with Corslettes go to the making of a just battaille from an hundred, to twenty thousand, also an approved way to arme a battaile with Harkabuzers and Winges of Horsemen. Trans. 1588.

Childe, L. A Short Compendium of the new and much enlarged Sea-Book, or Pilot's Sea Mirror: containing the distances and thwart courses of the Eastern, Northern, and Western Navigation. 1663. (The copy in Brit. Mus. contains a catalogue of works on Navigation.)

Clark, S. The Life and Death of Sir Francis Drake. 1671.

Colson, Nathaniel. The Mariner's New Kalendar, with Description and use of the Sea-Quadrant, a Rutter for the coasts of England, France, etc. and directions for Sailing into some Principal Harbours. 1697.

Columne, Jacob. The Fierie Sea-Columne, wherein are shewed the Seas, and Sea-Coasts, of the Northern, Eastern, and Western Navigation, manifestly inlightened, and the failings and mistakes of the former Licht or Sea-Mirrour amended. 1640.

Coryate, Thomas. Coryats Crudities, Hastilie gobled up in five Moneths Travells in France, Savoy, Italy, Rhetia . . . Helvetia . . . Germany and the Netherlands, newly digested in the hungrie aire of Odcombe in the County of Somerset and now dispersed to the nourishment of the travelling members of this kingdome. 1611. Rptd., 2 vols. Glasgow, 1905.

—— Coryats Cramb, or his Colwort twise sodden, and now served with other Macaronicke dishes as the second course to his Crudities. 1611.

—— The Odcombian Banquet: Dished foorth by Thomas the Coriat, and served in by a number of Noble Wits in praise of his Crudities and Cramb, too. Asinus, Portans, Mysteria. 1611.

—— Thomas Coriate, Traveller for the English Wits: Greeting. From the Court of the Great Mogul, Resident at the Towne of Asmere, in Easterne India. 1616.

Coverte, Robert. A True and Almost Incredible Report of an Englishman, that (being cast away in the good ship, called the Assention, in Cambaya, the farthest part of the East Indies,) travelled by lande through many unknowne Kingdomes, and great Cities. With a discoverie of a Great Emperor, called the Great Mogull, a Prince not till now known to our English nation. 1614.

Crosfeild, Robert. England's Glory Revived, demonstrated in several pre-positions, showing an easy method for fully manning the Royal Navy with saylers without charge or obstruction to trade. 1693.

Cumberland, Earl of. Voyage to the Azores, etc. 1599.

Davies, John (trans.). The Voyages and Travels of the Ambassadors from the Duke of Holstein to the Duke of Moscovy and King of Persia, 1632 to 1639, containing a complete Historie of Moscovy, Tartary, Persia, and other adjacent countries By Adam Olearius. 1662.

—— (trans.). The Voyage and Travels of J. Albert de Mendelslo into the East Indies, 1638 to 1640, containing a Description of the Great Mogul's Empire, Philippine and other Islands, Japan, etc. 1662.

—— (trans.). The History of Algiers, and its Slavery, with many Remarkable Particularities of Africk, written by the Sieur Emanuel D'Aranda, some time a Slave there. 1666.

Davys, John. The Seaman's Secrets. Divided into 2 partes, wherein is taught the three kindes of sayling, horizontell, paradoxall and sayling upon a great circle. 1594, 1607, 1626.

—— The Worlde's Hydrographical Description, wherein is proved . . . that the worlde in all his zones . . . is habitable . . . and in seas . . . navi-gable . . . whereby appears that . . . there is a short . . . passage into the South Seas to China . . . and India by Northerly Navigations, etc. 1595.

Dee, John. The Perfect Arte of Navigation. 1577.

De Palacio Garcia. Instrucion Nauthica, Para El Buen Uso, y regimiento de las Naos, fu traça, y govierno conforme à la altura de Mexico. 1587. (The first printed book on shipbuilding.)

Drake, Sir Francis, Bart. Sir Francis Drake Revived, who is or may be a pattern to stir up all heroicke and active spirits of these times . . . being a summary and true relation of four severall voyages made by the said Sir Francis Drake to the West Indies. 1626.

Drayton, Michael. Poly-Olbion. 1613. Second part. 1622.

Dunton, John. A True Journall of the Sally Fleet, with the proceedings of the voyage. 1637. (Annexed is a list of the names of the captives in Sallee.)

Eden, Richard. A Treatyse of the newe India with other new founde landes and Islands, as well eastwarde as westwarde, as they are knowen and founde in these our dayes, after the description of Sebastian Munster. 1553. (Translated from the Latin.)

—— The Decades of the Newe Worlde or West India; conteyning the Navigations and Conquestes of the Spanyardes; with particular description of the most ryche and large Landes and Islandes lately found in the West Ocean perteyning to the inheritance of the Kinges of Spayne; written in the Latine tounge by Peter Martyr of Angleria, and translated into Englysshe, 1555. Imprynted in Lumbard streete at the signe of the Cradle by Edwarde Sutton. 1555. [See also Lok.]

—— The Arte of Navigation, conteyning a compendious description of the Sphere with the makynge of certen Instrumentes and Rules for Navigations. 1561. (Translated from the Spanish of Martin Cortes.)

—— The History of Travayle in the West and East Indies, and other Countreys lying either way, towards the fruitfull and ryche Moluccaes; as Moscovia, Persia, Arabia, Syria, Ægypte, Ethiopia, Guinea, China in Cathayo and Giapan; with a discourse of the Northwest Passage; . . . finished by Richarde Willes. 1577.

Elton, Richard, and Rudd, Thomas. The Complete Body of the Art Military, in three bookes, by Richard Elton. To which are added the Arming and Exercising of Cavalry, the Practick Part of the Art of Gunnery, etc., by Captain Thomas Rudd. 1668.

Erondelle, Peter. Nova Francia: or the Description of that part of New France, which is one continent with Virginia. Translated from the French of M. Lescarbot. 1609.

Esquemeling, John. The Bucaniers of America, or a True Account of the most remarkable Assaults committed upon the Coasts of the West Indies By the bucaniers of Jamaica and Tortuga. (Translated from the Spanish.) 1684. (The original in Dutch was first published in 1678. The second edition, published in the same year, contains additional matter.)

Evelyn, John. Navigation and Commerce, their Original and Progress. Containing a Succinct Account of Traffick in General . . . with special Regard to the English Nation: their several Voyages and Expeditions, to the Beginning of our late Differences with Holland, etc. 1674.

Everett, George. Encouragement for Seamen and Mariners. Being a method for the more speedy and effectual furnishing their Majesties' Navy with Seamen and Mariners, etc. 1695.

Fletcher, Francis. The World Encompassed, by Sir Francis Drake, being his next voyage to that to Nombre de Dios, formerly imprinted; carefully collected out of the notes of Master Francis Fletcher. 1628. (Reprinted in 1635 and 1653, and also by the Hakluyt Society.)

Fletcher, Giles. Of the Russe Common Wealth. 1591.

Fox, Luke. North-West Fox, or, Fox from the North-west passage . . . with briefe Abstracts of the Voyages of Cabot, Frobisher, Davis, Waymouth, Knight, Hudson, Button, Gibbons, Bylot, Baffin, Hawkridge . . . Mr. James Hall's three Voyages to Groynland. . . . Demonstrated in a Polar Card. . . With the Author, his owne Voyage, being the XVIth. 1635.

Frobisher, Martin.   A True Reporte of the Laste Voyage (the Second) into the West and Northwest Regions, etc., in 1577, worthily atchieved by Captaine Frobisher of the Sayde Voyage the First Finder and Generall 1577.

—— A True Reporte of the Third and Last Voyage into Meta incognita; 1578.   Written by Thomas Ellis, Sailer.   Imprinted at the Three Cranes in the Vintree by Thos. Dawson.   1578.

—— A Prayse and Reporte of Maister Martyne Forboishers (*sic*) Voyage to Meta Incognita. . . . Now Spoken of by Thomas Churchyarde, Gentleman.   1578.

Frobisher, Sir Martin.   De Martini Forbisseri Angli Navigatione in Regiones Occidentis et Septentrionis Narratio historica, Ex Gallico sermone in Latinum translata per D. Joan.   1580.   (The first Latin edition of Frobisher's second voyage in 1577.)

Gage, Thomas.   A New Survey of the West Indies, or the English American, his Travail by Sea and Land, etc.   1648.

Gellibrand, Henry.   An Epitome of Navigation, containing the doctrine of plain and spherical triangles, and their use and application in plain sailing.   1674.

Gilbert, Sir Humphrey.   A Discourse of a Discoverie for a new passage to Cataia.   1576.

Godolphin, John.   View of the Admiral Jurisdiction, also divers of the Laws, Customs, Rights, and Privileges of the High Admiralty of England. 1685.

Gorges, William.   Observations and Overtures for a Sea Fight upon our own Coast.   1618.

Grassi, Giacomo.   Gia Coco Di Grassi His True Arte of Defence, plainlie teaching by infallable Demonstrations, apt Figures and Perfect Rules the manner and forme how a man without other Teacher or Master may safelie handle all sorts of Weapons as well offensive as defensive.   Englished by I. G.   Printed at London for I. I. and are to be sold within Temple Barre at the Signe of the Hand and Starre.   1594.

Gray, D.   The Storehouse of Brevitie in Woorkes of Arithmetic, Containyng as well the soundrie Parts of the Science in whole and broken Numbers, with the Rules of proportion, furthered to profitable use.   1577.   (Mentioned by Hawkins.)

Guildford, Sir R.   Pilgrimage to the Holy Land.   1506.   Ed. Ellis, Sir H. Camden Soc.   1851.

Gunter, Edmund.   Workes, containing the Description of the Sector, Crossstaff, and other instruments: with a cannon of Artificial Sines and Tangents.   Together with a new Treatise on Fortification.   1653.

Hagthorpe, John.   England's Exchequer; or, a Discourse of the Sea and Navigation.   1625.

Hakluyt, Richard.   Divers Voyages touching the Discoverie of America and the Islands adjacent unto the same, made first of all by our Englishmen and afterwards by the Frenchmen and Britons.   1582.

—— A notable historie containing foure voyages made by certayne French captains unto Florida . . . newly trans. . . . by R. H.   1587.

—— The Principall Navigations, Voiages and Discoveries of the English Nation made by Sea or Over Land to the most remote and farthest distant quarters of the earth at any time within the compasse of these 1500 yeeres, . . . devided into three severall partes . . . whereunto is added the last most renowned English Navigation, round about the whole globe of the earth. Geo. Bishop and R. Newberie deputies to Chr. Barker. 1589. New ed. The navigations at any time within the compass of these 1600 yeeres. Vol. I, 1598; vol. II, 1599; vol. III, 1600. Later editions 1809–12 (5 vols.), 1884–90 (16 vols.). Hakluyt Society, extra series, 1903 *et seq.* (12 vols.), and Glasgow, 1903–5.

—— The Discoverie of the world from their originall unto the yeere of our Lord, 1555, trans. from the Portuguese of Antonio Galvano, published in English by Richard Hakluyt. 1601.

—— Virginia Richly valued, by the description of the maine land of Florida, her next neighbour: out of the foure yeeres continuall travell and discoverie, . . . of Don Ferdinando de Soto . . . wherein are truly observed the riches and fertilitie of those parts, abounding with things necessarie, pleasant, and profitable for the life of man: with the natures and dispositions of the Inhabitants, . . . trans. by Richard Hakluyt, . . . 1609.

Hale, Thomas. An Account of New Inventions and Improvements made necessary for England, relating to English Shipping, Naval Philosophy, etc. 1691.

Hammond, W. A Paradox, proving that the Inhabitants of the Isle called Madagascar or Saint Laurence (in Temporall Things) are the Happiest People in the World, . . . with most Probable Arguments of a Hopeful and Fit Plantation of a Colony there in respect of the fruitfulnesse of the Soyle, the benignity of the ayre, and the Relieving of our English Ships, both to and from the East Indies. 1640.

Harcourt, Robert. A Relation of a Voyage to Guiana. Describing the Climat, Situation, Fertilitie, Provisions, and Commodities, of that Country, containing Seven Provinces, and other Signiories within that Territory: together with the manners, customs, behaviour, and dispositions of the people. 1613.

Harwood, Sir Edward. The Advice of that worthy commander. Written by King Charles his command upon occasion of the French King's Preparation. Also a relation of his life and death, (by Hugh Peters) with divers remarkable instructions written by the late and ever famous Earl of Essex. All tending to the Securing and Fortifying of this Kingdom, both by sea and land. 1642.

Hawkins, John. A True Declaration of the troublesome Voyage of M. John Haukins to the Partes of Guynea and the West Indies, in the Yeares of Our Lord 1567 and 1568. 1569.

Hawkins, Sir Richard. The Observations of Sir Richard Hawkins, Knight, in his Voiage into the South Sea, 1593. 1622.

Hellowes, E. The Art of Navigation. 1560. (Trans. of the work of A. Guevara.)

Heylyn, Peter. Microcosmus. A little description of the Great World, augmented and revised. 1625, etc.

Heywood, Thomas. A True Description of His Majesty's Royall Ship, built this yeare at Woolwich. 1637.

Hickeringill, E. Jamaica Viewed with all the Ports, Harbours and their Several Soundings, Towns and Settlements thereunto belonging, together with the nature of its climate, fruitfulness of the soile, and its suitablenesse to English Complexions, etc. 1661.

Hodges, William. Ruin to Ruin after Misery to Misery, wherein is shown that tens of thousands of men have five or six years pay due, with proposals for paying them. 1699.

Hodgetts, John. Terra Australis Incognita; or a new Southerne Discoverie, containing a fifth part of the World. Lately found out by Ferdinand De Quir, a Spanish captaine. 1617.

Hood, Thomas. The Mariner's Guide. 1592.

Hynde, S. Iter Lusitanicum: or the Portugal Voyage, with what Memorable Passages Intervened at the shipping, and in the transportation of Queen Catherine from Lisbon to England. 1662.

James, Captain Thomas. Strange and Dangerous Voyage, . . . in his intended discovery of the North West Passage into the South Sea, etc. 1633.

James, Duke of York and Albany, Lord High Admiral. Instructions for the better ordering H. M. Fleet in Sailing. 1660.

—— Orders establisht for the well government of H. M. ships. 1670.

Jenner, Thomas. A Description and Plate of the Sea Coasts of England, from London, up all the River of Thames, all along the coast to Newcastle and so to Edinburgh, all along Scotland, the Orchades, and Hitland, where the Dutch Begin their Fishing. Unto which is added, a list containing the monthly wages of all officers, sea-men, and others serving in the States' ships at sea; and as to the wages to common sea-men, to their share in Prizes, etc. 1653.

Jobson, Richard. The Golden Trade: or a discovery of the River Gambra and the trade of the Aethiopians. 1623. (Early travel and trade on the west coast of Africa.)

Johnson, Robert. The Traveller's Breviat, or an Historicall Description of the most famous Kingdomes in the World, . . . trans. 1601. (The countries described are Poland, Turkey, Spain, Netherland, England, France, Japan, China, etc.)

—— Nova Britannia. Offering most excellent fruits by Planting in Virginia. 1609. Second part. 1612.

Josselyn, John. An account of two voyages to New England. Wherein you have the setting out of a ship, with the charges, the prices of all necessaries for furnishing a Planter and his family at his first coming; etc. 1674.

Knolles, Richard. The General Historie of the Turkes from the first beginning of that nation to the rising of the Othoman Familie. 1603.

Lea, James. An Answer to the Untruthes published and printed in Spaine in glory of their supposed Victorie achieved against our English Navie and Charles Lord Howard, Lord High Admiral. 1589.

Leybourn, William. Nine Geometrical Exercises for Young Seamen and others that are studious in mathematical practices. 1669.

—— Pan Organon, or an Universal Instrument performing all such conclusions Geometrical and Astronomical as are usually wrought by the Globes, Spheres, Sectors, Quadrants, Planispheres, or other the like instruments, yet in being, with ease and exactness in the practice of Geometry, Astronomy, Dialling, Geography, Trigonometry, Projection, etc. 1672.

Linton, A. Newes of the Complement of the Art of Navigation, and of the Mighty Empire of Cataya, together with the Strait of Anian. 1609.

Lok, M. De Novo Orbe, or the Historie of the West Indies, Contayning the actes and adventures of the Spanyardes, which have conquered and peopled those Countries: inriched with varietie of pleasant relations of the Manners, Ceremonies, Lawes, Governments, and Warres of the Indians. Comprised in eight decades. Written by Peter Martyr, a Millanoise of Angleria, chief secretary to the Emperor. Whereof three, have beene formerly translated into English by R. Eden, whereunto the other five, are newly added by M. Lok. 1612, 1620.

Manwayring, Sir H. The Sea-Man's Dictionary: or, an Exposition and Demonstration of all the parts and things belonging to a ship. 1644.

Marten, Anthony. An Exhortation to stirre up the mindes of all her Majesties faithfull Subjects, to Defend Their Countrey, in this dangerous time, from the invasion of enemies, . . . Imprinted by John Windet, and are to be sold in Paules Church-yard, at the Brasen Serpent. 1588.

Maydman, Henry. Naval Speculations and Maritime Politicks: being a Modest and Brief Discourse of the Royal Navy of England; of its Oeconomy and Government, and a Projection for an everlasting Seminary of Seamen, by a Royal Maritime Hospital, etc. 1691.

Medows, Sir P. Observations concerning the Dominion and Sovereignty of the Seas. 1689.

Molloy, Charles. De Jure Maritimo et Navali, or a Treatise of Affairs Maritime and of Commerce in three Books. 1676.

Moryson, F. An Itinerary, containing his Ten Years' Travell through the Twelve Dominions of Germany, France, England, Scotland and Ireland, etc. 1617. Rptd., 4 vols. Glasgow, 1907.

Moxon, Joseph. A Tutor to Astronomie and Geographie. Or an Easie and Speedy Way to know the Use of both the Globes, celestial and terrestrial. 1670.

Moyle, John. Chirurgus Marinus, or, the Sea Chirurgion, being instructions to junior Chirurgic Practitioners who design to serve at sea in this imploy. 1699.

Narborough, Sir John. The Mariner's Jewel, a dictionary of naval terms. 1695.

Navy List. Gloria Britannica, or The Boast of the British Seas, containing a True and Full Account of the Royal Navy of England, Shewing where each Ship was Built, by whom, and when, its Length, Breadth, Depth, Draught of Water, Tons, the Number of Men and Guns, both in Peace and War, at Home and Abroad, together with every Man's Pay, from a Captain to a Cabin-Boy, truly calculated and Cast up, for a Day, a Week, a Month, and a Kalendar Year, or 13 Months and 1 Day. Carefully Collected and Digested by a True Lover of the Seamen. 1689. (Probably the first Navy List.)

Newhouse, Captain. The Whole Art of Navigation. 1685.

Nicholas, T. The Pleasant Historie of the Conquest of the Weast India, now called Newe Spayne. Trans. by T. Nicholas. 1578.

Nicholl, John. An Houre Glasse of Indian Newes. 1607.

Nixon, Anthony (fl. 1602). The Three English Brothers. Sir Thomas Sherley his Travels. 1607. (For other pamphlets, see D. of N. B.)

Norman, Robert. The Safeguard of Sailors: or Great Rutter. Containing the Courses, Distances, Depthes, Soundings, Floudes and Ebbes, with the markes for the entringes of sundry Harboroughs bothe of England, France, Spaine, Ireland, Flaunders, and the Sounds of Denmark, with other necessarye Rules of common Navigation. Trans. 1587.

Norton, Robert. The Gunner: showing the whole practice of Artillery by Sea and Land. 1628.

Norwood, Richard. The Sea-Man's Practice, Contayning a Fundamentall Probleme in Navigation, experimentally verified, etc. 1644.

Nye, Nathaniel. The Art of Gunnery. 1648.

Oughtred, William. Mathematical Recreations: or, a collection of Many Problems extracted out of the Ancient and Modern Philosophers: as, Secrets and Experiments in Arithmetick, Geometrie, Horologiography, Navigation, Chymistry, Water-Works, Fire-Works, etc. 1674.

Palmer, Roger, Earl of Castlemaine. A Short and True Account of the material passages in the war between the English and the Dutch. 1671.

Pepys, Samuel. Memoirs relating to the State of the Royal Navy of England for ten years, determined December, 1688. 1690.

Perkins, Peter. The Seaman's Tutor: explaining Geometry, Cosmography, and Trigonometry. . . . Compiled for the Use of the Mathematical School in Christ's Hospital London. (This is the first navigation class-book used in the Bluecoat school, and has for a frontispiece a plate of "One of the Children Educated in Xts Hospitall.")

Phillip, William. John H. van Linschoten. His Discours of Voyages into ye Easte and Weste Indies. An English translation. 1598.

—— The True and Perfect Description of Three Voyages, so Strange and Wonderful that the like hath never been heard of before. The voyages of Barents. Translated from the Dutch. 1609.

Phillippes, Henry. The Geometrical Sea-Man, or the Art of Navigation, performed by Geometry, shewing how all the three kinds of Sayling, viz., by Plain Chart, Mercator's Chart, or a Great Circle, may be easily and exactly performed by a Plain Ruler and a Pair of Compasses without Arithmeticall Calculation. 1652.

Polter, R. The Pathway to Perfect Sayling. 1605.

Purchas, Samuel. Hakluytus Posthumus, or Purchas His Pilgrimes, con-tayning a History of the World, in Sea voyages and lande Travells, by Englishmen and others, etc. 1625. Rptd., 20 vols. Glasgow, 1905.

—— His Pilgrimage, or Relations of the World and the Religions, observed in all Ages and Places Discovered. 1613.

Ralegh, Sir Walter. [See bibliography to Chap. III.]

Recorde, Robert. The Whetstone of Witte, whiche is the seconde parte of Arithmeticke: containyng thextraction of rootes: the Cossike practice with the rule of Equation: and the woorkes of Surde numbers. 1557. (Early English book on Algebra.)

Rich, Barnabe. Allarme to England, foreshowing what Perilles are Pro-cured, where the people live without regarde of Martiall Lawe, with a short discourse conteyning The Decay of Warlike Discipline convenient to be perused by Gentlemen, such as are desirous by Service to seeke their owne deserved prayse, and the Preservation of their Countrey. 1578.

Rich, Richard. Newes from Virginia. 1610. Rptd. 1865, 1874.

Robinson, Richard. A Learned and True Assertion of the Original Life, Actes and Death of the most Noble, Valiant, and Renouned Prince Ar-thure, King of Great Brittaine, who succeeding his Father Uther Pen-drageon, and right nobly governing this Land six and twentie yeares, then dyed of a mortall wounde receyved in battell, together with victory over his enemies, as appeareth cap. 9, and was buried at Glastonbury, cap. 12, an. 543; trans. from the Latin of John Leyland. 1582.

Rosier, James. A True Relation of the most prosperous voyage made this present year 1605, by Captain George Waymouth in the discoverie of the land of Virginia, etc. 1605.

St. Lo, Captain George, R. N. England's Safety: or a Bridle to the French King. 1693.

—— England's Interest: or, a Discipline for Seamen. 1694.

Saltonstall, Wye. Historia Mundi, or Mercator's Atlas, containing his Cosmographicall Description of the Fabricke and Figure of the World. 1637.

Sandys, George. A Relation of a Journey Begun An. Dom. 1610. Foure Bookes, containing a Description of the Turkish Empire, of Aegypt, of the Holy Land, of the Remote Parts of Italy and Islands Adjoyning, etc. 1615 ff.

Savery, Thomas. Navigation Improved, or the Art of Rowing Ships of all Rates in Calms, with a more easy, swift, and steady motion than Oars can. Also Description of the Engine that performs it. 1698.

Saville, Captain Henry. A Libell of Spanish Lies: found at the Sacke of Cales, discoursing the fight in the West Indies twixt the English Navie, being fourteene Ships and Pinasses and a fleete of twentie saile of the King of Spaine, and of the death of Sir Francis Drake. With an answer briefely confuting the Spanish lies, and a short Relation of the fight according to Truth. 1596.

Selden, John. Mare Clausum: (the Right and Dominion of the Seas) 1635. Translated into English by M. N. 1652.

Seller, John. Atlas Maritimus, or Sea Atlas, describing most of the known parts of the world. 1675.

—— Coasting Pilot, describing the coasts of England, Flanders, and Holland. 1673.

—— The English Pilot. 1671.

Smith, Captain John. The Generall Historie of Virginia, New England, and the Summer Isles: with the names of the Adventurers, Planters, and Governours from their first beginning, An: 1584 to this present 1624. . . . Also the Maps and Descriptions of all those Countryes, their Commodities, people, Government, Customes, and Religion yet knowne. 1624 ff. (See ed. Arber, E., 1884; rptd., Glasgow, 1907; and also cf. Captain John Smith, by Bradley, A. G., 1905.)

—— The Sea Grammar and Accidence for Young Seamen. 1626–7. (Amplified into The Seaman's Grammar: containing most pleasing and easie directions, etc., 1653.)

Smith, Sir T. Voiage and Entertainment in Rushia. 1605.

Smythe, Sir John. Certain Discourses, written by Sir John Smythe, Knight, concerning the formes and effects of divers sorts of weapons, and other verie important matters militarie, greatlie mistaken by divers of our men of war in these daies; and chiefly of the Mosquet, the Caliver and the Longbow; as also of the great sufficiencie, excellencie and wonderful effects of archers. 1590.

Speed, John. The Theatre of the Empire of Great Britain, presenting an Exact Geography of the Kingdom, together with a Prospect of the most famous parts of the World. 1676.

Sturmy, Samuel. The Mariner's Magazine, stor'd with these Mathematical Arts, Navigation and Geometry, Mathematical Instruments, Doctrine of Triangles, Art of Navigation, etc. 1669. Second edition, 1679.

Terry, Edward. A Voyage to East India. 1655.

Tosier, John, Captain, R.N. A Narrative of his Embassye and Command
to the Captain General and Governor of Havannah to demand His
Majesty of Great Britain's subjects kept prisoners there. 1679.

Vaughan, Sir William. The Golden Fleece. Divided into Three Parts.
Transported from Cambrioll Colchos, out of the Southernmost Part of
the Iland, commonly called the Newfoundland, by Orpheus Junior. 1626.

Venn, Captain Thomas. Military and Maritime Discipline, etc., and the
Compleat Gunner. 1683.

Wafer, Lionel. A New Voyage and Description of the Isthmus of America,
giving an Account of the Author's Abode there, etc. 1699.

Warren, George. An Impartial Description of Surinam, upon the Continent of Guiana, in America. With a history of several strange Beasts,
Birds, Fishes, Serpents, Insects, and Customs of that Colony, etc. 1667.

Welwood, William. An Abridgement of All Sea Lawes, etc. 1613.

Wheeler, George. A Journey into Greece, with a Voyage to Constantinople, and Adjacent Places. 1682.

Whitbourne, Richard. A Discourse and Discovery of Newfoundland, with
many reasons to prove how worthy and beneficial a Plantation may
there be made, etc. 1620.

Whitehorne, Peter. The Arte of Warre, written in Italian, by Nicholas
Machiavel, and set foorth in English by Peter Whitehorne. 1588.

—— Certain Waies for the Ordering of Soldieurs in Battleray, and setting of
Battailes after divers fashions, with their manner of marching, also how
to make Saltpetre, Gunpowder, and divers sortes of Fireworkes, or Wilde
Fire. . . . 1588.

Williams, Edward, and Farrer, John. Virgo Triumphans: or, Virginia
Richly and Truly Valued; more especially the South part thereof, viz.,
the fertile Carolana, and no lesse excellent Isle of Roanoak, etc. 1650.

Williams, Sir Roger. A Brief Discourse of War. 1590.

Wilson, Samuel. An Account of . . . Carolina, etc. 1682.

Wright, Edward. The Haven-Finding Art. Trans. from the Dutch. 1599.

—— Certain Errors in Navigation. 1599.

Yarranton, Andrew. England's Improvement by Sea and Land, to Out-do
the Dutch without Fighting, to Pay Debts without Moneys, to Set to
Work all the Poor of England with the Growth of our own Lands, etc.,
a Method of Improving the Royal Navy, and lessening the Growing
Power of France, etc. 1677.

[See also the publications of the Hakluyt Society and Commander Robinson's own works: The British Fleet, 1894; and (with John Leyland) The
British Tar in fact and fiction, 1909; Arber's English Garner, "Voyages
and Travels," 2 vols., 1903; Froude, J. A., English Seamen in the 16th
century, 1901; Traill, H. D., Social England, vol. III, 1902. A. R. W.]

CHAPTER VI

THE SONG-BOOKS AND MISCELLANIES

I. Song-books

The growth of English song from the earliest days to the period of the
song-books, with its prominent features, "Sumer is icumen in," the Agincourt Song, the hymn "Quene of Evene," the influence of John of Dunstable

and his School, etc., may be studied in Chappell, W., Popular Music of the Olden Time, ed. Wooldridge, H. E., 1893; Rockstro, W. S., A general History of Music, 1886; The Oxford History of Music, ed. Hadow, W. H., 1891; Davey, Henry, History of English Music [1895]; Grove's Dictionary of Music and Musicians, ed. Fuller Maitland, J. A., 1904. For John of Dunstable see also D. of N. B. *s.v.*; for "Sumer is icumen in" see also Country Life, 11 April, 1908, p. 510, where the music will be found; and for "Quene of Evene," British Museum, Arundell MS., 245.

Adson, John. Courtly Masquing Ayres, Composed to 5. and 6. Parts, for Violins, Consorts, and Cornets. 1621.

Alison, Richard. An howres recreation in Musicke, apt for Instrumentes and Voyces. 1606.

Amner, John. Sacred Hymnes. Of 3.4.5 and 6 parts for Voyces & Vyols. [1615.]

Attey, John. The First Booke Of Ayres Of Foure Parts, with Tableture for the Lute. 1622.

Barley, William. A new Booke of Tabliture. 1596.

Bartlet, John. A Booke Of Ayres With a Triplicitie of Musicke. 1606.

Bateson, Thomas. The first set of English Madrigales: to 3. 4. 5. and 6. voices. 1604. Ed. Rimbault, E. F. 1846.

—— The Second Set Of Madrigales to 3. 4. 5. and 6. Parts: Apt for Viols and Voyces. 1618.

Bennet, John. Madrigalls To Foure Voyces. M.D.XC.IX. Ed. Hopkins, E. J. 1845.

Byrd, William. Psalmes, Sonets, & songs of sadnes and pietie, made into Musicke of five parts. 1588.

—— Songs of sundrie natures, some of gravitie, and others of myrth, fit for all companies and voyces. Lately made and composed into Musicke of 3. 4. 5. and 6. parts. 1589. Another edition, 1610.

—— Psalmes, Songs, and Sonnets: some solemne, others joyfull, framed to the life of the Words: Fit for Voyces or Viols of 3. 4. 5. and 6. Parts. 1611.

—— Madrigales translated of foure, five and six parts, chosen out of divers excellent Authors, with the first and second part of La Verginella, made by Maister Byrd, upon two Stanz's of Ariosto and brought to speake English with the rest. Published by N. Yonge, in favour of such as take pleasure in Musick of voices. 1588.

—— Musica Transalpina. The Second Booke of Madrigalles, to 5. and 6. voices: translated out of sundrie Italian Authors. 1597.

Campion, Thomas. [See bibliography to Chapter VIII.]

Carlton, Richard. Madrigals to Five voyces. 1601.

Coperario (*i. e.* Cooper), John. Funeral Teares, For the death of the Right Honorable the Earle of Devonshire. Figured In seaven songes. 1606

—— Songs of Mourning: Bewailing the untimely death of Prince Henry. Worded by Tho. Campion. And set forth to bee sung with one voyce to the Lute, or Violl: By John Coprario. 1613.

Corkine, William. Ayres, To Sing And Play To The Lute And Basse Violl. With Pavins, Galliards, Almaines, and Corantos for the Lyra Violl. 1610.

—— The Second Booke Of Ayres, Some, to Sing and Play to the Base-Violl alone: Others, to be sung to the Lute and Basse Violl. With new Coran toes, Pavins, Almaines; as also divers new Descantes upon old Grounds, set to the Lyra-Violl. 1612.

Danyel, John.   Songs For the Lute Viol and Voice.   1606.

Dowland, John.   The First Booke of Songes or Ayres of fowre parts with
    Tableture for the Lute: So made that all the partes together, or either
    of them severally may be song to the Lute, Orpherian or Viol de gambo.
    1597, etc.   Second Booke.   1600.   Third And Last Booke.   1603.

—— A Pilgrimes Solace.   Wherein is contained Musicall Harmonie of
    3. 4. and 5. parts, to be sung and plaied with the Lute and Viols.
    1612.

Dowland, Robert.   A Musicall Banquet.   Furnished with varietie of delicious
    Ayres, Collected out of the best Authors in English, French, Spanish and
    Italian.   1610.

Este, Michael.   Madrigales To 3. 4. and 5. parts: apt for Viols and voices.
    1604.   Second set.   1606.   Third set . . . Wherein are Pastorals, An-
    themes, Neopolitanes, Fancies, and Madrigales, to 5. and 6. parts.   1610.
    Fourth set.   1619.   Fift set . . . Wherein are Songs full of Spirit and
    delight.   1618.   Sixt Set.   1624.   Seventh set.   1638.

Farmer, John.   The First Set Of English Madrigals: To Foure Voices.   1599.

Farnaby, Giles.   Canzonets To Fowre Voyces, With a Song of eight parts.
    M.D.XCVIII.

Ferrabosco, Alfonso.   Ayres.   1609.

Ford, Thomas.   Musicke of Sundrie Kindes, Set forth in two Bookes.   1607.

Gibbons, Orlando.   The first set Of Madrigals And Mottets of 5. Parts: apt
    for Viols and Voyces.   1612.   Ed. Smart, G.   1841.

—— Parthenia or The Maydenhead of the first musicke that ever was printed
    for the Virginalls.   Composed by three famous Masters: William Byrd,
    Dr. John Bull, and Orlando Gibbons.   [1611.]   Also 1655.

Greaves, Thomas.   Songes of sundrie kindes: First, Aires to be sung to the
    Lute, and Base Violl.   Next, Songes of Sadnesse, for the Viols and
    Voyces.   Lastly, Madrigalles, for five voyces.   1604.

Hilton, John.   Ayres, or Fa las for three voyces.   1627.   Rptd. by the
    Musical Antiquarian Society, 1844.

—— Catch that Catch can.   A Choice Collection of Catches, Rownds, &
    Canons.   1652.

Hume, Tobias.   The First Part of Ayres, French, Pollish, and others to-
    gether, some in Tabliture, and some in Pricke-Song.   1605.

Jones, Robert.   The First Booke Of Songes & Ayres Of foure parts with
    Tableture for the Lute.   1600.   First And Second Booke.   1601.

—— Ultimum Vale or The Third Book of Ayres.   [1608.]   [No title-page.
    Unique copy in the library of the Royal College of Music, with MS. note
    by Edward F. Rimbault.]

—— A Musicall Dreame.   Or The Fourth Booke Of Ayres.   1609.

—— The Muses Gardin for Delights.   Or the fift Booke of Ayres, onely for
    the Lute, the Base-voyll, and the Voyce.   1610.

—— The First Set of Madrigals, of 3. 4. 5. 6. 7. 8. Parts, for Viols and Voices,
    or for Voices alone, or as you please.   1607.

Kirbye, George.   The first set Of English Madrigalls, to 4. 5. & 6. voyces.
    1597.

Lichfield, Henry.   The First Set Of Madrigals of 5. Parts: apt both for
    Viols and Voyces.   1613.

Mason, George, and Easden, John.   The Ayres That Were Song and Played,
    at Brougham Castle in Westmerland, in the Kings Entertainment.
    1618.

Morley, Thomas. Canzonets. Or Little Short Songs To Three Voyces. 1593.

—— The first booke of Canzonets to two voyces. 1595.

—— Canzonets. Or Little Short Songs To Foure Voyces: Celected out of the best and approved Italian Authors. 1597.

—— Canzonets or Litle Short Aers To Five and Six Voices. 1597.

—— Madrigalls to foure voyces. The first booke. 1594.

——Madrigals To five voyces. Celected out of the best approved Italian Authors. 1598.

—— Madrigals to Foure Voices . . . with some Songs added. 1600.

—— The First Booke of Balletts To Five Voyces. 1595. [Also 1600.]

—— A Plaine And Easie Introduction To Practicall Musicke, set downe in forme of a dialogue: Devided into three partes, With new songs of 2. 3. 4. and 5. parts. 1597.

—— The First Booke of Ayres. Or Little Short Songs, to sing and play to the Lute, with the Base Viole. 1600.

—— Madrigales The Triumphes of Oriana, to 5. and 6. voices: composed by divers severall aucthors. 1601. Ed. Hawes, W. 1815.

—— The Canzonets And Madrigals For Three and Four Voices. Ed. Holland, W. W. and Cooke, W. Oxon. and London (1808?).

Mundy, John. Songs and Psalmes composed into 3. 4. and 5. parts. 1594.

Peerson, Martin. Private Musicke. Or The First Booke of Ayres and Dialogues: Contayning Songs of 4. 5. and 6. parts. 1620.

—— Mottects or Grave Chamber Musique. Containing Songs of five parts. Also, A Mourning Song of six parts for the Death of the late Right Honorable Sir Fulke Grevil. 1630.

Pilkington, Francis. First Booke Of Songs or Ayres of 4. parts. 1605.

—— The first set of madrigals and pastorals of 3. 4. and 5. Parts. 1613.

—— The Second Set Of Madrigals, and Pastorals, of 3. 4. 5. and 6. Parts; Apt for Violls and Voyces. 1624.

Ravenscroft, Thomas. Pammelia, Musicks Miscellanie. 1609. Also 1618.

—— Deuteromelia: or The second part of Musicks melodie, or melodious Musicke, Of Pleasant Roundelaies; K. H. Mirth, or Freemens Songs and such delightfull Catches. 1609.

—— Melismata. Musicall phansies. Fitting The Court, Citie, and Countrey Humours. To 3. 4. and 5. Voyces. 1611.

—— A briefe discourse Of the true (but neglected) use of Charract'ring the Degrees by their Perfection, Imperfection, and Dimunition in Measurable Musicke, against the Common Practise and Custome of these Times. 1614.

Robinson, Thomas. New Citharen Lessons. 1609.

Rosseter, Philip. A Booke of Ayres, Set foorth to be song to the Lute, Orpherian, and Base Violl. 1601.

Tomkins, Thomas. Songs of 3. 4. 5. and 6. parts. 1622.

Vautor, Thomas. The First Set: Beeing Songs of divers Ayres and Natures, of Five and Six parts: Apt for Vyols and Voyces. 1619.

Ward, John. The First Set of English Madrigals To 3. 4. 5. and 6. parts apt both for Viols and Voyces. With a Mourning Song in memory of Prince Henry. 1613.

Watson, Thomas. The first sett, Of Italian Madrigalls Englished. 1590

Weelkes, Thomas.   Madrigals To 3. 4. 5. & 6. voyces.   1597.   Ed. Hopkins, E. J.   1843.
—— Balletts and Madrigals To five voyces, with one to 6. voyces.   1598. Another edition, 1608.
—— Madrigals of 5. and 6. parts, apt for the Viols and voices.   1600.
—— Madrigals Of 6. parts, apt for the Viols and voices.   1600.
—— Ayeres or Phantasticke Spirites for three voices.   1608.
Whythorne, Thomas.   Songes of three, fower, and five voyces.   1571.
—— Of Duos, or Songs for two voices.   1590.
Wilbye, John.   The First Set Of English Madrigals To 3. 4. 5. and 6. voices. 1598.   Ed. Turle, J.   1840–1.
—— The Second Set Of Madrigales To 3. 4. 5. and 6. parts, apt both for Voyals and Voyces.   1609.   Ed. Budd, G. W.   1846.
Youll, Henry.   Canzonets To Three Voyces.   1608.

II.   LATER REPRINTS AND COLLECTIONS

Aikin, J.   Vocal Poetry; or, a select collection of English songs.   To which is prefixed an essay on song-writing.   1810.
Arber, E.   An English Garner.   Ingatherings from our History and Literature.   Vols. II (1879), III (1880), IV (1882), VI (1883) and VII (1883).
Bullen, A. H.   An English Garner, Shorter Elizabethan Poems.   1903.
—— Lyrics from the Song-Books of the Elizabethan Age.   1887.   More Lyrics from the Song-Books of the Elizabethan Age.   1888.   Lyrics from the Song-Books of the Elizabethan Age.   New and Revised Edition. 1889 and 1891.   (Selections from the two preceding volumes.)   Lyrics from the Dramatists of the Elizabethan Age.   1889 and 1890.   Poems, Chiefly Lyrical, from Romances and Prose-Tracts of the Elizabethan Age: With Chosen Poems of Nicholas Breton.   1890.
Carpenter, F. I.   English Lyric Poetry, 1500–1700.   1906.
Chambers, E. K.   English Pastorals.   1906.
Collier, J. P.   Seven English Poetical Miscellanies, Printed between 1557 and 1602.   1867.
—— Lyrics for old Lutenists in the reigns of Elizabeth and James I, Being Specimens of the Words of Airs intended for concerted performance, and social amusement.   1863.   (In Illustrations of Early English Popular Literature, vol. 1, 1863.)
—— Lyrical Poems, Selected from Musical Publications between the years 1589 and 1600.   Percy Society.   Vol. XIII.   1844.
Cox, F. A.   English Madrigals in the time of Shakespeare.   1899.
Crow, Martha F.   Elizabethan Sonnet Cycles.   1896–8.
Grosart, A. B.   Miscellanies of the Fuller Worthies' Library.   The Writings in verse and prose of Sir Edward Dyer, Knt.   (1540?–1607.)   1872.
—— Miscellanies of the Fuller Worthies' Library.   The Poems of Thomas, Lord Vaux (died 1562), Edward, Earl of Oxford (died 1604), Robert, Earl of Essex (died 1601); and Walter, Earl of Essex (died 1576). 1872.
Hannah, J.   The Courtly Poets from Raleigh to Montrose.   1870.
—— Poems by Sir Henry Wotton, Sir Walter Raleigh, and others.   1845.
[Hazlitt, W. Carew.]   Inedited Poetical Miscellanies, 1584–1700.   Selected from MSS. chiefly in private hands.   1870.
Linton, W. J.   Rare Poems of the Sixteenth and Seventeenth Centuries. A Supplement to the Anthologies.   1882.

Oliphant, T. La Musa Madrigalesca; or A Collection of Madrigals, Ballets, Roundelays, etc., chiefly of the Elizabethan Age. 1837.

Park, T. Heliconia. Comprising A Selection of English Poetry of the Elizabethan Age: Written or Published between 1575 and 1604. Three vols. 1815.

—— Nugae Antiquea: being a miscellaneous collection of original papers, in prose and verse; written during the reigns of Henry VIII. Edward VI. Queen Mary, Elizabeth, and King James. Vol. II. 1804.

Rimbault, E. F. The Ancient Vocal Music of England. A Collection of Specimens Referred to in a Series of Lectures, and Adapted to Modern Use.

—— Bibliotheca Madrigaliana. A Bibliographical Account of the Musical and Poetical Works published in England during the Sixteenth and Seventeenth Centuries, under the Titles of Madrigals, Ballets, Ayres, Canzonets, etc., etc. 1847.

Ritson, J. A select collection of English Songs, with their original airs: and a historical essay on the origin and progress of national song. 3 vols. Second edition. Ed. Park, T. 1813.

Schelling, F. E. A Book of Elizabethan Lyrics. Boston, 1895.

Scott, C. K. Euterpe. A Collection of Madrigals and other Vocal Music of the 16th and 17th Centuries. The Oriana Madrigal Society. In progress.

Smith, J. S. Musica Antiqua. A Selection of Music of this and other Countries, from the Commencement of the Twelfth to the beginning of the Eighteenth Century. 2 vols. [1812.]

Squire, W. B. Madrigals and Part Songs of the 16th and 17th Centuries. In progress.

III. MISCELLANIES

A Banquet of daintie Conceits: furnished with verie delicate and choyse Inventions, to delight their Mindes who take Pleasure in Musique; and there-withall to sing sweete Ditties, either to the Lute, Bandora, Virginalles, or anie other Instrument. Published at the desire of botne honorable and worshipful Personages, who have had Copies of divers of the Ditties heerein contained. Written by A. M. Servaunt to the Queenes most excellent Majestie. Honos alit Artes. At London, printed by J. C. for Edward White, and are to be sold at the signe of the Gunne, at the little North Doore of Paules. 1588. (In Harleian Miscellany, vol. IX, p. 219, 1812.)

The Phoenix Nest. Built up with the most rare and refined workes of Noble men, woorthy Knights, gallant Gentlemen, Masters of Arts, and brave Schollers. Full of Varietie, excellent invention, and singular delight. Never before this time published. Set foorth by R. S. of the Inner Temple Gentleman. Imprinted at London, by John Jackson. 1593.

Englands Parnassus: or The choycest Flowers of our Moderne Poets, with their Poeticall comparisons; Descriptions of Bewties, Personages, Castles, Pallaces, Mountaines, Groves, Seas, Springs, Rivers, &c. Whereunto are annexed other various discourses, both pleasant and profitable. Imprinted at London for N. L. C. B. and T. H. 1600. Rptd., Arber, E., English Garner, vol. I.

A badly edited, but very popular, volume of "Snippets" from contemporary poets, compiled by Allot, R.   The volume has recently been
exhaustively examined and corrected by Crawford, C., in Notes and
Queries, Series x., vol. IX. pp. 341, 401; vol. x, pp. 4, 84, 182, 262, 362,
444; vol. XI. pp. 5, 123, 204.

Belvedére Or The Garden Of The Muses.   Imprinted at London by F. K.
for Hugh Astley, dwelling at Saint Magnus Corner.   1600.

A Poetical Rapsody containing, Diverse Sonnets, Odes, Elegies, Madrigalls,
and other Poesies, both in Rime, and Measured Verse.   Never yet
published.   The Bee and Spider by a diverse power, Sucke Hony and
Poyson from the selfe same flower.   Printed at London by V. S. for
John Baily, and are to be solde at his Shoppe in Chancerie lane, neere
to the Office of the Six Clarkes.   1602.   Ed. Brydges, E.   Vol. I, 1814.
Vol. II, 1816.   Ed. Bullen, A. H.   2 vols.   1890.

Englands Helicon.   Casta placent superis, pura cum veste venite, Et manibus
puris sumite fontis aquam.   At London Printed by I. R. for John
Flasket, and are to be sold in Paules Church-yard, at the signe of the
Beare.   1600.   Second edition, 1614.   Ed. Bullen, A. H.   1887.

Love's Garland; or Posies for Rings, Hand-kerchiefs, and Gloves, and such
pretty Tokens that Lovers send to their Loves.   1624, etc.   See Arber's
An English Garner, Shorter Elizabethan Poems, 1903.

IV. SONG WRITERS

Barnfield, Richard.   The Affectionate Shepheard.   Containing the Complaint
of Daphnis for the love of Ganymede.   1594.   Ed.   Halliwell-Phillipps,
J. O. Percy Society.   1842.

—— Cynthia.   With certaine Sonnets, and the Legend of Cassandra.   Quod
cupio nequeo.   1595.   Beldornie Press, Ryde, Isle of Wight, 1841.

—— The Encomion of Lady Pecunia: Or The praise of Money.   Contains
also: The Complaint of Poetrie, for the Death of Liberalitie.   1598.

—— The Combat, betweene Conscience and Covetousnesse, in the minde of
Man.   1598.

—— Poems: In divers humors.   1598, 1605.   Ed. Boswell, A.   Roxburghe
Club.   1816.   Ed. Collier, J. P.   Illustrations of Old English Literature.
1866.

—— Poems.   Ed. Grosart, A. B.   1876.   See also, Arber, E., An English
Garner, Some Longer English Poems, ed. Bullen, A. H., 1903.

See, also, an English Miscellany, presented to Dr. Furnivall, Oxford, 1901,
p. 158, Barnfield's Ode: "As it fell upon a day," by Henneman, J. B.

Barnes, Barnabe.   Parthenophil and Parthenope.   Sonnettes, Madrigals,
Elegies and Odes.   [Entered in Stationers' register 10 May, 1593.]

—— A Divine Centurie of spiritual sonnets.   1595.

—— The Poems of Barnabe Barnes: Part I, Parthenophil and Parthenope,
1593.   Part II, A Divine Centurie of spiritual sonnets, 1595.   Ed.
Grosart, A. B.   1875.

Breton, Nicholas.   A flourish upon Fancie.   As gallant a Glose, upon so
trifling a text, as ever was written.   Compiled by N. B. Gent.   To which
are annexed The Toyes of an Idle head: Containing, many pretie Pamphlets, for pleasaunt heads to passe away Idle time withall.   By the same
Authour.   1582.

Breton, Nicholas. The Pilgrimage to Paradise, joyned with the Countesse of Penbrookes love. Oxford. 1592.

—— The Arbor of Amorous Devices; Wherein young Gentlemen may reade many pleasant fancies and fine devices: And thereon meditate divers sweete Conceites to court the love of faire ladies & Gentlewomen. 1597.

—— Brittons Bowre of Delights. Contayning. Many, most delectable and fine devises, of rare Epitaphes, pleasant Poems, Pastoralls and Sonnets. 1597.

—— Melancholike Humours, in verses of diverse Natures. 1600.

—— Pasquils Passe, and passeth not. Set downe in three Pees His Passe Precession, and Prognostication. 1600.

—— Pasquils Fooles-cap sent to such (to keep their weake braines warme) as are not able to conceive aright of his Mad-cap. With Pasquils Passion for the Worlds Waywardnesse. Begun by himselfe, and finished by his Friend Morphorius. 1600.

—— An excellent poeme, upon the longing of a blessed Heart: which loathing the world, doth long to be with Christ. With an addition, upon the definition of love. 1601.

—— A Divine Poeme, divided into two Partes: The Ravisht Soule, and the Blessed Weeper. 1601.

—— The Soules Harmony. . . . Numquam aut Nunc. 1602.

—— A true description of unthankfulnesse. Or an enemie to Ingratitude. 1602.

—— The Mothers Blessing. 1602.

—— The Passionate Shepheard, or the Shepheardes Love: set downe in Passions to his Shepheardesse Aglaia. With many excellent conceited Poems and pleasant Sonnets, fit for young heads to passe away idle houres. 1604.

—— The Honour of Valour. 1605.

—— The Soules immortall crowne consisting of, seaven glorious graces. 1. Vertue. 2. Wisedome. 3. Love. 4. Constancie. 5. Patience. 6. Humilitie. 7. Infiniteness. Devided into seaven dayes Workes. 1605.

—— I would and would not. 1614.

—— Pasquils Mad-cappe, Throwne at the corruptions of these times. With His Message to Men of all Estates. 1626.

—— The Works in Verse and Prose of Nicholas Breton. Ed. Grosart, A. B. Two volumes. 1879.

G., J., or C., J. Alcilia. Philoparthens Loving Follie. 1595. Ed. Wagner, W., in Jahrbuch der Deutschen Shakespeare-Gesellschaft, 1875, vol. x, and ed. Grosart, A. B., Manchester, 1879. Rptd. 1613.

—— Alcilia. Philoparthens loving Folly: Whereunto is added, Pigmalions Image: With the Love of Amos and Laura. And also, Epigrammes, by Sir I. H. and others. 1628. Ed. Arber, E., English Garner, vol. IV, 1882.

On the authorship of this work, see Wagner *ut sup.* and Grosart *ut sup.* A small collection of poems in rime.

Copley, Anthony. A Fig for Fortune. 1596. Rptd., Spenser Society, 1883.
Cutwode, Thomas. Caltha Poetarum: or the Bumble Bee. 1599. Rptd. by Roxburghe Club. (A fanciful, skilful and often charming poem, in stanzas of seven decasyllabic lines, by an author of whom nothing is known. On account of its supposed licentiousness (which is not remarkable), the book was burned by order of the archbishop of Canterbury in the year of its publication.)

Dickenson, John. The Shepheardes Complaint. A passionate Eclogue, written in English Hexameters: Whereunto are annexed other conceits, brieflie expressing the effects of Loves impressions, and the just punishment of aspiring beautie. n.d.

—— Arisbas, Euphues amidst his slumbers: Or Cupids Journey to Hell. Decyphering a Myrror of Constancie, a Touch-stone of tried affection, begun in chaste desires, ended in choise delights: And emblasoning Beauties glorie, adorned by Natures bountie. With the Triumph of True Love, in the foyle of false Fortune. 1594.

—— Greene in Conceipt. New raised from his grave to write the Tragique Historie of faire Valeria of London. Wherein is truly discovered the rare and lamentable issue of a Husbands dotage, a wives leudnesse, & childrens disobedience. 1598.

—— Prose and Verse by John Dickenson. Ed. Grosart, A.B. 1878.

Edwards, Thomas. Cephalus and Procris. Narcissus. Aurora musae amica. 1595. Rptd., Roxburghe Club, 1882.

Ovid's treatment is closely followed. Cephalus and Procris is in rimed heroics; Narcissus in stanzas of seven decasyllabic lines. Of the author little is known; but his poems are good.

Greene, Robert. The lyric poems of Robert Greene are to be found chiefly in the following works:

—— Perimedes The Blacke-Smith. A golden methode, how to use the mind in pleasant and profitable exercise: Wherein is contained speciall principles fit for the highest to imitate, and the meanest to put in practise, how best to spend the wearie winters nights, or the longest summers Evenings, in honest and delightfull recreation: Wherein we may learne to avoide idlenesse and wanton scurrilitie, which divers appoint as the end of their pastimes. Heerein are interlaced three merrie and necessarie discourses fit for our time: with certaine pleasant Histories and tragicall tales, which may breed delight to all, and offence to none. 1588.

—— Menaphon Camillas alarum to slumbering Euphues, in his melancholie Cell at Silexedra. Wherein are deciphered the variable effects of Fortune, the wonders of Love, the triumphes of inconstant Time. Displaying in sundrie conceipted passions (figured in a continuante Historie) the Trophees that Vertue carrieth triumphant, maugre the wrath of Envie, or the resolution of Fortune. A worke worthie the youngest eares for pleasure, or the gravest censures for principles. 1589.

—— Greenes Never too late. Or, A Powder of Experience: Sent to all youthfull Gentlemen; to roote out the infectious follies, that over-reaching conceits foster in the spring time of their youth. Decyphering in a true English historie, those particular vanities, that with their frothie vapours nip the blossoms of everie ripe braine, from atteining to his intended perfection. As pleasant, as profitable, being a right pumice-stone, apt to race out idlenesse with delight, and follie with admonition. 1590.

—— Franceicos Fortunes: or The second Part of Greenes Never too late. Wherein is discoursed the fall of Love, the bitter fruites of Follies pleasure, and the repentant sorrowes of a reformed man. 1590.

—— Greenes farewell to Folly. Sent to Courtiers and Schollers as a president to warne them from the vaine delights that drawes youth on to repentance. 1591.

Greene, Robert. Philomela. The Lady Fitzwaters Nightingale. 1592.
—— Greens Groats-worth of Wit, bought with a Million of Repentaunce.
Describing the follie of youth, the falshoode of makeshift flatterers, the
miserie of the negligent, and mischiefes of deceving Courtezans.
Written before his death, and published at his dying request. 1596.
—— Ciceronis Amor. Tullies Love. Wherein is discoursed the prime of
Ciceroes youth, setting out in lively portratures how young Gentlemen
that aime at honour should levell the ende of their affections, holding
the love of countrie and friends in more estecme then those faiding
blossomes of beauty, that only feede the curious survey of the eye. A
worke full of Pleasure as following Ciceroes vaine, who was as conceipted
in his youth as grave in his age, profitable as containing precepts worthy
so famous an Orator. 1597.
—— A Looking Glasse, for London and Englande. Made by Thomas Lodge
Gentleman, and Robert Greene. 1598.
—— Greenes Orpharion. Wherin is discovered a musicall concorde of
pleasant Histories, many sweet moodes graced with such harmonius
discords, as agreeing in a delightfull closse, they sound both pleasure
and profit to the eare. Heerein also as in a Diateheron, the branches
of Vertue, ascending by degrees: are counited in the glorious praise of
women-kind. With divers Tragicall and Comicall Histories presented by
Orpheus and Arion, beeing as full of profit as of pleasure. 1599.
—— Greenes Mourning Garment: given him by repentance at the Funerals
of Love; which he presents for a favour to all young Gentlemen, that wish
to weane themselves from wanton desires. Both Pleasant and Profitable. 1616.
—— Dramatic and Poetical Works of Greene and Peele. Ed. Dyce, A. 1861.
—— The Life and Complete Works in Prose and Verse of Robert Greene. In
Fifteen Volumes. Ed. Grosart, A. B. 1881–6.
Lodge, Thomas. The lyric poems of Thomas Lodge are to be found chiefly
in the following works:
—— Scillaes Metamorphosis: Enterlaced with the unfortunate love of Glau-
cus. Whereunto is annexed the delectable discourse of the discontented
Satyre: with sundrie other most absolute Poems and Sonnets. Contayn-
ing the detestable tyrannie of Disdaine, and Comicall triumph of
Constancie: Verie fit for young Courtiers to peruse, and coy Dames to
remember. 1589.
—— A Margarite of America. By T. Lodge. 1596.
—— Rosalynde. Euphues golden legacie: found after his death in his Cell
at Silexedra. Bequeathed to Philautus sonnes noursed up with their
father in England. Fetcht from the Canaries. 1590.
—— The Famous, true and historicall life of Robert second Duke of Nor-
mandy, surnamed for his monstrous birth and behaviour, Robin the
Divell. Wherein is contained his dissolute life in his youth, his devout
reconcilement and vertues in his age: Interlaced with many straunge and
miraculous adventures. Wherein are both causes of profite, and manie
conceits of pleasure. 1591.
—— Phillis: Honoured with Pastorall Sonnets, Elegies, and amorous delights.
Where-unto is annexed, the tragicall complaynt of Elstred. 1593.
—— A Looking Glasse. See above under Greene.
—— The Complete Works of Thomas Lodge [1580–1623?]. Hunterian Club.
Four volumes. 1883.

Munday, Anthony. A Banquet of daintie Conceits: furnished with verie delicate and choyse Inventions, to delight their Mindes who take Pleasure in Musique; and there-withall to sing sweete Ditties, either to the Lute, Bandora, Virginalles, or anie other Instrument. 1588. Harl. Misc. Vol. IX. 1812.

—— Metropolis Coronata, The Triumphes of Ancient Drapery: or, Rich Cloathing of England, in a second Yeeres performance. 1615.

—— The Famous and Renowned Historie of Primaleon of Greece. . . . Translated out of French and Italian. Three vols. 1619. See also Los tres libros del muy esforçado cauallero Primaleon et Polendos su hermano hijos del Emperador palmerin de Oliua, Seville, 1524; and Le troisiesme livre de Primaleon de Grece Traduit d'Espagnol en François (by Gabriel Chapuis), Lyons, 1579.

—— John a Kent and John a Cumber; a comedy. Ed. Collier, J. P. Shakspeare Society. 1851.

Peele, George. The Araygnement of Paris A Pastorall. 1584.

—— An Eglogue Gratulatorie. Entituled: To the right honorable, and renowned Shepheard of Albions Arcadia: Robert Earle of Essex and Ewe, for his welcome into England from Portugall. 1589.

—— Polyhymnia, describing the honourable Triumph at Tylt, before her Majestie, on the 17. of November last past, being the first day of the three and thirtith yeare of Her Highnesse raigne. 1590.

—— The Famous Chronicle of King Edward the first, sirnamed Edward Longshankes, with his returne from the holy land. Also the life of Llevellen rebell in Wales. Lastly, the sinking of Queene Elinor, who sunck at Charingcrosse, and rose againe at Potters-hith, now named Queenehith. 1593.

—— The Old Wives Tale. A pleasant, conceited Comedie, played by the Queenes Majesties players. 1595.

—— Dramatic and Poetical Works. See under Greene.

Roydon, Matthew. Son of T. Roydon, editor of the Gorgeous-Gallery of Gallant Inventions. His Elegy or friend's passion for his Astrophell is to be found in Spenser's Colin Clout, 1595, in The Phoenix Nest and in A gorgious Gallery. There are verses by him also in H. Gilbert's True Report, 1583.

Sabie, Francis. Pans Pipe, Three pastorall Eglogues, in English Hexameter. With other Poetical Verses delightfull. . . . 1595.

—— Adams Complaint. The Olde Worldes Tragedie. David and Bathsheba. 1596. (In rime. Versifications of Scripture.)

Sabie, who was a schoolmaster at Lichfield, also versified Greene's Pandosto under the titles The Fisher-mans Tale, 1595, and Floras Fortune, 1595, in blank verse.

Smith, William. Chloris, or The Complaint of the passionate despised Shepheard. 1596. Ed. Grosart, A. B. 1877.

Soowthern, John. Pandora. The Musyque of the beautie of his mistresse Diana. 1584.
    (Nothing in this volume of sonnets, based mainly on Ronsard, is so beautiful as its title.)

Storer, Thomas (1571–1604). Life and Death of Thomas Wolsey. 1599. [See England's Parnassus.]

Watson, Thomas. The ΕΚΑΤΟΜΠΑΘΙΆ or Passionate Centurie of Loue, Divided into two parts: whereof, the first expresseth the Author's sufferance in Love: the latter, his long farewell to Love and all his tyrannie. [1581?.]

—— Thomas Watson's "Italian Madrigals Englished," 1590. Ed. Carpenter, F. I. [1899.]

—— The Poems of Thomas Watson. Ed. Arber, E. 1895.

Willoby(?), Henry. Willobie his Avisa. Or, the true Picture of a modest Maid, and of a Chast and constant wife. In Hexameter verse. . . . 1594. Rptd. 1596, etc.

—— Willobie's Avisa, &c. Ed. Grosart, A. B. Manchester, 1880.

For the authorship of this work and its references to Shakespeare, see Grosart as above, Sidney Lee's Life of Shakespeare, 1903, and D. of N. B. *s.vv.* Willoughby or Willobie, Henry. The author was probably one Hadrian Dorrell.

Yates, James. The Castell of Courtesie, Whereunto is adjoyned the Holde of Humilitie, with the Chariot of Chastitie thereunto annexed. Also A Dialogue betweene Age and Youth and other matters herein conteined. [1582.]

Yong, Bartholomew. Los Sieste Libros de la Diana de Iorge de Mōtemayor. Valencia. [1559?.]

—— Diana of George of Montemayor. Trans. 1598.

V. Biography and Criticism

Barrett, W. A. English Glee and Madrigal writers. 1877.

Chappell, W. Some account of an Unpublished Collection of Songs and Ballads by King Henry VIII and his Contemporaries. Archaeologia, XLI, p. 371.

Courthope, W. J. A History of English Poetry. Vols. II (1904) and III (1903).

Elizabethan Lyric, The. Quarterly Review, No. 302, October 1902.

Erskine, J. The Elizabethan Lyric. A Study. New York and London, 1903. (Contains a bibliography on pp. 315–329.)

Furnivall, F. J. Robert Laneham's Letter; Describing a part of the entertainment unto Queen Elizabeth at the Castle of Kenilworth in 1575. 1907.

Grove's Dictionary of Music and Musicians. Ed. Maitland, J. A. F. 5 vols. 1904.

Greg, W. W. Pastoral Poetry and Pastoral Drama. A Literary Inquiry, with special reference to the Pre-Restoration Stage in England. 1906.

Hadow, W. H. The Oxford History of Music. 6 vols. Oxford, 1901–5.

Kastner, L. E. Thomas Lodge as an imitator of the Italian Poets. Modern Language Review, II, 2, p. 155, January, 1907.

Knaut, C. F. Über die Metrik Robert Greene's. 1890.

Lanier, S. Shakspere and his Forerunners. 2 vols. 1902.

Penner, E. Metrische Untersuchungen zu George Peele. 1890.

Ritson, J. Bibliographia Poetica. 1802.

Saintsbury, G. A History of Elizabethan Literature. 1890.

—— A History of English Prosody. Vols. I. (1906) and II (1908).

Schelling, F. E. Poetic and verse criticism of the reign of Elizabeth. **Publications** of the University of Pennsylvania. 1891.

Scott, C. K. Madrigal Singing. 1907.

Scott, M. A.   Elizabethan Translations from the Italian.   Modern Language
    Association of America, x, xi, xiii and xiv.   Baltimore, 1895, 1896, 1898
    and 1899.
Symonds, J. A.   In the key of blue and other prose essays.   1893.   (Lyrics
    from Elizabethan Song-Books, p. 265.)
—— Essays Speculative and Suggestive.   Third edition.   1907.   (A Com-
    parison of Elizabethan with Victorian Poetry, p. 365.)
Tappan, E. M.   Nicholas Breton.   Modern Language Association, xiii.
    Baltimore, 1898.
Tovey, D. C.   Reviews and Essays.   1897.
Warton, T.   The History of English Poetry.   3 vols.   1774–81.
Wood, Anthony à.   Athenae Oxonienses.   Ed. Bliss, P.   1820.

CHAPTER VII

ROBERT SOUTHWELL.   SAMUEL DANIEL

Andrews, John.   Anatomie of Basenesse.   1615.   Rptd. in Grosart's Fuller
    Worthies' Library, vol. ii.
Barret, Robert (*fl.* 1600).   For his epic The Sacred Warr, see D. of N. B.

ROBERT CHESTER

Loves Martyr: or Rosalins Complaint.   Allegorically shadowing the truth of
    Love, in the constant Fate of the Phœnix and Turtle.   A Poeme enter-
    laced with much varietie and raritie; now first translated out of the
    venerable Italian Torquato Cæliano, by Robert Chester.   With the true
    legend of famous King Arthur. . . . 1601.   Reissued as: The Annals of
    great Brittaine.   Or, A Most Excellent Monument, wherein may be
    seene all the antiquities of the kingdome. . . . 1611.   Ed. Grosart,
    A. B.   Occ. Issues, vol. vii.   1878.   [Cf. Nathaniel Baxter's Sir Philip
    Sydney's Ourania, 1606.]

Sir Robert Chester, Knight, 1566 (?)–1640 (?).   This extraordinary collection of poems displays much learning in natural history as understood in its
author's time, much ingenuity in the making of acrostics and very little
poetry.   The portions concerning the Phoenix and Turtle appear to relate
to Elizabeth and Essex.   For the title given to it on its reissue there is little
excuse, King Arthur being the only historical, or mythological, subject with
which it deals.   The translation from "Torquato Cæliano" appears to be a
pure fiction.

SAMUEL DANIEL

Syr P. S. His Astrophel and Stella.   Wherein the excellence of sweet Poesy
    is concluded.   To the end of which are added, sundry other rare Sonnets
    of divers Noble men and Gentlemen.   1591.   (2 issues.)
Delia.   Contayning certayne Sonnets.   1592.
Delia . . . with the complaint of Rosamond.   1592.
Delia and Rosamond augmented.   Cleopatra.   1594.   Ed. Arber, E.   1877.
The Tragedie of Cleopatra.   1594.
Daniel's Delia and Drayton's Idea.   Ed. Esdaile, A.   1908.   (Contains a
    bibliography of Delia.)

The first fowre Bookes of the civile wars between the two houses of Lancaster and Yorke. 1595. (Contains also the fifth book, pagination and signatures following consecutively.)

The Poeticall Essayes of Sam. Danyel. Newly corrected and augmented. 1599.

This volume contains: Musophilus: containing a generall defence of learning, 1599; A letter from Octavia to Marcus Antonius, 1599; The Tragedie of Cleopatra, 1599; The first fowre Bookes of the civile wars, etc., 1595.

The Works of Samuel Daniel Newly augmented. 1601, 1602.

This folio contains: A Defence of Ryme: Against a Pamphlet entituled: Observations in the Art of English Poesie, wherein is demonstratively proved, that Ryme is the fittest harmonie of words that comportes with our Language [n.d.], rptd. by Haslewood, J., in Ancient Critical Essays, 1815; and also: A panegyrike congratulatory Delivered to the Kings most excellent majesty at Burleigh Harrington in Rutlandshire; also certaine Epistles. With a Defence of Ryme, heertofore written, and now published by the Author [n.d.].

The Vision of the 12. Goddesses, presented in a maske the 8. of January, at Hampton Court. 1604.

Certaine small poems lately printed: with the Tragedie of Philotas. 1605, 1607.

The Queenes Arcadia. A Pastorall Trage-Comedie presented to her Majestie and her Ladies, by the Universitie of Oxford in Christs Church, in August last. 1605, 1606.

A Funerall Poeme uppon the Death of the late noble Earle of Devonshyre. [n.d., 1606.]

The Civile Wares betweene the Howses of Lancester and Yorke. 1609.

Tethys Festival: or The Queenes Wake. Celebrated at Whitehall, the fifth day of June 1610. 1610.

Hymens' Triumph. A Pastorall Tragicomaedie. Presented at the Queenes Court on the Strand at her Majesties magnificent intertainement of the Kings most excellent Majestie, being at the Nuptials of the Lord Roxborough. 1615.

The whole workes of Samuel Daniel Esquire in Poetrie. 1623.

The Complete Works in verse and prose of Samuel Daniel. Ed. Grosart, A. B. Five volumes. 1885.

A Selection from the Poetry of Samuel Daniel & Michael Drayton. Ed. Beeching, H. C. 1899.

Inedited poems of Samuel Daniel. Philobiblon Society. Bibliographical and Historical Miscellanies. Vol. II. 1854.

JOHN DAVIES OF HEREFORD

Mirum in modum. A Glimpse of Gods Glorie and the Soules Shape. Eyes must be bright, or else no eyes at all Can see this sight, much more then mysticall. 1602.

Microcosmos. The Discovery of the Little World, with the government thereof. Oxford, 1603.

Humours Heav'n on Earth; With the Civile Warres of Death and Fortune. As also The Triumph of Death: Or, The Picture of the Plague, according to the Life; as it was in Anno Domini. 1603. 1605.

Bien Venu. Greate Britaines Welcome to her greate friendes, and deere
    brethren the Danes. 1606.
Summa Totalis or, All in All, and the same for ever: Or, an Addition to
    Mirum in Modum. 1607.
The Holy Roode, or Christs Crosse: Containing Christ Crucified, described
    in Speaking-picture. 1609.
Humours Heav'n on Earth: With the Civile Warres of Death and
    Fortune. As also The Triumph of Death: Or, The Picture of
    the Plague, according to the Life; as it was in Anno Domini 1603.
    1609.
Wittes Pilgrimage, (by Poeticall Essaies) Through a World of amorous
    Sonnets, Soule-passions, and other Passages, Divine, Philosophicall,
    Morall, Poeticall and Politicall. [1610.]
The Scourge of Folly. Consisting of satyricall Epigrams, And others in honour
    of many noble Persons and worthy friends, together, With a pleasant
    (though discordant) Descant upon most English Proverbs and others.
    [1611–12?.]
The Muse's Sacrifice, or Divine Meditations. 1612.
The Muses Teares for the losse of their hope; heroick and nere-too-much
    praised, Henry, Prince of Wales, &c. Together with Times Sobs for
    the untimely death of his Glory in that his Darling: and lastly, his
    Epitaphs. Consecrated To the hight and mighty Prince, Frederick the
    fift, Count Palatine of Rhoyn. &c. Whereunto is added, Consolatory
    Straines to wrest Nature from her bent in immoderate mourning.
    1613.
A Select Second Husband for Sir Thomas Overburie's Wife, now a matchlesse
    widow. 1617.

The Complete Works of John Davies of Hereford (15..–1618). Ed. Grosart,
    A. B. 2 vols. 1878.
Les Oeuvres Poetiques et Chretiennes de G. de Saluste, Seigneur du Bartas.
    2 vols. [Paris.] 1598.
Chertsey Worthies' Library. The Complete works of Joshuah Sylvester.
    Ed. Grosart, A. B. 2 vols. 1880.

CHARLES FITZGEFFREY

A Cornish clergyman (1575?–1637) educated at Cambridge, who wrote
much Latin verse. His work was well known to, and much admired by, his
poetical contemporaries.

Sir Francis Drake, His Honorable lifes commendation, and his Tragicall
    Deathes lamentations. Oxford, 1596.
    A very long poem in rime royal, full of classical allusion; dignified
    and scholarly, rather than poetical.
The Blessed Birth-day, celebrated in some religious meditations on the
    Angels Anthem. Luc. 2. 14. Also Holy Transportations in contem-
    plating some of the most observable adjuncts about our Saviours
    Nativity. The second Edition with Additions. Oxford, 1636.
    In rimed couplets of decasyllables: a work of considerable accom-
    plishment and religious and poetical fervour.
Poems. Ed. Grosart, A. B. Manchester, 1881.

William Forest

The History of Joseph the Chaiste composed in balladde royall crudely: largely derived from the Testaments of the Twelve Patriarchs. In two parts. MS. Part I in the library of University College, Oxford; Part II in British Museum, Royal Library, 18. C. xiii. Partially ptd. in Second Grisilde, *v. inf.*

A Notable warke called the pleasaunt poesye of princelie practise, composed of late in meatre royall by the symple and unlearned sir William forrest preeiste, muche parte collecte owte of A booke entiteled The governaunce of noblemen, which booke the wise philosopher Aristotele wrote too his discyple Alexandre the great and mightie Conqueroure. 1548. British Museum, Royal Library, 17. D. iii. Partially ptd. in England in the Reign of King Henry VIII. Part 1. Starkey's Life and Letters. Ed. Herrtage, S. J. Early English Text Society. 1878.

A metrical version of fifty of the Psalms. British Museum, Royal Library. 17. A. xxi. Partially ptd. in Second Grisilde. *v. inf.*

A New Ballade of the Marigolde. Rptd. in Harl. Misc. x, 253, 1813.

Paternoster and Te Deum in English Verse. In Foxe's Actes and Monuments, 1563.

A true and moste notable Historye of a right noble and famous ladye produced in Spayne, intytuled, the Seconde Grisilde, practiced not longe out of this tyme, in muche parte tragedous, as delectable bothe to Heearers and Readers. MS. in Bodleian library. Ptd. by Roxburghe Club. Ed. Macray, W. D. 1875.

An Oration consolatorye to Marye oure Queene. In same MS. as preceding entry, and ptd. as above.

The Life of the Blessed Virgin Mary with other poems. British Museum, Harl. MSS. 1703. Ptd. as above.

William Forrest (*fl.* 1581) was a Catholic priest, chaplain to queen Mary, and probably holder of an office in Wolsey's new college of Christ Church, Oxford. His most important poem, the Seconde Grisilde, presented by him to Mary in 1558, is a narrative of the divorce of her mother, queen Catherine of Arragon. His poems are interesting rather for the light they throw on the theological and social history of his times than for their merits as poetry. Forrest was a friend of Alexander Barclay, whom he mentions in the prologue to the second part of the Pleasaunt poesye of princelie practise. He was a musician, and the owner of copies of much good music of his day; his collection is now at Oxford.

Abraham Fraunce

The Lamentations of Amintas for the Death of Phillis; paraphrastically translated out of Latine into English Hexameteres. 1587, etc.

The Countesse of Pembrokes Yvychurch. Conteining the affectionate life, and unfortunate death of Phillis and Amyntas; That in a Pastorall; This in a Funerall: both in English Hexameters. 1591.

The Countesse of Pembrokes Emanuel. Conteining the Nativity, Passion, Buriall, and Resurrection of Christ: togeather with certaine Psalmes of David. All in English Hexameters. 1591.

The third part of the Countesse of Pembrokes Yvychurch: entitled, Amintas
Dale. Wherein are the most conceited tales of the Pagan Gods in
English Hexameters: together with their auncient descriptions and
Philosophical explications. 1592.

See, also, D. of N. B., 1908, vol. VII, *s.v.* Fraunce, Abraham; and the
introduction to Victoria, a Latin comedy, ed. Moore Smith, G. C., 1906, in
Materialien zur Kunde des älteren englischen Dramas, vol. XIV.

ROBERT SOUTHWELL

Saint Peters Complaint, with other Poemes. 1595. Also Edinburgh, [1595?.]
Saint Peters Complaint, newly augmented with other Poems. I live to dy:
I dy to live. Printed by H. L. for William Leake: and are to be sold
at his shop in Paules Churchyard, at the signe of the holy Ghost. [n.d.]
Also 1602, 1620.
Mæoniae, or, certaine excellent Poems and spirituall Hymnes: Omitted in
the last Impression of Peters Complaint; being needefull thereunto to
be annexed, as being both Divine and Wittie. All composed by R. S.
1595.
[A?] Foure-fould meditation, of the foure last things: viz.

1		Houre of Death.
2	of the	Day of Judgement.
3		Paines of Hell.
4		Joyes of Heaven.

Shewing the estate of the Elect and Reprobate. Composed in a Divine
Poeme. 1606. Ed. Edwards, C. 1895. (Isham Reprints, No. 4.)
Poetical Works. Ed. Turnbull, W. B. 1856.
Complete Poems of Robert Southwell, S. J. Ed. Grosart, A. B. 1872.

WILLIAM WARNER

Albions England. Or Historical Map of the same Island: prosecuted from
the lives, Actes and Labors of Saturne, Jupiter, Hercules, and Æneas:
Originalles of the Bruton, and Englishmen, and occasion of the Brutons
their first aryvall in Albion. . . . With Historicall Intermixtures, Invention, and Varietie proffitably, briefly and pleasantly performed in
Verse and Prose. 1586. Revised and enlarged 1589, etc. and in 1612
with the addition of the Epitome (in prose) of the whole history of England. Rptd., Chalmers, Eng. Poets, vol. IV, 1810. [See, also, Letters of
Charles Lamb, ed. Ainger, A., 1888, II, 93.]

BIOGRAPHY AND CRITICISM

Courthope, W. J. A History of English Poetry. Vols. II (1904) and III
(1903).
Fleay, F. G. On the career of Samuel Daniel. Anglia, vol. XI, p. 619. 1889.
—— A Biographical Chronicle of the English Drama, 1559–1642. 2 vols. 1891.
Hannay, D. The Later Renaissance. Edinburgh. 1898.
Isaac, H. Wie weit geht die Abhängigkeit Shakspere's von Daniel als
Lyriker? Shakespere Jahrbuch, XVII, p. 165. 1882.
Prideaux, W. F. Daniel's Delia, 1592. Athenæum, No. 3952, 25 July, 1903.
Quiller-Couch, A. T. Adventures in Criticism. 1896.
Saintsbury, G. A History of Elizabethan Literature. 1890.
—— A History of English Prosody. Vols. I (1906) and II (1908.)

CHAPTER VIII

THOMAS CAMPION

Thomae Campiani Poemata. Ad Thamesin. Fragmentum Umbrae. Liber Elegiarum. Liber Epigrammatum. 1595.

A Booke of Ayres, Set foorth to be song to the Lute, Orpherian, and Base Violl, by Philip Rosseter, Lutenist: And are to be solde at his house in Fleetstreete neere to the Gray-hound. 1601.

Observations in the Art of English Poesie. Wherein it is demonstratively prooved, and by example confirmed, that the English toong will receive eight severall kinds of numbers, proper to it selfe, which are all in this booke set forth, and were never before this time by any man attempted. 1602. [For Daniel's reply, see *ante* Vol. III.]

The Discription Of A Maske, Presented before the Kinges Majestie at White-Hall, on Twelfth Night last, in honour of the Lord Hayes, and his Bride. . . . To this by occasion other small Poemes are adjoyned. 1607.

Songs of Mourning: Bewailing the untimely death of Prince Henry. Worded by Tho. Campion. And set forth to be sung with one voyce to the Lute, or Viol: by John Coprario. 1613.

A Relation Of the Late Royall Entertainment Given By the Right Honorable The Lord Knowles, At Cawsome-House neere Redding: to our most Gracious Queene, Queene Anne, in her Progresse toward the Bathe, upon the seven and eight and twentie dayes of Aprill, 1613. Whereunto is annexed the Description, Speeches, and Songs of the Lords Maske, presented in the Banquetting-house on the Marriage night of the High and Mightie, Count Palatine, and the Royally descended the Ladie Elizabeth. 1613.

Two Bookes of Ayres. The First Contayning Divine and Morall Songs: The Second, Light Conceits of Lovers. To be sung to the Lute and Viols, in two, three, and foure Parts: or by one Voyce to an Instrument. [n.d. *c.* 1613.]

The Description of a Maske: Presented in the Banqueting roome at White-hall, on Saint Stephens night last, At the Mariage of the Right Honourable the Earle of Somerset: And the right noble the Lady Frances Howard. Whereunto are annexed divers choice Ayres composed for this Maske that may be sung with a single voyce to the Lute or Base-Viall. 1614.

The Third and Fourth Booke of Ayres. So as they may be expressed by one Voyce, with a Violl, Lute, or Orpharion. [n.d. *c.* 1617.]

A New Way of Making Fowre parts in Counter-point by a most familiar and infallible Rule. Secondly, a necessary discourse of Keyes, and their proper closes. Thirdly, the allowed passages of all Concords perfect, or imperfect, are declared. Also by way of Preface, the nature of the Scale is expressed, with a briefe Method teaching to Sing. [n.d. *c* 1617.]

Tho. Campiani Epigrammatum libri II. Umbra. Elegiarum liber unus. Excudebat E. Griffin. 1619.

Bullen, A. H. (ed.). The works of Dr. Thomas Campion. 1889.

——(ed.). Songs and Masques with Observations in the Art of English Poesy. 1903.

Reyher, Paul. Les Masques Anglais. Paris, 1909.

Rhys, Ernest (ed.). Lyric Poems. (Lyric Poets Series.) n.d.

Vivian, Percival (ed.). Poetical Works (in English) of Thomas Campion. 1907.

—— (ed.). Complete Works of Thomas Campion. Oxford. [In preparation.]

See, also, Egerton MS. 2599 (British Museum), being the Account book of Augustine Steward.

CHAPTER IX

THE SUCCESSORS OF SPENSER

WILLIAM BASSE

The Pastorals and other Workes of W. B. Never before imprinted. Oxford, 1653. Ed. Collier, J. P. Oxford, 1870. (See, also, Collier, J. P., Illustrations of early English Popular Literature, vol. II, 1863 ff.)

The Poetical Works of William Basse, now for the first time collected and edited, with introduction and notes by Bond, R. W. 1893. (With an excellent bibliography.)

Great Brittaines Sunnes-set, bewailed with a shower of tears. Oxford, 1613. Facsimiled by Allnutt, W. H. Oxford, 1872.

William Basse was born c. 1583. He wrote, in close imitation of Spenser's lighter mood, Pastorals and a long poem Urania. Izaak Walton quotes his Angler's Song and mentions Tom of Bedlam and the Hunter in his careere with admiration. Full information on his life and writings may be found in Bond's edition.

WILLIAM BROWNE, OF TAVISTOCK

Works; containing Britannia's Pastorals. The Shepherd's Pipe. The Inner Temple Masque, and other poems. 3 vols. 1772.

Original Poems of W. B. never before published, ed. Brydges, S. E. Lee Priory, 1815.

The Whole Works of W. Browne now first collected. Hazlitt, W. C. Roxburghe Library. 1868.

The Poems of William Browne, of Tavistock, Ed. Goodwin, G. With an introduction by Bullen, A. H. 2 vols. 1894.

An Elegie on the never Inough Bewailed Death of the Worthy, Vertuous, glory of these, and wonder for ensuing times, Henry, Prince of Wales. 1613.

Britannia's Pastorals. The first book appeared in folio, without any date on title-page: but the address to the reader is dated 18 June 1613. Book II, Printed by Thomas Snodham for George Norton, and are to be sold at the signe of the Red Bull without Temple-barre, 1616. Books I and II, 1625, and ed. Thompson, W., 1845. Book III was printed for the first time in 1852, by Croker, T. Crofton, from the MS. in the library of Salisbury cathedral.

The Inner Temple Masque. Jan. 13, 1614.

The Shepheard's Pipe. (Other Eclogues by Mr. Brooke, Mr. Wither, and Mr. Davies.) 3 pts. 1614.

Authorities

Breton, N. Pastoral Poems. Pembroke Booklets, no. 3. 1906.

Gosse, E. The Jacobean Poets. 2nd ed. 1899.

Moorman, F. W.   William Browne.   His Britannia's Pastorals.   1897.

Prince, J.   The Worthies of Devon.   1701.

Sidney, P.   The Subject of All Verse: being an enquiry into the authorship of a famous epitaph.   1907.

Transactions of Devonshire Association, vol. VI, 531; vol. XIX, 219–237.

SIR JOHN DAVIES

Collected Works

The Poetical Works of Sir John Davies published from a corrected copy formerly in the possession of Mr. Thompson.   1773.

Works in verse and prose (including hitherto unpublished MSS.).   Ed. Grosart, A. B.   In Fuller Worthies' Library.   3 vols.   1869–79.

Complete Poems.   Ed. Grosart, A. B.   2 vols.   1876.

Works.   Ed. Morley, H.   The Carisbroke Library.   Vol. X.   1889 ff.

Single Works

Orchestra or a Poeme on Dauncing Judicially prooving the true observation of time and measure, in the Authenticall and laudable use of Dauncing. 1596.   Rptd. in Arber's An English Garner, vol. V, 1882.

Orchestra or A Poeme expressing the Antiquitie and Excellencie of Dauncing. In a Dialogue betweene Penelope and one of her Wooers.   Not finished. 1622.   (Contains also Nosce teipsum, Hymnes of Astroea.)

Nosce teipsum.   This oracle expounded in two elegies.   1.   Of humane knowledge.   2.   Of the soule of man and the immortalitie thereof.   1599 (rptd. in Arber's An English Garner, vol. V, 1882), 1602, etc.

A discoverie of the true causes why Ireland was never entirely subdued . . . untill the beginning of his Majesties happie raigne.   1612.

Le primer Report des cases et matters en Ley resolves adjudges en les Courts de Roy en Ireland.   1615.   Translated, Dublin, 1762.

Hymnes of Astroea in acrosticke verse.   Praises of his Soveraigne Queen Elizabeth.   1618.

England's Independency.   1674.

A Poem on the immortality of the soul.   To which is prefixed an essay on the same subject, by Dr. T. Sheridan.   Together with historical relations concerning Ireland, by Sir J. D.   2 pts.   Dublin, 1751.

The antiquity . . . and succession of the High Steward of England.   The antiquity . . . of the Earl Marshall of England.   Of the antiquity, use . . . of lawful combats in England.   In A collection of curious discourses.   Vol. II.   Hearne, T.   1771.

Historical Tracts.   1786.

A letter to the Earl of Salisbury.   In Collectanae de rebus Hibernicis. Vol. I.   1786.

Epigrammes, reprinted from a rare edition in the possession of Sir C. Isham. Isham Reprints.   1870 ff.

See Woolrych, H. W., Lives of eminent Serjeants-at-Law, 2 vols., 1869.

WILLIAM DRUMMOND, OF HAWTHORNDEN

Collected Works

Poems: Amorous, Funerall, Divine, Pastorall, in Sonnets, Songs, Sextains, Madrigals.   1616.

Poems, By that most famous Wit, William Drummond of Hawthornden.
1656. (With a preface by Edward Phillips, Milton's nephew. It contains
most of the poems previously published, and about sixty new poems,
two of which are certainly not by Drummond.) The title-page of the B.
M. copy of 1659 reads: The most Elegant and Elabourate Poems of that
Great Court Wit Mr. William Drummond, etc. Printed for William
Rands Bookseller, at his House over against the Beare Taverne in Fleet
street, 1659. There is also another title-page bound up with the same:
Poems, By that most Famous Wit, William Drummond of Hawthornden.
Printed by W. H. and are to be sold in the Company of Stationers, 1656.
It contains the introduction by Phillips.

The Works of William Drummond, of Hawthornden. Consisting of those
which were formerly Printed and those which were design'd for the
Press. Now Published from the Author's Original Copies. Edinburgh:
printed by James Watson, in Craig's-Closs, 1711. (Edited by Sage,
John, and Ruddiman, T. Contains about forty additional poems,
many of doubtful authenticity; various prose tracts and papers; a
further selection of Drummond's correspondence, and a memoir by
bishop Sage which is the principal early authority for the life of
Drummond.)

Poems. Ed. Maitland, T. Maitland Club. Edinburgh, 1832. Ed. Turnbull, W. B. 1856. Rptd. in Library of British Authors. 1890. Ed.
Ward, W. C., in The Muses Library. 2 vols. 1894. (Contains
bibliography.)

Single Works

Teares on the Death of Meliades. Edinburgh, printed by Andro Hart, and
are to bee sold at his shop on the north side of the high streete, a litle
beneath the Crosse. 1613. 3rd ed. 1614.

Forth Feasting. A Panegyricke to the Kings Most Excellent Majestie.
Edinburgh, 1617. Rptd. in The Muses Welcome to King James, Edinburgh, 1618, with the prefixed sonnet by Drummond, which does not
appear in original edition.

Flowers of Sion. To which is adjoyned Drummond's Cypresse Grove. 1623.
Edinburgh, 1630. (Contains four new poems, viz. An Hymn of the
Ascension; a Sonnet, Death's Last Will; The Shadow of the Judgment;
and a Sonnet to the Obsequies of King James.)

The Entertainment of the high and mighty Monarch Charles, King
of Great Britaine, France, and Ireland, into his auncient and
royall citie of Edinburgh, the fifteenth of June, 1633. Edinburgh,
1633.

To The Exequies of the Honourable Sr Antonye Alexander, Knight, etc. A
pastorall Elegie. Edinburgh, printed in King James his College, by
George Anderson. 1638.

The History of Scotland, from the year 1423 until the year 1542, containing
the lives and reigns of James I–V. With several memorials of state
during the reign of James VI and Charles I. 1655.

A Cypress Grove. The Venetian Series. 1905. Ed. Bullen, A. H. Stratford-on-Avon, 1907.

See Conversations of Ben Jonson with William Drummond of Hawthornden, Shakspr. Soc., 1842.

GILES FLETCHER (THE YOUNGER)

(See also under Phineas Fletcher)

Poems. Fuller Worthies' Library. Ed. Grosart, A. B. 1868.
Complete Poems. Ed. Grosart, A. B. Early English Poets. 1876.

Sorrowes Joy Or a Lamentation for our late deceased Soveraigne Elizabeth, with a triumph for the prosperous succession of our gratious King, James. Cambridge, 1603.
Christ's Victorie, and Triumph in Heaven, and Earth, over, and after death. Cambridge, 1610, 1632, 1640.
The Reward of the Faithfull. 1623.
See Hunter's Chorus Vatum MS., Brit. Mus. Addit. MS. 24487, f. 79.

PHINEAS FLETCHER

Poems, ed. Grosart, A. B. Fuller Worthies' Library. 1868.
Giles and Phineas Fletcher. Poetical Works. Ed. Boas, F. S. Cambridge English Classics. 2 vols. 1908, 1909.

Single Works

Locustae, vel pietas Jesuitica. (The Locusts or Apollyonists.) Cambridge, 1627.
Brittain's Ida written by that renowned Poët Edmond Spencer. 1628. (Attributed by Grosart and Boas to Phineas Fletcher.)
Sicelides; a piscatory. 1631.
Joy in Tribulation, or Consolations for Afflicted Spirits. 1632.
The Way to Blessedness, a treatise on the First Psalme. 1632.
Sylva Poetica. Cambridge, 1633.
The Purple Island: or the Isle of Man: together with Piscatorie Eclogs and other Poetical Miscellanies. Cambridge, 1633.
Elisa or An Elegie Upon the Unripe Decease, of Sr Antoine Irby. Cambridge, 1633.
A Father's Testament. Written long since for the benefit of the particular relations of the author. 1670.

See Cole's MS., History of King's College, Cambridge, MS. xv, 35, and Hunter's Chorus Vatum MS., Brit. Mus. Addit. MS. 24487, f. 80.

FULKE GREVILLE, LORD BROOKE

[For sonnets, see Vol. III of the present work]

Certaine learned and elegant workes of the Right Honourable Fulke, Lord Brooke, written in his youth and familiar exercise with Sir Philip Sidney. Printed by E. P. for Henry Seyle, and are to be sold at his shop at the signe of the Tygers head in St. Paules Churchyard. 1633.
The Remains of Sir Fulk Grevill Lord Brooke: Being Poems of Monarchy and Religion: Never before Printed. Printed by T. N. for Henry Herringman at the sign of the Blew Anchor in the Lower Walk of the New Exchange. 1670. (Contains Poems, Alaham, Mustapha, Coelica, a Letter to an Honourable Lady a Letter of Travell.)
The Works in verse and prose complete of the Lord Brooke. Ed. Grosart, A. B. 4 vols. Fuller Worthies' Library. 1868.

The Tragedy of Mustapha. 1609.
The life of the renowned Sr Philip Sidney. With the true interest of
England, as it then stood in relation to all forrain princes: and par-
ticularly for suppressing the power of Spain, stated by him. His
principall Actions, Counsels, Designes, and Death. Together with a
short account of the maxims and policies used by Queen Elizabeth in her
government. Written by Sir Fulke Grevil, Knight, Lord Brook, a
Servant to Queen Elizabeth, and his Companion and Friend. 1652. Ed.
Brydges, E. 2 vols. Lee Priory, 1816. Ed. Smith, N. Oxford, 1907.
[Fully annotated.]

   See Bolton, E., Hypercritica, 1622; Hunter's Chorus Vatum MS., Brit. Mus.
Addit, MS. 24492, f. 107; A Tractate called the Patron, Brit. Mus. Addit. MS.
4839, f. 131; Walpole, H., Royal and Noble Authors, II, 220, 1806.

GEORGE WITHER

Workes. Containing Satyrs, Epigrams, Eclogues, Sonnets, and Poems.
Whereunto is annexed a Paraphrase on the Creed and the Lords Prayer.
1620.
Juvenilia. A Collection of those Poemes which were heretofore imprinted.
1622. Ed. Gutch, J. M. Bristol, 1820.
Divine Poems (by way of Paraphrase) on the Ten Commandments. Ed.
Elizabeth Barry (Wither's daughter). 1688.
Poems. Ed. Morley, H. 1891.

Epithalamia; or Nuptiall Poems. 1612. Rptd. 1633.
Prince Henrie's Obsequies, or Mournefull Elegies upon his death. 1612.
Abuses Stript and Whipt: or satyricall essayes. Divided into two bookes.
1613, 1617. Also 1632, containing Epithalamia and The Shepheards
Hunting.
Fidelia. 1615. Newly corrected and augmented. 1619. A rpt. of the 1615
edition in Arber's An English Garner, vol. VI, 1883.
Shepherds Hunting, The: being certaine Eglogues written during the time
of the Authors Imprisonment in the Marshalsey. 1615.
Wither's Motto, Nec habeo, nec Careo, nec Curo. London (?) 1621(?).
Faire-Virtue, the Mistresse of Phil'arete. A Miscelany of Epigrams, Sonnets,
Epitaphs, etc. 1622. Rptd. in Arber's An English Garner, vol. IV, 1882.
Verses intended to the King's Majesty, by Major G. W., whilst he was
prisoner in Newgate. 1622.
The Hymnes and Songs of the Church, divided into two parts. 1624?.
Ed. Farr, E., in Library of Old Authors. 1857–8.
Schollers Purgatory, The, discovered in the Stationers Commonwealth, and
described in a Discorse Apologeticall. 1625(?).
Britain's Remembrancer, containing a narration of the Plague lately past; a
declaration of the mischiefs present, and a prediction of judgments to
come, if repentence prevent not. 1628.
Collection of Emblemes, A, ancient and modern. 1634–5.
Halelujah, or Britans second Remembrancer bringing to Remembrance
(in praisefull and Poenitentiall Hymns, Spirituall Songs, and Morall
Odes) Meditations, advancing the glory of God, in the practise of Pietie
and Vertue; and applyed to easie Tunes, to be sung in Families, etc.
Composed in a threefold Volume, by George Wither. The first, contains
Hymns Occasionall. The second, Hymns Temporary. The third, Hymns

Personall. That all Persons, according to their Degrees, and Qualities, may at all Times, and upon all eminent Occasions, be remembered to praise God; and to be mindfull of their Duties. One woe is past, the second, passing on; Beware the third, if this, in vain be gone. 1641. Ed. Farr, E., in Library of Old Authors. 1857-8.

Campo-Musae, or the field-musings of Captain George Wither, touching his Military Engagement for the King and Parliament, the justnesse of the same, and the present distractions of these Islands. 1643.

Wither's prophesie of the downfal of Antichrist. 1644.

Letter of Advice touching the choice of Knights and Burgesses for the Parliament. 1645.

Vox Pacifica; a Voice tending to the Pacification of God's wrath. 1645.

Justifiarius justificatus: Justice justified. 1646.

Opobalsamum Anglicanum: an English Balme, lately pressed out of a shrub, and spread upon these papers. 1646.

Carmen expostulatorium, or a timely expostulation with those both of the city of London and the present armie. 1647.

Carmen Eucharisticon: a private thank-oblation exhibited to the glory of the Lord of Hosts. 1649.

British Appeals with Gods mercifull replies, on the behalfe of the Common-Wealth of England. 1651.

Dark Lantern, The, containing a dim discoverie. 1653.

Three private Meditations. 1655.

Epistolium-vagum-prosa-metricum; or an Epistle at randome, in prose and metre. 1659.

Petition, The, and narrative of G. W. Esq. concerning his many grievances and long sufferings. 1659.

Fides-Anglicana. Or, a plea for the publick-faith of these nations. 1660.

Speculum Speculativum: or a considering glass. 1660.

Tudor-Poeticus. A Poetick-Phrensie. 1660.

Paralellogrammaton. An epistle to the three nations of England, Scotland, and Ireland. 1662.

Echoes from the Sixth Trumpet. Reverberated by a review of neglected remembrances. 1666.

Nil Ultra; or, the Last Works of Captain G. W. 1668.

Vox Vulgi. A poem in censure of the Parliament of 1661. Macray, W. D. Anecdota Bodleiana. Pt. 2. 1879 ff.

Authorities

Arber, E. An English Garner. Vol. IV. 1882. Vol. VI. 1883.

Aubrey, J. Brief Lives. Ed. Clarke, A. Vol. I, 221; vol. II, 306-7. Oxford, 1898.

Hunter's Chorus Vatum MS., Brit. Mus. Addit. MS. 24491, f. 24.

Lamb, C. See works, ed. Lucas, E. V., 7 vols. 1903-5.

Spenser Society. The reprints of Wither's Works between 1870 and 1883. 20 pts.

Wood, A. à. Athenae Oxonienses. Ed. Bliss, P. Vol. III, 761-75. 1813.

Sir Henry Wotton

Works

Poems. Ed. Dyce, A. 1842.

Poems of Sir H. Wotton, Sir W. Raleigh and others. Ed. Hannah, J. 1845 ff.

A panegyrick of king Charles; being observations upon the inclination, life, and government of our sovereign lord the King. 1649.

Reliquiae Wottonianae; or a collection of lives, letters, poems; with characters of sundry personages: and other incomparable pieces of language and art Ed. with life by Walton, Izaak. 1651. Third edition with large additions. 1672. Fourth edition with additions and several letters to Lord Zouch, never publish'd till now. 1685.

The State of Christendom; or a most exact and curious discovery of many secret passages and hidden mysteries of the Times. 1657.

Letters to Sir Edmund Bacon. 1661.

Ad regem e Scotia reducem H. Wottoni plausus et vota. Monarchia Britannica. 1681.

A short view of the life and death of George Villiers Duke of Buckingham. Harleian Miscellany, vol. VIII. 1744.

Letter to John Milton, in Comus, a mask. 1747.

The elements of Architecture. In A second collection of scarce and valuable Tracts, vol. I, 1750. Ed. Prideaux, S. T. 1903.

A parallel between the Earl of Essex and the Duke of Buckingham. 1753.

Authorities

Smith, L. P. The Life and Letters of Sir Henry Wotton. 2 vols. 1907.

Walton, Izaak. The Life of Sir Henry Wotton. 1670. Also in the 1651 and earlier editions of Reliquiae Wottonianae.

Ward, A. W. Sir Henry Wotton: a biographical sketch. 1898.

CHAPTER X

MICHAEL DRAYTON

The Harmonie of the Church. Containing, The Spirituall Songes and holy Hymnes, of godly men, Patriarkes and Prophetes: all, sweetly sounding, to the praise and glory of the highest. Now (newlie) reduced into sundrie kinds of English Meeter: meete to be read or sung, for the solace and comfort of the godly. 1591. Rptd. 1610 as A Heavenly Harmonie of Spirituall Songes. Ed. Dyce, A., Percy Soc., vol. VII, 1843. In Poems, ed. Collier, J. P., Roxburghe Club, 1856. In Works, ed. Hooper, R., 1876.

[dea The Shepheards Garland, Fashioned in nine Eglogs. Rowlands Sacrifice to the Nine Muses. . . . By Peace Plenty. By Wisdome Peace. T. O. 1593. Rptd., ed. Collier, Roxburghe Club, 1856, and facsimiled, ed. Collier [1870?]. Revised and printed as Eglogs, in Poemes Lyrick and Pastoral [1606.] Rptd., Spenser Soc., 1891. Again revised and printed as Pastorals Containing Eglogues, in Poems, 1619 and 1620. Rptd. in Works, 1748, etc. Ed. Arber, E., in An English Garner, vol. VIII, 1896. Songs from editions of 1593, 1605 and 1606 in Minor Poems of M. D., ed. Brett, C., 1907.

Peirs Gaveston Earle of Cornwall. His life, death, and fortune. [1593 or 1594.] Rptd. 1595 (?); and revised in The Tragicall Legend of Robert, Duke of Normandy, etc., 1596; and in Poems of 1605, etc.; in Works, 1748, etc.; and Spenser Soc., Poems, 1888.

Matilda. The faire and chaste Daughter of the Lord Robert Fitzwater. The True Glorie Of The Noble House Of Sussex. 1594. Rptd. 1594; and in 1596 to 1888 as Peirs Gaveston above.

The Tragicall Legend of Robert, Duke of Normandy, surnamed Shortthigh, eldest sonne to William Conqueror. With the legend of Matilda. . . . And the Legend of Piers Gaveston. 1596. Rptd. in Poems, 1605, etc.; in Works, 1748, etc.; and in Spenser Soc., Poems, 1888.

The Legend of Great Cromwel. 1607. Rptd. 1609; in A Mirour for Magistrates, 1610, and ed. Haslewood, 1815; in Poems, 1619, 1620; and in Works, 1748, etc.

Ideas Mirrour. Amours in Quatorzains. 1594. Rptd. in Poems, ed. Collier, Roxburghe Club, 1856. Second edition, revised, in Englands Heroicall Epistles, 1599. Third edition, revised, in Eng. Her. Ep., 1600. Fourth edition, revised, in Eng. Her. Ep., 1602; rptd. with alterations in The Barrons Wars, 1603. Fifth edition, revised, in Poems, 1605; rptd. 1608, etc.; in Poems, Spenser Soc., 1888. Sixth edition in Poems, 1619; rptd. 1620, etc.; in Works, 1748, etc.; ed. Arber and Lee in An English Garner, 1883, 1904; ed. Morley in The Barons' Wars, 1887; ed. Crow in Elizabethan Sonnet-Cycles, 1897; Collier's Roxburghe Club Poems, 1856, contains also the sonnets from editions later than 1594; and Brett's Minor Poems, 1907, gives all the sonnets from all editions in the form in which they were first published, with others, not from Idea, in the appendix. Daniel's Delia and Drayton's Idea, ed. Esdaile, A., 1908, contains the 63 sonnets of 1619, with 11 others, and a bibliography of Ideas Mirrour.

Endimion and Phœbe. Ideas Latmus. n.d. [1595]. Rptd., ed. Collier, Roxburghe Club, 1856, and facsimiled, ed. Collier, 1870 (?). Portions incorporated in The Man in the Moone, 1606, q.v.

Mortimeriados. The Lamentable cruell warres of Edward the Second and the Barrons. 1596. Rptd., ed. Collier, Roxburghe Club, 1856. Later rewritten and published as

The Barrons Wars in the raigne of Edward the second, with Englands Heroicall Epistles. 1603. Rptd. in Poems, 1605, etc.; in Works, 1748, etc.; ed. Morley, 1882; Spenser Soc., Poems, 1888.

Englands Heroicall Epistles. 1597. Enlarged in 1598, in 1599 (? rptd. 1600), in 1602 (rptd. in The Barrons Wars, 1603), and in Poems, 1605; rptd. in Poems, 1608, etc.; rptd. alone [169-], 1697, 1737, [1758?]; in Works, 1738, etc.; and in Spenser Soc., Poems, 1888.

To the Majestie of King James. A gratulatorie Poem. 1603.

The Owle. Noctuas Athenas. 1604. Rptd. in Poems, 1619; in Works, 1748, etc.

A Pæan Triumphall composed for the Societie of the Goldsmiths of London: congratulating his Highnes magnificent entring the citie. 1604. Rptd. in Nichols, J., The Progresses . . . of King James the First, 1828.

Moyses in a Map of his Miracles. 1604. Altered and published as

Moses, his Birth and Miracles, in The Muses Elizium, 1630 (rptd. Spenser Soc., 1892); rptd. in Works, 1748, etc.

Poemes Lyrick and Pastorall. Odes, Eglogs, The Man in the Moone. [1606?.] Rptd. in Poems, ed. Collier, Roxburghe Club, 1856; Spenser Soc., 1891.

Odes. In Poemes Lyrick and Pastorall, 1606 (?); with additions in Poems, 1619, 1620; in Works, 1748, etc.; in Arber's English Garner, 1896 and 1903; in Minor Poems, ed. Brett, C., 1907.

The Man in the Moone. In Poemes Lyrick and Pastorall, 1606 (?); in Poems, 1619, 1620; in Works, 1748, etc.

Poly-Olbion or A Chorographicall Description of Tracts, Rivers, Mountaines, Forests, and other Parts of this renowned Isle of Great Britaine, With intermixture of the most Remarquable Stories, Antiquities, Wonders, Rarityes, Pleasures, and Commodities of the same: Digested in a Poem by Michael Drayton, Esq. With a Table added, for direction to those occurrences of Story and Antiquitie whereunto the Course of the Volume easily leads not. 1613.

A Chorographicall Description. . . . Divided into two Bookes; the latter containing twelve Songs, never before Imprinted. 1622. Before Song XIX is another title-page: The second part, or A Continuance Of Poly-Olbion From The Eighteenth Song. . . . 1622. Rptd. in Works, 1748, etc.; ed. Southey, in Select works of the British Poets, 1831; in Works, ed. Hooper, 1876; and Spenser Soc., 1890.

An Elegie on the Lady Penelope Clifton, by M. Dr.

An Elegie on the death of the three sonnes of the Lord Sheffield, drowned neere where Trent falleth into Humber.

These two are in Certain Elegies done by Sundrie Excellent Wits, 1618 and 1620. For later reprints, see The Battaile of Agincourt, 1627, etc.

Elegies upon sundry Occasions. In The Battaile of Agincourt, 1627, rptd. 1631; in Works (with omissions), 1748, etc. Rptd. in full from the edition of 1627 in Brett, C., Minor Poems, 1907.

The Battaile of Agincourt. . . . The Miseries of Queene Margarite, the infortunate wife of that most infortunate King Henry the sixt. Nimphidia, the Court of Fayrie. The Quest of Cinthia. The Shepheard's Sirena. The Moone-Calfe. Elegies upon sundry occasions. 1627. Rptd. 1631; in Works, 1748, etc.; ed. Garnett, R., 1893.

The Miseries of Queene Margarite. In The Battaile of Agincourt, 1627, and all subsequent editions.

Nimphidia. In the Battaile of Agincourt, 1627, and all subsequent editions. Also as the History of Queen Mab, 1751. Also ed. Brydges, E., 1814; in Selections, ed. Bullen, 1883; in The Barons' Wars, ed. Morley, 1887; in Selections, ed. Beeching, 1899; in Minor Poems, ed. Brett, C., 1907; and in Sidgwick, F., Sources and Analogues of A Midsummer-Night's Dream, Shakespeare Library, 1908, and elsewhere.

The Shepheards Sirena. In the Battaile of Agincourt, 1627, and all subsequent editions. Also in Minor Poems, ed. Brett, C., 1907.

The Moone-Calfe. In the Battaile of Agincourt, 1627, and all subsequent editions.

The Quest of Cynthia. In The Battaile of Agincourt, 1627, and all subsequent editions. Also in Minor Poems, ed. Britt, C., 1907.

The Muses Elizium, Lately discovered, By A New Way Over Parnassus. The passages therein, being the subject of ten sundry Nymphalls, Leading three Divine Poemes, Noahs Floud, Moses, his Birth and Miracles, David and Goliah. 1630. Rptd. in Works, 1748, etc.; Spenser Soc., 1892; in The Barons' Wars, ed. Morley, 1887; in Minor Poems, ed. Brett, C., 1907.

Noahs Floud. In The Muses Elizium, 1630; rptd. in Works, 1748, etc.

David and Goliah. In The Muses Elizium, 1630; rptd. in Works, 1748, etc.

Fugitive Pieces

In Morley, T., A First Book of Ballets, 1595; England's Helicon, 1600 and 1614, rptd., ed. Bullen, 1887; Middleton, C., Legend of Humphrey Duke of Gloucester, 1600; Geffe, N., The Perfect Use of Silk-Wormes, 1607;

Davies, J., of Hereford, The Holy Roode, 1609; Murray, D., Sophonisba, 1611· Coryate, T., Crudities, 1611; Chapman, G., The Georgicks of Hesiod, 1618; Munday, A., Primaleon, 1619; Naumachia or Hollands Sea-fight, 1622; Beaumont, Sir J., Bosworth-field, 1629; Annalia Dubrensia, 1636, rptd., ed. Grosart, A. B., 1877; Elton, O., Michael Drayton, 1905, p. 210. Some of these are collected by Brett, C., Minor Poems. For others of doubtful authenticity, see Elton, *ut supra*, pp. 203, 204.

Collected Works

1.   Editions published in Drayton's life-time

Poems: By Michaell Draiton Esquire.   London, Printed for N. Ling, 1605.

Poems: by Michael Drayton, Esquire.   1608, 1610, 1613.

Poems: by Michael Drayton Esquire, Viz. The Barons Warres, Englands Heroicall Epistles, Idea, Odes, The Legends of Robert, Duke of Normandie, Matilda, Pierce Gaveston And, Great Cromwell, The Owle, Pastorals, Contayning Eglogues, with the Man in the Moone.   n.d.

> This volume contains separate title-pages for certain sections, all dated 1619.   Rptd. in 1620.

Poems.   Newly Corrected and Augmented.   n.d., but 2 separate title-pages are dated 1620.

Poems: Newly Corrected by the Author.   n.d.   [1631 ?.]

2.   Editions published after Drayton's death

Poems, 1637.   Works (in one volume), 1748; rptd in four volumes, 1753; in British Poets; ed. Anderson, R., vol. III, 1795; in English Poets, 1810.

Poems.   By Michael Drayton, From The Earliest And Rarest Editions. Or From Unique Copies.   Ed. Collier, J. P.   Roxburghe Club.   1856,

The Complete Works of Michael Drayton.   Ed. Hooper, R.   3 vols.   1876 (unfinished).

Poems.   Spenser Soc.   1888.   (A reprint of the Poemes of 1606.)

Minor Poems of Michael Drayton.   Ed. Brett, C.   Oxford, 1907.

Selections

Selections from the Poems of Michael Drayton.   Ed. Bullen, A. H.   1883.

The Barons' Wars, Nymphidia, And Other Poems By Michael Drayton. Ed. Morley, H.   1887.

A Selection from the Poetry Of Samuel Daniel and Michael Drayton.   Ed. Beeching, H. C.   1899.

Biography and Criticism

Historical Essay in Works of 1748 and 1753.

Beeching, as under Selections, *supra*.

Brett, as under Collected Works (2), *supra*.

Bullen, as under Selections, *supra*.

Collier, as under Collected Works (2), *supra*.

Courthope, W. J.   History of English Poetry, vol. III.

Elton, O.   Michael Drayton.   A Critical Study With a Bibliography (which see for fuller details than can be given here).   Spenser Soc. 1895.   Second edition, enlarged and revised.   1905.

Esdaile, A., as under Ideas Mirrour, *supra*.

Fleay, F. G.   Biographical Chronicle of the English Drama.   1891.

CHAPTER XI

JOHN DONNE

I. Poems

An Anatomy of the World. Wherein By Occasion of the untimely death of Mistris Elizabeth Drury the frailty and the decay of this whole world is represented. Printed for Samuel Macham and are to be solde at his shop in Paules Churchyard, at the signe of the Bul-head. 1611. (Contains only the first Anniversary and A Funeral Elegie.) Second edition with addition of Of the Progresse of the Sowle Wherein By occasion of the Religious death of Mistris Elizabeth Drury, the incommodities of the Sowle in this life, and her exaltation in the next, are contemplated. The second Anniversarie. 1612. Rptd. 1621, 1625.

Lachrymae Lachrymarum. By Joshua Sylvester. Third edition. 1613. (Contains Donne's Elegie upon The Untimely Death of the Incomparable Prince Henry.)

Coryat's Crudities. 1611. [Among the Panegyricke Verses upon the Author and his Booke appears one headed "Incipit Joannes Donne."

> "Oh to what heigth will love of greatness drive
> Thy leavened spirit, sesqui-superlative."

It has a macaronic verse ("In eundum Macaronicon") as a kind of post-script, and is terminated by the words "Explicit Joannes Donne."

Farther on, the phrase "Incipit Joannes Dones" introduces the piece of verse beginning:

> "Loe her's a man worthy indeed to travell."]

Coryat's Crudities. 1776. (The two former poems reappear. Also, among the "Extracts relating etc." is another piece of verse assigned to Donne.

> "Another here thy Booke doth much commend
> That none can study it to any end," etc.

It repeats the conceits of the first poem.)

Poems, by J. D. With Elegies on the Author's Death. 1633, 1635 (with new arrangement, and several new poems, some of which are not Donne's), 1639, 1649 (very scarce).

Poems. With Elegies on the Author's Death. To which Is added divers Copies under his own hand never before in print. 1650, 1654, 1669.

Poems on several Occasions. 1719.

Satires (versified) by Alexander Pope. 1735.

Poetical Works. With life by Izaak Walton. 3 vols. Bell's Poets. Vols. XXIII–XXV. 1779. See also Anderson's Poets, vol. IV, 1793; and Chalmers's English Poets, vol. V, 1810.

Two elegies by Dr. Donne not in any edition of his works. In Waldron's Shakespearean Miscellany, part III, 1802. (Probably not by Donne.)

Unpublished poems. Ed. Simeon, Sir J. Philobiblon Society Miscellanies. 1856. (All doubtful or spurious.)

Complete Poems. Ed. Grosart, A. B. 2 vols. Fuller Worthies' Library. 1872–3.

Poems. From the Text of the Edition of 1633. Revised, Lowell, J. R. With the various readings of the other Editions, etc. By Norton, C. E. 2 vols. The Grolier Club. New York, 1895.

Love-Poems. Ed. Norton, C. E. Boston. MDCCCCV.

Poems. Ed. Chambers, E. K., with an introduction by Saintsbury, G. 2 vols. 1896.

II. MISCELLANEOUS PROSE WORKS

Pseudo-Martyr. Wherein out of Certaine Propositions and Gradations, this Conclusion is evicted that those which are of the Romane Religion in this Kingdome may and ought to take the Oath of Allegiance &c. 1610.

Conclave Ignatii: sive ejus in nuperis Inferni comitiis inthronisatio: Accessit et Apologia pro Jesuitis etc. [1611.]

Ignatius his Conclave: or his Inthronisation in a late election in Hell: wherein many things are mingled by way of Satyr. Translated out of Latin. 1611, etc.

Devotions upon Emergent Occasions, and severall Steps in my Sickness, etc. 1624, 1638.

Juvenilia: or Certaine Paradoxes and Problemes. 1633.

BIAΘANATOΣ. A Declaration of that Paradox or Thesis that selfe-homicide is not so naturally sinne that it may never be otherwise. 1648, 1700 (dedicatory Epistle by John Donne, the son).

Paradoxes, Problemes, Essayes, Characters, . . . to which is added a Book of Epigrams. 1652. (The Epigrams are not by Donne.)

Essayes in Divinity, being several disquisitions, interwoven with meditations and prayers, before he entered into Holy Orders. Now made publick by his son. 1651. Ed. Augustus Jessopp, 1855.

Letters to severall Persons of Honour. 1651, 1657.

A Collection of Letters made by Sir Tobie Mathews. 1660. (Includes several by Donne.)

III. SERMONS

A Sermon . . . preached to the honourable Company of the Virginian Plantation, 13th November, 1622.

A Sermon upon the xv verse of the xx chapter of the Book of Judges. 1622.

A Sermon . . . Preached at the Crosse the 15th of Sept. 1622.

Encœnia. The Feast of Dedication. Celebrated at Lincolne's Inne in a sermon At the dedication of a new Chapell there, etc. 1623.

The first sermon preached to King Charles, 3rd April, etc. 1625.

A Sermon of commemoration of the Lady Dävers. . . . 1627.

A Sermon preached to the Kings Mtie at Whitehall, 24 Feb. 1625. 1626.

Death's Duell, or a Consolation to the Soule against the dying Life and living Death of the body. Delivered in a sermon at Whitehall, before the King's Majesty in the beginning of Lent 1630, etc. . . . Being his last Sermon and called by his Majesties household The Doctor's owne Funerall Sermon. 1632, 1633.

Six Sermons . . . preached before the King and elsewhere. 1634.

LXXX Sermons. 1640/1.

Fifty Sermons. Second Volume. (The LXXX Sermons forming the first.) 1649.

XXVI Sermons never before published. The Third Volume. 1660/1.

IV. Biographies and Appreciations

Alford, H., in Collected Works of Donne. 6 vols. 1839.

Courthope, W. J. A History of English Poetry. Vol. III, chap. VIII, The School of Metaphysical Wit—John Donne. 1903.

Gosse, Edmund. The Life and Letters of John Donne, Dean of St. Paul's. Now for the first time revised and collected. 2 vols. 1899.

Harrison, John Smith. References to Donne's conceptions of Love and Woman in Platonism in English Poetry of the sixteenth and seventeenth centuries. Columbia University Press, New York, 1903.

Jessopp, Augustus. John Donne. (See, also, D. of N. B.) 1897.

Johnson's Lives of the Poets. (Cowley.) Vol. I. 1779.

Lightfoot, J. B. Donne, the Poet-Preacher. 1877.

Melton, Wightman Fletcher. The Rhetoric of John Donne's Verse. Johns Hopkins University. 1906.

Phillips, Edward. Theatrum Poetarum, or a Compleat Collection of the Poets, etc. 1674.

Walton, I. The Life and Death of Dr. Donne. Prefixed to LXXX Sermons, and signed Iz. Wa. 1640–. Also much enlarged in 1658, 1670, etc.

Articles

Dowden, Edward, The Poetry of John Donne. The Fortnightly Review, New Series, vol. XLVII, p. 791. Reprinted in New Studies in Literature, 1895.

Fathers of Literary Impressionism. Quarterly Review, vol. CLXXXV, p. 173.

Gosse, Edmund. The Poetry of John Donne. The New Review, vol. IX, p. 236.

John Donne and His Contemporaries. Quarterly Review, vol. CXCII, p. 217.

Minto, William. John Donne. The Nineteenth Century, vol. VII.

Stephen, Leslie. John Donne. National Review, vol. XXXIV, p. 595.

Symons, Arthur. John Donne. The Fortnightly Review, New Series, vol. LXVI, p. 734.

CHAPTER XII

THE ENGLISH PULPIT FROM FISHER TO DONNE

I. History of Preaching

The best complete survey of Christian preaching is the art. Predigt by Schian in Hauck-Herzogs Realencyklopädie, vol. XV. A good outline is given in A History of Preaching, A.D. 70–1572, by Dargan, E. C., 1905.

For the later medieval sermon see Gasquet, F. A., The Eve of the Reformation (3rd ed., 1905), and The Old English Bible (2nd ed., 1908); Neale, J. M., Mediaeval Preachers (1856); Baring Gould, S., Post-Mediaeval Preachers (1865): and the ridicule by Erasmus in Encomium Moriae.

For the reformation period: of general ecclesiastical historians, Dixon gives most attention to the preachers. The best special account is Sketches of the Reformation and Elizabethan age taken from the contemporary Pulpit, by Haweis, J. O. W., 1844. See also Puritan Preaching in England, by Brown, John. The most important regulations about preaching are given in Documents illustrative of English Church History, compiled by Gee, H., and Hardy, W. J., 1896.

Contemporary views of the proper methods of preaching may be found in Erasmus, Ecclesiastes sive concionator Evangelicus, Basel, 1535; Amandi Polani De Concionum sacrarum methodo, Basel, 1574; William Perkins, Prophetica, sive de sacra et unica ratione concionandi, Cambridge, 1592 (translated as The Art of Prophesying, 1606); Matthaei Sutlivii (*i.e.* Sutcliffe, 1550?–1629), De concionum formulis, 1602. For a later criticism see Bishop Burnet, Of the Pastoral Care, chap. IX.

II. SERMONS

Andrewes, Lancelot. XCVI Sermons . . . published by his Majesties speciall Command. Folio. 1629. 2nd ed., 1631; 3rd, 1635.

—— The Moral Law expounded . . . whereunto is annexed 19 Sermons . . . upon Prayer. . . . Also 7 Sermons on our Saviours Tentations. 1642.

—— 'Αποσπασμάτια Sacra; or a collection of posthumous & orphan Lectures delivered at St. Paul's and St. Giles his church. 1657.

—— Collected Edition by Wilson, I. P. (Anglo-Catholic Library.) 5 vols. Oxford, 1841–3.

—— Index of texts, & general index to sermons, by Bliss, J. (Anglo-Cath. Libr.) Oxford, 1854.

See, also, a lecture by Church, R. W., in Masters in English Theology, 1877, and biographies by Ottley, R. L., 1894, and Whyte, A., 1896.

Bancroft, Richard (1544–1610). A Sermon preached at Paules Crosse the 9 of Februarie, being the first Sunday in the Parliament, anno 1588.

Becon, Thomas (1512–67). A new Postil conteinyng most godly & learned sermons upon all the Sonday Gospelles. 1566.

Bilson, Thomas (1547–1616), bishop of Winchester. The effect of certain Sermons touching the full Redemption of Mankind. 1599.

Bradford, John. A Sermon on Repentance. 1553.

—— Two Sermons. (The above, with one on the Lord's Supper.) 1574.

—— Writings. Parker Soc., ed. Townshend, A. Cambridge, 1848.

Broughton, Hugh (1549–1612). An Exposition upon the Lord's Prayer . . . preached in a Sermon at Oatelands. . . . Aug. 13, 1603. 1613 (?).

—— The Works of the great Albionean divine renownd in many nations for rare skill in Salems and Athens tongues, & familiar acquaintance with Rabbinical learning. 4 tomes, folio. 1662.

Cole, Thomas (d. 1571). A godly & learned sermon, made . . . before the Queens majestie, the first of Marche, 1564. 1564.

Colet, John. Oratio . . . ad Clerum in Convocatione, anno 1511.

—— The Sermon . . . made to the Convocacion at Paulis. Berthelet, T., 1511 (?). See Maitland's Early Printed Books, p. 239. Rptd. as A Sermon of Conforming & Reforming, with extracts from Andrewes and Hammond, and notes by Smith, T., Cambridge, 1661; also in The Phoenix, 1708, vol. II; in Life by Knight, Samuel, 1724 and 1823; and in Life by Lupton, J. H., 1887; 2nd ed., 1909.

Valuable information in Erasmi Epistolae (Leyden ed.), III, no. ccccxxxv, and especially in annotated edition of the same by Lupton, J. H., The Lives of Vitrier & Colet, written in Latin by Erasmus of Rotterdam, in a Letter to Justus Jonas, 1883.

Dering, Edward. A Sermon preached at the Tower of London the xi day of December, 1569.

Dering, Edward. A Sermon preached before the Quenes Majestie the 25 Februarie, anno 1569.
—— Maister Derings Workes. 3 vols. 1590 and 1614.
Donne, John. See bibliography to Chap. xi.

See also, article on Izaak Walton's Life of Donne in Religio Laici by Beeching, H. C., 1902, and Lightfoot, J. B., in Classic Preachers of the English Church, ed. Kempe, J. E., 1877.

Drant, Thomas (d. 1578?). A fruitfull . . . Sermon, specially encouraging Almes giving. 1572. [For his Latin verses, see D. of N. B.]
—— Three godly & learned sermons. 1584.
Fisher, John. This treatyse concernynge the fruytful saynges of Davyd the kynge & prophete in the seven penytencyall psalmes. Devyded in seven sermons was made & compyled . . . at the exortacion and sterynge of . . . Margarete, countesse of Rychemount & Derby, etc. Wynkyn de Worde, 1508 and 1509. Reprints in 1714, 1876 (Mayor), and 1888 (Vaughan, K.).
—— This sermon folowynge was compyled & sayd in the Cathedrall chyrche of saynt Poule . . . , the body beynge present of . . . kynge Henry the VII the x day of Maye . . . mccccix. Wynkyn de Worde. 1509.
—— Hereafter followeth A Mornynge Remembraunce had at the moneth minde of the noble prynces Margarete countesse, etc. Wynkyn de Worde, without date [1509]. Reprints edited by Baker, T., 1708; Hymers, J., 1840; Ashbee, C. R., 1906.
—— The sermon of . . . made agayn yᵉ pernicyous doctryn of Martin luuther, 1521. Wynkyn de Worde, 1521 (?). Reprints 1528 (?), 1554, 1556, 1876 (Mayor).
—— A Sermon had at Paulis by the cōmandment of . . . my lorde legate, & sayd by Johñ the byshop of Rochester, upō quīquagesom sonday concernynge certayne heretickes, whiche thā were abjured for holdynge the heresies of Martyn Luther. Berthelet, T., 1525 (?).

(This sermon is sometimes confused with the preceding sermon. It is not included in any modern edition. The Brit. Mus. copy (C 53 b. 15) has several corrections, made in a contemporary hand, not Fisher's, but perhaps at his instance.)
—— The English Works, now first collected by Mayor, John E. B. (E.E.T.S. Ex. Ser. xxvii), Part i. (No other Part published.) 1876.
See, also, John Fisher, sein Leben und Wirken by Kerker, M., Tubingen, 1860; Vie du beinheureux Martyr J. F., texte anglais et traduction latine du xviᵉ siècle, publiés par Fr. von Ortroy, Brussels, 1893; and Life by Bridgett, T. E., 1888; 2nd ed., 1890.

Gilpin, Bernard. A Godly Sermon preached in the court at Greenewich the first Sonday after the Epiphanie An. Do. 1552. 1581. Rptd. in Life by Carleton, bp. G., 1629, and in Life by Gilpin, W., 1752. See Leaders in the Northern Church by Lightfoot, J. B., 1890.

Gosson, Stephen. The Trumpet of Warre. A sermon preached at Paules Crosse the seventh of Maie, 1598.

Grindal, Edmund (1519–83). A Sermon, at the ffuneral solemnitie of the most high & mighty Prince Ferdinandus. 1564. Rptd. in Remains, edited for the Parker Soc. by Nicholson, W., Cambridge, 1843.

Harspfield, John (1516–78). Concio quaedam habita coram Patribus et Clerⁱⁿ ecclesia Paulina Londini, 26 Oct. 1553.

Harpsfield, John. A notable & learned sermon or Homilie upon S. Andrewes Daye last past. 1556.

Hooker, Richard. See bibliography to Chap. xviii in Vol. III.

See, also, Puritan and Anglican, by Dowden, E., 1900; Religio Laici, by Beeching, H. C., 1902; and Notes on English Divines, by Coleridge, S. T., 1853.

Hooper, John. An oversighte and deliberacion uppon the holy prophet Jonas: . . . Comprehended in seven Sermons. 1550.

—— A funerall oratyon made the xiiii day of January . . . 1549.

—— Early Writings of. Ed. Carr, S. Parker Soc. Cambridge, 1843.

Hutchinson, Roger (d. 1555). A faithful Declaration of Christes holy supper, comprehended in thre Sermons preached at Eaton Colledge . . . 1552. 1560.

—— Works. Edited for the Parker Soc. by Bruce, J. Cambridge, 1842.

Jewel, John. The Copie of a Sermon pronounced by the Byshop of Salisburie at Paules Crosse the second Sondaye before Easter . . . 1560. (The famous challenge was first given in a sermon at Paul's Cross on 26 Nov., 1559; it was repeated in substance at court on 17 Mar., 1560, and at Paul's Cross again on 31 Mar. It was then printed, as above.)

—— Certaine sermons preached before the Queens Majestie and at Paules Crosse. 1583.

—— Seven godly and learned sermons. 1607.

—— Works. With Life by Featley, D. 1609.

—— Works. Ed. for Parker Soc. by Ayre, J. 4 vols. Cambridge, 1845–50.

—— Works. Ed. by Jelf, R. W. 8 vols. Oxford, 1848.

Latimer, Hugh. See bibliography to Chap. ii in Vol. III and add

—— Concio quam habuit . . . ēpus Worcestrie in cōuētu spiritualiū nono Junii, ante inchoationē Parlamenti celebrati anno 28 . . . Regis Henrici octaui. Southwarke, 1537. (An English translation also in 1537.)

—— Certain Sermons made . . . before . . . Katherine, duchess of Suffolk, 1552, 1562 (edited by Latimer's Helvetian Secretary, Augustine Bernher).

—— Sermons. (Everyman's Library). With Introduction by Beeching, H. C. 1906.

See, also, on Latimer's preaching, The Jewel of Joy (1553) by Thomas Becon, and chap. iii in Leaders of the Reformation by John Tulloch, Edinburgh, 1883.

Lever, or Leaver, Thomas. A fruitfull Sermon made in Poules churche at London in the Shroudes the seconde daye of Februari. 1550.

—— A Sermon preached ye fourth Sunday in Lent before the Kynges Majestie . . . 1550.

—— A Sermon preached at Poules Crosse, the xiiii day of Decembre. 1550.

—— Three fruitfull sermons . . . made 1550, and now newlie perused by the authour. 1572. The only reprint is Edward Arber's, 1870, 1901.

Longland, John. Johannis Longlondi dei gratia Lincolniensis Episcopi, Tres Conciones. (The first was delivered in the presence of Wolsey and the legate, 10 Jan., 1519, the second at the foundation of Cardinal college in 1525, the third before an assembly of bishops in Westminster Abbey on 27 Nov., 1527.) Printed by Pynson, R., 1527 (?).

—— Quinque Sermones, sextis quadragesimae feriis habiti coram illustrissimi regis Henrici VIII, 1517. Printed by Pynson, R. Re-issued with the preceding, 1527. Both are translated from the original English, probably by Thomas Caius.

Longland, John. A Sermōd made before the kynge hys hyghenes at Rychemunte uppon good fryday, . . . MCCCCCXXXVI (Petyt?, 1536?). (An imperfect copy, without imprint, in the library of Trin. Coll. Camb.)
—— A Sermonde made before the Kynge, his majestye at grenewiche, upon good Frydaye, . . . MDXXXVIII. Thomas Petyt, undated, [1538?]. (The Brit. Mus. copy, C 53 k. 14, has on the flyleaf, Tho. Baker coll: Jo: Socius ejectus, "liber rarissimus," and other MS. notes.)
Perkins, William. A godly and learned exposition upon the whole epistle of Jude, containing threescore & sixe sermons, preached at Cambridge. 1606.
—— A . . . exposition of Christ's Sermon in the Mount. Cambridge, 1608.
—— The Workes . . . gathered. 3 vols. Cambridge, 1616–18.
Rainolds, or Reynolds, John. The prophecie of Obadiah opened & applyed in sondry sermons. Oxford, 1613. (Edited by Hinde, W., after Rainolds's death, apparently from H.'s own MS. notes.) Rptd. Edinburgh, 1864.
—— The Discovery of the Man of Sinne . . . first preached in divers sermons to the Universitie & Cittie of Oxon. (Ed. by Hinde, W.) Oxford, 1614.
—— The Prophesie of Haggai interpreted & applied in sundry Sermons. Never before printed. 1649.
See Hallam's appreciation of Rainolds in Hist. Eur. Lit. II, 86.
Sandys, or Sandes, Edwin. Sermons. (The Epistle to the Reader is not by the preacher.) 1585 and 1616.
—— Sermons. Edited for Parker Soc. by Ayre, J. Cambridge, 1842.
Smith, Henry. The Examination of Usurie in two sermons, taken by characterie, & after examined. (With a short preface, signed, Thine H. S.) 1591. These and several other sermons were printed in the author's lifetime, and for twenty years after his death there was a remarkably large output of his sermons, singly, in small sets and in collected editions. On the use of shorthand for taking down sermons, see Encycl. Brit., art. Shorthand (Keith-Falconer, I.) and Watson, Foster, The English Grammar Schools, Cambridge, 1908.
—— The Sermons . . . gathered into one volume. 1592. Another edition, ed. by Thomas Fuller (with a short memoir). 1657. Reprint, 1866.
—— A selection of the Sermons. Edited by Brown, John. Cambridge. 1908.
Udall, or Uvedale, John (1560?–92). Amendment of Life, in three sermons. 1584. Reprint, 1596.
—— Obedience to the Gospell. Two Sermons. 1584 and 1596.
—— Peters Fall: two sermons. 1584.
Whitgift, John (1530?–1604). A Godlie Sermon preached before the Queenes Majestie at Grenewiche the 26 of March last past. 1574. Reprint in Parker Soc.'s ed., 1853.

III. Devotional Writings

Alcock, John (1430–1500), bishop of Ely. Mons perfectionis, otherwyse in Englysshe, The Hylle of perfeccyon. Wynkyn de Worde, 1497, 1499 and 1501.
Andrewes, Lancelot. A manual of the private devotions of . . . , Translated out of a fair Greek MS. of his amanuensis by R. D[rake]. 1648.
—— Preces Privatae, Graecè & Latinè. (Ed. by Lamphire, John.) Oxonii, 1675. Important modern editions: Newman, J. H., 1842; Meyrick, F., 1865–73; Medd, P. G., 1892 and 1899, and especially Brightman, F. E., 1903.

Babington, Gervase (1550?–1610), bishop of Worcester. A briefe Conference betwixt mans Frailty and Faith. 1584.

Bayly, Lewes (d. 1631), bishop of Bangor. The Practice of Piety. 1612. 51 editions by 1714. Printed also in French (1625), German (1629) and Welsh (1630). Modern edition by Webster, G., 1842.

Becon, Thomas. Davids Harpe ful of moost delectable armony newely strynged & set in tune by Theodore Basille [i.e. Becon, T.]. Mayler, J., 1541.

—— The Pomaunder of Prayer. 1558. (Another Book with this title was printed by W. de Worde in 1532.)

Bradford, John. Godlie Meditations. Hall, R. 1562.

Bull, Henry (d. 1575?). Christian Prayers & holie meditations . . . gathered. 1566 and 1570. Parker Soc. 1842.

Byfield, Nicholas (1579–1622). The Marrow of the Oracles of God. 1620.

Catherine Parr, queen of England. Prayers or Medytacions . . . collected out of holy woorkes. 1545.

Daye, Richard (1552–1607?). A Booke of Christian Prayers, collected out of the aunciēt writers, and best learned in our tyme. 1569.

Donne, John. Devotions upon emergent occasions, & severall steps in my sicknes. 1624. Pickering's ed. 1840.

Elyot, Sir Thomas. A swete & devoute sermon of holy saynct ciprian of mortalitie of men. The rules of a christian life made by Picus erle of Mirandola, both translated into englyshe. 1539.

Featley, Daniel (1582–1645). Ancilla Pietatis, or, The Hand-Maid to Private Devotion. 1626.

Fisher, John. A spirituall consolation . . . to hys sister Elizabeth, at suche tyme as hee was prisoner. 1535 and 1577. Paris, 1640. E.E.T.S. 1876.

—— The wayes to perfect Religion, made by . . . being Prysoner in the Tower of London. 1535. E.E.T.S. 1876.

—— A godlie Treatisse declaryng the benefites, fruites, & great commodities of prayer. 1560. Modernised version, 1887. (De Fructu Orationis, 1575.)

Hunnis, William (d. 1579). The Seven Sobs of a Sorrowful Soule for Sinne. 1583.

Norden, John (fl. 1600). A pensive mans practise. 1584.

—— The Progresse of Piety, whose Jesses lead into the Harborough of heavenly Hearts-ease. 1591. Parker Soc. 1847.

Parsons, or Persons, Robert (1546–1610), S.J. The first booke of the Christian Exercise appertayning to resolution. (Preface signed R. P.) Rouen, 1582. Rptd. with additions, as A Christian Directorie, guiding men to their salvation, commonly called the Resolution . . . with Reproofe of the corrupt & falsified edition . . . by E. Buny. Rouen (?), 1585. [Edmund Bunny edited several protestant editions, from 1584 onwards, which Parsons described as "punished & plumed (which he termeth purged)."]

Primers, reformed and unreformed. See bibliography in Sarum and York Primers, with kindred books, by Edgar Hoskins, 1901.

Prose lives of Women Saints. Ed. Horstmann, C. E.E.T.S. 1886.

Rogers, Thomas (d. 1616). A pretious book of heavenly meditations, called a private talke of the soule with God. Written, as some thinke, by . . . S. Augustine, and not translated only, but purified also . . . by T. R. 1581.

Southwell, Robert, S.J. Mary Magdalens Teares. 1591.
—— The Triumph over Death; or, A consolatorie Epistle. 1596.
—— A hundred Meditations on the Love of God. Ed. Morris, J. 1873.
Sutton, Christopher (1565?–1629). Disce Mori. 1600. Ed. Newman, J. H., 1839.
—— Disce Vivere. 1603.
Symon, "the Anker of London Wall" (*fl.* 1512–29). (Sometimes identified with Whytford, R.) The Fruyte of Redempcyon . . . compyled . . . in Englysshe for your ghostly conforte that understande no latyn. W. de Worde, 1514.
Whytford, Richard (*fl.* 1495–1555?), "wretch of Syon." A Werke for Housholders, or for them that have the gydyng or governaunce of any company. W. de Worde, 1530.
—— A werke of preparation . . . unto communion. Redman, R. (*c.* 1531).
—— The folowyng of Christ. (Based on version of Atkynson, W., 1503.) 1535 (?). Cawood, 1556. Edited by Raynal, W., 1872 and 1908.
—— (attributed to). The Psalter of Jesus. The earliest printed copy yet found is at the end of a Salisbury Primer, printed by Thielman Kerver, Paris, 1532. But, for earlier authority, see The Psalter of Jesus: from a MS. of the fifteenth century, preface signed H. G[ough], 1885. Also (written without knowledge of H. G.'s tract), Jesus Psalter: what it was at its origin, by Sole, S. H., 1888.

CHAPTER XIII

ROBERT BURTON, JOHN BARCLAY AND JOHN OWEN

I. BURTON

i. *Biography, and Burton's Library*

MSS. Marshall, 132 (Bodleian), an early fourteenth century volume of Statuta Angliae, at one time in the possession of Burton's ancestor, William Burton, who fell in the battle of Towton, 1461. It has been used for memoranda, and contains a pedigree of the Burton family, medical recipes and notes by Burton's father.

The original will of Robert Burton, proved in May, 1640, in the Prerogative Court of Canterbury, is now at Somerset house. (See, also, Stephen Jones's Life of Burton in the 1800 edition of the Anatomy, and often in later reprints.)

MSS. Seld. *supra* 80 (Bodleian). Among the contents is "A Note of Mr. Robert Burton's books, given to the Library by his Last Will and testament A° Dni. 1639." The Bodleian contains many books with Burton's autograph. In some, passages are marked by his pen. Those of his books which belong to the library of Christ Church have, through Osler's liberality, been brought together and placed in a special case, with editions of the Anatomy.

Burton, William. Description of Leicester Shire, 1622, pp. 173–9. On the engraved title is a bird's-eye view of Lindley, the house in which Robert Burton was born. The Brit. Mus. copy (at one time Peter le Neve's) has MS. notes on the Burton pedigree.

Hearne, Thomas. His edit. of Benedictus, Abbas Petroburgensis, Oxford, 1735, Appendix ad Praefationem, pp. lv, lvi.
—— Reliquiae Hearnianae. Ed. Bliss, P. 2nd ed. Vols. I, 282; III, 113, 114–5. 1869.
Kennet, White. A Register and Chronicle. Vol. I (all published), 320. 1728.
Lluelyn, Martin. Elegie: On the Death of Master R. B., in Men-Miracles, with other Poemes by M. Ll., p. 124. Oxford, 1646.
Macray, W. D. Annals of the Bodleian Library, pp. 46, 90–92, 159. 1890.
Nichols. J. The History and Antiquities of the County of Leicester. Vols. III, 415–9, 557–9, 1137; IV, 635, 668. 1795–1811.
Thompson, H. L. Christ Church (College Histories, University of Oxford), pp. 245, 254. Oxford, 1898.
Wood, Anthony à. Athenae Oxonienses. Ed. Bliss, P. Vol. II, cols, 652–4. 1815.
—— Fasti Oxonienses. Ed. Bliss, P. Part I, cols. 296, 305, 357.

ii. *Philosophaster, and Occasional Latin Verse*

A MS. of Philosophaster was formerly in the possession of W. E. Buckley. Another is in Lord Mostyn's library.

Philosophaster, Comoedia; Poemata adhuc sparsim edita, nunc in unum. collecta. Ed. Buckley, W. E. Roxburghe Club. Hertford, 1862. The poems had appeared in Academiae Oxoniensis Pietas erga Jacobum Regem, Oxford, 1603; Musa Hospitalis, Ecclesiae Christi, Oxon., Oxford, 1605; Justa Oxoniensium (in memory of Henry, Prince of Wales, London, 1612); Death Repealed, Verses on Lord Bayning, Oxford, 1638; and similar collections. Buckley did not give all Burton's Latin verse. At the beginning of the 1617 ed. of Rider's Dictionarie, corrected by Francis Holyoake, are some Latin elegiacs by Burton addressed to the editor.

An edition of Philosophaster by Bensly, E., is announced as in preparation in W. Bang's Materialien zur Kunde des älteren Englischen Dramas (Louvain).

iii. *The Anatomy of Melancholy*

The Anatomy of Melancholy, What it is. With all the Kindes, Causes, Symptomes, Prognostickes, and Severall Cures of it. In Three Maine Partitions with their severall Sections, Members, and Subsections. Philosophically, Medicinally, Historically, Opened and Cut up. By Democritus Junior, With a Satyricall Preface, conducing to the following Discourse. Macrob. Omne meum, Nihil meum. 4to. Oxford, 1621. The next seven editions are in folio. The first edition of the Anatomy contains the Conclusion of the Author to the Reader, signed in Burton's own name. Second ed., Oxford, 1624. Third (first with engraved frontispiece explained in English verses, and introductory poems in English and Latin), Oxford, 1628. Fourth, Oxford, 1632. Fifth (begun at Edinburgh and stopped by Burton's printers), Oxford, 1638. Sixth, Oxford, 1651, and London, 1652. Seventh, 1660. Eighth (double columns), 1676. Editions of 1728 and 1738, mentioned in Watt's Bibliotheca Britannica, appear to be imaginary. Ninth edition, 2 vols., 1800. For this reprint see Lamb, C., Detached thoughts on Books and Reading, and Coleridge, S. T., Letters, ed. by Coleridge, E. H., vol. I, 428. The 1800 ed. was reprinted several times, and so was that published in 1845.

The Anatomy of Melancholy. Ed. by Shilleto, A. R., with introduction by
    Bullen, A. H. 1893. Supplies many references, chiefly for quotations
    from well known authors. Text, apparently, from seventh ed. Re-
    viewed in Academy, 15 Sept., 1894, by Robert Steele, also Athenæum,
    6 Jan., 1894; Saturday Review, 17 Feb., 1894; Spectator, 6 Oct., 1894.
    Reprinted in 1896, etc.; with some corrections, 1904.

W. Aldis Wright has made a collation of all the editions from 1621 to
1676; his work is not yet published.

iv. *The Anatomy of Melancholy abridged*

Melancholy . . . Drawn chiefly from . . . Burton's Anatomy of Melancholy.
    1801. A careless reprint was published in 1824 and in 1827. Further
    eds., 1865, 1881.

v. *Comment, Criticism and Imitation*

Bensly, E. A hitherto unknown source of Montaigne and Burton. Athen-
    æum, 5 Sept. 1908 (see 6 June and 13 June).
—— Burton's Anatomy of Melancholy. N. & Q. Ser. IX, vols. XI, XII; Ser. X,
    vols. I, II, III, IV, V, VI, VII, X. (Passages from earlier authors identified.)
—— Burton's Anatomy of Melancholy. Presentation Copy of the First
    Edition. N. & Q. Ser. X, vols. VIII, XI.
—— Burton and Fletcher. N. & Q. Ser. X, vol. VI.
—— Burton and Jacques Ferrand. N. & Q. Ser. X, vol. XI.
—— The Scene of Burton's Philosophaster. N. & Q. Ser. X, vol. XII.
—— The title of R. Burton's Anatomy of Melancholy. Mod. Lang. Rev.vol.IV.
—— Theodorus Prodromus, John Barclay and Robert Burton. N. & Q.
    Ser. X, vol. XI.
Blackwood's Edinburgh Magazine, vol. XC, 323–342. Burton's Anatomy of
    Melancholy.
Boswell, James. Life of Johnson. Ed. Hill, G. Birkbeck. Vols. II, 121,
    440; III, 415. Oxford, 1887 ff.
Brown, T. E. Robert Burton (Causerie). New Review, vol. XIII (1895),
    257–266. (A curiously perverse and unsympathetic treatment.)
Byron, Lord. Letters and Journals. Ed. Prothero, R. E. Vols. II, 383;
    V, 184, 392. 1898–1901. Poetry. Ed. Coleridge, E. H. Vol. II, 236.
    1898–1904. Letters and Journals with notices of his life, by Moore, T.
    Vol. 1, 98. 1830.
Dieckow, Fritz. John Florio's Englische Übersetzung der Essais Mon-
    taigne's und Lord Bacon's [*sic*], Ben Jonson's und Robert Burton's
    Verhältnis zu Montaigne. Diss. Strassburg, 1903.
Ferriar, John. Illustrations of Sterne. 2nd ed. Vol. I. 82–120. 1812.
Fuller, Thomas. The Worthies of England. Part II, 134. 1662.
Greenwood, William. Ἀπογραφὴ στοργῆς Or, A Description Of The Passion
    of Love. 1657.
Herring, Thomas (archbishop of Canterbury). Letters to William Duncombe,
    pp. 148–150. 1777. (Among the wits whom Herring thought to have
    been beholden to Burton were probably Swift, and possibly Addison.
    Compare No. 1 of the Spectator with the beginning of Democritus to the
    Reader.)
Johnson, Samuel. Letters. Ed. Hill, G. Birkbeck. Vol. 1, 293, 383. Ox-
    ford, 1892.

Jusserand, J. J.   Hist. lit. du peuple Angl.   Part II, livr. 5, sect. 2, 873–9. Paris, 1894.

Keats, John.   Poetical Works and other Writings.   Ed. Forman, H. Buxton.   Vol. II, 40.   1883.   See, also, Complete Works, vol. III, 266–275, Glasgow, 1901; Marginal notes on B's Anatomy of Melancholy, vol. II of ed. 1813.

Lake, Bernard.   A General Introduction to Charles Lamb, together with a Special Study of his Relation to Robert Burton.   Diss. 49–91.   Leipzig, 1903.

Lamb, Charles.   Curious Fragments, extracted from a Common-place Book which belonged to Robert Burton, the Famous Author of the Anatomy of Melancholy, in John Woodvil, A Tragedy, to which are added Fragments of Burton, the Author of the Anatomy of Melancholy.   Reprinted with alterations in Lamb's Works, 1818.   See the Works of Charles and Mary Lamb, ed. by Lucas, E. V., vol. I, 31–36 and notes (an imitation of Burton, by Craigie, W. J.), 394–8, 1903–5.

—— Letters in Lucas's Edition.   Vol. VI, 159, 161, 173.

—— Essays of Elia, and Last Essays of Elia.   Lucas's ed., vol. II, 40, 67, 174.   See, also, vols. I, 175, 452, and V, 27, 29.

Nichols, John.   Illustrations of the Literary History of the Eighteenth Century.   Vol. IV, 210.   1822.

ΠΕΡΙΑΜΜΑ 'ΕΠΙΔΗ'ΜΙΟΝ: Or, Vulgar Errours in Practice Censured. 1659.   See N. & Q. Ser. x, vol. IV, 123.   (J. T. Curry.)

Steevens, George.   MS. notes in a 1632 copy of the Anatomy.   See Nichols's Leicestershire, III, pt. I, 558.

Toynbee, Paget.   Dante in English Literature from Chaucer to Cary.   Vol. I, 114–116.   1909.

Warton, Thomas,   Poems upon several occasions . . . by John Milton.   2nd ed.; esp. 94–96.   1791.

Whibley, Charles.   Literary Portraits.   Robert Burton, pp. 251–288.   1904.

II. Barclay

[At the end of P. A. Becker's article (see below, iv) is a general bibliography of Barclay's works, translations of his works, and productions that have been attributed to him on dubious grounds.   See, also, pp. 34 and 114, 115 of the same essay.   Dukas (see below, iv) supplies a bibliography of Euphormio; Collignon, one of Icon Animorum in his Le Portrait des Esprits de Jean Barclay, and one of Argenis in his Notes sur l'Argenis.   The fullest and best bibliography of the last work is to be found in John Barclay's Argenis, by Schmid, K. F.   The following select list is necessarily based in great part on these authorities.]

i. *Biography*

(A useful summary of the original sources for Barclay's life and a list of later biographical works and articles is given by Becker, pp. 109–111 and 114, 115.)

Abram, Nicolas.   Historia Universitatis et Collegii Mussipontani quam conscripsit P. Abram S.J. ab institutione ad annum 1650.   In MS. A copy is in the municipal library at Nancy, another in the library at Épinal.   A French translation of the parts dealing with John Barclay and Euphormio is printed on pp. 9–21 of Collignon's Notes sur l'Euphormion.

Bayle, Pierre. Dictionnaire historique et critique. (For a criticism of the article on Jean Barclai see R. Garnett's life of J. B. in the D. of N. B.).

Bugnot, Louis Gabriel. Joannis Barclaii Vita in Bugnot's ed. of Argenis. Leyden, 1659.

Dalrymple, Sir David (Lord Hailes). Sketch of the life of John Barclay. 1786.

Gassendi, Pierre. Vita Peireskii. 1655.

Irving, David. Lives of Scottish Authors. Vol. I, 371–384. Edinburgh, 1839.

Mackenzie, George. The Lives and Characters of the most eminent Writers of the Scots nation. Vol. III, 476. Edinburgh, 1822.

Ménage, Gilles. Vita Petri Aerodii. Paris, 1675.

Peiresc, Nicolas Claude Fabri de. Lettres. Ed. by Larroque, Ph. Timizey de. Vol. VII. Paris, 1898.

Scaliger, J. J. Epistres françoises de M. J. J. de la Scala. Harderwyck, 1624. Three letters by Barclay on pp. 15, 198, 361.

Thorie, Ralph. In obitum Jo. Barclaii Elegia. Signed R. Th. 1621.

Tomasinus, J. Ph. Elogia. 1644.

Urbain, Charles. Apropos de J. de Barclay. In the Bulletin du Bibliophile, 1891, pp. 315–330 (contains some hitherto unpublished letters of Barclay from the Bibliothèque Nationale).

References to Barclay are found in Isaac Casaubon's Ephemerides (where we have a glimpse of Barclay in England), the *epistolae* of J. J. Scaliger, Grotius, Claude Morisot and elsewhere. For a mention of Barclay in Gilbert Gaulmin's ed. of Theodorus Prodromus, see N. & Q. Ser. x, vol. XI, 101.

ii. *Works*

Euphormionis Lusinini Satyricon. (London?), 1603. (See Dukas, p. 29. No copy of this edition is known to exist.)

Euphormionis Lusinini Satyricon nunc primùm recognitum, emendatum, et varijs in locis auctum. Paris, 1605.

Euphormionis Lusinini Satyricon Pars Secunda Nunc primum in lucem edita. Paris, 1607.

Both parts of Euphormio and Apologia were first published together, with separate titles and pagination, in 1610–11 (s.l.). These three, with Icon Animorum, were first published together in 1616 (s.l.) in the same way. The 1628 (Rouen) ed. first added pt. v (Morisot's continuation) which had appeared separately in 1625; the annotated edition of Bugnot with pt. vi (Aletophilus Castigatus) was published in 1674 (Leyden).

The Clavis is first found in the editions of 1623.

Euphormionis Satyrici Apologia Pro Se. Paris, 1610.

In Phaethonta Gallicum (signed I. B.). Paris.

In P. Statii Papinii Thebaidos libros IIII commentarii et in totidem sequentes notae, cum argumentis. Pont-à-Mousson, 1601.

Ioannis Barclaii Argenis. Parisiis, Apvd Nicolavm Bvon, in via Iacobaea, sub signis S. Claudij, & Hominis Siluestris. MDCXXI.

The Elzevir ed. of 1627 (Leyden) is the first that contains Discursus in Io. Barclaii Argenidem (Clavis). The Elzevir of 1630 (Leyden) is the first that contains Discursus de Autore Scripti (Schmid, pp. 13–17).

For Tabula Nominum fictorum, see Schmid, pp. 9 and 16, 17.

Io Barclaii Argenis. Nunc primum Illustrata. Leyden, 1659. (The notes are by Bugnot.)

Joannis Barclaii Icon Animorum. 1614.

Johannis Barclaii Pietas, sive publica regum ac principum, et privata Guil. Barclaii sui parentis defensio adversus Roberti S. R. E. Card. Bellarmini Tractatum. Paris, 1612. (Replied to by Andreas Eudaemon-Joannes in Epistola Monitoria ad Joannem Barclaium Guillelmi filium. Cologne, 1613.)

Paraenesis ad Sectarios. Rome, 1617.

Poematum Libri Duo. 1615. (Dedicated to prince Charles.)

Poematum Libri II cum l. III ex Argenide. Cologne, 1626.

Preface to William Barclay's De Potestate Papae, an et quatenus in reges et principes sæculares jus et imperium habet (printed in London, some copies s.l., some with imprint of Pont-à-Mousson). 1609. (Bellarmine attacked this work in Tractatus de Potestate summi Pontificis in temporalibus adversus Gulielmum Barclaium.)

Regi Jacobo primo, carmen gratulatorium, auct. Joanne Barclaio. Paris, 1603. (See Becker, p. 36.)

Series Patefacti Divinitus Parricidii in Ter maximum Regem regnumque Britanniae cogitati et instructi: Nonis ixbribus MDCV. Illo ipso novembri Scripta, nunc demum edita. Printed at the end of the 1628 (Amsterdam) ed. of Euphormio.

Sylvae. 1606. (Dedicated to Christian IV of Denmark.)

According to Fr. Pona (Life of Barclay in his Italian trans. of Argenis), Barclay left in MS. De Bello sacro, dealing with the same subject as Tasso's Gerusalemme, and some pages of a History of Europe.

iii. *Translations into English*

Argenis. A trans. by Ben Jonson was entered at Stationers' hall, 2 Oct., 1623.

Barclay His Argenis: Or, The Loves of Poliarchus and Argenis: Faithfully translated out of Latine into English, By Kingsmill Long, Gent. 1625 and 1636. (The verse is by May.)

John Barclay His Argenis, Translated out of Latine into English: The Prose upon His Majesties Command: By Sir Robert Le Grys, Knight: And the Verses by Thomas May, Esquire. 1629. (Southey's copy with MS. notes by Coleridge is in the Brit. Mus.)

Icon Animorum. The Mirrour of Mindes, Englished by Thomas May. 1633.

The Adventures of Poliarchus And Argenis. Translated from the Latin of John Barclay. By the Revd. Mr. John Jacob. Dublin, 1734. (For this English abridgment of Argenis, not mentioned in the bibliographies of Barclay, see Bensly, E., Mod. Lang. Rev. vol. IV, 392–5.)

The Phoenix; or, the History of Polyarchus and Argenis, translated from the Latin, By a Lady. 4 vols. London and York, 1772. (By Clara Reeve.)

(For translations of Argenis in other languages, and continuations, see Schmid, K. F. For dramatisations, see Collignon. For translations of Euphormio and Icon Animorum, see Dukas.)

iv. *Criticism, etc.*

Becker, Ph. Aug. Johann Barclay, 1582–1621. Zeitschrift für vergleichende Litteraturgeschichte, Neue Folge, Band XV, 33–118. Berlin, 1903.

Boucher, Léon. De Joannis Barclaii Argenide. Paris, 1874.

Censura Euphormionis auctore Anonymo. Paris, 1620. (Pierre Musnier's
    Censura Censurae Euphormionis in same vol.)
Coleridge, Samuel Taylor. Literary Remains. Vol. I, 255–258. 1836.
Collignon, Albert. Le Portrait des Esprits (Icon animorum) de Jean
    Barclay. Nancy, 1906. (Extrait des Mémoires de l'Académie de
    Stanislas, 1905–6.) (On pp. 68, 69 is a list of Ouvrages relatifs à l'Icon
    animorum.)
—— Note complémentaire sur l'Argenis. Appendix to C.'s Le Portrait des
    Esprits de J. B.
—— Notes Historiques, Littéraires et Bibliographiques sur l'Argenis de
    Jean Barclay. (Extrait des Mémoires de l'Académie de Stanislas,
    1901–2.) Paris and Nancy, 1902.
—— Notes sur l'Euphormion de Jean Barclay. (Extrait des Annales de
    l'Est.) Nancy, 1901.
Dukas, Jules. Étude Bibliographique et Littéraire sur le Satyricon de Jean
    Barclay. Paris, 1880.
Dupond, Albert. L'Argénis de Barclai. Étude Littéraire. Paris, 1875.
Fournel, Victor. La Littérature independante et les écrivains oubliés, essais
    de critique et d'érudition sur le XVIIᵉ siècle, pp. 212–4. Paris, 1862.
Körting, Heinrich. Geschichte des französichen Romans im XVII Jahrhun-
    dert. 2 vols. Leipzig and Oppeln, 1885–7.
Schmid, Karl Friedrich. John Barclays Argenis. Eine literarhistorische
    Untersuchung. 1. Ausgaben der Argenis, ihrer Fortsetzungen und
    Übersetzungen. Berlin and Leipzig, 1904. (Heft XXXI of Josef Schick
    and M. v. Waldberg's Literarhistorischen Forschungen.)

    (For 17th and 18th cent. works on Argenis see Schmid, pp. 167–174.)

III. Owen

i. *Biography*

Archaeologia Cambrensis. New Series, vol. IV, 130. 1853.
Colvile, F. L. Worthies of Warwickshire. Warwick and London, 1870.
Dwnn, Lewys. Heraldic Visitations of Wales and Part of the Marches.
    Ed. by Meyrick, Sir S. R. Vol. II, 180. Llandovery, 1846.
Hughes of Kinmel, H. R. The Two Hugh Owens. Y Cymmrodor, vol. XVI.
    1903.
Leach, A. F. History of Warwick School, pp. 124–134. (See Bensly, E.,
    John Owen the Epigrammatist, N. & Q. Ser. x, vol. XI, 21.)
Williams, W. Ll. The Two Hugh Owens. Appendix H to Welsh Catholics
    on the Continent. Trans. Hon. Soc. Cymmrodorion, Session 1901–2,
    pp. 128–144.
Wood, Anthony à. Athenae Oxonienses. Ed. Bliss, P. Vol. II, cols. 320–2.

ii. *Works*

Epigrammatum Ioannis Owen Cambro-Britanni Libri Tres. Ad Illus-
    trissimam D. Mariam Neuille, Comitis Dorcestriae filiam Patronam
    suam. Editio Tertia, prioribus emendatior. 1607. (The first two eds.
    had appeared in 1606.)
Epigrammatum Ioannis Owen Cambro-Britanni Ad Excellentissimam &
    doctissimam Heroïnam, D. Arbellam Stuart, Liber Singularis. Editio
    Prima. 1607. (Uniform with the above.) (Fourth ed. of Owen's first
    volume was published in 1612. Lond. ex off. Joh. Legati, sumtibus
    Simonis Waterson, and also the two following.)

Epigrammatum Ioannis Owen Oxoniensis, Cambro-Britanni, Libri Tres.
Ad Henricvm Principem Cambriae Dvo. Ad Carolvm Eboracensem
unvs. Editio prima. 1612.

Epigrammatum Ioannis Owen Cambro-Britanni Oxoniensis. Ad Tres Me-
caenates, Libri Tres. Ad Edoardum Noel equitem & Baronetum, vnus.
Ad Guilielmum Sidley equitem & Baronetum, alter. Ad Rogerum
Owen equitem auratum, Tertius. Editio Prima. 1612. (Uniform with
the above.)

Additional epigrams are printed in the Leyden ed. of 1628 and in
Ioannis Oweni libellus epigrammatum, etc., ed. by Ebert, F. A., Leipzig,
1824.

iii. *Translations*

English.

Vicars, John. Epigrams Of That most wittie and worthie Epigrammatist
Mr. John Owen, Gentleman. Translated by John Vicars. 1619.

Hayman, Robert. Qvodlibets, Lately Come Over From New Britaniola, Old
Newfound-land. Epigrams and other small parcels, both Morall and
Divine. The first foure Bookes being the Authors owne: the rest trans-
lated out of that Excellent Epigrammatist, Mr. John Owen, and other
rare Authors. With two Epistles of that excellently wittie Doctor,
Francis Rablais: Translated out of his French at large. All of them
Composed and done at Harbor-Grace in Britaniola, anciently called
Newfound-Land. By R. H. Sometimes Governour of the Plantation
there. 1628.

Pecke, Thomas. Parnasi Puerperium: or, Some Wellwishes to Ingenuity,
in the Translation of Six Hundred, of Owen's Epigrams; Martial de
Spectaculis, or of Rarities to be seen in Rome; and the most Select, in
Sir Tho. More. To which is annext A Century of Heroick Epigrams,
(Sixty whereof concern the Twelve Caesars; and the Forty remaining,
several deserving Persons.) By the Author of that celebrated Elegie
upon Cleeveland: Tho. Pecke of the Inner Temple, Gent. 1659.

Harvey, Thomas. John Owen's Latin Epigrams, Englished by Tho. Harvey,
Gent. 1677.

Cowper, William. Epigrams translated from the Latin of Owen. Life and
Works, ed. Grimshawe, T. S. Vol. VIII, 368–9.

Translations of isolated epigrams of Owen occur in various collections.

Harflete, Henry. A Banquet of Essayes, Fetcht out of Famous Owens
Confectionary, Disht out, and serv'd up at the Table of Mecoenas. By
Henry Harflete, sometime of Grayes-Inne, Gent. 1653. (Essays on
Ep. 1, 2, with a trans. of that Epigram.)

German.

(For early German translators and very numerous imitators of Owen, see
Erich Urban's treatise. For translations in other languages, see Brit. Mus.
Cat.)

iv. *Criticisms and Literary History*

Gervinus, Georg Gottfried. Geschichte der Deutschen Dichtung. Vol.
III (ed. 5), IX, 4. Epigramme und Satiren, pp. 396–423. Leipzig, 1872.

Lafenestre, Pierre. François Maynard. Révue d'Histoire littéraire de la
France, pp. 457–477. 1903.

Lessing, Gotthold Ephraim. Zerstreute Anmerkungen über das Epigramm, und einige der vornehmsten Epigrammatisten, pp. 214 sqq. in vol. xi, 3rd ed. (Stuttgart, 1895) of Karl Lachmann's ed. of Lessing's Sämtliche Schriften.

Urban, Erich. Owenus und die deutschen Epigrammatiker des xvii Jahrhunderts. Berlin, 1900. (Heft xi in Literarhistorische Forschungen ed. by Josef Schick and M. v. Waldberg.)

v. Mention and imitation of Owen in Latin epigrammatists

(A selection)

Barth, Caspar. Amphitheatrum seriorum Jocorum. Hanau, 1613. (Several references.)

Bauhuis, Bernard, Epigrammatum Libri v, ed. altera. Antwerp, 1620. (1st ed. 1615.) (Slight touches of imitation.)

Bruch, Richard. Epigrammatum Hecatontades duae authore R. B. 1627. (Imitations of Owen.)

Cabilliau, Baldwin. Epigrammata Selecta. Antwerp, 1620. (Slight touches.)

Dunbar, John. Epigrammaton Ioannis Dvnbari Megalo-Brittani Centvriae Sex, Decades totidem. 1616. (Imitations of Owen.)

Harder, H. Epigrammata, in Deliciae Poetarum Danorum ed. Rostgaard, F. Leyden, 1693. Tom. ii. (Much imitation of Owen.)

Paterson, Ninian, Epigrammatum Libri Octo. Edinburgh, 1678. (Imitation of Owen.)

Stradling, John. Epigrammatum Libri Quatuor. 1607. (Owen addressed in lib. iv, 91.)

Owen's epigrams are freely quoted in such books as Caroli A. S. Antonio Patavino, Anconitani, de Arte Epigrammatica Libellus, Cologne, 1650, and Nic. Mercer's De Conscribendo Epigrammate, Paris, 1653.

[For the writings of Thomas Newton (1542?-1607), see D. of N. B. A. R. W.]

CHAPTER XIV

THE BEGINNINGS OF ENGLISH PHILOSOPHY [1]

FRANCIS BACON

Philosophical Works (Spedding's arrangement)

i. Parts of the Instauratio Magna

Instauratio magna. 1620. (After two pages beginning "Franciscus de Verulamio sic cogitavit," an epistle dedicatory to the king, preface, distributio operis and a page announcing "deest pars prima instaurationis, quae complectitur partitiones scientiarum," there follows a second title-page: Pars Secunda Operis, quae dicitur Novum Organum, sive Indicia Vera de interpretatione naturae. The same volume also contains: Parasceve ad Historiam Naturalem et Experimentalem.)

Opera. Tomus primus. Qui continet De Augmentis Scientiarum libros ix. 1623. (The second title is: de Dignitate et Augmentis Scientiarum libri ix.)

[1] For scholastic works, see bibliography to Chap. x, Vol. I, of the present work.

Historia Naturalis et Experimentalis ad condendam philosophiam: sive Phaenomena Universi: quae est Instaurationis Magnae pars tertia. 1622. (This volume contains Historia Ventorum, also titles and "aditus" to five other Historiae, namely, Densi et Rari, Gravis et Levis, Sympathiae et Antipathiae Rerum, Sulphuris Mercurii et Salis, Vitae et Mortis.)

Historia Vitae et Mortis. Sive Titulus Secundus in Historia Naturali et Experimentali ad condendam philosophiam: quae est Instaurationis Magnae pars tertia. 1623.

Historia Densi et Rari (1658).[1]

Sylva Sylvarum: or A Natural History. In ten centuries. Written by the Right Honourable Francis Lord Verulam, Viscount St. Alban. Published after the author's death by William Rawley. 1627.

Scala intellectus, sive Filum Labyrinthi (1653) (a preface intended for the fourth part of the Instauratio).

Prodromi, sive Anticipationes Philosophiae Secundae (1653) (a preface intended for the fifth part of the Instauratio).

ii. **Works connected with the Instauratio, but not intended to be included in it**

Cogitationes de natura rerum (1653).

De Fluxu et Refluxu Maris (1653).

De Principiis atque Originibus secundum Fabulas Cupidinis et Coeli (1653).

New Atlantis; a work unfinished. (First published by Rawley at the end of the volume containing Sylva Sylvarum in 1627.)

iii. **Works originally designed for parts of the Instauratio, but superseded or abandoned**

Cogitationes de Scientia Humana. (A series of fragments of uncertain date, first published by Spedding (Bacon's Works, vol. III), who supplied the title.)

Valerius Terminus of the Interpretation of Nature; with the annotations of Hermes Stella (1734).

The Twoo Bookes of Francis Bacon of the Proficience and Advancement of Learning Divine and Humane. 1605.

Filum Labyrinthi, sive Formula Inquisitionis (1734) (little else than an English version of the Cogitata et Visa).

De Interpretatione Naturae Prooemium (1653).

Temporis Partus Masculus sive Instauratio Magna Imperii Humani in Universum (1653).

Partis Instaurationis Secundae Delineatio et Argumentum, et Redargutio philosophiarum (1653, in part).

Cogitata et Visa: de Interpretatione Naturae, sive de Scientia Operativa (1653).

Filum Labyrinthi; sive Inquisitio Legitima de Motu (1653.)

Sequela Cartarum; sive Inquisitio Legitima de Calore et Frigore (1734).

Historia et Inquisitio Prima de Sono et Auditu, et de Forma Soni et Latente Processu Soni; sive Sylva Soni et Auditus (1658).

Phaenomena Universi; sive Historia Naturalis ad Condendam Philosophiam (1653).

---

[1] Writings published for the first time in posthumous collections have the date of the collection given in parentheses. Titles will be found under "Editions."

Descriptio Globi Intellectualis et Thema Coeli (1653).
De Interpretatione Naturae Sententiae XII (1653).
Aphorismi et Consilia (1653).

Literary Works

Essayes. Religious Meditations. Places of perswasion and disswasion. Seene and allowed. 1597. (There are ten essays in this volume. The Religious Meditations are in Latin and are entitled Meditationes Sacrae; the Places of perswasion and disswasion are in English and are entitled Coulers of Good and Evill; a fragment. Reprinted in 1598, 1604 and 1606.)

The Essaies of Sir Francis Bacon Knight the kings solliciter generall. 1612. (This volume contains essays only—thirty-eight in number, twenty-nine of them new, and the rest corrected and enlarged.)

The Essayes or Counsels, Civill and Morall, of Francis Lo. Verulam, Viscount St. Alban. 1625. (This volume contains fifty-eight essays, twenty of them being new and most of the rest altered and enlarged.)

De Sapientia Veterum Liber, ad inclytam academiam Cantabrigiensem. 1609.

The Historie of the Raigne of King Henry the Seventh. 1622.

Advertisement touching an Holy Warre. Written in the year 1622. 1629.

Of the True Greatness of the Kingdom of Britain (1734).

Apothegmes new and old. 1625.

Promus of Formularies and Elegancies (begun 1594, published 1882, and in part by Spedding, vol. VII).

Translation of Certaine Psalmes into English Verse. 1625.

Professional Works

Maxims of the Law (written about 1597; first printed 1630).

Reading on the Statute of Uses (read at Gray's Inn in the Lent vacation, 1600; first printed in 1642).

The Arguments of Law of Sir Francis Bacon, Knight, The King's Solicitor-General, in certain great and difficult cases. (Revised by Bacon in 1616, but not published by him; first printed by Blackbourne in 1730.)

Argument in Chudleigh's Case. (Easter Term, 1594.) (Translated from Law French and printed in Spedding's edition, vol. VII.)

The Argument of Sir Francis Bacon, Knight, His Majesty's Solicitor-general, in the Case of the Post-Nati of Scotland. (Delivered before Easter Term, 1608; first printed in 1641.)

The Argument of Sir Francis Bacon, Knight, Attorney-General in the King's Bench, in the Case De Rege Inconsulto. (Delivered Jan. 25, 1616; first printed in Collectanea Jurid.)

A Preparation towards the Union of Laws.

Occasional Writings (a selection)

An Advertisement touching the Controversies of the Church of England (written 1589; first published as pamphlet, 1640).

A Declaration of the Practices and Treasons attempted and committed by Robert, late Earle of Essex. 1601.

A Brief Discourse touching the Happy Union of the Kingdoms of England and Scotland (written 1603).

Certain Considerations touching the better Pacification and Edification of the
    Church of England (written 1603).
Sir Francis Bacon his Apologie, in certaine imputations concerning the late
    Earle of Essex.   1604.
A Proposition to His Majesty . . . touching the Compiling and Amendment
    of the Laws of England (written 1616, first published 1653).

Editions

1. Collections chiefly of works unpublished in his life-time:
    (a)   Collected by Rawley, W.:—Certaine Miscellany works.   1629.
          Operum moralium et civilium tomus primus.   1638.   Re-
          suscitatio.   1657.   Opuscula varia posthuma.   1658.
    (b)   Collected by Gruter, I.:—Scripta in naturali et universali
          philosophia.   Amsterdam, 1653.
    (c)   Collected by Stephens, R.:—Letters written during the reign of
          King James.   1702.   Letters and Remains.   1734.
2. Editions of collected works; by Schönwetter and Gruter, Frankfort,
    1665; Mallet, 4 vols., 1740; Stephens, Locker and Birch, 5 vols., 1765;
    Lasalle, A., French translation, 15 vols., Dijon, 1801–4; Montagu,
    16 vols., 1825–36; Spedding, J., Ellis, R. L. and Heath, D. D., 14 vols.,
    1857–74. In the last-named edition, vols. I–III contain the Philosophical
    Works, vols. IV–V translations of the same, vols. VI–VII Literary and
    Professional Works, vols. VIII–XIV the Letters and the Life. The
    Philosophical Works were edited in one volume by Robertson, J. M., 1905.
3. Among editions of separate works mention may be made of the editions of
    the Advancement of Learning by Wright, W. A., Oxford, 1869, 5th ed.,
    1900, and by Case, T., Oxford, 1906, and of the Novum Organum by
    Fowler, T., Oxford, 1878, 2nd ed., 1889.

Works on Bacon's Life and Philosophy

Abbott, E. A.   Bacon and Essex.   1877.
—— Bacon: an account of his life and works.   1885.
Adamson, R.   In Encyclopaedia Britannica, ninth ed.
Blunt, H. W.   Bacon's Method.   Proc. of Aristotelian Soc.   N. S. IV.
Cassirer, E.   In his Erkenntnisproblem in der Phil. u. Wissenschaft.
Church, R. W.   Bacon.   1884.
Ellis, R. L.   General Preface to the Philosophical Works, Bacon's Works,
    vol. I.   1857.
Fisher, Kuno.   Francis Bacon und seine Schule.   Entwicklungsgeschichte
    der Erfahrungsphilosophie.   Vol. x. of the Jubiläumsausgabe of his
    Gesch. d. neuern Phil.   Heidelberg, 1904.   (Third revised edition of a
    work originally published in 1856, translated into English by Oxenford,
    J., 1857.)
Fowler, T.   Bacon.   1881.
Gardiner, S. R.   In D. of N. B.
Hallam, H.   Introduction to the Literature of Europe.   Chap. xx.
Lee, Sidney.   Great Englishmen of the Sixteenth Century.   1904.
Liebig, J. v.   Ueber Francis Bacon und die Methode der Naturforschung.
    Munich, 1863.
Macaulay, T. B.   In Edinburgh Review, July, 1837.
Nichol, J.   Bacon.   Edinburgh, 1888–9.

Rémusat, C. de. Bacon: sa vie, son temps, sa philosophie, et son influence jusqu'à nos jours. Paris, 1857.

Whewell, W. Philosophy of Discovery. Chaps. xv, xvi. 1860.

[See, also, Craik's English Literature, 1869, vol. 1, p. 617.]

WILLIAM BALDWIN

Treatise of moral Phylosophie, contayning the Sayinges of the Wyse. 1547.

SIR RICHARD BARCKLEY

A Discourse of the Felicitie of Man: or his *Summum bonum*. 1598.

NATHANAEL CARPENTER

Philosophia libera, triplici exercitationum Decade proposita, in qua adversus hujus temporia Philosophos dogmata quaedam nova discutiuntur. Ed. secunda. Oxford, 1622. (1st ed. in 1621.)

JOHN CASE

Summa veterum interpretum in universam Dialecticam Aristotelis. 1584.
Oxford, 1592. Frankfort, 1593.

Speculum moralium questionum in universam ethicen Aristotelis. Oxford, 1585. Frankfort, 1589.

Sphaera civitatis. Oxford, 1588.

Reflexus speculi moralis. Oxford, 1596.

Thesaurus Oeconomicae. Oxford, 1597.

Lapis philosophicus. Oxford, 1599. London, 1612.

Ancilla philosophiae. Oxford, 1599.

EVERARD DIGBY

Theoria analytica, Viam ad Monarchiam Scientiarum demonstrans, totius Philosophiae et reliquarum Scientiarum, necnon primorum postremorumque Philosophorum mysteria arcanaque dogmata enucleans. 1579.

De duplici methodo libri duo, unicam P. Rami methodum refutantes. 1580.

Everardi Digbei Cantabrigiensis admonitioni Francisci Mildapetti . . . responsio. 1580.

De Arte Natandi. 1587. [Believed to be the earliest treatise on swimming published in England; trans. Middleton, C., 1595.]

Cf. Freudenthal, J., Beiträge zur Geschichte der englischen Philosophie (two articles) in Archiv für Geschichte der Philosophie, vol. iv, 1891.

WILLIAM FULKE

An Almanack and Prognostication. 1560.

Antiprognosticon contra inutiles astrologorum praedictiones. 1560. (English trans., 1560.)

A Goodly Gallerie, with a most pleasant prospect into the garden of naturall contemplation, to behold the naturall causes of all kynde of Meteors. 1563.

And other works, chiefly theological.

Robert Fludd

Utriusque Cosmi majoris scilicet et minoris, Metaphysica, physica atque technica Historia. Frankfort, 1617.

Clavis Philosophiae et Alchymiae. Frankfort, 1633.

Medicina Catholica, seu mysticum artis medicandi sacrarum (Integrum Morborum mysterium). Frankfort, 1629.

Philosophia Moysaica. Gouda, 1638 (in English, 1659).

William Gilbert

Guilielmi Gilberti Colcestrensis, medici londinensis, de Magnete, magneticisque corporibus, et de magno magnete tellure; Physiologia nova, plurimis et argumentis, et experimentis demonstrata. 1600.

De Mundo nostro Sublunari Philosophia Nova. Opus posthumum. Amsterdam, 1651.

Edward Herbert

De Veritate, prout distinguitur a Revelatione, a Verisimili, a Possibili, et a Falso. Paris. 1624.

De Religione Gentilium, errorumque apud eos causis. Amsterdam, 1663. Eng. transl. 1709.

(For the non-philosophical works, see Vol. VII of the present work.)

Works on Herbert's Philosophy

Güttler, C. Lord Herbert von Cherbury. 1897.

Lechler, G. V. Geschichte des englischen Deismus. 1841.

Rémusat, C. de. Lord Herbert de Cherbury. 1874.

Sorley, W. R. In Mind, October, 1894.

Thomas Harriot

A Brief and True Report of the new-found Land of Virginia. 1588.

Artis Analyticae Praxis ad aequationes algebraicas resolvendas. 1631.

John Napier of Merchiston

Mirifici Logarithmorum Canonis Descriptio. Edinburgh, 1614. (English trans., 1616.)

Rabdologiae seu numerationis per virgulas libri duo. Edinburgh, 1617.

Mirifici Logarithmorum Canonis Constructio. Edinburgh, 1619.

Robert Norman

The Newe Attractive, containing a short discourse of the Magnes or Lodestone. 1581.

John Sanderson

Institutionum dialecticarum libri quatuor. Antwerp, 1589. Oxford, 1594. 1602.

William Temple

Francisci Mildapetti Navarreni ad Everardum Digbeium Anglum Admonitio de unica P. Rami Methodo rejectis ceteris retinenda. 1580.

Pro Mildapetti de unica methodo defensione contra Diplodophilum, commentatio Gulielmi Tempelli, e Regio Collegio Cantabrigiensis. Huc accessit nonnullarum e physicis et ethicis quaestionum explicatio, una cum epistola de Rami dialectica ad Joannem Piscatorem Argentinensem. 1581. Frankfort, 1584.

P. Rami Dialecticae libri duo, scholiis G. Tempelli Cantabrigiensis illustrati. Cambridge, 1584. Frankfort, 1591, 1595.

Jacobi Martini Scoti Dunkeldensis philosophiae professoris publici, in Academia Taurinensi, de prima simplicium et concretorum corporum generatione disputatio. Cambridge, 1584. Frankfort, 1591, 1595. (Martin's book was first published at Turin, 1577.)

Cf. Freudenthal, J., Beiträge zur Geschichte der englischen Philosophie in Archiv für Geschichte der Philosophie, vol. v, 1892.

CHAPTER XV

EARLY WRITINGS ON POLITICS AND ECONOMICS

Alexander, Sir W. An Encouragement to Colonies, 1621-8. Rptd., Bannatyne Club, 1867.

Andrewes, L. De usuris, theologica determinatio, habita in publica schola theologica Cantabrigiae. 1593.

The Anti-projector, or, the history of the Fen project. London (?), 1646 (?).

Ashley, W. J. An Introduction to English Economic History and Theory. Pt. I, The Middle Ages. Pt. II, The End of the Middle Ages. 1889-93.

Aubrey, J. The Natural History of Wiltshire. Ed. Britton, J. 1847.

—— in Rawlinson's The natural history and antiquities of the county of Surrey, 1719.

Awdeley, J. Fraternitye of Vacabones, 1561. Ed. Viles, E. and Furnivall, F. J. 1907.

Aylmer, J. An Harborowe for faithfull and trewe Subjectes, against the late blowne Blaste, concerninge the governmēt of Wemen. Strasborowe, 1559.

Bardes, Walter de. Tractatus novae monetae. Brit. Mus. Lansd. MS. LXXI.

Battie, J. The Merchants Remonstrance. 1648.

Bell, T. The Speculation of Usurie. 1596. (A copy of this tract, believed to be unique, is in the Cambridge University Library.)

Best, H. Rural economy in Yorkshire in 1641. Ed. Robinson, C. B., for Surtees Soc. 1857.

Blith, W. The English improver, or a new survey of husbandry. 1649.

Bodin, J. Consilia de Principe recte instituendo. Cum praeceptis cujusdam principis politicis. 1603.

—— The six bookes of a Commonweale. 1606.

Britain's Buss, or A Computation as well of the Charge of a Buss or Herring Fishing Ship. 1615. In Arber's An English Garner, vol. II, 621 ff., 1880.

Buchanan, G. Ane admonition direct to the trew Lordis mantenaris of justice and obedience to the Kingis graces authorite. 1571.

—— De Jure Regni apud Scotos, Dialogus. Edinburgh, 1579.

Bullock, W. Virginia impartially examined. 1649.

Caesar, P. A general discourse against the damnable sect of Usurers. Trans. by Rogers, T. 1578.

Calvin, J. Institutio Christianiae religionis nunc vere demum suo titulo respondens. Argentorati, 1545.

Camden, W. Annales Rerum Anglicarum et Hibernicarum, regnante Elizabetha. 1615–27.

Carew, R. The Survey of Cornwall. 1602.

Caxton, W. The Game and Playe of the chesse. Bruges, c. 1475.

Cecil, W. Lord Burghley. Draft of the Queen's Proclamation to her subjects to withhold corn and munition from the Spaniard. 1591. Brit. Mus. Lansd. MS. CIV, 47.

—— Letter to Isabella Countess of Rutland complaining of her waste of the timber in Sherwood Forest. 28 July, 1594. Brit. Mus. Lansd. MS. CIII, 80.

—— Memorial on the question of preparing for the Spanish invasion. 1587. Brit. Mus. Cotton. MS. Vesp. C. VIII, 4.

—— A treatise touching the traffic of the East Countries into Spain. 1591. Brit. Mus. Lansd. MS. CIV, 30.

Chamberlen, P. The Poore Mans Advocate. 1649.

Coke, J. The Debate Betwene the Heraldes of Englande and Fraunce. 1550.

Cooke, Sir J. Unum Necessarium, or the Poore Man's Case. 1648.

Cowell, J. The Interpreter; or Booke containing the signification of Words . . . and Termes . . . mentioned in the Lawe-Writers or Statutes . . . requiring any exposition. Cambridge, 1607.

Culpepper, Sir T. A Tract against Usurie. 1621.

Davies, Sir John. A discoverie of the true causes why Ireland was never entirely subdued . . . untill the beginning of his Majesties happie raigne. 1612.

Dekker, T. The Seven Deadly Sinnes of London. 1606.

Digges, Sir D. The defence of Trade, in a letter to Sir T. Smith. 1615.

Drake, Sir F. The World Encompassed by Sir Francis Drake, Being his next voyage to that to Nombre de Dios formerly imprinted; Carefully collected out of the notes of Master Francis Fletcher, Preacher in this employment, and divers others his followers in the same. 1628.

Dudley, E. The Tree of the Common Wealth; a treatise . . . Written by him while a prisoner in the Tower, in the years 1509 and 1510, and under sentence of death for High Treason. Manchester, 1859.

Dugdale, Sir W. The History of Imbanking and drayning of divers Fenns and Marshes, both in foreīn parts and in this Kingdom; and of the improvements thereby. 1662.

Fenton, R. A treatise of Usurie. 1612.

Fish, S. A Supplicacyon for the Beggars. 1529 (?). Ed. Maskell, W. 1845.

Fisher, J. The Book of John Fisher. 1580–8. Ed. Kemp, T. 1900.

Fitzherbert, Sir A. The new booke of Justyces of Peas. 1541.

Fitzherbert, John. [The Book of Surveying] Here begynneth a ryght frutefull mater; and hath to name the boke of surveying and improuve-mētes. 1523.

—— The boke of husbandry. 1534.

(These books have been generally attributed to Sir Anthony Fitzherbert, Justice of the Common Pleas, but good reason has been shown for believing that they were written by his brother, John Fitzherbert of Norbury. See Fitzherbert, R. H. C., English Historical Review, XII, 225, and Cunningham's Growth of Eng. Industry and Commerce, vol. I, 553. 1905.)

Fitz-Neale, or -Nigel, R.   Dialogus de Scaccario.   Ed. Hughes, A., Crump, C. G. and Johnson, C.   Oxford, 1902.   [See, also, The Ancient Dialogue of the Exchequer, trans. by a gentleman of the Inner Temple (Rayner, J.), 1658.]

Fortescue, Sir J.   De Laudibus Legum Angliae.   1616.

Fuller, T.   The History of the Worthies of England.   1662.

Gardiner, S. R.   The political element in Massinger.   Contemporary Review, XXVIII.   1876.

Gentleman, Tobias.   England's way to win wealth, and to employ ships and mariners.   1614.   Rptd. in Arber's An English Garner, vol. IV, 1882.

Goodman, C.   How Superior Powers ought to be obeyed of their Subjects: and wherein they may lawfully by Gods worde be disobeyed and resisted. Wherein also is declared the cause of all this present miserie in England, and the onely way to remedy the same.   Geneva, 1558.

Googe, B.   Foure bookes of husbandry.   1577 ff.

Grosseteste, see Walter of Henley.

[Hales, J.]   A Discourse of the Common Weal of this realm of England. First printed in 1581.   Ed. Lamond, E.   Cambridge, 1893.

Hall, Joseph.   Virgidemiarum.   1597.

Harrison, William.   Description of England, in Holinshed's Chronicles. 1577–8, 1587.

—— An historicall description of the Islande of Britayne.   1577.

(Samuel) Hartlib his Legacie; or, an enlargement of the Discourse of husbandry used in Brabant and Flaunders.   1651.   This is generally attributed to Cressy Dymock.   [See Growth of English Industry and Commerce, Part I, 568, Cunningham, W., 1907.]

Hayward, Sir J.   An Answer to the first Part of a certaine conference concerning Succession.   1603.

Heath, Sir R.   Propositions showing the great utility of a bank, and recommendation for erecting one in London.   1622.   In State Papers, Domestic, James I, cxxx, 30.

Heronis, W. A. S.   English Trade and Finance chiefly in the Seventeenth Century.   1892.

Hitchcock, R.   A Pollitique Platt for the honour of the Prince, the greate profite of the publique state, relief of the poore, preservation of the riche, reformation of Roges and Idle persones, and the wealthe of thousandes that knowes not how to live.   1580.

Homilies.   Certayne Sermons appoynted by the Quenes Majestie to be declared and read, by all Persones, Vycars and Curates, every Sonday and holy daye, in theyr churches.   1559–63.   Ed. Corrie, G. E.   Cambridge, 1850.

Hooker, R.   Of the Lawes of Ecclesiasticall Politie.   1622.

I., R.   Nova Britannia.   Offring most excellent fruites by Planting in Virginia.   1609.

James I.   The true Law of Free Monarchies; or the reciprock and mutuall dutie betwixt a free king and his naturall subjects.   1603.   Works. 1616.

Jeninges, E.   A brief Discovery of the damages that happen to this realme by disordered and unlawfull diet.   The benefites and commodities that otherwise might ensue.   With a perswasion of the people, for a better maintenance to the Navie.   1593.

Keymor, J. Booke of Observations, in Sir W. Raleigh's Works, vol. VIII, 206. Oxford, 1829.
—— J. Keymor's observations made upon the Dutch fishing, about the year 1601. Demonstrating that there is more wealth raised out of herrings and other fish in his Majesties Seas by the neighbouring nations in one year, then the King of Spain hath from the Indies in four. 1604.
Knox, J. The first Blast of the Trumpet against the Monstruous Regiment of women. 1558.
—— The source and bounds of Kingly power. Sermon in History and Repository of Pulpit Eloquence, vol. II. Fish, H. C. 1857.
Knyveth, Sir H. Defence of the Realme, 1596. Ed. Hughes, C. Oxford, 1906.
Latimer, H. See bibliography to Chap. XII.
Leland, J. The Itinerary of John Leland the Antiquary, 9 vols. Oxford, 1710-2. Ed. Smith, L. T. 1906 ff.
Lodge, T. An Alarum against Usurers. 1584.
Lyndsay, Sir D. Works. 1568. Ed. Laing, D. Edinburgh, 1879.
Malynes, G. de. St. George for England, allegorically described. 1601.
—— A Treatise of the Canker of England's Commonwealth. 1601. (In the proportion between money and landed property.)
—— England's View in the unmasking of two Paradoxes. 1603.
—— Consuetudo vel Lex Mercatoria, or, the Ancient Law Merchant. Divided into three parts: according to the essentiall parts of Trafficke. 1622.
—— The Maintenance of Free Trade, according to the three essentiall parts of traffique; . . . or, an answer to a treatise of Free Trade [by Misselden, E.], lately published. 1622.
—— The Centre of the Circle of Commerce. Or, a refutation of a Treatise intituled The Circle of Commerce, or the Ballance of Trade, lately published by E. M. 1623.

(The original MS. notes embodied in a portion of the above works are to be found in Brit. Mus. Cotton. MS. Otho E. x. 65 ff.)

Markham, Gervase. See bibliography to Chap. XVII.
May, J. A Declaration of the Estate of Clothing now used within this realme of England . . . with an Apologie for the Alneger, shewing the necessarie use of his Office. 1613.
McCulloch, J. R. The Literature of Political Economy. 1845.
Milles, T. The Replie, Or Second Apologie. That is to say, an Answer to a confused Treatise of Publicke Commerce. 1604.
—— The Custumer's Alphabet and Primer. Conteining their creed . . . their Ten Commandments . . . and Forme of Prayers. 1608.
—— The Customer's Apologie. 1609 (?).
Misselden, E. Free Trade; or, The Means to make trade flourish. 1622.
—— The Circle of Commerce. Or the Ballance of Trade, in defence of Free Trade: opposed to Malynes Little fish and his Great Whale, and poized against them in the Scale. 1623.
More, T. A fruteful and pleasaunt worke of the beste state of a publyque weale, and of the newe yle called Utopia. 1551. Ed. Lumby, J. R. Cambridge, 1879 ff.
Mosse, M. The Arraignment and Conviction of Usurie. 1595.
Mun, T. A Discourse of Trade from England into the East Indies. 1621.
—— England's Treasure by forraign trade; or, the ballance of our forraign trade is the rule of our treasure. 1664.

Nashe, T. See bibliography to Chap. XVI.

Norden, J. The Surveyors Dialogue. 1607.

Oresme, N. Treatise of the beginning of nature's lawe and Right and change of money. (A fifteenth century translation marked O. 3. 11 in the library of Trinity College, Cambridge.)

Parker, H. Of a Free Trade. 1648.

Parsons, R. A Conference about the next Succession to the Crowne of Ingland. 1594.

Phillips, Sir T. A letter . . . to King Charles i concerning the Plantations of the Londoners. In Hibernica. Harris, W. 1757.

Pindar, Paul. Letter to Lord Salisbury on erecting a Bank for the Crown, occasioned upon the King's want of a Loan from the City. Brit. Mus. Lansd. MS. CVIII, 90.

Platt, Sir H. The Jewell House of Art and Nature. 3 pts. 1594.

Prynne, W. The Antipathie of the English . . . Prelacie, both to Regall Monarchy and Civill Unity. 2 pts. 1641.

Respublica, A.D. 1553. A play on the social condition of England at the accession of Queen Mary. Ed. Magnus, L. A. From Gurney's unique Macro MS. E.E.T.S. CXV. 1905.

Roberts, L. The Merchants Mappe of Commerce; wherein the Universal Manner and Matter of Trade, is compendiously handled. 1638.

—— The Treasure of Traffike; or, a Discourse of Forraigne Trade. 1641.

Robinson, H. England's Safety in Trade's Encrease. 1641.

—— Briefe Considerations concerning the advancement of Trade and Navigation . . . tendred unto all ingenious patriots. 1649.

Roscher, W. Zur Geschichte der Englischen Volkwirthschaftslehre, in Abhandlungen der phil. hist. Classe der k. sächs. Gesellschaft d. Wissen. Vol. II. Leipzig, 1857.

S., M. Greevous Grones for the Poore done by a Well-Willer who wisheth that the poore of England might be so provided for as none should neade to go a begging. 1622.

Sanderson, R. Logicae Artis Compendium. 1618. Ten Sermons: (i) ad Clerum 3; (ii) ad Magistratum 3; (iii) ad Populum 4. 1627.

Sandys, E. Sermon 4. Parker Soc. 1841.

Selden, J. Titles of Honor. 1614.

Shaw, W. A. Select Tracts and Documents Illustrative of English Monetary History. 1896.

Smith, H. Examination of Usury, in two sermons. 1591.

Smith, Capt. J. Advertisements for the unexperienced Planters of New-England, or any where. Or The Path-way to experience to erect a Plantation. 1631.

Smith, Sir T. De Republica Anglorum. 1583. Ed. Alston, L. and Maitland, F. W. Cambridge, 1906.

Spenser, E. The Faerie Queene, book V. 1596.

—— View of the State of Ireland. 1633. [Globe ed. 1869 ff.]

Stanley'es remedy; or, the way to reform wandring beggers, theeves, highway-robbers and pick-pockets. 1646.

Starkey, T. A dialogue between Cardinal Pole and T. Lupset. Ed. Cowper, J. M. E.E.T.S. Ex. Ser. XII.

Symonds, W. Virginia; a sermon . . . preached . . . in the presence of . . . the Adventurers and Planters for Virginia. 1609.

Tusser, T. A hundreth good pointes of husbandrie. 1557.

—— Five hundreth pointes of good husbandry. 1573. Ed. Payne, W. and Herrtage, S. J. 1878.

Ussher, J. The Power communicated by God to the Prince, and Obedience required of the subject. 1683.

Vaughan, R. Most approved and long experienced Water-Workes. Containing the manner of Winter and Summer drowning of medow and pasture . . . thereby to make those grounds . . . more fertile, ten for one. 1610.

Vehse, E. Shakspeare als Protestant, Politiker, Psycholog and Dichter. 2 vols. Hamburg, 1851.

Vintners, The retayling, their answer to a Petition against the said Retaylors. 1641.

Walter of Henley's Husbandry, together with an anonymous Husbandry, Seneschancie and Robert Grosseteste's Rules. The transcripts, translation and glossary by Lamond, E. 1890.

Westcote, T. A view of Devonshire in 1630 and pedigrees of most of our Devonshire families. Edd. Oliver, G. and Jones, P. Exeter, 1845.

Wheeler, J. The Lawes, Customes and Ordinances of the Fellowshippe of Merchantes Adventurers of the Realme of England. 1608. In Univ. of Pennsylvania Translations and Reprints. Lingelback, W. E. 1902.

—— A treatise of commerce, wherein are shewed the commodities arising by a wel ordered . . . Trade . . . such as that of Merchantes Adventurers is proved to bee. 1601.

Wilson, T. A Discourse uppon usurye. 1572.

CHAPTER XVI

LONDON AND THE DEVELOPMENT OF POPULAR LITERATURE

Henry Chettle

The batynge of Dyogens. Licensed 27 Sep., 1591 (identified by Collier, J. P., with A satirycall Dialogue or a Sharplye-invective conference, betweene Alexander the great and that truelye Woman-hater Diogenes 1616(?), an invective against women).

Englande's Mourning Garment. n.d., but with address to reader signed Hen. Chettle. 1st ed. certainly appeared 1603. Rptd. 1603, etc.; 1744 et seq., Harl. Misc.; 1874, Ingleby, C. M., New Shakspr. Soc. Allusion-bks. pt. I.

Kind-Hart's Dreame. n. d. (Licensed Dec., 1592.) Rptd. 1842, Rimbault, E. F., Percy Soc.; 1874, Ingleby, C. M., New Shakspr. Soc. Allusion-bks. pt. I. (The tract, though of slight merit, illustrates the style and literary form which was most fashionable at the moment. It is a dream vision: five popular celebrities (including Greene: see Harvey-Nashe Controversy) are introduced; they present complaints which expose existing abuses and gratify the people's insatiable appetite for tales of deception.)

Pierce Plainnes seaven yeres Prentiship. 1593. See ante, Vol. III, Chap. XVI, p. 417.

Beginning of the reaction from Euphuism

Greenes Mourning Garment . . . which he presents for a favour to all Young
Gentlemen that wish to weane themselves from wanton desires . . .
licensed 2 Nov., 1590, published same year.

Greenes Never too Late. Or a Powder of Experience: sent to all Youthful
Gentlemen. 1590.

Greenes farewell to Folly: sent to Courtiers and Schollers as a president to
warne them from the vaine delights that drawes youth on to repentance
Licensed 11 June, 1587, published 1591.

A Maiden's Dreame. 1591.

Coney-Catching Pamphlets

(Professionalism betrayed in the fabrication of pretentious titles and the
claim to disinterested motives in publishing.)

A Notable Discovery of Coosnage. Now daily practised by sundry lewd
persons called Connie-catchers and Crosse-biters. 1591. Rptd. 1592
and 1859 by Halliwell, J. O. Second part, 1591. Third part entered in
Stationers' register, 7 Feb. 1591/2.

The Defence of Conny-catching. By Cuthbert Cony-catcher. 1592. Rptd.
1859 by Adlard, J. E.

A Disputation Betweene a Hee Conny-catcher and a Shee Conny-catcher
whether a Theefe or a Whoore is most hurtfull in Cousonage to the
Common-wealth. . . . 1592. Rptd. with additions in 1617 as Theeves
falling out, True Men come by their Goods, and in 1637 with sub-title
The Belman wanted a clapper. A Peale of new Villanies rung out.
(See Belman of London under Dekker.)

The Black Bookes Messenger. Laying open the Life and Death of Ned
Browne, one of the most notable Cutpurses, Crosbiters, and Conny-
catchers, that ever lived in England. 1592. (Thomas Middleton
followed Greene's idea with The Blacke Booke, 1604.)

(Cf. the imitations entitled: Questions concerning Conie-hood and the
nature of the Conie, n.d.; Nihil Munchance, n.d. See, also, Chandler, F. W.,
The Literature of Roguery, 1907, vol. I, chap. III. For origins of genre,
see Vol. III, Chap. V of the present work.)

Social Tracts and Confessions

Philomela. The Lady Fitzwaters Nightingale. . . . 1592.

A Quip for an Upstart Courtier: or, a quaint dispute between Velvet-breeches
and Cloth-breeches. Wherein is plainely set downe the disorders in all
Estates and Trades. Licensed 20 July, 1592. Rptd. 1606, etc.; 1871,
Hindley, C., Miscellanea Antiqua Anglicana, pt. III.

Greens Groatsworth of Wit, bought with a Million of Repentance. . . .
Written before his death, and published at his dying request. Licensed
20 Sept., 1592. Edited by Chettle, H. Earliest extant ed. 1596. Rptd.
1600, etc.; 1813, Brydges, Sir E. (privately printed); 1874, Shakspere
Allusion Bks. pt. I; 1889, The Bookworm's Garner, No. VI; 1871, Hindley,
C., Miscellanea Antiqua Anglicana.

Authorities:

Bernhardi, W. Robert Greenes Leben und Schriften. Leipzig, 1874.
Collins, J. Churton: General Introduction to Plays and Poems. Oxford, 1905.
Grosart, A. B. Greene's Complete Works. Huth Library. 1881–6.
Schelling, Felix E. The Queen's Progress. n.d.
Storojenko, N.: Life of R. Greene. 1878. See vol. I of Huth Lib. ed.

THOMAS NASHE

(For The Unfortunate Traveller and Nashe's Marprelate tracts, see *ante*, Vol. III, Chaps. XVI and XVII.)

The Anatomie of Absurditie: contayning a breefe confutation of the slender imputed prayses to feminine perfection, with a short description of the severall practises of youth, and sundry follies of our licentious times. 1589. (Licensed 19 Sept., 1588.) Rptd. 1590; 1866, Collier, J. P., Illustrations of Old Eng. Lit.

Pierce Penilesse his Supplication to the Divell. Describing the over-spreading of Vice, and suppression of Vertue. 1592 (licensed 8 Aug.). Rptd. 1592, etc.; 1842, Collier, J. P., Shakspr. Soc.; 1870, Miscellaneous Tracts, Temp. Eliz. and Jac. I.

Strange Newes, of the intercepting certaine Letters, and a convoy of Verses, as they were going Privilie to victuall the Low Countries. 1592. Rptd. 1592, etc.; 1870, Misc. Trs., Temp. Eliz. and Jac. I. (In page headings the book is entitled Foure Letters Confuted and is licensed (12 Jan., 1592) as The Apologie of Pierce Penilesse.)

Cnrists Teares over Jerusalem. Whereunto is annexed a comparative admonition to London. 1593. (Licensed 8 Sep.) Rptd. 1594; 1613; 1815, Brydges, Sir E., Archaica. (The Terrors of the Night was licensed three months earlier but not published till 1594.)

The Terrors of the Night, or, A Discourse of Apparitions. 1594. (Licensed 30 June, 1593 and 15 Oct., 1594.)

Have with you to Saffron-walden. Or, Gabriell Harveys Hunt is up. Containing a full Answere to the eldest sonne of the Halter-maker. Or, Nashe his Confutation of the sinfull Doctor. 1596. (No entry in register.) Rptd. 1870, Collier, J. P., Misc. Trs., Temp. Eliz. and Jac. I.

Nashes Lenten Stuffe, Containing, The Description and first Procreation and Increase of the towne of Great Yarmouth in Noffolke: With a new Play never played before, of the praise of the Red Herring. 1599 (licensed 11 Jan., 1598–9). Rptd. 1745; 1809–10, Harl. Misc.; 1871, Hindley, C., Miscellanea Antiqua Anglicana.

The choise of Valentines. (In MS.; see McKerrow, R. B., Works, vol. III, A piece of pornography not devoid of literary art.)

Complete Works:

Grosart, A. B. Huth Library. 1883, 1885.
McKerrow, R. B.: Text 1904–5, Notes 1908. (4 vols. 5th vol. with memoir in preparation.)

(Cf. Cunningham, P., New Facts in the Life of Nashe, Shakspr. Soc. Papers, III, 178, and Upham, A. H., French Influence in English Literature, 1908.)

REPRESENTATIONS OF THE SEVEN DEADLY SINS

For representations previous to Nashe, see Rogers, F., The Seven Deadly

Sins in Literature, 1907, and Schofield, W. H., Eng. Lit. from the Norman Conquest, p. 416, 1906. See also Dekker, T., The Seven Deadly Sins; Lodge, T., Wits Miserie and the Worlds Madnesse: discovering the Devils incarnat of this Age, 1596; More, Sir T., Treatise on the Four Last Things; Nashe, T., Pierce Penilesse; Rowlands, S., The Seaven deadly Sins all Horst and riding to Hell (satire appended to The Knave of Spades); Tom Tel-Troths Message and his Pens Complaint, 1600, rptd. 1876, Furnivall, F. J., New Shakspr. Soc. A modified form of this classification is also used by Anton, R., Rankins, W., Rowlands, S., Times Whistle.

BURLESQUE ENCOMIA

Origins:

Βατραχομυομαχία, then supposed to be by Homer, Eng. trans., Crowne of all Homers Works. Batrachomyomachia, or the Battaile of Frogs and Mise, George Chapman; Catullus's poem on his yacht and two on Lesbia's sparrow; Vergil's Culex, trans. Spenser, E., published 1591; Lucian, Μυίας ἐγκώμιον (Muscae encomium), trans. in Works by Fowler, H. W. and F. G., 1905.

German:

The collection in the Nymwegen Pallas, 1666. See Herford, C. H., Literary Relations, 1886, chap. VII.

English:

The Noblenesse of the Asse . . . by A. B., 1595; Cornwallis, Sir W., Essayes of certaine Paradoxes, 1616 (2nd impression "inlarged," 2 pts., 1617), contains mock-encomia on Richard III, etc.; Nashe, T., Lenten Stuffe; Pimlyco or Runne Red Cap; Randall, Thomas (*i.e.* Randolph), The High and mightie commendation of the Vertues of a Pot of Good Ale, full of Wit, 1642 (published with The Battle fought betweene the Norfolk Cock and the Wisbich Cock), rptd. 1661; Pills to Purge Melancholly as The Ex-Ale-tation of Ale (Ebsworth, J. W., in his ed. of the Pills assigns the song to Rowlands), 1783, Ritson, J., English Song, vol. II; Skelton, J., Prayse of Phylyp Sparrow (*ante*, Vol. III, Chap. IV); The Treatyse Answerynge the boke of Berdes (*ibid.*, Chap. V., bibl. p. 560); Taylor, J., The Praise of Antiquity and the Commodity of Beggery, 1621 (verse and prose), The Praise and Vertue of a Jayle and Jaylers, 1623 (verse), The Praise of Cleane Linnen, 1624, The Needles Excellency, 1640.

Grobianism, as Herford has pointed out (Literary Relations), should also be regarded as a development, in which satire soon blended with burlesque.

FLYTINGS

Origins:

See *ante*, Vol. III, Chap. V, bibl. p. 557; Beowulf; Brotanek, R., Alex. Montgomerie, 1896; Christie, R. C., Étienne Dolet, 2nd ed., 1899; Nisard, M. E. C., Les Gladiateurs de la République des Lettres aux XVe, XVIe, XVIIe Siècles, 1860; Schipper, T., William Dunbar, 1884; Sandys, J. E., Harvard Lectures on the Revival of Learning, 1905 (chap. VI).

Gabriel Harvey

For sketch of Harvey-Nashe Controversy, see *ante*, Vol. III, Chap. XVII, bibl. pp. 615, 616.

Brydges, Sir E. Restituta. Vol. III. 1814-6.
Collier, J. P. Rpts. of both Nashe's and Harvey's pamphlets. 1870.

Disraeli, I.   Quarrels of Authors.   1814 ff.
Grosart, A. B.   Introduction to works of Harvey.   Huth Lib.   1884-5.
Morley, H.   Hobbinol.   Fortnightly Review, vol. v, pp. 274-283.   (Attempt
     to rehabilitate Harvey's character.)
Smith, G. C. Moore.   Introduction to Pedantius.   Louvain, 1905.

Subsequent Controversies

Vide Greene's attacks on Marlowe: Gosson, Lodge and the stage-contro-
versy (Vol. V of present work); Ben Jonson's war with the Poetasters (Penni-
man, J. H., The War of the Theatres, Boston, 1897; Small, R. A., The Stage-
quarrel, Breslau, 1899), also with Inigo Jones, Nath. Butter and Alex. Gill.

Marston, J.   Scourge of Villanie.   1598.   Answered by W. I. (William
     Ingram or John Weever?) in The Whipping of the Satyre, 1601, which
     provoked The Whipper of the Satyre, his Pennance in a White Sheet,
     1610 (by Marston?).
Rowlands, S.   Tis mery when knaves mete.   1600.   Rptd. 1609, expurgated
     as Knave of Clubs.   Rowlands severely criticised Belman of London,
     1608, in Martin Mark-all, . . . his Defence and Answere to the Belman of
     London, 1610.
Davies, J.   Scourge of Folly.   1611.   Amongst other personal attacks,
     represents himself submitting Nefarius (no doubt easily recognisable at
     the time) to the indignities of a school flogging (Epig. 212).
Taylor, John, attacked Thomas Coryate in the Sculler, 1612, Laugh and be
     Fat, 1613, W. Fennor, H. Walker, G. Wither and other contemporaries.
Stephens, J., attacked the stage in the character of A Common Player in
     Essays and Characters, 1615, which was answered by the character of an
     Excellent Actor in the Overbury Collection and in Ignoramus, 1630
     (Latin Comedy by Ruggles, G., answered by Cocke, J., in 3rd ed. of
     Stephens's Essayes and Characters, 1631).

EPIGRAMS AND SATIRES

For Barclay, J., Skelton, J., Cock Lorell's Bote, etc., see *ante*, Vol. III,
Chaps. IV and V.

For tracts on Usury see: Coplands, W., Newes come from Hell of love
unto all her welbeloved frendes, 1565; Wilson, Sir T., Discourse upon Usurye,
1572; Lodge, T., An Alarum against Usurers containing tryed experiences
against worldly abuses, 1584, rptd. 1853, Shakspr. Soc., 1883, Complete works,
Hunterian Club; Morse, M., The Arraignment and Conviction of usurie, 1595.

For more general satire: Hake, Edward, Newes out of Paules Churcheyarde, A Trappe for Syr Monye, 1567, Touchestone for this time present,
1574, Of Golds Kingdome and this unhelping age, 1604; Wilcox, T., A glasse
for gamesters: and namelie for such as delight in cards and dice, 1581;
Salter, T., A contention betwene three brethren; that is to say the whore-
monger, the drunkarde and the dice-player, 1581; R[ankins], W[illiam],
The English Ape, the Italian Imitation, the Foote-steppes of Fraunce, 1588;
Timme, T., Discoverie of Ten Lepers, 1592; Gosson, S., An excellent newe
ballad, declaringe the monstrous abuse in apparell, 1594, A glasse for
vaynglorious women, 1594-5, Quippes for upstart new fangled Gentlewomen,
1595, rptd. 1866, Hazlitt, W. C., E.E.P.P. (issued anonymously, authorship
assigned by Collier, J. P., on evidence of 2nd ed. inscribed "authore Stephen
Gossen").

Prynne, W., began his turbulent career with an attempt to reform the fashions of the day in Health's Sicknesse, The Unlovelinesse of Lovelocks, 1628.
For Origins and Development of Classical Epigram and Satire see:
Boissier, G.   L'opposition sous les Césars.   1875.
Butler, H. E.   Post-Augustan Poetry from Seneca to Juvenal.   1909.
Croiset, A. and M.   Histoire de la Littérature Grecque.   1899.   Tomes i, ii, v.
Mackail, J. W.   Latin Literature.   1891.
Martha, C.   Les Moralistes sous l'Empire Romain.   1865.
Murray, G.   A History of Ancient Greek Literature.   1897.
Nettleship, H.   Essays in Latin Literature.   1885.   Lectures and Essays.
2nd series.   1895.
Nisart, J. M. N. D.   Études de Mœurs et de Critique sur les Poëtes latins de
la Décadence.   1849.
Sellar, W. Y.   The Roman Poets of the Augustan Age.   1892.

Heywood, John.   A dialogue conteyning the number of the effectuall
proverbes in the Englishe tounge. . . . With one hundred of Epigrammes
and three hundred of Epigrammes upon three hundred of proverbes;
and a fifth hundred of Epigrams.   Whereunto are now newly added a
syxt hundred of Epigrams by the sayde John Heywood.   1562.   Rptd.
1576, etc.; 1867, Spenser Soc.; 1874, the Proverbs ed. by Sharman, J.;
1906, Proverbs, Epigrams and Miscellanies ed. by Farmer, J. S., Early
Eng. Drama Soc.
Drant, Thomas.   Medicinable Morall, that is the two bookes of Horace his
Satyres englyshed.   1566.
Gascoigne, George.   Steele Glas.   1576.   (*Ante*, Vol. III, Chap. x, p. 235.)
Kendall, Timothy.   Flowres of Epigrammes.   1577.
D[avies], [J.] and M[arlowe], C.   Epigrammes and Elegies.   1590.
Lodge, Thomas.   A Fig for Momus: containing pleasant Varietie, included
in Satyres, Eclogues, and Epistles.   1595.   Rptd. 1883, Gosse, E., Works.
Donne, John.   Satires.   (See *ante*, Chap. xi.)
Hall, Joseph.   Virgidemiarum.   Sixe Bookes.   First three bookes of Tooth-
lesse Satyrs.   1597.   Sixe Bookes, three last bookes of byting Satyres.
1598.   Rptd. 1599; 1602; 1879, Grosart, A. B., Complete Poems, Man-
chester.   [For Hall's indebtedness to Scaliger, J. C., see article by
Bensly, E., shortly to appear in Modern Language Review.   See, also,
Hall's works, ed. Pratt, J., 1808; ed. Hall, P., Oxford, 1837; ed. Wynter,
P., Oxford, 1863.]
Guilpin, Edward.   Skialetheia, on a Shadowe of Truth in certain Epigrams
and Satyres.   1598.   Rptd. 1878, Grosart, A. B.
Marston, John.   The Metamorphosis of Pygmalion's Image, and certain
Satyres.   1598 (published anonymously).   The Scourge of Villanie,
three Bookes of Satyres.   1598.   Rptd. 1856, Halliwell, J. O., Library of
Old Authors; 1879, Grosart, A. B.
Rankins, William.   Seaven Satyres applyed to the weeke.   1598.
Anon.   Tyros Roving Megge.   Planted against the walles of Melancholy.
Bastard, Thomas.   Chrestoleros; Seven bookes of Epigrammes.   1598.
Rptd. 1880, Grosart, A. B.
Barnfield, Richard.   Encomion of Lady Pecunia.   1598.   Rptd. 1605.   (*Vide*
Collier, J. P., Bibl. Cat., 1865, vol. 1, pp. 47–50.)
Weever, John.   Epigrammes in the oldest Cut and Newest Fashion.   1599.

M., T.   (Possibly Thomas Middleton, prob. Thomas Moffat).   Micro-cynicon,
Sixe Snarling Satyres.   1599.

(1 June, 1599, edict of Jo[hn Whitgift] Cantuar. and Ric[hard Bancroft]
London entered in Stationers' register to the effect that Virgidemiarum,
Pigmalion with certaine other Satyres, The Scourge of Villanye, The Shadowe
of Truthe in Epigrams and Satyres, Snarlinge Satyres, Caltha Poetarum,
Davyes Epigrams with Marlowes Elegyes, the booke againste woemen,
viz. of marriage and wyvinge, the xv joyes of marriage, should be burnt
and "that noe Satyres or Epigrams be printed hereafter . . . that all
Nasshes bookes and Doctor Harveyes bookes be taken wheresoever they
maye be found and that none of theire bookes be ever printed hereafter."
Pygmalion, The Scourge of Villany, Skialetheia, Snarling Satires, Davies's
Epigrams, Marriage and Wyving, xv Joyes of Marriage, and the Harvey-
Nashe books were burnt.   Hall's Satires and Caltha Poetarum (by Cutwode,
T., mostly love poems, rptd. 1815, Roxburghe Club) were "staied.")

Rowlands, Samuel.   The letting of humours blood in the Head Vaine.   1600.
Humors Looking-glasse.   1608.   (Anonymous, attributed to Rowlands.)
Thynne, Francis.   Emblems and Epigrames.   1600.   1876, Furnivall, F. J.
Breton, Nicholas.   Pasquils Mad-Cappe and his Message.   Pasquil's Fooles-
cap.   Pasquils Mistresse, or the Worthy and Unworthy Woman.   Pas-
quil's Passe and Passeth Not, set downe in three pees, his Passe, Pre-
cession, and Prognostication.   All in 1600.
Woodhouse, Peter.   The Flea.   1605.   Rptd. 1877.
P[arrot], H[enry].   Mous-Trap.   1606.   Epigrams by H. P.   1608.   Laquei
Ridiculosi, or Springes to catch Woodcocks.   1613.   The Mastive, or
Young-Whelpe of the Old-Dogge.   Epigrams and Satyres.   1615.   VIII.
Cures for the Itch.   Characters, Epigrams, Epitaphs, by H. P.   1626.
Walkington, T. (d. 1621).   The Optick Glasse of Humors.   1607.   [A pre-
decessor of Burton.]
West, Richard.   The Court of Conscience or Dick Whippers Sessions.   1607.
A Century of Epigrams.   1608.   (*Vide* Warton's Hist. of Eng. Poetry,
vol. IV.)   [See D. of N. B. for other works by, or attributed to him.]
Anon.   Epigrams or Humours Lottery.   1608.
Tofte, Robert.   Translation of Ariosto's Satyres.   1608.
Heath, John.   Two Centuries of Epigrammes.   1610.
Sharpe, Roger.   More fooles yet.   1610.   (Epigrams.)
Scot, T.   Philomythie or Philomythologie.   Wherein outlandish birds, beasts
and fishes are taught to speake true English verse.   1610, 1616.
Davies, John, of Hereford.   The Scourge of Folly.   (See *ante*, p. 542.)
Taylor, John.   The Scoller . . . or Gallimawfry of Sonnets, Satyres and
Epigrams.   1612.   Rptd. 1614.   Taylor's Water-Worke. Epigrammes
. . . being ninety in number, besides two new made Satyres.   1651.
Wither, George.   Abuses Stript and Whipt.   1613 ff.
Freeman, Thomas.   Rubbe and a Great Cast: and Runne and a Great Cast.
The second Bowle.   In 200 Epigrams.   1614.
C., R.   The Times Whistle: or A Newe Daunce of Seven Satires, and other
Poems.   *c.* 1614.   Rptd. 1871, Cowper, J. M., E.E.T.S.
Brathwaite, Richard.   A Strappado for the Divell.   Epigrams and Satyres
alluding to the time.   1615.   Rptd. 1878, Ebsworth, J. W. (with intro.).
Natures Embassie: or, the Wilde-mans Measures: Danced naked by
twelve Satyres.   1621.   [See Hales, J. W., Folia Litteraria, 1893.]

Goddard, William. A Neaste of Waspes latelie found out and discovered in the Law (Low) Countreys yealding as sweete hony as some of our English bees. 1615. A Satyricall Dialogue, or a sharplye-invective Conference betweene Alexander the Great and that trulye woman-hater Diogynes. Imprinted in the Lowe Countryes for all such gentlewomen as are not altogether Idle nor yet well ocupyed. n.d. A Mastif Whelp, with other ruff-Island-lik Currs fetcht from amongst the Antipodes. Which bite and barke at the fantasticall humorists and abusers of the time. . . . Imprinted amongst the Antipodes and are to be sould where they are to be bought. n.d. (Assigned by Collier, J. P., Poetical Decameron, to T. M. and dated *c.* 1600.)

Anton, Robert. Philosophers Satyrs. 1616. Of which a 2nd ed. was produced as Vices Anotimie scourged and corrected in new satirs. 1617.

Harington, Sir John. The most elegant and witty Epigrams of Sir John Harrington. 1618. Rptd. 1625, etc. (A few had been appended to Alcilia by J. C., 1613. For miscellaneous remnants in prose and verse and especially for letters, *vide* Harington, R. H., Nugae Antiquae, 1769. Rptd. 1779; 1792; 1804, re-ed. by Park, T.)

Jonson, Ben. Epigrams. Published with Works. 1616.

Hutton, Henry, Dunelmensis: Follie's Anatomie or Satyres and Satyricall Epigrams with a Compendious History of Ixion's Wheele. 1619. Rptd. 1842, Rimbault, E. F., Percy Soc.

Wroth, Thomas. An Abortive of an idle Hour, or a century of Epigrams. 1620.

Peacham, Henry. Thalia's Banquet. 1620.

Martyn, Joseph. Newe Epigrams, having in their Company a mad Satyre. Licensed to George Eld, 1619. Earliest extant copy, 1621.

Hayman, Robert. Quolibets. 1628.

Randolph, Thomas. Aristippos or, The Joviall Philosopher. 1630.

Anon. Epigrammes, mirrour of New Reformation. 1634.

The following books should be consulted:

Alden, R. M. The Rise of Formal Satire in England. Philadelphia. 1899.

Collier, J. P. Poetical Decameron. 1820. 3rd, 4th, 5th conversations.

Seccombe, T. and Allen, J. W. The age of Shakespeare. 1904. Vol. I, bk. I, § 9.

Shade, O. Satiren u. Pasquille, a. d. Reformationszeit. 1862–3.

Warton, T. History of English Poetry from the Twelfth to the close of the Sixteenth century. Ed. by Hazlitt, W. C. 1871. Vol. IV, sections LXII—LXVI.

CHARACTER WRITERS

Anticipations of the Genre

Vision concerning Piers the Plowman (allegorical portraits, *ante*, Vol. II, Chap. I); Bartholomaeus Anglicus and Higden (description of national and social types, *ibid.* Chap. III); Skelton (Bowge of Court: types of courtiers, Vol. III, Chap. IV); Barclay (Ship of Fools: types of folly discussed rather than portrayed, *ibid.*); Cock Lorell (glimpses of individual types of lower classes, Chap. v); Mock Testaments (classification according to some dominant characteristic, *ibid.*); Copland's Hye Waye to the Spittel Hous (vivid descriptions of character and appearance from the view of failure in life, *ibid.*);

Fraternitye of Vagabonds, Caveat and xxv Orders of Knaves (precise definitions of rogue-nomenclature, *ibid.*); T. Lodge's Wits Miserie (portrayal of devils as impersonations of specific vices, see above); T. Greene's Quip; T. Nashe, especially Pierce Penilesse.

Classical Sources

Aristotle: Rhetoric, Bk. II.   Ed. Cope, E. M., and Sandys, J. E., 1877. Ethics, Bk. IV.   Ed. Grant, Sir A., 1857–8.   (Except in the case of Earle and Bacon, Aristotle's influence can be traced only through Theophrastus.) Theophrastus.   Trans.: Casaubon, I., 1592; Editio ultima recognita . . . aucta et locupletata, 1617; Healey, J., 1616; Jebb, R. C., revised by Sandys, J. E., 1909.

English Writers

Ormerod, Oliver. The Picture of a Papist, and a Discourse of Popish Pagan-
      isme.   1605.   The Picture of a Puritane.   1605.
Hall, Joseph. Characters of Virtues and Vices.   1608.
Anon. The Cobler of Canterburie.   1608.   ("The exposition of the eight
      degrees of Cuckolds.")
M., W. The Man in the Moone telling Strange Fortunes.   1609.   Rptd.
      1849, Halliwell, J. O., Percy Soc.
Overbury, Thomas. A Wife: now the Widdow of Sir Thomas Overburye.
      Being a most exquisite and singular Poem of the Choice of a Wife.
      Whereunto are added many witty characters, and conceited Newes,
      written by himself and other learned Gentlemen his friends.   1614 ff.
      (There had already appeared in the same year A wife, now a Widowe,
      without characters.)   Note contemporary imitations, The Husband, with
      commendatory verses by Ben Jonson, 1614; A second Select Husband, by
      John Davies of Hereford, in 1616; The Description of a Good Wife, by
      Brathwaite, and the Happy Husband, by Patrick Hannay, 1619; Picturae
      loquentes, by Saltonstall, W., with a Poem of a Maid, 1631 (?); A Wife
      not ready made but bespoken, Robert Aylett, 1653.   (See D. of N. B.
      art. Overbury.)   1890, Rimbault, E. F., Library of Old Authors, rpt. of
      ninth ed. (*i.e.* in 1616).   See Fox, A. W., A Book of Bachelors, 1899.
Stephens, John. Satyrical Essayes, characters and others.   1615. New
      Essayes and Characters.   With a new Satyre in defence of the Common
      Law and Lawyers: mixt with reproofe against their enemy Ignoramus.
      1631.   (*Vide* Brydges, Restituta, vol. IV, 503 ff. (N. & Q. Ser. IV, vol. III,
      550).)
Breton, Nicholas. Characters upon Essayes, morall and divine.   1615.   The
      Good and the Badde, or Descriptions of the Worthies and Unworthies of
      this Age.   1616.   2nd ed. 1643, under title England's selected characters.
Mynshul, Geffray. Essayes and Characters of a Prison and Prisoners.
      1618.   Rptd. 1638; 1821, Edinburgh.
P[arrot], H. Cures for the Itch. Characters, Epigrams, Epitaphs.   1626.
Earle, John. Microcosmographie or a Piece of the World discovered; in
      Essays and Characters.   1628 (54 characters).   Re-ed. 1811, Bliss, P.,
      with bibliography of Character writers; 1871, Fowler, J. T. (ed. from
      a MS. among Hunter MSS. in Durham Cath., dated 14 Dec., 1627, with
      46 characters of which 3 are unique, collated with printed eds. from which
      it frequently differs.   *Vide* N. & Q. Ser. IV, vols. VIII & IX); 1897, West,
      A. S., with excellent introduction and notes.

M., R. Micrologia. Characters or Essayes of Persons, Trades and Places.
1629.

Alexandrinus, Clitus [Richard Brathwaite]. Whimzies, or, A new Cast of
Characters. 1631. Rptd. 1859, Halliwell, J. O.

Saltonstall, Wye. Picturae Loquentes. 1631. 2nd ed. 1635.

Lupton, Donald. London and Country Carbonadoed and quartered into
severall Characters. 1630. (See British Bibliographer, vol. 1, 464.)
Rptd. Harl. Misc. (ed. Park), vol. IX.

Anon. A Strange Metamorphosis of Man, transformed into a Wildernesse.
Deciphered in Characters. 1634. (Noticed by Haslewood in Censura
Literaria, vol. VIII, 284.)

Habington, William. Castara. 2nd ed. 1635, has characters of A mistris, A
wife, A friend; 3rd ed., 1640, has further addition, The Holy Man.

Anon. A Brown Dozen of Drunkards (ali-ass Drinkhards) whipt and shipt
to the Isle of Gulls. 1648.

For adaptation of the character sketch to party politics, its subsequent
development as social satire, especially in the hands of John Cleveland
and Samuel Butler, its application to moral instruction, especially by William
Law (Serious Call to the Unconverted, 1729), see later vols. of present
work.

Works to be consulted:

Baldwin, C. S. Modern Language Association of America, June, 1904.

Cross, W. L. Development of the English Novel. 1899.

Greenough, C. N. Studies in the Development of Character-writing in
England. Harvard, 1898. Larger work in preparation.

Halliwell, J. O. Books of Characters. Illustrating habits and manners of
Englishmen, from the reign of James 1st to the Restoration. 1857.
Confused Characters. 1860.

Lee, E. Selections from La Bruyère and Vauvenargues. 1902.

Raleigh, W. A. The English Novel. 1891.

Seccombe, T. and Allen, J. W. Age of Shakespeare. Vol. 1, bk. II, § 4.

Whibley, C., in Blackwood's Magazine, June, 1909.

English character writing should be distinguished from French *portraits*,
which may have been imitated from Holland or copied from the famous
relazioni in which the Venetian ambassadors depicted the most important
personalities of the court to which they might be attached; see M. de Boislisle
Ann.-Bulletin de la Soc. de l'Hist. de France, t. XXXIII, 1896. The French
portrait consists in a description of the physiognomy, complexion, figure,
appearance and mannerisms of an individual designated under a pseudonym.
This art was cultivated in the salons which flourished during the first half
of the 16th cent., in such romances as Le Grand Cyrus and Clélie and in
the collection of *portraits* made under the auspices of Mlle. de Montpensier.
After the appearance of Charles Sorel's Description de l'isle de Portraiture,
1659, the art, as a social amusement, began to decay, but reached its consummation in the memoir-writers, especially Saint Simon, and started on a new
stage of development in La Bruyère. Owing to the absence of salons in
England, this style of writing has remained undeveloped, though there are
a few striking exceptions, such as Philautus's description to Psellus of the
Gentlewoman in Euphues and his England (p. 340 of Arber's ed.), Nashe's
portrait of Harvey in Have with you, the pictures of low-class passengers
in the Cobler of Canterburie and Westward for Smelts, the portrait of

Colonel Hutchinson by his wife and the historical portraiture of the second half of the 17th cent. On the other hand, the cultivation of portraits, maxims, etc., have left French 17th cent. literature poor in character sketches of the English type, Le Moine's Peintures Morales, 1643, being the nearest parallel in this period. It should also be noted that the same influence which favoured the *portrait* and starved the generic character also hindered the development of the discursive essay, in spite of Montaigne's example, but encouraged the *maxime* and the *pensée*, *i.e.* condensed and aphoristic reflections, of which the most accomplished master was La Rochefoucauld.

See Cousin, V., La Société française au XVIIᵉ Siècle, 1854–1869; Fournel, V., La litt. indépendante et les écrivains oubliés au XVII siècle; Franz, A., Das literarische Porträt in Frankreich im Zeitalter Richelieus und Mazarins, 1906; Lee, E., Intro. to selections from La Bruyère and Vauvenargues, 1903; Petit de Julleville, Hist. de la langue et de la litt. française, 1897, vol. IV, chap. II; Sainte-Beuve, Portraits de Femmes, 1840, Causeries du Lundi, 1853, vols. XI, XIV, Nouveaux Lundis, 1863, vols. V, X.

ESSAY

Sources:

Epictetus. Dissertationes. Text. Shenkl, H. 1898. Trans. Healey, John. 1610.

Plutarch's Moralia. Bernardakis. 1888–96. Trans. Holland, P. 1603. Vitae Parallelae. Trans. North, T. 1579.

Lucius Annaeus Seneca (not the dramatist). Dialogi; De Beneficiis; Epistolae morales. Text. Haase, F. 1853. Trans. Lodge, Thomas: The Workes, both Morrall and Natural, of Lucius Annaeus Seneca. 1614.

Montaigne. First appearance of essays, 1580. Revises and expands his work and adds a third book, 1588. Early trans. by Florio, John, 1603, 2nd ed. 1613.

See Becker, P. A., Montaignes geistige Entwicklung in Deutsche Literaturzeitung, 4 Sept., 1909; Bond, R. W., Montaigne, 1907; Dieckow, F. A. F., John Florio's englishe Übersetzung der Essais Montaigne's und Lord Bacon's, Ben Jonson's und Robert Burton's Verhältnis zu Montaigne, 1903; Dowden, E., Montaigne, 1907; Texte, J., Études de Litt. Européenne, 1898; Villey, P., Les sources et l'évolution des Essais de Montaigne, 1908.

Anticipations in English Literature

Caxton's prefaces (*ante*, Vol. III, Chap. XIV). Jest-books (especially Merrie Tales and quicke answers, *ibid.* Chap. V). Andrew Boorde, William Bullein (*ibid.*). Disquisitions on Women (especially the Scholehouse for Women). Lord Burghley, Precepts or Directions for the well ordering and carriage of a man's life (printed 1637, though composed in 16th cent. See Peck's Desiderata Curiosa, and Kippis's ed. of Biographia Britannica.)

English Essays

Remedies against Discontentment, drawn into severall Discourses from the writinges of auncient Philosophers. 1596. (See Arber, E., A Harmony of the Essays, etc., 1895, Prologue, pp. ix and x.)

Greeneham. Diverse sermons and tracts uppon severall textes. 1598.

Essayes by Sir William Corne-waleys.   1600, etc.   Essayes of certaine Para-
    doxes.   1616.   Essayes.   Newlie corrected.   Discourses upon Seneca the
    tragedian.   1632.
Johnson, Robert.   Essaies or Rather Imperfect Offers.   1601, etc.
J., H.   The Mirrour of Worldly fame.   1603.   Rptd. Harl. Misc. 1808, ii, 515.
Anon.   Essays of conjecture.   1607.
T[uvill], D[avid].   Essaies Politicke and Morall.   1608.   Essayes Morall and
    Theologicall.   1609, 1629, etc.
Stephens, John.   Satyricall Essayes.   1615.
A Discourse against flattery.   1620.
Brathwaite, Richard.   Essaies upon the five Senses.   1620.   Rptd. 1635; 1815.
Horae Subsecivae.   Observations and Discourses.   1620.   (See N. & Q. Ser.
    x, vol. xii, Nos. 293 and 296 for attempt to father the essays on
    Bacon.   Generally attributed to lord Chandos or Gilbert Cavendish.
    See Brydges, Sir S. E., Censura literaria, 2nd ed., 1815.)
Mason, William.   A handfull of Essaies or Imperfect Offers.   1621.
Bacon, Francis.   Essays.   1597–1625.   For the development of the essays
    and the addition of new ones in the different editions, for reprints of the
    Religious Meditations and Places of perswasion and disswasion, see
    Arber, E., A Harmony of the Essays, etc., 1895.   (Among other modern
    commentators and editors may be mentioned: Abbott, E. A., 1885
    (attempt to trace influence of B.'s scientific research on the Essays);
    Spedding, J., Ellis, R. L., Heath, D. D., 1857 (highly appreciative); West,
    A. S., 1897; Whateley, R., 6th ed., 1864; Wright, W. Aldis, 1862 ff.
Felltham Owen.   Resolves.   n.d. (1620?).   First complete ed.   1628.   Rptd.
    1631, etc.   See also Retrospective Review, vol. x, 343–355.
Peacham, H. (the younger).   The Truth of our Times.   Revealed out of one
    Man's Experience by way of Essay.   1638.
Jonson, Ben.   Timber; or Discoveries made upon Men and Matter as they
    have flowed out of his daily readings; or had their refluxe to his peculiar
    Notion of the Times.   [Published posthumously in vol. ii of fol. ed.
    1640–1.   Among modern editors and commentators are: Castelain, M.
    Discoveries, a critical edition, with an introduction and notes on the
    true purport and genesis of the book, 1906 (contends that Timber was
    extra title added by publisher: suggests that Discoveries was a note-book
    begun after the burning of B. J.'s library, 1623, and that some, at least,
    of the notes were destined to be put into verse; Castelain was the first
    thoroughly to investigate the extent of B. J.'s indebtedness to other
    writers); Ben Jonson.   L'homme et l'œuvre.   1572–1637, 1907 (in chap.
    iii constructs character and habit of thought of the writer out of Dis-
    coveries); Gifford, W., Works of Ben Jonson, 1816, re-ed. Cunningham,
    F., 1875; Schelling, F. E., Timber; or Discoveries made upon Men
    and Matter, Boston, 1892 (intro. contains careful analysis of Jonson's
    style); Spingarn, J. E., The sources of Jonson's Discoveries, 1905
    (traces some thoughts to Heinsius, de Tragoediae constitutione, 1611,
    and Jacobus Pontanus, Poeticarum Institutionum Libri iii, 1594);
    Swinburne, A. C., A study of Ben Jonson, 1889; Whalley, P., Jonson's
    Works, 1756 (first pointed out the fact, admitted in sub-title of Discover-
    ies, that the book was not original).]

(Cf. Littleboy, A. L., Relations between French and English Literature in
    the sixteenth and seventeenth centuries, 1895; Maiberger, M., Studien über

d. Einfluss Frankreichs auf d. Elizabethan Literatur, 1903; Upham, A. H.,
French Influence in English Literature, 1908.)

TREATISES AND DISSERTATIONS AKIN TO THE ESSAY

The development of the Baconian essay was retarded by the age's love of
more formal literature, especially of dialogues, which covers almost exactly
the same ground as the Jacobean essayists, with the added attractions of
style, and influenced Addison and his circle no less than Cornwallis, R.
Johnson, Bacon, Felltham, etc.)

The Booke of Honor and Armess Wherein is discoursed the causes of Quarrell,
and the nature of Injuries, with their repulses. Also the Meanes of
satisfaction and pacification. 1590.

Brathwaite, Richard. The English Gentleman. 1630, 1641, 1652. The
English Gentlewoman. 1631, 1641. Ar't asleepe Husband? 1640.
(Prose. Bolster lectures on moral themes and a novelette.)

—— The Schollers Medley. Rptd. 1638 as A Survey of History, or a Nursery
for Gentry, and in 1651.

Breton, Nicholas. [See D. of N. B. for fuller bibliography.]

——Wits Trenchmour, in a Conference betwixt a Scholler and an Angler.
1597. (A trenchmour (i.e. riotous dance) of repartees, similes and
reflections beginning as a dialogue on angling and developing into
tales and discourses delivered by a scholar.)

—— The Wil of wit, Wits Wil, or Wils Wit, chuse you whether. 1599.
Rptd. 1606; 1860, Halliwell-Phillipps, J. O.

—— The Figure of Foure. Registered 1597 and 1607. Only The Second
Part of ed. 1636 (rptd. 1654) exists. (Proverbial utterances, each describing four things united under some common similarity.)

—— Wonders Worth the Hearing which being read or heard in a Winters
evening by a good fire, or a Summers morning . . . may serve both to
purge melancholy from the minde, and grosse humours from the body.
1602.

—— A Poste with a Packet of Mad Letters. 1603, 1609, 1637. (Letters
mostly addressed to typical figures. It should be remembered that
letter-writing had already become an art under the influence of Cicero,
Seneca and Guevara. Angell Day's English Secretary (1586), had been
followed by many other manuals of letter-writing. J. Hall had
published Six Decads of Epistles (1607–10), and the letters of J. L.
Guez de Balzac had been translated by W. T[yrwhit] and R. B. (Sir R.
Baker?).)

—— Strange Newes out of divers countries. 1622. (Facetious satire against
society under the guise of news.) Cf. Overbury's Newes.

—— The Court and Country, or, a Briefe Discourse betweene the Courtier
and Country-man. 1618.

—— Fantasticks: serving for a perpetual Prognostication. 1626.

Bryskett, Ludowick. Discourse of Civil Life. 1606. (Composed 1584–9;
dialogue on moral philosophy in which Spenser takes part.)

Munday, Anthony. The Mirrour of Mutabilitie: or principal Part of the
Mirrour of Magistrates. 1579.

—— The Paine of Pleasure, profitable to be perused of the Wise, and necessary to be by the Wanton. 1580.

—— The Defence of Contraries. Translated out of French. 1593.

Peacham, Henry (the elder). The Garden of Eloquence, conteyning the Figures of Grammar and Rhetorick, from whence may bee gathered all manner of Flowers, Coulors . . . Formes and Fashions of speech. 1577.

Peacham, Henry (the younger). (See, also, under English Essays.) The Art of Drawing with the Pen, and limming in water colours . . . with the true manner of painting upon glasse, the order of making your furnace. . . . 1606. Rptd. 1612 as Graphice, etc. The Compleat Gentleman, fashioning him absolute in the most necessary and commendable qualities concerning Minde or Bodie. . . . 1622. Rptd. 1634; 1661; 1906, intro. by Gordon, G. S. Tudor and Stuart lib. (Peacham treats of the details of a nobleman's education. Criticises flogging in schools, strongly recommends travel and insists on the study of heraldry.) The Worth of a Peny: or a caution to keep money. With the causes of the scarcity and misery of the want hereof in these hard and mercilesse times. 1647 (misprint for 1641?), etc. Rptd. 1903, in Arber's English Garner.

Powell, Thomas. Tom of All Trades or The Plaine Path-way to Preferment. 1631. Rptd. 1876, Furnivall, F. J., New Shakspr. Soc.
　　Cf. Ducci, L., Ars Aulica, trans. Blount, E., 1607; de Refuge, E., Traité des Cours, 1617, trans. Reynolds, J., 1642; Faret, N., Des Vertus nécessaries à un prince, 1623; L'Honnête Homme ou l'art de plaire, 1630.

Rich, Barnabe. Opinion Diefied. Discovering the Ingins, Traps and Traynes that are set in this age, whereby to catch opinion. 1613. The Honestie of this Age, proving by good circumstance that the world was never honest till now. 1614 ff. (Rptd. 1844, Cunningham, P., Percy Soc.) The Irish Hubbub, or the English Hue and Crie. 1617. (General denunciation of society.)

Wits Common-Wealth. (Generic title for Politeuphuia, Wits Common-Wealth, by John Bodenham, 1597 (18 eds. before Restoration). Palladis Tamia. Wits Treasury, . . . by Meres, F., 1598. Wit's Theatre of the Little World, 1599. Palladis Palatium, 1604. These four books contain quotations and maxims from various writers. See Ingleby, C. M., Shaks. Allusion-Bks. Part I, 1874; New Shakspr. Soc., and cf. Theatrum Virtutis et Honoris; oder Tugend Büchlein aus etlichen . . . Griechischen und Lateinischen Scribenten ins Teutsch gebracht, durch W. Pirckheymern, . . . Nürmberg, 1606.)

THOMAS DEKKER

Canaans Calamitie, Jerusalems Misery, or the dolefull destruction of faire Jerusalem by Tytus. (Verse. Ascribed to Dekker by Grosart, A. B.)

The wonderfull Yeare 1603, wherein is shewed the Picture of London, lying sicke of the Plague. 1603.

The Batchelor's Banquet. 1603, etc. (Founded on the Quinze Joyes de Mariage (see ante, Vol. III, Chap. v, bibl. p. 551). Important as evidence of the interest still taken in satires on women and married life (see ibid., pp. 98–102, bibl. pp. 551–554). Cf. Tom Tell-Trothes New-yeares Gift, 1593, a satire on jealousy, The passionate Morrice, 1593, a review of the art of wifing as exemplified by eight typical couples dancing a morris-dance. See also The praise of Vertuous Ladies in Breton's The Wil of Wit, and Rowlands's pamphlets. Cf. Vol. III, Chap. v, pp. 98–102, bibl. pp. 551–554.)

The seven deadly Sinnes of London: drawne in seven severall Coaches through the seven severall Gates of the Citie, bringing the Plague with them. 1606. Rptd., Arber, E., 1879, The English Scholar's Lib., no. 7.

Newes from Hell; brought by the Divel's Carriers. 1606. Rptd. 1607, enlarged and entitled A Knights Conjuring done in Earnest discovered in Jest; 1842, Rimbault, E. F., Percy Soc. (For earlier conceptions of visions of Hell, Heaven and Purgatory, see Homer: Odyssey, XI (trans. Chapman, G.); Aristophanes: Frogs; Plato: picture of the infernal judges at the end of the Gorgias, of Tartarus in Phaedo and the vision of Er the Armenian in the Republic (trans. Jowett, B., 1871, 3rd ed. revised, 1892); Plutarch: vision of Timarchus in Περὶ τοῦ Σωκράτους δαιμονίου in Moralia (trans. Holland, P., 1603); Vergil: Georgics IV and Aeneid VI; Lucian: the Κατάπλους and the Μένιππος (trans. Necromantia . . . interlocutors, Menippus and Philonidas; ptd. by Rastell, J., n.d.) in Dialogues of the Dead; Dante: Inferno, Paradiso, Purgatorio; Staunton, W.: St. Patrick's Purgatory, 1409; Damerval: Sensuit le grãt dyablerie qui traicte coment Sathan fait demõstrance a Lucifer de tous les maulx que les mõdains font selon leurs estatz vacations et mestiers . . .; Dunbar, William: The Dance of the Sevin Deidly Synnis, 1503–8; Lyndsay, Sir David, Ane Satyre of the Three Estaits, 1540; Rabelais: Pantagruel. Bk. II, chap. 30 (imitated in Le Nouveau Panurge, Gaillard, Michel); Ford, J.: 'Tis Pity she's a Whore, act III, sc. 6; Tarlton's Newes out of Purgatorie, c. 1589; Tell-Trothes New-yeares Gift, 1593 (represents Robin Goodfellowe as just returning from Hell whence he brought an oration on jealousy). Cf. also title Greenes Newes both from Heaven and Hell, 1593, by Barnabe Rich, and Dekker His Dreame (below). See Wright, T.: St. Patrick's Purgatory, an essay on the legends of Purgatory, Hell and Paradise, current during the Middle Ages, 1844; Becker, E.: Visions of Heaven and Hell, 1898, Johns Hopkins Univ. Diss.)

The Double P.P., a Papist in Armes, Bearing Ten severall Sheilds, encountered by the Protestant. . . . 1606. (Verse attack on the Roman Catholics ascribed to Dekker by Collier, J. P. (Bibl. Cat. I, 197).)

Jests to make you merie. Written by T. D. and George Wilkins. 1607. (Jest-book: ascribed to Dekker.)

The Dead Terne or Westminster's Complaint for long Vacations and short Termes. Written in manner of a Dialogue betweene the two Cityes London and Westminster. 1608. (A compilation of history, anecdotes, comment, satire, conceits, descriptions, exposures and complaints all dealing with London mostly anticipating the themes which he treated more fully in subsequent works.)

The Belman of London: Bringing to Light the most notorious Villanies that are now practised in the Kingdome. 1608. 2nd and 3rd eds. (with additions) in same year. Re-edited 1612 as O per se O, or a newe Cryer of Lanthorne and Candle Light.

Lanthorne and Candle Light: or, the Bell-Mans Second Nights Walke. In which he brings to light a Brood of more strange Villanies than ever were till this yeare discovered. 1608. Rptd. 1609 (twice); 1612 as O per se O, or a new cryer of Lanthorne and Candlelight Being an addition or Lengthening of the Bell-mans Second Night-walke.

(Both rogue-pamphlets frequently rptd. under such titles as English Villanies six severall Times prest to death, but still reviving again, are now the seventh time discovered. . . . 1632; English Villanies seven severall Times prest to Death by the Printers . . . are now the eighth time, etc. . . . 1637.)

The Ravens Almanacke, Foretelling of a Plague, Famine and Civill Warre. 1609. (Parody on prognostications.)

Foure Birdes of Noahs Arke; the Dove, the Eagle, the Pelican and the Phoenix. 1609. Rptd. 1857, Halliwell, J. O. (A devotional work.)

Worke for Armorours, or the Peace is broken. Open Warres likely to happen this yeare 1609. 1609. (Allegorical description of the rising of poverty against wealth.)

The Gulls Horne-booke or Fashions to please all sorts of Guls. 1609. Rptd. 1812, Nott, Dr., Bristol; 1892, Saintsbury, G., Eliz. and Jac. Pamphlets; 1902, McKerrow, R. B., King's Lib. (For Friedrich Dedekind's Grobianus *vide* Goedeke, K., Grundriss zur Gesch. der deuts. Dichtung, 2e Aufl., 1886, Bd II, Buch IV, § 158, and Herford, C. H., Literary Relations, 1886, chap. VIII. A Nuremberg poet at the end of the 15th cent. parodied German poems on courtesy and manners into instructions for negligence. Seb. Brant in Narrenschiff (*ante*, Vol. III, Chap. IV) invented St. Grobianus as a suitable figure-head for the ill-mannered character. Dedekind, F., produced, 1549, Grobianus, De morum simplicitate (Latin poem), ed. 1903, by Bömer, A., in Lateinische Litteraturdenkmäler des XV und XVI Jahrhts., English trans. 1605, The Schoole of Slovenrie or, Cato turnd wrong side outward, by R. F.

A strange Horse Race, at the End of which comes in the Catch-pols Masque. And after that the Bankrouts Banquet: which done, the Divell falling sicke, makes his last Will and Testament this present yeare, 1613. 1613.

Dekker His Dreame: in which beeing rapt with a Poeticall Enthusiasme, the great volumes of Heaven and Hell to him were opened, in which he read many wonderfull Things. 1620. Rptd. 1860, Halliwell-Phillipps, J. O., see The Bookworm, vol. II, p. 349, 1888.

Rod for Run-awayes. 1625. (Satire on those who desert London in plague-time.)

Authorities:

Grosart, A. B., in Non-Dramatic Works of T. Dekker. Huth Lib., 1881.
Swinburne, A. C. Nineteenth Century. Jan. 1887.

SAMUEL ROWLANDS [for full bibliography, see D. of N. B.].

The Betraying of Christ, Judas in Despaire with other poems on the Passion. 1598.

Tis mery when Knaves mete. 1600, and later years under differing titles. Contains humorous tales of knavery and burlesque adventure, reminiscent of *fabliaux* and jest-books, narrated in bright easy verse.)

The Letting of Humours Blood in the Head-vaine; with a new Morisco daunced by seaven Satyres upon the bottome of Diogenes Tubbe. 1600. (Suppressed.) Rptd., Edinburgh, 1815.

Humors Ordinarie, where a Man may be verie merrie, and exceeding well used for his Sixepence. n.d.

Greenes Ghost haunting Cony-catchers, With the Merry Conceits of Doctor Pinchbacke a notable Makeshift. 1602. Rptd. 1626. (Marks another step in the fusion of the rogue pamphlet into the picaresque novel; the anecdotes illustrating triumphs of ingenuity and mother wit rather than a felonious professionalism. For another example of trading on Greene's name, see Barnabe Rich, Greenes Newes, 1593.

'T is Merrie when Gossips meete. 1602 ff. (For previous literature of this type see *ante*, Vol. III, Chap. v, bibl. pp. 551–554.)

Looke to it: for Ile stabbe ye. 1604.

Hell 's broke loose. 1605. (Epic on John of Leyden.)

A terrible Battell betweene the two consumers of the whole world; Time and Death. n.d. (1606 according to Gosse, see below, Collected Works.) Rptd. 1841, Utterson, E. V., Beldornie Tower Press.

Diogenes Lanthorne. 1607. (Copied from Lodge: Catharos Diogenes in his Singularity, 1591. Consists of misanthropic monologue of Diogenes in streets of Athens and ends with jest-book fables in verse.)

Democritus or Doctor Merryman his Medicines against melancholy Humours by S. R. 1607. Rptd. 1609, etc.

Famous History of Guy, Earl of Warwick. 1608.

Humors Looking-glasse. 1608. (Epigrams on London characters and incidents similar to Humours Blood.)

Whole crew of Kind Gossips. 1609. (Six wives discuss their husbands in the usual Elizabethan spirit. The husbands afterwards pass equally severe strictures on them.)

The Knave of Clubbs. 1609. (See above, Tis mery when Knaves mete.)

Martin Mark-all, Beadle of Bridewell; his Defence and Answere to the Belman of London. Discovering the long concealed Originall and Regiment of Rogues, when they first began to take head, and how they have succeeded one the other successively unto the sixe and twentieth yeare of King Henry the eight, gathered out of the Chronicle of Crackeropes, and (as they term it) the Legend of Lossels. 1610. (The last part, the Runnagates Race tells of the foundation of the order of vagabonds by Jack Mendall (J. Cade) and of their cooperation in the risings of the North (cf. Jusserand, J., La Vie Nomade, trans. Smith, L. T., 8th ed., n.d.). The tract ends with an unhistorical sketch of the subsequent vagabond leaders who were now becoming proverbial, and in some sort shared in the popular imagination the place occupied by the older and not less questionable heroes such as Robin Hood, Sir Bevis, etc. The list includes Hugh Roberts, Jenkin Cowdiddle, Spysing, Puffing Dicke, Laurence Crosbiter, and Cock Lorell (*ante*, Vol. III, Chap. v, bibl. p. 548).)

The Knave of Harts. Haile Fellow, well met. 1612. (Verse portraits of types of knaves and anecdotes of knavery.)

More Knaves yet. The Knaves of Spades and Diamonds, with new Additions. 1613. (Verse anecdotes, etc., mostly dealing with rogues.) Rptd. 1843, Rimbault, E. F., Percy Soc.; 1841, Utterson, E. V., Beldornie Tower Press.

A Fooles Bolt is soone shott. 1614. (Jests and Tales in verse mostly recording the blunders of fools.)

The Melancholic Knight, by S. R. 1615.

The Night Raven. 1620. Rptd. 1634; 1841, Utterson, E. V., Beldornie Tower Press. (Purports to represent scenes after dark, but presents the usual sketches of knavery.)

A Paire of Spy-knaves. n.d. (1620?).

Good Newes and bad Newes. 1622. Rptd. 1841, Utterson, E. V., Beldornie Tower Press. (Another verse jest-book.)

Heavens Glory, seeke it. Earths Vanitie, flye it. Hells Horror, fere it. 1628. (The vol. contains The Common Cals, Cryes and Sounds of the Bell-man; or, divers Verses to put us in Minde of our Mortalitie.)

See Gosse, E., Complete Works of S. Rowlands, Hunterian Club, 1880. (Contains an admirable appreciation of Rowlands's work.)

ROGUE PAMPHLETS AND PRISON TRACTS

(See footnote to p. 111, Chap. v, Vol. III, and cf. Ben Jonson's masque The Gipsies Metamorphosed, 1621.)

S., E. The Discoverie of the Knights of the Poste: or the Knights of the post, or common baylers newly Descried. Wherein is shewed and plainely laide open many lewde actions and subtill devises, which are daily practised by them: to the great abuse of most honorable Councelers, learned Judges and other grave Majestrates: And also to the defrauding and utter undoing of a greate no. of her Majesties good and loyall subjects. 1597. (E. S., supposed by G. C. Moore Smith to be Edward Sharpham, vide N. & Q. 11 July 1908.)

Hutton, Luke. Luke Hutton's Lamentation. 1597 (?) (Hazlitt).

Hutton, Luke. The Blacke Dogge of Newgate. c. 1600. 1638 enlarged as The Discovery of a London Monster.

The Life and Death of Gamaliel Ratsey, a famous thief of England. 1605. Rptd. 1866, Collier, J. P., Illus. of Old Engl. Lit., vol. III.

Johnson, R. Looke on me, London. I am an honest Englishman, ripping up the Bowels of Mischiefe, lurking in thy sub-urbs and Precincts. 1613. Rptd. 1864, Collier, J. P., Illus. of Early Engl. Pop. Lit., vol. II.

Anon. The severall notorious and lewd cousonages of John West and Alice West, . . . who were convicted in the Old Baily. . . . 1613. (Narrates impostures and confidence tricks. The gold finding and necromancy are strikingly similar to the deceits exposed by Erasmus, Colloquia Familiaria Alcumistica and Exorcismus sive Spectrum, and Scot, R., Discoverie of Witchcraft. The soothsaying and clairvoyance illustrate the tales told by Doctor Burcot and William Cuckoe in Chettle's Kind-Hart's Dreame, and the pranks played by Dr. Pinchbacke in Rowlands's Greenes Ghost.)

Fennor, William. Comptors Common-Wealth. 1617. Rptd. 1619; 1629.

Mynshul, Geffray. Essayes and Characters of a Prison and Prisoners. 1618. (Cf. Ashton, J., The Fleet, its rivers, prison and marriages, 1888.)

Anon. A briefe collection of the exactions, extortions, oppressions . . . towards the lives, bodies and goods of prisoners, done by Alexander Harris. . . . 1620–1 (broadsheet). Rptd. 1879, Camden Soc.

Clavell, John. Recantation of an ill led Life: a discoverie of the High-way Law. 1628. See Collet, S., Reliques of Literature, 1823; Granger, J., Biog. History of Great Britain, 5th ed., vol. III; Caulfield, J., Portraits and Memoirs, 1813, vol. I.

Anon. Frogges of Egypt, or the Catterpillars of the Commonwealth Truly Dissected and Laid open. 1641.

A Whip for the Marshal's Court by Robert Robins. 1647.

See Chandler, F. W., The Literature of Roguery, 1907, chap. III. The writer of the present chapter is indebted to this book in many ways.

TOBACCO PAMPHLETS

(The whole output of literature on tobacco is eminently characteristic of the age in its elaborate titles, far-fetched conceits and bitter invective. The spirit of criticism is so strong that even the partisans of the weed satirise the habits of the smoker.)

Frampton, John. Joyfull newes oute of the newe founde worlde. . . . Englished by 1577. According to Arber, E., the earliest detailed account of the herb. See also Athenæum, 27 June, 1 Aug., 1857.

Buttes, Henry. Dyets Dry Dinner. That is, varietie of Fare: provided, prepared and ordered, at Dyets own prescription: Prandium, without Wine, but Accipitrimum, without all drinke except Tobacco (which also is but Dry Drinke): . . . 1599. (Recommends tobacco as a sedative, narcotic, purge, but adds A Satyricall Epigram, upon the wanton, and excessive use of Tobacco.)

Anon. The Metamorphosis of Tobacco. 1602. (Dedicated To my loving Friend Master Michael Drayton.)

Anon. Work for Chimney-sweepers: or A warning for Tabacconists. Describing the pernicious use of Tobacco. . . . As much to say, Better be chokt with English hemp, then poisoned with Indian Tobacco. Written by Philaretes. 1602.

Anon. A Defence of Tobacco: with a friendly answer to the late printed Booke called Worke for Chimney-sweepers. 1602.

King James. A Counter Blaste to Tobacco. 1604; 1616. Ed. Arber, E., 1895 (good introduction). [For King James's other works, see D. of N. B. and Rait, R. S., Lusus Regius, 1902.]

G[ardiner], E[dmund]: The Triall of Tabacco. Wherein his worth is most worthily expressed. 1610. (A medical defence.)

Anon. Perfuming of Tobacco, and the great Abuse committed in it. 1611.

Barclay, William. Nepenthes; or, the vertues of Tobacco. Edinburgh, 1614. Rptd. 1841, Miscellany of the Spalding Club, vol. I.

Sylvester, Joshua. Tobacco battered; and the Pipes shattered (about their ears that idlely Idolize so base and barbarous a Weed; or at least-wise over-love so loathsome Vanitie:) by a Volley of holy Shot thundered from Mount Helicon. 1614 (verse).

T., C. An Advice how to plant Tobacco in England. 1615.

Deacon, John. Tobacco tortured, or the filthie fume of tobacco refined. 1616.

Rich, Barnabe. The Irish Hubbub, or the English Hue and Crie. 1617. (Denounces tobacco-smoking in a general attack on society.)

Brathwaite, Richard. The Smoaking Age, or the Man in the Mist. Dedicated to those three renowned and inparallel'd heroes, Captain Whiffe, Captain Pipe and Captain Snuffe; to whom the Author wisheth as much content as this smoaking age can afford them. At the signe of Teare-nose. 1617. Rptd. 1703. Vide Corser's Collectanea, pt. II, p. 361.

Bennett, E. A treatise . . . touching the inconveniences, that the importation of tobacco out of Spaine, hath brought into this land. (About 1620.)

Thorius, R. Hymnus tabaci. 1626.

Authorities:

Bragge, W. Bibliotheca nicotiana. Birmingham, 1880.

Cleland, H. W. On the History and Properties, Chemical and Medical, of Tobacco. Glasgow, 1840.

Fairholt, F. W.   Tobacco: its history and Associations.   1859.

Tiedeman, F.   Geschichte des Tabaks.   1854.

JEST-BOOKS AND MISCELLANEOUS TRACTS ON LONDON

Barclay, Sir R.   Discourse of the Felicitie of Man: or his Summum Bonum 1598.   (Amusing histories and anecdotes.)

Tarlton, Richard.   Tarlton's Jigge of a horse loade of Fooles.   (Composed before 1588.)   1884, Halliwell, J. O., Tarlton's Jests, Shakspr. Soc. (Verse.   Idea of the Ship of Fools converted into journey in cart down Fleet Street for a puppet show.   Types suggested by contemporary London society.   See Herford, C. H., Literary Relations, chap. VI, pp. 372 ff.)

Anon.   Tarlton's Newes out of Purgatorie, n.d.   (Ptd. before The Cobler of Canterburie, 1590.)

The Cobler of Canterburie.   1590.   Rptd. 1862, Ouvry, F. (privately ptd.). (Coll. of prose stories, mostly about cuckolds.)

Anon.   Tarlton's Jests, drawn into three parts.   1.   His Court-witty Jests. 2.   His sound city jests.   3.   His Countrey Pretty Jests.   1611 (earliest ext. ed., but 1st series mentioned by Nashe 1592 and 2nd series licensed 1609).   Rptd. 1864, Hazlitt, W. C., Shakespr. Jest-books, vol. II (illustrates the universal fame of Tarlton by quotations from contemporary authors); 1876 (?), Ashbee, E. W., Fac-simile reproduction (privately printed); 1884, Halliwell, J. O., with notes and life, Shakspr. Soc.

Anon.   Maroccus extaticus.   Or Bankes bay horse in a trance.   A discourse set downe in a merry dialogue between Bankes and his beast;   Anatomising some abuses and tricks of this age.   1595.   (Dialogue between the animal and its master is a satire on the abuses of London life.   The horse's description of the hypocrisy of the puritan and of the landlord particularly noteworthy, and foreshadow the character writers.)

Jack of Dover, his quest of Inquirie, or His Privy Search for the Veriest Foole in England.   1604.   1842, Percy Soc.; 1864, Hazlitt, W. C., *ibid.*, vol. II.

Pasquils Jests, mixed with Mother Bunches Merriments.   1604, etc.; Rptd. 1864, Hazlitt, *ibid.*

Newes from Graves End.   1604.   (Assigned by Collier, J. P., to Dekker.)

Jests to make you merie . . . written by T. D. (Dekker?) and George Wilkins. 1607.

Johnson, Richard.   The Pleasant Walkes of Moore-fields.   1607.   Rptd. 1864, Collier, J. P., Illus. of Early Engl. Pop. Lit., vol. II.   Pleasant Conceites of Old Hobson.   1607.   Rptd. 1843, Percy Soc.; 1864, Hazlitt, *op. cit.*

Anon.   Merrie Conceited Jests of George Peele.   1607, etc.   1864, Hazlitt, *ibid.*

Munday, Anthony.   Song of Robin Hood in Metropolis.   (Verses on the Guildhall Gate (see Stow's Survey, bk. III).)

The Great Frost.   Cold doings in London, except it be at the Lottery.   With news out of the Country.   1608.   Rptd. 1903, Social Engl. Illus., An Engl. Garner.   (An excellent piece of journalism describing the amusements and accidents connected with the freezing of the Thames, etc.)

Armin, Robert.   A nest of Ninnies.   1608.   Rptd. 1842, Collier, J. P., Fools and Jesters, Shakspr. Soc.   (Records a number of jests perpetrated by court fools.   See Herford, *op. cit.* chap. VI, p. 375, for relation of Nest to Ship literature of the 16th cent., and Fool literature of the 17th.)

Pimlyco, or, Runne Red-Cap. Tis a mad world at Hogsdon. 1609. Rptd. 1891, Bullen, A. H., Antient Drolleries (no. 2).

Rowley, W. A search for money, or the lamentable complaint for the Losse of the wandring Knight, Mounsieur l'Argent. 1609. 1840, Percy Soc.

Anon. Westward for Smelts, or, the Waterman's fare of mad merry Western wenches whose tongues, albeit like Bell-clappers they never leave ringing, yet their tales are sweet, and will much content you. Written by Kinde Kit of Kingstone. 1620. Rptd. 1848, Halliwell, J. O.

Taylor, John. [See D. of N. B. for full list.]

—— Cold Tearme . . . or the Metamorphosis of the River of Thames. 1621 (Ballad ascribed to Taylor, J.)

—— The World runnes on Wheeles, or oddes betwixt carts and coaches. 1623. (Review of the new modes of locomotion in the city where were starving the waterman's profession. Cf. A pleasant Dispute between Coach and Sedan. 1636.)

—— The Fearefull Sommer. 1625. Rptd. 1869, Spenser Soc. (Description of the plague.)

—— Wit and mirth. Chargeably collected Out of Taverns, Ordinaries, Innes, Bowling-Greenes and allyes, ale-houses, Tobacco-shops, Highwayes and Water-passages. Made up and fashioned into Clinches, Bulls, Quirkes, Yerkes, Quips and Jerkes. Apothegmatically bundled up and garbled at the request of old John Garretts Ghost. 1629. Appeared in collected ed. of Taylor, . . . 1630. Rptd. 1864, Hazlitt, op. cit. vol. III.

—— John Taylor the Water-Poet's Travels through London to visit all the Taverns. 1636. Rptd. 1870–7, Spenser Soc.

Anon. Robin Good-Fellow; his mad pranks and merry jests. Earliest ext. ed. 1628. Some version probably existed in the 16th cent., see intro. to rpt. 1841, Collier, J. P., Percy Soc.; 1845, Halliwell, J. O., Illustrations of the Fairy Mythology of a Midsummer Night's Dream, Shakspr. Soc.; 1875, Hazlitt, W. C., Fairy Mythology of Shakespeare. Early in the 17th cent. a number of incidents drawn from the book were versified and sold as a chap-book with the title The merry pranks of Robin Good-Fellow; cf. The merry Prankes of Robin Goodfellow in Percy's Reliques. (Begins as a jest-book copied from Eulenspiegel (ante, Vol. III, Chap. v, p. 105 and bibl. p. 555) and develops into the jests and tricks played by a fairy. The Second Part of Robin Good-Fellow, commonly called Hob-Goblin: with his mad Prankes and merry Jests, published the same year, contains a proportion of songs and catches inserted among the tricks. The legend of Robin Good-Fellow, according to Wright, T. (Foreign Quarterly Review, no. 35), dates from the 13th cent. at least. It is frequently alluded to in Eliz. literature (e.g. Tarlton's Newes out of Purgatorie, Munday's The Two Italian Gentlemen, Guilpin's Skialetheia, Midsummer Night's Dream, etc.).)

P[eacham], H. The Art of Living in London. 1642. Rptd. Harl. Misc. vol. IX. For supplementary list of Jest-books, see Hazlitt, W. C., Handbook to Early Engl. Lit., 1867, p. 300.

BURLESQUE AND WAGERING VOYAGES

The most dangerous and memorable adventure of Richard Ferris, . . . who departed from Tower Wharf, on Midsummer Day last past . . . who undertook, in a small wherry boat, to row, by sea, to the city of Bristow. . . . 1590. Rptd. 1903, Social England Illustrated. An English Garner.

Kemp's nine days' wonder. Performed in a dance from London to Norwich.
1600. Rptd. 1840, Dyce, A., Camden Soc.; 1903, Social England
Illustrated. Alluded to by Marston, The Scourge of Villanie, 1599;
Jonson, B., Every Man out of his Humour (acted 1599); Rowley, W.,
A Search for Money, 1609; Brathwaite, R., Remains after Death, 1618.
Kemp figures in The Returne from Parnassus, 1606, and The Travailes of
The three English Brothers, 1607 (?).

Taylor, John. The Pennyles Pilgrimage, or the Money-lesse perambulation
. . . from London to Edenborough (prose and verse). 1618.

—— A Very Merry Wherry-Ferry-Voyage; or Yorke for my Money (verse).
1622. Rptd., Hindley, C., Misc. Antiq. Angl. See Halliwell-Phillipps,
J. O., Lit. of the 16th and 17th cents. illustrated, 1851.

Brathwaite, R. Barnabae Itinerarium. Barnabees Journall, under the
Names of Mirtilus & Faustulus shadowed. 1638. Rptd. 1820, by Haslewood, J., with elaborate bibl.; 1876, W. C. Hazlitt's rpt. of Haslewood.

MISCELLANEOUS BURLESQUES AND GOLIARDIC EXTRAVAGANCES

Harington, Sir John. A New Discourse of a stale subject called the Metamorphosis of Ajax. 1596.

Ulysses upon Ajax. 1596. (Davies, J., of Hereford speaks of Ulysses upon
Ajax as being the work of a different hand (Wits Bedlam, 1617) but the
similarity of style is unmistakable.)

An Anatomie of the Metamorpho-sed Ajax. By T. C. . . . Rpt. of all three
tracts, 1814, from press of Whittingham, C., Chiswick. Vide Collier, J. P.
Poetical Decameron, 1820. (Ajax is meiosis for "a jakes" and the series
of pamphlets, probably all published in the same year, exemplify the
nearest approach in English literature to the humour of Rabelais.
Marston in The Scourge of Villanie, Bk. III, Sat. 11, speaks of
         loathsome brothel rime,
      that stinks like Ajax froth, or muck-pit slime.)

The Knight of the Sea. 1600.

Anton, R. Meriomachia. 1613. Rptd. 1909, Becker, G., in Archiv für das
Studium der neueren Sprachen etc., Vol. CXXII.

Brathwaite, Richard. A Solemne Joviall Disputation. 1617. (On the laws
of drinking.)

Pasquils Palmodia, and His progresse to the Taverne. Rptd. 1620; 1634;
1866, Collier, J. P., Illus. of Old Engl. Lit., vol. I.

Taylor, J. A Dogge of Warre, or, the Travels of Drunkard (mostly verse)
1630.

—— Drinke and welcome: or, the Famous Historie of . . . Drinks. 1637.
Rptd. 1871, no. 17 of Ashbee's Occasional Fac-simile Reprints.

PROGNOSTICATIONS, SERIOUS AND BURLESQUE

(Cf. Pantagrueline Pronostication, 1533, and the Fool's prophecy in Lear
(act III, sc. 2).)

Nashe, T. A wonderfull, strange and miraculous Astrologicall Prognostication for this yeer of our Lord God, 1591 . . . by Adam Fouleweather,
student in Assetronomy. Rptd. 1892, Saintsbury, G., Eliz. and Jac.
Pamphlets. (Parody of soothsayers' pamphlets. (Ante, Vol. III,
Chap. v, pp. 123, 124.) No entry in Stationers' register.)

Breton, N. Pasquil's Passe and Passeth Not, set downe in three pees, his
Passe, Precession, and Prognostication. 1600.

Waldegrave, R. (publisher). The whole prophecie of Scotland, England and
some part of France and Denmark, prophesied bee mervellous Merling,
Beid, Bertlington, Thomas Rymour, Waldhave, Eltraine, Banester, and
Sibbilla, all according to one. Containing many strange and mervelous
things. 1603. See also Laing, D., A Collection of Ancient Scottish
Prophecies, 1833; and The Romance and Prophecies of Thomas of Ercel-
doune, intro. by Murray, J. A. H., E.E.T.S. 1875, no. 61.

A Piece of Friar Bacon's Brazen-heads Prophecie. By William Terilo.
1604. Rptd. 1844, Halliwell, J. O., Percy Soc. (The pamphlet is a satire
contrasting the distrust and artificiality of the 17th cent. with the
simplicity and industry of the former generation.)

Newes from Rome of two mightie armies . . . also certaine prophecies of a
Jew called Cabel, Shilock. . . . Translated out of Italian by W. W. 1606.
(See N. & Q. 24 July 1909.)

The Raven's Almanacke; foretelling of a Plague, Famine and Civill Warre,
that shall happen this present year 1609. 1609. (A parody, ascribed to
Dekker.)

Cobbes Prophecies, his signes and tokens, his Madrigalls, Questions, and
Answeres, with his spirituall lesson. 1614. Rptd. 1890 (private).

The Owles Almanacke; prognosticating many strange accidents that shall
happen. 1618 . . . by Jocundary Merrie-braines. 1618.

Wither, G. Fragmenta Prophetica. 1669. Rptd. 1872, Spenser Soc.

WITCH-CONTROVERSY

The public agitation over supernatural questions continued to form a
background to popular thought, as is seen in the tracts of Nashe and Dekker,
broadsides, news-sheets and in the dramatists. For origins of this phase of
superstition in the social disorders of the late 15th and 16th cents., and for the
beginning of daemonology in Jacob Sprenger's Malleus Maleficarum, see
ante, Vol. III, Chap. v, pp. 125 ff. For bibl. see ibid. p. 562 and N. & Q. Ser. x,
vol. XI, no. 286, pp. 491 ff., also Lecky, W. E. H., Rationalism in Europe, 4th
ed. 1870, vol. I, chap. I. Subsequent to R. Scot's Discoverie of Witchcraft,
the following works may be noted:

Gifford, G., Discourse of the Subtill Practices of Devilles, 1587. Holland, H., A Treatise against Witchcraft, 1590. Nashe, T., The Terrors
of the Night, 1594. King James, Daemonologie, 1597 (Edinburgh), 1603
(London). Chamber, J., Treatise against Judicial Astrologie, 1601.
Heydon, Sir C., A Defence of Judicial Astrologie in answer to Mr. J.
Chamber, 1603. Gifford, G., Dialogue of Witches and Witchcraft, 1603
(rptd. 1842, Wright, T., Percy Soc.). Perkins, P., Discoverie of the
Damned Art of Witchcraft, 1610. Cotta, J., The Triall of Witchcraft,
1616. Roberts, Alexander, Treatise of Witchcraft, 1616. Cooper, Rev.
Thomas, The Mystery of Witchcraft, 1617. Goodcole, H., The wonderful
Discovery of Elizabeth Sawyer . . . her conviction . . . together with
the Devil's Access to her. . . . 1621. (Source of The Witch of Edmon-
ton.) Vicars, T., The Madnesse of Astrologers, 1624. Bernard, R.,
Guide to Jurymen, 1627.

The whole dispute was enhanced by controversies over particular cases of
witchcraft, such as the paper war waged between John Darrell and George

More on the one side, and by Samuel Harsnet, John Deacon and John Walker on the other, over the possession and dispossession of William Somers, and over "the strange and grevous vexation by the Devil" of seven persons in Lancashire. The whole country was thrown into excitement over the Lancashire trials of 1612 (the case is reported in a pamphlet by Thomas Potts, 1612) and great interest was aroused by cases of imposture, of which the most celebrated was that of the "Boy of Bilson." He feigned fits and "cast out of his mouth rags, thred, straw, crooked pins" when in the presence of a certain woman, who was promptly arrested as a witch. These episodes led to the production of such works as: Witches apprehended, examined and executed, for notable villanies. . . . With a strange and true triall how to know whether a woman be a Witch or not, 1613; A Treatise of Witchcraft . . . with a true narration of the witchcrafts which Mary Smith . . . did practise . . . and lastly of her death and execution, 1616; The Wonderful Discoverie of the Witchcrafts of Margaret and Philip Flower, . . . 1618.

For fuller examination of the subject and its continuation through the 17th cent. see later vols. of present work.

BROADSIDES, STREET BALLADS, NEWS-SHEETS AND POLITICAL PAMPHLETS

News-agents and Political Journalists

Elderton, W.   The true fourme and shape of a monsterous chyld. . . . 1565. A new Yorkshyre song. 1584 etc.

Tarlton, Richard.   A very lamentable and wofull Discours of the fierce Fluds, whiche lately flowed in Bedford shire . . . and in many other places . . . the 5 of October 1570. A newe booke in English Verse, entitled, Tarltons Toyes. 1576. Tarltons devise uppon the unlooked for great snowe. 1578. Tarltons Farewell. 1588. A Sorrowful newe Sonnette Intituled Tarltons Recantation. 1589. Tarltons Repentance, or his Farewell to his Frendes in his Sicknes a little before his Deathe. 1589. A pleasant Dyttye, Dialogue wise betweene Tarltons Ghost and Robyn Good Fellowe. 1590.

Rich, Barnabe.   Besides novels and romances (see ante, Vol. III, Chap. xvi) and numerous tracts on Ireland, he produced: A right exelent and pleasant Dialogue betwene Mercury and an English Souldier, contayning his application to Mars, 1574 (1st part exposes the ill-treatment of English soldiers and enters a plea for archery); Greenes Newes both from Heaven and Hell, 1593, rptd. 1624 as A New Irish Prognostication (purports to be printed from Greene's papers but is really a treatise on Ireland. It may have been Rich who also published a booklet of sonnets with title Greenes Funeralls by R. B. . . . A Martiall Conference pleasantly discoursed between two Souldiers only practised in Finsbury Fields. . . . 1598).

Munday, A.   [For fuller bibliography, see D. of N. B.]
——— A Watch-word to Englande, to beware of Traytors and tretcherous Practises, which have beene the Overthrowe of many famous Kingdomes and Commonweales. 1584. (Arising from the Campion affair but of a more general character.) View of Sundry Examples. n.d. Rptd., Collier, J. P., Shakspr. Soc., 1851. (Relates murders, strange incidents and prodigies occurring 1570–80.)
[See, also, Pollard, A. F., Tudor Tracts, 1532–1588. 1903.]

Collections of Songs and Broadsides

(See *ante*, Vol. III, Chap. v, bibl. p. 558, and Chap. viii, bibl. pp. 579, 580. The greater number of extant broadsides are subsequent to the Civil War, but the following collections contain specimens of our period.)

Antidote Against Melancholy. 1661. Rptd. 1876, Ebsworth, J. W.

Ashton, J. A Century of Ballads. 1887. Humour, Wit and Satire of the Seventeenth Century. 1883.

Bagford Ballads. 1876. Ebsworth, J. W. Ballad Soc.

Bullen, A. H. Carols and Poems from the fifteenth century to the present time. 1886.

Collier, J. P. A Collection of Old Ballads anterior to the reign of Charles I. 1840. Percy Soc. A Book of Roxburghe Ballads. 1868. Broadside, black-letter Ballads printed in the Sixteenth and Seventeenth Centuries. 1868. Twenty-five old Ballads and Songs. 1869. (Coll. of MSS., temp. Eliz. and Jac. Probably copies of broadsides.) Illustrations of Early English Popular Literature. 1863. (Contains songs, ballads and murder pamphlets, together with political tracts.)

Deloney, T. Strange Histories, n.d. Garland of Good Will. Earliest known ed., a fragment dated 1604.

Deuteromelia, or the second Part of Musick's Melodie. 1609. (Sequel to Pammelia.)

Evans, Robson. Old Ballads. 1810.

Farmer, J. S. Merry Songs and Ballads prior to the year 1800. 1897.

Furnivall, F. J. Love-poems and humourous Ones. 1874. Ballad Soc.

Goldsmid, E. Quaint Gleanings from Ancient Poetry. 1884.

Huth, H. Ancient Ballads and Broadsides published in England in the Sixteenth Century. 1867. Philobiblon Soc.

Johnson, Richard. Besides a number of romantic and narrative ballads of which the Nine Worthies of London, 1592, is best known, he produced: The Crowne Garland of Golden Roses, 1612, etc., rptd. 1845, Chappell, W., Percy Soc.: The Golden Garland of Princely Pleasures and Delicate Delights, 3rd ed., 1620.

Lemon, R. Catalogue of a Collection of Printed Broadsides in the Possession of the Society of Antiquaries of London. 1866. (Title-pages, reproduction of wood-cut illustrations, descriptions of contents.)

Munday, A. Banquet of Dainty Conceits. 1581. (Songs and ditties for popular tunes.)

Pammelia. Musicks Miscellanie. 1606.

Percy, Bp. Reliques of Ancient Poetry. 1765. Ed. Wheatley, H. B., 1876. Percy Folio Manuscript, Hales, J. W. and Furnivall, F. J.; Ballads and Romances, 1867–8; Loose and humorous Songs, 1867, E.E.T.S.

Roxburghe Ballads. Ed. Ebsworth, J. W. Ballad Soc. 1869.

Shirburn Ballads. Ed. Clarke, A. Oxford, 1907.

CHAPTER XVII

WRITERS ON COUNTRY PURSUITS AND PASTIMES

The following is a brief list of the more important books. Fuller lists, and details of the various editions, will be found in the bibliographical books noted below. See, also, D. of N. B.

Amherst, A.   A History of Gardening in England.   2nd ed.   1896.

Brydges, E.   Censura Literaria.   Vol. v.   1815.

Cockle, J. D.   A bibliography of English Military Books up to 1642 and of contemporary foreign works.   1900.

Donaldson, John.   Agricultural biography.   1854.

Gatfield, G.   Guide to printed books and manuscripts relating to Heraldry and Genealogy.   1892.

Harting, J. E.   Bibliotheca Accipitraria.   1891.

Hazlitt, W. C.   Gleanings in old garden literature.   1887.

—— Old cookery books and ancient cuisine.   1886.

Huth, F. H.   Works on Horses and Equitation.   1887.

Jackson, B. D.   Guide to the literature of Botany.   Index Soc.   1881.

McDonald, D.   Agricultural writers, 1200–1800.   1908.

Marston, R. B.   Walton and some earlier writers on fish and fishing. 1894.

Moule, T.   Bibliotheca Heraldica Magnae Britanniae.   1822.

Old English Cookery.   Quarterly Review, Jan. 1894.

The Master of Game, ed. by Baillie-Grohmann, W. A. and F.   1904.   (Bibliographical notes on early hunting literature.)

Westwood, T. and Satchell, T.   Bibliotheca Piscatoria.   1883.

GERVASE MARKHAM

Country Books

Cavelarice, or the English horseman. . . . 1607.

Cheape and Good Husbandry for the well-ordering of all beasts, and fowles, and for the generall cure of their diseases. . . . Together, with the use and profit of bees; the making of fish-ponds, and the taking of all sorts of fish.   1614, etc.

The Complete Farriar, or the kings high-way to horsmanship. . . . 1639.

The Compleat Husbandman and gentleman's recreation: or the whole art of husbandry.   1707.

Country Contentments; or the husbandmans recreations.   1611.   (Contains the first book only.)   Country Contentments, in two bookes: the first containing the whole art of riding great horses. . . . Likewise . . . the arts of hunting, hawking, etc.   The second intituled, The English Huswife; containing the inward and outward vertues which ought to be in a compleate woman. . . . 1615, etc.

The Country Housewifes Garden . . . together with the husbandry of bees . . . with divers new knots for gardens.   1617, etc.

The Country-mans Recreation, or the art of planting, grafting, and gardening, in three bookes.   (i. The art of planting, grafting, and gardening.   ii. A perfect platforme of a hoppe garden.   iii. The expert gardener.)   1640, etc.)

A cure for all diseases in horses.   1610.   (As Markhams Method, 1616, etc.)

A discource of Horsemanshippe.   Wherein the breeding and ryding of horses for service, in a brefe manner is more methodically sett downe then hath been heeretofore. . . . Also the manner to chuse, trayne, ryde and dyet, both hunting-horses, and running-horses.   1593, 1595, etc.

The English Husbandman. The first part: contayning the knowledge of the true nature of every soyle within this kingdome. . . . Together with the art of planting, grafting, and gardening after our latest and rarest fashion. . . . 1613. Second booke. . . . Contayning the ordering of the kitchin-garden, and the planting of strange flowers: the breeding of . . . cattell. . . . Whereunto is added a treatise, called Good mens recreation: contayning a discourse of the generall art of fishing. . . . Together with the . . . breeding and dyeting of the fighting cocke. 1614, etc.

The Gentlemans Academie, or The Booke of St Albans, compiled by Juliana Barnes . . . and now reduced into a better method by G. M. 1595.

The Gentlemen's Accomplish'd Jockey: with the compleat horseman and approved farrier. . . . 1722.

The Horsemans Honour, or the beautie of horsemanship as the choise, natures, breeding, breaking, riding, and dieting, whether outlandish or English horses. With the true, easie, cheape, and most approved manner, how to know and cure all diseases in any horse whatsoever. 1620. (Anon., but possibly by Markham.)

How to trayne and teach horses to amble. 1605.

Hungers Prevention: or the whole arte of fowling. . . . 1621, etc.

The Husbandman's Jewel, directing how to improve land . . . destroy vermin, etc. 1707.

The Inrichment of the Weald of Kent. 1625, etc.

Maison Rustique, or, the countrey farme. Compyled in the French tongue by Charles Stevens, and John Liebault . . . translated into English by Richard Surflet . . . reviewed, corrected, and augmented. By Gervase Markham. 1616.

Le Marescale, or the horse marshall, containing those secrets which I practice, but never imparted to any man. (Manuscript: in possession of Sir Clements R. Markham.)

Markhams Faithfull Farrier. 1630, etc.

Markhams Farwell to Husbandry: or, the inriching of all sorts of barren and sterill grounds. . . . 1620, etc.

Markhams Maister-peece, or what doth a horse-man lacke, containing all possible knowledge whatsoever which doth belong to any smith, farrier or horse-leech, touching the curing of all maner of diseases or sorrances in horses, . . . with an addition of 130 most principal chapters, and 340 most excellent medicines receits and secrets worthy every mans knowledge. 1610, etc.

The Perfect Horseman; or, the experienc'd secrets of Mr. Markham's fifty years practice . . . now published by Launcelot Thetford. 1655, etc.

A Way to get Wealth: containing the sixe principall vocations or callings in which everie good husband or house-wife may lawfully imploy themselves. . . . 1631, etc. (A collection containing: 1. Cheap and Good Husbandry; 2. Country Contentments; 3. The English House-wife; 4. The Inrichment of the Weald of Kent; 5. Markhams farewell to Husbandry; 6. Lawson's New Orchard and Garden, with The Country House-wifes Garden, Harward's Art of propagating Plants, and The Husbandmans Fruitefull Orchard.)

The Whole Art of Husbandrie, by C. Heresbach, translated by B. Googe, 1577, enlarged by Gervase Markham. 1631.

The Young Sportsman's Instructor. In angling, fowling, hawking, hunting, ordering singing birds, hawks, poultry, coneys, hares, and dogs, and how to cure them. By G. M. Sold at the Gold Ring, in Little Britain. Price 6*d*. Rptd. 1820; also by Gamidge, S., Worcester (n.d.).

Poems and Plays

Devoreux. Vertues teares for the losse of King Henry III of Fraunce, etc., paraphrastically translated into English by Jervis Markham. 1597.

The Dumbe Knight. A pleasant comedy, acted sundry times by the children of his Majesties Revels. Written by Jarvis Markham [and L. Machin]. 1608, 1633. Rptd. in Dodsley's Collection, vol. IV.

The Famous Whore, or noble curtizan: conteining the lamentable complaint of Paulina, the famous Roman curtizan. 1609. Ed. by Ouvry, F., 1868.

The most honorable tragedie of Sir Richard Grinvile, Knight. 1595. Rptd. by Arber, E., 1871.

The true tragedy of Herod and Antipater: with the death of faire Marriam. . . . As it hath beene, of late, divers times publiquely acted (with great applause) at the Red Bull, by the Company of his Majesties Revels. Written by Gervase Markham and William Sampson. 1622.

Marie Magdalens Lamentations for the losse of her master Jesus. 1601, 1604. Ed. Grosart in Miscell. of the Fuller Worthies' Library, vol. II, 1871.

The Poem of Poems; or Sions muse; contayning the divine song of king Salomon, devided into eight eclogues. 1595, 1596.

Rodomonths Infernall, or the divell conquered. Ariostos conclusions of the marriage of Rogero with Bradamanth, etc., paraphrastically translated by G. M. 1607. (Entered in Stationers' register, 15 Sept., 1598.)

The Teares of the Beloved: or, the lamentations of Saint John. 1600. Ed. Grosart in Miscellanies of the Fuller Worthies' Library, vol. II, 1871.

Thyrsis and Daphne. By Gervis Mackwm. (Entered in Stationers' register, 23 April, 1593.)

Miscellaneous

The Art of Archerie. 1634. Dedication signed Gervase Markham. In the Huth Catalogue is described a similar copy dated 1633.

Conceyted letters, newly layde open: or a most excellent bundle of new wit, wherein is knit up together all the perfections or arte of episteling. 1618, etc. (Preface signed I. M.)

Death triumphant. (Entered in Stationers' register, 16 Nov., 1621.)

The English Arcadia alluding his beginning from Sir Philip Sydnes ending. 1607. Second part, 1613.

Hobsons Horse-load of Letters; or a president for epistles. By G. M. 1613. ("A presidente for epistles by Gervase Markham" was entered in the Stationers' register, 23 Sept., 1613.)

Honour in his perfection. 1624.

A second parte to the Mothers blessing, or a cure against misfortunes. (Entered in Stationers' register, 7 May, 1622.)

The Souldiers Accidence. Or an introduction into military discipline, containing the first principles and necessary knowledge meete for captaines, muster-masters, and all young souldiers of the infantrie, or foote bandes. Also the cavallarie or formes of trayning of horse-troopes. 1625. Rptd. in The Souldiers Exercise, 1643. See also Brit. Mus. Stowe MSS. 438.

The Souldiers Grammar. . . . By G. M.   1626, etc.   Second part, 1627, etc.

Verus pater, or health of body.   (Entered in Stationers' register, 4 May, 1620.)

Wittes only wealth.   (Entered in Stationers' register, 4 May, 1620.)

Doubtful Works

Ariostos satyres, by Gervase Markham.   1608.   (Generally attributed to Robert Tofte.)

A Health to the gentlemanly profession of serving-men.   1598.   (Sometimes attributed to Markham, but probably not by him.)

The Pastoralls of Julietta.   (Entered in Stationers' register, 11 Nov., 1609, as "translated out of Ffrench by Jarvis Markham," but published in 1610 as the work of Robert Tofte.)

A schoole for yonge schollers contayneing a briefe table to teach and learne to trayne and to be trayned, by Master Markeham.   (Entered in Stationers' register, 26 Sept., 1615.)

Vox militis, by G. M.   1625.   (This re-issue of Barnabe Rich's Allarme to England, sometimes attributed to Markham, is believed to be by Marcelline, G.)

The best account of Markham is that given in the D. of N. B. The following books may also be consulted; Langbaine's Dramatic Poets, Ritson's Bibliographica Poetica, Brydges's Restituta, Grosart's uncritical memoir, prefixed to his reprint of Teares of the Beloved (Miscellanies of Fuller Worthies' Library, vol. II), D. F. Markham's History of the Markham Family, 1854, and the bibliographical works mentioned above.

Other Writers

Horses

Astley, J.   The art of riding, set foorthe . . . out of Xenophon and Gryson. 1584.

Baret, M.   An hipponomie or vineyard of horsemanship, with the art of breeding and dieting horses.   1618.

Bedingfield, T.   The art of riding . . . written in the Italian tong by Maister Claudio Corte.   1584.

Blundeville, T.   A newe booke, containing the arte of ryding, and breakinge greate horses.   1560 (?).

—— The fower chiefyst offices belongyng to horsemanshippe. . . . The office of the breeder, of the rider, of the keper, and of the ferrer.   1565-6.

Browne, T.   Fiftie years practice: or an exact discourse concerning snaffle-riding.   1624.

C., L. W.   A very perfect discourse and order, how to know the age of a horse, and the diseases that breed in him, with the remedies to cure the same.   1610.

Clifford, C.   The schoole of horsmanship.   1585.

Malbie, N.   A plaine and easie way to remedy a horse that is foundered in his feete.   1576.

—— Remedies for diseases in horses.   1576.

Maroccus extaticus. Or, Bankes bay horse in a trance. A discourse set downe in a merry dialogue, between Bankes and his beast. 1595. (Rptd. by Percy Soc. in Early English Poetry, vol. IX, 1844.)

For an account of this horse and the references to him in contemporary literature see Halliwell-Phillipps's Memoranda on Love's Labour's Lost. 1879.

Mascall, L. The first booke of cattell, wherein is shewed the government of oxen, kine, calves, and how to use bulls and other cattell to the yoake and fell; the seconde booke intreating of the government of horses. 1587.

Morgan, N. The perfection of horsemanship, drawn from nature, arte, and practise. 1609.

Propertees and medcynes for a horse. Wynkyn de Worde (about 1500).

Hunting, Hawking, Angling, etc.

Book of St. Albans. St. Albans (about 1486).

This edition contained only the three treatises on hawking, hunting and coat-armour. The treatise on fishing with an angle was added to the second edition, printed by Wynkyn de Worde in 1496.

Bert, E. An approved treatise of hawkes and hawking. 1619.

Caius, J. Of English dogges, the diversities, the names, the natures, and the properties. Trans. Fleming, A. 1576.

Cokayne, T. A short treatise of hunting, compyled for the delight of noble-men and gentlemen. 1591.

Dennys, J. The secrets of angling. . . . By I. D. Esquire. 1613.

Gryndall, W. Hawking, hunting, fowling and fishing, with the true measures of blowing. 1596.

Latham, S. Falconry: or the faulcons lure and cure. 1615.

—— New and second booke of faulconry. 1618.

Manwood, J. A brefe collection of the lawes of the forest. 1592.

Mascall, L. A booke of fishing with hooke and line. . . . Another of sundrie engines and trappes to take polcats, buzards, rattes, mice and all other kindes of vermine. . . . Made by L. M. 1590.

S., T. A jewell for gentrie. Being an exact dictionary . . . all the art, secrets and worthy knowledges belonging to hawking, hunting, fowling and fishing. Together with all the true measures for winding of the horne. 1614.

Taverner, J. Certaine experiments concerning fish and fruit. 1600.

Turbervile, G. The Booke of faulconrie or hawking. 1575.

—— The noble arte of venerie or hunting. 1575. [1576 ed. rptd. Oxford, 1909.]

Wilson, G. The commendation of cockes and cock-fighting. Wherein is shewed, that cocke-fighting was before the comming of Christ. 1607.

York, Edward, second Duke of. The master of game. Written about 1406, and first printed in 1904; ed. by Baillie-Grohman, W. A. and F.

Husbandry

Bellot, J. The booke of thrift, containing a perfite order and right methode to profite lands and other things belonging to husbandry. 1589.

C., R. An olde thrift newly revived . . . the manner of planting, preserving, and husbanding yong trees. 1612.

Fitzherbert. J. A newe tracte or treatyse moost profytable for all husband-
men. Pynson (not later than 1523). Ed. Skeat, W. W., English Dialect
Soc., 1882. [See Eng. Hist. Review, XII, 225 (1897).]
—— The boke of surveying. Pynson, 1523.
Henley, Walter of. Boke of Husbandry. Ed. by Lamond, E. and Cunning-
ham, W. 1890.
Mascall, L. The husbandlye ordring and governmente of poultrie. 1581.
Plat, H. The jewell house of art and nature. Conteining divers rare and
profitable inventions, together with sundry new experimentes in the art
of husbandry, distillation, and moulding. 1594.
—— The new and admirable arte of setting corne. (About 1596.)
—— Sundrie new and artificiall remedies against famine. 1596.
Standish, A. The commons complaint. . . . The generall destruction and
waste of woods in this kingdome. . . . 1611.
—— New directions of experience to the commons complaint . . . for the
planting of timber and fire-wood. 1613.
Surflet, R. Maison rustique or the countrie-farme. 1600.
Tusser, T. (See bibl. to Vol. III, Chap. VIII.)

Gardening, Bees, etc.

Butler, C. The feminine monarchie, or a treatise concerning bees. Oxford,
1609.
F., N. The fruiterers secrets. 1604.
Gardiner, R. Profitable instructions for the manuring, sowing, and planting
of kitchen gardens. 1599.
Harward, S. The art of propagating plants, in Lawson's New Orchard. 1626.
Hill, T. (Didymus Mountain). A most briefe and pleasaunt treatyse, teachynge
how to dress, sowe, and set a garden. 1563, 1568, etc.
—— A pleasaunt instruction of the parfit ordering of bees. 1568.
—— The gardeners labyrinth (completed by Henry Dethick). 1577.
Lawson, W. A new orchard and garden. 1618.
Mascall, L. A booke of the arte and maner, howe to plant and graffe all
sortes of trees. 1572.
Orchard (The), and the garden: containing certaine necessarie, secret, and
ordinarie knowledges in grafting and gardening. . . . 1602.
Parkinson, J. Paradisi in sole, paradisus terrestris, or a garden of all sorts of
pleasant flowers . . . with a kitchen garden . . . and an orchard.
1629.
Passe, C. de. A garden of flowers. (Trans. by E. W.) Utrecht, 1615.
Platt, H. Floraes paradise, beautified and adorned with sundry sorts of
delicate fruites and flowers. 1608.
Scot, R. A perfite platforme of a hoppe-garden. 1574.

Herbals

Andrew, L. The vertuose boke of distyllacyon of the waters of all maner of
herbes. 1527.
Ascham, A. A little herball. 1550.
C., W. (W. Copland?). A boke of the propreties of herbes. 1549 (?). A re-
issue of A newe mater, 1525.
Gerard, J. The herball, or generall historie of plantes. 1597. (Revised
and enlarged by Thomas Johnson, 1633.)

Grete herball (The).   P. Treveris, Southwark, 1526.

Hollybush, J.   A most excellent and perfecte homish apothecarye, or a homely physick booke.   Cologne, 1561.

Langham, W.   The garden of health, conteyning the sundry rare and hidden vertues and properties of all kindes of simples and plants.   1579.

Lyte, H.   A niewe herball or historie of plantes . . . set foorth in the Doutche or Almaigne tongue by . . . Rembert Dodoens. . . . Nowe first translated out of French.   1578.

Macers herbal practysid by Doctor Linacro.   (About 1530.)

—— A new herball of Macer.   (About 1535.)

Parkinson, J.   Theatrum botanicum.   The theater of plants, or an universall and compleate herball.   1640.

Ram, W.   Rams little Dodeon.   A briefe epitome of Lyte (see above).   1606.

Turner, W.   The names of herbes in Greke, Latin, Englishe, Duche and Frenche, with the commune names that herbaries and apotecaries use.   (About 1548.)

—— A new herball.   1551.   Second part.   Cologne, 1562.

Tobacco

(See bibliography to Chap. xvi.)

Natural History, etc.

Bacon, F.   Sylva sylvarum: or a naturall historie.   1627.

Goffe, N.   The perfect use of silk-wormes.   1607.

Maplet, J.   A greene forest, or, naturall historie: wherein may bee seene first the most sufferaigne vertues in all the whole kinde of stones and mettals: next of plants . . . lastly of brute beastes, foules, etc.   1567.

Moffet, T.   Insectorum sive minimorum animalium theatrum.   1634.

S., W.   Instructions for the increasing of mulberie trees, and the breeding of silke-wormes for the making of silke in this kingdome.   1609.

Topsell, E.   The historie of foure-footed beastes . . . collected out of all the volumes of Conradus Gesner, etc.   1607.

—— The historie of serpents, or the second book of living creatures.   1608.

Housewifery

Boke of cookery.   Pynson, 1500.

Butts, H.   Dyets dry dinner.   1599.

Closet (A) for ladies and gentlewomen, or, the art of preserving, conserving, and candying.   1608.

Dawson, T.   The good huswifes jewell . . . most excellent and rare devices for conceites in cookery.   1596.

Murrell, J.   A delightfull daily exercise for ladies and gentlewomen.   Whereby is set foorth the secrete misteries of the purest preservings in glasses and other confrictionaries.   1621.

—— A new booke of cookerie, with the newest art of carving and serving.   (About 1630.)

Plat, H.   Delightes for ladies, to adorne their persons, tables, closets, and distillatories.   With beauties, bouquets, perfumes, and waters.   1602.

Tasso, T.   The householders philosophie.   1558.

Xenophon's treatise of householde.   1534.   (Translated by Gentian Hervet.)

Heraldry

Bolton, E. The elements of armories. 1610.

Book of honor and arms. 1590. (Sir Wm. Segar ?.)

Book of St. Albans. St. Albans (about 1486). (Part III treats of coat-armour.)

Bossewell, J. Workes of armorie. 1572.

Brooke, R. A catalogue and succession of the kings, princes, dukes, marquesses, earles, and viscounts of this realme . . . with their armes, wives, and children. 1619.

Favine, A. The theater of honour and knight-hood. 1623.

Ferne, J. The blazon of gentrie. 1586.

Guillim, J. A display of heraldrie. 1611 (1610).

Holland, H. Basiliologia . . . effigies of all our English kings . . . with their severall coats of arms, impresses, and devices. 1618.

Legh, G. The accedens of armory. 1562.

Milles, T. The catalogue of honor, or tresury of true nobility. 1610.

Peacham, H. The compleat gentleman. 1622. (Contains chapters on heraldry.)

Robinson, R. A rare, true, and proper blazon of coloures in armoryes and ensigns. 1583.

Segar, W. Honor military and civill. 1602.

Wyrley, W. The true use of armorie. 1592. (See, also, Camden, Selden, etc.)

CHAPTER XVIII

THE BOOK TRADE, 1557–1625

Arber, E. A transcript of the registers of the Company of Stationers of London, 1554–1640. 5 vols. Privately printed, 1875–94.

British Museum catalogue of books printed in England, Scotland and Ireland, and of books in English printed abroad to the year 1640. 3 vols. 1884.

Dibdin, T. F. Typographical antiquities. Begun by Joseph Ames, augmented by William Herbert. 4 vols. 1810–19.

Hazlitt, W. C. Hand-book to the popular, poetical, and dramatic literature of Great Britain. 1867. Bibliographical Collections and Notes. 6 vols. 1876–1903. Index by Gray, G. J. 1893.

Herbert, W. Typographical antiquities: or an historical account of printing in Great Britain and Ireland. Begun by Joseph Ames. 3 vols. 1785–90.

Sayle, C. E. Early English printed books in the University Library, Cambridge (1475–1640). 4 vols. Cambridge, 1900–7.

Arber, E. A list of 837 London publishers between 1553 and 1640. Birmingham, 1890. (An advance issue of part of vol. v of the Transcript of the Stationers' register.)

Ballads. See bibliography to Chap. XVI.

Bibliographical Society. Transactions and Monographs. 1893 ff.

Bigmore, E. C. and Wyman, C. W. H. A bibliography of printing. 3 vols. 1880–6.

Chatto, W. A. and Jackson, J. A treatise on wood engraving. 1861.

Colvin, S. Early engraving and engravers in England (1545–1695). 1905.

Contributions towards a dictionary of English book-collectors. Parts I–XIII.
      Quaritch, B., 1892–9.
Duff, E. G.   A century of the English book trade, 1457–1557.   Bibliographical
      Society.   1905.
—— Notes on stationers from the Lay Subsidy Rolls of 1523–4.   The Library,
      1908, pp. 257–266.
—— The printers, stationers and bookbinders of Westminster and London
      from 1476 to 1535.   Cambridge, 1906.
—— The stationers at the sign of the Trinity.   Bibliographica, vol. I,
      1895.
Elton, C. I. and M.A.   The great book-collectors.   1893.
Fletcher, W. Y.   English book collectors.   1902.
Greg, W. W.   A list of English plays written before 1643 and printed before
      1700.   Bibliographical Society.   1900.
—— A list of masques, pageants, etc.; supplementary to A list of English
      plays.   Bibliographical Society.   1902.
—— On certain false dates in Shakespearian quartos.   The Library, 1908,
      pp. 113–131, 381–409.   See also Athenæum, 1908, vol. I, 544, 574,
      669.
Griffiths, L. M.   Evenings with Shakspere.   1887.   (For printers and
      publishers of Shakespeare's works.)
Hand-lists of English printers, 1501–1556.   3 parts.   Bibliographical Society.
      1895–1905.
Lee, S.   Life of William Shakespeare.   1908.
Nichols, J. G.   Notices of the Stationers' Company.   Lond. and Middlesex
      Archaeological Soc. Trans. II, 1864.
Plomer, H. R.   A short history of English printing.   1900.
—— Abstracts from the wills of English printers and stationers, 1492–1630.
      Bibliographical Society.   1903.
—— Bishop Bancroft and a catholic press.   The Library, 1907, pp. 164–176.
—— New documents on English printers and booksellers of the 16th century.
      Bibliographical Soc. Trans. IV, 1898.
—— Notices of English stationers in the archives of the city of London.
      Bibliographical Soc. Trans. VI, 1901.
—— Notices of printers and printing in the State Papers.   Bibliographica,
      vol. II, 1896.
—— Some notes on the Latin and Irish stocks of the Company of Stationers.
      The Library, 1907, pp. 286–297.
—— The Long Shop in the Poultry.   Bibliographica, vol. II, 1896.
—— The printers of Shakespeare's plays and poems.   The Library, 1906,
      pp. 149–166.
Pollard, A. W.   Early illustrated books.   1893.
—— English books printed abroad.   Bibliographical Soc. Trans. III, 1896;
      and in Old Picture Books, 1902.
—— Some notes on English illustrated books.   Bibliographical Soc. Trans.
      VI, 1903.
—— Woodcuts in English plays, printed before 1660.   The Library, 1900,
      pp. 71–88.
Reed, T. B.   A History of the old English letter foundries.   1887.
"Richard Robinson's Eupolemia, Archippus, and Panoplia."   1603.   (A
      manuscript containing an account of his literary earnings.)   Gentleman's
      Mag. ccc, 277 (April, 1906).

Rivington, C. R. A short account of the worshipful Company of Stationers. Privately printed, 1903.

—— Notes on the Stationers' Company. The Library, 1903, pp. 355–366.

—— The records of the worshipful Company of Stationers. Lond. and Middlesex Archaeological Soc. Trans. VI, 1885: also published separately, 1883, and in vol. V of Arber's Transcript.

Rogers, J. E. T. A history of agriculture and prices in England. Vols. IV and V. Oxford, 1882–7. (For the prices of books, paper, etc.)

Sayle, C. E. Initial letters in early English printed books. Bibliographical Soc. Trans. VII, 1904.

Scintilla, or a light broken into darke warehouses. With observations upon the monopolists of seaven severall patents and two charters. Practised and performed by a mistery of some printers, sleeping stationers, and combining book-sellers. 1641. Rptd. in Arber's Transcript, vol. IV.

Sheavyn, Ph. Patrons and professional writers under Elizabeth and James I. Writers and the publishing trade, c. 1600. The livelihood of the professional writer, c. 1600. Writers and official censors under Elizabeth and James I. The Library, 1906–7. Four articles.

Smith, G. The Frankfort book-mart. The Library, 1900, pp. 167–179.

Steele, R. The earliest English music printing. Bibliographical Society. 1903.

Strype, J. Life and acts of Matthew Parker. 3 vols. Oxford, 1821.

—— Life and acts of John Whitgift. 3 vols. Oxford, 1822.

Taylor, John. All the workes of John Taylor the water-poet. Being sixty and three in number. 1630. Rptd. by the Spenser Society. 3 vols. 1863–9.

—— Works, not included in the folio volume of 1630. 5 vols. Spenser Society. 1870–8.

—— Works. Ed. by Hindley, C. 1872. (Contains 21 of the principal works.)

For list of Taylor's pieces see D. of N. B. and Hindley's edition of the works. See, also, Southey, R., Essay on the lives and works of our uneducated poets (prefixed to Attempts in verse by John Jones, 1831.)

Timperley, C. H. A dictionary of printers and printing. 1839.

Watt, R. Bibliotheca Britannica; or a general index to British and foreign literature. 4 vols. Edinburgh, 1824.

Welch, C. St. Paul's Cathedral and its early literary associations. Lond. and Middlesex Archaeological Soc. Trans., N.S., I, 1905.

Wheatley, H. B. Signs of booksellers in St. Paul's Churchyard. Bibliographical Soc. Trans. IX, 1908.

—— The dedication of books to patron and friend. 1887.

Williams, J. B. A history of English journalism. 1908. (For early newspapers.)

Wither, G. The schollers purgatory, discovered in the stationers' commonwealth. Imprinted for the Honest Stationers [c. 1624].

Worman, E. J. Alien members of the book-trade during the Tudor period. Bibliographical Society. 1906.

INDIVIDUAL PRINTERS AND STATIONERS

Thomas Berthelet, royal printer and bookbinder to Henry VIII. By Davenport, C. Caxton Club. Chicago, 1901.

—— Notes on the types, borders, etc., used by Thomas Berthelet. By Greg, W. W. Bibliographical Soc. Trans. VIII, 1907.

Edward Blount. An Elizabethan bookseller. By Lee, S. Bibliographica, vol. I, 1895.

Henry Bynneman, printer, 1566–83. By Plomer, H. R. The Library, 1908, pp. 225–244.

Robert Copland (printer and translator). By Plomer, H. R. Bibliographical Soc. Trans. III, 1896.

John Day, the printer. By Nichols, J. G. Gentleman's Mag., Nov., 1832.

Henry Denham, printer. By Plomer, H. R. The Library, 1909, pp. 241–250.

Thomas East, printer. By Plomer, H. R. The Library, 1901, pp. 298–310.

William Pickering, the earliest bookseller on London Bridge, 1556–71. By Gray, G. J. Bibliographical Soc. Trans. IV, 1896–8.

John Rastell and his contemporaries. By Plomer, H. R. Bibliographica, vol. II, 1896.

Peter Short, printer, and his marks. By Thompson, S. P. Bibliographical Soc. Trans. iv, 1898.

Richard Tottel. By Plomer, H. R. Bibliographica, vol. III, 1897.

—— Tottel's Miscellany. By Greg, W. W. The Library, 1904, pp. 113–133.

Robert Wyer, printer and bookseller. By Plomer, H. R. Bibliographical Society. 1897.

The D. of N. B. should also be consulted for notices of the more important stationers and sources of fuller information.

THE PROVINCES. SCOTLAND. IRELAND

Allnutt, W. H. English provincial presses. Bibliographica, vol. II, 1896.

Bowes, R. A catalogue of books printed at or relating to Cambridge, 1521–1893. With Index by Worman, E. J. 2 vols. Cambridge, 1894.

—— Biographical notes on the [Cambridge] University printers. Cambridge Antiquarian Soc. Communications, v, 1886.

Bowes, R. and Gray, G. J. John Siberch, bibliographical notes, 1886–1905. Cambridge, 1906.

Bradshaw, H. Bibliographical introduction to facsimile of Henrici Bulloci Oratio, Cambridge, 1521. Cambridge, 1886. (Notes on Siberch's press. See, also, Cambridge Antiq. Soc. Proc. VII, 104, 188; VIII, 31; IX, 1.)

Burton, J. R. Early Worcestershire printers and books. Associated Architectural Societies' Reports, XXIV, 197–206. 1897.

Cotton, H. Typographical gazetteer. 2 vols. 1831–66.

Davies, R. A memoir of the York press. Westminster, 1868.

Duff, E. G. Notes on a book printed at York in 1579. Edinburgh Bibliographical Soc. Papers, III, 1899.

—— The printers, stationers and bookbinders of York up to 1600. Bibliographical Soc. Trans. v, 1901.

Gibson, S. Abstracts from the wills of binders, printers, and stationers of Oxford, 1493–1638. Bibliographical Society. 1907.

Gray, G. J. The earlier Cambridge stationers and bookbinders and the first Cambridge printer. Bibliographical Society. 1904.

Madan, F. A brief account of the University Press at Oxford. Oxford, 1908.

—— A chart of Oxford printing, "1468"–1900. Bibliographical Society. 1904.

—— The early Oxford press, "1468"–1640. Oxford, 1895.

Pierce, W. An historical introduction to the Marprelate tracts. 1908.

Plomer, H. R. A secret press at Stepney in 1596. The Library, 1903, p. 236.

Proctor, R. The French royal Greek types and the Eton Chrysostom. Bibliographical Soc. Trans. VII, 1904.

Wilson, J. D. A new tract from the Marprelate press. The Library, 1909, pp. 225–240. See also Chap. XVII and bibliography in Vol. III.

Aldis, H. G. A list of books printed in Scotland before 1700. Edinburgh Bibliographical Society. 1904.

—— Scottish Bibliography. Scottish Review, XXIX, 1897.

—— Thomas Finlason and his press. Edinburgh Bibliographical Soc. Papers, I, 1896.

Bannatyne Miscellany, vol. 2. Bannatyne Club. Edinburgh, 1836. (For wills and inventories of Edinburgh printers and stationers.)

Cowan, W. Andro Hart and his press. Edinburgh Bibliographical Soc. Papers, I, 1896.

Dickson, R. and Edmond, J. P. Annals of Scottish printing to the beginning of the 17th century. Cambridge, 1890.

Dobson, W. T. History of the Bassandyne Bible. Edinburgh, 1887.

Edinburgh Bibliographical Society. Papers. 1896 ff.

Edmond, J. P. The Aberdeen printers, 1620–1736. Aberdeen, 1886. Last notes on the Aberdeen printers. 1888.

—— Notes on the inventories of Edinburgh printers, 1577–1603. Edinburgh Bibliographical Soc. Papers, I, 1896.

History of the art of printing. James Watson, Edinburgh, 1713. (For the history of Scottish printing.)

Lee, J. Memorial for the Bible Societies in Scotland. Edinburgh, 1824. Additional memorial. Edinburgh, 1826. (Contain much information relating to early Scottish printers.)

Dix, E. R. McC. Catalogue of early Dublin-printed books, 1601–1700. Dublin, 1898–1905.

—— List of books, pamphlets, &c., printed wholly, or partly, in Irish. Dublin, 1905.

—— The earliest Dublin printers and the Company of Stationers of London. Bibliographical Soc. Trans. VII, 1904.

—— The earliest Dublin printing. Dublin, 1901.

—— The ornaments used by John Franckton, printer at Dublin. Bibliographical Soc. Trans. VIII, 1907.

Printing in the Irish character. (Letters from Bradshaw, H., to Reed, T. B.) The Bibliographical Register, 1905.

EARLY TRADE CATALOGUES

Maunsell, A. The first part of the catalogue of English printed bookes: which concerneth such matters of divinitie, as have bin either written in our owne tongue, or translated out of anie other language. 1595.

—— The seconde parte of the catalogue of English printed bookes . . . which concerneth the sciences mathematicall, as arithmetick, geometrie, astronomie, astrologie, musick, the arte of warre, and navigation: and also, of phisick and surgerie. 1595.

Catalogus universalis pro nundinis Francofurtensibus vernalibus, de anno
M.DC.XVII. John Bill, London, 1617.

This list was published twice a year, in April and October, and at least
twenty-four numbers (April, 1617, to October, 1628) are known to have been
issued. From October, 1622, to October, 1626, a supplement of Books printed
in English was appended to each number.

A catalogue of such English bookes, as lately have bene, and now are in
printing for publication. From the ninth day of October, 1618, untill
Easter terme next ensuing. And . . . to be continued for every half
year. W. Jaggard, London, 1618. (No further issue has been found.)

A catalogue of certaine bookes which have been published, and (by authoritie)
printed in England, both in Latine and English, since the yeare 1626,
untill November this present yeare 1631. Now published for supply
since the intermission of the English Catalogue, with intention hereafter
to publish it exactly every yeare. London, 1631. (No further issue has
been found.)

Arber, E. Contemporary printed lists of books produced in England.
Bibliographica, vol. III, 1897.

Growoll, A. Three centuries of English booktrade bibliography. New
York, 1903. (Contains a list, by Eames, W., of the catalogues, etc.,
published for the English book trade from 1595–1902.)

BOOKBINDING

Bagford's Notes on bookbindings. Ed. Davenport, C. Bibliographical
Soc. Trans. VII, 1904.

Brassington, W. S. Historic bindings at the Bodleian Library. 1892.

Catalogue of the exhibition of bookbindings at the Burlington Fine Arts
Club. 1891.

Davenport, C. English embroidered bookbindings. 1899.

—— English heraldic book stamps. 1909.

—— Little Gidding bindings. Bibliographica, vol. II, 1896.

—— Royal English bookbindings. Portfolio monographs. 1896.

Fletcher, W. Y. English armorial book stamps and their owners. Bibliographica, vol. III, 1897.

—— English bookbindings. 1896. Rptd. from The Portfolio, 1893.

—— English bookbindings in the British Museum. 1895.

Gibson, S. Early Oxford bindings. Bibliographical Society. 1903.

—— The localization of books by their bindings. Bibliographical Soc.
Trans. VIII, 1907.

Gray, G. J. The earlier Cambridge stationers and bookbinders. Bibliographical Society. 1904.

Holmes, R. R. Specimens of royal, fine, and historical bookbinding selected
from the Royal Library, Windsor Castle. 1893.

Horne, H. P. The binding of books, an essay in the history of gold-tooled
bindings. 1894.

Prideaux, S. T. An historical sketch of bookbinding. 1893. (Contains a
chapter on early stamped bindings by Duff, E. G.)

Quaritch, B. Facsimiles of choice examples of historical and artistic bookbinding in the 15th and 16th centuries. 1889.

Weale, W. H. J. Bookbindings and rubbings of bindings in the National
Art Library South Kensington Museum. 2 parts. 1894–8.

Wheatley, H. B. Remarkable bindings in the British Museum. 1889.

Chapter XIX

THE FOUNDATION OF LIBRARIES

Abbot, T. K. The Book of Trinity College, Dublin (1591–1891). Belfast and Dublin, 1892. Chap. VII.

Becker, G. Catalogi Bibliothecarum antiqui. Bonn, 1885.

Botfield, B. Catalogi veteres Librorum Ecclesiae Cathedralis Dunelm. (Edited by B. Botfield.) Surtees Society. Vol. VII. 1840.

—— Notes on the Cathedral Libraries of England. 1849.

Bowes, Robt. Catalogue of Books printed at or relating to the University, Town and County of Cambridge from 1521 to 1893. Cambridge, 1894.

Bradley, J. W. Dictionary of Miniaturists, Illuminators, Calligraphers and Copyists. 3 vols. 1887–9.

Bradshaw, H. Collected Papers. Cambridge, 1889.

Camdeni et illustrium Virorum Epistolae. Ed. Smith, T. 1691.

Carlisle, Nich. Endowed Grammar Schools. 2 vols. 1818. Vol. I, pp. 435–6.

Catalogue of MSS. in Cambridge University Library. 5 vols. 1856–61.

Catalogue of MSS. in Bodleian collected by Clarke, E. D. 2 vols. 1812–15.

Catalogue of MSS. in Bodleian. 13 vols. 1848–56.

Catalogue of the manuscripts in the libraries of Peterhouse, Clare, Pembroke, Gonville and Caius, Trinity Hall, King's, Queens', Jesus, Christ's, Trinity, Emmanuel and Sidney Sussex colleges, Cambridge, ed. James, M. R. Cambridge, v.d.

Clark, J. W. Ancient Libraries: Christ Church, Canterbury. Camb. Antiq. Soc. Proceedings, vol. VIII, p. 359.

—— The Architectural History of the University and Colleges of Cambridge. 4 vols. Cambridge, 1886.

—— Libraries in the Medieval and Renaissance Periods. Cambridge, 1894.

—— The Care of Books. 2nd edition. Cambridge, 1902. (Incorporates a large proportion of the information respecting libraries in the three preceding works and also traces the development of libraries from antiquity to the end of the 18th century.)

Coxe, H. O. Catalogus Codicum MSS. qui in Collegiis aulisque Oxoniensibus hodie adservantur. 2 pts. 4to. Oxonii, 1852.

Durie, John. The Reformed Librarie Keeper. 1650.

Edwards, Edward. Memoirs of Libraries; including a Handbook of Library Economy. 2 vols. 1859. (A work descriptive of ancient and medieval libraries and also of the collections subsequently incorporated in the British Museum; those of the Faculty of Advocates and Writers to the Signet at Edinburgh; the university and town libraries of Scotland; the library of Trinity college, Dublin; and the minor libraries of London; those of the United States and the continent.)

Gasquet, Dom F. A. Some Notes on Medieval Monastic Libraries. [See his Old English Bible and other Essays (pp. 1–34, and 35–53), 1908.]

Gottlieb, Theodor. Ueber Mittelalterliche Bibliotheken. Leipzig, 1890. (Supplies useful corrections of and additions to the researches of Edwards: see supra.)

Hales, John. Works. Vol. I. Glasgow, 1765. (Contains his Oration on Bodley.)

Hardy, Sir T. D. Descriptive Catalogue of Manuscripts relating to the History of Great Britain and Ireland. 4 vols. (Rolls Series.)

James, M. R. On the Abbey of St. Edmund at Bury. (Cambridge Publications, Octavo Series, No. xxviii.)

—— The Ancient Libraries of Canterbury and Dover. Cambridge, 1903.

James, Thomas (1573?–1629). Bodley's first librarian. [For his works, see
D. of N. B.]

Macray, W. D. Annals of the Bodleian Library, 2nd ed. 1890.

Pietas Oxoniensis in memory of Sir Thomas Bodley, Knt., and the Foundation of the Bodleian Library. Oxford, 1902.

Reid, T. D. (d. 1624). "Founder of the first public reference library in
Scotland," now part of Aberdeen university library. [For his works,
see D. of N. B.]

Sandys, J. E. A History of Classical Scholarship. Vol. ii. From the
Revival of Learning to the end of the 18th century (in Italy, France,
England, and the Netherlands). Cambridge, 1908.

Traube, L. Die Bibliotheken. In Vorlesungen u. Abhandlungen (ed. Boll.),
i, 103–127.

Westminster Abbey, The Manuscripts of. By Robinson, J. Armitage and
James, Montague Rhodes. Cambridge, 1909.

TABLE OF PRINCIPAL DATES

877 Death of Johannes Scotus Erigena.

1274 Death of Thomas Aquinas.

1294 Death of Roger Bacon.

1308 (?) Death of Johannes Scotus
Duns.

1349 (?) Death of William of Ockham.

1413–1422 King Henry V.

1418 Peterhouse library catalogued.

1422–1471 King Henry VI.

1461–1483 King Edward IV.

c. 1470 Fortescue's *De Laudibus
Legum Angliae.*

1478 (?) First book printed at Oxford.

1483 King Edward V.

1483–1485 King Richard III.

1485–1509 King Henry VII.

1486 Bartolommeo Diaz circum-
navigates the Cape.

c. 1486 *The Book of St. Albans.*

1488 Library given by Humphrey,
duke of Gloucester to Oxford
opened.

1492 Columbus sets sail from Spain
and discovers the West Indies.

1494 Sebastian Brant's *Narrenschiff*
printed at Basel.

1497 John Cabot discovers the
mainland of America.

1499 Pinzon and Amerigo Vespucci
rediscover America.

1504 The Lady Margaret's preachership founded at Cambridge.

1504 Colet appointed dean of St.
Paul's.

1506 Death of Columbus.

1508 Chepman and Myllar print in
Edinburgh.

1509–1547 King Henry VIII.

1513 Macchiavelli's *Prince* (published, 1532).

1515 Earliest known ed. of *Eulenspiegel.*

1516 Ariosto's *Orlando Furiosa.*

1519 Cortes reaches the capital of
Mexico.

1520 Straits of Magellan crossed.

1521–1522 John Siberch prints
books at Cambridge.

1525 Tindale's New Testament,
Worms.

c. 1526 A C. Mery Talys.

1527 Death of Macchiavelli.

1528 Simon Fish's *Supplication for
the Beggars.*

1528 Castiglione's *Il Cortegiano.*

c. 1529 Latimer's *Sermons on the
Card.*

1532–1564 Rabelais's *Pantagruel.*

1533 Death of Ariosto.

1534 Fitzherbert's *Husbandry.*

1535 Execution of Fisher.

1535 First complete English Bible
(Coverdale's 1st ed.) printed.

1537 First Bible (Coverdale's 2nd
ed.) printed in England.

1539 "The Great Bible."

1546 Leland's *Laboriouse Journey
and Serche.*

1547–1553 King Edward VI.

1549 Hales's *Commonweal* written
(published, 1581).

1549 Dedekind's *Grobianus.*

1549 The first prayer-book of Edward VI.

1550 Lever: Three Sermons.

1551 More's *Utopia.*

1551 *Book of Common Prayor* printed in Dublin.

1551–1552 Turner's *New herball*

1590–1592 Sylvester's *Du Bartas.*

1590 *The Faerie Queene,* Books I–III.

1591 Harington's *Ariosto.*

1591 Greene's *Notable Discovery of Coosnage.*

1592 Samuel Daniel's *Delia* and *The Complaynt of Rosamond.*

1592 Greene's *A Quip for an Upstart Courtier,* and *Groatsworth of Wit* (licensed).

1592 Nashe's *Pierce Pennilesse.*

1592 Death of Montaigne.

1592 Plague revives in London.

1593 Sir Richard Hawkins voyages into the South Sea.

1593 *The Phoenix Nest.*

1593 Drayton's *Idea.*

1593 Nashe's *Christs Teares over Jerusalem.*

1594 Drayton's *Ideas Mirrour.*

1594 Nashe's *Terrors of the Night.*

1595 (?) Drayton's *Endimion and Phoebe.*

1595 Daniel's *The Civil Wars.*

1595 Execution of Robert Southwell.

1595 Southwell's *St. Peters Complaint.*

1595 Lodge's *A Fig for Momus.*

1595 Maunsell's *Catalogue of English Printed Books.*

1595 Davys's *Worlde's Hydrographical Description.*

1595 Ralegh's first expedition to Guiana.

1595–1596 *The Faerie Queene,* Books IV–VI.

1596 Danett's *Commines.*

1596 Ralegh's *Fight about the Iles of the Açores.*

1596 Drayton's *Mortimeriados.*

1596 Nashe's *Have With You to Saffron Walden.*

1597 Bacon's *Essays* (1st ed.).

1597 Drayton's *Heroicall Epistles.*

1597 Hall's *Virgidemiarum.*

1597 *Discoverie of the Knights of the Poste.*

1597 Gerard's *Herball.*

1597 National scheme for relief of the poor formulated.

1598 Meres's *Palladis Tamia.*

1598 Florio's *A Worlde of Wordes.*

1598 Chapman's *Iliad.*

1598 Death of Burghley.

1598 Bedingfield's trans. of Macchiavelli's *Florentine Historie.*

1598 Restoration of the University library, Oxford, by Sir Thomas Bodley.

1599 Nashe's *Lenten Stuffe.*

1599 Daniel's *Musophilus.*

1599 *The Passionate Pilgrim.*

1599 Death of Spenser.

1599 Sir John Davies's *Nosce Teipsum.*

1599 Marston's *Scourge of Villanie.*

1600 Gilbert's *De Magnete.*

1600 *England's Helicon.*

1600 Execution of Giordano Bruno.

1600–1601 Cornwallis's *Essays.*

1600 Rowlands's *The Letting of Humours Blood in the Head Vaine.*

1600 Foundation of the East India Company.

1601 Campion's *Booke of Ayres* (also 1612 and 1617).

1602 Davison's *Poetical Rapsody.*

1602 Bodleian library opened.

1602 Rowlands's *Tis Merrie when Gossips meete.*

1602 Campion's *Observations in the Art of English Poesy.*

1602 (?) Daniel's *Defence of Ryme.*

1603 Florio's *Montaigne.*

1603 Dekker's *The Wonderfull Yeare.*

1603 Holland's trans. of Plutarch's *Morals.*

1603 Knolles's *Generall Historie of the Turkes.*

1603 Barclay's *Euphormionis Satyricon,* 1st part.

1603–1625 King James I of England.

1603 King James's *The true Law of Free Monarchies.*

1603 Plague in London.

1605 Bacon's *Advancement of Learning.*

1605 Gunpowder Plot.

1605–1615 *Don Quixote.*

1606 Drayton's *Odes*.

1606 Owen's 1st vol. of *Epigrammata*.

1606 Dekker's *The Seven Deadly Sinnes of London*.

1606 Dekker's *Newes from Hell*.

1607 Gervase Markham's *Cavelarice, or the English Horseman*.

1607 Topsell's *Fourefooted Beastes*.

1607 First permanent English colony in Virginia.

1608 Hall's *Characters*.

1608 Dekker's *The Belman of London*.

1609 Dekker's *The Guls Hornebooke*.

1609 *Pimlyco, or Runne Red Cap*.

1610 John Davies of Hereford's *The Scourge of Folly*.

1610 Donne's *Pseudo-Martyr*.

1610 Giles Fletcher's *Christs Victorie*.

1610 Phineas Fletcher's *The Purple Island*.

1610 Markham's *Maister-peece*.

1610–1613 Chrysostom printed at Sir Henry Savile's press, Eton.

1611 *Coryats Crudities*.

1611 Ralegh's *History of the World* entered on Stationers' register; published 1614 or 1615.

1611 The "*Authorised Version*."

1612 Death of prince Henry.

1614 Thomas Lodge's *Seneca*.

1614 Barclay's *Icon Animorum*.

1611–1612 Donne's *The Anatomy of the World*.

1612 Campion's *Two Bookes of Ayres*.

1612 Shelton's *Don Quixote*, 1.

1612 Marriage of princess Elizabeth.

16.. Drummond of Hawthornden's *Tears on the Death of Moeliades*.

1613 Wither's *Abuses stript and whipt*.

1613–1616 Browne's *Britannia's Pastorals*.

1613–1622 Drayton's *Poly-Olbion*.

1614 The Overbury *Characters* published.

1615 Wither's *The Shepherd's Hunting*.

1615 Stephens's *Satyricall Essayes*.

1615 Sandys's *Relation of a Journey*.

1616 Death of Shakespeare.

1616 Death of Cervantes.

1618 Ralegh executed.

1618 Beginning of the Thirty Years' War.

1620 The Pilgrim Fathers land in New England.

1620 Bacon's *Novum Organum*.

1621 Burton's *Anatomy of Melancholy*.

1621 Barclay's *Argenis*.

1623 First folio of Shakespeare.

1623 Drummond of Hawthornden's *Flowers of Sion*.

1624 Bacon's *New Atlantis* written.

1624 Herbert's *De Veritate*.

1624 Donne's ΒΙΑΘΑΝΑΤΟΣ.

1624 Smith's *General History of Virginia*.

1625 *Purchas His Pilgrimes*.

1625–1649 King Charles I.

1626 Death of Lancelot Andrewes.

1627 Drayton's *Nimphidia*.

1627 Phineas Fletcher's *The Locusts or Apollyonists*.

1628 Owen Feltham's *Resolves*.[1]

1628 Earle's *Microcosmographie*.

1629 Parkinson's *Paradisi in sole Paradisus terrestris*.

1630 Drayton's *The Muses Elizium*.

1631 Phineas Fletcher's *Sicelides*.

1633–1635. Collections of Donne's poems.

1639 Death of Sir Henry Wotton.

1640 Parkinson's *Theatrum Botanicum*.

1640 1649, 1669 Donne's *Sermons* published.

1641 Ben Jonson's *Timber*.

1651 *Reliquiae Wottonianae*.

1652 Fulke Greville's *Life of Sir Philip Sidney*.

[1] First complete edition.

[The table of dates in Volume III should, also, be consulted.]

CORRIGENDA AND ADDENDA

THE CAMBRIDGE HISTORY OF ENGLISH LITERATURE

VOLUME IV. PROSE AND POETRY. SIR THOMAS NORTH TO MICHAEL DRAYTON

p. 157, ll. 10–12 *for* Warner's poem . . . very successful; *read* Warner's poem which is written in the old 'fourteeners,' rimed in couplets, was very successful;

p. 196, ll. 19–27 *for* Were this . . . in 1610. *and footnotes read* The statement, long current, that the book was confiscated in the year of its publication has been proved erroneous.[1] Drayton reissued the work in 1610 under the title, *A Heavenly Harmonie of Spirituall Songes.*

[1] By R. B. McKerrow in *The Library*, 3rd Series, October, 1910, pp. 348–350.

p. 499, *in respect of the Bibliographies generally, consult* The Modern Language Review, General Index to volumes I–X, Cambridge, 1915.

Add to the bibliography of chapter I:

Satire Ménippée. A pleasant Satyre or Poesie, wherein is discovered the Catholicon of Spain, etc. 1595.

Add to the bibliography of chapter II:

Bowen, F. A Layman's Study of the English Bible. New York, 1894.

Cook, A. S. Words in the Bible. The Nation. New York, 1912.

Prothero, R. E. The Psalms in Human Life. 1903.

Wordsworth, C. Shakespeare's Knowledge and Use of the Bible. 1864, etc.

Add to the bibliography of chapter III:

Buchan, John. Sir Walter Raleigh. Oxford, 1897.

Hume, Martin A. S. Sir Walter Raleigh. 1897.

Rodd, Sir Rennell. Sir Walter Raleigh. 1904.

Add to the bibliography of chapters IV and V:

Arber, E. The Story of the Pilgrim Fathers. 1897.

Beazley, C. R. The Dawn of Modern Geography. 3 vols. Oxford, 1904, 1906.

Douady, J. La mer et les poètes anglais. Paris, 1912.

Jusserand, J. J. Histoire Littéraire du Peuple anglais. Vol. II, Bk. v, chapters I and IX. Paris, 1904.

Payne, E. J. [ed.]. Voyages of Elizabethan Seamen to America. Select Narratives from . . . Hakluyt. 2 vols. 2nd edn. Oxford, 1893, 1900.

Raleigh, W. English Voyages of the Sixteenth Century. First printed as an introduction to Messrs. MacLehose's edition of Hakluyt, 1905. Revised and reissued separately. Glasgow, 1906.

Wright, T. Early Travels in Palestine. 1848.

Add to the bibliography of chapter VI:

Stopes, C. C. William Hunnis and the Revels of the Chapel Royal. Bang's Materialien, 1910.

2

Add to the bibliography of chapter VII:
[See, also, Mod. Lang. Rev. vols. VII and XI, 1912 and 1916.]
Add to the bibliography of chapter IX under William Drummond of Hawthornden
Ed. Kastner, L. E. Manchester, 1913.
Add to the bibliography of chapter XI:
[See Bibliography by Keynes, G., Cambridge and London, 1914.]
Poems. Ed. Grierson, H. J. C. 2 vols. Oxford, 1912.
Conversations of Ben Jonson with William Drummond of Hawthornden. Shakspr. Soc. 1842.
Smith, G. C. M. Donniana. Mod. Lang. Rev. vol. VIII, 1913.
Add to the bibliography of chapter XII:
Gray, G. J. Fisher's sermon against Luther. London, 1912.
Spearing, E. M., Mod. Lang. Rev. vols. VII and VIII, 1912, 1913.
Add to the bibliography of chapter XIII:
An edition of Burton's Anatomy of Melancholy with a full commentary by W. Aldis Wright and E. Bensly is in preparation and will be published by the Clarendon Press.
Osler, Sir W. The Library of Robert Burton. See the news sheet of the Bibliographical Society; December, 1909.
Add to the bibliography of chapter XIV under Bacon:
Steeves, G. W. Francis Bacon. A Sketch of his Life, Works and Literary Friends. [Bibliographical.] 1910.
Add to the bibliography of chapter XVI:
Smith, G. C. Moore. Gabriel Harvey's Marginalia. Stratford-upon-Avon, 1913.
The Bride, by S. R[owlands]. 1617. Ed. Porter, A. C. Boston, 1905.
Smith, C. F. John Dee (1527–1608). 1909.
Dixon, J. H. Ballads and Songs of the Peasantry of England. 1846.
Ingledew, C. J. D. The Ballads and Songs of Yorkshire. 1860.
Add to the bibliography of chapter XVII:
Einstein, L. The Italian Renaissance in England. 1902.
Add to the bibliography of chapter XVIII:
Estienne, H. Francofordiense Emporium. Geneva, 1574. The Frankfort Book-Fair, the Francofordiense Emporium of Henri Estienne. Edited, with historical introduction, translation, and notes, by Thompson, J. W. The Caxton Club, Chicago, 1911.
McKerrow, R. B. A dictionary of printers and booksellers in England, Scotland and Ireland, and of foreign printers of English books. 1557–1640. Ed. by McKerrow, R. B. Bibliographical Society. 1910.
—— Notes on bibliographical evidence for literary students and editors of English works of the 16th and 17th centuries. 1914. (Trans. of the Bibliographical Society, vol. XII.)
—— Printers' and publishers' devices in England and Scotland 1485–1640. Bibliographical Society. 1913.
Pollard, A. W. Shakespeare Folios and Quartos: a study in the bibliography of Shakespeare's plays 1594–1685. 1909.
—— Shakespeare's fight with the pirates and the problems of the transmission of the text. (Sandars Lectures, 1915.) 1917.
Spirgatis M. Englische Litteratur auf der Frankfurter Messe von 1561–1620. (Dziatzko, K. Sammlung Bibliothekswissenschaftlicher Arbeiten. Heft 15. Leipzig, 1902.)

INDEX

[**Ff** after an entry implies that there are references to the same subject on at least two immediately succeeding pages.]

"A. B.," 136
Abbot, George (1562–1633), archbishop of Canterbury, 73, 304, 485
Aberdeen Breviary, 470
Aberdeenshire, 290
Abingdon, 466
Abishag, queen, 265
Abram, Père, *Histoire de l'université et du Collège de Pont-à-Mousson*, 294
Abrey Hatch, 275
Acapulco, 117
Achaians, 37
Achilles, 25
Acignius, in *Euphormio*, 293, 296
Actaeon, 225
Adams, Clement (1519?–1587), 84
—— Francis (printer), 441
—— William, 116 ff.
Addison, J., 34, 244, 383
Adelard, 79
Adelbright, king of Diria, in *Albion's England*, 157
Adlington, William, 3, 11; *Golden Ass, The*, 3
Admonition to the Parliament, An, 469
Adonijah, 264
Adonis (Shakespeare's), 223
Aegeon of Syracuse, in *The Comedy of Errors*, 91
Aelfric, 42, 453, 485; *Homilies*, ed. Thorpe, 42, 453; *Lives of the Saints*, 485
Aeschylus, 4, 284
Aesop, 488
Affonso, Pedro, 82
Agatho, 286
Agincourt, battle of, 343
Agra, 105, 116
Ajmere, 105
Alanius (Yong's), 142
Alcalà, 80
Alcock, John, 562
Alcofribas, Messer, 10
Alcuin of York, 309
Alderton, Suffolk, 189, 190
Aleppo, 97, 105

Alexander the Great, 160, 225
—— of Hales, 309, 312
—— Hieronymus, 297
—— Sir William, 357
—— Sir William, earl of Stirling, 175, 471
Aleman, M., *The Rogue, or the Life of Guzman de Alfarache*, 451
Alfred, king, 85
Alison, Richard, 132
Alkmaar, Holland, 282
Allot, Robert (*fl.* 1600), 449; *England's Parnassus*, 449
Allde, Edward, 438, 445
Alleyn, Edward (1566–1626), 467
Alps, the, 6
Amada, Philip, 98
Amadis, 10
Amalteo, Hieronimo, 303
Amatus Lusitanus, in **Burton's** *Anatomy*, 282
Amazons, the, 66, 71
Amboina, 115
America, 85, 86, 100, 111, 112, 118
—— discovery of, 79, 80, 87
—— English books relating to, 80
Amsterdam, 459, 460
Amyot, Jacques, 3, 11, 12
Anacreon, 143 ff., 213
Ancient Pistol in *Henry IV*, 91
Ancor, river, 194, 199 ff., 218
Andreae, 285; *Menippus*, 285
Andreos, in *The Purple Island*, 191
Andrews, John, 540
Andrewes, Lancelot (1555–1626), bishop of Winchester, 261, 272 ff.; *Private Devotions*, 273
Androphilus, in *The Purple Island*, 191
Anglicus, Bartholomaeus, 366; *Proprietatibus Rerum, De*, 366
Angling, writers on, 612
Anian, strait of, 90
Annals of England, 485
Anne, queen, 289, 495
—— queen of Denmark, 154, 165
Antenorius, in *Argenis*, 297
Anti-papa, Felix, 369

Index